PRACTICAL ENGLISH USAGE

Michael Swan

PRACTICAL ENGLISH USAGE

Second Edition

Oxford University Press

Oxford University Press
Great Clarendon Street, Oxford OX2 6DP

Oxford New York
Athens Auckland Bangkok Bogotá Buenos Aires Cape Town
Chennai Dar es Salaam Delhi Florence Hong Kong Istanbul Karachi
Kolkata Kuala Lumpur Madrid Melbourne Mexico City Mumbai Nairobi
Paris São Paulo Shanghai Singapore Taipei Tokyo Toronto Warsaw

and associated companies in
Berlin Ibadan

OXFORD and OXFORD ENGLISH
are trade marks of Oxford University Press

ISBN 0 19 431197 x (paperback)
ISBN 0 19 431198 8 (hardback)

© Michael Swan 1980, 1995

First published 1980 (reprinted twenty-six times)
Second edition 1995
Thirteenth impression 2001

Typeset in Adobe Utopia and Franklin Gothic by
Tradespools Ltd. Frome, Somerset

Printed in China

Dedication

To John Eckersley, who first encouraged my interest in this kind of thing.

Contents

page

Acknowledgements   ix

Introduction   xi

List of entries   xiii

Language terminology   xxi

Phonetic alphabet   xxx

Practical English Usage   1

Index   635

Acknowledgements

So many people have helped me to write this revised edition that I am no longer totally sure of my claim to be its author.

Keith Mitchell and Gareth Watkins both gave the typescript meticulous attention; their line-by-line comments, and their help with difficult problems of analysis and description, were invaluable, and have resulted in a large number of important corrections and improvements. I am no less grateful to the other scholars who were kind enough to read and comment on the entire typescript, and who have made an enormous contribution to the clarity, accuracy and completeness of the finished text: Mike McCarthy, Ian Thompson, Catherine Walter, John Algeo and Sharon Hilles. The latter three deserve my additional thanks for dealing so patiently and tactfully with my attempts to describe American English. Ray Woodall, Frank Keenan, Jeremy Clear and David Lott of the Oxford University Press were kind enough to give me access to data from the British National Corpus; this material helped to solve a number of problems (if sometimes invalidating my solutions to others).

I am also deeply indebted to Norman Coe and Michio Kawakami, whose detailed comments on the first edition have helped me very substantially with the preparation of the second; and to the many other colleagues and correspondents without whose suggestions and advice almost every page of this book would have less to offer. To the following, and those others whose names have not survived the rigours of my filing system, my most grateful thanks: Gerry Abbott, Spencer Allman, Rune Andersen, Tsutomu Aoi, Piotr Bąkowski, David Banks, Reinald Baumhauer, Joshua Bear, Franz J Braun, G Brisou, J Brondel, Lilijana Burcar, María Cecilia Carattoli, Jung Chang, J F Chapin, Javier Chico, K K Roy Choudhury, Doreen Cooper, Sven-Inge Dahlman, Jo-Ann Delaney, Zhou Di, Michel Dupagne, John Eastwood, John Eckersley, M T Edwards, Ralph Erkelenz, Tim Eyres, Rauf Farouquee, Blake Finley, Steve Flinders, Yoshiteru Fuku, Agatha Gewirtz, Sue Girolami, J G Goble, Lucyna Gołebiowska, Huang Yao Hai, Sylvia Harratt, Rita Hartono, J Hatch, Jill and Charlie Hadfield, Yvonne Haueter, Stephan Hegglin, Mark Helme, Liesel Hermes, Hanns Höfer, Mavis Holstein, Kenji Hosoda, Takahiro Hosokawa, Françoise Houdart, Rudi Huber, Kyoichi Iwase, Zador Jeno, Pierre Juge, Franz Keller, David Keyho, Roy Kingsbury, Szilvia Komlódi, Július Korbaš,Turnay Korna, S Kumar, Kikuko Kunikata, Shirley Larsen, Charles Lowe, Richard MacAndrew, Neil P MacPhee, Jonathan Marks, Maurizio Martorelli, Barbara Mather, Greg Matheson, James P McDonnell, Kirk McElhearn, Mary McIntosh, Shin-ichi Miura, Jill Moore, Tatsuhide Mori, Ray Murphy, Kieran O'Halloran, Ali Ihsan Özeroğlu, Lewis Paines, Christine Pasani, Stefano Piantino, Simon Pocock, Siegfried Pokorny, Chan Pui-yim, Lam Pun, Angus Rose, Raul Rueda, E Santos, J Sauvanet, Silke Schade, Baby Sebastian, Yu Sheng-zhen, Christiane Sieche, Ottmar K Siegrist, Guido Smanio, E Stabetsi, R Sundaresan, Aira Suormala, H A Swan, Ruth Swan, Edmund Swylan, Santiago Tho, F Tsuchiya, Hideko Uezono, Penny Ur, Isabelle Vay, Koichi Watanabe, Annie Watson, Paul Westney,

J Williams, L Winkel, D V Woodman, Hiroko Yamamoto, Chao Yang, Shigeto Yawata, Zeng Yiting, Tao Zhanyong.

I must reacknowledge my debt to those whose help with the preparation of the first edition continues as a contribution to the second: Jonathan Blundell, Anthony Cowie, Alan Duff, Christine Forster, Michael Macfarlane, Nigel Middlemiss, Jonathan Price, Christina Ruse, Loreto Todd, Philip Tregidgo and Catherine Walter.

There is not enough space to mention all the grammarians and other linguists on whose work I have drawn, even if I had a complete record of my borrowings; but I must at least pay homage to the monumental *Comprehensive Grammar of the English Language*, by Quirk, Greenbaum, Leech and Svartvik (Longman 1985), whose authoritative account of the facts of English structure and usage constitutes an essential source of information for anyone writing pedagogic grammar materials today.

It is with particular pleasure that I express my affectionate and deeply-felt gratitude to Stewart Melluish of Oxford University Press. Without his deployment of the many qualities that distinguish editors from authors, including heroic calm, unfailing courtesy and monumental patience, this book would still be far from finished.

Finally, my thanks to Catherine, Mark and Helen for their support and tolerance during the writing of this book, which has separated me from them for too many hours over too many years.

NOTE
The author and publisher owe a special debt of thanks to Teruo Motoyama for his invaluable help in the correction of the text for the eighth impression.

Introduction

The purpose of this book

English, like all languages, is full of problems for the foreign learner. Some of these points are easy to explain – for instance, the formation of questions, the difference between *since* and *for,* the meaning of *after all.* Other problems are more tricky, and cause difficulty even for advanced students and teachers. How exactly is the present perfect tense used? When do we use past tenses to be polite? What are the differences between *at, on* and *in* with expressions of place? We can say *a chair leg* – why not **a girl leg*? What are the real rules for the use of *like* and *as*? When can we use the expression *do so*? When is *the* used with superlatives? Is *unless* the same as *if not*? What are the differences between *come* and *go,* between *each* and *every,* between *big, large* and *great,* between *fairly, quite, rather* and *pretty*? Is it correct to say *There's three more bottles in the fridge*? How do you actually say *3 × 4 = 12*? And so on, and so on.

This book is a practical reference guide to questions of this kind. It deals with over 600 points which regularly cause problems for foreign students of English. Most of the points treated are grammatical, but there are also explanations of a certain number of common vocabulary problems.

Level

The book is intended for intermediate and advanced students, and for teachers of English. Being a reference book, it contains information at various levels, ranging from relatively simple points to quite advanced problems.

Organisation

Problems are mostly explained in short separate entries; the book is more like a dictionary than a grammar in form. This makes it possible to give a clear complete treatment of each point, and enables the user to concentrate just on the question he or she needs information about. Entries are arranged alphabetically by title and numbered in sequence; a comprehensive index shows where each point can be found.

Approach and style

I have tried to make the presentation as practical as possible. Each entry contains an explanation of a problem, examples of correct usage, and (when this is useful) examples of typical mistakes. More complicated items are divided into separate entries: a general explanation first, followed by more complete information for advanced students and teachers. Explanations are, as far as possible, in simple everyday language. Where it has been necessary to use grammatical terminology, I have generally preferred to use traditional terms that are well known and easy to understand. Some of these terms (e.g. *future tense*) would be regarded as unsatisfactory by academic grammarians, but I am not writing for specialists. There is a dictionary of the language terminology used in the book on pages xxi–xxix.

The kind of English described

The explanations deal mainly with standard modern British English, and the examples are as realistic as I can make them. Stylistic differences (e.g. between formal and informal usage, or spoken and written language) are mentioned where this is appropriate. A good deal of information is given about American usage, but the book is not intended as a systematic guide to American English.

Correctness

If we say that a form is 'incorrect', we can mean two different things. We may be referring to a form like *I have seen her yesterday,* which normally only occurs in the English of foreigners; or we may be talking about a form like *ain't,* which is used in speech by many British and American people, but which does not occur in the standard dialects and is not usually written. In this book, I am mainly concerned with the first sort of 'incorrectness' (the differences between British or American English and 'foreign' English), but I have mentioned a few examples of the second kind. Sometimes a form is used by some educated people, but considered wrong by others (e.g. *me* in *It was me that found your keys*). When this is the case, I have said so, but I have not usually tried to suggest who is right.

How to use the book

This is a reference book, not a systematic course in English grammar. It will be most useful to a student who has made a mistake and wants to find out why it is wrong, or to a teacher who is looking for a clear explanation of a difficult point of grammar or vocabulary. The best way to find a point is to look in the index at the back: most problems are indexed under several different names, so it is not usually difficult to locate quickly the entry you need. (For instance, if you want to know why we say *I'm not used to driving on the left* instead of *I'm not used to drive on the left,* you can find the number of the section where this is explained by looking in the index under 'used', 'be used', 'to' or '-*ing* forms'.)

Other reference books

This book gives explanations of individual points of usage, but does not show how the separate points 'fit together'. For a systematically organised account of the whole of English grammar, students should consult a book such as *A Student's Grammar of the English Language,* by Greenbaum and Quirk (Longman), the *Longman English Grammar,* by L.G. Alexander, or the *Oxford Guide to English Grammar,* by John Eastwood. For a detailed treatment of English vocabulary, see the *Oxford Advanced Learner's Dictionary of Current English,* the *Longman Dictionary of Contemporary English* or the *Collins Cobuild English Language Dictionary.*

List of entries

1 **abbreviated styles**
2 **abbreviations and acronyms**
3 **able**
4 **about** and **on**
5 **about to**
6 **above** and **over**
7 **accept** and **agree**
8 **according to**
9 **across, over** and **through**
10 **active verb forms**
11 **actual(ly)**
12 **adjectives**: complementation
13 **adjectives ending in -ed**: pronunciation
14 **adjectives**: order before nouns
15 **adjectives**: position
16 **adjectives**: position after **as, how, so, too**
17 **adjectives** with **and**
18 **adjectives without nouns**
19 **adverb particles**
20 **adverbs of manner and adjectives**
21 **adverbs or adjectives?** confusing cases
22 **adverbs**: position (general)
23 **adverbs**: position (details)
24 **affect** and **effect**
25 **afraid**
26 **after** (adverb)
27 **after** (conjunction)
28 **after all**
29 **afternoon, evening** and **night**
30 **age**
31 **ago**
32 **alike**
33 **all** (1): introduction
34 **all** (2): subject, object or complement; **all, everybody** and **everything**
35 **all** (3): **all (of)** with nouns and pronouns
36 **all** (4): with verbs
37 **all** and **every**
38 **all** and **whole**
39 **all right** and **alright**
40 **allow, permit** and **let**
41 **almost** and **nearly**
42 **alone, lonely, lonesome** and **lone**
43 **along**
44 **already** and **all ready**
45 **also, as well** and **too**
46 **also, as well, too** and **either** in negative clauses
47 **alternate(ly)** and **alternative(ly)**
48 **although** and **though**
49 **altogether** and **all together**
50 **American and British English**
51 **and**
52 **and** after **try, wait, go** etc
53 **another** and **other(s)**
54 **any**
55 **any** and **every**
56 **any** and **no**: adverbs
57 **any more**
58 **appear**
59 **arise** and **rise**
60 **(a)round** and **about**
61 **arouse** and **rouse**
62 **articles** (1): introduction
63 **articles** (2): summary of the rules
64 **articles** (3): countable and uncountable nouns
65 **articles** (4): **the** (details)
66 **articles** (5): **a/an** (details)
67 **articles** (6): the difference between **some/any** and no article
68 **articles** (7): talking in general
69 **articles** (8): special rules and exceptions
70 **as ... as ...; as much/many as**
71 **as** and **though**: special word order
72 **as, because, since** and **for**
73 **as, when** and **while** (simultaneous events)
74 **as if** and **as though**
75 **as long as**
76 **as usual**
77 **as well as**
78 **ask**
79 **at/in** and **to**
80 **at, on** and **in** (place)
81 **at, on** and **in** (time)
82 **at all**
83 **at first** and **first**

84 **auxiliary verbs**
85 **(a)wake** and **(a)waken**

86 **back** and **again**
87 **bath** and **bathe**
88 **be**: progressive forms
89 **be** with auxiliary **do**
90 **be** + infinitive
91 **be** and **have**
92 **beat** and **win**
93 **because** and **because of**
94 **been** meaning 'come' or 'gone'
95 **before** (adverb)
96 **before** (conjunction)
97 **before** (preposition) and **in front of**
98 **begin** and **start**
99 **below** and **under**
100 **beside** and **besides**
101 **besides, except** and **apart from**
102 **bet**
103 **better**
104 **between** and **among**
105 **big, large** and **great**
106 **a bit**
107 **born** and **borne**
108 **borrow** and **lend**
109 **both (of)** with nouns and pronouns
110 **both** with verbs
111 **both ... and**
112 **bring** and **take**
113 **bring up** and **educate**
114 **Britain, the United Kingdom, the British Isles** and **England**
115 **broad** and **wide**
116 **but** = **except**
117 **by** (method, agent) and **with** (tools etc)
118 **by**: time
119 **by** and **near**

120 **call**
121 **can** and **could** (1): introduction
122 **can** and **could** (2): ability
123 **can** and **could** (3): possibility and probability
124 **can** and **could** (4): interpersonal uses (permission, requests etc)
125 **can** and **could** (5): with **see, hear** etc
126 **can't help**

127 **care: take care (of)**, **care (about)** and **care for**
128 **change**
129 **changes**
130 **city** and **town**
131 **cleft sentences**
132 **close** and **shut**
133 **cloth** and **clothes**
134 **come** and **go**
135 **comparison** (1) structures
136 **comparison** (2): comparative and superlative adjectives
137 **comparison** (3): comparative and superlative adverbs
138 **comparison** (4): using comparatives and superlatives
139 **comparison** (5): **much, far** etc with comparatives and superlatives
140 **complements**
141 **conditional**
142 **conjunctions** (1): general points
143 **conjunctions** (2): problems
144 **contractions**
145 **contrary**
146 **control**
147 **copular verbs**
148 **countable and uncountable nouns**
149 **country**

150 **dare**
151 **dates**
152 **dead** and **died**
153 **degree** (1): modification of adjectives and adverbs
154 **degree** (2): modification of nouns
155 **degree** (3): modification of verbs
156 **degree** (4): modification of other words
157 **determiners**
158 **different**
159 **discourse markers**
160 **disinterested**
161 **distancing**
162 **do** (1): introduction
163 **do** (2): auxiliary verb
164 **do** (3): general-purpose verb; **do** and **make**
165 **do** (4): substitute verb
166 **do so/it/that**
167 **doubt**
168 **dress**
169 **drown**

170 **due to** and **owing to**
171 **during** and **for**
172 **during** and **in**

173 **each**
174 **each** and **every**: the difference
175 **each other** and **one another**
176 **east** and **eastern**, **north** and **northern** etc
177 **efficient** and **effective**
178 **either**: determiner
179 **either ... or**
180 **elder** and **eldest**
181 **ellipsis** (1): general
182 **ellipsis** (2): with **and**, **but** and **or**
183 **ellipsis** (3): at the beginning of a sentence
184 **ellipsis** (4): in noun phrases
185 **ellipsis** (5): after auxiliary verbs
186 **ellipsis** (6): infinitives
187 **else**
188 **embedding and comprehension problems**
189 **emphasis**
190 **enable**
191 **end** and **finish** (verbs)
192 **enjoy**
193 **enough**
194 **especial(ly)** and **special(ly)**
195 **even**
196 **eventual(ly)**
197 **ever**
198 **ever so**, **ever such**
199 **every (one)**
200 **except (for)**
201 **exclamations**: structures
202 **expect**, **hope**, **wait** and **look forward**
203 **experiment** and **experience**
204 **explain**

205 **fairly**, **quite**, **rather** and **pretty**: adverbs of degree
206 **far** and **a long way**
207 **farther** and **further**
208 **feel**
209 **female** and **feminine**; **male** and **masculine**
210 **finally**, **at last**, **in the end** and **at the end**
211 **finished**

212 **fit** and **suit**
213 **for**: purpose and cause
214 **for**, **in**, **from** and **since** (time)
215 **forget** and **leave**
216 **formality and politeness**
217 **fronting**
218 **fun** and **funny**
219 **future** (1): introduction
220 **future** (2): present progressive and **be going to**
221 **future** (3): **shall/will** (information and prediction)
222 **future** (4): **shall** and **will** (interpersonal uses)
223 **future** (5): simple present
224 **future** (6): future perfect
225 **future** (7): future progressive
226 **future** (8): future in the past

227 **gender** (references to males and females)
228 **get**
229 **get** and **go** (movement)
230 **give** with action-nouns
231 **go/come for a ...**
232 **go/come ...ing**
233 **gone** with **be**

234 **had better**
235 **half**
236 **happen**
237 **hardly**, **scarcely** and **no sooner**
238 **have** (1): introduction
239 **have** (2): auxiliary verb
240 **have** (3): actions
241 **have** (4): **have (got)** – possession, relationships and other states
242 **have** (5): + object + verb form
243 **have** (6): **have (got) to**
244 **hear** and **listen (to)**
245 **hear**, **see** etc + object + verb form
246 **hear**, **see** etc with **that**-clause
247 **help**
248 **here** and **there**
249 **high** and **tall**
250 **holiday** and **holidays**
251 **home**
252 **hope**
253 **hopefully**
254 **how**
255 **how** and **what ... like**

256 -ic and -ical
257 **idioms and collocations**
258 **if** (1): introduction
259 **if** (2): ordinary tense-use
260 **if** (3): special tense-use
261 **if** (4): other points
262 **if** (5): other words with the same meaning
263 **if** (6): meaning 'although'
264 **if I were you**
265 **if only**
266 **ill** and **sick**
267 **immediately, the moment** etc. (conjunctions)
268 **imperatives**
269 **in** and **into, on** and **onto** (prepositions)
270 **in** and **to**
271 **in case** and **if**
272 **in front of, facing** and **opposite**
273 **in spite of**
274 **indeed**
275 **infinitives** (1): introduction
276 **infinitives** (2): forms
277 **infinitives** (3): without **to**
278 **infinitives** (4): using perfect infinitives
279 **infinitive clause** as subject, object or complement of sentence
280 **infinitive clause** introduced by **for** + noun/pronoun
281 **infinitive clauses of purpose**
282 **infinitive clauses**: other uses
283 **infinitive complements** (1): after verbs
284 **infinitive complements** (2): after verb + object
285 **infinitive complements** (3): after adjectives
286 **infinitive complements** (4): after nouns and pronouns
287 **infinitive complements** (5): active and passive infinitive with similar meaning
288 **infinitive complements** (6): after **who, what, how** etc
289 **information structure**
290 **-ing forms** ('gerunds' and 'participles'): introduction
291 **-ing forms used as modifiers**
292 **-ing forms used like nouns** (1): subject, object or complement
293 **-ing forms used like nouns** (2): after verbs
294 **-ing forms used like nouns** (3): after nouns and adjectives
295 **-ing forms used like nouns** (4): after prepositions
296 **-ing forms used like nouns** (5): -ing form or infinitive?
297 **instead (of)**
298 **inversion** (1): auxiliary verb before subject
299 **inversion** (2): whole verb before subject
300 **irregular verbs**
301 **it** (1): preparatory subject
302 **it** (2): preparatory object
303 **its** and **it's**
304 **it's time**

305 **just**

306 **know**

307 **last** and **the last**
308 **later** and **in**
309 **lay** and **lie**
310 **learn**
311 **least** and **fewest**
312 **left**
313 **less** and **fewer**
314 **lest**
315 **let** introducing imperatives
316 **let**: structures
317 **letters**
318 **life**: countable or uncountable noun
319 **like** (verb)
320 **like** and **as** (similarity, function)
321 **likely**
322 **(a) little** and **(a) few**
323 **long** and **(for) a long time**
324 **look**
325 **lose** and **loose**
326 **a lot, lots, plenty, a great deal, a large number, the majority**

327 **make**
328 **make**: prepositions

329 **marry** and **divorce**
330 **may** and **might** (1): introduction
331 **may** and **might** (2): possibility
332 **may** and **might** (3): permission
333 **may** and **might** (4): **may** in wishes and hopes
334 **may** and **might** (5): **may/might … but**
335 **may** and **might** (6): **may/might as well**
336 **may** and **might** (7): **might** (requests, suggestions and criticisms)
337 **maybe** and **perhaps**
338 **meals**
339 **mean**
340 **means**
341 **measurements**: marked and unmarked forms
342 **mind**
343 **miss**
344 **modal auxiliary verbs**: introduction
345 **modal auxiliary verbs**: meanings
346 **more**
347 **most**
348 **much** and **many**
349 **must** (1): introduction
350 **must** (2): concluding that something is certain
351 **must** (3): necessity and obligation
352 **must** (4): **must** and **have (got) to**

353 **names and titles**
354 **nationalities, countries and regions**
355 **near (to)**
356 **nearest** and **next**
357 **need**
358 **negative structures** (1): basic rules
359 **negative structures** (2): transferred negation
360 **negative structures** (3): negative questions
361 **negative structures** (4): double negatives
362 **negative structures** (5): ambiguous sentences
363 **neither (of)**: determiner
364 **neither, nor** and **not … either**
365 **neither … nor**
366 **newspaper headlines**

367 **next** and **the next**
368 **no** and **none**
369 **no/none** and **not a/any**
370 **no doubt**
371 **no matter**
372 **no more, not any more, no longer, not any longer**
373 **no one** and **none**
374 **non-assertive words**
375 **not** and **no**
376 **not only**
377 **noun complementation**
378 **noun modifiers**
379 **nouns in groups** (1): introduction and general rules
380 **nouns in groups** (2): classifying expressions
381 **nouns in groups** (3): the **'s** structure and the **of** structure
382 **nouns in groups** (4): special cases
383 **now (that)**
384 **nowadays**
385 **numbers**

386 **of course**
387 **often**
388 **older English verb forms**
389 **once** (adverb)
390 **once** (conjunction)
391 **one**: substitute word
392 **one, you** and **they**: indefinite personal pronouns
393 **one of …**
394 **only** (focusing adverb)
395 **open**
396 **opportunity** and **possibility**
397 **opposite**: position
398 **ought**
399 **out of**
400 **own**

401 **paragraphs**
402 **part**
403 **participles (-ing** and **-ed** forms) (1): introduction
404 **participles** (2): active and passive
405 **participles** (3): details
406 **participles** (4): clauses
407 **passives** (1): passive structures and verb forms
408 **passives** (2): agent

409 **passives** (3): choice of passive structures
410 **passives** (4): verbs with two objects
411 **passives** (5): infinitive and clause objects
412 **passives** (6): verbs with object + infinitive
413 **passives** (7): object complements
414 **passives** (8): finished-result verbs
415 **past time** (1): talking about the past in English
416 **past time** (2): the simple past tense
417 **past time** (3): the past progressive tense
418 **past time** (4): the simple present perfect tense
419 **past time** (5): simple present perfect and simple past (advanced points)
420 **past time** (6): the present perfect progressive tense
421 **past time** (7): the past perfect tenses
422 **past verb form** with present or future meaning
423 **perfect verb forms**
424 **personal pronouns** (1): general
425 **personal pronouns** (2): subject and object forms
426 **piece- and group-words**
427 **place**
428 **play** and **game**
429 **please** and **thank you**
430 **point of view**
431 **politics** and **policy**
432 **possessive 's**: forms and grammar
433 **possessives: my, mine** etc
434 **possessives** with **of** (**a friend of mine** etc)
435 **prefer**
436 **prepositions** (1): introduction
437 **prepositions** (2): after particular words and expressions
438 **prepositions** (3): before particular words and expressions
439 **prepositions** (4): expressions without prepositions.
440 **prepositions** (5): at the ends of clauses
441 **prepositions** (6): before conjunctions
442 **prepositions** (7): **-ing** forms and infinitives
443 **present tenses** (1): introduction
444 **present tenses** (2): the simple present tense
445 **present tenses** (3): the present progressive tense
446 **present tenses** (4): stories, commentaries and instructions
447 **presently**
448 **price** and **prize**
449 **principal** and **principle**
450 **progressive verb forms** (1): general
451 **progressive verb forms** (2): non-progressive verbs
452 **progressive verb forms** (3) with **always** etc
453 **punctuation** (1): apostrophe
454 **punctuation** (2): colon
455 **punctuation** (3): comma
456 **punctuation** (4): dash
457 **punctuation** (5): full stop, question mark and exclamation mark
458 **punctuation** (6): quotation marks
459 **punctuation** (7): semi-colon
460 **question words**
461 **questions** (1): basic rules
462 **questions** (2): declarative questions
463 **questions** (3): reply questions
464 **questions** (4): rhetorical questions
465 **questions** (5): question tags (basic information)
466 **questions** (6): question tags (advanced points)
467 **quite**
468 **rather** (1): adverb of degree
469 **rather** (2): preference
470 **reason**
471 **reflexive pronouns**
472 **reinforcement tags**
473 **relatives** (1): relative clauses and pronouns (introduction)
474 **relatives** (2): identifying and non-identifying clauses
475 **relatives** (3): **whose**
476 **relatives** (4): **what** and other nominal relative pronouns
477 **relatives** (5): advanced points
478 **remind**

479 **repetition**
480 **reporting** (1): introduction
481 **reporting** (2): basic rules for indirect speech
482 **reporting** (3): advanced points
483 **requests**
484 **(the) rest**
485 **road** and **street**

486 **(the) same**
487 **say** and **tell**
488 **see**
489 **see, look (at)** and **watch**
490 **seem**
491 **sensible** and **sensitive**
492 **shade** and **shadow**
493 **short answers**
494 **should** (1): the difference between **should** and **would**
495 **should** (2): obligation, deduction etc
496 **should** (3): **should, ought** and **must**
497 **should** (4): in subordinate clauses
498 **should** (5): **should/would**
499 **since**: tenses
500 **singular and plural** (1): regular plurals
501 **singular and plural** (2): irregular and special plurals
502 **singular and plural** (3): pronunciation of regular plurals
503 **singular and plural** (4): singular nouns with plural verbs
504 **singular and plural** (5): plural expressions with singular verbs
505 **singular and plural** (6): **they** with singular reference
506 **singular and plural** (7): mixed structures
507 **singular and plural** (8): distributive plural
508 **singular and plural** (9): noun modifiers
509 **singular and plural** (10): miscellaneous points
510 **slang**
511 **small** and **little**
512 **smell**
513 **so** (degree adverb, substitute word)
514 **so** after **say** and **tell**
515 **so** and **not** with **hope, believe** etc

516 **so am I, so do I** etc
517 **so** and **then**
518 **so much** and **so many**
519 **so that** and **in order that**
520 **'social' language**
521 **some**
522 **some** and **any**
523 **somebody, someone, anybody, anyone** etc
524 **some time, sometime** and **sometimes**
525 **soon, early** and **quickly**
526 **sort of, kind of** and **type of**
527 **sound**
528 **speak** and **talk**
529 **spelling** (1): capital letters
530 **spelling** (2): **-ly**
531 **spelling** (3): **-ise** and **-ize**
532 **spelling** (4): hyphens
533 **spelling** (5): final **e**
534 **spelling** (6): **y** and **i**
535 **spelling** (7): doubling final consonants
536 **spelling** (8): **ch** and **tch, k** and **ck**
537 **spelling** (9): **ie** and **ei**
538 **spelling and pronunciation**
539 **still, yet** and **already**
540 **stress, rhythm and intonation**
541 **subjunctive**
542 **substitution**
543 **such**
544 **such** and **so**
545 **suggest**
546 **suppose, supposing** and **what if**
547 **supposed to**
548 **surely**
549 **sympathetic**

550 **taboo words and swearwords**
551 **take**
552 **taste**
553 **technique** and **technology**
554 **telephoning**
555 **telling the time**
556 **tense simplification** in subordinate clauses
557 **than, as** and **that**
558 **thankful** and **grateful**
559 **that**-clauses
560 **that**: omission
561 **the matter (with)**
562 **there**

563   **there is**
564   **think**
565   **this** and **that** (demonstrative pronouns and determiners)
566   **this/that** and **it** in discourse
567   **through** (time)
568   **time**
569   **tonight**
570   **too**
571   **too much** and **too many**
572   **travel, Journey, trip** and **voyage**
573   **turning verbs into nouns**

574   **unless**
575   **until**
576   **up** and **down**
577   **used** + infinitive
578   **(be) used to**

579   **verb complementation**: what can follow a verb?
580   **verb + object + complement**
581   **verbs of movement**
582   **verbs with prepositions and particles**
583   **verbs with two objects**

584   **wait**
585   **want**
586   **-ward(s)**
587   **way**
588   **weak and strong forms**
589   **well**
590   **when** and **if**
591   **where (to)**
592   **whether ... or ...**
593   **whether** and **if**
594   **which, what** and **who** : question words
595   **who ever, what ever** etc
596   **whoever, whatever** etc
597   **whose** (question word)
598   **whose** and **who's**
599   **why** and **why not**
600   **will**
601   **wish**
602   **with**
603   **worth**
604   **would**

605   **yes** and **no**

Language terminology

The following words and expressions are used in this book to talk about grammar and other aspects of language. For more information about their meaning, see the sections where they are discussed.

abstract noun (the opposite of a **concrete noun**) the name of something which we experience as an idea, not by seeing, touching etc. *doubt*; *height*; *geography*.

active An active verb form is one like *breaks, told, will help* (not like *is broken, was told, will be helped*, which are **passive** verb forms). The subject of an active verb is usually the person or thing that does the action, or is responsible for what happens.

adjective a word like *green, hungry, impossible*, which is used when we describe people, things, events etc. Adjectives are used in connection with nouns and pronouns. *a **green apple**; **she's hungry**.*

adverb a word like *tomorrow, once, badly, there, also*, which is used to say, for example, when, where or how something happens. There are very many kinds of adverbs with different functions; see sections 20–23.

adverb particle a word like *up, out, off*, used as part of a phrasal verb. *clean **up**, sold **out**, tell **off**.*

adverbial a group of words that does the same job as an adverb.

affirmative An affirmative sentence is one that makes a statement – not a negative sentence or a question. Compare *I agree* (affirmative); *I don't agree* (negative).

agent In a passive sentence, the agent is the expression that says who (or what) an action is done by. *This picture was probably painted by **a child**.*

article *A, an* and *the* are called 'articles'. *A/an* is called the 'indefinite article'; *the* is called the 'definite article'.

assertive The words *some, somebody* etc are used most often in affirmative sentences. In other kinds of sentence, they are often replaced by *any, anybody* etc. *Some, somebody* etc are called 'assertive forms'; *any, anybody* etc are called 'non-assertive forms'. Other non-assertive forms are *yet, ever*.

attributive Adjectives placed before nouns are in 'attributive position'. *a **green** shirt*; *my **noisy** son*. See also **predicative**.

auxiliary verb a verb like *be, have, do* which is used with another verb to make tenses, passive forms etc. *She **was** writing; Where **have** you put it?* See also **modal auxiliary verb**.

bare infinitive the infinitive without *to*. *Let me **go**.*

clause a part of a sentence which contains a subject and a verb, usually joined to the rest of the sentence by a conjunction. ***Mary said** that **she was tired***. The word *clause* is also sometimes used for structures containing participles or infinitives (with no subject or conjunction). ***Not knowing what to do**, I telephoned Robin; I persuaded her **to try a new method**.*

cleft sentence a sentence in which special emphasis is given to one part (e.g. the subject or the object) by using a structure with *it* or *what*. *It was you that caused the accident; What I need is a beer.*

collective noun a singular word used to refer to a group. *family; team.*

comparative the form of an adjective or adverb made with *-er* (*older, faster*), also the structure *more* + adjective/adverb, used in the same way (*more useful; more politely*).

complement (1) a part of a sentence that gives more information about the subject (after *be, seem* and some other verbs), or, in some structures, about the object. *You're **the right person to help**; She looks **very kind**; The President appointed Bristow **his confidential adviser**.* (2) structure or words needed after a noun, adjective, verb or preposition. *the intention **to invest**; full **of water**; try **phoning**; down **the street**.*

compound A compound noun, verb, adjective, preposition, etc is one that is made of two or more parts. *bus-driver; get on with; one-eyed; in spite of.*

concrete noun (the opposite of an **abstract noun**) the name of something which we can experience by seeing, touching etc. *cloud; petrol; raspberry.*

conditional (1) a verb form made by using the modal auxiliary *would* (also *should* in the first person). *I would run; she would sing; I should think.* (2) a clause or sentence containing *if* (or a word with a similar meaning), and often containing a conditional verb form. *If you try you'll understand; I should be surprised if she knew; What would you have done if the train had been late?*

conjunction a word like *and, but, although, because, when, if,* which can be used to join clauses together. *I rang **because I** was worried about you.*

continuous the same as **progressive**.

contraction a short form in which a subject and an auxiliary verb, or a verb and the word *not*, are joined together into one word. *I'm; who'll; can't.*

co-ordinate clause one of two or more clauses of equal 'value' that make up a sentence. A co-ordinate clause does not function as a subject, object, complement or adverbial in another clause. ***Shall I come to your place or would you like to come to mine? It's cooler today and there's a bit of a wind.*** See also **subordinate clause**.

copular verb *be, seem, feel* and other verbs which link a subject to a complement which describes it. *My mother **is in Jersey**; He **seems unhappy**; This **feels** soft.*

countable noun a noun like *car, dog, idea,* which can have a plural form, and can be used with the indefinite article *a/an*. See also **uncountable noun**.

dangling participle the same as **misrelated participle**.

declarative question a question which has the same grammatical form as a statement. *That's your girl-friend?*

definite article *the*.

degree saying 'how much' something is true. Adverbs of degree are, for example, *quite, rather, very, too.*

demonstrative *this/these; that/those.*

determiner one of a group of words that are normally used at the beginning of noun phrases. Determiners include *a/an, the, my, this, each, either, several, more, both, all.*

direct object see **object**.

direct speech speech reported 'directly', in the words used by the original speaker (more or less), without any changes of tense, pronouns etc. *She looked me straight in the eye and said, **'This is my money.'*** See also **indirect speech**.

discourse marker a word or expression which shows the connection between what is being said and the rest of the 'discourse' (e.g. what came before or after, or the speaker's attitude to what he/she is saying). *on the other hand; frankly; as a matter of fact.*

duration the length of time something lasts. The preposition *for* can be used with an expression of time to indicate duration.

ellipsis leaving out words when their meaning can be understood from the context. *(It's a) Nice day, isn't it? It was better than I expected (it would be).*

emphasis giving special importance to one part of a word or sentence (for example by pronouncing it more loudly; by writing it in capital letters; by using *do* in an affirmative clause; by using special word order).

emphatic pronoun reflexive pronoun (*myself, yourself, himself* etc) used to emphasise a noun or pronoun. *I'll tell him **myself**; **I** wouldn't sell this to the King **himself**.* See also **reflexive pronouns**.

ending something added to the end of a word, e.g. *-er, -ing, -ed.*

first person see **person**.

formal the style used when talking politely to strangers, on special occasions, in some literary writing, in business letters, etc. For example, *commence* is a more formal word than *start.*

frequency Adverbs of frequency say how often something happens. *often; never; daily; occasionally.*

fronting moving a part of a clause to the beginning in order to give it special emphasis. ***Jack** I like, but **his wife** I can't stand.*

future tense a verb form made with the auxiliary verb *shall/will*. *I **shall arrive**; **Will** it **matter**?*

future perfect tense a verb form made with *shall/will* + *have* + past participle. *I **will have finished** by lunchtime.*

future progressive a verb form made with *shall/will* + *be* + ...*ing*. *I **will be needing** the car this evening.*

gender the use of different grammatical forms to show the difference between masculine, feminine and neuter, or between human and non-human. *he, she, it; who, which.*

genitive the form of a noun made with *'s* or *s'*, used to show (for instance) possession. Also called *possessive. the **earth's** gravity; **birds'** nests.*

gradable *Pretty, hard* or *cold* are gradable adjectives: things can be *more* or *less* pretty, hard or cold. Adverbs of degree (like *rather, very*) can be used with gradable words. *Perfect* or *dead* are not gradable words: we do not usually say that something is more or less perfect, or very dead.

grammar the rules that say how words are combined, arranged and changed to show different meanings.

hanging participle the same as **misrelated participle**.

hypothetical Conditional verbs and structures are often used to talk about *hypothetical* situations – that is to say, situations which may not happen, or which are not real. *What would you do if you had three months free?*

identifying relative clause a relative clause which identifies the noun it refers to – that is to say, it tells us which person or thing is being talked about. *There's the woman **who tried to steal your cat**.* (The relative clause *who tried to steal your cat* identifies the woman – it tells us which woman is meant.) See also **non-identifying relative clause**.

imperative the form of a verb used to give orders, make suggestions, etc. ***Bring** me a pen; **Have** a good holiday.*

indefinite article *a/an.*

indirect object see **object**.

indirect speech a structure in which we report what somebody said by making it part of our own sentence (so that the tenses, word order, and pronouns and other words may be different from those used by the original speaker). Compare: *He said, 'I'm tired'* (the original speaker's words are reported in direct speech); *He said **that he was tired*** (the original speaker's words are reported in indirect speech).

infinitive the 'base' form of a verb (usually with *to*), used after another verb, after an adjective or noun, or as the subject or object of a sentence. *I want to go home*; *It's easy **to sing***; *I've got a plan **to start** a business*; ***To err** is human, **to forgive** divine.*

informal the style used in ordinary conversation, personal letters, etc, when there is no special reason to speak politely or carefully. *Get* is used mostly in an informal style; *start is* a more informal word than *commence*.

-ing form the form of a verb ending in *-ing*. *finding*; *keeping*; *running*; *firing*.

initial at the beginning. *Sometimes* is an adverb that can go in initial position in a sentence. ***Sometimes** I wish I had never been born.*

intensifying making stronger, more emphatic. *Very* and *terribly* are intensifying adverbs.

interrogative Interrogative words and structures are used for asking questions. In an interrogative sentence, there is an auxiliary verb before the subject (e.g. ***Can you** swim?*). *What, who* and *where* are interrogative words.

intransitive An intransitive verb is one that cannot have an object or be used in the passive. *smile*; *fall*; *come*; *go*.

inversion a structure in which a verb (or part of a verb) comes before its subject. *Here **comes John***; *Under no circumstances **are visitors** allowed to feed the animals.*

irregular not following the normal rules. An irregular verb has a past tense and/or past participle that does not end in *-ed* (e.g. *swam, taken*); *children* is an irregular plural.

main clause, subordinate clause Some sentences consist of a main clause and one or more subordinate clauses. A subordinate clause acts like a part of the main clause (e.g. like a subject, or an object, or an adverbial). ***Where she is** doesn't matter.* (The subordinate clause *Where she is* is the subject of the main clause.) *I told you **that I didn't care**.* (The subordinate clause *that I didn't care* is the direct object in the main clause.) ***Wherever you go, you'll find Coca-cola.*** (The subordinate clause *Wherever you go* acts like an adverb in the main clause; compare *You'll find Coca-cola **anywhere**.*)

main verb the verb which is used as the basis for the main clause in a sentence. In the sentence *Running into the room, she **started** to cry*, *started* is the main verb.

manner an adverb of manner describes how something happens. *well*; *suddenly*; *fast.*

mid-position If an adverb is in *mid-position* in a sentence, it is between the subject and the main verb. *I **definitely** agree with you.*

misrelated participle a participle which does not have a subject in the sentence. ***Looking out of the window**, the mountains seemed very close.* · The construction is usually avoided, because of the possibility of misunderstanding.

modal auxiliary verb one of the verbs *can, could, may, might, must, will, shall, would, should, ought.*

modify An adjective is said to 'modify' the noun it is used with: it adds to or changes its meaning. An adverb can modify a verb (e.g. *run **fast***), an adjective (e.g. ***completely** ready*) or other words or expressions. In ***sports car***, the first noun modifies the second.

negative a negative sentence is one in which the word *not is* used with the verb. *I **don't** know.*

nominal relative clause a relative clause (usually introduced by *what*) which acts as the subject, object or complement of a sentence. *I gave him **what he needed**.*

non-assertive see **assertive**.

non-identifying relative clause a relative clause which does not identify the noun it refers to (because we already know which person or thing is meant). *There's Hannah Smith, **who tried to steal my cat**.* (The relative clause, *who tried to steal my cat*, does not identify the person – she is already identified by the name *Hannah Smith*.) See also **identifying relative clause**.

noun a word like *oil, memory, arm*, which can be used with an article. Nouns are most often the names of people or things. Personal names (e.g. *George)*, and place-names (e.g. *Birmingham)* are called 'proper nouns'; they are usually used without articles.

noun phrase a group of words (e.g. article + adjective + noun) which acts as a subject, object or complement of a clause. *the last bus.*

number the way in which differences between singular and plural are shown grammatically. The differences between *house* and *houses, mouse* and *mice, this* and *these* are differences of number.

object a noun or pronoun that normally comes after the verb, in an active clause. The direct object refers to a person or thing affected by the action of the verb. In the sentence *Take **the dog** for a walk, the dog* is the direct object. The indirect object usually refers to a person who receives the direct object. In the sentence *Ann gave **me** a watch*, the indirect object is *me*, and the direct object is *a watch*.

participle see **present participle** and **past participle**.

participle clause a clause-like structure which contains a participle, not a finite verb form. ***Discouraged by his failure**, he resigned from his job; **Having a couple of hours to spare**, I went to see a film.*

passive a passive verb form is made with *be* + past participle (e.g. *is broken, was told, will be helped* – not *breaks, told, will help,* which are active verb forms). The subject of a passive verb is usually the person or thing that is affected by the action of the verb. Compare: ***They sent Lucas** to prison for five years* (active); ***Lucas was sent** to prison for five years* (passive).

past participle a verb form like *broken, gone, stopped*, which can be used to form perfect tenses and passives, or as an adjective. (The meaning is not necessarily past, in spite of the name.)

past perfect tense a verb form made with *had* + past participle. *I **had forgotten**; The children **had arrived**; she **had been working**; It **had been raining**.* The first two examples are past perfect simple; the last two (with *had been* + ...*ing*) are past perfect progressive.

past progressive tense a verb form made with *was/were* + ...*ing*. *I **was going**; They **were stopping**.*

past simple tense see **simple past tense**.

perfect a verb form made with the auxiliary *have* + past participle. *I **have forgotten**; She **had failed**; **having arrived**; **to have finished**.*

perfect conditional *should/would have* + past participle. *I **should/would have agreed**; He **would have known**.*

perfect infinitive *to have* + past participle. *to have arrived; to have gone.*

person the way in which, in grammar, we show the difference between the person speaking (*first person*), the person spoken to (*second person*), and the people or things spoken about (third person). The differences between *am, are* and *is* are differences of person.

personal pronouns the words *I, me, you, he, him* etc.

phrase two or more words that function together as a group. *dead tired; the silly old woman; would have been repaired; in the country.*

phrasal verb a verb that is made up of two parts: a 'base' verb followed by an adverb particle. *fill up; run over; take in.*

plural grammatical form used to refer to more than one person, thing etc. *we; buses; children; are; many; these.* See also **singular**.

possessive a form used to show possession and similar ideas. *John's; our; mine.*

possessive pronoun *Mine, yours, hers* etc are usually called *'possessive pronouns'. My, your, her* etc are often called *'possessive adjectives'* (although in fact they are determiners, not adjectives).

postmodifier a word which comes after the word which it modifies, e.g. *invited* in *The people **invited** all came late.* See also **premodifier**.

predicative adjectives placed after a verb like *be, seem, look* are in *predicative position. She looks **happy**; The house is **enormous**.* See also **attributive**.

premodifier a word that comes before the noun it modifies, e.g. *invited* in *an **invited** audience.* See also **postmodifier**.

preparatory subject, preparatory object When the subject of a sentence is an infinitive or a clause, we usually put it towards the end of the sentence and use the pronoun *it* as a preparatory subject (e.g. ***It** is important **to get enough sleep**). There* can also be used as a kind of preparatory subject (usually in the structure *there is*); and *it* can be used as a preparatory object in certain structures (e.g. *He made **it** clear **that he disagreed**).*

preposition a word like *on, off, of, into,* normally followed by a noun or pronoun.

prepositional verb a verb that has two parts: a 'base' verb and a preposition. *insist on; care for.*

present participle the verb-form ending in *-ing. She was **running**; **Opening** his newspaper, he started to read; I hate the noise of **crying** babies.* (The meaning is not necessarily present, in spite of the name.)

present perfect tense a verb form made with *have/has* + past participle. *I **have forgotten**; The children **have arrived**; **I've been working** all day; **It has been raining**.* The first two examples are present perfect simple; the last two (with *have been* + ...*ing*) are present perfect progressive.

present progressive tense a verb form made with *am/are/is* + ...*ing. **I'm going**; She **is staying** for two weeks.*

present simple tense see **simple present tense**.

progressive A verb form made with *be* + ...*ing* (e.g. *to **be going**; we **were wondering**)* is called *progressive.*

progressive infinitive a form like *to be going*; *to be waiting*.

pronoun a word like *it, yourself, their,* which is used instead of a more precise noun or noun phrase (like *the cat, Peter's self, the family's*). The word *pronoun* can also be used for a determiner when this 'includes' the meaning of a following noun which has been left out. *'Which bottle would you like?' – 'I'll take* **both**.*' (Both* stands for *both bottles,* and we can say that it is used as a pronoun.)

proper noun a noun (normally with no article) which is the name of a particular person, place, organization, etc. *Andrew; Brazil; Marks and Spencer.*

quantifier a word or expression like *many, few, little, several, plenty, a lot,* which is used in a noun phrase to show how many or how much we are talking about. Most quantifiers are determiners.

question tag an expression like *isn't it?* or *don't you?* (consisting of auxiliary verb + pronoun subject) put on to the end of a sentence. *It's a nice day,* **isn't it?**

reflexive pronouns *myself, yourself, himself* etc. *I cut* **myself** *shaving this morning.* See also **emphatic pronoun**.

regular following the normal rules. *Hoped is* a regular past tense; *cats* is a regular plural. See also **irregular**.

reinforcement tag a tag which repeats (and so reinforces or strengthens) the meaning of the subject and verb. *You're a real idiot,* **you are**.

relative clause a clause introduced by a relative pronoun, like *who or which. I like people* **who like me**. See also **identifying relative clause**; **non-identifying relative clause**.

relative pronoun one of the pronouns *who, whom, whose, which* and *that* (and sometimes *what, when, where* and *why*). A relative pronoun is used to repeat the meaning of a previous noun; at the same time, it connects a relative clause to the rest of the sentence (so it acts as a conjunction and a pronoun at the same time). *Is this the child* **that** *was causing all that trouble?*

reply question a question (similar in structure to a question tag) used to reply to a statement (for instance to express interest). *'I've been invited to spend the weekend in London.' – '***Have you, dear?***'*

second person see **person**.

sentence a group of words that expresses a statement, command, question or exclamation. A sentence consists of one or more clauses, and usually has at least one subject and verb. In writing, it begins with a capital letter and ends with a full stop, question mark or exclamation mark.

's genitive a form like *John's, the earth's, our parents'*.

short answer an answer consisting of a subject and an auxiliary verb. *'Who's ready for more?' – 'I am.'*

simple past tense a past verb form made without an auxiliary verb. *I* **stopped**; *You* **heard**; *We* **saw**.

simple present tense a present verb form made without an auxiliary verb. *He* **goes** *there often; I* **know**; *I* **like** *chocolate.*

simple tense a tense that is not progressive. *I* **went**; *she* **wants**; *they* **have arrived**.

singular a grammatical form used to talk about one person, thing, etc, or about an 'uncountable' quantity or mass. *me; bus; water; is; much; this.* See also **plural**.

slang a word, expression or special use of language found mainly in very informal speech, especially in the usage of particular groups of people. *thick* (= 'stupid'); *lose one's cool* (= 'get upset').

split infinitive structure in which an adverb comes between *to* and the infinitive verb form (sometimes considered 'incorrect'). *to easily understand.*

standard A standard form of a language, or a standard accent, is one that is usually used by the most educated or influential people in a country, and is therefore considered more widely acceptable or 'correct' than other forms, and taught in schools. The standard language is the one normally used for writing. *I'm not* is standard English; *I ain't* is non-standard, or sub-standard.

statement a sentence which gives information. *I'm cold*; *Philip stayed out all night.*

stress the way in which one or more parts of a word, phrase or sentence are made to sound more important than the rest (by using a louder voice and/or higher pitch). In the word *particular,* the main stress is on the second syllable /pə'tɪkjələ/. In the sentence *'Where's the 'new 'secretary?* there are three stresses.

strong form Certain words can be pronounced in two ways: slowly and carefully ('strong form'), or with a quicker pronunciation with the vowel /ə/ or /ɪ/ ('weak form'). *can* (/kæn/, /kən/); *was* (/wɒz/, /wəz/); *he* (/hiː/, /hɪ/).

subject a noun or pronoun that comes before the verb in an ordinary affirmative sentence. It often says (in an active sentence) who or what does the action that the verb refers to. **Helen** *broke another glass today*; **Oil** *floats on water.*

subject-tag a tag which repeats or identifies the subject. *She's an idiot,* ***that girl.***

subjunctive a verb form (not very common in British English) used in certain structures. *If I* ***were*** *you, ...*; *It's important that he* ***be*** *informed immediately.*

subordinate clause a clause which functions as part of another clause (e.g. as subject, object or adverbial in the main clause of a sentence). *I thought* ***that you understood***; ***What I need*** *is a drink*; *I'll follow you* ***wherever you go.*** See also **clause**, **main clause**.

sub-standard not in the standard language, and considered 'incorrect'. *I* ***ain't*** *ready*; *She* ***don't*** *agree*; *He already* ***done*** *it.*

superlative the form of an adjective or adverb made with the suffix *-est* (e.g. *oldest, fastest*); also the structure *most* + adjective/adverb, used in the same way (e.g. *most intelligent, most politely*).

swearword a taboo word used (usually with a change of meaning) to express strong emotion or emphasis. *Fuck!*

taboo word a word (e.g. *fuck*) connected with a subject (e.g. sex) which is not talked about freely, so that some of its vocabulary is considered shocking, is not used in formal speech or writing, and is avoided altogether by many people. See also **swearword**.

tag a short phrase (e.g. auxiliary verb + pronoun subject) added on to the end of a sentence. *She doesn't care,* ***does she?*** See also **question tag**, **reinforcement tag**, **subject tag**.

tense a verb form which shows the time of an action or event. *will go* (future); *is sitting* (present); *saw* (past).

third person see **person**.

transitive A transitive verb is one that can have an object. *eat (a meal)*; *drive (a car)*; *give (a present)*. See also **intransitive**.

uncountable noun a noun which has no plural form and cannot normally be used with the article *a/an. mud; rudeness; furniture*.

verb a word like *ask, wake, play, be, can,* which can be used with a subject to form the basis of a clause. Most verbs refer to actions or states. See also **auxiliary verb, modal auxiliary verb**.

verb phrase a verb that has several parts. *would have been forgotten*.

weak form see **strong form**.

Phonetic alphabet

It is necessary to use a special alphabet to show the pronunciation of English words, because the ordinary English alphabet does not have enough letters to represent all the sounds of the language. The following list contains all the letters of the phonetic alphabet used in this book, with examples of the words in which the sounds that they refer to are found.

Vowels and diphthongs (double vowels)

iː	seat /siːt/, feel /fiːl/		eɪ	take /teɪk/, wait /weɪt/
ɪ	sit /sɪt/, in /ɪn/		aɪ	mine /maɪn/, light /laɪt/
e	set /set/, any /'eniː/		ɔɪ	oil /ɔɪl/, boy /bɔɪ/
æ	sat /sæt/, match /mætʃ/		əʊ	no /nəʊ/, open /'əʊpən/
ɑː	march /mɑːtʃ/, after /'ɑːftə(r)/		aʊ	house /haʊs/, now /naʊ/
ɒ	pot /pɒt/, gone /gɒn/		ɪə	hear /hɪə(r)/, deer /dɪə(r)/
ɔː	port /pɔːt/, law /lɔː/		eə	air /eə(r)/, where /weə(r)/
ʊ	good /gʊd/, could /kʊd/		ʊə	tour /tʊə(r)/, endure /ɪn'djʊə(r)/
uː	food /fuːd/, group /gruːp/			
ʌ	much /mʌtʃ/, front /frʌnt/			
ɜː	turn /tɜːn/, word /wɜːd/			
ə	away /ə'weɪ/, collect /kə'lekt/, until /ən'tɪl/			

Consonants

p	pull /pʊl/, cup /kʌp/		tʃ	cheap /tʃiːp/, catch /kætʃ/
b	bull /bʊl/, rob /rɒb/		dʒ	jail /dʒeɪl/, bridge /brɪdʒ/
f	ferry /'feriː/, life /laɪf/		k	case /keɪs/, take /teɪk/
v	very /'veriː/, live /lɪv/		g	go /gəʊ/, rug /rʌg/
θ	think /θɪŋk/, bath /bɑːθ/		m	my /maɪ/, come /kʌm/
ð	then /ðen/, with /wɪð/		n	no /nəʊ/, on /ɒn/
t	take /teɪk/, set /set/		ŋ	sing /sɪŋ/, finger /'fɪŋgə(r)/
d	day /deɪ/, red /red/		l	love /lʌv/, hole /həʊl/
s	sing /sɪŋ/, rice /raɪs/		r	round /raʊnd/, carry /'kæriː/
z	zoo /zuː/, days /deɪz/		w	well /wel/
ʃ	show /ʃəʊ/, wish /wɪʃ/		j	young /jʌŋ/
ʒ	pleasure /'pleʒə(r)/, occasion /ə'keɪʒn/		h	house /haʊs/

The sign (') shows stress (see 540).

1 abbreviated styles

Some styles of writing and speech have their own special grammar rules,
often because of the need to save space or time.

1 advertisements and instructions

Small ads and instructions often leave out articles, subject or object
pronouns, forms of *be* and prepositions.

> *Cars wanted for cash. Contact Evans, 6 Latton Square.*
> (NOT ~~*Cars are wanted for cash*~~...)
> *Single man looking for flat Oxford area. Phone 806127 weekends.*
> *Job needed urgently. Will do anything legal. Call 312654.*
> *Pour mixture into large saucepan, heat until boiling, then add three*
>   *pounds sugar and leave on low heat for 45 minutes.*
> *Can be assembled in ten minutes. Easy to clean. Simple controls. Batteries*
>   *not included.*

2 notes

Informal notes, diary entries etc often follow similar rules.

> *Gone to hairdresser. Back 12.30.*
> *Book tickets   phone Ann   see Joe 11.00   meeting Sue lunch*

The same style may be used in postcards and short informal letters.

> *Dear Gran*
> *Watching tennis on TV. A good book. Three meals a day. No washing-up.*
> *Clean sheets every day. Everything done for me. Yes, you've guessed – in*
> *hospital!!*
> *Only went to doctor for cold – landed up in hospital with pneumonia!! If*
> *you have time please tell the others – would love some letters to cheer me up.*
> *Hope to see you.*
> *Love, Pam*

3 commentaries

Commentaries on fast-moving events like football matches also have their
own grammar. Less important verbs are often left out.

> *Goal kick ... And the score still Spurs 3, Arsenal 1 ... that's Pearce ... Pearce*
> *to Coates ... good ball ... Sawyer running wide ... Billings takes it, through*
> *to Matthews, Matthews with a cross, oh, and Billings in beautifully, a good*
> *chance there – and it's a goal!*

4 titles, notices etc

Titles, labels, headings, notices and slogans usually consist of short phrases,
not complete sentences. Articles are often left out, especially in the names of
buildings and institutions.

> *ROYAL HOTEL*
> *SUPER CINEMA*
> *INFORMATION OFFICE*
> *BUS STOP*
> *POLICE OUT!*
> *MORE MONEY FOR NURSES!*

5 headlines

Newspaper headlines have their own special grammar and vocabulary. For details, see 366.

> *RECORD DRUGS HAUL AT AIRPORT: SIX HELD*
> *FOUR DIE IN M6 BLAZE*

For other rules about leaving words out ('ellipsis'), see 181–186.

2 abbreviations and acronyms

1 punctuation

We usually write abbreviations without full stops in modern British English. Full stops (US 'periods') are normal in American English.

> *Mr* (US *Mr.*) = *Mister* (not usually written in full)
> *Ltd* (US *Ltd.*) = *Limited (company)*   *kg* (US *kg.*) = *kilogram*

2 initial-letter abbreviations

Some abbreviations are made from the first letters of several words. This often happens with the names of organisations.

> *the BBC* = *the British Broadcasting Corporation*
> *UNESCO* = *United Nations Educational, Scientific and Cultural Organisation*

Some initial-letter abbreviations are pronounced letter by letter (e.g. *the BBC*). Others are pronounced like words (e.g. *UNESCO*) – these are often called *acronyms*.

3 letter-by-letter abbreviations: pronunciation

These abbreviations are most often stressed on the last letter.

> *the BBC* /ðə biː biː 'siː/   *the USA* /ðə juː es 'eɪ/

If one of these abbreviations has an article (*a/an* or *the*), the form and pronunciation of the article depend on the pronunciation of the first letter of the abbreviation. Compare:

- *an IRA* attack
  a US diplomat /ə juː .../ (NOT *an US* ...)
- *a BA* degree
  an MP /ən em .../ (NOT *a MP*)
- *the USA* /ðə juː .../ (NOT /ðiː juː.../)
  the RSPCA /ðiː aːr .../ (NOT /ðə aːr.../)

4 acronyms: articles

Articles are usually dropped in acronyms (abbreviations that are pronounced like words).

> *UNESCO* (NOT *the UNESCO*)

5 plurals

An apostrophe (') is sometimes used before the *s* in the plurals of abbreviations: *MP's* or *MPs*; *CD's* (= 'compact discs') or *CDs*.

3 able

We use *able* especially in the structure ***be able*** + **infinitive**. This often has the same meaning as *can*. There is a negative form *unable*.

*Some people **are able to / can** walk on their hands.*
*I **am unable to / can't** understand what she wants.*

Can is preferred in the sense of 'know how to', and in expressions like *can see, can hear* etc (see 125).

***Can** you knit?* (More natural than *Are you able to knit?*)
*I **can** see a ship.* (More natural than *I **am able** to see a ship.*)

Be able is used in cases (e.g. future, present perfect) where *can/could* is not grammatically possible.

*One day scientists **will be able** to find a cure for cancer.*
(NOT ... ~~will can find~~ ...)
*What **have** you **been able** to find out?* (NOT ~~What have you could~~ ...?)
*I **might be able** to help you.* (NOT ~~I might can~~ ...)

Able is not usually followed by passive infinitives.

He can't be understood. (NOT ~~He's not able to be understood.~~)

For the use of *can* for ability, see 122.
For other differences between *could* and *was able*, see 122.3.
For other uses of *able*, see a good dictionary.

4 about and on

Compare:
– *a book for children **about** Africa and its peoples*
  *a textbook **on** African history*
– *a conversation **about** money*
  *a lecture **on** economics*

We use *about* to talk about ordinary, more general kinds of communication. *On* suggests that a book, lecture, talk etc is serious or academic, suitable for specialists.

For some other uses of *about*, see 5, 60.
For some other uses of *on*, see 80–81.

5 about to

About + **infinitive** means 'going to very soon'; 'just going to'.

*Don't go out now – we're **about to have** lunch.*
*I was **about to go** to bed when the telephone rang.*

In informal American English, *not about to* can mean 'unwilling to'.

*I'm **not about to** pay 100 dollars for that dress.*

6 above and over

1 'higher than': *above* or *over*

Above and *over* can both mean 'higher than'.

*The water came up **above/over** our knees.*
*Can you see the helicopter **above/over** the palace?*

▶

2 'not directly over': *above*

We prefer *above* when one thing is not directly over another.
*We've got a little house **above** the lake.*

3 'covering': *over*

We prefer *over* when one thing covers and / or touches another.
*There is cloud **over** the South of England.*
*He put on a coat **over** his pyjamas.*
We use *over* or *across* (see 9) when one thing crosses another.
*The plane was flying **over/across** Denmark.*
*Electricity cables stretch **over/across** the fields.*

4 measurements: *above*

Above is used in measurements of temperature and height, and in other
cases where we think of a vertical scale.
*The temperature is three degrees **above** zero.*
*The summit of Everest is about 8000 metres **above** sea level.*
*She's well **above** average in intelligence.*

5 ages, speeds, 'more than': *over*

We usually use *over*, not *above*, to talk about ages and speeds, and to mean
'more than'.
*You have to be **over** 18 to see this film.*
*The police said she was driving at **over** 110 mph.*
*There were **over** 100,000 people at the festival.*

6 *see above/over*

In a book or a paper, *see above* means 'look at something written before'; *see
over* means 'look on the next page'.

The difference between *below* and *under* is similar. See 99.
For other meanings of *over*, see a good dictionary.

7 accept and agree

Before an infinitive, we usually use *agree*, not *accept*.
*I **agreed** to meet them here.* (More normal than *I **accepted** . . .*)

8 according to

According to X means 'If what X says is true'. Note that *after* is not used in
this sense.
According to Harry, it's a good film. (NOT *After Harry . . .*)

We do not usually give our own opinions with *according to*. Compare:
- **According to** Joan, the people across the road are moving.
    (= If what Joan says is true, . . .)
  According to the timetable, the train gets in at 8.27.
- **In my opinion**, she's sick. (NOT ~~According to me,~~ . . .)

For other uses of *according to* , see a good dictionary.

9 across, over and through

1 on/to the other side of (line): *across* and *over*

Across and *over* can both be used to mean 'on or to the other side of a line, river, road, bridge etc'.
> *His village is just **across/over** the border.*
> *See if you can jump **across/over** the stream.*

2 high things: *over* preferred

We prefer *over* to say 'on / to the other side of something high'.
> *Why are you climbing **over** the wall?* (NOT . . .~~across the wall?~~)

3 on flat areas; in water: *across* preferred

We usually prefer *across* to say 'on / to the other side of a flat area or surface', or to talk about movement in water.
> *He walked right **across** the desert.* (NOT . . .~~over the desert.~~)
> *Let's swim **across** the river.* (NOT . . .~~over the river.~~)

But *over* is sometimes used in British English if there is no idea of arriving at the other side.
> *We often walk **over** the fields in the evening.*

4 the adverb *over*

Note that the adverb *over* has a wider meaning than the preposition *over*. You cannot say ~~Let's swim over the river to the church~~, but you can say *Let's swim over to the church.*

5 *across* and *through*

The difference between *across* and *through* is like the difference between *on* and *in*. *Through*, unlike *across*, is used for a movement in a three-dimensional space, with things on all sides. Compare:
- *We walked **across** the ice.* (We were **on** the ice.)
  *I walked **through** the wood.* (I was **in** the wood.)
- *We drove **across** the desert.*
  *We drove **through** several towns.*

For *over* and *above*, see 6.
For other uses of these words, see a good dictionary.

10 active verb forms

This is a list of all the active affirmative forms of an ordinary English verb, with their names.

simple future *I will/shall work, you will work, he/she/it will work,*
    we will/shall work, they will work
future progressive *I will/shall be working, you will be working* etc
simple future perfect *I will/shall have worked, you will have worked* etc
future perfect progressive *I will/shall have been working, you will have been*
    working etc
simple present *I work, you work, he/she/it works, we work, they work*
present progressive *I am working, you are working* etc
simple present perfect *I have worked, you have worked, he/she/it has worked* etc
present perfect progressive *I have been working, you have been working* etc
simple past *I worked, you worked, he/she/it worked* etc
past progressive *I was working, you were working* etc
simple past perfect *I/you/etc had worked*
past perfect progressive *I/you/etc had been working, you had been working* etc
infinitives *(to) work, (to) be working, (to) have worked, (to) have been working*
-ing forms *working, having worked*
past participle *worked*

Progressive forms are called 'continuous' in some grammars.
Shall is rare in American English (see 221.1).

For more information about the forms and their uses, see the entry for each one.
For question forms, see 461. For negatives, see 358.
For progressive forms, see 450.
For verbs that are not used in progressive forms, see 451.
For perfect forms, see 423.
For 'conditional' forms, see 141 and 260–261.
For irregular verbs, see 300.
For auxiliary verbs, see 84.
For verb forms constructed with modal auxiliary verbs, see 344 and the entry for each modal
    auxiliary.
For passive verb forms, see 407.

11 actual(ly)

1 meaning and use

Actual means 'real'; *actually* means 'really' or 'in fact'.
They can be used to correct mistakes or misunderstandings.
    *The book says she died aged 47, but her **actual** age was 43.*
    *'Hello, John. Nice to see you.' '**Actually**, my name's Andy.'*
They are also used to make things clearer or more precise, or to introduce
unexpected information.
    *I've got a new job. **Actually**, they've made me sales manager.*
    *She was so angry that she **actually** tore up the letter.*
British people often use *actually* to break bad news gently.
    *'How did you get on with my car?' 'Well, **actually**, I'm terribly sorry, I'm*
        afraid I had a crash.'

Actually can suggest either that the hearer's expectations were wrong (see above examples), or that they were correct (especially in British English).
> *'Did you enjoy your holiday?' 'Very much, **actually**.'*

2 'false friends'

Actual and *actually* are 'false friends' for people who speak some languages of European origin. They do not mean the same as *actuel(lement), aktuell, attual(ment)e* etc. We express these ideas with *present, current, up to date; at this moment, now, at present.*
> *What's our **current** financial position?*
> (NOT . . . ~~our **actual** financial position?~~)
> *In 1900 the population of London was higher than it is **now**.*
> (NOT . . . ~~than it **actually** is.~~)

For *actually, in fact, as a matter of fact* and *to tell the truth* as discourse markers, see 159.

12 adjectives: complementation

Many adjectives can be followed by 'complements' – other words and expressions that 'complete' their meaning. Not all adjectives are followed by the same kind of complement. Some can be followed by **preposition + noun/-ing**.
> *I'm **interested in cookery**.*
> *I'm **interested in learning** to cook.*

Some can be followed by infinitives.
> *You don't look **happy to see** me.*
> *The soup is **ready to eat**.*

An infinitive may have its own subject, introduced by *for* (see 280).
> *I'm anxious **for her to get** a good education.*
> (= *I'm anxious that she should get . . .*)

Some adjectives can be followed by clauses.
> *I'm **glad that you were able to come**.*
> *It's **important that everybody should feel comfortable**.*

And many adjectives can have more than one kind of complement.
> *I'm **pleased about** her promotion.*
> *I'm **pleased to see** you here.*
> *I'm **pleased that** we seem to agree.*

We rarely put **adjective + complement** before a noun.
> *He's a **difficult** person **to understand**.*
> (NOT ~~He's a **difficult to understand** person.~~)

For complementation in general, see 140.
For more information about *-ing* forms after adjectives, see 294.
For infinitives after adjectives, see 285.
For *should* in clauses after adjectives, see 497.
For subjunctives in clauses after adjectives, see 541.1.
For the prepositions that are used after some common adjectives, see 437.
For prepositions with clauses after adjectives, see 441.
For structures with 'preparatory it' (e.g. *It is **important that** we move fast, She made **it clear that** she distrusted all of us*), see 301–302.

13 **adjectives ending in -ed**: pronunciation

A few adjectives ending in *-ed* have a special pronunciation: the last syllable is pronounced /ɪd/ instead of /d/ or /t/. They are:

aged /'eɪdʒɪd/ (= *very old*)	*naked* /'neɪkɪd/
beloved /bɪ'lʌvɪd/	*ragged* /'rægɪd/
blessed /'blesɪd/	*rugged* /'rʌgɪd/
crooked /'krʊkɪd/	*sacred* /'seɪkrɪd/
cursed /'kɜːsɪd/	*wicked* /'wɪkɪd/
dogged /'dɒgɪd/	*wretched* /'retʃɪd/
learned /'lɜːnɪd/	*one/three/four-legged* /'legɪd/

Note that *aged* is pronounced /eɪdʒd/ when it means 'years old' (as in *He has a daughter **aged** ten*), or when it is a verb.

Other adjectives ending in *-ed* always have the normal pronunciation, with /ɪd/ only after *d* or *t*.

   tired /taɪəd/   *hunchbacked* /'hʌntʃbækt/   *undecided* /ʌndɪ'saɪdɪd/

14 **adjectives**: order before nouns

When several adjectives come before a noun (or when nouns are used to modify another noun), they usually have to be put in a particular order. For instance, we say *a **fat old** lady*, not ~~an **old fat** lady~~; *a **small shiny black leather** handbag*, not ~~a **leather black shiny small** handbag~~. Unfortunately, the rules for adjective order are very complicated, and different grammars disagree about the details. Here are some of the most important rules:

1 **colour, origin, material and purpose**

Adjectives (or modifying nouns) of **colour**, **origin**, **material** and **purpose** usually go in that order.

	colour	origin	material	purpose	noun
	red	Spanish	leather	riding	boots
a	brown	German		beer	mug
a		Venetian	glass	flower	vase

2 **other adjectives**

Other adjectives usually go before words of colour, origin, material and purpose. It is impossible to give exact rules, but adjectives of **size**, **length** and **height** often come first.

   *the **round glass** table* (NOT ~~the **glass round** table~~)
   *a **big, modern brick** house* (NOT ~~a **modern, big** brick house~~)
   ***long, flexible steel** poles*   *a **tall, ancient** oak-tree*

3 **judgements and attitudes**

Adjectives which express judgements or attitudes usually come before all others. Examples are *lovely, definite, pure, absolute, extreme, perfect, wonderful, silly*.

   *a **lovely, long, cool** drink*   *Who's that **silly fat** man over there?*

4 numbers

Numbers usually go before adjectives.
> *six large* eggs   the *second big* shock

First, next and *last* most often go before *one, two, three* etc.
> the *first three* days (more common than the *three first* days)
> my *last two* jobs

5 commas

Before nouns, we generally use commas between adjectives (especially in longer sequences) which give similar kinds of information, for example in physical descriptions.
> a *lovely, long, cool, refreshing* drink
> an *expensive, ill-planned, wasteful* project

But commas can be dropped before short common adjectives.
> a *tall(,) dark(,) handsome* cowboy

For *and* with adjectives, see 17. For commas with *and*, see 455.1.

15 adjectives: position

1 attributive and predicative position

Most adjectives can go in two main places in a sentence:

before a noun ('attributive position')
> The *new* secretary doesn't like me.
> He's going out with a *rich* businesswoman.

after *be, seem, look, become* and other 'copular' verbs ('predicative position')
> That dress is *new*, isn't it?   She looks *rich*.   I feel *unhappy*.

For adjectives with pronouns (e.g. *Poor you!*), see 424.3.
For details of the verbs that can be followed by adjectives ('copular verbs'), see 147.

2 adjectives used only in attributive position

Some adjectives are used only (or mostly) in attributive position. After a verb, other words must be used. Common examples of such adjectives are:

elder and **eldest** (mainly British English – see 180) Compare:
> My *elder* sister is a pilot.   She's three years *older* than me.

live (meaning 'not dead') Compare:
> a *live* fish   It's still *alive*.

old (referring to relationships that have lasted a long time)
> an *old* friend (not the same as *a friend who is old*)

little (see 511) Compare:
> a nice *little* house   The house is quite *small*.

intensifying (emphasising) adjectives
> He's a *mere* child. (BUT NOT *That child is mere.*)
> It's *sheer* madness. (BUT NOT *That madness is sheer.*)
> You *bloody* fool! (BUT NOT *That fool is bloody.*)

▶

3   adjectives used only in predicative position

Some adjectives beginning with *a-*, and a few others, are used mainly in predicative position – after a verb. Common examples: *afloat, afraid, alight, alike, alive, alone, asleep, awake.* Compare:
- *The baby's* **asleep**.
  a **sleeping** *baby* (NOT *an asleep baby*)
- *The ship's still* **afloat**.
  a **floating** *leaf*
- *He was* **afraid**.
  a **frightened** *man*

The adjectives *ill* and *well* are most common in predicative position. Before a noun, many people prefer other words. Compare:
- *He's very* **well**.
  a **healthy/fit** *man*
- *You look* **ill**.
  Nurses look after **sick** *people.*

For other uses of *well*, see 589.
For more information about *ill* and *sick*, see 266.
For *very* with *afraid*, see 25.3.

4   attributive adjectives after nouns

In older English (see 388), it was quite common to put attributive adjectives after nouns, especially in poetry and songs.
   He came from his palace **grand**.
In modern English, this is only possible in a few cases. It happens in some fixed phrases.

Secretary **General**	*court* **martial** (= *military court*)
Poet **Laureate**	*President* **elect**
God **Almighty!**	*Attorney* **General**

Some adjectives can be used after nouns in a similar way to relative clauses. This is common with adjectives ending in *-able/-ible*.
   Send all the tickets **available**. (= . . .*tickets which are available.*)
   It's the only solution **possible**.
Some adverbs can also be used like this.
   the woman **upstairs**   *the people* **outside**
Before a noun, *present* refers to time; after a noun it means 'here/there', 'not absent'. Compare:
   the **present** *members* (= *those who are members now*)
   the members **present** (= *those who are/were at the meeting*)
Before a noun, *proper* means 'real', 'genuine' (especially GB). After a noun it refers to the central or main part of something. Compare:
   Snowdon's a **proper** *mountain, not a hill.*
   After two days marching through the foothills, they found themselves at the base of the mountain **proper**.

For the position and meaning of *opposite*, see 397.

5   *something, everything* etc

Adjectives come after *something, everything, anything, nothing, somebody, anywhere* and similar words.

>   Have you read **anything interesting** lately?
>   Let's go **somewhere quiet**.

6   **expressions of measurement**

Adjectives come after the measurement noun in most expressions of measurement.

>   two metres **high**
>   two miles **long**
>   ten years **older**
>   six feet **deep**

For word order with *worth*, see 603.

7   **attributive adjectives with complements**

When an adjective has its own complement (e.g. *skilled **at design***), the whole expression normally comes after the noun in attributive position.

>   We are looking for people **skilled at design**.
>   (NOT ... ~~skilled at design people~~.)

A relative clause is often more natural.

>   We are looking for people **who are skilled at design**.

In some cases an adjective can be put before a noun and its complement after it. This happens with *different, similar, the same*; *next, last, first, second* etc; comparatives and superlatives; and a few other adjectives like *difficult* and *easy*.

>   a **different** life **from this one**
>   the **next** house **to the Royal Hotel** (especially GB)
>   the **second** train **from this platform**
>   the **best** mother **in the world**
>   a **difficult** problem **to solve**

8   **verb + object + adjective**

Another possible position for adjectives is after the object, in the structure **verb + object + adjective**.

>   I'll get the car **ready**.
>   Do I make you **happy**?
>   Let's paint the kitchen **yellow**.

For information about noun modifiers (e.g. *a **leather** jacket*), see 378.
For the order of adjectives and other modifiers before nouns, see 14.
For the use of *and* between adjectives, see 17.
For commas between adjectives, see 14.5.

16 **adjectives**: position after **as, how, so, too**

Normally adjectives go after the article *a/an*.
> *a **beautiful** voice*

But after *as, how, so, too* and *this/that* meaning *so*, adjectives go before *a/an*. This structure is common in a formal style.

> *as/how/so/too/this/that* + adjective + *a/an* + noun

> *I have **as good a voice** as you.*
> ***How good a pianist** is he?*
> *It was **so warm a day** that I could hardly work.*
> *She is **too polite a person** to refuse.*
> *I couldn't afford **that big a car**.*

The structure is not possible without *a/an*.
> *I like your country – it's so beautiful.*
> (NOT *I like your ~~so beautiful country~~.*)
> *Those girls are too kind to refuse.* (NOT *~~They are **too kind girls** to refuse.~~*)

For structures with *such* and *what* + adjective + noun, see 543.3, 544.1 and 201.2.
For the structure with adjective + *as* in expressions like *tired as I was...*, see 71.

17 **adjectives** with **and**

When two or more adjectives (or other modifiers) come together, we sometimes put *and* before the last one and sometimes not. It depends partly on their position in the sentence.

1 **after a verb**

When adjectives come in predicative position (after *be, seem* and similar verbs – see 147), we usually put *and* before the last one.
> *He was tall, dark **and** handsome.*
> *You're like a winter's day: short, dark **and** dirty.*

In a very literary style, *and* is sometimes left out.
> *My soul is exotic, mysterious, incomprehensible.*

2 **before a noun**

In attributive position (before a noun), *and* is less common.
> *a tall, dark, handsome cowboy*

However, *and* is possible when the adjectives describe the same kind of thing (for example appearance or character).
> *a cruel (**and**) vicious tyrant*
> *a tall (**and**) elegant lady*

And has to be used when two or more adjectives (or other modifiers) refer to different parts of something.
> *a yellow **and** black sports car*
> *a concrete **and** glass factory*

For more information about the use of *and*, see 51.
For commas with adjectives, see 14.5.

18 adjectives without nouns

We cannot usually leave out a noun after an adjective.

*Poor little **boy!*** (NOT *Poor little!*)
*The most important **thing** is to be happy.*
    (NOT *The most important is to be happy.*)

But there are some exceptions.

1 well-known groups

The + **adjective** is used to talk about certain well-known groups of people, especially those in a particular physical or social condition.

*He's collecting money for **the blind**.*
***The unemployed** are losing hope.*

The meaning is usually general, but occasionally a more limited group is referred to.

*After the accident, **the injured** were taken to hospital.*

The most common expressions of this kind are:

the blind	the old
the dead	the poor
the deaf	the rich
the handicapped	the unemployed
the jobless	the young
the mentally ill	

The above expressions are always plural: *the dead* means 'all dead people' or 'the dead people', but not 'the dead person'.

Note that these expressions cannot be used with a possessive *'s.*

the problems of the poor OR *poor people's problems*
    (NOT *the **poor's** problems*)

Adjectives are not normally used in this way without *the.*

*This government doesn't care about **the poor**.* (NOT *...about **poor**.*)

However, adjectives without *the* are sometimes possible after quantifiers like *many* and *more*, in paired structures with *and* or *or*, and after possessives.

*There are **more unemployed** than ever before.*
*opportunities for **both rich and poor***
*Give me **your tired**, **your poor**, ...*

2 adjectives of nationality

A few adjectives of nationality ending in *-sh* or *-ch* (see 354.3) are used after *the* without nouns. They include *Irish, Welsh, English, British, Spanish, Dutch, French.*

***The Irish** are very proud of their sense of humour.*

These expressions are plural; singular equivalents are for example *an Irishwoman, a Welshman* (NOT *a **Welsh***).

Where nouns exist, these are preferred to expressions with *the ...ish*: we say *the Danes* or *the Turks*, not *the **Danish*** or *the **Turkish***.   ▶

3 singular/plural examples

In a few formal fixed phrases, ***the*** + **adjective** can have a singular meaning. These include *the accused, the undersigned, the deceased, the former* and *the latter.*

    The accused *was released on bail.*

    ... Mr Gray and Mrs Cook; ***the latter*** *is a well-known designer.*

Plural meanings are also possible (e.g. ***The accused were*** *released on bail*).

4 abstract ideas

Adjectives are sometimes used after *the* to refer to general abstract ideas, especially in certain kinds of philosophical writing. (Examples: *the beautiful, the supernatural, the unreal.*) These expressions are singular.

    She's interested in ***the supernatural****.*

5 leaving out nouns

We often leave out a noun that has already been mentioned, or which does not need to be mentioned, when thinking about a choice between two or more different kinds of thing.

    'Have you got any bread?' 'Do you want ***white*** *or* ***brown?****'*

    I'd like two three-hour video-cassettes and one ***four-hour****.*

Superlatives are often used in this way.

    I'm the ***tallest*** *in my family.*

    We bought the ***cheapest****.*

Colour adjectives can sometimes have a plural *-s* in this situation.

    Wash the ***reds*** *and* ***blues*** *separately.* (= *red and blue clothes*)

For other cases where nouns are left out after adjectives and determiners, see 184.

19 adverb particles

1 adverb particles and prepositions

Words like *down, in, up* are not always prepositions. Compare:

  – *I ran* ***down*** *the road.*
    Please sit ***down****.*
  – *He's* ***in*** *his office.*
    You can go ***in****.*
  – *Something's climbing* ***up*** *my leg.*
    She's not ***up*** *yet.*

In the expressions *down the road, in his office* and *up my leg*, the words *down, in* and *up* are prepositions: they have objects (*the road, his office* and *my leg*).

In *sit down, go in* and *She's not up*, the words *down, in* and *up* have no objects. They are adverbs, not prepositions.

Small adverbs like these are usually called 'adverb(ial) particles'. They include *above, about, across, ahead, along, (a)round, aside, away, back, before, behind, below, by, down, forward, in, home, near, off, on, out, over, past, through, under, up.* Many words of this kind can be used as both adverb particles and prepositions, but there are some exceptions: for example *back, away* (only adverb particles); *from, during* (only prepositions).

2 phrasal verbs

Adverb particles often join together with verbs to make two-word verbs, sometimes with completely new meanings (e.g. *break down, put off, work out, give up*). These are often called 'phrasal verbs'.

Note that, unlike most other adverbs, adverb particles can come just before the object of a verb (if the object is a noun – see 582.3).
> *Could you switch **off** the light?*

For details of phrasal and prepositional verbs, see 582.
For information about the position of adverbs, see 22–23.

3 adverb particles with *be*

Adverb particles are often used, rather like adjectives, as complements of the verb *be*.
> *Why **are** all the lights **on**?*
> *Hello! You**'re back**!*
> *The match **will be over** by 4.30.*

For inverted word order in sentences beginning with an adverb particle (e.g. *Out walked Sarah*), see 299.

20 adverbs of manner and adjectives

1 adverbs of manner with verbs

Adverbs of manner say **how something happens or is done**.
Examples: *quickly, happily, terribly, fast, badly, well.*
These adverbs should not be confused with adjectives (*happy, quick* etc).
We use adverbs, not adjectives, to modify verbs.

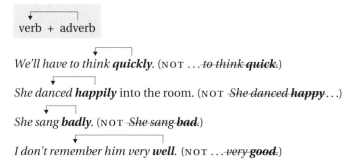

verb + adverb

*We'll have to think **quickly**.* (NOT *...to think **quick**.*)

*She danced **happily** into the room.* (NOT *She danced **happy**...*)

*She sang **badly**.* (NOT *She sang **bad**.*)

*I don't remember him very **well**.* (NOT *...very **good**.*)

▶

But note that adjective forms are sometimes used as adverbs in an informal style, especially in American English (see 21).

> *She talks **funny**.*

For the use of adjectives after copular verbs like *look* or *seem*, see 147.

2 other uses

These adverbs can also modify adjectives, past participles, other adverbs and adverbial phrases.

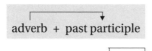

*It's **terribly** cold today.* (NOT ... *terrible cold.*)

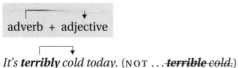

*This steak is very **badly** cooked.* (NOT ... *bad cooked.*)

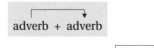

*They're playing **unusually** fast.* (NOT ... *unusual fast.*)

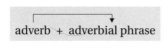

*He was **madly** in love with her.* (NOT ... *mad...*)

For adjectives ending in -*ly,* see the next section.
For adverbs and adjectives with the same form, see the next section.
For the adjective *well,* see 589.
For the position of adverbs of manner, see 23.6, 23.10, 23.14.
For spelling rules, see 530.

21 adverbs or adjectives? confusing cases

1 adjectives ending in -*ly*

Some words ending in -*ly* are adjectives, and not normally adverbs.
Common examples: *costly, cowardly, deadly, friendly, likely, lively, lonely, lovely, silly, ugly, unlikely.*

> *She gave me a **friendly** smile.*
> *Her singing was **lovely**.*

There are no adverbs *friendly/friendlily, lovely/lovelily* etc.

> *She smiled **in a friendly way**.* (NOT *She smiled friendly.*)
> *He gave **a silly laugh**.* (NOT *He laughed silly.*)

Daily, weekly, monthly, yearly, early and *leisurely* are both adjectives and adverbs.

> *It's a **daily** paper.   It comes out **daily**.*
> *an **early** train   I got up **early**.*

2   adjectives and adverbs with the same form; adverbs with two forms

Some adjectives and adverbs have the same form: for example, a *fast* car goes *fast*; if you do *hard* work, you work *hard*. In other cases, the adverb may have two forms (e.g. *late* and *lately*), one like the adjective and the other with *-ly*. There is usually a difference of meaning or use. Some examples follow; for more detailed information, check in a good dictionary.

bloody Some swearwords (see 550), including *bloody* (GB only), can be used both as adjectives and as adverbs.

> *'You **bloody** fool. You didn't look where you were going.' 'I **bloody** did.'*

clean The adverb *clean* means 'completely' before *forget* (informal) and some expressions of movement.

> *Sorry I didn't turn up – I **clean forgot**.*
> *The explosion blew the cooker **clean through the wall**.*

dead The adverb *dead* is used in certain expressions to mean 'exactly', 'completely' or 'very'. Examples:

> ***dead** ahead, **dead** certain, **dead** drunk, **dead** right, **dead** slow* (GB only),
> ***dead** straight, **dead** sure, **dead** tired*

Note that *deadly* is an adjective, meaning 'fatal', 'causing death'. The adverb for this meaning is *fatally*. Compare:

> *Cyanide is a **deadly** poison.*
> *She was **fatally** injured in the crash.*

direct *Direct* is often used as an adverb in British English, referring to journeys and timetables.

> *The plane goes **direct** from London to Houston without stopping.*

easy *Easy* is used as an adverb in some informal expressions.

> *Take it **easy**! (= Relax!)   **Easier** said than done.*
> *Go **easy**! (= Not too fast!)   **Easy** come, **easy** go.*

fair *Fair* is used as an adverb after a verb in some expressions.

> *to play **fair**   to fight **fair**   to hit something **fair** and square*

For the adverb of degree *fairly*, see 205.

fast *Fast* can mean both 'quick' and 'quickly' (a *fast* car goes *fast*). *Fast* means 'completely' in the expression *fast asleep*, and it means 'tight', 'impossible to remove' in expressions like *hold fast, stick fast, fast colours*.

fine The adverb *fine* (= 'well') is used in some informal expressions.

> *That suits me **fine**.   You're doing **fine**.*

The adverb *finely* is used to talk about small careful adjustments and similar ideas.

> *a **finely** tuned engine   **finely** chopped onions (= 'cut up very small')*   ▶

flat *Flat* can be used as an adverb in a musical sense (*to sing flat* means 'to sing on a note that is too low'). In most other cases, the adverb is *flatly*.

free The adverb *free* (used after a verb) means 'without payment'; *freely* means 'without limit or restriction'. Compare:
> *You can eat free in my restaurant whenever you like.*
> *You can speak freely – I won't tell anyone what you say.*

hard The adverb *hard* has a similar meaning to the adjective.
> *Hit it hard.*   *Don't work too hard.*
Hardly means 'almost not'.
> *I've hardly got any clean clothes left.*
For the use of *hardly ... when* in clauses of time, see 237.

high *High* refers to height; *highly* expresses an extreme degree (it often means 'very much'). Compare:
– *He can jump really high.*
> *Throw it as high as you can.*
– *It's highly amusing.*
> *I can highly recommend it.*

just *Just* is an adverb with several meanings (see 305). There is also an adjective *just*, meaning 'in accordance with justice or the law'; the adverb is *justly*.
> *He was justly punished for his crimes.*

late The adverb *late* has a similar meaning to the adjective *late*; *lately* means 'recently'. Compare:
> *I hate arriving late.*   *I haven't been to the theatre much lately.*

loud *Loud* is often used informally as an adverb after a verb.
> *Don't talk so loud – you'll wake the whole street.*

low *Low* is an adjective and adverb (*a low bridge, a low voice, bend low*).

most *Most* is the superlative of *much*, and is used to form superlative adjectives and adverbs (see 136).
> *Which part of the concert did you like most?*
> *This is the most extraordinary day of my life.*
In a formal style, *most* can be used to mean 'very' (see 153).
> *You're a most unusual person.*
Mostly means 'mainly', 'most often' or 'in most cases'.
> *My friends are mostly non-smokers.*

pretty The informal adverb of degree *pretty* is similar to *rather* (see 205, 468). *Prettily* means 'in a pretty way'. Compare:
> *I'm getting pretty fed up.*   *Isn't your little girl dressed prettily?*

quick In an informal style, *quick* is often used instead of *quickly*, especially after verbs of movement.
> *I'll get back as quick as I can.*

real In informal American English, *real* is often used instead of *really* before adjectives and adverbs.
> *That was real nice.*   *He cooks real well.*

right *Right* with adverb phrases means 'just', 'exactly' or (GB only) 'all the way'.
>*She arrived **right** after breakfast.*
>*The snowball hit me **right** on the nose.*
>*Turn the gas **right** down.* (GB)

Right and *rightly* can both be used to mean 'correctly'. *Right* is only used after verbs, and is usually informal. Compare:
>*I **rightly** assumed that Henry was not coming.*
>*You guessed **right**.*   *It serves you **right**.* (. . .~~rightly~~ is not possible.)

sharp *Sharp* can be used as an adverb to mean 'punctually'.
>*Can you be there at six o'clock **sharp**?*

It also has a musical sense (*to sing sharp* means 'to sing on a note that is too high'), and is used in the expressions *turn **sharp** left* and *turn **sharp** right* (meaning 'with a big change of direction').
In other senses the adverb is *sharply*.
>*She looked at him **sharply**.*   *I thought you spoke to her rather **sharply**.*

short *Short* is used as an adverb in the expressions *stop **short*** (= 'stop suddenly') and *cut **short*** (= 'interrupt'). *Shortly* means 'soon'; it can also describe an impatient way of speaking.

slow *Slow* is used as an adverb in road signs (e.g. *SLOW – DANGEROUS BEND*), and informally after *go* and some other verbs (especially in American English). Examples: *go **slow**, drive **slow**.*

sound *Sound* is used as an adverb in the expression *sound **asleep**.* In other cases, *soundly* is used (e.g. *She's sleeping **soundly***).

straight The adverb and the adjective are the same. A *straight* road goes *straight* from one place to another.

sure *Sure* is often used to mean 'certainly' in an informal style, especially in American English.
>*'Can I borrow your tennis racket?' '**Sure**.'*

Surely (not) usually expresses surprise (see 548 for details).
>***Surely** you're not going out in that old coat?*

tight After a verb, *tight* can be used instead of *tightly*, especially in an informal style. Typical expressions: *hold **tight**, packed **tight*** (compare ***tightly** packed*).

well *Well* is an adverb corresponding to the adjective *good* (a *good* singer sings *well*). *Well* is also an adjective meaning 'in good health' (the opposite of *ill*). For details, see 589.

wide The normal adverb is *wide*; *widely* suggests distance or separation. Compare:
>*The door was **wide** open.*   *She's travelled **widely**.*
>*They have **widely** differing opinions.*

Note also the expression *wide awake* (the opposite of *fast asleep*).

wrong *Wrong* can be used informally instead of *wrongly* after a verb. Compare:
>*I **wrongly** believed that you wanted to help me.*   *You guessed **wrong**.*   ▶

3 comparatives and superlatives

Informal uses of adjective forms as adverbs are especially common with comparatives and superlatives.

*Can you drive a bit **slower**?*
*Let's see who can do it **quickest**.*

4 American English

In informal American English, many other adjective forms can also be used as adverbs of manner.

*Drive **friendly**.*
*He looked at me real **strange**.*

22 adverbs: position (general)

Different kinds of adverbs go in different positions in a clause. Here are some general rules; for more details, see 23.

Note: in the following explanations, the word *adverb* is generally used both for one-word adverbs (e.g. *here, often*) and for longer adverb phrases (e.g. *in this house, once every six weeks*).

1 verb and object

We do not usually put adverbs between a verb and its object.

> ...adverb + verb + object

*I **often** get headaches.* (NOT *I get **often** headaches.*)

> ...verb + object + adverb

*She speaks English **well**.* (NOT *She speaks **well** English.*)
But an adverb particle (see 19, 582) can go between a verb and a noun object.
*Could you switch **off** the light?*

2 initial, mid- and end position

There are three normal positions for adverbs:

initial position (at the beginning of a clause)

> ***Yesterday morning** something very strange happened.*

mid-position (with the verb)

(For exact position, see 23.10–13.)

> *My brother **completely** forgot my birthday.*
> *I have **never** understood her.*

end position (at the end of a clause)

*What are you doing **tomorrow**?*
Many adverbs can go in all three of these positions, and some others can go in both mid- and end position. Longer adverb phrases cannot usually go in mid-position. Compare:

*He **quickly** got dressed.   He got dressed **quickly**.*

(*Quickly* can go in mid- or end position.)

*He got dressed **in a hurry**.* (NOT *He **in a hurry** got dressed.*)

(*In a hurry* cannot go in mid-position.)

However, a few very common short adverb phrases like *at once* can go in mid-position; and adverbs of degree like *very, quite* can be added to mid-position adverbs.

*She **at once** realised her mistake.*
*I **very much** enjoy skiing.*
*We were **quite often** invited to parties at the weekends.*

3   **What goes where?**

initial position

Connecting adverbs (which join a clause to what came before).
Time adverbs can also go here (see 23.8).

***However**, not everybody agreed.* (connecting adverb)

***Tomorrow** I've got a meeting in Cardiff.* (time adverb)

Some negative adverbial expressions (e.g. *under no circumstances*) can go in initial position with 'inverted' word order (see 298.5).

***Under no circumstances are children** allowed in the bar.*

mid-position

Focusing adverbs (which emphasise one part of the clause); adverbs of certainty and completeness; adverbs of indefinite frequency; comment adverbs; some adverbs of manner (see 23.6).

*She's done everything – she's **even** been a soldier.* (focusing)

*It will **probably** rain this evening.* (certainty)

*I've **almost** finished painting the house.* (completeness)

*My boss **often** travels to America.* (indefinite frequency)

*I **stupidly** forgot my keys.* (comment)

*She **quickly** got dressed.* (manner)

end position

Adverbs of manner (how), place (where) and time (when) most often go in end position. (For details, see 23.7, 23.8, 23.14.)

*She brushed her hair **slowly**.* (manner)

*The children are playing **upstairs**.* (place)

*I phoned Alex **this morning**.* (time)

23 **adverbs**: position (details)

(It is best to read section 22 before studying this.)

1 connecting adverbs

These adverbs **join** a clause to what came before.
Examples: *however, then, next, besides, anyway*
Position: beginning of clause
> *Some of us want a new system;* **however**, *not everybody agrees.*
> *I worked until five o'clock.* **Then** *I went home.*
> **Next**, *I want to say something about the future.*

Mid-position is often possible in a more formal style.
> *I* **then** *went home.*

2 indefinite frequency

These adverbs say **how often** something happens.
Examples: *always, ever, usually, normally, often, frequently, sometimes, occasionally, rarely, seldom, never.*
Position: mid-position (after auxiliary verbs and *am/are/is/was/were*; before other verbs – see paragraph 10 for more details).

> auxiliary verb + adverb

> *I* **have never** *seen a whale.*
> *You* **can always** *come and stay with us if you want to.*
> **Have** *you* **ever** *played American football?*

> *am/are/is/was/were* + adverb

> *My boss* **is often** *bad-tempered.*
> **I'm seldom** *late for work.*

> adverb + other verb

> *We* **usually go** *to Scotland in August.*
> *It* **sometimes gets** *very windy here.*

When there are two auxiliary verbs, these adverbs usually come after the first.
> *We* **have never been** *invited to one of their parties.*
> *She* **must sometimes have** *wanted to run away.*

Usually, normally, often, frequently, sometimes and *occasionally* can also go at the beginning or end of a clause. *Always, ever, rarely, seldom* and *never* cannot normally go in these positions.
> **Sometimes** *I think I'd like to live somewhere else.*
> **Usually** *I get up early.*
> BUT NOT ~~Always I get up early~~; ~~Never I get up early.~~
> *I go there* **occasionally**.
> *I go there* **quite often**. (BUT NOT ~~I go there always.~~)

However, *always* and *never* can begin imperative clauses.
> **Always** *look in the mirror before starting to drive.*
> **Never** *ask her about her marriage.*

For adverbs of definite frequency (e.g. *daily, weekly*), see paragraph 8 below.
For inversion after *rarely, seldom* and *never,* see 298.5.

3   focusing adverbs

These adverbs '**point to**' one part of a clause.
Examples: *also* (see 45–46), *just* (see 305), *even* (see 195), *only* (see 394), *mainly, mostly, either* (see 179), *or, neither* (see 364), *nor* (see 364).
Position: mid-position (see paragraph 10 for more details). They can also go in other places in a clause, directly before the words they modify.

auxiliary verb + adverb

*He's been everywhere – he's **even** been to Antarctica.*
***We're only** going for two days.*

am/are/is/was/were + adverb

*She's my teacher, but she**'s also** my friend.*
*The people at the meeting **were mainly** scientists.*

adverb + other verb

*Your bicycle **just needs** some oil – that's all.*
*She **neither said** thank-you **nor looked** at me.*

adverb directly before word(s) modified

***Only you** could do a thing like that.*
*I feel **really tired.***
*He always wears a coat, **even in summer**.*

Too and *as well* are focusing adverbs that usually go in end position (see 45).
Either goes in end position after *not* (see 364).

4   adverbs of certainty

We use these adverbs to say **how sure** we are of something.
Examples: *certainly, definitely, clearly, obviously, probably.*
Position: mid-position (see paragraph 10 for more details).

auxiliary verb + adverb

*It will **probably** rain this evening.*
*The train **has obviously** been delayed.*

am/are/is/was/were + adverb

*There is **clearly** something wrong.*
*She **is definitely** older than him.*

adverb + other verb

*He **probably thinks** you don't like him.*
*I **certainly feel** better today.*

Maybe and *perhaps* usually come at the beginning of a clause.
***Perhaps** her train is late.*
***Maybe** I'm right and **maybe** I'm wrong.*

▶

5   adverbs of completeness

These adverbs say **how completely** something happens or is true.
Examples: *completely, practically, almost, nearly, quite, rather, partly, sort of, kind of, more or less, hardly, scarcely.*
Position: mid-position (see paragraph 10 for more details).

> auxiliary verb + adverb

I **have completely** forgotten your name.   Sally **can practically** read.

> am/are/is/was/were + adverb

It **was almost** dark.   The house **is partly** ready.

> adverb + other verb

I **kind of hope** she wins.   It **hardly matters**.

6   adverbs of manner; comment adverbs

Adverbs of manner say **how** something happens or is done.
Examples: *angrily, happily, fast, slowly, suddenly, well, badly, nicely, noisily, quietly, hard, softly.*
Position: most often at the end of a clause, especially if the adverb is important to the meaning of the verb and cannot be left out (see paragraph 14). Adverbs in *-ly* can go in mid-position if the adverb is not the main focus of the message (for details of the exact position, see paragraph 10).

> end position

He drove off **angrily**.   You speak English **well**.
She read the letter **slowly**.

> mid-position

She **angrily** tore up the letter.   I **slowly** began to feel better again.

Mid-position is especially common with passive verbs.
Her books **are** always **well written**.
(BUT NOT ~~She always **well writes** her books.~~)
Comment adverbs (which give the speaker's opinion of an action) most often go in mid-position.
I **stupidly** forgot my keys.

For more information about adverbs of manner, see 20–21.

7   adverbs of place

These adverbs say **where** something happens.
Examples: *upstairs, around, here, to bed, in London, out of the window.*
Position: at the end of a clause.
The children are playing **upstairs**.   Come and sit **here**.
Don't throw orange peel **out of the window**.
She's sitting **at the end of the garden**.
Initial position is also possible, especially in literary writing and if the adverb is not the main focus of the message.
At the end of the garden there was a very tall tree.

Adverbs of direction (movement) come before adverbs of position.
  *The children are running **around upstairs**.*
Here and *there* often begin clauses. Note the word order in *Here/There is, Here comes* and *There goes*.

> *Here/There* + verb + subject

  Here comes your bus. (NOT *Here your bus comes.*)
  There's *Alice.*   ***There goes*** *our train!*
Pronoun subjects come directly after *here* and *there*.
  Here *it comes.* (NOT *Here comes it.*)   ***There*** *she is.* (NOT *There is she.*)

8 adverbs of time and definite frequency

These adverbs say **when** or **how often** something happens.
Examples: *today, afterwards, in June, last year, finally, before, eventually, already, soon, still, last, daily, weekly, every year.*
Position: mostly in end position; initial position is also common if the adverb is not the main focus of the message. Some can go in mid-position (see below). Adverbs of indefinite frequency (*often, ever* etc) go in mid-position (see paragraph 2).
  *I'm going to London **today**. / **Today** I'm going to London.*
  *She has a new hair style **every week**. / **Every week** she has a new hair style.*
Finally, eventually, already, soon and *last* can also go in mid-position; *still* and *just* only go in mid-position.
  *So you **finally** got here.*   *When did you **last** see your father?*
  *I've **already** paid the bill.*   *I **still** love you.*
  *We'll **soon** be home.*   *She's **just** gone out.*

9 emphasising adverbs

These adverbs modify particular words or expressions in a clause, and go just before them.
Examples: *very, extremely, terribly, just, almost, really, right.*
  *I'll see you in the pub **just before** eight o'clock.*
  *She walked **right past** me.*   *We all thought she sang **very well**.*

10 mid-position: detailed rules

Mid-position adverbs usually go after auxiliary verbs, after *am/are/is/ was/were*, and before other verbs.
  *She **has never** written to me.*   *The discussion **was mainly** about money.*
  *It **certainly looks** like rain.*
When there are two or more auxiliaries, the adverb usually goes after the first.
  *You **have definitely been** working too hard.*
  *She **would never have been promoted** if she hadn't changed jobs.*
But other positions are possible, especially when the first part of the verb phrase is a modal auxiliary (see 344), *used to* or *have to*.
  *They **sometimes must** be bored.* (OR *They **must sometimes** be bored.*)
  *She **could have easily been** killed.* (OR *She **could easily have been** killed.*)
  *We **always used** to go to the seaside in May.* (OR *We **used always to go** . . .*
    OR *We **used to always** go . . .*)

▶

When adverbs of completeness or manner go in mid-position, they are normally put after all auxiliary verbs.

> I **will have completely** finished by next June.
> Do you think the repair **has been properly** done?
> When I saw her, she **was being well** looked after.
> This time next week I'll **be happily** working in my garden.

When an auxiliary verb is used alone instead of a complete verb phrase (see 185), a mid-position adverb comes before it.

> 'Are you happy?' 'I **certainly am**.'
> I don't trust politicians. I **never have**, and **I never will**.

11 mid-position adverbs with negative verbs

In negative sentences, adverbs generally come before *not* if they emphasise the negative; otherwise they come after. Compare:

> I **certainly do not** agree.
> I **do not often** have headaches.

Both positions are possible with some adverbs, often with a difference of meaning. Compare:

> I **don't really** like her. (mild dislike)
> I **really don't** like her. (strong dislike)

When adverbs come before *not*, they may also come before the first auxiliary verb; they always come before *do*.

> I **probably will** not be there. (OR I **will probably not** be there.)
> He **probably does** not know. (NOT ~~He **does probably not** know.~~)

Only one position is possible before a contracted negative.

> I **probably won't** be there.

12 mid-position adverbs with emphatic verbs

When we emphasise auxiliary verbs or *am/are/is/was/were*, we put most mid-position adverbs before them instead of after. Compare:

> – She **has certainly made** him angry.
>   She **certainly HAS made** him angry!
> – I'm **really** sorry.
>   I **really AM** sorry.
> – 'Polite people **always say** thank-you.'
>   'Yes, well, I **always DO** say thank-you.'

13 mid-position in American English

In American English (see 50), mid-position adverbs are often put before auxiliary verbs and *am/are/is/was/were*, even when the verb is not emphasised. Compare:

> He **probably has** arrived by now. (US normal, GB emphatic)
> He **has probably** arrived by now. (GB normal)

As an extreme example, here are four sentences in a journalistic style taken from an American newspaper article on crime in Britain. The most normal British equivalents are given in brackets.

> – 'Britain **long has** been known as a land of law and order.'
>   (GB Britain **has long** been known …)

– '... but it **probably will** lead to a vote ...'
(GB ... but it **will probably** lead ...'
– '... the Labor Party **often has** criticized police actions.'
(GB ... the Labour Party **has often** criticised ...)
– '... he **ultimately was** responsible for the treatment ...'
(GB ... he **was ultimately** responsible ...)

14 end position: detailed rules

Some sentences are incomplete without adverb complements. For example,
a sentence with *put, go* or *last* may not make sense unless one says **where**
something is put, **where** somebody goes or **how long** something lasts. To say
how well somebody does something, one is likely to need an adverb of
manner. These 'essential complements' usually go in end position, and
before other adverbs.
*Put the butter **in the fridge** at once.* (NOT ... ~~at once **in the fridge**.~~)
*Let's go **to bed** early.* (NOT ... ~~early **to bed**.~~)
*His speech lasted **about three hours**.*   *You sang **very well** last night.*
Except for essential complements, adverbs in end position usually come in
the order **manner, place, time**.
*I worked **hard yesterday**.*
*She sang **beautifully in the town hall last night**.*

24 affect and effect

Affect is a verb. It means 'cause a change in' or 'influence'.
*The cold weather **affected** everybody's work.*
Effect is usually a noun meaning 'result' or 'change'. The expression *have an
effect on* is similar to *affect*. Compare:
*The war seriously **affected** petrol prices.*
*The war **had** a serious **effect** on petrol prices.*
In a formal style, *effect* can also be used as a verb, meaning 'carry out', 'cause
to happen'.
*We did not **effect** much improvement in sales last year.*

For more information about these words, see a good dictionary.

25 afraid

1 *afraid* and *fear*

In an informal style, *be afraid* is more common than *fear*.
*Don't **be afraid**.* (NOT ~~Don't fear.~~)   *Are you **afraid of** the dark?*
*She's **afraid that** I might find out.*

2 *I'm afraid* = 'I'm sorry'

I'm afraid (that) often means 'I'm sorry to tell you (that)'. It is used to
introduce apologetic refusals and bad news.
***I'm afraid (that)** I can't help you.*
***I'm afraid that** there's been an accident.*

▶

I'm afraid so/not are used as 'short answers' (see 493).
> '*Can you lend me a pound?*' ***I'm afraid not.***
> '*It's going to rain.*' '*Yes,* ***I'm afraid so.***'

3 not used before a noun

Afraid is one of the adjectives that are not usually used before a noun in 'attributive position' (see 15). Compare:
> *John's* ***afraid.***
> *John's a* ***frightened*** *man.* (NOT ...*an afraid man.*)

We often use *very much* instead of *very* before *afraid*, especially when *I'm afraid* means 'I'm sorry to tell you'.
> *I'm* ***very much afraid*** *he's out.*

For information about -*ing* forms and infinitives after *afraid*, see 296.13.

26 **after** (adverb)

1 *after* in adverb phrases

After is often used in adverb phrases like *shortly after, long after, a week after, a few days after* etc.
> *We had oysters for supper.* ***Shortly after,*** *I began to feel ill.*
> *They started the job on 17 June and finished* ***a week after.***

2 *after* not used alone

After is not normally used alone as an adverb. Instead, we use other expressions like *afterwards, then* or *after that*.
> *I'm going to do my exams, and* ***afterwards*** *I'm going to study medicine.* (NOT ...*and* ***after, I'm going***...)

For *after* (conjunction), see 27.
For *after* and *according to*, see 8.

27 **after** (conjunction)

> clause + *after* + clause
> *after* + clause, + clause

1 use and position

The conjunction *after* joins one clause to another. *After* and its clause can come either after or before the other clause.
> – *I went to America* ***after I left school.***
> ***After I left school,*** *I went to America.*
> > (In both cases the speaker left school first and then went to America. Note the comma in the second structure.)
> – *He did military service* ***after he went to university.***
> > (He went to university first.)
> ***After he did military service,*** *he went to university.*
> > (He did military service first.)

2 present with future meaning

In a clause with *after*, we use a present tense if the meaning of the clause is future (see 556).

> *I'll telephone you **after I arrive**.* (NOT ...~~after I will arrive.~~)

3 perfect tenses

In clauses with *after*, we often use present and past perfect tenses to show that one thing is completed before another starts.

> *I'll telephone you **after I've seen** Jake.*
> ***After I had finished school**, I went to America.*

4 *after...ing*

In a formal style, we often use the structure ***after + -ing. After having + past participle** is also possible, especially when talking about the past.

> ***After completing** this form, give it to the secretary.*
> (More natural than ***After having completed**...*)
> *He wrote his first book **after returning / having returned** from Mongolia.*

For *after* (adverb), see 26.

28 after all

1 two meanings

After all can mean 'in spite of what was said before' or 'contrary to what was expected'. Position: usually at the end of a clause.

> *I'm sorry. I can't come **after all**.*
> *I expected to fail the exam, but I passed **after all**.*

Another meaning is 'we mustn't forget that ...', introducing an important argument or reason which may have been forgotten. Position: at the beginning or end of a clause.

> *I think we should let Sylvia go camping with her boyfriend. **After all**, she's a big girl now.*
> *Of course you're tired. **After all**, you were up all night.*
> *Let's finish the cake. Somebody's got to eat it, **after all**.*

2 not used for 'finally'

After all does NOT mean 'finally', 'at last', 'in the end'.

> *After the theatre we had supper and went to a night club; then we **finally** went home.* (NOT ...~~after all we went home.~~)

29 afternoon, evening and night

1 *afternoon* and *evening*

In most people's speech, *afternoon* starts after lunch and changes to *evening* after work (or after normal working hours).

▶

2 *evening* and *night*

Evening changes to *night* more or less at bedtime. But note that
Good evening usually has the sense of 'Hello' and *Good night* of 'Goodbye' –
Good night is not used to greet people.
>A: **Good evening**. *Terrible weather, isn't it?*
>B: *Yes, dreadful.*
>A: *Hasn't stopped raining for weeks. Well, I must be going.* **Good night**.
>B: **Good night**.

30 age

1 use of *be*

We most often talk about people's ages with ***be* + number**.
>*He **is** thirty.* (NOT ~~*He **has** thirty.*~~)

or ***be* + number + *years old*** (more formal *... of age*).
>*He **is** thirty **years old** / **of age*** (NOT *...thirty **years**.*)

We ask *How old are you?*, not normally *What is your age?*

2 *be* + ... *age*

Note the structure ***be* + ... *age*** (without a preposition).
>*When I **was your age** I was working.* (NOT ~~*When I was **at your age**...*~~)
>*The two boys **are the same age**.*
>*She's **the same age** as me.*

3 prepositions

In other structures, *at* is common before *age*.
>*He could read **at** the age of three.* (NOT *...~~in the age~~...*)

31 ago

1 position

>| expression of time + *ago* |
>| :--- |

>*I met her **six weeks ago**.* (NOT *...~~ago six weeks.~~*)
>***a long time ago***

2 tenses

An expression with *ago* refers to a finished time, and is normally used with a
past tense, not a present perfect (see 418.7).
>*She **phoned** a few minutes ago.* (NOT ~~*She **has phoned**...*~~)
>*'Where's Mike?' 'He **was working** outside ten minutes ago.'*

However, a present perfect tense is used with *since ... ago* (as with *since* +
any other time expression).
>*We've **been living** here since about eight years ago.*
>*I **haven't bought** any since a week ago.*

3   the difference between *ago* and *for*

Ago says **how long before the present something happened**; *for* (with a past tense) says **how long it lasted**. Compare:

> *He died **three years ago**.* (= three years before now)
> (N O T ~~*He died for three years.*~~ O R *...~~for three years ago.~~*)
> *He was ill **for three years** before he died.* (= His illness lasted three years.)

4   the difference between *ago* and *before*

counting back

Ago is used with a past tense and a time expression to 'count back' from the present; to say **how long before the present** something happened. *Before* is used in the same way (with a past perfect tense) to count back from a past moment (see also 95). Compare:

> *I **met** that woman in Scotland **three years ago**.*
> (N O T *...~~three years before / before three years.~~*)
> *When we got talking, I found out that I **had been** at school with her husband **ten years before**.* (N O T *...~~ten years ago.~~*)

'at any time before now / then'

We can also use *before*, with a present or past perfect tense and no time expression, to mean 'at any time before now / then' (see 95.2).

> *'**Have** you **been** here **before**?' 'Yes, I was here a year ago.'*
> *As soon as I saw her I knew that I **had met** her **before**.*

For other uses of *before*, see 96–97.

32   alike

Alike means 'like each other'. Compare:

> *The two boys are **alike** in looks, but not in personality.*
> *He's **like** his brother.* (N O T ~~*He's alike his brother.*~~)

Alike is mainly used in predicative position (see 15). Compare:

> *His two daughters are very much **alike**.*
> *He's got two very **similar-looking** daughters.* (N O T *...**~~alike daughters.~~***)

For *like*, see 320.

33   **all** (1): introduction

1   three or more items

All refers to three or more items. Compare:

> *I'll take **all** three shirts, please.*
> *I'll take **both** shirts.* (N O T *...**~~all two shirts.~~***)

▶

2 subject, object or complement

All can be the subject, object or complement of a sentence.
> **All** *that matters is to be happy.*   *I gave her **all** she asked for.*
> *That's **all**.*

For more detailed rules, see 34.

3 *all* with nouns and pronouns

All can modify a noun or pronoun. Two positions are possible:
with the noun or pronoun:
> **All (of) the people** *were singing.*   *I haven't read **all of it**.*
> *Give my love to **them all**.*
with the verb:
> *The people **were all singing**.*

For more detailed rules, see 35.

4 *all* with adjectives, adverbs etc

All can be used to emphasise some adjectives, adverbs, prepositions and
conjunctions.
> *You're **all wet**.*   *I was **all alone**.*
> *I looked **all round**, but I couldn't see anything.*
> *Tell me **all about** your holiday.*   *It's **all because** of you.*
For more examples, see a good dictionary.

All, both and *half* follow similar grammar rules. For *both*, see 109–110; for *half*, see 235.
For *all but*, see 116.1.

34 all (2): subject, object or complement; all, everybody and everything

1 *all* and *everybody*

We do not normally use *all* to mean 'everybody'. Compare:
> **All the people** *stood up.*   **Everybody** *stood up.* (NOT ~~All stood up.~~)

2 *all* and *everything*

All can mean 'everything', but usually only in the structure ***all* + relative
clause** (*all that . . .*). Compare:
– **All (that) I have** *is yours.*
  Everything *is yours.* (NOT ~~All is yours.~~)
– *She lost **all she owned**.*
  *She lost **everything**.* (NOT ~~She lost all.~~)
This structure often has a rather negative meaning, expressing ideas like
'nothing more' or 'the only thing(s)'.
> *This is **all I've got**.*
> **All I want** *is a place to sit down.*
> **All that happened** *was that he went to sleep.*
Note also *That's all* (= 'It's finished'; 'There's no more').

3 older English

In older English, *all* could be used alone to mean 'everybody' or 'everything' (e.g. *Tell me **all**; **All** is lost; **All** are dead*). This only happens regularly in modern English in dramatic contexts like newspaper headlines (e.g. SPY TELLS *ALL*).

35 all (3): all (of) with nouns and pronouns

1 *all* and *all of*

All (of) can modify nouns and pronouns.

Before a noun with a determiner (for example *the, my, this*), *all* and *all of* are both possible. American English usually has *all of*.
   *She's eaten **all (of) the cake**.   **All (of) my friends** like riding.*
Before a noun with no determiner, we do not normally use *of*.
   ***All children** can be difficult*. (NOT ~~*All of children*~~...)

For more about *of* in noun phrases, see 157.4.

2 *all of* + personal pronoun

With personal pronouns, we use ***all of*** + object form.
All of us/you/them can be the subject or object of a clause.
   ***All of us** can come tomorrow*. (NOT ~~*All we*~~...)
   *She's invited **all of you**.   Mary sent **all of them** her love.*

3 pronoun + *all*

We can put *all* after pronouns used as objects.
   *She's invited **you all**.*
   *Mary sent her love to **them all**.*
   *I've made **us all** something to eat.*
This does not happen with complement pronouns or in short answers.
   *Is that **all of them**?* (NOT ~~*Is that them all?*~~)
   *'Who did you invite?' '**All of them**.'* (NOT ~~*'Them all.'*~~)
All can follow a subject pronoun (e.g. ***They all** went home*), but in this case it belongs grammatically with the verb (see 36) and may be separated from the pronoun (e.g. ***They have all** gone home*).

For the American plural pronoun *you all*, see 424.2.

4 types of noun

All is used mostly before uncountable and plural nouns.
   all the water   all my friends
However, *all* can be used before some singular countable nouns referring to things that can naturally be divided into parts.
   all that week   all my family   all the way
With other singular countable nouns, it is more natural to use *whole* (e.g. *the **whole** story*). For details, see 38.

For the difference between *all* and *every*, see 37.   ▶

5   negative verbs

It is not very common to use **all** + **noun** as the subject of a negative verb
(e.g. *All Americans don't like* hamburgers). We more often use **not all** +
noun + **affirmative verb**.

   Not all Americans like hamburgers.

Note the difference between *not all* and *no*. Compare:

   Not all birds can fly.   *No* birds can play chess.

6   leaving out *the*

It is sometimes possible to drop *the* after *all* (e.g. *all day, all three brothers*).
See 69.6 for details.

36   all (4): with verbs

When *all* refers to the subject of a clause, it can go with the verb, in 'mid-
position' (like some adverbs – see 15).

> auxiliary verb + *all*
> *am/are/is/was/were* + *all*

We **can all** *swim.*
The guests **have all** *arrived.*
Those apples **were all** *bad.*

> *all* + other verb

My family **all work** *in education.*
They **all liked** *the soup.*

Note that these meanings can also be expressed by using **all (of)** +
noun/pronoun as the subject (see 35).

All of us can swim.   *All (of) the guests have arrived.*

37   all and every

All and *every* can both be used to talk about people or things in general, or
about all the members of a group. There is little difference of meaning; *every*
often suggests 'without exception'. The two words are used in different
structures.

1   *every* with singular nouns; *all* with plurals

Every is used with a singular noun. To give the same meaning, *all* is used
with a plural noun. Compare:

–   *every* + singular

   Every child needs love. (NOT *All child needs love.*)
   Every light was out.

–   *all* + plural

   All children need love.
   All the lights were out.

2 *all* with determiners

We can use *all*, but not normally *every*, with certain determiners (articles, possessives or demonstratives). Compare:

– *all* + determiner + plural

   All the lights *were out.*
   I've written to **all my friends.**

– *every* + singular

   Every light *was out.* (NOT ~~*The every light*...~~)
   I've written to **every friend I have.**
      (NOT ~~*every my friend / my every friend.*~~)

3 *all* with uncountables

We can use *all*, but not *every*, with uncountable nouns.
   I like **all music.** (NOT ...~~*every music.*~~)

4 *all* = 'every part of'

We can use *all* with place names and some singular countable nouns to mean 'every part of', 'the whole of'.
   All London *was talking about her affairs.*
   I've been round **all the village** *looking for the cat.*
Note the difference between *all day/week* etc and *every day/week* etc.
   She was here **all day.** (= from morning to night)
   She was here **every day.** (Monday, Tuesday, Wednesday, ...)

For the difference between *all* and *whole,* see 38.
For detailed rules for the use of *all,* see 33–36.
For the difference between *every* and *each,* see 174.

38 **all** and **whole**

1 pronunciation

   all /ɔːl/   *whole* /həʊl/

2 word order

All (of) and *whole* can both be used with singular nouns to mean 'complete', 'every part of'. The word order is different.

   determiner + *whole* + noun
   all (of) + determiner + noun

– *Julie spent* **the whole week** *at home.*
   Julie spent **all (of) the week** *at home.*
– **my whole** *life*
   all (of) my *life*

3 indefinite reference

All is not generally used before indefinite articles.
   She's eaten **a whole** *loaf.* (NOT ...~~*all a loaf.*~~)

▶

4   uncountable nouns

With most uncountable nouns we prefer *all (of)*.
> *I've drunk **all (of) the milk**.* (NOT ...~~the whole milk~~.)

5   *the whole of*

Instead of *whole* we can generally use *the whole of.*
> *Julie spent **the whole of** the summer at home.*
> ***the whole of** my life*
Before proper nouns (names) and pronouns we always use *the whole of,* not
whole. All (of) is also possible.
> ***The whole of / All of** Venice was under water.* (NOT ~~Whole Venice~~...)
> *I've just read **the whole of / all of** 'War and Peace'.*
> *I've read **the whole of / all of** it.*

6   plural nouns

With plural nouns, *all* and *whole* have different meanings. *All* is like *every*;
whole means 'complete', 'entire'. Compare:
> ***All Indian tribes** suffered from white settlement in America.*
> (= ***Every Indian tribe** suffered ...*)
> ***Whole Indian tribes** were killed off.*
> (= ***Complete tribes** were killed off; nobody was left alive in these tribes.*)

39   all right and alright

The standard spelling is *all right. Alright* is common, but many people
consider it incorrect.

40   allow, permit and let

1   *allow* and *permit*

These words have similar meanings and uses. *Permit* is more formal.
Both words can be followed by **object + infinitive**.
> *We do not **allow/permit people to smoke** in the kitchen.*
When there is no personal object, an *-ing* form is used.
> *We do not **allow/permit smoking** in the kitchen.*
Passive structures are common; personal subjects and gerund (*-ing* form)
subjects are both possible.
> ***People are not allowed/permitted** to smoke in the kitchen.*
> ***Smoking is not allowed/permitted** in the kitchen.*
The passive structure with *it* is only possible with *permit.*
> ***It is not permitted** to smoke in the kitchen.*
> (BUT NOT ~~It is not allowed to smoke~~...)
Allow, but not *permit,* can be used with adverb particles.
> *She wouldn't **allow** me **in**.*
> *Mary isn't **allowed out** at night.*

2 *let*

Let is the least formal of these three words, and is followed by **object + infinitive without** *to*. Compare:

> *Please **allow me to buy** you a drink.* (polite and formal)
> ***Let me buy** you a drink.* (friendly and informal)

Let is not usually used in the passive.

> *I **wasn't allowed** to pay for the drinks.* (NOT ~~I wasn't let~~ ...)

Let can be used with adverb particles; passives are possible.

> *She wouldn't **let** me **in**.*
> *I've been **let down**.*

For more about *let*, see 315–316.

41 **almost** and **nearly**

1 meaning: progress, measurement and counting

Almost and *nearly* can both express ideas connected with progress, measurement or counting. *Nearly* is less common in American English.

> *I've **almost/nearly** finished.*
> *There were **almost/nearly** a thousand people there.*

Sometimes *almost* is a little 'nearer' than *nearly*. Compare:

> *It's **nearly** ten o'clock.* (= perhaps 9.45)
> *It's **almost** ten o'clock.* (= perhaps 9.57)

Very and *pretty* can be used with *nearly* but not *almost*.

> *I've **very/pretty nearly** finished.* (NOT ... ~~very almost~~ ...)

2 other ideas

Nearly mostly suggests progress towards a goal or closeness to a figure. We prefer *almost* for other ideas like 'similar to, but not exactly the same', and to make statements less definite.

> *Jake is **almost** like a father to me.*
> *Our cat understands everything – he's **almost** human.*
> (NOT ... ~~he's nearly human.~~)
> *My aunt's got a strange accent. She **almost** sounds foreign.*
> (NOT ... ~~She nearly sounds foreign.~~)
> *I **almost** wish I'd stayed at home.* (NOT ~~I nearly wish~~ ...)

3 negative words

We do not usually use *nearly* before negative or non-assertive words: *never, nobody, nothing, any* etc. Instead, we use *almost*, or we use *hardly* with *ever, anybody, anything* etc (see 374.2).

> *She's **almost never** / **hardly ever** at home.* (NOT ... ~~nearly never~~ ...)
> ***Almost nobody** / **hardly anybody** was there.*
> *He eats **almost anything**.*

42 alone, lonely, lonesome and lone

Alone suggests that a person or thing is separate – there are no others around. *Lonely* (and informal US *lonesome*) refers to unhappiness caused by being alone. Compare:

*I like to be **alone** for short periods.*
*But after a few days I start getting **lonely/lonesome**.*

Alone can be emphasised by *all*.

*After her husband died, she was **all alone**.*

Alone is not used before a noun (see 15.3). *Lone* and *solitary* can be used instead; *lone* is rather literary.

*The only green thing was a **lone/solitary** pine tree.*

43 along

The preposition *along* is used with nouns like *road, river, corridor, line*: words that refer to things with a long thin shape.

*I saw her running **along the road**.*
*His office is **along** the corridor.*

To talk about periods or activities, we prefer *through*.

through *the centuries* (NOT ~~**along** the centuries~~)
*all **through** the journey* (NOT ~~all **along** the journey~~)
*right **through** the meal*

Note the special use of *along* as an adverb particle in expressions like *Come **along*** (= 'Come with me') or *walking **along*** (= 'walking on one's way').

44 already and all ready

Already is an adverb of time, meaning 'by now', 'sooner than expected'.
All ready simply means the same as *all + ready*. Compare:

*'When's Jane coming?' 'She's **already** arrived.'*
*'Are you **all ready**?' 'No, Pete isn't.'*

For more about *already*, see 539.

45 also, as well and too

1 position

Also, as well and *too* have similar meanings, but they do not go in the same position in clauses. *Also* usually goes with the verb, in 'mid-position' (see 23.3); *as well* and *too* usually go at the end of a clause. *As well* is less common in American English.

*She not only sings; she **also** plays the piano.*
*She not only sings; she plays the piano **as well**.*
*She not only sings; she plays the piano **too**.*

2 reference

These words can refer to different parts of a clause, depending on the meaning. Consider the sentence *We have meetings on Sundays **as well***. This can mean three different things:

a *(Other people have meetings on Sundays, and)* ***we*** *have meetings on Sundays **as well***.

b *(We do other things on Sundays, and)* *we **have meetings** on Sundays **as well***.

c *(We have meetings on other days, and)* *we have meetings **on Sundays as well***.

When we speak, we show the exact meaning by stressing the word or expression that *also/as well/too* refers to.

3 imperatives and short answers

As well and *too* are used in imperatives and 'short answers', but not usually *also*.

Give me some bread ***as well***, please. (More natural than ***Also** give me ...*)
'She's nice.' 'Her sister is ***as well***.' (More natural than 'Her sister is ***also***.')
'I've got a headache.' 'I have ***too***.' (More natural than 'I ***also** have*.')

In very informal speech, we often use *Me too* as a short answer.
'I'm going home.' '***Me too***.'

More formal equivalents are *So am I* or *I am too*, but not ~~I also~~.

4 *also* referring to a whole clause

Also can be used at the beginning of a clause to refer to the whole clause.
It's a nice house, but it's very small. ***Also***, it needs a lot of repairs.

5 *too* in a formal style

In a formal or literary style, *too* can be placed directly after the subject.
I, ***too***, have experienced despair.

For *also, as well, too* and *either* in negative clauses, see 46.
For *also* and *even*, see 195.3.
For *as well as*, see 77.

46 also, as well, too and either in negative clauses

1 negative + negative: *either*

After mentioning a negative idea or fact, we can add another negative point by using *not ... either*. *Also*, *as well* and *too* are not normally used with *not* in this way.

Peter ***isn't*** here today. John ***isn't*** here ***either***.
    (NOT ~~John isn't here also.~~)
I know you ***don't*** like me. I ***don't*** like you ***either***.
    (NOT ~~I don't like you too.~~) ▶

2 affirmative + negative: *also/as well/too*

After mentioning an affirmative (non-negative) fact or idea, we can add a related negative idea by using *not ... also, not ... as well* or *not ... too*.

> He **smokes** too much, but at least he **doesn't also drink** too much.
> That day, for the first time since her husband **had died** a year before, she was glad that she **had not died as well**.
> You **can have** an apple, but you **can't have** an orange **too**.

47 alternate(ly) and alternative(ly)

Alternate(ly) means 'every second', 'first one and then the other', 'in turns'.

> We spend **alternate** weekends at our country cottage.
> I'm **alternately** happy and depressed.

Alternative(ly) is similar to 'different', 'instead', 'on the other hand'.

> Janet's not free on the 27th. We'll have to find an **alternative** date for the meeting.
> You could go by air, or **alternatively** you could drive there.

48 although and though

(al)though + clause, + clause
clause, + (al)though + clause
clause + though

1 conjunctions

Both these words can be used as conjunctions, with the same meaning. In informal speech, *though* is more common.

> **(Al)though** the government refuses to admit it, its economic policy is in ruins.
> **(Al)though** I don't agree with him, I think he's honest.
> I'd quite like to go out, **(al)though** it is a bit late.

We use *even though* to emphasise a contrast. (*Even although* is not possible.)

> **Even though** I didn't understand a word, I kept smiling.

2 *though* used as an adverb

We can use *though* as an adverb, to mean 'however'.

> 'Nice day.' 'Yes. Bit cold, **though**.'
> The strongest argument, **though**, is economic and not political.

For the difference between *even* and *even though*, see 195.4.
For *even though* and *even so*, see 195.4–5.
For *as though*, see 74.
For sentences like *Cold though it was, I went out*, see 71.

49 altogether and all together

Altogether means 'completely' or 'everything considered'.

> My new house isn't **altogether** finished.
> **Altogether**, she decided, marriage was a bit of a mistake.

Altogether can also be used to give totals.
> *That's £4.38 **altogether**.*
> *I'd like three dozen **altogether**.*
All together usually means 'everybody / everything together'.
> *Come on, everybody sing. **All together** now. . .*
> *Put the plates **all together** in the sink.*
> *They **all** went to the cinema **together**.*

50 American and British English

These two varieties of English are very similar. There are a few differences of grammar and spelling, and rather more differences of vocabulary and idiom. Modern British English is heavily influenced by American English, so some of the contrasts are disappearing. Pronunciation is sometimes very different, but most American and British speakers can understand each other without great difficulty.

1 grammar

Here are examples of the most important differences. Note that in many cases, two different forms are possible in one variety of English, while only one of the forms is possible or normal in the other variety. For more details, look up the sections in other parts of the book where these structures are discussed.

American English	**British English**

*He just **went** home.*
  OR *He's just **gone** home.*
	*He's just **gone** home.*
	  (See 419.5, 305.2.)

***Do you have** a problem?* OR ***Have you got** a problem?*	***Have you got** a problem?* (See 241.6.)
*I've never really **gotten** to know her.*	*I've never really **got** to know her.* (See 228.7.)
*I **(can)** see a car coming.*	*I **can see** a car coming.* (See 125.1.)
*Her feet were sore because her shoes **fit** badly.*	*Her feet were sore because her shoes **fitted** badly.* (See 300.3.)
*It's important that he **be** told.*	*It's important that he **should be** told.* (See 541.)
*'Will you buy it?' 'I **may**.'*	*. . . 'I **may (do)**.'* (See 165.)
*The committee **meets** tomorrow.*	*The committee **meet/meets** tomorrow.* (See 503.1.)
(on the phone) *Hello, is **this** Susan?*	*Hello, is **that** Susan?* (See 565.5.)
*It looks **like** it's going to rain.*	*It looks **as if / like** it's going to rain.* (See 74.3.)

*He looked at me **real strange**.*
  (very informal) OR *He looked at me **really strangely**.*
	*He looked at me **really strangely**.*
	  (See 21.)

▶

American English	British English
*One should get to know **his** neighbours.* (formal)	*One should get to know **one's** neighbours.* (formal) (See 392.6.)
*He **probably has** arrived by now.* OR *He **has probably** arrived . . .*	*He **has probably** arrived by now.* (See 23.13.)

Besides *get* and *fit*, some other irregular verbs have different forms in British and American English. For details, see 300.3.

For the Southern US second person plural pronoun *you all*, see 424.2.

2   vocabulary

There are very many differences. Sometimes the same word has different meanings (GB *mad* = 'crazy'; US *mad* = 'angry'). And very often, different words are used for the same idea (GB *lorry* = US *truck*). Here are a few examples, with very brief information about the words and their meanings. (For a larger list with more complete information, see *The British/American Dictionary* by Norman Moss, published by Hutchinson.)

American English	British English
airplane	aeroplane
anyplace, anywhere	anywhere
apartment	flat / apartment
area code	dialling code (*phone*)
attorney, lawyer	barrister, solicitor
busy	engaged (*phone*)
cab / taxi	taxi
call collect	reverse the charges (*phone*)
can	tin
candy	sweets
check / bill	bill (*in a restaurant*)
coin-purse	purse
cookie, cracker	biscuit
corn	sweet corn, maize
crib	cot
crazy	mad
cuffs	turn-ups (*on trousers*)
diaper	nappy
doctor's office	doctor's surgery
dumb, stupid	stupid
elevator	lift
eraser	rubber, eraser
fall, autumn	autumn
faucet, tap	tap (*indoors*)
first floor, second floor etc	ground floor, first floor etc
flashlight	torch
flat (tire)	flat tyre, puncture
french fries	chips

American English	British English
garbage, trash	rubbish
garbage can, trashcan	dustbin, rubbish bin
gas(oline)	petrol
gear shift	gear lever (*on a car*)
highway, freeway	main road, motorway
hood	bonnet (*on a car*)
intersection	crossroads
mad	angry
mail	post
mean	nasty
movie, film	film
one-way (ticket)	single (ticket)
pants, trousers	trousers
pavement	road surface
pitcher	jug
pocketbook, purse, handbag	handbag
(potato) chips	crisps
railroad	railway
raise	rise (*in salary*)
rest room	public toilet
round trip	return (journey/ticket)
schedule, timetable	timetable
sidewalk	pavement
sneakers	trainers (= *sports shoes*)
spigot, faucet	tap (*outdoors*)
stand in line	queue
stingy	mean (*opposite of 'generous'*)
store, shop	shop
subway	underground
truck	van, lorry
trunk	boot (*of a car*)
two weeks	fortnight, two weeks
vacation	holiday(s)
windshield	windscreen (*on a car*)
zee	zed (*the name of the letter 'z'*)
zipper	zip

Expressions with prepositions and particles

American English	British English
different **from/than**	different **from/to** (see 158)
check something (**out**)	check something
do something **over/again**	do something **again**
live **on** X street	live **in** X street
on a team	**in** a team
Monday **through/to** Friday	Monday **to** Friday

►

3   spelling

A number of words end in *-or* in American English and *-our* in British English (e.g. *color/colour*). Some words end in *-er* in American English and *-re* in British English (e.g. *center/centre*). Many verbs which end in *-ize* in American English (e.g. *realize*) can be spelt in British English with *-ize* or *-ise* (see 531). Some of the commonest words with different forms are:

American English	**British English**
aluminum	aluminium
analyze	analyse
catalog(ue)	catalogue
center	centre
check	cheque (*issued by a bank*)
color	colour
defense	defence
honor	honour
jewelry	jewellery
labor	labour
pajamas	pyjamas
paralyze	paralyse
practice, practise	practise (*verb*)
program	programme
realize	realise / realize
theater	theatre
tire	tyre (*on a wheel*)
trave(l)ler	traveller (*see 535*)
whiskey	(Scotch) whisky; (Irish) whiskey

4   pronunciation

There are, of course, many different regional accents in both Britain and America. The most important general differences between American and British speech are as follows:

a   Certain vowels are nasal (pronounced through the nose and mouth at the same time) in some varieties of American English, but not in most British accents.

b   British English has one more vowel than American English. This is the rounded short *o* (/ɒ/) used in words like *cot, dog, got, gone, off, stop, lost.* In American English these words are pronounced either with /ɑ/, like the first vowel in *father*, or with /ɔ:/, like the vowel in *caught.* (This vowel is also pronounced rather differently in British and American English.)

c   Some words written with *a* + **consonant** (e.g. *fast, after*) have different pronunciations: with /ɑ:/ in standard southern British English, and with /æ/ in American and some other varieties of English.

d   The vowel in *home, go, open* is pronounced /əʊ/ in standard southern British English, and /oʊ/ in American English. The two vowels sound very different.

e   In standard southern British English, *r* is only pronounced before a vowel sound. In most kinds of American English, *r* is pronounced in all positions where it is written in a word, and it changes the quality of a vowel that comes before it. So words like *car, turn, offer* sound very different in British and American speech.

f   In many varieties of American English, *t* and *d* both have a very light voiced pronunciation /d/ between vowels – so *writer* and *rider*, for example, can sound the same. In British English they are quite different: /ˈraɪtə(r)/ and /ˈraɪdə(r)/.

g   Some words which are pronounced with /uː/ in most varieties of American English have /juː/ in British English. These are words in which *th, d, t* or *n* (and sometimes *s* or *l*) are followed by *u* or *ew.*

    enthusiastic US /ɪnˈθuːziˈæstɪk/ GB /ɪnˈθjuːziˈæstɪk/
    duty US /ˈduːti/ GB /ˈdjuːti/
    tune US /tuːn/ GB /tjuːn/
    new US /nuː/ GB /njuː/
    illuminate US /ɪˈluːmɪneɪt/ GB /ɪˈljuːmɪneɪt/

h   Words ending in unstressed *-ile* (e.g. *fertile, reptile, missile, senile*) are pronounced with /aɪl/ in British English; some are pronounced with /l/ in American English.

    fertile US /ˈfɜːrtl/ (rhyming with *turtle*)
    GB /ˈfɜːtaɪl/ (rhyming with *her tile*)

i   Some long words ending in *-ary, -ery* or *-ory* are pronounced differently, with one more syllable in American English.

    secretary US /ˈsekrəteri/ GB /ˈsekrətri/

j   *Borough* and *thorough* are pronounced differently.

    US /ˈbʌroʊ, ˈθʌroʊ/ GB /ˈbʌrə, ˈθʌrə/

k   Words borrowed from French are often stressed differently, especially if their pronunciation ends with a vowel sound. The final vowel is usually stressed in American English but not in British English.

    paté US /pæˈteɪ/ GB /ˈpæteɪ/
    ballet US /bæˈleɪ/ GB /ˈbæleɪ/

51 and

1 use

When we join two or more grammatically similar expressions, we usually put *and* before the last.

    bread **and** cheese
    We drank, talked **and** danced.
    I wrote the letters, Peter addressed them, George bought the stamps **and** Alice posted them.

And is sometimes left out in a very literary or poetic style, but this is unusual.

    My dreams are full of darkness, despair, death.

For rules about the use of commas, see 455.1, 5.

2 fixed expressions

Some common expressions with *and* have a fixed order which cannot be changed. The shortest expression often comes first.

bread and butter (NOT ~~butter and bread~~)
hands and knees (NOT ~~knees and hands~~)
young and pretty   *thunder and lightning*
black and white   *cup and saucer*
knife and fork

3 adjectives before a noun

We do not usually use *and* with adjectives (or other modifiers) before a noun (see 17.2).

*Thanks for your **nice long** letter.* (NOT *... **nice and long** letter.*)
*a **tall, dark, handsome** cowboy*   ***cheap wooden garden** furniture*

However, *and* is used in certain cases, for example when the modifiers refer to different parts of the same thing.

***red and yellow** socks*   *a **metal and glass** table*

We also use *and* when we say that something belongs to two or more different classes.

*It's a **social and political** problem.*   *She's a **musical and artistic** genius.*

And is common, too, when we are 'piling up' favourable or unfavourable descriptions.

*You're a **good and generous** person.*
*She's an **intelligent and strong-minded** woman.*
*It's an **ill-planned, expensive and wasteful** project.*

4 *nice and*

In an informal style, the expression *nice and* is often used before another adjective or an adverb. It means something like 'pleasantly' or 'suitably'.

*It's **nice and warm** in front of the fire.* (= pleasantly warm)
*The work was **nice and easy**.*
*Now just put your gun down **nice and slow**.*

5 meanings

When two clauses are joined by *and*, there are many possible relationships between them – for example time, cause and effect, contrast, condition.

*I lay down **and** went straight to sleep.* (time)
*She won the prize **and** astonished them all.* (cause and effect)
*She's a bank manager **and** I'm just a road-sweeper.* (contrast)
*Do that again **and** I'll hit you.* (condition: = If you do that again ...)

Note: *and* is usually pronounced /ən(d)/, not /ænd/ (see 588).
For ellipsis after *and*, in expressions like *the bread and (the) butter*, see 182.
For singular and plural verbs after subjects with *and*, see 504.5.
For *and* after *try, wait, go, come* etc, see 52.
For *both ... and*, see 111.

52 **and** after **try, wait, go** etc

1 *try/be sure/wait and ...*

We often use *try and ...* instead of *try/be sure to ...* This is informal.
> ***Try and** eat something – you'll feel better if you do.*
> *I'll **try and** phone you tomorrow morning.*
> ***Be sure and** ask Uncle Joe about his garden.*

We only use this structure with the simple base forms *try/be sure*. It is not possible with *tries, tried, trying* or *am/are/is/was/were sure*. Compare:
> ***Try and** eat something.*
> *I **tried to** eat something.* (NOT ~~I tried and ate something.~~)

Note also the common expression *Wait and see*.
> *'What's for lunch?' '**Wait and see**.'*

2 *come/go/etc and ...*

Come and ..., *go and ...*, *run and ...*, *hurry up and ...*, *stay and ...* are often used informally with similar meanings to infinitive structures.
> ***Come and** have a drink.*
> ***Stay and** have dinner.*
> ***Hurry up and** open the door.*

With these verbs, the structure is not only used with the base form.
> *He often **comes and spends** the evening with us.*
> *She **stayed and played** with the children.*
> *She thought of **going and getting** him.*

3 **American English**

In informal American English, *and* is sometimes dropped after the base forms *go* and *come*.
> *Let's **go see** if Anne's home.*
> ***Go jump** in the river.*
> ***Come sit** on my lap.*

53 **another** and **other(s)**

1 **spelling of *another***

Another is one word.
> *He's bought **another** car.* (NOT ~~...an other car.~~)

2 'additional, extra'

Another can mean 'an additional, extra'. It is used with singular countable nouns.
> *Could I have **another** piece of bread?*

Another can be used as a pronoun without a noun, or with *one*, if the meaning is clear from what has come before.
> *Those cakes are wonderful. Could I have **another (one)**?*

With uncountable and plural nouns, we normally use *more*, not *other*.
> *Would you like some **more** meat?* (NOT ~~...other meat?~~)
> *Would you like some **more** peas?* (NOT ~~...other peas?~~)

▶

However, we can use *another* before a plural noun in expressions with *few* or a number.

*I'm staying for **another few weeks**.*   *We need **another three chairs**.*

For other cases where *a(n)* is followed by a plural, see 509.6.

3 'alternative'

(An)other can also mean '(an) alternative', 'besides this / these'.
*I think we should paint it **another** colour.*
*Have you got any **other** cakes, or are these the only ones?*
Other people often means 'people besides oneself'.
*Why don't you think more about **other** people?*

4 *other* and *others*

When *other* is used with a noun it has no plural form.
*Where are the **other** photos?* (NOT *...~~the **others** photos?~~*)
But used alone, without a noun, it can have a plural form.
*I've got one lot of photos. Where are **the others**?*
*These are too small. Have you got any **others**?*
Normally, *other(s)* is only used alone if it refers to a noun that has been mentioned before. An exception is the common plural use of *(the) others* to mean *(the) other people*.
*He never thinks of **others**.*   *Jake's arrived – I must tell **the others**.*
BUT NOT ~~*On the telephone, one cannot see **the other***~~ OR
~~*He never listens to **another***~~.

5 not used to mean 'different'

Other is not used as an adjective to mean 'different'.
*I'd prefer a completely **different** colour.*
(NOT *...~~a completely **other** colour.~~*)
*It would print better on **different paper**.* (NOT *...~~other paper.~~*)
*You look **different** with a beard.* (NOT *~~You look **other**~~...*)

For *one another*, see 175.

54 any

1 the meaning of *any*

Any is a determiner (see 157). It generally suggests an indefinite amount or number, and is used when it is not important to say how much / many we are thinking of. Because of its 'open', non-specific meaning, *any* is often used in questions and negative clauses, and in other cases where there is an idea of doubt or negation.

*Have you got **any** beer?*
*We didn't have **any** trouble going through customs.*
*You never give me **any** help.*
*The noise of the party stopped me getting **any** sleep.*
*I suddenly realised I'd come out without **any** money.*

Any is common after *if*.
>*If you find **any** blackberries, keep some for me.*

Sometimes *any* means 'if there is / are any' or 'whatever there is / are'.
>***Any** fog will clear by noon.* (= ***If there is any** fog, it will clear by noon.*)
>*Perhaps you could correct **any** mistakes I've made.*

Any can be used to emphasise the idea of open choice: 'it doesn't matter who / what / which'. For details, see paragraph 6 below.
>*You can borrow **any** book you like.*

2   *any* and *some*

Any often contrasts with *some*, which is most common in affirmative clauses. Compare:
>*I need **some** razor blades.*
>*Have you got **any** razor blades?*
>*Sorry, I haven't got **any** razor blades.*

For details, see 522.

3   *any, not any* and *no*

Any alone does not have a negative meaning. It is only negative when used with *not*.
>*She's unhappy because she has**n't** got **any** friends.*
>   (NOT *... because she **has** got **any** friends.*)

No (see 369) means the same as *not any*, but is more emphatic.
>*She's got **no** friends.*

Not any cannot begin a sentence; *no* is used instead.
>***No** cigarette is harmless.* (NOT *Not any cigarette...*)
>***No** tourists came to the town that year.*

For more details, see 369.

4   *any* and *a/an*

Any is very often used with uncountable and plural nouns. It can have the same kind of meaning as the indefinite article *a/an* has with singular countable nouns (see 66.1a).
>*I haven't got **a** car, and I haven't got **any** money to buy one.*
>*Is there **a** tin-opener in the house? And are there **any** plates?*

With this meaning *any* is unusual with singular countable nouns.
>*She hasn't got **a** job.* (NOT *She hasn't got **any** job.*)
>*Do you know **a** good doctor?* (NOT *Do you know **any** good doctor?*)

Note that the fixed expressions *any idea* and *any difference* are used as if the nouns were uncountable (see 148.5).
>*Have you got **any idea** what she wants?*
>*Is there **any difference** between 'close' and 'shut'?*

For the use of *any* meaning 'it doesn't matter who / what / which' with singular countable nouns, see paragraph 6 below.   ▶

5   *any* and no article

With an uncountable or plural noun, *any* usually suggests the idea of an indefinite amount or indefinite number. When there is no idea of quantity or number, we generally use **no article**. For details, see 67. Compare:
– *Is there **any water** in that can?*
  *Is there **water** on the moon?*
       (The interest is in the existence of water, not its amount.)
– *Dad hasn't got **any hair**.* (He has lost the amount he had.)
  *Birds have feathers, not **hair**.* (No idea of amount.)

6   *any* = 'it doesn't matter who/which/what'

Any can be used to emphasise the idea of free choice, with the meaning of 'it doesn't matter who/which/what'. With this meaning, *any* is common in affirmative clauses as well as questions and negatives, and is often used with singular countable nouns as well as uncountables and plurals. In speech, it is stressed.
  *Ask **any** doctor – they'll all tell you that alcohol is a poison.*
  *She goes out with **any** boy who asks her.*
  *'When shall I come?' '**Any** time.'*
  *Can I get a meal here at **any** time of the day?*
  *I don't do just **any** work – I choose jobs that interest me.*
Note that we use *either* (see 178), not *any*, to talk about a choice between two alternatives.
  *I can write with **either** hand.* (NOT ...~~any hand.~~)

7   *any* and *any of*; *any* as a pronoun

Before a determiner (definite article, demonstrative or possessive word) or a pronoun, we use *any of* (see 157.4). Compare:
– *I didn't go to **any** lectures last term.* (NOT ...~~any of lectures~~...)
  *I wasn't interested in **any of the** lectures.* (NOT ...~~any the lectures.~~)
– *Do **any** books here belong to you?*
  *Do **any of these** books belong to you?*
– *I don't think **any staff** want to work tomorrow.*
  *I don't think **any of us** want to work tomorrow.*
Note that when *any of* is followed by a plural subject, the verb can be singular or plural. A singular verb is more common in a formal style.
  *If **any of your friends is/are** interested, let me know.*
A noun can be dropped after *any*, if the meaning is clear.
  *'Did you get the oil?' 'No, there wasn't **any** left.'*
Instead of *not any*, *none* (see 368) can be used. This is often more emphatic.
  *There was **none** left.*

8   *at all*

At all (see 82) is often used to emphasise the meaning of *(not) any*.
  *I'll do **any** job **at all** – even road-sweeping.*
  *Do you play **any** games **at all**?*
  *She does**n't** speak **any** English **at all**.*
  *Is there **any** difference **at all** between 'begin' and 'start'?*

9 compounds

Many of the rules given above also apply to the compounds *anybody*, *anyone*, *anything* and *anywhere*. For more information about these, see 523.

For the use of *any* and *no* as adverbs, see 56.
For *any . . . but*, see 116.
For *any* and *every*, see 55.
For *some*, see 521–522.
For *any more/longer*, see 372.

55 **any** and **every**

Any and *every* can both be used to talk in general about all the members of a class or group.

   Any/Every *child can learn to swim.*

The meaning is not quite the same. *Any* looks at things one at a time: it means 'whichever one you choose', 'this or that or the other'. *Every* looks at things together: its meaning is closer to 'all', 'this and that and the other'. Compare:

   *'Which newspaper would you like?' 'It doesn't matter. **Any** one.'*
      (= 'one or another or another') (N O T *. . . Every one.*)
   *On the stand there were newspapers and magazines of **every** kind.*
      (= 'one and another and another') (N O T *. . . magazines of any kind.*)

For more information about *any*, see 54.
For *every*, see 199.

56 **any** and **no**: adverbs

> *any/no* + comparative
> *any/no different*
> *any/no good/use*

1 *any* and *no* with comparatives

Any can modify comparatives. This can happen in questions and negative sentences, and after *if* (see also 374.2).

   *Can you go **any faster**?*
   *You don't look **any older** than your daughter.*
      (= *You don't look at all older . . .*)
   *If I were **any younger**, I'd fall in love with you.*

No can also be used in this way (but not *some*).

   *I'm afraid the weather's **no better** than yesterday.*

2 *any/no different*

We can also use *any* and *no* with *different*.

   *This school isn't **any different** from the last one.*
   *'Is John any better?' '**No different**. Still very ill.'*

▶

3 *any/no good; any/no use*

Note the expressions *any good/use* and *no good/use*.
> *Was the film **any good**?*
> *This watch is **no use**. It keeps stopping.*

57 any more

In British English, *any more* is usually written as two separate words. In American English, it is often written as one word *anymore* when it refers to time (= 'any longer'). It usually comes in end position.
> *She doesn't work in New York **anymore**.*
> (NOT *She doesn't **any more** work in New York.*)

58 appear

1 copular verb: 'seem'

Appear can be a copular verb (see 147), used to say how things look (like *seem*). It is used in similar ways to *seem*: see 490 for details.
> *He **appears** (to be) very **angry** today.* (NOT *He **appears** very **angrily** today.*)
> *It **appears** to be some kind of bomb.*
> *She **appears** to have enough money to live on.*
> *They do not **appear** to be at home.* `
> *It **appears** that we may be mistaken.*
> *There **appears** to be a problem with the oil pressure.*

2 *appear* and *seem*: differences

Seem can be used to talk both about objective facts and about subjective impressions and feelings (see 490 for examples). *Appear* is mostly used to talk about objective facts. Compare:
> *The baby **seems/appears** (to be) hungry.*
> *She doesn't want to go on studying. It **seems** a pity.* (NOT *It **appears** a pity.*)
Seem is often used with *like*. This is not normal with *appear*.
> *It **seemed like** a good idea.*
> (More natural than *It **appeared like** a good idea.*)
Seem can be used in a special structure with *can't* (see 490.4). This is not possible with *appear*.
> *I **can't seem** to make him understand.*
> (BUT NOT *I **can't appear** to make him understand.*)
Appear is also rather more formal than *seem*.

3 'come into sight'

Appear can also mean 'come into sight' or 'arrive'. In this case it can be modified by an adverb.
> *She **suddenly appeared** in the doorway.*

For *appear* with introductory *there*, see 563.5.

59   arise and rise

Arise means 'begin', 'appear', 'come to one's notice'. It is used mostly with abstract nouns as subjects.

> *A discussion **arose** about the best way to pay.*
> *I'm afraid a difficulty has **arisen**.*

Rise usually means 'get higher', 'come / go up'.

> *Prices keep **rising**.*
> *What time does the sun **rise**?*
> *My hopes are **rising**.*

Note that we usually say that people *get up* in the morning. *Rise* is only used with this meaning in a very formal style.

Arise and *rise* are irregular verbs.

> *(a)rise – (a)rose – (a)risen*

For the difference between *rise* and *raise,* see 300.2.
For *arouse* and *rouse,* see 61.

60   (a)round and about

1   circular movement etc

In British English, we usually use *round* for movement or position in a circle or a curve.

> *She walked **round** the car and looked at the wheels.*
> *We all sat **round** the table.*
> *'Where do you live?' 'Just **round** the corner.'*

2   touring; distribution

British people also use *round* to talk about going to all (or most) parts of a place, or giving things to everybody in a group.

> *We walked **round** the old part of the town.*
> *Can I look **round**?*
> *Could you pass the cups **round**, please?*

3   indefinite movement and position

We use *around* or *about* to refer to movements or positions that are not very clear or definite: 'here and there', 'in lots of places', 'in different parts of', 'somewhere in' and similar ideas.

> *The children were running **around/about** everywhere.*
> *Stop standing **around/about** and do some work.*
> *'Where's John?' 'Somewhere **around/about**.'*
> *I like doing odd jobs **around/about** the house.*

We also use these words to talk about time-wasting or silly activity.

> *Stop fooling **around/about**. We're late.*

And *around/about* can mean 'approximately', 'not exactly'.

> *There were **around/about** fifty people there.*
> *'What time shall I come?' '**Around/About** eight.'*   ▶

4 American English

Note that in American English, *about* is mostly used to mean 'approximately', 'not exactly'; for the other meanings discussed in paragraphs 1–3, Americans normally use *around*.

For more details and examples, see a good dictionary.

61 arouse and rouse

To *rouse* somebody is to wake them up, make them interested, make them excited etc.
> *It is extremely difficult to rouse my father in the mornings.* (In an informal style, . . . *to wake my father up . . .* would be much more natural.)
> *Professor Bognor's speech failed to rouse his audience.*

Arouse is often used with an abstract word as an object: you can *arouse* somebody's interest, suspicions, sympathy etc.
> *When he kept saying he was working late at the office, it began to arouse her suspicions.*

Arouse can be used in a sexual sense.
> *Most men are aroused by pictures of naked women.*

Arouse and *rouse* are both regular verbs.

For *arise* and *rise*, see 59.
For *(a)wake* and *(a)waken*, see 85.

62 articles (1): introduction

1 How much do articles matter?

The correct use of the articles (*a/an* and *the*) is one of the most difficult points in English grammar. Fortunately, most article mistakes do not matter too much. Even if we leave all the articles out of a sentence, it is usually possible to understand it.
> ~~Please can you lend me pound of butter till end of week?~~

However, it is better to use the articles correctly if possible. Sections 63–69 give the most important rules and exceptions.

2 speakers of Western European languages

Most languages of Western European origin, and one or two others, have article systems very like English. So a student does not need to know the whole contents of sections 63–69 if he/she already speaks one of the following languages, for example, perfectly or very well: French, German, Dutch, Danish, Swedish, Norwegian, Icelandic, Spanish, Italian, Portuguese, Greek, Romanian. However, some of the rules in these sections will probably be useful. Note especially the following.

a In English, when we are talking about people or things **in general** we do not usually use *the* with uncountable or plural nouns. (See 68 for more details.)
> **Life** *is complicated.* (NOT ~~The life is complicated.~~)
> *My sister loves horses.* (NOT . . . ~~the horses.~~)

b In English, we normally put *a/an* with a noun that is used for **classifying** – saying what class, group or type somebody or something belongs to, what job, role or position somebody or something fills, etc. (See 66.1c for more details.)

> *She's **a dentist**.* (NOT ~~She's **dentist**.~~)
> *I'm looking forward to being **a grandmother**.*
>   (NOT ...~~to being **grandmother**.~~)
> *I used my shoe as **a hammer**.* (NOT ...~~as **hammer**.~~)

3 speakers of other languages

If a student does not already have a very good knowledge of one of the languages listed in paragraph 2 (or a related language), he or she may have more difficulty with the correct use of articles. Most of the important problems are dealt with in the following sections.

63 articles (2): summary of the rules

1 articles are determiners

The articles *a/an* and *the* belong to a group of words called 'determiners'. (Determiners also include possessives like *my*, demonstratives like *this* and quantifiers like *all*. For more information, see 157.) Articles normally come at the beginning of noun phrases, before adjectives.

For the word order in structures like *How strange an idea*, see 16.
For the word order in *quite a ...* , see 154.2,5; for *rather a ...* , see 154.2; for *such a ...* , see 544.1; for *what a ...* , see 201.2.

2 What are articles used for?

A/an is called the 'indefinite article'. *The* is called the 'definite article'. *Some/any* is often used as the plural of *a/an*. And if we use **no article**, this has a different meaning from all the others. So there are really four articles.

Articles are used to show whether we are referring to things that are known both to the speaker/writer and to the listener/reader ('definite'), or that are not known to them both ('indefinite').

Articles can also show whether we are talking about things in general or particular things.

3 *the* = 'we know which one(s)'

We say *the doctor*, *the salt* or *the dogs* (for example), when we expect the listener/reader to **know which** doctor, salt or dogs we are talking about. In other cases, we use *a/an*, *some/any* or **no article**. Compare:
– *I've been to **the doctor**.* (You know which one: my doctor.)
   A doctor must like people. (= any doctor at all)
– *Could you pass me **the salt**?*
      (The listener knows that it is the salt on the table that is meant.)
   *We need **some more salt**.* (not particular 'known' salt)   ▶

– *Have you fed **the dogs**?*
   (The listener obviously knows which dogs are meant.)
   *Do you like **dogs**?* (= dogs in general)

For more details, see 65.

4 particular and general

We can use articles to show whether we are talking about particular things or
things in general. Compare:
– *There are **some children** in the garden.* (= particular children)
   ***Children** usually start walking at around one year old.*
      (= children in general)
– *They're delivering **the oil** tomorrow.* (= particular oil)
   ***Oil** has nearly doubled in price recently.* (= oil in general)
Note that with plural and uncountable nouns we use **no article**, and not ***the***,
to talk about people or things in general.
   ***Oil** has nearly doubled in price.* (NOT ~~The oil~~...)
   ***Children** usually start walking...* (NOT ~~The children~~...)
But we can sometimes use ***the* + singular countable noun** to generalise.
   *Who invented **the telephone**?*

For more details, see 68.
For more information about *some* and *any*, see 54, 521 and 522.

64 articles (3): countable and uncountable nouns

Articles are used in different ways with countable and uncountable nouns.

1 the difference

Countable nouns are the names of separate objects, people, ideas etc which
we can count.
   a cat   three cats
   a secretary   two secretaries
   a plan   two plans
Uncountable nouns are the names of materials, liquids and other things
which we do not usually see as separate objects.
   water (NOT ~~a water, two waters~~)
   wool (NOT ~~a wool, two wools~~)
   weather (NOT ~~a weather, two weathers~~)
   energy (NOT ~~an energy, two energies~~)

2 use of articles

A singular countable noun normally has an article or other determiner (see
157) with it. We can say *a cat, the cat, my cat, this cat, any cat, either cat* or
every cat, but not just *cat.* (There are one or two exceptions – see 69.) Plural
and uncountable nouns (e.g. *cats, water*) can be used with or without an
article or other determiner.

3   *a/an*

Plural nouns cannot be used with *a/an* (because *a/an* has a similar meaning to 'one'), and uncountable nouns are not generally used with *a/an*, though there are a certain number of exceptions (see paragraph 4).

4   exceptions: uncountable nouns treated as countable

Many normally uncountable nouns can be treated as countable to express the meaning 'a type of' or 'a portion of'.

> *Have you got **a shampoo** for dry hair?*
> ***Three coffees**, please.*

Many other normally uncountable nouns can have 'partly countable' uses: they do not have plurals, but can be used with *a/an*. This can happen when the meaning is particular rather than general.

> *We need a secretary with **a knowledge** of English.*
> *You've been **a** great **help**.*
> *I need **a** good **sleep**.*

But some uncountable nouns (e.g. *weather, progress*) cannot normally be used in this way.

> *We're having **terrible weather**.* (NOT ...*a terrible weather.*)
> *You've made **very good progress**.* (NOT ...*a very good progress.*)

Note also:

> *She speaks **very good English**.* (NOT ...*a very good English.*)

Some nouns that are countable in other languages are uncountable in English. Examples are *information* (NOT *an information*), *advice* (NOT *an advice*); see 148.3 for a more complete list.

For detailed information about countable and uncountable nouns, see 148.

65   articles (4): **the** (details)

1   *the* = 'you know which one(s)'

The usually means something like 'you know which one(s) I mean'. We use *the* before a noun when our listener / reader knows (or can work out) which particular person(s), thing(s) etc we are talking about. Compare:

> *Did you lock **the car**?* (The listener knows very well which car is meant.)
> *We hired **a car** to go to Scotland.* (The listener does not know which one.)

The listener / reader may know which one(s) we mean because:

a   we have mentioned it / them before

> *She's got two children: **a boy** and **a girl**. **The boy**'s fourteen and
> **the girl**'s eight.*
> *'So what did you do then?' 'Gave **the money** straight back to **the
> policeman**.'* (The speaker uses *the* because the listener has already heard about the money and the policeman.)

b   we say which one(s) we mean

> *Who's **the girl over there with John**?*
> *Tell Pat **the story about John and Susie**.*
> *What did you do with **the camera I lent you**?*

▶

c   it is clear from the situation which one(s) we mean
> *Could you close **the door**?* (Only one door is open.)
> *Ann's in **the kitchen**.   Did you enjoy **the party**?*
> *What's **the time**?*

2   *the* = 'the only one(s) around'

The listener may know **which one(s)** we mean because there is no choice –
we are talking about something unique, like *the sun*, or something that is at
least unique in our environment, like *the Government, the police.*
> *I haven't seen **the sun** for days.*
> ***the** moon   **the** stars   **the** planets   **the** earth   **the** world*
> ***the** unions   **the** railways*
> ***the** Japanese* (There is only one Japanese nation.)

This use of *the* (to show that there is no choice) is possible even when we are
talking about somebody / something that the listener knows nothing about.
> *You don't know **the Aldersons**, do you?* (The use of *the* makes it clear that
> there is only one Alderson family in the speaker's social environment.)
> *Have you never heard of **the Thirty Years' War**?* (There was only one.)

3   physical environment

The is also used with a number of expressions referring to our physical
environment – the world around us and its climate – or to other common
features of our lives. The use of *the* suggests that everybody is familiar with
what we are talking about. Examples are:

***the** town*	***the** mountains*	***the** fog*	***the** future*
***the** country*	***the** rain*	***the** weather*	***the** universe*
***the** sea*	***the** wind*	***the** night*	***the** sunshine*
***the** seaside*			

> *Do you prefer **the town** or **the country**?*
> *My wife likes **the seaside**, but I prefer **the mountains**.*
> *I love listening to **the wind**.*

Note that **no article** is used with *nature, society* or *space* when these have a
'general' meaning (see 68).

4   superlatives

We usually use *the* with superlatives (see 138.12) because there is normally
only one *best, biggest* etc individual or group (so it is clear **which one(s)** we
are talking about). For the same reason, we usually use *the* with *first, next,
last, same* and *only.*
> *I'm **the oldest** in my family.   Can I have **the next** pancake?*
> *We went to **the same** school.*

5   *the* meaning 'the well-known'

After a name, an identifying expression with *the* is often used to make it clear
that the person referred to is 'the well-known one'.
> *She married Richard Burton, **the actor**.*
> *I'd like you to meet Cathy Parker, **the novelist**.*

6 possessives and demonstratives

We do not use *the* with possessives or demonstratives.
> *This is **my** uncle.* (NOT *...~~the my uncle.~~*)
> *I like **this** beer.* (NOT *...~~the this beer.~~*)

7 proper names

We do not usually use *the* with singular proper names (there are some exceptions – see 69.18–19).
> ***Mary** lives in **Switzerland**.* (NOT ~~*The Mary lives in the Switzerland.*~~)

But note the use of *the* (pronounced /'ði:/) with a person's name to mean 'the well-known'.
> *'My name's James Bond.' 'What, not **the** James Bond?'*

8 things in general

We usually use **no article**, not *the*, to talk about things in general – *the* does not mean 'all'.
> ***Books** are expensive.* (NOT ~~*The books are expensive.*~~)

For details and exceptions, see 68.

9 pronunciation

The is pronounced /ði:/ before a vowel and /ðə/ before a consonant. Compare:
> *the ice* /ði: aɪs/   *the snow* /ðə snəʊ/

The choice between /ði:/ and /ðə/ depends on pronunciation, not spelling. We pronounce /ði:/ before a vowel **sound**, even if it is written as a consonant.
> *the **hour*** /ði: aʊə/   *the **MP*** /ði: em pi:/

And we pronounce /ðə/ before a consonant **sound**, even if it is written as a vowel.
> *the **university*** /ðə juːnɪ'vɜːsəti/
> *the **one-pound** coin* /ðə 'wʌn 'paʊnd 'kɔɪn/

We sometimes pronounce a stressed /ði:/ before a hesitation, or when we want to stress the following word, even if it begins with a consonant.

66 articles (5): **a/an** (details)

1 *a/an*

a   We can use *a/an* to talk about one particular person or thing, when the listener / reader does not know **which one** is meant, or when it does not matter **which one**.
> *My brother's going out with **a French girl**.*
> 　　(The listener does not know which particular French girl it is.)
> *She lives in **a nice big house**.*
> *Could you lend me **a pen**?*

b   We can also use *a/an* to talk about **any one member** of a class.
> ***A doctor** must like people.* (= *any doctor*)
> ***A spider** has eight legs.*

▶

c   And we can use *a/an* after a copular verb or *as* to classify people and things –
to say what class, group or type they belong to.
> She's **an architect**. (NOT ~~She's architect.~~)
> I'm looking forward to being **a grandmother**.
> 'What's that noise?' 'I think it's **a helicopter**.'
> He decided to become **an engineer**.
> He remained **a bachelor** all his life.
> Don't use your plate as **an ashtray**. (NOT ... ~~as ashtray.~~)

2   *a/an, some/any* and no article

A/an is mainly used with singular countable nouns. (The original meaning of
a/an was 'one'.) Before plural and uncountable nouns, we normally express
similar meanings (see paragraph 1) with *some/any* or **no article**.

> plural nouns

> We met **some nice French girls** on holiday. (NOT ... ~~a nice French girls~~...)
> Have you got **any matches**?
> **Doctors** generally work long hours. (NOT ~~A doctors~~...)
> Both my parents are **architects**.

> uncountable nouns

> I think there's **some butter** in the fridge.
> **Whisky** is made from barley.
> 'What's that on your coat?' 'It looks like **paint**.'

For the difference between *some/any* and **no article**, see 67.
For more information about *some* and *any*, see 54 and 522–523.
For structures like *a happy three days*, see 509.6.

3   adjectives

A/an cannot normally be used with an adjective alone (without a noun).
Compare:
> It's **a good car**.
> It's **good**. (NOT ~~It's a good.~~)

For *a* + **adjective** + *one*, see 391.

4   possessives

A/an cannot be used together with a possessive. Instead, we can use the
structure **a ... of mine/yours/etc** (see 434).
> He's **a friend of mine**. (NOT ~~He's a my friend.~~)

5   when *a/an* cannot be dropped

Note that *a/an* is not normally left out in negative expressions, after
prepositions or after fractions.
> 'Lend me your pen.' 'I haven't got **a pen**.' (NOT ~~'I haven't got pen.'~~)
> You mustn't go out without **a coat**. (NOT ... ~~without coat.~~)
> three-quarters of **a pound** (NOT ~~three-quarters of pound~~)

For exceptions, see 69.2.

6 *a* and *an*

We do not normally pronounce the sound /ə/ before a vowel. So before a vowel, the article *a* (/ə/) changes to *an*. Compare:

a *rabbit*   **a** *lemon*
an *elephant*   **an** *orange*

The choice between *a* and *an* depends on pronunciation, not spelling.
We use *an* before a vowel **sound**, even if it is written as a consonant.
    an *hour* /ən ˈaʊə/   **an** *MP* /ən em ˈpiː/
And we use *a* before a consonant **sound**, even if it is written as a vowel.
    a *university* /ə juː . . ./   **a** *one-pound coin* /ə wʌn . . ./
Some people say *an*, not *a*, before words beginning with *h* if the first syllable is unstressed.
    an *hotel* (*a hotel* is more common)
    an *historic occasion* (*a historic . . .* is more common)
    (BUT NOT ~~*an housewife*~~ – the first syllable is stressed.)
A is sometimes pronounced /eɪ/ before a hesitation, when we want to emphasise the following word, or when we want to make a contrast with *the*.
    *It's **a** /eɪ/ reason – it's not the only reason.*

67 **articles** (6): the difference between **some/any** and no article

1   use with uncountable and plural nouns

Uncountable and plural nouns can often be used either with *some/any* or with **no article**. There is not always a great difference of meaning.
    *We need (**some**) cheese.   I didn't buy (**any**) eggs.*
Some is used especially in affirmative sentences; *any* is more common in questions and negatives (see 54 and 522).

2   the difference

We use *some/any* when we are thinking about limited but rather indefinite vague numbers or quantities – when we don't know, care or say exactly how much / many. We use **no article** when we are thinking about unlimited numbers or quantities, or not thinking about numbers / quantities at all. Compare:
–   *We've planted **some roses** in the garden.*
        (A limited number; the speaker doesn't say how many.)
    *I like **roses**.* (No idea of number.)
–   *We got talking to **some students**.* (A limited number.)
    *Our next-door neighbours are **students**.*
        (The main idea is classification, not number.)
–   *Would you like **some more beer**?*
        (An indefinite amount – as much as the listener wants.)
    *We need **beer, sugar, eggs, butter, rice and toilet paper**.* (The speaker is
        thinking just of the things that need to be bought, not of the amounts.)
–   *Is there **any water** in the fridge?* (The speaker wants a limited amount.)
    *Is there **water** on the moon?*
        (The interest is in the existence of water, not the amount.)   ▶

– *This engine hardly uses **any petrol**.* (The interest is in the amount.)
*This engine doesn't use **petrol**.*
(The interest is in the type of fuel, not the amount.)

We do not use *some/any* when it is clear exactly how much/many is meant.
Compare:

– *You've got **some great books**.*
*You've got **pretty toes**.* (A definite number – ten. *You've got **some pretty toes*** would suggest that the speaker is not making it clear how many –
perhaps six or seven!)

For full details of the different uses of *some* and *any*, see 54 and 522–523.

68 articles (7): talking in general

1 *the* does not mean 'all'

We do not use *the* with uncountable or plural nouns to talk about things in general – to talk about all books, all people or all life, for example. *The* does not mean 'all'. Instead, we use **no article**. Compare:

– *Move **the books** off that chair and sit down.* (= particular books)
***Books** are expensive.* (NOT ~~*The books are expensive*~~. The sentence is about books in general – all books.)
– *I'm studying **the life** of Beethoven.* (= one particular life)
***Life** is complicated.* (NOT ~~*The life*~~... The sentence is about the whole of life.)
– *'Where's **the cheese**?' 'I ate it.'*
*I love **cheese**.*
– *Why has **the light** gone out?*
*Nothing can travel faster than **light**.*

Note that *most* (meaning 'the majority of') is used without *the*.
***Most** birds can fly.* (NOT ~~*The most*~~...)
***Most** of the children got very tired.* (NOT ~~*The most*~~...)

2 generalisations with singular words

Sometimes we talk about things in general by using *the* with a singular countable noun.
*Schools should pay less attention to examination success, and more attention to **the child**.*

This is common with the names of scientific instruments and inventions, and musical instruments.
*Life would be quieter without **the telephone**.*
***The violin** is more difficult than **the piano**.*

We can also generalise by talking about one example of a class, using *a/an* (meaning 'any') with a singular countable noun.
***A baby deer** can stand as soon as it's born.*   ***A child** needs plenty of love.*

Note that we cannot use *a/an* in this way when we are generalising about all of the members of a group together.
***The tiger** is in danger of becoming extinct.*
(NOT ~~*A tiger is in danger of becoming extinct*~~. The sentence is about the whole tiger family, not about individuals.)
*Do you like **horses**?* (NOT ~~*Do you like a horse?*~~)

3   difficult cases: 'general' + 'known'

We use **no article** to generalise with uncountable and plural words (see paragraph 1 above); but we use *the* to show that the listener/reader knows which people or things we are talking about (see 65). Sometimes both these meanings come together, and it is difficult to know whether or not to use *the*.

a   *the sea, the weather* etc

The is used with a lot of general expressions that refer to our physical environment – the world around us and its climate – or to other common features of our lives. The use of *the* seems to suggest shared experience or knowledge: the listener/reader 'has been there too'.

> *Do you prefer **the town** or **the country**?*
> *My wife likes **the sea**, but I prefer **the mountains**.*
> *English people always talk about **the weather**.*
> *I wish **the trains** were cleaner and more punctual.*
> *He's always after **the girls**.*

Note that we use **no article** with *nature, society, space* and other abstract nouns when these have a general meaning.

> *I love **nature**. (NOT ...~~the nature~~.)*
> *It isn't always easy to fit in with **society**. (NOT ...~~the society~~.)*
> *We are just taking our first steps into **space**. (NOT ...~~the space~~.)*

b   *the Russians* etc

We often use *the* to refer to well-known, well-defined groups of people (e.g. nationalities), even when we are talking about these in general.

> ***The Russians** have a marvellous folksong tradition.*
> ***The Irish** have their own language.*
> *Should **the police** carry guns?*

For more details of the grammar of nationality words, see 354.

Note also the use of ***the* + adjective** (e.g. *the blind, the old*) to talk about certain groups (see 18).

4   difficult cases: 'half-general'

Some expressions are 'half-general' – in the middle between general and particular. If we talk about *eighteenth-century history, sixties music* or *poverty in Britain*, we are not talking about all history, music or poverty, but these are still rather general ideas (compared with *the history I did at school, the music we heard last night* or *the poverty I grew up in*). In these 'half-general' expressions, we usually use **no article**. However, *the* is often used when the noun is followed by a limiting, defining phrase, especially one with *of*. Compare:

– *eighteenth-century **music***
  ***the music of** the eighteenth century*
– *African **butterflies***
  ***the butterflies of** Africa*

69 **articles** (8): special rules and exceptions

1 **common expressions without articles**

In some common fixed expressions to do with place, time and movement, normally countable nouns are treated as uncountables, without articles. Examples are:

> *to school   at school   in school* (US)   *from school*
> *to/at/from university/college* (GB)   *to/in/from college* (US)
> *to/at/in/into/from church   to/in/into/out of bed/prison*
> *to/in/into/out of hospital* (GB)   *to/at/from work*
> *to/at sea   to/in/from town   at/from home   leave home*
> *leave/start/enter school/university/college*
> *by day   at night*
> *by car/bus/bicycle/plane/train/tube/boat   on foot*
> *by radio/phone/letter/mail*

With place nouns, similar expressions with articles may have different meanings. Compare:

– *I met her **at college**.* (when we were students)
  *I'll meet you **at the college**.* (The college is just a meeting place.)
– *Jane's **in hospital**.* (as a patient)
  *I left my coat **in the hospital** when I was visiting Jane.*
– *Who smokes **in class**?* (= ... *in the classroom?*)
  *Who smokes **in the class**?* (= *Who is a smoker ...?*)

In American English, *university* and *hospital* are not used without articles.

> *She was unhappy **at the university**.*

2 **double expressions**

Articles are often dropped in double expressions, particularly with prepositions.

> *with knife and fork   on land and sea   day after day*
> *with hat and coat   arm in arm   husband and wife*
> *from top to bottom   inch by inch*

But articles are not usually dropped when single nouns follow prepositions (for exceptions, see paragraph 1 above).

> *You can't get there **without a car**.* (NOT *...~~without car.~~*)

For cases like *the bread and (the) butter*, see 182.

3 **'s genitives**

A noun that is used after an *'s* genitive (like *John's, America's*) has no article (just like a noun used after a possessive).

> ***the** coat that belongs to John = John's coat*
>   (NOT *~~John's the coat~~* OR *~~the John's coat~~*)
> ***the** economic problems of America = America's economic problems*
>   (NOT *~~the America's economic problems~~*)

But the genitive noun itself may have an article.

> *the wife of **the** boss = **the** boss's wife*

4 *the ... of a ...*

In classifying expressions of this kind, the first article is definite even if the meaning of the whole expression is indefinite.

> *Lying by the side of the road we saw **the** wheel of a car.*
> (N O T *... a wheel of a car.*)

5 noun modifiers

When a noun modifies another noun, the first noun's article is dropped.

> ***guitar** lessons = lessons in how to play **the guitar***
> (N O T *the guitar lessons*)
> *a **sun**spot = a spot on **the sun***

6 *both* and *all*

We often leave out *the* after *both*.

> ***Both (the)** children are good at maths.*

And we often leave out *the* between *all* and a number.

> ***All (the) three** brothers were arrested.*

We usually leave out *the* after *all* in *all day, all night, all week, all year, all winter* and *all summer*.

> *We've been waiting to hear from you **all week**.*
> *I haven't seen her **all day**.*

7 *kind of* etc

We usually leave out *a/an* after *kind of, sort of, type of* and similar expressions.

> *What **kind of (a)** person is she?*
> *Have you got a cheaper **sort of** radio?*
> *They've developed a new **variety of** sheep.*

For more information about *kind of, sort of* etc, see 159.16–17, 526.

8 *amount* and *number*

The is dropped after *the amount/number of*.

> *I was surprised at **the amount of money** collected.*
> ***The number of unemployed** is rising steadily.*

9 *man* and *woman*

Unlike other singular countable nouns, *man* and *woman* can be used in a general sense without articles.

> ***Man** and **woman** were created equal.*

But in modern English we more often use *a woman* and *a man*, or *men* and *women*.

> *A **woman** without **a man** is like a fish without a bicycle.* (old feminist joke)
> ***Men** and **women** have similar abilities and needs.*

Man is also commonly used to mean 'the human race', though many people regard this usage as sexist and prefer to avoid it (see 227.6).

> *How did **Man** first discover fire?* ▶

10 days, months and seasons

We use articles with the names of days of the week and months when we are talking about particular days or months.

*We met on **a wet Monday** in June.*
*She died on **the Tuesday** after the accident.*
*We're having **a very wet April**.*
*It was **the January** after we went to Greece.*

But articles are not used when the meaning is 'the day/month before or after this one'.

*See you on **Thursday**.*   *See you in **April**.*
*Where were you last **Saturday**?*   *We're moving next **September**.*

To talk about the seasons in general, we can say *spring* or *the spring, summer* or *the summer*, etc. There is little difference. *The* is always used in *in the fall* (US).

*Rome is lovely in **(the) spring**.*
*I like **(the)** winter best.*

When we are talking about particular springs, summers etc, we are more likely to use *the*.

*I worked very hard in **the summer** that year.*

11 musical instruments

We often use ***the* + singular** when we talk about musical instruments in general, or about playing musical instruments.

***The violin** is really difficult.*
*Who's that on **the piano**?*

But *the* is often dropped when talking about jazz or pop, and sometimes when talking about classical music.

*This recording was made with Miles Davis **on trumpet**.*
*She studied **oboe** and **saxophone** at the Royal Academy of Music.*

12 *television, (the) radio, (the) cinema and (the) theatre*

When we talk about television as a form of entertainment, we do not use articles.

*It's not easy to write plays for **television**.*
*Would you rather go out or watch **TV**?*

But articles are used when *television* means 'a television set'. Compare:

*What's on **TV**?*
*Look out! The cat's on **the TV**!*

Articles are generally used with *radio, cinema* and *theatre*.

*I always listen to **the radio** while I'm driving.*
*It was a great treat to go to **the cinema** or **the theatre** when I was a child.*

But the article can be dropped when we talk about these institutions as art forms or professions.

***Cinema** is different from **theatre** in several ways.*
*He's worked in **radio** all his life.*

13   jobs and positions

We normally use *a/an* when we say what job somebody has (see 66.1c).
> She's **an architect**. (NOT ~~She's architect.~~)

The is not used in titles like *Queen Elizabeth, President Lincoln*. Compare:
> **Queen Elizabeth** had dinner with **President Kennedy**.
> **The Queen** had dinner with **the President**.

And *the* is not usually used in the complement of a sentence, when we say that somebody has or gains a unique position (the only one in the organisation). Compare:
– *They appointed him* **Head Librarian**.
 He's **a librarian**.
– *He was elected* **President** *in 1879.*
 I want to see **the President**.

14   exclamations

We use *a/an* with singular countable nouns in exclamations after *What*.
> **What a** lovely dress! (NOT ~~What lovely dress!~~)

Note that *a/an* cannot be used in exclamations with uncountable nouns.
> *What nonsense!* (NOT ~~What a nonsense!~~)
> *What luck!* (NOT ~~What a luck!~~)

15   illnesses

The names of illnesses are usually uncountable in standard British English (for more details, see 148.4). *The* can be used informally before the names of some common illnesses such as *the measles, the flu*; others have **no article**. American usage is different in some cases.
> *I think I've got* **(the) measles**.
> *Have you had* **appendicitis**?
> *I'm getting* **toothache**. (US . . . *a toothache*.)

Exceptions: **a** *cold,* **a** *headache* (US also *an earache, a backache*).
> *I've got* **a** *horrible cold.*
> *Have you got* **a** *headache?*

16   parts of the body etc

When talking about parts of someone's body, or about their possessions, we usually use possessives, not *the*.
> *Katy broke* **her** *arm climbing.* (NOT ~~Katy broke the arm climbing.~~)
> *He stood in the doorway,* **his** *coat over* **his** *arm.*
>   (NOT . . . ~~the coat over the arm.~~)

However, when talking about parts of the body we generally prefer *the* in prepositional phrases related to the object of a clause (or the subject of a passive clause).
> *She hit* **him in the stomach**.
> *Can't you look* **me in the eye**?
> **He** *was shot* **in the leg**.

This can also happen in prepositional phrases after *be* + adjective.
> *He's broad across* **the** *shoulders.*   ▶

17   measurements

Note the use of *the* in measuring expressions beginning with *by*.
> *Do you sell eggs **by the kilo** or **by the dozen**?*
> *She drinks cough medicine **by the litre**.*
> *He sits watching TV **by the hour**.   Can I pay **by the month**?*

A/an is used to relate one measuring unit to another.
> *sixty pence **a** kilo   thirty miles **an** hour* (OR *... miles per hour*)
> *twice **a** week, on average   a third of **a** pint*

18   place names

We use *the* with these kinds of place names:
> seas (**the** *Atlantic*)
> mountain groups (**the** *Himalayas*)
> island groups (**the** *West Indies*)
> rivers (**the** *Rhine*)
> deserts (**the** *Sahara*)
> most hotels (**the** *Grand Hotel*)
> most cinemas and theatres (**the** *Odeon;* **the** *Playhouse*)
> most museums and art galleries (**the** *British Museum;* **the** *Frick*)

We usually use **no article** with:
> continents, countries, states, counties, departments etc (*Africa, Brazil,*
>   *Texas, Berkshire, Westphalia*)
> towns (*Oxford*)
> streets (*New Street, Willow Road*)
> lakes (*Lake Michigan*)

Exceptions: places whose name is (or contains) a common noun like
republic, state, union (e.g. **the** *People's* **Republic** *of China,* **the** *United*
Kingdom, **the** *United* **States**). Note also **the** *Netherlands,* and its seat of
government **The** *Hague*.

In British English, *the* is unusual in the titles of the principal public buildings
and organisations of a town.
> *Oxford University* (NOT ~~**the** Oxford University~~)
> *Hull Station* (NOT ~~**the** Hull Station~~)
> *Salisbury Cathedral*
> *Birmingham Airport*
> *Bristol Zoo*
> *Manchester City Council*
> *Cheltenham Football Club*

In American English, *the* is more often used in such cases.
> *The San Diego Zoo   The Detroit City Council*

Names of single mountains vary. Most have no article.
> *Everest   Kilimanjaro   Snowdon   Table Mountain*

But definite articles are usually translated in the English versions of
European mountain names, except those beginning *Le Mont*.
> **The** *Meije* (= **La** *Meije*)   **The** *Matterhorn* (= **Das** *Matterhorn*)
> *Mont Blanc* (NOT ~~**the** Mont Blanc~~)

19 newspapers and magazines

The names of newspapers usually have *the*.
>*The* Times   *The* Washington Post

The names of magazines do not always have *the*.
>*New Scientist*

20 abbreviated styles

We usually leave out articles in abbreviated styles (see 1).

newspaper headlines	*MAN KILLED ON MOUNTAIN*
headings	*Introduction*
	Chapter 2
	Section B
picture captions	*Mother and child*
notices, posters etc	*SUPER CINEMA, RITZ HOTEL*
instructions	*Open packet at other end*
numbering and	*Go through door A*
labelling	*Control to Car 27: can you hear me?*
	Turn to page 26. (NOT ... ~~the page 26.~~)
dictionary entries	**palm** *inner surface of hand ...*
lists	*take car to garage; pay phone bill; ...*
notes	*J thinks company needs new office*

For the use of articles with abbreviations (*NATO, the USA*), see 2.3–4.
For the use of *the* in double comparatives (**the** more, **the** better), see 138.4.
For *a* with *few* and *little*, see 322.
For *a* with *hundred, thousand* etc, see 385.10.
For *the blind* etc, see 18.1.
For *the Japanese* etc, see 18.2.
For *next* and *the next*, see 367; for *last* and *the last*, see 307.
For *the* instead of *enough*, see 193.7.
For *another two days, a good three weeks* etc, see 509.6

70 as ... as ...; as much / many as

> *as* + adjective / adverb + *as* + noun / pronoun / clause / etc
> *as much / many* (+ noun) + *as* + noun / pronoun / clause / etc

1 use

We use *as ... as ...* to say that two people or things are equal in some way.
>She's **as** tall **as** her brother.
>Is it **as** good **as** you expected?
>She speaks French **as** well **as** the rest of us.

2 negative structures

After *not*, we can use *so ... as ...* instead of *as ... as ...* This structure is more common than *less than* in informal English.
>He's not **as/so** successful **as** his sister.   ▶

3   *as ... as* + adjective / adverb

Note the structure *as ... as* + **adjective / adverb**.
> *Please get here **as** soon **as possible**.*
> *I'll spend **as** much **as necessary**.*
> *You're **as** beautiful **as ever**.*

4   pronouns after *as*

We can use object pronouns (*me, him* etc) after *as*, especially in an informal style.
> *She doesn't sing as well **as me**.*

In a formal style, we prefer **subject + verb** after *as*.
> *She doesn't sing as well **as I do**.*

Note that a subject form without a verb (e.g. *as well as he*) is unusual in this structure in modern English.

5   *as much/many ... as*

We can use *as much/many ... as ...* to talk about quantity.
> *I haven't got **as much** money **as** I thought.*
> *We need **as many** people **as** possible.*

As much/many can be used as pronouns, without following nouns.
> *I ate **as much** as I could.*
> *She didn't catch **as many** as she'd hoped.*

And *as much ...* can be used as an adverb.
> *You ought to rest **as much** as possible.*

6   *half as ... as* etc

Note the structure *half as ... as ...; twice as ... as ...; three times as ... as ...;* etc.
> *You're not **half as** clever **as** you think you are.*
> *I'm not going out with a man who's **twice as** old **as** me.*
> *It took **three times as** long **as I had expected**.*
> > (OR ... ***three times** longer **than** I had expected* – see 138.7)

7   modification

Expressions with *as ... as ...* can be modified by *(not) nearly, almost, just, nothing like* (GB), *every bit, exactly, not quite*.
> *It's **not nearly as** cold **as** yesterday.*
> *He's **just as** strong **as** ever.*
> *You're **nothing like as** bad-tempered **as** you used to be.*
> *She's **every bit as** beautiful **as** her sister.*
> *I'm **not quite as** tired **as** I was last week.*

8   infinitives

Where *as ... as* is used with two infinitives, *to* is often dropped from the second.
> *It's as easy **to do** it right as **(to) do** it wrong.*

9 tenses

In *as . . . as*-clauses (and other kinds of *as*-clauses), a present tense is often used to refer to the future, and a past tense is often used with a conditional meaning (see 556).

> *We'll get there as soon as you **do/will**.*
> *If you married me, I'd give you as much freedom as you **wanted**.*

10 ellipsis

The second part of the *as . . . as* or *so . . . as* structure can be left out when the meaning is clear from what comes before.

> *The train takes 40 minutes. It'll take you twice **as long** by car.*
> *I used to think he was clever. Now I'm not **so sure**.*

In cases like this, *not so* is much more common than *not as*.

11 *as* replacing subject or object

As takes the place of the subject or object in a clause, rather like a relative pronoun (see 473.5).

> *We've got food for as many people **as** want it.* (NOT *. . .as they want it.*)
> *I gave him as much **as** he could eat.* (NOT *. . .as he could eat it.*)

12 traditional expressions

We use the structure *as . . . as . . .* in a lot of traditional comparative expressions.

> **as** cold **as** ice   **as** black **as** night
> **as** hard **as** nails   **as . . . as** hell

The first *as* is sometimes dropped in these expressions, especially in American English.

> *She's **hard as nails**.*
> *I'm **tired as hell** of listening to your problems.*

Note that *as* is usually pronounced /əz/ (see 588).
For *as long as*, see 75.
For *as well as*, see 77.
For the word order in sentences like *She's **as good a dancer** as her brother*, see 16.
For other comparative structures, see 135–139.

71 **as** and **though**: special word order

Adjective / adverb + *as* + clause

As and *though* can be used in a special structure after an adjective or adverb. In this case they both mean 'although', and suggest an emphatic contrast.

> ***Cold as/though it was**, we went out.* (= *Although it was very cold, . . .*)
> ***Tired as/though I was**, I went on working.* (= *Although I was very tired, . . .*)
> ***Bravely as/though they fought**, they had no chance of winning.*
> ***Much as/though I respect** your point of view, I can't agree.*
> *We can't come and see you this weekend, **much as we'd like to**.*
> ***Strange though it may seem**, I don't like watching cricket.* ▶

Occasionally *as* can be used in this construction to mean 'because'.
> *Tired as she was, I decided not to disturb her.*

In American English, *as ... as* is normally used in this structure.
> *As cold as it was, we went out.*

For the word order in structures like *I did **as good a job** as I could*, see 16.

72 as, because, since and for

All four of these words can be used to refer to the reason for something. They are not used in the same way.

1 *as* and *since*

As and *since* are used when the reason is already known to the listener / reader, or when it is not the most important part of the sentence. *As*- and *since*-clauses often come at the beginning of sentences.
> ***As it's raining again**, we'll have to stay at home.*
> ***Since he had not paid his bill**, his electricity was cut off.*

As- and *since*-clauses are relatively formal; in an informal style, the same ideas are often expressed with *so*.
> *It's raining again, **so** we'll have to stay at home.*

2 *because*

Because puts more emphasis on the reason, and most often introduces new information which is not known to the listener / reader.
> ***Because I was ill for six months**, I lost my job.*

When the reason is the most important part of the sentence, the *because*-clause usually comes at the end. It can also stand alone. *Since* and *as* cannot be used like this.
> *Why am I leaving? I'm leaving **because I'm fed up**!*
> (NOT ... ~~I'm leaving as/since I'm fed up!~~)
> *'Why are you laughing?' '**Because you look so funny**.'*

A *because*-clause can be used at the end of a sentence to say how one knows something.
> *You didn't tell me the truth, **because** I found the money in your room.*
> (= ... **I know because** I found ...)

3 *for*

For introduces new information, but suggests that the reason is given as an afterthought. A *for*-clause could almost be in brackets. *For*-clauses never come at the beginning of sentences, and cannot stand alone. *For*, used in this sense, is most common in a formal written style.
> *I decided to stop and have lunch – **for I was feeling hungry**.*

73 **as**, **when** and **while** (simultaneous events)

To talk about actions or situations that take place at the same time, we can use *as, when* or *while*. There are some differences.

1 'backgrounds': *as, when* or *while*

We can use all three words to introduce a longer 'background' action or situation, which is / was going on when something else happens / happened.

As I was walking down the street I saw Joe driving a Porsche.
*The telephone always rings **when you are having a bath**.*
***While they were playing cards**, somebody broke into the house.*

As-, when- and *while*-clauses can go at the beginning or end of sentences, but *as*-clauses usually introduce less important information, and most often go at the beginning.

A progressive tense is usually used for the longer 'background' action or situation (*was walking; are having; were playing*). But *as* and *while* can be used with a simple tense, especially with a verb like *sit, lie,* or *grow* which refers to a continuous action or state.

***As I sat** reading the paper, the door burst open.*

2 simultaneous long actions: *while; as*

We usually use *while* to say that two longer actions or situations go / went on at the same time. We can use progressive or simple tenses.

***While you were reading** the paper, **I was working**.*
***John cooked** supper **while I watched** TV.*

As is used (with simple tenses) to talk about two situations which develop or change together.

***As I get** older I **get** more optimistic.*

We prefer *when* to refer to ages and periods of life.

***When I was a child** we lived in London.* (NOT ~~As/While I was a child~~ ...)
*His parents died **when** he was twelve.* (NOT ... ~~while he was twelve.~~)

3 simultaneous short actions: *(just) as; (just) when*

We usually use *(just) as* to say that two short actions or events happen / happened at the same time.

***As** I opened my eyes I heard a strange voice.*
*Mary always arrives **just as** I start work.*

(Just) when is also possible.

*I thought of it **just when** you opened your mouth.*

4 reduced clauses with *when* and *while*

It is often possible to leave out **subject + be** after *when* (especially when it means 'whenever'), and after *while*.

*Don't forget to signal **when turning** right.*
  (= ... *when you are turning right.*)

▶

*Climb **when ready**.*
  (= ... **when you are** ready.)
***While in Germany**, he got to know a family of musicians.*
  (= **While he was** ...)

Note that *as* is usually pronounced /əz/ (see 588).
For the use of present tenses to refer to the future with *as, when, while* and other
  conjunctions, see 556.

74 as if and as though

1 meaning

As if and *as though* mean the same. We use them to say what a situation
seems like.
  *It looks **as if/though** it's going to rain.*
  *I felt **as if/though** I was dying.*
  *She was acting **as if/though** she was in charge.*

2 tenses

We can use a past tense with a present meaning after *as if/though*. This
shows that a comparison is 'unreal'. Compare:
– *She looks as if **she's** rich.*
    (Perhaps she is rich.)
  *He talks as if he **was** rich.*
    (But he is not.)
– *You look as though you **know** each other.*
  *Why is she looking at me as though she **knew** me? I've never seen her before
    in my life.*
In a formal style, *were* can be used instead of *was* in an 'unreal' comparison.
This is normal in American English.
  *He talks as if he **were** rich.*

3 informal use of *like*

In an informal style, *like* is often used instead of *as if/though*, especially in
American English. This is not considered correct in a formal style.
  *It seems **like** it's going to rain.*
  *He sat there smiling **like** it was his birthday.*

For the difference between *like* and *as*, see 320.

75 as long as

1 tenses

After *as long as*, we use a present tense to express a future idea.
  *I'll remember that day **as long as I live**.*
    (NOT ...*as long as I will live*.)
For other conjunctions which are used in this way, see 556.

2 conditions

As/So long as is often used to state conditions.
> *You can take my car **as/so long as** you drive carefully.*
> (= ... **on condition that** *you drive carefully*.)

76 as usual

Note that in this expression we use the adjective *usual*, not the adverb *usually*.
> *The train's late, **as usual**.* (NOT ... ~~as usually~~.)

77 as well as

1 meaning

As well as has a similar meaning to 'not only ... but also'.
> *She's got a car **as well as** a motorbike.*
> (= ... *not only a motorbike, but also a car*.)
> *He's clever **as well as** good-looking.*
> (= *He's not only good-looking, but also clever*.)
> *She works in television **as well as** writing children's books.*

Note the 'information structure': usually *as well as* introduces information which is already known to the listener / reader; the rest of the sentence gives new information.
> *They speak French **in parts of Italy as well as France**.*
> (NOT ~~They speak French in France as well as parts of Italy~~.
> Everybody knows that French is spoken in France, so this information is introduced by *as well as*.)

2 verbs after *as well as*

When we put a verb after *as well as*, we most often use the *-ing* form.
> *Smoking is dangerous, **as well as making** you smell bad.*
> (NOT ... ~~as well as it makes you smell bad~~.)
> ***As well as breaking** his leg, he hurt his arm.*
> (NOT ... ~~as well as he broke his leg~~, ...)

After an infinitive in the main clause, an infinitive without *to* is possible.
> *I have to feed the animals **as well as look after** the children.*

Note the difference between:
> *She sings **as well as playing** the piano.*
> (= *She not only plays, but also sings*.)
> *She sings **as well as she plays** the piano.*
> (= *Her singing is as good as her playing*.)

▶

3 subjects

It is possible to connect two subjects with *as well as* before a verb. If the
first subject is singular, the verb is also likely to be singular, especially if
as well as . . . is separated by commas.

> **Alice, as well as Paula,** *was shocked by the news.*
> (NOT ~~*Alice, as well as Paula, were shocked . . .*~~)

With longer singular subjects, a plural verb is more likely, especially if
commas are not used.

> **His appearance as well as his strange way of talking make** *me*
> *suspicious.*

However, this is not a common structure. It is more normal to put
as well as . . . after the main clause; with pronoun subjects, this almost
always happens.

> *Alice was shocked by the news* **as well as Paula.**
> *He's ill* **as well as me.**
> (NOT ~~*He, as well as I/me, is ill.*~~)

For *as well*, *also* and *too*, see 45–46.

78 ask

1 *ask* and *ask for*

> *Ask for*: ask somebody to give something
> *Ask* without *for*: ask somebody to tell something

Compare:
– *Don't* **ask** *me* **for** *money.*
  (NOT ~~*Don't ask me money.*~~)
  Don't **ask** *me my name.*
  (NOT ~~*Don't ask me for my name.*~~)
– **Ask for** *the menu.*
  Ask *the price.*

Ask is sometimes used without *for* when talking about asking for sums of
money, especially in connection with buying, selling and renting.

> *They're* **asking** *£500 a month rent.*
> *'How much is the car?' 'I'm* **asking** *fifteen hundred.'*

Note also the expressions *ask a lot of somebody, ask too much of somebody,
ask a favour of somebody* and *ask (for) permission*.

2 direct and indirect objects

Ask can be followed by either a direct or an indirect object.

> *Ask* **his name.**   *Ask* **him.**

When *ask* is followed by two objects, the indirect object (the person)
normally comes first, without a preposition.

> *I'll ask* **that man** *the time.* (NOT ~~*I'll ask the time to that man.*~~)
> *Can I ask* **you** *a favour?*

A structure with **direct object** + *of* + indirect object is also possible, especially in American English.

> *I want to ask **a question of that man** over there.*
> *She's never asked **a favour of anybody**.*

3 infinitive structures

We can use infinitive structures after *ask* (see 283–284).

> ask + infinitive

> *I asked **to go** home.* (= *I asked permission to go home.*)

> ask + object + infinitive

> *I asked **John to go** home.* (= *I told John I would like him to go home.*)

> ask + *for* + object + infinitive

> *I asked **for the children to have** extra milk.*
> *I asked **for the parcel to be sent** to my home address.*

Note the difference between these two sentences:

> *I asked John **to go home**.* (I wanted John to go home.)
> *I asked John **if I could go home**.* (I wanted to go home myself.)

79 **at/in** and **to**

1 the difference

At and *in* are generally used for position (see 80); *to* is used for movement or direction. Compare:

– *He works **at** the market.*
 *He gets **to** the market by bike.*
– *My father lives **in** Canada.*
 *I go **to** Canada to see him whenever I can.*

2 expressions of purpose

If we mention the purpose of a movement before we mention the destination, we usually use *at/in* before the place. Compare:

– *Let's go **to** Marcel's for coffee.*
 *Let's go and have coffee **at** Marcel's.*
  (N O T ~~Let's go and have coffee to Marcel's.~~)
– *I went **to** Canada to see my father.*
 *I went to see my father **in** Canada.*
  (N O T ~~I went to see my father to Canada.~~)

3 targets

After some verbs, *at* is used to indicate the 'target' of a perception or non-verbal communication. Common examples are *look, smile, wave, frown, point.*

> *Why are you **looking at** her like that?*
> *Because she **smiled at** me.*

▶

At is also used after some verbs referring to attacks or aggressive behaviour.
Common examples are *shoot, laugh, throw* and *shout.*

> *It's a strange feeling to have somebody **shoot at** you.*
> *If you can't **laugh at** yourself, who can you **laugh at**?*
> *Stop **throwing** stones **at** the cat, darling.*
> *You don't need to **shout at** me.*

Throw to and *shout to* are used when there is no idea of attack.

> *Please do not **throw** food **to** the animals.*
> *Could you **shout to** Phil and tell him it's breakfast time?*

Arrive is generally followed by *at* or *in*; never by *to.*

> *We should arrive **at** Pat's in time for lunch.* (NOT ...~~arrive to Pat's~~...)
> *When did you arrive **in** New Zealand?* (NOT ...~~to New Zealand?~~)

For *in* and *into*, see 269.

80 **at**, **on** and **in** (place)

1 *at*

At is used to talk about position at a point.

> *It's very hot **at the centre of the earth**.*
> *Turn right **at the next corner**.*

Sometimes we use *at* with a larger place, if we just **think** of this as a point: a
stage on a journey or a meeting place, for example. Compare:

> – *The plane stops for an hour **at Frankfurt**.* (a point on a journey)
> *She lives **in Frankfurt**.* (somebody's home)
> – *Let's meet **at the club**.* (a meeting point)
> *It was warm and comfortable **in the club**.* (a place to spend time)

We very often use *at* before the name of a building, when we are thinking not
of the building itself but of the activity that happens there.

> *There's a good film **at the cinema in Market Street**.*
> *Eat **at the Steak House** – best food in town.*
> *Sorry I didn't phone last night – I was **at the theatre**.*

At is particularly common with proper names used for buildings or
organisations. Compare:

> – *I first met your father **at/in Harrods**.*
> *I first met your father **in a shop**.*
> – *She works **at Legal and General Insurance**.*
> *She works **in a big insurance company**.*

At is used to say where people study.

> *He's **at the London School of Economics**.*

And *at* is used before the name of a city to refer to that city's university.
Compare:

> *He's a student **at** Oxford.*
> *He lives **in** Cambridge.*

At is also used before the names of group activities.

> ***at** a party   **at** a meeting   **at** a concert*
> ***at** a lecture   **at** the match*

2 *on*

On is used to talk about position on a line (for example a road or a river).
> *His house is **on the way** from Aberdeen to Dundee.*
> *Stratford is **on the river Avon**.*

But *in* is used to talk about the position of things which actually form part of the line.
> *There's a misprint **in line 6** on page 22.*
> *Who's the good-looking boy **in the sixth row**?*

On is used for position on a surface.
> *Hurry up – supper's **on the table**!*
> *That picture would look better **on the other wall**.*
> *There's a big spider **on the ceiling**.*

On can mean 'attached to'.
> *Why do you wear that ring **on** your first finger?*
> *There aren't many apples **on** the tree this year.*

On is also used for position by a lake or sea.
> *Bowness is **on Lake Windermere**.*   *Southend-**on-Sea***

3 *in*

In is used for position inside large areas, and in three-dimensional space (when something is surrounded on all sides).
> *She grew up **in Swaziland**.*
> *I don't think he's **in his office**.*
> *He lived **in the desert** for three years.*
> *Let's go for a walk **in the woods**.*
> *I last saw her **in the car park**.*

4 public transport

We use *on* (and *off*) to talk about travel using buses, planes and trains, as well as (motor)cycles and horses.
> *He's arriving **on the 3.15 train**.* (NOT ...~~in/with the 3.15 train~~.)
> *We're booked **on flight 604**.*
> *There's no room **on the bus**; let's get **off** again.*
> *It took five days to cross the Atlantic **on** the Queen Elizabeth.*

But we use *in* and *out (of)* to talk about private cars, planes and boats.
> *Jump **in** and I'll drive you to the station.*
> *He fell into the river when he was getting **out of** his canoe.*

5 addresses

We generally use *at* to talk about addresses.
> *Are you still **at the same address**?*
> *She lives **at 73 Albert Street**.*

We use *in* (US *on*) if we just give the name of the street.
> *She lives **in Albert Street**.*

We use *on* for the number of the floor.
> *She lives in a flat **on the third floor**.*

At can be used with a possessive to mean 'at somebody's house or shop'.
> *'Where's Jane?' 'She's round **at Pat's**.'*
> *You're always **at the hairdresser's**.*   ▶

6 special expressions

Note these expressions:

> **in/at** church   **at** home/work
> **at** school/college
> **in** school/college (American English)
> **in** a picture   **in** the sky   **in** the rain   **in** a tent   **in** a hat
> The map is **on page 32**. (BUT I opened the book **at page 32**.)
> **in** bed/(the) hospital/prison
> **on** a farm   working **on** the railway

Note that *at* is usually pronounced /ət/, not /æt/ (see 588).
For the difference between *at/in* and *to*, see 79.
For *smile at* etc, *shoot at* etc and *arrive at*, see 79.3.
For other uses of *at, on* and *in*, see a good dictionary.

81 **at, on** and **in** (time)

> *at* + clock time
> *in* + part of day
> *on* + particular day
> *at* + weekend, public holiday
> *in* + longer period

1 clock times: *at*

> I usually get up **at six o'clock**.
> I'll meet you **at 4.15**.
> Phone me **at lunch time**.

At is usually left out before *what time* in an informal style (see paragraph 7).

> **What time** does your train leave?

2 parts of the day: *in*

> I work best **in the morning**.
> three o'clock **in the afternoon**
> We usually go out **in the evening**.

Note the difference between **in** the night (= during one particular night) and **at** night (= during any night). Compare:

> I had to get up **in the night**.
> I often work **at night**.

In an informal style, plurals without a preposition can be used to refer to repeated activity.

> Would you rather work **nights** or **days**?

We use *on* if we say which morning/afternoon/etc we are talking about, or if we describe the morning/afternoon/etc.

> See you **on Monday morning**.
> We met **on a cold afternoon** in early spring.

3   **days: *on***

> *I'll ring you **on Tuesday**.*
> *My birthday's **on March 21st**.*
> *They're having a party **on Christmas Day**.*

In an informal style we sometimes leave out *on*. This is especially common in American English.

> *I'm seeing her **Sunday morning**.*

Note the use of plurals (*Sundays, Mondays* etc) when we talk about repeated actions.

> *We usually go and see Granny **on Sundays**.*

4   **public holidays and weekends: *at***

We use *at* to talk about the whole of the holidays at Christmas, New Year, Easter and Thanksgiving (US).

> *We're having the roof repaired **at Easter**.*

But we use *on* to talk about one day of the holiday.

> *Come and see us **on Christmas Day**.*
> *What are you doing **on Easter Monday**?*

British people say *at the weekend*; Americans use *on*.

> *What did you do **at the weekend**?*

5   **longer periods: *in***

> *It happened **in the week after Christmas**.*
> *I was born **in March**.*
> *Our house was built **in the 15th century**.*
> *Kent is beautiful **in spring**.*
> *He died **in 1616**.*

6   **other uses of *in***

In can also be used to say how soon something will happen, and to say how long something takes to happen.

> *Ask me again **in three or four days**.*
> *I can run 200 metres **in about 30 seconds**.*

The expression *in . . .'s time* is used to say how soon something will happen, not how long something takes. Compare:

> *I'll see you again **in a month's time**.*   *It'll be ready **in three weeks' time**.*
> *He wrote the book **in a month**.* (NOT *. . .in a month's time*.)

In American English, *in* can be used, like *for*, to talk about periods up to the present (British English only *for*).

> *I haven't seen her **in years**.*

7   **expressions with no preposition**

At/on/in are not normally used in expressions of time before *next, last, this, that* (sometimes), *one, any* (in an informal style), *each, every, some, all*.

> *See you **next week**.*   *Come **any time**.*
> *Are you free **this morning**?*   *I'm at home **every evening**.*
> *I didn't feel very well **that week**.*   *We stayed **all day**.*
> *Let's meet **one day**.*   ▶

These prepositions are not normally used, either, before *yesterday, the day before yesterday, tomorrow* or *the day after tomorrow.*
> *What are you doing **the day after tomorrow**?*

And prepositions are usually dropped in questions beginning **What/Which + expression of time**, and in answers which only contain an expression of time.
> ***What day** is the meeting?*
> ***Which week** did you say you're on holiday?*
> *'**What time** are you leaving?' '**Eight o'clock.**'*

Note that *at* is usually pronounced /ət/, not /æt/ (see 588).
For the difference between *in* and *during*, see 172.

82 at all

1 *at all* with a negative

We often use *at all* to emphasise a negative idea.
> *I didn't understand anything **at all**.* (= *I didn't understand even a little.*)
> *She was hardly frightened **at all**.*

2 questions etc

At all can also be used in questions, and with 'non-assertive' words like *if, hardly, ever* and *any.*
> *Do you play poker **at all**?* (= *... even a little?*)
> *He'll come before supper **if** he comes **at all**.*   *I **hardly** know her **at all**.*
> *You can come whenever you like – **any** time **at all**.*

3 'Not at all'

The expression *Not at all* is used (especially in British English) as a rather formal answer to *Thank you* – see 520.19.

83 at first and first

We use *at first* to talk about the beginning of a situation, when we are making a contrast with what happens/happened later. *At first ...* is often followed by *but.*
> ***At first** they were very happy, **but** then things started going wrong.*
> *The work was hard **at first**, **but** I got used to it.*

In other cases, we usually prefer *first.*
> *That's mine – I saw it **first**!* (NOT *... I saw it at first.*)
> *We lived there when we were **first** married.* (= *... in the early days of our marriage.*) (NOT *... when we were at first married.*)
> *I **first** met her at a party in Oxford.* (= *... for the first time ...*)
> ***First**, I want to talk about the history of the problem; then I'll outline the situation today; and then we'll discuss possible solutions.*
> (NOT *At first, I want to talk ...*)

Note that *at last* is not the opposite of *at first* – see 210.

For *first(ly)* as a discourse marker, see also 159.10.
For information about other uses of *first*, see a good dictionary.

84 auxiliary verbs

1 the need for auxiliary verbs

In English sentences, a lot of important meanings are expressed by the form of the verb phrase – for example questioning, negation, time, completion, continuation, repetition, willingness, possibility, obligation. But English verbs do not have many different forms: the maximum (except for *be*) is five (e.g. *see, sees, seeing, saw, seen*). So to express all these meanings, a number of 'auxiliary' (or 'helping') verbs are added to other verbs. There are two groups.

2 *be, do* and *have*

Be is added to other verbs to make progressive and passive forms.
>*Is* it raining?
>She **was** imprisoned for three years.

Do is used to make questions, negatives and emphatic forms of non-auxiliary verbs.
>**Do** you smoke?
>It **didn**'t matter.
>**Do** come in.

Have is used to make perfect forms.
>What **have** you done?
>I realised that I **hadn**'t turned the lights off.

See the Index for details of entries on these forms and their uses, and on non-auxiliary uses of *be, do* and *have*.

3 modal auxiliary verbs

The verbs *will, shall, would, should, can, could, may, might, must* and *ought* are usually called 'modal auxiliary verbs'. They are used with other verbs to add various meanings, mostly to do with degrees of certainty or obligation. For details, see 344–345 and the entries for each verb.

4 other verbs

Other verbs (e.g. *seem*) which are used in **verb + verb** structures are not usually called 'auxiliary verbs'. One important difference is grammatical. In auxiliary verb structures, questions are made by simply changing the order of the auxiliary verb and the subject, while in other **verb + verb** structures the auxiliary *do* has to be added to the first verb. Negatives are also constructed differently. Compare:
– **She ought** to understand.
  Ought she to understand?
– **She seems** to understand.
  Does she seem to understand?
– **He is** swimming.
  He is not swimming
– **He likes** swimming.
  He doesn't like swimming.

85 (a)wake and (a)waken

1 forms

The verbs *awake* and *wake* are irregular in British English, but can be regular in American English.
(a)wake – (a)woke – (a)woken GB / US
(a)wake – (a)waked – (a)waked US
(A)waken is regular.
(a)waken – (a)wakened – (a)wakened

2 use

Wake is the most common of these four verbs. It can mean 'stop sleeping' or 'make (somebody else) stop sleeping'. It is often followed by *up*, especially when it means *stop sleeping*.
*I **woke up** three times in the night.*
*Could you **wake** me (**up**) at half past six?*
Waken is a more literary alternative to *wake (up)*.
*The princess did not **waken** for a hundred years.*
*Then the prince **wakened** her with a kiss.*
Awake and *awaken* are also rather literary words. They can be used to mean 'wake (up)', but are more often used figuratively, to talk not about waking from sleep, but about the waking of emotions, understanding etc.
*I slowly **awoke** to the danger that threatened me.*
*At first I paid little attention, but slowly my interest **awoke**.*
*The smell of her perfume **awakened** the gipsy's desire.*

3 *awake* and *asleep* (adjectives)

Note that in informal British English the adjective *awake* is more common (in predicative position) than the verb form *waking*; and *asleep* is more common than *sleeping*.
*Is the baby **awake** yet?*   *You were **asleep** at ten o'clock.*

For *arouse* and *rouse*, see 61.

86 back and again

Back and *again* can be used with similar meanings, but there are some differences.

1 *back* with a verb

Back is an adverb particle (see 19). With a verb, we use *back* to suggest a return to an earlier situation, a movement in the opposite direction to an earlier movement, and similar ideas. *Again* is not normally used in this way with a verb.
*Give me my watch **back**.* (NOT ~~Give me my watch **again**.~~)
*I'm **taking** this meat **back** to the shop.*
  (NOT ~~I'm **taking** this meat to the shop **again**.~~)

2 *again* with a verb

With a verb, *again* usually suggests repetition. Compare:
- *That was lovely. Can you **play** it **again**?*
  *When I've recorded your voice I'll **play** it **back**.*
- *Eric was really bad-mannered. I'm never going to **invite** him **again**.*
  *She comes to our parties but she never **invites** us **back**.*
- *I don't think he got your letter. You'd better **write again**.*
  *If I write to you, will you **write back**?*

Note the difference between *sell back* (to the same person) and *sell again*.
  *The bike you sold me is too small. Can I **sell** it **back** to you?*
  If we buy this house and then have to move somewhere else, how easy will it
      *be to **sell** it **again**?*

3 cases when *back* is not used

When the verb itself already expresses the idea of 'return to an earlier situation' or 'movement in the opposite direction', *back* is not used, but *again* can be used to emphasise the idea of 'return'.
  *Stefan can never **return** to his country (**again**).*
      (NOT ~~Stefan can never **return back**...~~)
  *Who opened the window? Could you **close** it (**again**), please?*
      (NOT ...~~**close it back**...~~)

4 adverb particles etc

With adverb particles and prepositional phrases, we can use both *back* and *again* to suggest 'return to an earlier situation' etc.
  *I stood up, and then I sat (**back**) **down** (**again**).*
  *He tasted the apple and spat it (**back**) **out** (**again**).*
  *Go (**back**) **to sleep** (**again**).*
  *I'll be (**back**) **in the office** (**again**) on Monday.*

5 *ring/call back*

Note that *ring back* (GB only) and *call back* can be used to mean both 'return a phone call' and 'repeat a phone call'.
  *'She's not here just now.' 'Ask her to **ring** me **back**.'* (= return my call)
  *'I haven't got time to talk now.' 'OK, I'll **ring back** later.'* (= ring again)

6 word order

Back, as an adverb particle, can usually go between a verb and its object, unless this is a pronoun (see 582.3). *Again* cannot.
  *Take **back** your money – I don't want it.* (OR *Take your money **back**...*)
  *Count the money **again**, please.* (NOT ~~Count **again** the money...~~)

For other uses of *back* and *again*, see a good dictionary.

87 · bath and bathe

1 *bath*

Pronunciation: *bath* /bɑːθ/
                       bathing /'bɑːθɪŋ/
                       bathed /bɑːθt/

The verb *bath* is used (in British English) to mean 'wash oneself in a bath (tub)'.

*Children have to be made to **bath** regularly.*

The verb is rather formal, and is not used is American English; in an informal style, we usually say *have a bath* (British) or *take a bath* (British and American).

*I'm feeling hot and sticky; I think I'll **take a bath**.*

Bath can also be used with an object (in British English).

*It's your turn to **bath** the baby.* (US . . . *to bathe the baby*.)

2 *bathe*

Pronunciation: *bathe* /beɪð/
                       bathing /'beɪðɪŋ/
                       bathed /beɪðd/

Bathe (in British English) can mean 'swim for pleasure'. It is rather formal in this sense (and is not used like this in American English); in an informal style, we usually say *have a swim, go for a swim, go swimming* or just *swim*.

*Let's **go for a swim** in the river.*

In American English, *bathe* is commonly used to mean 'take a bath'.

*I always **bathe** before I go to bed.*

Bathe can also be used (in both British and American English) with an object, to talk about putting water on a part of the body that hurts (for instance sore eyes).

*Your eyes are very red – you ought to **bathe** them.*

To lie in the sun is to *sunbathe* (NOT ~~sunbath~~).

88   be: progressive forms

> *I am being / you are being* etc + adjective / noun

We can use this structure to talk about actions and behaviour, but not usually to talk about feelings. Compare:

– *You're **being** stupid.* (= You're doing stupid things.)
  *I **was being** very careful.* (= I was doing something carefully.)
  *Who's **being** a silly baby, then?*
– *I'm happy just now.* (NOT ~~I'm being happy just now.~~)
  *I **was** very depressed when you phoned.*
    (NOT ~~I was being very depressed . . .~~)

Note the difference between *He's **being** sick* (GB = *He's vomiting*) and *He's sick* (= *He's ill*).

For the use of *am being* etc in passive verb forms, see 407.2.

89 **be** with auxiliary **do**

Normally, *be* is used without the auxiliary *do*.
> *I'm not often sick.* (NOT *I don't often be sick.*)

But *do* is used to make negative imperative sentences with *be* (when we tell somebody not to do something).
> ***Don't be*** *silly!*   ***Don't be*** *such a nuisance!*

And *do be* is used to begin emphatic imperatives.
> ***Do be*** *careful!*   ***Do be*** *quiet, for God's sake!*

In an informal style, people sometimes use *do* with *be* in one or two other structures which have a similar meaning to imperative sentences.
> *Why* ***don't*** *you* ***be*** *a good boy and sit down?*
> *If you* ***don't be*** *quiet you'll go straight to bed.*

For other auxiliary uses of *do*, see 163.

90 **be** + infinitive

> *I am to … you are to …* etc

1 **plans and arrangements**

We use this structure in a formal style to talk about plans and arrangements, especially when they are official.
> *The President* ***is to visit*** *Nigeria next month.*
> *We* ***are to get*** *a 10 per cent wage rise in June.*
> *I felt nervous because I* ***was*** *soon* ***to leave*** *home for the first time.*

A perfect infinitive can be used to show that a planned event did not happen.
> *I* ***was to have started*** *work last week, but I changed my mind.*

2 'fate'

Another use is to talk about things which are / were 'hidden in the future', fated to happen.
> *I thought we were saying goodbye for ever. But we* ***were to meet*** *again, many years later, under very strange circumstances.*

3 **pre-conditions**

The structure is common in *if*-clauses, when the **main clause** expresses a pre-condition – something that must happen first **if something else is to happen**.
> *If we* ***are to get*** *there by lunchtime we had better hurry.*
> *He knew he would have to work hard if he* ***was to pass*** *his exam.*

4 **orders**

We also use the structure to give orders. Parents often use it when speaking to children.
> *You* ***are to do*** *your homework before you watch TV.*
> *She can go to the party, but she's* ***not to be*** *back late.*

▶

5   *be* + passive infinitive

***Be* + passive infinitive** is often used in notices and instructions.

> *am/are/is (not) to be* + past participle

> *This cover is **not to be removed**.*

Sometimes only the passive infinitive is used.

> ***To be taken** three times a day after meals.* (on a medicine bottle)

Some other common expressions with ***be* + passive infinitive**:

> *There's nothing **to be done**.*
> *She was nowhere **to be found**.*
> *I looked out of the window, but there was nothing **to be seen**.*

6   tenses

Note that this structure exists only in present and past tenses, not present perfect or future. We cannot say that somebody ~~*has been to go somewhere*,~~ or ~~*will be to go somewhere*.~~ Participle structures (~~***being to go***~~) are not possible either.

For other ways of talking about the future, see 219–226.

91   **be** and **have**

1   physical conditions etc

To talk about experiencing hunger, thirst, heat, cold and certain other common physical conditions we normally use ***be*** (or *feel*) + **adjective**, not ***have* + noun**. Note the following expressions:

> *be hungry* (NOT ~~*have hunger*~~)   *be thirsty*   *be warm*
> *be hot*   *be cold*   *be sleepy*   *be afraid*

Note also:

> *be right*   *be wrong*   *be lucky*

2   age, height, weight, size and colour

Be is also used to talk about age, height, length, weight, size, shape and colour.

> *I'm nearly thirty.* (NOT ~~*I have nearly thirty.*~~)
> *She is nearly my age.*
> *He is six feet tall.*
> *I wish I was ten kilos lighter.*
> *The room is ten metres long.*
> *What size are your shoes?*
> *What colour are his eyes?*
> *She is the same height as her father.*

Be heavy is not usually used in measuring expressions.

> *It weighs 37 kilos.* (NOT ~~*It's 37 kilos heavy.*~~)

For the use of *have* in expressions like *have a bath, have a drink, have a walk*, see 240.

92 **beat** and **win**

You can *win* (in) a game, a race, a battle, an argument etc, and you can *win* a prize, money etc. You can *beat* a person that you are playing / arguing / fighting etc against. Compare:

>*My girlfriend **wins** when we play poker.*
>*My girlfriend **beat** me at poker the first time we played.*
>   (NOT ~~My girlfriend **won** me at poker~~…)

Both verbs are irregular:

>*beat – beat – beaten*
>*win – won – won*

93 **because** and **because of**

1 the difference

Because is a conjunction. It is used at the beginning of a clause, before a subject and verb. *Because of* is a two-word preposition, used before a noun or a pronoun. Compare:

– *We were late **because** it rained.* (NOT …~~**because of** it rained.~~)
  *We were late **because of** the rain.* (NOT …~~**because** the rain.~~)
– *I'm happy **because** I met you.*
  *I'm happy **because of** you.*

2 position of *because*-clauses

Because and its clause can go after or before the main clause.

>*I finished early **because I worked fast**.*
>***Because I worked fast**, I finished early.*

Because-clauses can stand alone as answers or after hesitations, but not usually in other cases.

>*'Why are you crying?' '**Because John and I have had a row**.'*
>*I don't think I'll go to the party after all, actually … **Because I'm feeling a bit tired**.*

Note that after *reason* we usually use *that* or *why*, not *because* (see 470).

For the differences between *because, as, since* and *for*, see 72.

94 **been** meaning 'come' or 'gone'

Been is often used as a past participle of *come* and *go*.

>*Granny has **been** to see us twice since Christmas.*
>*I haven't **been** to the theatre for ages.*
>*Have you ever **been** to Northern Ireland?*

Note that *been* is only used for completed visits. Compare:

– *The postman's already **been**.* (He has come and gone away again.)
  *Jane's **come**, so we can start work.* (She has come and is still here.)
– *I've **been** to London three times this week.*
  *'Where's Lucy?' 'She's **gone** to London.'*

For *be gone*, see 233.

95 before (adverb)

1 'at any time before now/then'

We can use *before* to mean 'at any time before now'. In British English, a present perfect tense is normally used.

I think I've seen this film before.   ***Have** you ever **been** here **before?***

Before can also mean 'at any time before then – before the past moment that we are talking about'. In this case a past perfect tense is used.

*She realised that she **had seen** him **before**.*

2 counting back from a past time

We also use *before* after a time expression to 'count back' from a past moment – to say how much earlier something else had happened. A past perfect tense is normally used.

*When I went back to the town that I **had left eight years before**, everything was different.* (NOT *...that I **had left before eight years**...*)

To count back from the present, we use *ago*, not *before* (see also 31).

*I left school **four years ago**.* (NOT *...**four years before / before four years**.*)

3 *before, before that* and *first*

Before is not generally used to mean 'before that' or 'first'.

*I want to get married one day. But **before that/first**, I want to travel.*
(NOT *...**But before, I want to travel.***)

For the difference between *before* and *ever*, see 197–198.
For *before* as a conjunction and preposition, see 96–97.

96 before (conjunction)

> clause + *before* + clause
> *before* + clause, + clause

1 position of *before*-clause

The conjunction *before* joins one clause to another. *Before* and its clause can come either after or before the other clause, depending on what is to be stressed.

– *I always feed the cat **before I have breakfast**.*
  ***Before I have breakfast**, I always feed the cat.*
  (The meaning is similar: the speaker feeds the cat and then has breakfast. Note the comma in the second structure.)
– *He did military service **before he went to university**.*
  (He did military service first.)
  ***Before he did military service**, he went to university.*
  (He went to university first.)

2 present tense with future meaning

In a clause with *before*, we use a present tense if the meaning is future (see 556).

*I'll telephone you **before I come**.* (NOT *...**before I will come**.*)

3 perfect tenses

In clauses with *before,* we often use present perfect and past perfect tenses to emphasise the idea of completion.

*You can't go home **before I've signed** the letters.*
(= ... *before the moment when I have completed the letters.*)
*He went out **before I had finished** my sentence.*
(= ... *before the moment when I had completed my sentence.*)
(Note that in sentences like the last, a past perfect tense can refer to a time **later** than the action of the main verb. This is unusual: see 421.)

4 *before ... ing*

In a formal style, we often use the structure ***before ... ing***.
*Please put out all lights **before leaving** the office.*
***Before beginning** the book, she spent five years on research.*

For the use of *before* as an adverb, see 95.
For the use of *before* as a preposition, see 97.

97 **before** (preposition) and **in front of**

before: time
in front of: place

Compare:
*I must move my car **before nine o'clock**.*
*It's parked **in front of the post office**.* (NOT ... ~~before the post office.~~)
Before is normally used to refer to time, but it can refer to place in a few cases:

a to talk about the order in which people or things come in queues, lists, written documents etc
*Do you mind? I was **before/in front of** you!*
*Her name comes **before** mine in the alphabet.*
*We use 'a' **before** a consonant and 'an' **before** a vowel.*

b to mean 'in the presence of (somebody important)'
*I came up **before the magistrates** for dangerous driving last week.*

c in the expressions *right **before** one's eyes, **before** one's very eyes.*

For the difference between *in front of* and *facing/ opposite*, see 272.
For the use of *before* as a conjunction, see 96.
For the use of *before* as an adverb, see 95.
For *by* meaning 'at/on or before', see 118.

98 **begin** and **start**

1 formality

There is usually little or no difference between *begin* and *start*.
> *I **began/started** teaching when I was 24.*
> *If Sheila doesn't come soon, let's **begin/start** without her.*

We generally prefer *begin* when we are using a more formal style. Compare:
> *We will **begin** the meeting with a message from the President.*
> *Damn! It's **starting** to rain.*

2 cases where *begin* is not possible

Start (but not *begin*) is used to mean:

a 'start a journey'
> *I think we ought to **start** at six, while the roads are empty.*

b 'start working' (for machines)
> *The car won't **start**.*

c 'make (machines) start'
> *How do you **start** the washing machine?*

For infinitives and *-ing* forms after *begin* and *start*, see 296.10.

99 **below** and **under**

1 'lower than': *below* or *under*

The prepositions *below* and *under* can both mean 'lower than'.
> *Look in the cupboard **below/under** the sink.*

2 not directly under: *below*

We prefer *below* when one thing is not directly under another.
> *The climbers stopped 300m **below** the top of the mountain.*
> *A moment later the sun had disappeared **below** the horizon.*

3 covered: *under*

We prefer *under* when something is covered or hidden by what is over it, and when things are touching.
> *I think the cat's **under** the bed.*
> *What are you wearing **under** your sweater?*
> *The whole village is **under** water.*

4 measurements: *below*

Below is used in measurements of temperature and height, and in other cases where we think of a vertical scale.
> *The temperature is three degrees **below** zero.*
> *Parts of Holland are **below** sea level.*
> *The plane came down **below** the clouds.*
> *She's well **below** average in intelligence.*

5 'less than': *under*

We usually use *under*, not *below*, to mean 'less than' or 'younger than'.
> *There were **under** twenty people at the lecture.*
> *You can't see this film if you're **under** 18.*

6 underneath

Underneath is sometimes used as a preposition instead of *under*, but only for physical position. Compare:
> *There's a mouse **under(neath)** the piano.*
> *He's still **under** 18.* (NOT *...underneath 18.*)

7 adverbs

Below can be used as an adverb. *Under* can be used as an adverb particle (see 19) with some verbs, but in other cases we prefer *underneath* for adverbial use.
> *We looked over the cliff at the waves crashing on the rocks **below**.*
> *A lot of businesses are **going under** because of the economic crisis.*
> *I can't take my sweater off – I haven't got anything on **underneath**.*

In a book or a paper, *see below* means 'look at something written later'.

The difference between *above* and *over* is similar to the difference between *below* and *under*. See 6 for details.

100 **beside** and **besides**

Beside is a preposition meaning 'at the side of', 'by', 'next to'.
> *Who's the big guy sitting **beside** Jane?*

Besides can be used as a preposition with a similar meaning to *as well as* (see 77), to add new information to what is already known.
> ***Besides** literature, we have to study history and philosophy.*
> *Who was at the party **besides** Jack and the Bensons?*

Besides can also be used as a discourse marker (see 159.11) meaning 'also', 'as well', 'in any case'. It is often used to add a stronger, more conclusive argument to what has gone before. In this case, *besides* usually goes at the beginning of a clause.
> *I don't like those shoes; **besides**, they're too expensive.*
> *It's too late to go out now. **Besides**, it's starting to rain.*

For the difference between *besides*, *except* and *apart from*, see 101.

101 **besides**, **except** and **apart from**

These expressions are sometimes confused.
Besides usually adds: it is like saying *with*, or *plus* (+).
> ***Besides** the violin, he plays the piano and the flute.*
> (He plays three instruments.)

Except subtracts: it is like saying *without*, or *minus* (–).
> *I like all musical instruments **except** the violin.*

▶

Apart from can be used in both senses.

> **Apart from** *the violin, he plays the piano and the flute.*
>> (= **Besides the** *violin . . .*)
>
> *I like all musical instruments* **apart from** *the violin.*
>> (= *. . .* **except** *the violin.*)

After *no, nobody, nothing* and similar negative words, the three expressions can all have the same meaning.

> *He has* **nothing besides / except / apart from** *his salary.*
>> (= *He only has his salary.*)

For the use of *besides* as an adverbial discourse marker, see 159.11.
For *beside*, see 100.
For *except* and *except for*, see 200.
For *nothing but*, see 116.

102 bet

1 use

I bet (you) can be used in an informal style to mean 'I think it's probable that'. *That* is usually dropped.

> **I bet** *(you) she's not at home.*
>> (More natural than *I bet (you) that she's not at home.*)

2 tenses

After *I bet (you)*, we often use a present tense to refer to the future.

> **I bet** *(you) they* **don't** *come this evening.* (OR *I bet (you) they* **won't** *come . . .*)
> **I bet** *(you) the Conservatives (will)* **lose**.

3 two objects

When *bet* is used to talk about real bets, it can be followed by two objects: the person with whom the bet is made, and the money or thing that is bet.

> *I bet* **you £5** *it doesn't rain this week.*
> *My father bet* **my mother dinner at the Ritz** *that she would marry him. He won, but she never bought him the dinner.*

103 better

1 'recovered'

When *better* means 'recovered from an illness', it can be used with *completely* or *quite* (unlike other comparative adjectives).

> *Don't start work again until you're* **quite better**.

2 correcting mistakes

We do not normally use *better* to correct mistakes.

> *She's gone to Hungary – or* **rather**, *Poland.* (NOT *. . . or* **better, Poland.**)

For the structure *had better*, see 234.

104 between and among

1 the difference

We say that somebody or something is *between* two or more clearly separate people or things. We use *among* when somebody or something is in a group, a crowd or a mass of people or things which we do not see separately. Compare:
– *She was standing **between** Alice and Mary.*
*She was standing **among** a crowd of children.*
– *Our house is **between** the woods, the river and the village.*
*His house is hidden **among** the trees.*
Between can be used to talk about intervals and time limits.
*We need two metres **between** the windows.*
*I'll be at the office **between** nine and eleven.*

2 things on two sides: *between*

We use *between* to say that there are things (or groups of things) on two sides.
*a little valley **between** high mountains*
*I saw something **between** the wheels of the car.*

3 *divide* and *share*

Before a series of singular nouns we usually use *divide between* and *share between*. Before a plural noun, we can say *between* or *among*. Compare:
*He **divided** his money **between** his wife, his daughter and his sister.*
*I **shared** the food **between/among** all my friends.*

4 *difference between*

We use *between*, not *among*, after *difference*.
*What are the main **differences between** crows, rooks and jackdaws?*

5 'one of' etc

Among can mean 'one of', 'some of' or 'included in'.
***Among** the first to arrive was the ambassador.*
*He has a number of criminals **among** his friends.*

6 *between each*

Some people feel that expressions like *between each window* or *between each birthday* are incorrect. They prefer *between each ... and the next.*
*We need two metres **between each window (and the next)**.*
*There seems to be less and less time **between each birthday (and the next)**.*

105 big, large and great

1 concrete nouns: *big* and *large*

Big and *large* are used mostly with concrete nouns–the names of things you can see, touch etc. *Big* is most common in an informal style.
*Get your **big** feet off my flowers.*
*I'm afraid my daughter has rather **large** feet.*
*It was a **large** house, situated near the river.*

▶

2 abstract nouns: *great*

Great is used mostly with abstract nouns – things you cannot see, touch etc.
> *You are making a **great** mistake.*
> *Her work showed a **great** improvement last year.*
> *I have **great** respect for her ideas.*

3 *big* with countable abstract nouns

Big can be used with countable abstract nouns in an informal style. *Large* is
not normally used with abstract nouns.
> *You're making a **big** mistake.* (NOT ... ~~a large mistake.~~)

Big is not used with uncountable abstract nouns (except in a few fixed
expressions like *big business, big trouble*).
> *His work shows **great** intelligence.* (NOT ... ~~big intelligence.~~)

4 uncountable concrete nouns

With uncountable concrete nouns, none of these three words is usual.
> *You've got **a lot of** luggage!* (NOT ... ~~big/large/great luggage!~~)

5 other uses of *great*

We also use *great* to mean 'famous' or 'important'.
> *Do you think Napoleon was really a **great** man?*

And in an informal style, *great* can mean 'wonderful'.
> *I've just got a **great** new job.*

Great is used in some informal expressions to emphasise the idea of size.
> *Then this **bloody great** dog came after me.*   *He's just a **great big** baby.*

6 *large* and *wide*

Large is a 'false friend' for speakers of some languages. It does not mean 'wide'.
> *The river is 100 metres **wide**.* (NOT ... ~~100 metres large.~~)

For *tall* and *high*, see 249.
For *broad* and *wide*, see 115.
For *small* and *little*, see 511.

106 a bit

1 use

A bit is often used as an adverb with the same meaning as *a little*, especially
in informal British English.
> *She's **a bit** old to play with dolls, isn't she?*
> *Can you drive **a bit** slower?*   *Wait **a bit**.*

Note that when *a bit* and *a little* are used with non-comparative adjectives,
the meaning is usually negative or critical.
> *a bit tired   a bit expensive   a little (too) old*
> (BUT NOT ~~a bit kind, a little interesting~~)

2   *a bit of a*

A bit of a can be used before some nouns in an informal style. The meaning
is similar to *rather a* (see 468).

>   He's *a bit of a* fool, if you ask me.   I've got *a bit of a* problem.

3   *not a bit*

The informal expression *not a bit* means 'not at all'.

>   I'm *not a bit* tired.
>   'Do you mind if I put some music on?' '*Not a bit.*'

Note that *not a bit* is not the same as the rather rare literary expression *not a
little* (= 'quite').

For *a bit* and other modifiers with comparative adjectives and adverbs, see 139.
For *a little* and *little*, see 322.

107   **born** and **borne**

1   *be born*

To talk about coming into the world at birth, we usually use the passive verb
to be born.

>   Hundreds of children *are born* deaf every year.

To give somebody's place or date of birth, we use the simple past tense
was/were born.

>   I *was born* in 1936. (NOT *~~I am born in 1936.~~*)
>   My parents *were born* in Scotland.

2   the verb *bear*

There is also a verb *bear* (*bore, borne*). This verb is most often used in the
expression *can't bear* (= 'hate', 'can't stand').

>   I *can't bear* her voice.

In a very formal style, *bear* can be used with other meanings, including
'carry' and 'give birth to'.

>   They *bore* the king's body away on a stretcher.
>   She *has borne* six children in seven years.
>   (More normal: *She has **had** six children . . .*)

For more details of the verb *bear*, see a good dictionary.

108   **borrow** and **lend**

> *borrow* something *from* somebody
> *lend* something *to* somebody
> *lend* somebody something

Borrow is like *take*.

>   Can I *borrow* your bicycle? (NOT *~~Can I lend your bicycle?~~*)

You borrow something *from* somebody.

>   I *borrowed* a pound *from* my brother.
>   (NOT *~~I borrowed my brother a pound.~~*)

▶

Lend (US also *loan*) is like *give*. You lend something *to* somebody, or lend somebody something.

>*I **lent** my coat **to** Steve, and I never saw it again.*
>***Lend** me your comb for a minute, will you?* (NOT ~~***Borrow me your*...**~~)

For *lend* in passive structures, see 410.

109 **both (of)** with nouns and pronouns

1 nouns with determiners: *both (of)*

Before a noun with a determiner (e.g. *the, my, these*), *both* and *both of* are both possible. In American English, *both of* is usual.

>*She's eaten **both (of) the chops**.*
>***Both (of) my parents** like riding.*
>***Both (of) these oranges** are bad.*

We often drop *the* or a possessive after *both*.

>*She's eaten **both chops**.*
>*He lost **both parents** when he was a child.*

2 personal pronouns: *both of*

With personal pronouns, we use *both of* (followed by the object form of the pronoun). *Both of us/you/them* can be the subject or object of a clause.

>***Both of them** can come tomorrow.*
>*She's invited **both of us**.*
>*Mary sends **both of you** her love.*

We can put *both* after pronouns used as objects.

>*She's invited **us both**.*
>*Mary sends **you both** her love.*

But this structure is not used with complement pronouns or in short answers.

>*'Who broke the window – Sarah or Alice?' 'It was **both of them**.'*
> (NOT *...~~them both.~~*)
>*'Who did you invite?' '**Both of them**.'* (NOT ~~*'Them both.'*~~)

When *both* is used after a subject pronoun (e.g. ***They both** wanted to marry him*) it goes in mid-position (see 22), and follows an auxiliary.

>***They have both** been invited.*

3 *the* not used before *both*

Note that we do not put *the* before *both*.

>***both (the)** children* (NOT ~~*the **both** children*~~)

4 negative structures

Instead of *both ... not*, we normally use *neither* (see 363).

>***Neither** of them is here.* (NOT ~~***Both of them are not** here.*~~)

For the use of *both* with verbs, see 110.

110 **both** with verbs

When *both* refers to the subject of a clause, it can go with the verb, in 'mid-position' (like *all* and some adverbs – see 36, 22.3).

> auxiliary verb + *both*
> *are/were* + *both*

*We **can both** swim.*   *The children **have both** gone to bed.*
*Those oranges **were both** bad.*

> *both* + other verb

*My parents **both work** in education.*   *They **both liked** the flowers.*
Note that these meanings can also be expressed by using ***both (of)** +*
noun/pronoun as the subject (see 109).
***Both of us** can swim.*   ***Both of the children** have gone to bed.*

111 **both ... and**

> *both* + adjective + *and* + adjective
> *both* + noun + *and* + noun
> etc

People usually 'balance' this structure, so that the same kind of words or expressions follow *both* and *and*.
*She's both **pretty** and **clever**.* (adjectives)
*I spoke to both **the Director** and **her secretary**.* (nouns)
*She both **dances** and **sings**.* (verbs)
The following sentences, which are not 'balanced' in this way, are possible in standard English. However, many people would feel that the style was bad.
*She both **dances** and **she sings**.* (*both* + verb; *and* + clause)
*She both **plays the piano** and **the violin**.* (*both* + verb + noun; *and* + noun)
*I both **spoke to the Director** and **her secretary**.*

See also *either ... or* (179), *neither ... nor* (365) and *not only ... but also* (376).

112 **bring** and **take**

1 speaker's/hearer's position

In British English, we use *bring* for movements to the place where the speaker or hearer is, but we use *take* for movements to other places. Compare:
– *This is a nice restaurant. Thanks for **bringing** me here.*
      (NOT ... ~~thanks for **taking** me here.~~)
   *Let's have another drink, and then I'll **take** you home.*
      (NOT ... ~~and then I'll **bring** you home.~~)
– (on the phone) *Can we come and see you next weekend? We'll **bring** a picnic.*
   *Let's go and see the Robinsons next weekend. We can **take** a picnic.*   ▶

2 speaker's/hearer's past or future position

We can also use *bring* for a movement to a place where the speaker or hearer already was or will be. Compare:

– *I'll be arriving at the hotel about six o'clock. Can you **bring** the car round at six-thirty?*
*Can you **take** the car to the garage tomorrow? I won't have time.*
(NOT ~~Can you **bring** the car to the garage tomorrow?~~ ...)

– *'Where's that report?' 'I **brought** it to you when you were in Mr Allen's office. Don't you remember?'*
*I **took** the papers to John's office.*

Note that these rules are not always followed in American English.
The difference between *come* and *go* is similar. See 134.
For other uses of *take*, see 551.

113 **bring up** and **educate**

Bring up and the noun *upbringing* are mostly used for the moral and social training that children receive at home. *Educate* and *education* are used for the intellectual and cultural training that people get at school and university.

*Lucy was **brought up** by her grandparents and **educated** at the local secondary school.*
*Their kids are very badly **brought up** – always screaming and fighting.*
(NOT ~~Their kids are very badly **educated**~~ ...)
*Would you rather have a good **upbringing** and a bad **education**, or the opposite?*

114 **Britain**, the **United Kingdom**, the **British Isles** and **England**

Britain (or *Great Britain*) and *the United Kingdom* (or *the UK*) are both used to include England, Scotland, Wales and Northern Ireland. (Sometimes *Britain* or *Great Britain* is used just for the island which includes England, Scotland and Wales, without Northern Ireland. Irish people generally use the words *Britain* and *British* in this way.)

The British Isles is the name for England, Scotland, Wales, the whole of Ireland (which includes both Northern Ireland and the Republic of Ireland, also called 'Eire'), and the smaller islands round about.

England is only one part of Britain. Scotland and Wales are not in England, and Scottish and Welsh people do not like to be called 'English'.

A very informal word for a British person is *Brit*. *Britisher* is used only by non-British people; *Briton* is hardly used except in news reports and newspaper headlines (e.g. THREE BRITONS DIE IN AIR CRASH), and to refer to the ancient inhabitants of Britain.

115 **broad** and **wide**

Wide is used for the physical distance from one side of something to the other.

> *We live in a very **wide** street.*   *The car's too **wide** for the garage.*

Broad is used in this physical sense in a few common expressions like **broad** *shoulders,* and in descriptions of landscape in a formal style.

> *Across the **broad** valley, the mountains rose blue and mysterious.*

But *broad* is mostly used in abstract expressions. Some examples:

> **broad** *agreement* (= agreement on most important points)
> **broad**-*minded* (= tolerant)   **broad** *daylight* (= full, bright daylight)

116 **but** = 'except'

1 use

We use *but* to mean 'except' after *all, none, every, any, no* (and *everything, everybody, nothing, nobody, anywhere* etc).

> *He eats **nothing but** hamburgers.*   *I've finished **all** the jobs **but** one.*
> ***Everybody**'s here **but** George.*   *She's done **nothing but** cry all day.*

Note the expressions *next but one, last but two* etc (GB).

> *Jackie lives **next** door **but** one.* (= two houses from me)
> *I was **last but two** in the race yesterday.*

The expression *but for* expresses the idea of 'if something had not existed / happened'.

> *I would have been in real trouble **but for** your help.*
> ***But for** the storm, I would have been home before eight.*

Note also the structure *Who should . . . but* (used to talk about surprising appearances, meetings etc).

> *I was just coming out of the supermarket, when **who should** I see **but** old Beryl?*

2 pronouns after *but*

After *but,* we usually use object pronouns (*me, him* etc). Subject pronouns (*I, he* etc) are possible in a more formal style.

> *Nobody **but her** would do a thing like that.* (More formal: *Nobody **but she** . . .*)

3 verbs after *but*

The verb form after *but* usually depends on what came before. Infinitives are normally without *to.*

> *That child **does** nothing but **watch** TV.* (*does . . . watch*)
> *She's not **interested in** anything but **skiing**.* (*interested in . . . skiing*)

***Cannot but** +* **infinitive** or ***cannot help but** +* **infinitive** is sometimes used with the meaning of 'can't help . . . ing' (see 126). *Cannot but . . .* is very formal; *can't help but . . .* is especially common in American English.

> *One **cannot (help) but admire** his courage.* (= *One has to admire . . .*)
> *I **can't help but wonder** what's going to happen to us all.*   ▶

4 *but* meaning 'only'

In older English, *but* was used to mean 'only', but this is now very unusual.
> *She is **but** a child.*

Note: *but* is usually pronounced /bət/, not /bʌt/ (see 588).
For *except*, see 200.
For *but* as a conjunction and ellipsis after *but*, see 182.

117 **by** (method, agent) and **with** (tools etc)

1 the difference

By and *with* can both be used to say how somebody does something, but there is an important difference.

We use *by* when we talk about an action – what we **do** to get a result. We use *with* when we talk about a tool or other object – what we **use** to get a result. Compare:
> *I killed the spider **by hitting** it.* (Note the -*ing* form after *by*.)
> *I killed the spider **with a shoe**.* (NOT *...by a shoe.*)
> *'I got where I am **by hard work**.' 'No you didn't. You got there **with your wife's money**.'*

Note that *without* is used as the opposite of both *with* and *by* in these cases. Compare:
- *I got her to listen **by shouting**.*
  *It's difficult to get her to listen **without shouting**.*
- *We'll have to get it out **with a screwdriver**.*
  *We can't get it out **without a screwdriver**.*

By is also used to refer to means of transport (*by bus*, *by train* etc). See 69.1.

2 passive clauses

In passive clauses, *by* introduces the agent – the person or thing that does the action (see 408).
> *I was interviewed **by three directors**.*
> *My car was damaged **by a falling branch**.*

We generally prefer *with* to refer to a tool or instrument used by somebody. Compare:
> *He was killed **by a heavy stone**.*
>> (This could mean 'A stone fell and killed him'.)
> *He was killed **with a heavy stone**.*
>> (This means 'Somebody used a stone to kill him'.)

118 **by**: time

By can mean 'not later than'.
> *I'll be home **by five o'clock**.* (= at or before five)
> *'Can I borrow your car?' 'Yes, but I must have it back **by tonight**.'*
>> (= tonight or before)

By can also suggest the idea of 'progress up to a particular time'.
> ***By** the end of the meal, everybody was drunk.*

By the time (that) is used with a verb, to mean 'not later than the moment that something happens'.

> *I'll be in bed **by the time** you get home.*
> ***By the time that** the guards realised what was happening, the gang were already inside the bank.*

For the difference between *by* and *until*, see 575.6.

119 **by** and **near**

By means 'just at the side of'; something that is *by* you may be closer than something that is *near* you. Compare:

> *We live **near** the sea.* (perhaps five kilometres away)
> *We live **by** the sea.* (We can see it.)

For *on the sea* (meaning 'by the sea'), see 80.2.

120 **call**

Call (with no object) can mean 'telephone'; in British English it can also mean 'visit'. This sometimes causes confusion.

> *'Alice **called** while you were out.' 'You mean she came round or she phoned?'*

For other meanings of *call*, see a good dictionary.

121 **can** and **could** (1): introduction

1 **grammar**

Can and *could* are modal auxiliary verbs (see 344–345).

a There is no *-s* in the third person singular..
> *She **can** swim very well.* (NOT ~~*She cans*~~...)

b Questions and negatives are made without *do*.
> ***Can you** swim?* (NOT ~~*Do you can swim?*~~)
> *I **couldn't** understand her.* (NOT ~~*I didn't could*~~...)

c After *can* and *could*, we use the infinitive without *to* of other verbs.
> *I **can speak** a little Arabic.* (NOT ~~*I can to speak*~~...)

Progressive, perfect and passive infinitives are also possible (see 276).
> *Do you think she **can** still **be working**? It's very late.*
> *You **could have let** me know you were going out tonight.*
> *This sweater **can't be washed** in the machine.*

d *Can* and *could* have no infinitives or participles (~~*to can, canning, I have could*~~ do not exist). When necessary, we use other words, for example forms of *be able* (see 3) or *be allowed* (see 40).
> *I'd like to **be able** to stay here.* (NOT ...~~*to can stay*~~...)
> *You'll **be able** to walk soon.* (NOT ~~*You'll can*~~...)
> *I've always **been able** to play games well.* (NOT ~~*I've always could*~~...)
> *She's always **been allowed** to do what she liked.*

▶

e *Could* is sometimes used as the past of *can*. However, it can also be used as a less definite or conditional form of *can*, referring to the present or future. For details, see 122.5, 123.2 and 124.1,3.

f Certain past ideas can be expressed by *can* or *could* followed by a perfect infinitive (***have + past participle***). For details, see 122.8, 123.6 and 124.6.
   *I don't know where she **can have gone**.*
   *That was dangerous – he **could have killed** somebody.*

g *Can* has two pronunciations: a 'strong' form /kæn/ and a 'weak' form /k(ə)n/. *Could* has a strong form /kʊd/ and a weak form /k(ə)d/. The weak pronunciation is used in most cases. For more details of strong and weak pronunciations, see 588.

h Contracted negative forms (see 144) are *can't* (pronounced /kɑːnt/ in standard British English and /kænt/ in standard American English) and *couldn't* (/ˈkʊdnt/). *Cannot* is usually written as one word.

2 meanings

Can and *could* are both used to talk about ability and possibility, to ask for and give permission, and to make requests and offers. And they can be used in a special way with *see, hear* and some other verbs to give a kind of 'present progressive' meaning.
   ***Can** you speak French?* (ability)
   *It **could** rain this afternoon.* (possibility)
   *Do you think she **could** be lying?* (possibility)
   *You **can** stop work early today.* (permission)
   ***Could** I have some more tea?* (request)
   ***Can** I help you?* (offer)
   *I **can hear** the sea.* ('present progressive' meaning)

For more details of this and other uses of *can* and *could*, see the following sections.

122 **can** and **could** (2): ability

1 present

We use *can* to talk about present or 'general' ability.
   *Look! I **can** do it!*
   *I **can** read Italian, but I **can't** speak it.*
Be able can often be used with similar meanings – see 3.

2 future

We normally use *will be able* to talk about future ability.
   *I'll **be able** to speak good French in a few months.*
   *One day people **will be able** to go to the moon on holiday.*
However, we use *can* if we are deciding now about the future.
   *I haven't got time today, but I **can** see you tomorrow.*
   ***Can** you come to a party on Saturday?*

3 past

We use *could* for 'general ability' – to say that somebody could do something at any time, whenever he/she wanted. (*Was/were able* is also possible.)
> *She **could** read when she was four.* (OR *She **was able** to read . . .*)
> *My father **could** speak ten languages.*

We do not normally use *could* to say that somebody managed to do something on one occasion. Instead, we use *was/were able, managed* or *succeeded (in . . .ing).*
> *How many eggs **were** you **able** to get?* (NOT *. . . could you get?*)
> *I **managed** to find a really nice dress in the sale.* (NOT *I could find . . .*)
> *After six hours' climbing, we **succeeded** in getting to the top of the
> mountain.* (NOT *. . . we could get to the top . . .*)

4 *could* used for particular occasions in the past

In certain cases, it is possible to use *could* to say that somebody was able to do something on one occasion. This happens with *see, hear, taste, feel, smell, understand, remember* and *guess* (see 125).
> *I **could smell** burning.*
> *I **could understand** everything she said.*

It also happens in some subordinate clauses.
> *I'm so glad that you **could** come.*

In negative clauses, and with negative or limiting adverbs like *only* and *hardly*, we also use *could* to refer to one occasion.
> *I **managed** to find the street, but I **couldn't** find her house.*
> *I **could only** get six eggs.*
> *She **could hardly** believe her eyes.*

5 conditional

We can use *could* to mean 'would be able'.
> *You **could** get a better job if you spoke a foreign language.*

This structure can be used to criticise people for not doing things.
> *You **could** ask me before you borrow my car.*

For the use of *might* in this sense, see 336.

6 reported speech

Could is used in past reported speech constructions, when *can* was used in direct speech.
> *'**Can** you phone me this evening?' 'What did you say?' 'I asked if you **could**
> phone me this evening.'*

7 passive structures

Note the use of *can* with a passive infinitive. (*Be able* is not normally used in passive structures.)
> *This game **can be played** by two or more players.*
> (NOT *. . . is able to be played . . .*)
> *Gold **can be found** in the Welsh mountains.*
►

8 *could have ...*

We use a special structure to talk about unrealised past ability – to say that somebody was able to do something, but did not try to do it.

> *could have* + past participle

> *I **could have married** anybody I wanted to.*
> *I was so angry I **could have killed** her!*

This structure can be used to criticise people for not doing things.

> *You **could have helped** me – why did you just sit and watch?*

The meaning can also be conditional (= 'would have been able').

> *I **could have won** the race if I hadn't fallen.*

Negative sentences suggest that somebody would not have been able to do something even if they had wanted or tried to.

> *I **couldn't have won**, so I didn't go in for the race.*
> *I **couldn't have enjoyed** myself more – it was a perfect day.*

9 *speak, play*

We often leave out *can* when we are talking about the ability to speak languages or to play instruments or games.

> *She **speaks** Greek. / She **can speak** Greek.*   *Do/Can you **play** the piano?*

123 **can** and **could** (3): possibility and probability

Can is used mostly to talk about 'theoretical' or 'general' possibility, not about the chances that something will actually happen or is actually true at this moment (this meaning is usually expressed by *may, might* or *could*).

1 **theoretical or general possibility**

We use *can* to say whether situations and events are possible theoretically, in general.

> *Anybody who wants to **can** join the club.*   *Can gases freeze?*
> *I don't think the car **can** be repaired.*

We use *could* to talk about past possibility.

> *It was a place where anything **could** happen.*

We predict future possibilities with *will be possible* or *will be able*.

> *One day, it **will be possible** to travel to the stars.*
> (OR *... people **will be able** to travel ...*)

We often use *can* and *could* to say what is / was common or typical.

> *Scotland **can** be very warm in September.*
> *It **could** be quite frightening if you were alone in our big old house.*

2 **choices and opportunities**

Can is often used in this way to talk about the choices that somebody has (now or in the future), or to suggest opportunities.

> *There are three possibilities: we **can** go to the police, we **can** talk to a lawyer, or we **can** forget all about it.*
> *'What shall we do?' 'We **can** try asking Lucy for help.'*

Could is also used, like *can*, to talk about present and future choices and opportunities, especially when we want to make suggestions sound less definite.

> *'What shall we do tomorrow?' 'Well, we* **could** *go fishing.'*
> *When you're in Spain, you* **could** *go and see Alex.*

3 future probability: *can* not used

We do not use *can* to talk about future probability – the chances that something will happen. We express this idea with *may* or *might* (see also 331).

> *We* **may/might** *go camping this summer.* (NOT ~~We~~ ~~*can go*~~...)
> *There* **may/might** *be a strike next week.* (NOT ~~*There can be*~~...)
> *I* **might** *be given a new job soon.*

Could is also used in this sense – it suggests a less definite possibility.

> *It* **could** *rain later this evening.*
> *War* **could** *break out any day.*

Note the difference between *can/could* and *may/might* in negative sentences. Compare:

> *It* **may/might** *not rain tomorrow.* (= *Perhaps it will not rain.*)
> *It* **can't/couldn't** *possibly rain tomorrow.* (= *It will certainly not rain.*)

4 present ('logical') possibility

We use *can* in questions and negative sentences, to talk about the logical possibility that something is true or that something is happening.

> *'There's the doorbell. Who* **can** *it be?' 'Well, it* **can't** *be your mother. She's in Edinburgh.'*

Can is not usually possible in affirmative sentences with this meaning. Instead, we use *could, may* or *might*.

> *'Where's Sarah?' 'She* **could/may/might** *be at Joe's place.'*
> (NOT ~~*She can be*~~...)

But *can* is possible in affirmative sentences with words like *only, hardly* or *never*, which have a limiting or negative meaning.

> *'Who's that at the door?' 'It* **can only** *be the postman.'*

(*Can only* is similar to *must* here – see 350.2.)

Note the difference between *may/might not* and *can/could not*.

> *It* **may not** *be true.* (= *Perhaps it is not true.*)
> *It* **can't be** *true.* (= *It is certainly not true.*)

5 reported speech

Could is used in past reported speech constructions, when *can* was used in direct speech.

> *'Anybody* **can** *join the club.' 'What?' 'I said anybody* **could** *join the club.'*

6 *can/could have* ...

We use *can/could have* + **past participle** to guess or speculate about what has happened, whether things (have) happened etc. *Can* is only used in ▶

questions and negative sentences, or with 'limiting' words like *only*, *hardly* or *never*. In other cases we use *could/may/might*.

> *Where **can** she **have gone**? She **can't have gone** to school – it's Saturday. And she **can hardly have gone** to church. She **could/may/might** have gone swimming, I suppose.* (NOT ~~She **can have gone**...~~)

Could have + past participle is also used to say that something was possible, but did not happen.

> *That was a bad place to go skiing – you **could have broken** your leg.*
> *Why did you throw the bottle out of the window? Somebody **could have been** hurt.*

The structure can refer to present situations which were possible but have not been realised.

> *He **could have** been Prime Minister now if he hadn't decided to leave politics.*

Compare *may/might have* ... and *can/could have* ... in negative sentences.

> *He **may/might not** have understood.* (= Perhaps he did not understand.)
> *He **can't/couldn't** have understood.* (= He certainly did not understand.)

For more about *may* and *might*, and the difference between *can/could* and *may/might*, see 331.10–11.

For ***must have* + past participle**, see 350.4.

124 can and could (4): interpersonal uses (permission, requests etc)

1 asking for and giving permission

We use *can* to ask for and give permission; *can't* is used to refuse permission.

> *'**Can** I ask you something?' 'Yes, of course you **can**.'*
> *'**Can** I have some more cake?' 'No, I'm afraid you **can't**.'*
> *You **can** go now if you want to.*

We also use *could* to ask for permission; it is more polite or formal than *can*. We do not use *could* to give or refuse permission (it suggests respect, so is more natural in asking for permission than in giving it.)

> *'**Could** I ask you something, if you're not too busy?' 'Yes, of course you **can**.'* (NOT ...~~of course you **could**.~~)

May and *might* are also used to ask and give permission (see 332). They are more formal than *can/could*. Some people consider them more 'correct', but in fact *can* and *could* are normally preferred in informal educated usage, especially in British English.

2 reporting permission

Can and *could* are also used to talk about permission that has already been given or refused, and about things that are (or are not) allowed by rules and laws. (Note that *may* is not normally used to talk about rules and laws – see 332.3.)

> *She said I **could** come as often as I liked.*
> ***Can** you park on a double yellow line on Sundays?* (NOT ~~**May you park**...?~~)

In talking about the past, we use *could* to say that somebody had permission to do something at any time ('general permission'), but we do not use *could* to talk about permission for one particular action in the past. Compare:

>*When I was a child, I **could** watch TV whenever I wanted to.*
>*Yesterday evening, Peter **was allowed** to watch TV for an hour.*
>(NOT ... *Peter **could** watch TV for an hour.*)

But *could not* can be used to talk about one particular action that was not allowed.

>*Peter **couldn't** watch TV yesterday because he was naughty.*

(The difference between *could* and *was/were allowed* is similar to the difference between *could* and *was/were able* – see 122.3.)

3 permission: conditional uses of *could*

Could has a conditional use (= 'would be allowed').

>*He **could** borrow my car if he asked.*

The structure ***could have*** + **past participle** means 'would have been allowed'.

>*I **could have kissed** her if I'd wanted to.*

4 offers

We often use *can* when we offer to do things for people.

>*'**Can** I carry your bag?' 'Oh, thanks very much.'*
>*'I **can** baby-sit for you this evening if you like.' 'No, it's all right, thanks.'*

Could is possible if we want an offer to sound less definite.

>*I **could** mend your bicycle for you, if that would help.*

5 requests, orders and suggestions

We can use *can* and *could* to ask or tell people to do things. *Could* is more polite, more formal or less definite, and is often used for making suggestions.

>***Can** you put the children to bed?*
>***Could** you lend me five pounds until tomorrow?*
>*Do you think you **could** help me for a few minutes?*
>*When you've finished the washing up you **can** clean the kitchen. Then you **could** iron the clothes, if you like.*
>*If you haven't got anything to do you **could** sort out your photos.*

6 criticisms

Could can be used to criticise people for not doing things. ***Could have*** + **past participle** is used to talk about the past.

>*You **could** ask before you borrow my car.*
>*You **could have told** me you were getting married.*

For the use of *might* in similar cases, see 336.

7 reported speech

Could is used in past indirect speech constructions (see 481), when *can* was used in direct speech.

>*'**Can** you give me a hand?' 'What?' 'I asked if you **could** give me a hand.'*

125 **can** and **could** (5): with **see, hear**, etc

1 *see, hear, feel, smell, taste*

When these verbs refer to perception (receiving information through the eyes, ears etc), we do not normally use progressive forms. To talk about seeing, hearing etc at a particular moment, we often use *can see, can hear* etc (especially in British English).

> I **can see** Susan coming. (NOT *I'm seeing*...)
> **Can** you **hear** somebody coming up the stairs?
> What did you put in the stew? I **can taste** something funny.
> Suddenly she realised she **could smell** something burning.

In American English, *I see/hear* etc are common in this sense.

2 *guess, tell*

Can and *could* are often used with *guess* and with *tell* (meaning *see, know*). *Can/could* are not normally used with *know* (see 306.5).

> I **could guess** what she wanted.
> You **can tell** he's Irish from his accent. (NOT *You can know*...)

3 *understand, follow, remember*

Can/could is often used with these verbs too. It does not always add very much to the meaning.

> I **can't**/don't **understand** what she's talking about.
> Do/**Can** you **follow** what he's saying?
> I **(can) remember** your grandfather.

126 **can't help**

If you say that you *cannot/can't help doing* something, you mean that you can't stop yourself doing it: something makes you, even though you are being careful not to, or should be trying not to.

> She's a selfish woman, but somehow you **can't help** liking her.
> Excuse me – I **couldn't help** overhearing what you said.
> Sorry I broke the cup – I **couldn't help** it.

Can't help is sometimes followed by **but + infinitive without to** (see 116); the meaning is the same as *can't help ...ing*. This is a common structure in American English.

> I **can't help but wonder** what I should do next.

127 **care: take care (of), care (about)** and **care for**

1 *take care of*

Take care of normally means 'look after'.

> Nurses **take care of** people in hospital.
> It's no good giving Peter a rabbit: he's too young to **take care of** it properly.
> Ms Savage **takes care of** marketing and publicity, and I'm responsible for production.

Take care (without a preposition) means 'be careful'. Some people use it as a formula when saying goodbye.

> **Take care** *when you're crossing the road, children.*
> *'Bye, Ruth.' 'Bye, Mike.* **Take care.***'*

2 *care (about)*

Care (about) is used to say whether or not you feel something is important, or whether it interests or worries you. It is most common in questions and negative sentences. *About* is used before an object, but is usually left out before a conjunction.

> *I don't* **care about** *your opinion.*
> > (N O T ~~I don't take care of your opinion.~~)
> > (N O T ~~I don't care for your opinion.~~)
> *I don't* **care** *whether it rains – I'm happy.*
> *'I'll never speak to you again.' 'I don't* **care***.'*
> *'Your mother's very upset with you.' 'I couldn't* **care** *less.'*
> > (= *'I don't care at all.'*)

3 *care for*

Care for can be used to mean 'look after'. This is rather formal or literary.

> *He spent years* **caring for** *his sick mother.*

A more common use is to mean 'like' or 'be fond of'.

> *Would you* **care for** *a cup of tea?*
> *I don't much* **care for** *strawberries.*
> *I really* **care for** *you, Sandra.*

128 change

When we talk about changing one thing for another, we often use *change* with a plural object.

> *We have to* **change trains** *at York.*
> *I'm thinking of* **changing jobs.**

For the differences between *change, turn, become* etc, see 129.

129 changes

Become, get, go, come, grow and *turn* can all be used with similar meanings to talk about change. The differences between them are complicated – they are partly grammatical, partly to do with meaning, and partly matters of conventional usage.

1 *become* with adjectives and noun phrases

Become can be used before adjectives and noun phrases.

> *It was* **becoming** *very* **dark.**
> *What do you have to do to* **become a pilot?**

Become is not usually used to talk about deliberate actions.

> *Please* **get ready** *now.* (N O T ~~Please **become ready now.**~~)   ▶

2   *get* with adjectives

Get can be used before adjectives (without nouns). It is less formal than
become.
> *It was **getting** very **dark**.* (informal)
> *You **get younger** every day.* (informal)

Get is not usually used (with this meaning) before nouns.
> *What do you have to do to **become a pilot?*** (N O T . . . ~~to get a pilot~~)

Get can also be used before past participles like *lost, broken, dressed, married.*
> *They **got married** in 1986, and **got divorced** two years later.*

For *get used to*, see 578.

3   *get* + infinitive

We can sometimes use *get* with an infinitive to talk about a gradual change.
> *After a few weeks I **got to like** the job better.*
> *She's nice when you **get to know** her.*

For *get* as a passive auxiliary and other uses of *get*, see 228.

4   *go*

Go can be used before adjectives to talk about change, especially in an
informal style. This is common in two cases.

a   colours

Go (and not *get*) is used to talk about changes of colour, especially in British
English.
> *Leaves **go brown** in autumn.* (US . . . *turn brown* . . .)
>> (N O T ~~Leaves get brown~~. . .)
> *She **went white** with anger.*
> *Suddenly everything **went black** and I lost consciousness.*

Other examples (mainly British English):
> ***go blue** with cold / **red** with embarrassment / **green** with envy*

Turn can also be used in these cases (see below), and so can *grow* when the
change is gradual. *Go* is more informal than *turn* and *grow*.

b   changes of quality

Go (and not usually *get*) is used before adjectives in a number of common
expressions that refer to changes for the worse. People *go mad/crazy/deaf/
blind/grey/bald*; horses *go lame*; machines *go wrong*; iron *goes rusty* (GB);
meat, fish or vegetables *go bad*; cheese *goes mouldy*; milk *goes off* (GB) or
sour; bread *goes stale*; beer, lemonade, musical instruments and car tyres
go flat.
> *He **went bald** in his twenties.*   *The car keeps **going wrong**.*

Note that we use *get*, not *go*, with *old, tired* and *ill*.

5   *come*

Come is used in a few fixed expressions to talk about things finishing up all
right. The most common are *come true* and *come right*.
> *I'll make all your dreams **come true**.*
> *Trust me – it will all **come right** in the end.*

Come + **infinitive** can be used to talk about changes in mental state or attitude.

> *I slowly **came to realise** that she knew what she was doing.*
> *You will **come to regret** your decision.*

6 *grow*

Grow is used before adjectives especially to talk about slow and gradual changes. It is more formal than *get* or *go*, and can sound a little old-fashioned or literary.

> *Without noticing it he **grew old**.*
> *When they **grew rich** they began to drop their old friends.*
> *As the weather **grows colder**, your thoughts naturally turn to winter holidays in the sun.*

Grow + **infinitive** can be used (like ***come* + infinitive**) to talk about changes in attitude, especially if these are gradual.

> *He **grew to accept** his stepmother, and she hoped that one day he would **grow to love** her.*

7 *turn*

Turn is used mostly for visible or striking changes of state. It is common before colour words (and is not so informal as *go*).

> *She **turned** bright red and ran out of the room.*
> *He **turns nasty** after he's had a couple of drinks.*

Turn into is used before nouns, to talk about a dramatic change in the nature of somebody or something.

> *He's a lovely man, but when he gets jealous he **turns into** a monster.*
> *A girl has to kiss a lot of frogs before one of them **turns into** a prince.*

Turn to and *turn into* can both be used before the names of materials.

> *His worry **turned (in)to** fury.*
> *Everything that King Midas touched **turned (in)to** gold.*
> *They stood there as if they had been **turned (in)to** stone.*

To talk about people changing their occupation, religion, politics etc, we sometimes use ***turn*** with a noun (with no preposition or article) or an adjective.

> *He worked in a bank for thirty years before **turning painter**.*
> *Towards the end of the war he **turned traitor**.*
> *At the end of her life she **turned Catholic**.*

Turn (in)to can also be used as a transitive verb with an object, to talk about causing change.

> *In the Greek legend, Circe **turned** men **into** pigs.*

8 *fall*

Fall is used to mean 'become' in a few fixed expressions such as *fall ill*, *fall asleep* and *fall in love*. ▶

9 verbs related to adjectives

A number of verbs which are related to adjectives have meanings like 'get more ...' or 'make more ...'. Many of them end in *-en*. Examples:

*The fog **thickened**.*
*The weather's beginning to **brighten** up.*
*His eyes **narrowed**.*
*Could you **shorten** the sleeves on this jacket?*
*They're **widening** the road here.*

10 absence of change: *stay, keep, remain*

To talk about things not changing, we can use *stay, keep* or *remain* before adjectives. *Remain* is more formal.

*How do you manage to **stay** young and fit?*
***Keep** calm.*
*I hope you will always **remain** so charming.*

Stay and *remain* are also sometimes used before noun phrases.

*Promise me you will always **stay/remain** my little boy.*

Keep can be used before *-ing* forms.

***Keep smiling** whatever happens.*

For other uses of the words discussed in this section, see a good dictionary.

130 city and town

According to the legal definition, a 'city' is a town that has been given a special status by a royal charter (in Britain) or by the State (in the US). However, most people simply use *city* to talk about large and important towns – examples in Britain are Belfast, Cardiff, Edinburgh, Glasgow, Manchester, Liverpool and London.

131 cleft sentences

We can emphasise particular words and expressions by putting everything into a kind of relative clause except the words we want to emphasise: this makes them stand out. These structures are called 'cleft sentences' by grammarians (*cleft* means 'divided'). They are useful in writing (because we cannot use intonation for emphasis in written language), but they are also common in speech.

1 *the person who, the thing that* etc

The words to be emphasised are joined to the relative clause by *is/was* and an expression like *the person who, what* (= *the thing that*), *the place where, the day when/that, the reason why*. We can put the words to be emphasised first or last in the sentence. Compare:

– MARY *keeps a pig in the garden shed.*
*Mary is **the person who** keeps a pig in the garden shed.*
***The person who** keeps a pig in the garden shed is Mary.*

– *Mary keeps A PIG in the garden shed.*
  *A pig is **what** Mary keeps in the garden shed.*
  ***What** Mary keeps in the garden shed is a pig.*
– *Mary keeps a pig IN THE GARDEN SHED.*
  *The garden shed is **(the place) where** Mary keeps a pig.*
  ***(The place) where** Mary keeps a pig is the garden shed.*
– *Phil is THE SECRETARY.*
  *The secretary is **what** Phil is.*
  ***What** Phil is is the secretary.*
– *Jake went to London ON TUESDAY to see Colin.*
  *Tuesday was **(the day) when/that** Jake went to London to see Colin.*
  ***(The day) when** Jake went to London to see Colin was Tuesday.*
– *Jake went to London on Tuesday TO SEE COLIN.*
  *To see Colin was **(the reason) why** Jake went to London on Tuesday.*
  ***(The reason)** why Jake went to London on Tuesday was to see Colin.*

The place, the reason etc can be dropped, but this is rather informal, especially at the beginning of a sentence.

> ***Why** I'm here is to talk about my plans.*
> (More formal: ***The reason why** I'm here is . . .*)
> *Spain's **where** we're going this year.*

Instead of *the person, the place, what* etc, we can use less general expressions.

> *You're **the woman (that)** I'll always love best.*
> *Paris is **the city (that)** I feel most at home in.*

A *what*-clause is normally considered to be singular; if it begins a cleft sentence it is followed by *is/was*. But a plural verb is sometimes possible before a plural noun in an informal style.

> *What we want **is/are** some of those cakes.*

For more information about *what*-clauses, see 476.

2 emphasising verbs

When we want to emphasise a verb, we have to use a more complicated structure with *what . . . do*. Various verb forms are possible.

> *He SCREAMED.*
> ***What** he **did** was (to) scream/screamed.*

This structure can be used to emphasise the verb together with other words that follow it. Compare:

> *She **writes** science fiction.*
> ***What** she **does** is (to) write/writes science fiction.*

3 emphasising a whole sentence

A whole sentence can be given extra emphasis by using a cleft structure with *what* and the verb *happen*. Compare:

> *The car broke down.*
> ***What happened** was (that) the car broke down.*

▶

4   preparatory *it*

We can use preparatory *it* (see 301) in cleft sentences. In this case, the words
to be emphasised are usually joined to the relative clause by *that*. Compare:

> *My secretary sent the bill to Mr Harding yesterday.*
> ***It was my secretary that*** *sent the bill to Mr Harding yesterday.*
>   (not somebody else)
> ***It was the bill that*** *my secretary sent to Mr Harding yesterday.*
>   (not something else)
> ***It was Mr Harding that*** *my secretary sent the bill to yesterday.*
>   (not to somebody else)
> ***It was yesterday that*** *my secretary sent the bill to Mr Harding.*
>   (not another day)

Negative structures are also possible.

> ***It wasn't my husband that*** *sent the bill . . .*

Who is possible instead of *that* when a personal subject is emphasised.

> ***It was my secretary who*** *sent . . .*

When a plural subject is emphasised, the verb is plural.

> *It was the students that **were** angry . . .* (NOT *. . . that was angry . . .*)

When the emphasised subject is a pronoun, there are two possibilities.
Compare:

– *It is **I who am** responsible.* (formal)
   *It's **me that's** responsible.* (informal)
– *It is **you who are** in the wrong.* (formal)
   *It's **you that's** in the wrong.* (informal)

To avoid being either too formal or too informal in this case, we could say,
for example, *I'm the person/the one who's responsible.* Note that the verb
cannot be emphasised with the preparatory *it* structure: we cannot say
It was sent that my secretary the bill . . .

For more about subject and object forms of pronouns, see 425.
For formal and informal language, see 216.

5   other structures

All (that), and expressions with *thing,* can be used in cleft sentences rather
like *what.*

> ***All*** *I want is a home somewhere.*
> ***All*** *I did was (to) touch the window, and it broke.*
> ***All*** *you need is love.*
> *The only **thing** I remember is a terrible pain in my head.*
> *The first **thing** was to make some coffee.*
> *My first journey abroad is **something** I shall never forget.*

Time expressions can be emphasised with *It was not until . . .* and *It was
only when . . .*

> ***It was not until I met you*** *that I knew real happiness.*
> ***It was only when I read her letter*** *that I realised what was happening.*

At the beginning of a cleft sentence, *this* and *that* often replace emphasised
here and *there.* Compare:

– *You pay **here**.*
   This *is where you pay.* (OR ***Here*** *is where you pay.*)

  – *We live **there**.*
    ***That**'s where we live.* (OR ***There**'s where we live.*)

For more about question-word clauses, see 460.
For more general information about sentence structure and the arrangement of information
  in sentences, see 289.

132 close and shut

1 use

Close and *shut* can often be used with the same meaning.
  *Open your mouth and **close/shut** your eyes.*
  *I can't **close/shut** the window. Can you help me?*
  *The shop **closes/shuts** at five o'clock.*

2 past participles

The past participles *closed* and *shut* can be used as adjectives.
  *The post office is **closed/shut** on Saturday afternoon.*
Shut is not usually used before a noun.
  *a **closed** door* (NOT *a shut door*)   *closed eyes* (NOT *shut eyes*)

3 cases where *close* is preferred

We prefer *close* for slow movements (like flowers closing at night), and *close*
is more common in a formal style. Compare:
  *As we watched, he **closed** his eyes for the last time.*   ***Shut** your mouth!*
We *close* roads, railways etc (channels of communication). And we *close*
(= 'end') letters, bank accounts, meetings etc.

133 cloth and clothes

Cloth (pronounced /klɒθ/) is material made from wool, cotton etc, used for
making clothes, curtains, soft furnishings and so on. (In modern English, it is
more common to say *material* or *fabric*.)
  *His suits were made of the most expensive **cloth**.*
A cloth is a piece of material used for cleaning, covering things etc.
  *Could you pass me **a cloth**? I've spilt some milk on the floor.*
Clothes (pronounced /kləʊ(ð)z/) are things you wear: skirt, trousers etc.
Clothes has no singular; instead of *a clothe*, we say *something to wear* or
an article / a piece of clothing.
  *I must buy some new **clothes**; I haven't got anything to wear.*

134 come and go

1 speaker's/hearer's position

We use *come* for movements to the place where the speaker or hearer is.
  *'Maria, would you **come** here, please?' 'I'm **coming**.'* (NOT *...I'm going.*)
  *When did you **come** to live here?*   *Can I **come** and sit on your lap?*   ▶

We use *go* for movements to other places.
> *I want to **go** and live in Greece.   Let's **go** and see Peter and Diane.*
> *In 1577, he **went** to study in Rome.*

2 speaker's/hearer's past or future position

We can use *come* for a movement to a place where the speaker or hearer was
or will already be at the time of the movement. Compare:
- *What time did I **come** to see you in the office yesterday?*
  *I **went** to your office yesterday, but you weren't in.*
- *Will you **come** and visit me in hospital when I have my operation?*
  *He's **going** into hospital next week.*
- *Susan can't **come** to your birthday party.*
  *She's **going** to see her mother.*

Come (with) can be used to talk about joining a movement of the
speaker's/hearer's, even if *go* is used for the movement itself.
> *We're **going** to the cinema tonight. Would you like to **come with** us?*

3 *come to*

Come to can mean *arrive at*.
> *Carry straight on till you **come to** a crossroads.*

And *come from* is used (in the present) to say where people's homes are or were.
> *She **comes from** Scotland, but her mother's Welsh.*
> *Originally I **come from** Hungary, but I've lived here for twenty years.*
> (N O T *Originally I came from Hungary...*)

Note that these rules are not always followed in American English.
The difference between *bring* and *take* is similar. See 112.
For *come/go and . . .*, see 52.
For *come/go . . . ing*, see 232.
For *been = come/gone*, see 94.

135 comparison (1): structures

Several different grammatical structures can be used for comparing.

1 similarity and identity

If we want to say that people, things, actions or events are similar, we can use
as or *like* (see 320); *so/neither do I* and similar structures (see 516); or
adverbs such as *too*, *also* and *as well* (see 45). To say that they are identical,
we can use *the same (as)* (see 486).
> *It's best cooked in olive oil, **as** the Italians do it.*
> *Your sister looks just **like** you.   She likes music, and **so do I**.*
> *The papers were late and the post was **too**.*
> *His eyes are just **the same** colour as mine.*

2 difference

To talk about differences, we can use the negative forms of the structures
used for talking about similarity and identity.
> *The baby does**n't** look much **like** you.*
> *Its eyes are **not** at all **the same** colour **as** yours.*

3 equality

To say that people, things etc are equal in a particular way, we often use the structure *as (much/many) ... as* (see 70).

> *My hands were **as** cold **as** ice.*
> *I earn **as much** money **as** you.*

In negative comparisons, we can use *not so ... as* or *not as ... as*.

> *The baby's **not so/as** ugly **as** you.*

4 inequality: more

To say that people, things etc are unequal in a particular way, we can use comparative adjectives and adverbs, or *more (... than)* with adjectives, adverbs, verbs or nouns.

> *He's much **older** than her.*
> *The baby's **more attractive** than you.*
> *The car's running **more smoothly** since it had a service.*
> *I **worry more** and **more** every day.*
> *If I'm going to do **more work** I want **more money**.*

To say which one of a group is outstanding in a particular way, we can use *most*.

> *You're the **most annoying** person in the whole office.*

For the use of these structures ('comparative' and 'superlative'), and the difference between them, see the following sections.
For comparatives and superlatives ending in *-er/-est*, see 136.
For details of the use of *more* and *most*, see 346–347.

5 inequality: less

We can also talk about inequality by focusing on the 'lower' end of the scale, using *less (than)* or *least*.

> *The baby's **less ugly** than you.*
> *I've got **less energy** than I used to have.*
> *My ambition is to spend the **least possible time** working.*

Note that *not as/so ... as* is more common than *less ... than* in informal usage.

For the difference between *as* and *than*, see 557.
For pronouns after *as* and *than*, see 70.4, 138.8.
For tenses after *as* and *than*, see 556.
For more information about *less*, see 313. For *least*, see 311.

136 comparison (2): comparative and superlative adjectives

One-syllable adjectives normally have comparatives and superlatives ending in *-er*, *-est*. Some two-syllable adjectives are similar; others have *more* and *most*. Longer adjectives have *more* and *most*. ▶

1   one-syllable adjectives (regular comparison)

Adjective	Comparative	Superlative	
old	*older*	*oldest*	Most adjectives: + *-er, -est.*
tall	*taller*	*tallest*	
cheap	*cheaper*	*cheapest*	
late	*later*	*latest*	Adjectives ending in *-e*: + *-r, -st.*
nice	*nicer*	*nicest*	
fat	*fatter*	*fattest*	One vowel + one consonant: double consonant.
big	*bigger*	*biggest*	
thin	*thinner*	*thinnest*	

Note the pronunciation of:

younger /ˈjʌŋgə(r)/   *longest* /ˈlɒŋgɪst/
youngest /ˈjʌŋgɪst/   *stronger* /ˈstrɒŋge(r)/
longer /ˈlɒŋgə(r)/   *strongest* /ˈstrɒŋgɪst/

2   irregular comparison

Adjective	Comparative	Superlative
good	*better*	*best*
bad	*worse*	*worst*
ill	*worse*	
far	*farther/further* (see 207)	*farthest/furthest*
old	*older/elder* (see 180)	*oldest/eldest* (see 180)

The determiners *little* and *much/many* have irregular comparatives and superlatives:

little (see 322)   *less* (see 313)   *least* (see 311)
much/many (see 348)   *more* (see 346)   *most* (see 347)

Few has two possible comparatives and superlatives: *fewer/less* and *fewest/least*. See 313, 311.

3   two-syllable adjectives

Adjectives ending in *-y* have *-ier* and *-iest*.

happy   *happier*   *happiest*
easy   *easier*   *easiest*

Some other two-syllable adjectives can have *-er* and *-est*, especially adjectives ending in an unstressed vowel, /l/ or /ə(r)/.

narrow   *narrower*   *narrowest*
simple   *simpler*   *simplest*
clever   *cleverer*   *cleverest*
quiet   *quieter*   *quietest*

With many two-syllable adjectives (e.g. *polite, common*), *-er/-est* and *more/most* are both possible. With others (including adjectives ending in *-ing, -ed, -ful* and *-less*), only *more/most* is possible. To find out the normal comparative and superlative for a particular two-syllable adjective, check in a good dictionary.

4 longer adjectives

Adjectives of three or more syllables have *more* and *most*.

intelligent	*more intelligent*	*most intelligent*
practical	*more practical*	*most practical*
beautiful	*more beautiful*	*most beautiful*

Words like *unhappy* (the opposites of two-syllable adjectives ending in *-y*) are an exception.

unhappy	*unhappier*	*unhappiest*
untidy	*untidier*	*untidiest*

Some compound adjectives like *good-looking* or *well-known* have two possible comparatives and superlatives.

good-looking	*better-looking*	*best-looking*
	OR *more good-looking*	*most good-looking*
well-known	*better-known*	*best-known*
	OR *more well-known*	*most well-known*

5 *more, most* with short adjectives

Sometimes *more/most* are used with adjectives that normally have *-er/-est*. This can happen, for example, when a comparative is not followed immediately by *than*; forms with *-er* are also possible.

*The road's getting **more and more steep**.* (OR ... *steeper and steeper*.)

When we compare two descriptions (saying that one is more suitable or accurate than another), we use *more*; comparatives with *-er* are not possible.

*He's **more lazy** than stupid.* (NOT ~~He's **lazier than stupid**.~~)

In a rather formal style, *most* can be used with adjectives expressing approval and disapproval (including one-syllable adjectives) to mean 'very'.

*Thank you very much indeed. That is **most kind** of you.*

(NOT ... ~~That is kindest of you.~~)

Real, right, wrong and *like* always have *more* and *most*.

*She's **more like** her mother than her father.* (NOT ... ~~**liker her mother**...~~)

For information about how to use comparatives and superlatives, see 138.
For modification of comparatives and superlatives (e.g. *much older, far the best*), see 139.

137 comparison (3): comparative and superlative adverbs

Most comparative and superlative adverbs are made with *more* and *most*.
> *Could you talk **more quietly**?* (NOT ...*quietlier*)

Adverbs that have the same form as adjectives (see 21), and a few others, have comparatives and superlatives with *-er* and *-est*. The most common are: *fast, early, late, hard, long, near, high, low, soon, well* (*better, best*), *badly* (*worse, worst*), and in informal English *easy, slow, loud* and *quick*.
> *Can't you drive any **faster**?*
> *Can you come **earlier**?*
> *Talk **louder**.* (informal)
> *We've all got terrible voices, but I sing **worst** of all.*

Note also the irregular comparatives and superlatives of *far* (*farther/further, farthest/furthest*, see 207), *much* (*more, most*, see 346 and 347), *little* (*less, least*, see 313 and 311).

Often sometimes has comparative and superlative *oftener* and *oftenest*, but forms with *more/most* are more common.

For the use of comparatives and superlatives, see the following sections.

138 comparison (4): using comparatives and superlatives

1 the difference between comparatives and superlatives

We use the comparative to compare one person, thing, action, event or group with another person, thing etc. We use the superlative to compare somebody/something with the whole group that he/she/it belongs to. Compare:
- *Mary's **taller** than her three sisters.*
  *Mary's the **tallest** of the four girls.*
- *Your accent is **worse** than mine.*
  *Your accent is the **worst** in the class.* (NOT ...*the worse*...)
- *He plays **better** than everybody else in the team.*
  *He's **the best** in the team.*
- *She's **richer** than 90 per cent of her neighbours.*
  *She's one of the **richest** people in town.*

2 groups with two members

When a group only has two members, we sometimes use the comparative instead of the superlative.
> *I like Betty and Maud, but I think Maud's the **nicer/nicest** of the two.*
> *I'll give you the **bigger/biggest** steak: I'm not very hungry.*

Some people feel that a superlative is incorrect in this case.

3   comparative meaning 'relatively', 'more than average'

Comparatives can also suggest ideas like 'relatively', 'more than average'.
Used in this way, comparatives make a less clear and narrow selection than
superlatives. Compare:

> They put on two classes – one for the **cleverer** students and one for the
> **slower** learners.
> The **cleverest** students were two girls from York.

Comparatives are often used like this in advertising to make things sound
less definite.

> **less expensive** clothes for the **fuller** figure
> (Compare cheap clothes for fat women)

4   double comparatives

We can use double comparatives to say that something is changing.

> ...er and ...er
> more and more ...

> I'm getting **fatter and fatter.**   We're going **more and more slowly.**
> (NOT ... ~~more slowly and more slowly.~~)

5   the ... the ...

We can use comparatives with the ... the ... to say that things change or vary
together, or that two variable quantities are systematically related.

> **Word order (in both clauses):**
> the + comparative expression + subject + verb

> **The older** I get, **the happier** I am. (NOT ~~Older I get, more I am happy.~~)
> **The more** dangerous it is, **the more** I like it.
> (NOT ~~The more it is dangerous, ...~~)
> **The more** I study, **the less** I learn.

More can be used with a noun in this structure.

> **The more money** he makes, **the more useless things** he buys.

Sometimes that is used before the first verb.

> The more information **that** comes in, the more confused the picture is.

A short form of this structure is used in the expression The more the merrier,
and in sentences ending the better.

> 'How do you like your coffee?' '**The stronger the better.**'

Note that in this structure, the word the is not really the definite article – it
was originally a form of the demonstrative pronoun, meaning 'by that much'.

6   all/any/none the + comparative

Another use of the meaning 'by that much' is in **all/any/none the +
comparative.** This structure can be used when we say why something is or
should be 'more ...'

> The burglary was **all the more** upsetting because the burglars broke up a
> whole lot of our furniture.
> Sunday mornings were nice. I enjoyed them **all the more** because Sue
> used to come round to breakfast.   ▶

*I feel **all the better** for that swim.*
*Her accident made it **all the more important** to get home fast.*
*He didn't seem to be **any the worse** for his experience.*
*He explained it all carefully, but I was still **none the wiser**.*
Note that this structure is used only to express abstract ideas. We would
not say, for example, ~~Those pills have made him **all the slimmer**~~.

7   *three times...er* etc

Instead of *three/four* etc *times as much* (see 70.6), we can use ***three/four* etc
times + comparative**.
*She can walk **three times further** than you.*
*It was **ten times more difficult** than I expected.*
Note that *twice* and *half* are not possible in this structure.
*She's **twice as lively** as her sister.* (N O T ...~~twice **livelier**~~...)

8   pronouns after *than*

In an informal style, object pronouns are used after *than*. In a more formal
style, subject pronouns are used (usually with verbs).
*She's older than **me**.* (informal)
*She is older than **I (am)**.* (formal)
The use of object pronouns can occasionally cause confusion.
*'I love you more than **her**.' 'You mean more than you love her or more than
she loves me?'*

For more details of the use of subject and object pronouns, see 425.

9   prepositions after superlatives; possessive structure

After superlatives, we do not usually use *of* with a singular word referring to
a place or group.
*I'm the **happiest** man **in** the world.* (N O T ...~~**of the world**.~~)
*She's the **fastest** player **in** the team.* (N O T ...~~**of the team**.~~)
But *of* can be used before plurals, and before singular quantifiers like *lot*
and *bunch*.
*She's the **fastest** player **of** them all.*
*He's **the best of the lot**.*
Note also the structure with possessive *'s*.
*He thinks he's the **world's strongest** man.*

10   ellipsis

The second part of a comparative or superlative structure can be left out
when the meaning is given by what comes before.
*You can get there faster by car, but the train is **more comfortable**.*
    (=... more comfortable ***than going by car**.)*
*I like everybody who works here, but you're **the nicest** of all.*
*Look – which of these do you think is **the best**?*
Note that this is not possible when the meaning is not given by what comes
before.
*Love is the **most important thing** in the world.*
    (N O T ~~Love is the **most important** in the world.~~)

11 infinitives after superlatives

We often use an infinitive after a superlative, with the same meaning as a relative clause.

*She's the **youngest** person ever **to swim** the Channel.*
*(=... the youngest person **who has** ever **swum** ...)*

This structure is also common after *first, last* and *next.*

*Who was the **first** woman **to climb** Everest?*
*The **next to speak** was Mrs Fenshaw.*

Note that this structure is only possible in cases where the noun with the superlative has a subject relationship with the following verb. In other cases, infinitives cannot be used.

*Is this the **first time** that you have stayed here?*
*(NOT ... the **first time for you to stay** here?)*

12 *the* with superlatives

Nouns with superlative adjectives normally have the article *the* (unless there is a possessive).

*It's **the best book** I've ever read.*

Superlative adjectives in predicative position also tend to have *the*, though it is sometimes dropped in an informal style.

*I'm **the greatest**.*
*Which of the boys is **(the) strongest**?*
*This dictionary is **(the) best**.*

The is sometimes dropped before superlative adverbs in an informal style.

*Who can run **(the) fastest**?*

The cannot be dropped when a superlative in predicative position is used with a defining expression.

*This dictionary is **the best I could find**.*
*(NOT This dictionary is **best I could find**.)*
*She was **the quickest of all the staff**.*

The is not used with superlatives in predicative position or with superlative adverbs, when we compare the same person or thing.in different situations. Compare:

– *He's **nicest** when he's had a few drinks. (NOT He's **the nicest when**...)*
*I've got a lot of friends, but he's **(the) nicest**.*
– *She works **hardest** when she's doing something for her family.*
*(NOT She works **the hardest when**... – a woman's work is being compared in different situations.)*
*She works **(the) hardest**; her husband doesn't know what work is.*
(A woman is being compared with a man – the is possible.)

13 non-assertive words after superlatives

'Non-assertive' words like *ever, yet* and *any* are not generally used in affirmative clauses (see 374). However, they often follow comparatives and superlatives.

*You're **more stubborn** than **anybody** I know.*
*It's the **best** book I've **ever** read.*
*This is my **hardest** job **yet**.*   ▶

14   words left out after *than*

In comparative clauses, *than* often seems to replace a subject or object pronoun or adverbial expression, rather like a relative pronoun or adverb (see 557.3).

>*She spent more money **than** was sensible.* (NOT ...*than it was sensible.*)
>*There were more people **than** we had expected.*
>>(NOT ...*than we had expected them.*)
>*I love you more **than** she does.* (NOT ...*than how much she does.*)

(In some English dialects, the above sentences would be constructed with *than what*.)

For the formation of comparatives and superlatives, see 136.
For *as* and *than*, see 557.
For comparisons with *as*, see 70.
For tenses after *than*, see 556.
For pronouns after *than*, see 138.8.
For *more*, see 346.
For *most*, see 347.
For *less*, see 313.
For *least*, see 311.
For *the first/second/best/* etc + present/past perfect, see 419.7.

139   comparison (5): **much, far** etc with comparatives and superlatives

1   *much, far* etc with comparatives

We cannot use *very* with comparatives. Instead, we use, for example, *much, far, very much, a lot* (informal), *lots* (informal), *any* and *no* (see 56), *rather, a little, a bit* (informal), and *even*.

>*My boyfriend is **much/far older** than me.* (NOT ...*very older than me.*)
>*Russian is **much/far more difficult** than Spanish.*

***very much** nicer*	***a bit** more sensible* (informal)
***a lot** happier* (informal)	*Is your mother **any better**?*
***rather** more quickly*	*She looks **no older** than her daughter.*
***a little** less expensive*	*Your cooking is **even worse** than Harry's.*

Quite cannot be used with comparatives except in the expression *quite better*, meaning 'recovered from an illness' (see 103.1). *Any, no, a bit* and *a lot* are not normally used to modify comparatives before nouns.

>*There are **much/far nicer shops** in the town centre.*
>>(BUT NOT ...*a bit nicer shops*...)

2   *many more/less/fewer*

When *more* (see 346) modifies a plural noun, it is modified by *many* instead of *much*. Compare:

>***much**/far/a lot/etc more money*   ***many**/far/a lot/etc more opportunities*

Many is sometimes used to modify *less* (before a plural noun) and *fewer*, but this is unusual; *far, a lot* etc are more common.

>***far less** words* (more common than ***many less** words*)
>***a lot fewer** accidents* (more common than ***many fewer** accidents*)

3 *much, by far, quite* etc with superlatives

Superlatives can be modified by *much* and *by far*, and by other adverbs of degree such as *quite* (meaning 'absolutely'), *almost, practically, nearly* and *easily*.

He's **much** the most imaginative of them all.
She's **by far** the oldest.
We're walking **by far** the slowest.
He's **quite** the most stupid man I've ever met.
I'm **nearly** the oldest in the firm.
This is **easily** the worst party I've been to this year.

4 *very* with superlatives

Note the special use of *very* to emphasise superlatives and *first, next* and *last*.

Bring out your **very best** wine – Michael's coming to dinner.
You're the **very first** person I've spoken to today.
This is your **very last** chance.

For modification of *too*, see 570.2.

140 complements

1 subject and object complements

Some clauses consist of a subject, the verb *be*, and an expression that describes the subject.

Alice is **a ballet dancer**.
Philip is **depressed**.

The expression that describes the subject in clauses like these is often called the 'complement' of the clause, or a 'subject complement'. Subject complements can follow not only *be*, but also other 'copular verbs' (see 147) like *become, look, seem*.

Alice eventually **became a ballet dancer**.
Philip **looks depressed**.

In some structures, the object of a verb can have a complement. This happens, for example, after *make, elect* or *call*. For details, see 580.

You **make me nervous**.
Why ever did they **elect him chairman**?
Don't you **call my husband a liar**.

2 complements of verbs, nouns and adjectives

The word 'complement' is also used in a wider sense. We often need to add something to a verb, noun or adjective to complete its meaning. If somebody says *I want*, we expect to hear what he or she wants; the words *the need* obviously don't make sense alone; after hearing *I'm interested*, we may need to be told what the speaker is interested in. Words and expressions which 'complete' the meaning of a verb, noun or adjective are also called 'complements'.

I **want a drink**, and then I **want to go home**.
Does she understand the **need for secrecy**?
I'm **interested in learning to fly**.

▶

Many verbs can be followed by noun complements or -*ing* forms with no preposition ('direct objects'). But nouns and adjectives normally need prepositions to join them to noun or -*ing* form complements. Compare:
– *Alan **criticised the plan**.*
  *Alan's **criticism of the plan** made him very unpopular.*
  *Alan was very **critical of the plan**.*
– *I **resent working** on Saturdays.*
  *My **resentment of working**...*
  *I feel **resentful about working**...*
It is important to know what kinds of complements can come after a particular word. For example, *interested* can be followed by *in...ing* or by an infinitive, but *bored* is not used in the same way; *want* can be followed by an infinitive, but *suggest* cannot; on the other hand *suggest* can be followed by a *that*-clause, but *want* cannot.

Related verbs, nouns and adjectives often have the same kinds of complements.
  *I **worry about** you a lot.*
  *She ignored our **worries about** the weather.*
  *I'm very **worried about** Bill.*
However, this is not always the case. Compare:
– *I **sympathise with** her.*
  *I feel some **sympathy for** her.*
  *I feel quite **sympathetic towards** her.*
– *I **hope to see** you soon.*
  *He gave up **hope of seeing** her.* (NOT ~~He gave up hope to see her.~~)

For more details, see 579 (verbs), 377 (nouns) and 12 (adjectives).

141 conditional

1 conditional clauses

Clauses constructed with *if* (except in reported speech) are often called 'conditional clauses'.
  ***If you think I'm going to help you**, you're wrong.*
  *You wouldn't have crashed **if you'd looked where you were going**.*

For details of the different kinds of structures with *if,* see 258–265.

2 conditional verb forms

The word *conditional* is also sometimes used as a name for verb forms constructed with the auxiliary verb *should/would* (and sometimes *could* and *might*).
  *I **should/would like** to use the computer for an hour or two.*
  *It **would be** nice if he **would stop** talking for a bit.*

For details of these verb forms and their use, see 498.

142 **conjunctions** (1): general points

1 **What are conjunctions?**

Conjunctions are words that join clauses into sentences.

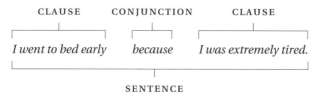

Conjunctions not only join clauses together; they also show how the
meanings of the two clauses are related.

*We brought the food **and** they supplied the drink.* (addition)
*She was poor **but** she was honest.* (contrast)
*We can go swimming, **or** we could stay here.* (alternative)
*People disliked her **because** she was so rude.* (cause)
*I'll phone you **when** I arrive.* (time)

2 **two kinds**

And, but and *or* are often called 'co-ordinating conjunctions'. They join pairs
of clauses that are grammatically independent of each other.

Other conjunctions, like *because, when, that* or *which*, are called
'subordinating conjunctions'. A subordinating conjunction together with its
following clause acts like a part of the other clause. Compare:
– *I'll phone you **when I arrive**.*
  *I'll phone you **tomorrow**.*
  (*When I arrive* is similar to *tomorrow* – it acts like an adverb in the
  clause *I'll phone you*.)
– *He told me **that he loved me**.*
  *He told me **a lie**.*
  (*that he loved me* is similar to *a lie* – it acts like the object in the clause
  He told me . . .)
– *It's a question **which nobody can answer**.*
  *It's an **unanswerable** question.*
  (*which nobody can answer* is similar to *unanswerable* – it acts like an
  adjective in the clause *It's a question*.)
Some conjunctions are made up of two or more words.

*I stayed an extra night **so that** I could see Ann.*
*Let me know **the moment that** you arrive.*

In grammars, clauses that follow subordinating conjunctions are called
'subordinate clauses' or 'dependent clauses'.

3 **position of subordinate clauses**

Adverbial subordinating conjunctions and their clauses can usually go either
first or last in a sentence (depending on what is to be emphasised).
– ***If you need help**, just let me know.*
  *Just let me know **if you need help**.*

▶

— *Although the bicycle was expensive*, she decided to buy it.
She decided to buy the bicycle *although it was expensive*.
— *While I was having a shower*, I slipped on the floor.
I slipped on the floor *while I was having a shower*.
— *Because she was too angry to speak*, Ann said nothing.
Ann said nothing, *because she was too angry to speak.*

4 punctuation

Commas are often used to separate longer or more complicated clauses.
Shorter pairs of clauses are often connected without commas. Compare:

I came home and the others went dancing.
I decided to come home earlier than I had planned, and the others spent
the evening at the local disco.

When a subordinate clause begins a sentence, it is more often separated by a
comma, even if it is short. Compare:

If you are passing, come in and see us.
Come in and see us if you are passing.

For more information about punctuation, see 455.
For punctuation in relative clauses, see 474.

5 leaving words out

Words for repeated ideas can often be left out in the second of two co-
ordinate clauses (see 182 for details), but not normally in a subordinate
clause. Compare:

*She was depressed, **and** didn't know what to do.*
   (= **and she** didn't know what to do.)
*She was depressed, **because she** didn't know what to do.*
   (NOT ~~She was depressed, because didn't know~~...)

However, after *if, when, while, until, once, unless* and *(al)though*, a pronoun
subject and the verb *be* can often be dropped, especially in common fixed
expressions like *if necessary.*

*I'll pay for you **if necessary**.* (= ... *if it is necessary.*)
If in doubt, wait and see. (= *If you are in doubt* ...)
When in Rome, do as the Romans do.
Cook slowly until ready.
Once in bed, I read for twenty minutes and then turned out the light.

Many conjunctions that express time relations (*after, before, since, when,*
while, whenever, once and *until*) can often be followed by -*ing* forms or past
participles instead of subjects and full verbs (see 406.6).

*I always feel better **after talking to you**.*
*Some things are never forgotten, **once learnt**.*

6 conjunctions in separate sentences

Normally a conjunction connects two clauses into one sentence. However,
sometimes a conjunction and its clause can stand alone. This happens, for
example, in answers.

'When are you going to get up?' 'When I'm ready.'
'Why did you do that?' 'Because I felt like it.'
'I'm going out, Mum.' 'As soon as you've brushed your hair.'

Writers and speakers can also separate clauses for emphasis.

*This government has got to go. **Before it does any more damage.***

Afterthoughts may also begin with conjunctions.

*OK, I did it. – **But I didn't mean to.***

For tenses in subordinate clauses, see 556.

For structures in which *that* is dropped, see 560.

See also 473–477 (relative pronouns and clauses), 480–482 (indirect speech), and the
individual entries on the various conjunctions.

143 **conjunctions** (2): problems

In most languages of European origin, clauses are joined together by
conjunctions in similar ways. However, students who speak non-European-
type languages may have some problems in using English conjunctions
correctly.

1 **one conjunction for two clauses**

One conjunction is enough to join two clauses – we do not normally use two.

– ***Although** she was tired, she went to work.*
*She was tired **but** she went to work.*
   (NOT *~~Although she was tired **but** she went to work.~~*)
– ***Because** I liked him, I tried to help him.*
*I liked him, **so** I tried to help him.*
   (NOT *~~Because I was tired, **so** I tried to help him.~~*)
– ***As** you know, I work very hard.*
*You know **that** I work very hard.*
   (NOT *~~As you know, **that** I work very hard.~~*)

However, two conjunctions can come together when two subordinate
clauses are connected with a co-ordinating conjunction.

*We came back **because** we ran out of money, **and because** Ann got ill.*

So and *yet* are like conjunctions in some ways, but they can be used together
with *and*.

*I forgot to post the letter, **and so** she never heard about my divorce.*
*He's not really nice-looking, **and yet** he has enormous charm.*

2 **Relative pronouns are also conjunctions**

Relative pronouns (*who, which* and *that* – see 473) join clauses like
conjunctions.

*There's the girl **who** works with my sister.*

A relative pronoun is like the subject or object of the verb that comes after it.
So we do not need another subject or object.

*I've got a friend **who** works in a pub.*
   (NOT *...~~**who he** works in a pub.~~*)
*The man **(that)** she married was an old friend of mine.*
   (NOT *~~The man **that** she married **him**...~~*)
*She always thanks me for the money **that** I give her.*
   (NOT *...~~the money **that** I give her **it**.~~*)

▶

3 *that, where* and *when*

That is often used instead of *which* or *who(m)* (see 473–474), but we do not usually use *that* instead of *when* or *where*.

> *August 31st is a national holiday,* **when** *everybody dances in the streets.*
> (NOT *...~~that everybody dances~~...*)
> *The house* **where** *I live is very small.*
> (NOT *~~The house~~* **that** *~~I live is very small.~~*)

But *that... in* can mean the same as *where*.

> *The house* **that** *I live* **in** *is very small.*

That can be used instead of *where* and *when* in a few special cases (e.g. after *place, day*); for details, see 477.3.

> *I'll always remember the day* **(that)** *I met you.*

For conjunctions after prepositions, see 441.
For *now* as a conjunction, see 383. For *once*, see 390. For *the moment* and *immediately*, see 267.

144 contractions

1 general rules

Forms like *I've, don't* are called 'contractions'. There are two kinds.

noun / pronoun / etc + (auxiliary) verb	(auxiliary) verb + *not*
I'm tired.	*They* **aren't** *ready.*
Do you know when **you'll** *arrive?*	*You* **won't** *be late, will you?*
I've no idea.	*I* **haven't** *seen him for ages.*
She'd like to talk to you.	**Can't** *you swim?*
Here's our bus.	
My **father's** *not very well.*	
Where's the station?	
There's a problem.	
Somebody's coming.	

Contractions are formed with auxiliary verbs, and also with *be* and sometimes *have* when these are not auxiliary verbs.

The short form *'s* (= *is/has*) can be written after nouns, question words, *here* and *now* as well as pronouns and unstressed *there*. The short forms *'ll*, *'d* and *'re* are commonly written after pronouns and unstressed *there*, but in other cases we more often write the full forms (especially in British English), even if the words would be contracted in pronunciation.

> *'Your mother will (/'mʌðərl/) be surprised', she said.*
> *I wondered what had (/'wɒtəd/) happened.*

Contractions are not usually written with double subjects.

> *John and* **I have** *decided to split up.* (NOT *~~John and I've decided~~...*)

The apostrophe (') goes in the same place as the letters that we leave out: *has not* = *hasn't* (NOT *~~ha'snt~~*). But note that *shan't* (= *shall not*) and *won't* (= *will not*) only have one apostrophe each.

Contractions are common and correct in informal writing: they represent the pronunciation of informal speech. They are not generally used in a formal style.

2   alternative contractions

Some negative expressions can have two possible contractions. For *she had not* we can say *she'd not* or *she hadn't*; for *he will not* we can say *he'll not* or *he won't*. The two negative forms of *be* (e.g. *she isn't* and *she's not*) are both common; with other verbs, forms with *n't* (e.g. *she hadn't*) are more common in most cases in standard southern British English and in American English. (Forms with *not* – e.g. *she'd not* – tend to be more common in northern and Scottish English.)

Double contractions are not normally written: ~~she'sn't~~ is impossible.

3   stress

Contractions in the first group (**noun / pronoun / question word + auxiliary verb**) are never stressed. When an auxiliary verb is stressed (for example at the end of a clause), a contraction is not possible. Compare:
–   *I'm* late.
     Yes, *you are*. (NOT ~~Yes, you're.~~)
–   *I've* forgotten.
     Yes, *you have*. (NOT ~~Yes, you've.~~)
However, negative contractions can be stressed, and we can use them at the ends of clauses.
     They really **aren't**.
     No, I **haven't**.

4   list of contractions

Contraction	Pronunciation	Meaning
I'm	/aɪm/	I am
I've	/aɪv/	I have
I'll	/aɪl/	I will
I'd	/aɪd/	I had / would
you're	/jɔː(r)/	you are
you've	/juːv/	you have
you'll	/juːl/	you will
you'd	/juːd/	you had / would
he's	/hiːz/	he is / has
he'll	/hiːl, hɪl/	he will
he'd	/hiːd/	he had / would
she's	/ʃiːz/	she is / has
she'll	/ʃiːl, ʃɪl/	she will
she'd	/ʃiːd/	she had / would
it's[1]	/ɪts/	it is / has
it'd (uncommon)	/ɪtəd/	it had / would
we're	/wɪə(r)/	we are
we've	/wiːv/	we have
we'll	/wiːl, wɪl/	we will
we'd	/wiːd/	we had / would

▶

Contraction	Pronunciation	Meaning
they're	/ðeə(r)/	they are
they've	/ðeɪv/	they have
they'll	/ðeɪl, ðel/	they will
they'd	/ðeɪd/	they had / would
there's	/ðəz/	there is / has
there'll	/ðəl /	there will
there'd	/ðəd/	there had / would
aren't [2]	/ɑːnt/	are not
can't [3]	/kɑːnt/	cannot
couldn't	/'kʊdnt/	could not
daren't [4]	/deənt/	dare not
didn't	/'dɪdnt/	did not
doesn't	/'dʌznt/	does not
don't	/dəʊnt/	do not
hadn't	/'hædnt/	had not
hasn't	/'hæznt/	has not
haven't	/'hævnt/	have not
isn't	/'ɪznt/	is not
mightn't	/'maɪtnt/	might not
mustn't	/'mʌsnt/	must not
needn't	/'niːdnt/	need not
oughtn't	/'ɔːtnt/	ought not
shan't [4]	/ʃɑːnt/	shall not
shouldn't	/'ʃʊdnt/	should not
usedn't [4]	/'juːsnt/	used not
wasn't	/'wɒznt/	was not
weren't	/wɜːnt/	were not
won't	/wəʊnt/	will not
wouldn't	/'wʊdnt/	would not

Notes

1   Do not confuse *it's* (= *it is/has*) and *its* (possessive).

2   *Am not* is only normally contracted in questions, to *aren't* (GB) (/ɑːnt/).
   *I'm late, **aren't** I?*

3   Note the difference in pronunciation of *can't* in British English (/kɑːnt/) and American English (/kænt/).

4   *Daren't, shan't* and *usedn't* are not often used in American English.

5   In non-standard English, *ain't* (pronounced /eɪnt/ or /ent/) is used as a contraction of *am not, are not, is not, have not* and *has not*.
   *I **ain't** going to tell him.   Don't talk to me like that – you **ain't** my boss.*
   *'It's raining.' 'No it **ain't**.'   I **ain't** got no more cigarettes.*
   *Bill **ain't** been here for days.*

6   For the contraction *let's*, see 315.

7   *May not* is not normally contracted: *mayn't* is very rare.

145 contrary

1 *on the contrary* and *on the other hand*

In modern English *on the contrary* is used to contradict – to say that what has been said is not true. If we want to give the other side of a question, we use *on the other hand*, not *on the contrary*. Compare:

> '*I suppose the job wasn't very interesting?*' '**On the contrary**, *it was fascinating. I loved it.*'
> *The job wasn't very interesting, but **on the other hand** it was well paid.*
> (NOT ... ~~on the contrary, it was well paid.~~)

2 *contrary* and *opposite*

We usually use *opposite*, not *contrary*, to talk about contrasting pairs of words.

> '*Short' is the **opposite** of 'tall', and also of 'long'.*
> (NOT ... ~~the contrary of 'tall'~~ ...)

For more information about *opposite*, see 397.

146 control

The word *control* is a 'false friend' for people who speak many languages of European origin. In English, *control* generally means *manage*, *direct*, not *check* or *inspect*. Compare:

> – *The crowd was too big for the police to **control**.* (=... *to keep in order*.)
> *The police were **checking** everybody's papers.*
> (NOT ... ~~controlling everybody's papers.~~)
> – *I found the car difficult to **control** at high speeds.*
> *I took the car to the garage and asked them to **have a look at** the steering.*
> (NOT ... ~~to control the steering.~~)

Note, however, that the noun *control* is used with the meaning of 'inspection point' in expressions like *passport/customs control*.

147 copular verbs

1 common copular verbs

We use a special kind of verb to join an adjective or noun complement to a subject. These verbs can be called 'copulas' or 'copular verbs'. Common copular verbs are: *be, seem, appear, look, sound, smell, taste, feel, become, get*.

> *The weather **is** horrible.*   *I do **feel** a fool.*
> *That car **looks** fast.*   *She **became** a racehorse trainer.*
> *The stew **smells** good.*   *It's **getting** late.*

2 adjectives after copular verbs

After copular verbs we use adjectives, not adverbs. Compare:

> *He spoke **intelligently**.* (*Intelligently* is an adverb. It tells you about how the person spoke.)
> *He looks **intelligent**.* (*Intelligent* is an adjective in predicative position (see 15). It tells you about the person himself – rather like saying *He **is** intelligent. Look* is a copular verb.)

▶

3 other uses

Note that some of these verbs are also used with other meanings as ordinary non-copular verbs. They are then used with adverbs, not adjectives. Compare:

The problem **appeared impossible**. (NOT ...~~impossibly.~~)

Isabel **suddenly appeared** in the doorway. (NOT ...~~sudden~~...)

Other verbs used in two ways like this are *look* (see 324), *taste* (see 552) and *feel* (see 208).

4 change

Some copular verbs are used to talk about change, or the absence of change. The most common are: *become, get, grow, go, turn, stay, remain, keep*.

It's **becoming** colder.
It's **getting** colder.
It's **growing** colder.
The leaves are **going** brown.
The leaves are **turning** brown.

How does she **stay** so young?
I hope you will always **remain** so happy.
Keep calm.

For the differences between these verbs, see 129.

5 other verbs followed by adjectives

Sometimes other verbs, too, can be followed by adjectives. This happens when we are really describing the subject of the sentence, and not the action of the verb. It is common in descriptions with *sit, stand, lie, fall*.

The valley **lay quiet and peaceful** in the sun.

She **sat motionless**, waiting for their decision.

He **fell unconscious** on the floor. (NOT ...~~unconsciously~~...)

Adjectives can also be used in the structure **verb + object + adjective**, in order to describe the object of the verb.

New *SUPER GUB* washes clothes *SUPER **WHITE**.* (NOT ...~~WHITELY~~...)

He pulled his belt **tight** and started off. (NOT ...~~tightly~~...)

See also the entries for particular copular verbs.
For more about verb complementation, see 579.

148 countable and uncountable nouns

1 the difference between countable and uncountable nouns

Countable nouns are the names of separate objects, people, ideas etc which can be counted. We can use numbers and the article *a/an* with countable nouns; they have plurals.

a cat
three cats

a newspaper
two newspapers

Uncountable (or 'mass') nouns are the names of materials, liquids, abstract qualities, collections and other things which we see as masses without clear boundaries, and not as separate objects. We cannot use numbers with uncountable nouns, and most are singular with no plurals. (For plural uncountable nouns, see paragraph 7 below.) We do not normally use *a/an* with uncountable nouns, though there are some exceptions (see paragraph 6 below).

> *water* (NOT ~~*a water, two waters*~~)
> *wool* (NOT ~~*a wool, two wools*~~)
> *weather* (NOT ~~*a weather, two weathers*~~)

Some determiners (see 157) can only be used with countable nouns (e.g. *many, few*); others can only be used with uncountables (e.g. *much, little*). Compare:

> How **many hours** do you work?
> How **much money** do you earn?

Note that not all nouns are either simply countable or simply uncountable. Many nouns have both countable and uncountable uses, sometimes with a difference of meaning. The following rules will help, but to know exactly how a particular noun can be used, it is necessary to check in a good dictionary.

2 problem cases

Usually it is easy to see whether a noun is countable or uncountable. Obviously *house* is normally a countable noun, and *sand* is not. But sometimes things are not so clear. For instance, *travel* and *journey* have very similar meanings, but *travel* is normally uncountable (it means 'travelling in general', and we do not talk about 'a travel'), while *journey* is countable (*a journey* is one movement from one place to another). And many things can be seen both as a collection of separate elements and as a mass; some names for things of this kind are countable, while others are uncountable. Compare:

Countable: *bean(s), pea(s), grape(s), lentil(s), fact(s)*
Uncountable: *rice, spaghetti, macaroni* (and other pasta foods), *sugar, salt, wheat, news*

3 English and other languages

Not all languages treat things in the same way. For example, *hair* can be uncountable in English, but is plural countable in many languages; *grapes* is a plural countable word in English, but uncountable in some other languages. Here is a list of some common words which are usually uncountable in English, but which have countable equivalents in some other languages. Corresponding countable expressions are also given.

Uncountable	**Countable**
accommodation	a place to live (NOT ~~an accommodation~~)
advice	a piece of advice (NOT ~~an advice~~)
baggage	a piece of baggage; a case / trunk / bag
bread	a piece of bread; a loaf; a roll
chess	a game of chess
chewing gum	a piece of chewing gum
equipment	a piece of equipment; a tool etc
furniture	a piece / article of furniture
grass	a blade of grass
information	a piece of information
knowledge	a fact

▶

Uncountable	Countable
lightning	a flash of lightning
luck	a bit/stroke of luck
luggage	a piece of luggage; a case/trunk/bag
money	a note; a coin; a sum
news	a piece of news
permission	—
poetry	a poem
progress	a step forward
publicity	an advertisement
research	a piece of research
rubbish	a piece of rubbish
spaghetti	a piece of spaghetti
thunder	a clap of thunder
traffic	—
travel	a journey/trip
work	a job; a piece of work

Note that when uncountable English words are borrowed by other languages, they may change into countable words with different meanings (for example French *parking* means 'car park', not 'parking').

4 illnesses

The names of illnesses are usually uncountable in English, including those ending in -*s*.

*If you've already had **measles**, you can't get **it** again.*
*There's a lot of **flu** around at the moment.*

The words for some minor ailments are countable: e.g. *a cold, a sore throat, a headache*. However, *toothache, earache, stomach-ache* and *backache* are more often uncountable in British English. In American English, these words are generally countable if they refer to particular attacks of pain. Compare:

*Love isn't as bad as **toothache**.* (GB)
*Love isn't as bad as **a toothache**.* (US)

5 mixed uses

Many nouns have both countable and uncountable uses, with some difference of meaning. Words for materials are uncountable, but we can often use the same word as a countable noun to refer to something made of the material. Compare:

– *I'd like some typing **paper**.*
  *I'm going out to buy **a paper** (= a newspaper)*
– *The window's made of unbreakable **glass**.*
  *Would you like **a glass** of water?*
– *Have you got any **coffee**?*
  *Could I have **two coffees**? (= cups of coffee)*

And normally uncountable nouns can often be used as countables if we are talking about different kinds of material, liquid etc.

*Not all washing **powders** are kind to your hands.*
*The 1961 **wines** were among the best this century.*

Many abstract nouns can have both uncountable and countable uses, corresponding to more 'general' and more 'particular' meanings. Compare:
- *Don't hurry – there's plenty of **time**.*
  *Have **a** good **time**.*
- *She hasn't got enough **experience** for the job.*
  *I had **a** really strange **experience** last week.*
- *It's hard to feel **pity** for people like that.*
  *It's **a pity** it's raining.*

Singular countable nouns are sometimes used as uncountables (e.g. with *much, enough, plenty of* or *a lot of*), in order to express the idea of amount.
> *I've got **too much nose** and not **enough chin**.*
> *If you buy a Volvo you get **plenty of car** for your money.*
> *We've got enough paint for about **20 square feet of wall**.*

Some countable abstract nouns can be used uncountably after *little, much* and other determiners. Common examples are *difference, point, reason, idea, change, difficulty, chance* and *question*.
> *There isn't **much difference** between 'begin' and 'start'.*
> *I don't think there's **much point** in arguing about it.*
> *We have **little reason** to expect prices to fall.*
> *I haven't got **much idea** of her plans.*
> *There isn't **any change** in his condition.*
> *They experienced **little difficulty** in stealing the painting.*
> *Do you think we have **much chance** of catching the train?*
> *There's **some question** of our getting a new Managing Director.*

Note the expression *have difficulty (in) . . .ing.*
> *I **have difficulty (in) remembering** faces.* (NOT ~~I have difficulties . . .~~)

A few uncountable nouns have plural uses in fixed expressions.
> *He goes running **in all weathers**.*
> *Did you meet anybody exciting **on your travels**?*
> ***Gulliver's Travels*** (novel by Jonathan Swift)

6 *a/an* with uncountable nouns

With certain uncountable nouns – especially nouns referring to human emotions and mental activity – we have to use *a/an* when we are limiting their meaning in some way.
> *We need a secretary with **a first-class knowledge** of German.*
> (NOT *. . .~~with first-class knowledge of German.~~*)
> *She has always had **a deep distrust** of strangers.*
> *That child shows **a surprising understanding** of adult behaviour.*
> *My parents wanted me to have **a good education**.*
> (NOT *. . .~~to have good education.~~*)

Note that these nouns cannot normally be used in the plural, and that most uncountable nouns cannot be used with *a/an* at all.
> *My father enjoys **very good health**.* (NOT *. . .~~a very good health.~~*)
> *We're having **terrible weather**.* (NOT *. . .~~a terrible weather.~~*)
> *He speaks **excellent English**.* (NOT *. . .~~an excellent English.~~*)
> *It's **interesting work**.* (NOT *. . .~~an interesting work.~~*) ▶

7 plural uncountables

Some uncountable nouns are plural. They have no singular forms with the same meaning, and cannot be used with numbers. Common examples are *groceries, arms, remains, goods, customs* (at a frontier), *clothes, thanks, regards, police*.

> *I've bought the **groceries**.* (BUT NOT *...a grocery.* OR *...three groceries.*)
> ***Many thanks** for your help.* (BUT NOT *Much thank...*)

Other plural uncountables include *trousers, jeans, pyjamas, pants, scissors, spectacles, glasses* (meaning *spectacles*), and the expressions *the British, the Dutch, the English, the French, the Irish, the Spanish* and *the Welsh*.

> *I need **some** new **jeans**.* (NOT *...a new jean.*)
> *In 1581 **the Dutch** declared their independence from Spain.*

For more information on the use of articles with countable and uncountable nouns, see 64.

149 country

1 countable use

Country (countable) = 'nation', 'land'.

> *Scotland is a cold **country**.*   *France is the **country** I know best.*
> *How many **countries** are there in Europe?*

2 uncountable use

Country (uncountable) = 'open land without many buildings'.

> *I like **wild country** best.*

With this meaning, we cannot say *a country* or *countries*.

> *My parents live in nice **country** near Belfast.* (NOT *...in a nice country...*)

The expression *the country* (the opposite of *the town*) is very common.

> *We live in **the country** just outside Manchester.*
> *Would you rather live in the town or **the country**?*

For similar general expressions with *the*, see 68.3a.
For information about countable and uncountable nouns, see 148.

150 dare

1 structures

Dare can be used in two ways:

a as an ordinary verb, followed by the infinitive with *to*

> *He's a man who **dares to say** what he thinks.*
> *She **didn't dare to tell** him what had happened.*

b as a modal auxiliary verb (see 344–345).

> ***Dare she tell** him?*   { (Question and negative without *do*;
> *I **daren't say** what I think.*   third person without *-s*;
>   following infinitive without *to*.)

In modern English, *dare* is not a very common verb. In an informal style, people generally use other expressions to express the same meaning.
>	He's **not afraid** to say what he thinks.

## 2	*dare* as an ordinary verb

When *dare* is used, it is usually as an ordinary verb, not a modal auxiliary. It is most common in negative sentences.
>	She **doesn't dare to** go out at night.
>	The old lady **didn't dare to** open the door.

The expressions *You dare!* (GB) and *Don't you dare!* are sometimes used to discourage people from doing unwanted things.
>	'Mummy, can I draw a picture on the wall?' '**You dare!**'

## 3	*dare* as a modal auxiliary

Modal auxiliary forms are common in a few present-tense uses. For instance, British people quite often use *daren't* to say that somebody is afraid to do something at the moment of speaking.
>	I **daren't** look.

How dare you? is sometimes used as an indignant exclamation.
>	**How dare you?** Take your hands off me at once!

And *I dare say* (sometimes written *I daresay*) is used in British English to mean 'I think probably', 'I suppose'.
>	I **dare say** it'll rain soon.	I **daresay** you're ready for a drink.

## 4	mixed structures

Occasionally mixed ordinary/modal structures are found.
>	**Do you dare put** your mind to the test? (advertisement)
>	He **didn't dare open** his eyes.	The bank **dares not try** to call in its debts.

## 5	*dare* + object + infinitive

Children use the expression *I dare you* + **infinitive** to challenge each other to do frightening things.
>	I **dare you to run** across the road with your eyes shut.

Need can also be used both as an ordinary verb and as a modal auxiliary. See 357.

# 151	dates

## 1	writing

In Britain, the commonest way to write the day's date is as follows. Note that the names of months always begin with capital letters.
>	*30 March 1995*	*27 July 1996*

The last two letters of the number word (*st, nd, rd* or *th*) are sometimes added. Some people write a comma before the year, but this is no longer very common in Britain except when the date comes inside a sentence.
>	*30th March(,) 1995*	*He was born in Hawick on 14 December, 1942.*	▶

The date may be written entirely in figures.

30/3/95   30-3-95   30.3.95

In the USA it is common to write the month first and to put a comma before the year.

March 30, 1995

All-figure dates are written differently in Britain and America, since British people put the day first while Americans generally start with the month. So for example, *6.4.94* means '6 April 1994' in Britain, but 'June 4, 1994' in the USA.

The longer names of the months are often abbreviated as follows:

Jan   Feb   Mar   Apr   Aug   Sept   Oct   Nov   Dec

The names of decades (e.g. *the nineteen sixties*) can be written like this: *the 1960s.*

For the position of dates in letters, see 317.

For full stops in abbreviations, see 2.

For words that are written with initial capital letters, see 529.

2   speaking

30 March 1993 = 'March the thirtieth, nineteen ninety-three'
(US 'March (the) thirtieth ...')
or 'the thirtieth of March, nineteen ninety-three'
1200 = 'twelve hundred'
1305 = 'thirteen hundred and five' or 'thirteen O (/əʊ/) five'
1498 = 'fourteen (hundred and) ninety-eight'
1910 = 'nineteen (hundred and) ten'
1946 = 'nineteen (hundred and) forty-six'
2000 = 'two thousand'
2005 = 'two thousand and five'

To announce the date, *It's* is used.

It's April the first.

To ask about dates, we can say for instance:

What's the date (today)?
What date is your birthday?

3   *BC* and *AD*

To distinguish between dates before and after the birth of Christ, we use the abbreviations *BC* (= 'Before Christ') and *AD* (= 'Anno Domini' – Latin for 'in the year of the Lord'). *BC* follows the date; *AD* can come before or after it.

*Julius Caesar first came to Britain in **55 BC**.*
*The emperor Trajan was born in **AD 53 / 53 AD**.*

152   **dead** and **died**

Dead is an adjective.

*a **dead** man*
*Mrs McGinty is **dead**.*
*That idea has been **dead** for years.*

Died is the past tense and past participle of the verb *die*.

> Shakespeare **died** in 1616. (NOT ~~Shakespeare **dead**...~~)
> She **died** in a car crash. (NOT ~~She **is dead** in...~~)
> So far 50 people **have died** in the fighting.

Note the spelling of the present participle *dying* (see 534).

For expressions like *the dead* (= 'dead people'), see 18.

153 **degree** (1): modification of adjectives and adverbs

1 **gradable and non-gradable**

Some adjectives and adverbs refer to qualities which are *gradable* – we can have more or less of them. For example, people can be more or less *interesting* or *old*; jobs can be more or less *difficult*; cars can go more or less *fast*. Other adjectives and adverbs refer to *non-gradable* qualities – we do not usually say that things are more or less *perfect*, *impossible* or *dead*.

2 **gradable adjectives and adverbs**

To add the idea of *degree* – 'how much' – to gradable adjectives and adverbs, we can use words and expressions like *too, as, so, enough, extremely, very, rather, pretty, quite* (British English), *fairly, a little, a bit* (informal), *not very, not at all, how.*

> The water's **too cold**.   I'm **extremely grateful** to you.
> It's going to be **very cold**.   You look **rather unhappy**.
> You're driving **a bit fast**, aren't you?
> I wasn't **at all enthusiastic** about the idea.
> I can't tell you **how pleased** I am about the result.
> **How well** do you speak Russian?

A little and *a bit* are mostly used before adjectives and adverbs that express negative ideas.

> I thought the house was **a little small**.
> You're looking **a bit tired**. (BUT NOT ~~You're looking **a bit happy**.~~)

A little and *a bit* are not used with adjectives in attributive position (= before nouns – see 15).

> I had a **rather unpleasant experience**.
>   (BUT NOT ~~I had an **a bit** unpleasant experience.~~)

Note that *enough* follows its adjective.

> He's not **tall enough** to be a policeman. (NOT ~~He's not **enough tall**...~~)

Indeed can be used for emphasis after **very + adjective/adverb**. It cannot normally be used without *very*.

> It's going to be **very cold indeed**. (BUT NOT ~~It's going to be cold **indeed**.~~)

Most is sometimes used (with the same meaning as *very*) before adjectives in a formal style.

> That's **most kind** of you.

For more information about *enough*, see 193.
For word order when *quite* and *rather* are used with **article + adjective + noun**, see 467–468.   ▶

3 *not very*

Not very expresses quite a low degree.
> It's **not very** warm – you'd better take a coat.
> That meal was**n't very** expensive. (=... **quite cheap**.)

Note that *little* cannot be used in this sense.
> He's **not very** imaginative. (BUT NOT ~~He's **little** imaginative.~~)

4 *very, too, so, as* and *how* without *much*

These words are normally used without *much* before adjectives and adverbs.
> The situation is **very serious**. (NOT ...~~very **much serious**.~~)
> I'm **very worried** about Angela. (NOT ...~~very **much worried**...~~)
> You're **too kind**. (NOT ~~You're **too much kind**.~~)
> I came **as quickly** as I could. (NOT ...~~as **much quickly**...~~)
> I don't care **how expensive** it is. (NOT ...~~how **much expensive**...~~)

However, *very much, too much, so much* etc are used before comparatives
(see paragraph 6 below), and often before *afraid* (especially when *I'm afraid*
means *I'm sorry to tell you*).
> I'm **very much afraid** that I can't come tomorrow.

Very much etc can be used before some participles that are used as
adjectives. For details, see 405.4.
> She was **very (much) annoyed** to find Jake in her room.

Before **adjective + noun**, we normally use *such*, not *so*. For details, see 544.
Compare:
> It's **so cold**.
> It's **such a cold day**.

For more about *so*, see 513.
For the use of *too, so, as* and *how* before **adjective + article + noun** (e.g. *so cold a day*), see 16.

5 special combinations

Some adjectives are commonly used with particular modifiers. For example,
as well as *very reliable* we can say *highly reliable*, but we cannot say *highly
old*; *grossly unfair* is possible, but not *grossly hot*. A good dictionary will give
information about the most common combinations.

6 comparatives

Different modifiers are used for comparatives. Compare:
> – It's **very cold**. (NOT ~~It's **(very) much cold**.~~)
>   It's **(very) much colder** than yesterday. (NOT ~~It's **very colder** than yesterday.~~)
> – The book's **quite interesting**.
>   The book's **a lot more interesting** than his last one.
>   (NOT ...~~**quite more interesting**.~~)

For full details of the modification of comparatives and superlatives, see 139.

7 non-gradable adjectives and adverbs

With non-gradable words, certain modifiers are used to stress the idea of completeness or to emphasise the meaning of the adjective or adverb.

*I'm **completely exhausted**.   The talk was **absolutely brilliant**.*
*He played **really superbly**.*
*Two minutes ago he was **fast asleep**, now he's **wide awake**.*

Quite is used with non-gradable words to mean 'completely'.

*The soup's not **quite ready**.*

See also the individual entries on *too, enough, quite* etc.

154 **degree** (2): modification of nouns

1 gradable nouns

Some nouns can be used gradably in descriptions, rather like adjectives.

*She's a **great nuisance**. (= She's **very annoying**.)*
*The meeting was a **relative success**. (= . . . **relatively successful**.)*

2 *quite/rather a ...*

Singular countable gradable nouns can be modified by *quite* or *rather* before the article.

*She's **quite/rather a nuisance**.   It was **quite/rather a success**.*

Note that this structure is not possible with uncountable or plural nouns. We would not say, for example, *~~It was quite luxury~~* or *~~They're rather fools~~*.

For more information about *quite*, see 467. For *rather*, see 468.

3 quantifiers with *of*

Another way of modifying a description is to use a quantifier with *of* before a singular countable noun.

*How **much of a mathematician** are you?*
*He's **very much of a family man**.*
*Between ourselves, I think she's **a bit of a fool**.*
*It was **more of a meeting** than a party.*
*She's **less of a scientist** than a technologist.*
*It's not **much of a place**, but it's home.*

A lot is not used in this structure.

*She's **very much of an intellectual**.*
    (BUT NOT *~~She's a lot of an intellectual.~~*)

This structure, too, is only used with singular countable nouns. One could not say *~~How much of mathematicians are they?~~*

For more information about the use of quantifiers, see the entries on individual words.

4 *such*

Such (see 543) can emphasise gradable nouns. It can be used with singular and plural countables and with uncountables.

*You've been **such a help**!   They're **such idiots**!*
*Don't talk **such nonsense**!*

For ***such* + adjective + noun**, see 543.3, 544.1.   ▶

5 *quite* **with non-gradables**

Quite (but not *rather*) can be used with singular countable non-gradable nouns to express the idea that something is remarkable or impressive.

> *She's **quite a girl**!*   *It was **quite a journey**!*
> *That's **quite a car**!*   *We had **quite a thunderstorm** last night!*

155 degree (3): modification of verbs

1 gradable verbs

Some verbs are 'gradable' – they refer to things that can happen more or less completely, fully, strongly etc. Various degree adverbs can be used with verbs of this kind. Examples:

> *I **entirely** agree.*   *I did**n't at all** want this to happen.*
> *She **very much** dislikes fish.*   *This weather **kind of** gets on my nerves.*
> *The boss **quite** enjoyed the party.*   *She's grown **a lot** since I last saw her.*
> *He **half** believed her story.*   *His letter annoyed me **a great deal**.*

Certain degree adverbs generally go together with certain verbs. For example, we can say *I fully understand*, but not *I fully like*; *I rather like*, but not *I rather understand*; *I firmly believe*, but not *I firmly think*. A good dictionary will give information about the most common combinations.

In a formal style, *much* can be used without *very* before certain verbs in mid-position (e.g. *I **much** admire, we **much** regret*), but not before all verbs in affirmative clauses (*I **much** like* is very unnatural). In end position, *much* is not used without *very* in affirmative clauses.

> *I like your new dress **very much**.* (BUT NOT *I like your new dress **much**.*)

For more about the use of *much*, see 348.

2 questions

Questions about degree are asked with *how much*.

> ***How much** do you want a Christmas holiday?*

But *how* is used with adjectives.

> ***How old** are your parents?*

And *how much of a* is used before singular countable nouns.

> ***How much of a job** would it be to rebuild the garage?*

3 word order

Quite, half, kind of and *sort of* usually go in mid-position (see examples above). Many other common degree adverbs can go either in mid-position or at the end of a clause. Longer and less common expressions usually go at the end. Adverbs do not normally go between a verb and its object.

> *I **very much** like skiing.* OR *I like skiing **very much**.*
>   (NOT *I like **very much** skiing.*)
> *We enjoyed the party **enormously**.*
>   (NOT *We enjoyed **enormously** the party.*)

For more details of the position of adverbs, see 22–23.

156 **degree** (4): modification of other words

1 **prepositions and particles**

Before prepositions and adverb particles referring to place and movement, we often use *right* to mean 'completely' or 'exactly'.

*I hit the target **right in** the middle.*

*We drove **right up** to Washington in two days.*

For the difference between prepositions and adverb particles, see 19.

2 **quantifiers**

Much, many, little and *few* can be modified by *too, so, as, very, rather* and *how*. (*Very much* and *very many* are mostly used in questions and negatives: see 348.)

*There's **too much** noise.*

***How many** people do you need to help you?*

*We've got **very little** time left.*

*We met **rather few** people who spoke English.*

A lot can be modified by *quite* and *rather*.

*His firm does **quite a lot** of business in Egypt.*

*You made **rather a lot** of mistakes.*

Quite a few is used with a similar meaning to 'rather a lot'.

*He speaks **quite a few** languages.*

Too much/many/little/few can be modified by *much, far* and *rather*, but not by *quite*.

*We bought **much too much** meat.*

*There are **far too many** weapons in the world.*

*I've been on **rather too many** planes and trains recently.*

    (NOT ...*quite too many*...)

Enough can be modified by *quite* (meaning 'fully').

*You've had **quite enough** to drink.*

For modification of *more* and *less*, see 139.

For more information about *much, many, few, little, quite, rather* and *enough*, see the entries for these words.

157 **determiners**

1 **What are determiners?**

Determiners are words like *the, a, my, this, some, either, every, enough, several*. Determiners come at the beginning of noun phrases, but they are not adjectives.

***the** moon*	***this** house*	***every** week*
***a** nice day*	***some** problems*	***enough** trouble*
***my** fat old cat*	***either** arm*	***several** young students*

There are two main groups of determiners. ▶

2   Group A determiners

These help to identify things – to say whether they are known or unknown to the hearer, which one(s) the speaker is talking about, whether the speaker is thinking of particular examples or speaking in general, etc.

articles*: a/an, the*
possessives*: my, your, his, her, its, our, your, their, one's, whose*
demonstratives: *this, these, that, those*

We cannot put two Group A determiners together. We can say *the* house, *my* house or *this* house, but not *the my* house, *the this* house, *this my* house or *my this* house. In order to put together the meanings of possessive and article / demonstrative, we have to use the structure *a/this . . . of mine/yours* etc (see 434).

Nouns with possessive *'s* can be used like determiners (e.g. *Britain's* weather).

For articles, see 62–69.
For possessives, see 433.
For demonstratives, see 565.
For articles with **noun + possessive *'s***, see 432.

3   Group B determiners

Most of these are 'quantifiers': they say how much or how many we are talking about.

some, any, no
each, every, either, neither
much, many, more, most; (a) little, less, least; a few, fewer, fewest;
    enough; several
all, both, half
what, whatever, which, whichever
one, two, three etc; *other*

Some Group B determiners are used with singular nouns (e.g. *each*), some with plurals (e.g. *many*), some with uncountables (e.g. *much*), and some with more than one kind of noun (e.g. *which*).

We can put two Group B determiners together if the combination makes sense.

*We meet **every few** days.*
*I've read **all six** novels by Jane Austen.*
*Have you got **any more** coffee?*

For details of the use of Group B determiners, look up the sections on particular words.

4   Group B + Group A: *of* with determiners

Group B determiners can be used directly before nouns, without *of.*

*Have you got **any sugar**?* (N O T *. . .**any of sugar.***)
***Most people** agree with me.* (N O T **Most of people** . . .)

But if we want to put a Group B determiner before a noun which has a Group A determiner (article, possessive or demonstrative), we have to use *of.*

Compare:
- *some* people   – *which* discs
  some of the people   *which of your* discs
- *each* child   – *enough* remarks
  each of my children   *enough of those* remarks
- *neither* door   – *six* green apples
  neither of these doors   *six of the* green apples
- *most* shops
  most of the shops

Of can be used directly before a noun with no Group A determiner in a few cases. This happens with proper nouns such as place names, and sometimes with uncountable nouns that refer to the whole of a subject or activity.

Most of Wales was without electricity last night.

Much of philosophy is concerned with questions that have no answers.

No and *every* are not used before *of*; instead we use *none* and *every one*. Compare:
- *no* friends   – *every* blouse
  none of my friends   *every one of* these blouses

We can leave out *of* after *all, both* and *half* when they are followed by nouns (but not when they are followed by pronouns).

all (of) his ideas
both (of) my parents
half (of) her income
BUT *all of* us (NOT ~~all us~~)

Note that when *each, every, either* and *neither* are used directly before nouns without *of,* the nouns are singular. Compare:
- *each* **tree**   – *neither* **partner**
  each of the **trees**   *neither of the* **partners**

5   determiner + *of* + pronoun

Group B determiners can also be used with *of* before pronouns.

neither of them   *which of* us   *most of* you

6   Group A + Group B

Certain Group B determiners can be used after Group A determiners. They are *many, most, little, least* and *few.*

his many friends   *these few* poems   *the least* time
the most money   *a little* time   *a few* questions

For the difference between *little* and *a little*, and between *few* and *a few*, see 322.

7   other determiners

There are a few other determiners that do not fit into Groups A and B. They are *other, such, what* (in exclamations) and *only. Other* and *only* come after Group A determiners (*another* is written as one word); *such* and *what* come before the article *a/an* (see 544.1, 69.14).

my other sister   *such a* nice day
the only possibility   *what a* pity   ▶

Other and *such* can also come after some Group B determiners.
many other *problems*   **most such** *requests*

For more information about *other*, see 53. For *such*, see 543. For *only*, see 394.

8 determiners without nouns

Nouns that have already been mentioned are often dropped after determiners.
*'Do you know Orwell's books?' 'I haven't read **any**.'*
*'Have we got any tomatoes?' '**A few**.'*
*'Which chair do you want?' '**This** will do.'*
Plural determiners are sometimes used without nouns to refer to people in general. This is formal and generally rather old-fashioned.
***Many** are called but **few** are chosen.* (The Bible)
***Some** say one thing, **some** say another.*
*OPEN MEETING NEXT TUESDAY EVENING. **ALL** (ARE) WELCOME.*
Possessives (except *whose* and *his*) have different forms when they are used without nouns: *mine, yours, hers, ours, theirs* (see 433). Compare:
*That's **my** coat.   That's **mine**.*
Its and *one's* are not used without nouns. (See 433.3.)

For *others* meaning 'other people', see 53.4. For *all* meaning *everything*, see 34.2.
For expressions like *a lot of, a heap of, the majority of*, see 326.
For more information about particular determiners, consult the entries for the individual words (see Index).
For singular and plural verbs after *any, either, neither* and *none*, see 509.5.

158 different

1 modifiers

Different is a little like a comparative (see 136, 139): unlike most adjectives, it can be modified by *any* and *no*, *little* and *not much*.
*I hadn't seen her for years, but she wasn't **any different**.*
*'How's the patient, doctor?' '**No different**.'*
*His ideas are **little different** from those of his friends.*
*The new school isn't **much different** from the old one.*
Quite different means 'completely different' (see 467.4).
*I thought you'd be like your sister, but you're **quite different**.*
Unlike comparatives, *different* can also be modified by *very*.
*She's **very different** from her sister.*

2 prepositions

From is generally used after *different*; many British people also use *to*. In American English, *than* is common.
*American football is very **different from/to** soccer.*
    (US ... *different **from/than*** soccer.)
Before a clause, *different than* is possible in British English.
*The job's **different than** I expected.*
    (OR ... ***different from/to what*** I expected.)

For the difference between *different* and *other*, see 53.5.

159 discourse markers

Discourse means 'pieces of language longer than a sentence'. Some words and expressions are used to show how discourse is constructed. They can show the connection between what a speaker is saying and what has already been said or what is going to be said; they can help to make clear the structure of what is being said; they can indicate what speakers think about what they are saying or what others have said. There are a very large number of these 'discourse markers', and it is impossible to give a complete list in a few pages. Here are a few of the most common examples. Some of these words and expressions have more than one use; for more information, look in a good dictionary. Some discourse markers are used mostly in informal speech or writing; others are more common in a formal style. Note that a discourse marker usually comes at the beginning of a clause.

1 focusing and linking

☐ *with reference to*; *talking/speaking of/about*; *regarding*; *as regards*; *as far as . . . is concerned*; *as for*

These expressions focus attention on what is going to be said, by announcing the subject in advance. Some of them also make a link with previous discourse, by referring back to what was said before.

With reference to is a very formal expression used mainly at the beginning of business letters.

> **With reference to** *your letter of 17 March, I am pleased to inform you that . . .*

Speaking/talking of/about . . . is used to make a link with what has just been said. It can help a speaker to change the subject.

> *'I saw Max and Lucy today. You know, she -' 'Talking of Max, did you know he's going to Australia?'*

Regarding can come at the beginning of a piece of discourse.

> *Hello, John. Now look, regarding those sales figures – I really don't think . . .*

As regards and *as far as . . . is concerned* usually announce a change of subject by the speaker/writer.

> *. . . there are no problems about production. Now as regards marketing . . .*
> *. . . about production. As far as marketing is concerned, I think the best thing is . . .*

People sometimes leave out *is concerned* after *as far as . . .* This is usually considered incorrect.

> *As far as the new development plan, I think we ought to be very careful.*

As for often suggests lack of interest or dislike.

> *I've invited Andy, Bob and Mark. As for Stephen, I don't care if I never see him again in my life.*

2 balancing contrasting points

☐ *on the other hand*; *while*; *whereas*

These expressions are used to balance two facts or ideas that contrast, but do not contradict each other.

> *Arranged marriages are common in many Middle Eastern countries. In the West, on the other hand, they are unusual.* ▶

*I like spending my holidays in the mountains, **while/whereas** my wife*
prefers the seaside.
While and *whereas* can be put before the first of the contrasting points.
   ***While/Whereas** some languages have 30 or more different vowel sounds,*
   others have five or less.

For a comparison of *on the other hand* and *on the contrary*, see 145.

3 emphasising a contrast

☐ *however*; *nevertheless*; *mind you*; *still*; *yet*; *in spite of this*

However and *nevertheless* emphasise the fact that the second point contrasts
with the first. *Nevertheless* is very formal.
   *Britain came last in the World Children's Games again. **However**, we*
   did have one success, with Annie Smith's world record in the egg and
   spoon race.
Mind you (less formal) and *still* introduce the contrasting point as an
afterthought.
   *I don't like the job much. **Mind you** / **Still**, the money's OK.*
Yet, still and *in spite of this* can be used to suggest that something is
surprising, in view of what was said before.
   *He says he's a socialist, and **yet** he owns three houses and drives a Rolls.*
   *The train was an hour late. **In spite of this**, I managed to get to the meeting*
   in time. (OR ... *I **still** managed to get ...*)

For other meanings of *yet*, see 539.

4 similarity

☐ *similarly*; *in the same way*

These are most common in a formal style.
   The roads are usually very crowded at the beginning of the holiday season.
   ***Similarly**, there are often serious traffic jams at the end of the holidays.*
   *James Carter did everything he could to educate his children. **In the same***
   ***way**, they in turn put a high value on their own children's education.*

5 concession and counter-argument

☐ **concession**: *it is true*; *of course*; *certainly*; *if*; *may*; stressed *do*
☐ **counter-argument**: *however*; *even so*; *but*; *nevertheless*; *nonetheless*; *all*
   the same; *still*

These expressions are used in a three-part structure: (1) the speaker/writer
mentions facts that point in a certain direction; (2) it is agreed (the
concession) that a particular contradictory fact points the other way; (3) but
the speaker/writer dismisses this and returns to the original direction of
argument.
   *... cannot agree with colonialism. **It is true** that the British **may** have done*
   *some good in India. **Even so**, colonialism is basically evil.*
   *... incapable of lasting relationships with women. **Certainly**, several*
   *women loved him, and he was married twice. **All the same**, the women*
   closest to him were invariably deeply unhappy.

*Very few people understood Einstein's theory. **Of course**, everybody had
    heard of him, and a fair number of people knew the word 'relativity'.
    But hardly anybody could tell you what he had actually said.*

*It was a successful party. The Scottish cousins, **if** a little surprised by the
    family's behaviour, were **nonetheless** impressed by the friendly welcome
    they received.*

*I'm glad to have a place of my own. **It's true** it's a bit small and it's a long
    way from the centre and it **does** need a lot of repairs done. **Still**, it's
    home.*

For other uses of *still*, see 539.
For other uses of *of course*, see 386.

6   contradicting

☐   *on the contrary*

On the contrary can be used to contradict a suggestion made by another
speaker.

> *'Interesting lecture?' '**On the contrary**, it was a complete waste of time.'*

The expression can also be used when a speaker / writer strengthens a
negative statement which he / she has just made.

> *She did not allow the accident to discourage her. **On the contrary**, she
>   began to work twice as hard.*

For a comparison of *on the contrary* and *on the other hand*, see 145.

7   dismissal of previous discourse

☐   *anyway; anyhow; at any rate; at least*

These expressions can be used to mean 'What was said before doesn't matter
– the main point is as follows'.

> *I'm not sure what time I'll arrive, maybe half past seven or a quarter
>   to eight. **Anyway/Anyhow/At any rate**, I'll certainly be there before
>   eight o'clock.*
>
> *What a terrible experience! **Anyway/Anyhow/At any rate**, you're safe,
>   that's the main thing.*

At least can suggest that one thing is certain or all right, even if everything
else is unsatisfactory.

> *The car's completely smashed up – I don't know what we're going to do.
>   **At least** nobody was hurt.*

Note that *anyway* is not the same as *in any way*, which means 'by any method'.

> *Can I help you **in any way**?*

8   change of subject

☐   *by the way; incidentally; right; all right; now; OK*

By the way and *incidentally* are used to introduce something one has just
thought of that is not directly connected with the conversation.

> *I was talking to Phil yesterday. Oh, **by the way**, he sends you his regards.
>   Well, he thinks ...*
>
> *Janet wants to talk to you about advertising. **Incidentally**, she's lost
>   a lot of weight. Anyway, it seems the budget ...*

▶

These two expressions can also be used to change the subject completely.

*'Freddy's had another crash.' 'Oh, yes? Poor old chap. **By the way**, have you heard from Joan recently?'*

*'Lovely sunset.' 'Yes, isn't it? Oh, **incidentally**, what happened to that bike I lent you?'*

(All) right, *now* and *OK* are often used by teachers, lecturers and people giving instructions, to indicate that a new section of the discourse is starting.

*Any questions? **Right**, let's have a word about tomorrow's arrangements.*

__Now__, I'd like to say something about the exam ...

*Is that all clear? **OK, now** has anybody ever wondered why it's impossible to tickle yourself? ...*

9 return to previous subject

☐ *as I was saying*

This is used to return to an earlier subject after an interruption or a brief change of subject.

*... on the roof – Jeremy, put the cat down, please. **As I was saying**, if Jack gets up on the roof and looks at the tiles ...*

10 structuring

☐ *first(ly), first of all, second(ly), third(ly)* etc; *lastly; finally; to begin with; to start with; in the first/second/third place; for one thing; for another thing*

We use these to show the structure of what we are saying.

*__First(ly)__, we need somewhere to live. **Second(ly)**, we need to find work. And __third(ly)__, ...*

*There are three reasons why I don't want to dance with you. **To start with**, my feet hurt. **For another thing**, you can't dance. And **thirdly**, ...*

Note that *firstly, secondly* etc are more formal than *first, second* etc, and are more common in British than American English.

For *at first*, see 83.
For *at last*, see 210.

11 adding

☐ *moreover* (very formal); *furthermore* (formal); *in addition; as well as that; on top of that* (informal); *another thing is; what is more; besides; in any case*

These expressions can be used to add information or arguments to what has already been said.

*The Prime Minister is unwilling to admit that he can ever be mistaken. **Moreover**, he is totally incapable ...*

*The peasants are desperately short of food. **In addition**, they urgently need doctors and medical supplies.*

*She borrowed my bike and never gave it back. And **as well as that / on top of that**, she broke the lawnmower and then pretended she hadn't.*

Besides and *in any case* can add an extra, more conclusive fact or argument.

*What are you trying to get a job as a secretary for? You'd never manage to work eight hours a day. **Besides / In any case**, you can't type.*

For *besides* as a preposition, see 101.

12 generalising

☐ *on the whole*; *in general*; *in all/most/many/some cases*; *broadly speaking*; *by and large*; *to a great extent*; *to some extent*; *apart from...*; *except for...*

These expressions say how far the speaker/writer thinks a generalisation is true.

On the whole, *I had a happy childhood.*
In general, *we are satisfied with the work.*
Broadly speaking, *teachers are overworked and underpaid.*
To a great extent, *a person's character is formed by the age of eight.*
In most cases, *people will be nice to you if you are nice to them.*

Apart from and *except for* introduce exceptions to generalisations. (For more information, see 101.)

Apart from *the starter, I thought the meal was excellent.*
Except for *Sally, they all seemed pretty sensible.*

13 giving examples

☐ *for instance*; *for example*; *e.g.*; *in particular*

These expressions introduce particular examples to illustrate what has been said.

People often behave strangely when they're abroad. Take Mrs Ellis, **for example / for instance**,*...*

In writing, the abbreviation *e.g.* (Latin *exempli gratia*), pronounced /iː ˈdʒiː/, is often used to mean 'for example'.

Some common minerals, **e.g.** *silica or olivine, ...*

In particular focuses on a special example.

We are not at all happy with the work you did on the new kitchen. **In particular**, *we consider that the quality of wood used for the cupboards ...*

14 logical consequence

☐ *therefore* (formal); *as a result* (formal); *consequently* (formal); *so*; *then*

These expressions show that what is said follows logically from what was said before.

She was **therefore** *unable to avoid an unwelcome marriage.*
So *she had to get married to a man she didn't like.*
*'The last bus has gone.' '***Then** *we're going to have to walk.'*

Therefore is used in logical, mathematical and scientific proofs.

Therefore $2x - 15 = 17y + 6.$

So is often used as a general-purpose connector, rather like *and*, in spoken narrative.

So *anyway, this man came up to me and said 'Have you got a light?'* **So** *I told him no, I hadn't.* **So** *he looked at me and ...*

For other uses of *so*, see 513–517. ▶

15 making things clear; giving details

☐ *I mean*; *actually*; *that is to say*; *in other words*

We use *I mean* when we are going to make things clearer, or give more details.

>*It was a terrible evening. **I mean**, they all sat round and talked politics for hours.*

Actually can introduce details, especially when these are unexpected.

>*Tommy's really stupid. You know, he **actually** still believes in Father Christmas.*

That is to say and *in other words* are used when the speaker/writer says something again in another way.

>*We cannot continue with the deal on this basis. **That is to say / In other words**, unless you can bring down the price we shall have to cancel the order.*

For more information about *I mean*, see 339.
For more about *actually*, see below and 11.

16 softening and correcting

☐ *I think*; *I feel*; *I reckon* (informal); *I guess* (American); *in my view/opinion* (formal); *apparently*; *so to speak*; *more or less*; *sort of* (informal); *kind of* (informal); *well*; *really*; *that is to say*; *at least*; *I'm afraid*; *I suppose*; *or rather*; *actually*; *I mean*

I think/feel/reckon/guess and *in my view/opinion* are used to make opinions and statements sound less dogmatic – they suggest that the speaker is just giving a personal opinion, with which other people may disagree.

>**I think** *you ought to try again.*   *I really **feel** she's making a mistake.*
>**I reckon/guess** *she just doesn't respect you, Bill.*
>**In my view/opinion**, *it would be better to postpone the decision until the autumn.*

Apparently can be used to say that the speaker has got his/her information from somebody else (and perhaps does not guarantee that it is true).

>*Have you heard? **Apparently** Susie's pregnant again.*

So to speak, *more or less* and *sort/kind of* are used to show that one is not speaking very exactly, or to soften something which might upset other people. *Well* and *really* can also be used to soften.

>*I **sort of** think we ought to start going home, perhaps, **really**.*
>*I **kind of** think it's **more or less** a crime.*
>*'Do you like it?' '**Well**, yes, it's all right.'*

That is to say and *at least* can be used to 'back down' from something too strong or definite that one has said.

>*I'm not working for you again. Well, **that's to say**, not unless you put my wages up.*
>*Ghosts don't exist. **At least**, I've never seen one.*

I'm afraid is apologetic: it can introduce a polite refusal, or bad news.

>**I'm afraid** *I can't help you.*   **I'm afraid** *I forgot to buy the stamps.*

I suppose can be used to enquire politely about something (respectfully inviting an affirmative answer).

>**I suppose** *you're very busy just at the moment?*

It can also be used to suggest unwilling agreement.
> '*Can you help me for a minute?*' '*I suppose so.*'
Or rather is used to correct oneself.
> *I'm seeing him in May – **or rather** early June.*
I mean can be used to correct or soften.
> *Let's meet next Monday – **I mean** Tuesday.*
> *She's not very nice. **I mean**, I know some people like her, but . . .*

For more information about *afraid*, see 25.
For more information about *sort of* and *kind of*, see 526.
For *actually* in corrections, see paragraph 20 below and 11.
See also 161 for 'distancing' structures.

17 gaining time

☐ *let me see*; *let's see*; *well*; *you know*; *I don't know*; *I mean*; *kind of*; *sort of*

Expressions of this kind (often called 'fillers') give the speaker time to think.
> '*How much are you selling it for?*' '*Well, **let me see** . . .*'
> '*Why did you do that?*' '*Oh, **well, you know, I don't know**, really, **I mean**, it just **sort of** seemed a good idea.*'

18 showing one's attitude to what one is saying

☐ *honestly*; *frankly*; *no doubt*

Honestly can be used to claim that one is speaking sincerely.
> ***Honestly**, I never said a word to him about the money.*
Both *honestly* and *frankly* can introduce critical remarks.
> ***Honestly**, John, why do you have to be so rude?*
> '*What do you think of my hair?*' '***Frankly**, dear, it's a disaster.*'
No doubt (see 370) suggests that the speaker/writer thinks something is probable, but does not know for certain himself/herself.
> ***No doubt** the Romans enjoyed telling jokes, just like us.*

19 persuading

☐ *after all*; *look*; *look here*; *no doubt*

After all suggests 'this is a strong argument that you haven't taken into consideration'. *Look* is more strongly persuasive.
> *I think we should let her go on holiday alone. **After all**, she is fifteen – she's not a child any more.*
> *You can't go there tomorrow. **Look**, the trains aren't running.*
Look here is an angry exclamation meaning 'You can't say/do that!'
> ***Look here!** What are you doing with my suitcase?*
No doubt can be used to persuade people politely to do things.
> ***No doubt** you'll be paying your rent soon?*

For more information about *after all*, see 28.

20 referring to the other person's expectations

☐ *actually* (especially GB); *in fact*; *as a matter of fact*; *to tell the truth*; *well*

These expressions are used when we show whether somebody's expectations have been fulfilled or not. *Actually* can be used to say that   ▶

somebody 'guessed right'.
> 'Did you enjoy your holiday?' 'Very much, **actually**.'

Actually, in fact and *as a matter of fact* can introduce additional information.
> The weather was awful. **Actually**, the campsite got flooded and we had to
> come home.
> 'Was the concert nice?' 'Yes, **as a matter of fact** it was terrific.'
> 'Did you meet the Minister?' 'Yes. **In fact**, he asked us to lunch.'

All four expressions are used when we say that the hearer's expectations
were *not* fulfilled.
> 'How was the holiday?' 'Well, **actually**, we didn't go.'
> 'How much were the carrots?' 'Well, **in fact / to tell the truth**, I forgot to buy
> them.'
> 'I hope you passed the exam.' 'No, **as a matter of fact**, I didn't.'

Actually is often used to introduce corrections.
> 'Hello, John.' '**Actually**, my name's Philip.'

Well can soften corrections, suggesting 'That's nearly right'.
> 'You live in Oxford, don't you?' '**Well**, near Oxford.'

After a new subject has been announced, *well* can suggest that something
new or surprising is going to be said about it.
> 'What did you think of her new boyfriend?' '**Well**, I was a bit surprised ...'
> You know that house we were looking at? **Well**, you'll never guess who's
> bought it.

For more information about *actually*, see 11.

21 summing up

☐ *in conclusion; to sum up; briefly; in short*

These expressions are most common in a formal style.
> ... **In conclusion**, then, we can see that Britain's economic problems were
> mainly due to lack of industrial investment.
> **To sum up**: most of the committee members supported the idea but a few
> were against it.
> He's lazy, he's ignorant and he's stupid. **In short**, he's useless.

160 disinterested

Disinterested is used to say that a person has no reason to support one side
or another in a disagreement or negotiation, because he / she will not get any
advantage if one side wins.
> I can't give you **disinterested** advice, because I'm a colleague of your
> employer.

Disinterested is also commonly used to mean 'uninterested'. Some people
consider this incorrect.
> I'm quite **disinterested** in politics.

161 distancing

Certain structures can be used to make a speaker's requests, questions
or statements seem less direct, more 'distant' from reality (and therefore
more polite).

1   requests and statements as *yes/no* questions

We usually make requests less direct by putting them in the form of *yes/no* questions. This suggests that the hearer can choose whether to agree or not.

> ***Could you tell** me the time, please?* (much more polite than *Please tell me the time.*)

Expressions of opinion can also be made less direct by turning them into questions. Compare:

> *It would be better to paint it green.* (direct expression of opinion)
> *Wouldn't it be better to paint it green?* (persuasive question – less direct)
> *Would it be better to paint it green?* (open question – very indirect)

2   distancing verb forms

We can make requests (and also questions, suggestions and statements) even less direct (and so more polite) by using verb forms that suggest 'distance' from the immediate present reality. Past tenses are often used to do this.

> *How much **did** you **want** to spend, sir?*
>   (meaning 'How much do you want to spend?')
> *How many days **did** you **intend** to stay?*
>   (meaning '… do you intend …')
> *I **wondered** if you **were** free this evening.*

Progressive forms can be used in the same way. They sound more casual and less definite than simple forms, because they suggest something temporary and incomplete.

> *I'm **hoping** you can lend me £10.* (less definite than *I **hope** …*)
> *What time **are** you **planning** to arrive?* (more casual-sounding than *Please let us know what time you **plan** to arrive.*)
> *I'm **looking** forward to seeing you again.*
>   (more casual than *I **look** forward …*)
> *I'm afraid we must **be going**.*

Past progressives give two levels of distancing.

> *Good morning. I **was wondering** if you had two single rooms.*
> ***Were** you **looking** for anything special?* (in a shop)
> *I **was thinking** – what about borrowing Jake's car?*

Another way to distance something is to displace it into the future. *Will need/have to* can be used to soften instructions and orders.

> *I'm afraid you'**ll need to** fill in this form.*
> *I'**ll have to** ask you to wait a minute.*

And *will* is sometimes used to say how much money is owed.

> *That **will** be £1.65, please.*

Future progressive verbs are often used to enquire politely about people's plans (see 225).

> ***Will** you **be going** away at the weekend?*

3   *would, could* and *might*

The modal verbs *would, could* and *might* also make questions, requests and suggestions less direct.

> *I thought it **would** be nice to have a picnic.*
> *Hi! I thought I'**d** come over and introduce myself. My name's Andy.*   ▶

Could you give me a hand?
Could I ask you to translate this for me?
We could ask Peter to help us.
*I was wondering if you **might** be interested in a game of tennis.*
*'I came in and ordered some shoes from you.' 'Oh yes, sir. When **would** that have been, exactly?'*

Would is very often used to form requests and offers with verbs like *like* and *prefer.*

*What **would** you **like** to drink?*

Note the common use of *would* before verbs of saying and thinking, to make a statement sound less definite.

*I **would say** we'd do better to catch the earlier train.*
*This is what I **would call** annoying.*
*I **would think** we might stop for lunch soon.*
*I'm surprised you didn't like the film. I **would have thought** it was just your kind of thing.*

4 conditional and negative expressions

Another way of distancing suggestions from reality is to make them conditional or negative.

*It would be better **if** we **turned** it the other way up.*
***What if** we **stayed** at home for a change?*
***Suppose** I **gave** Alice a call?*
***If** you **would come** this way ...*
*I wonder **if** you **could** lend me £5?*
*I **don't suppose** you want to buy a car, do you?*
*You **wouldn't like** to come out with us, by any chance?*

5 softening expressions etc

A further form of distancing is the use of softening expressions like *quite, kind of* etc. And yet another is to talk about planning or beginning things instead of about actually doing them. The following sentence (which could easily be heard at an English party) means 'I want to go', but distances the message in six different ways.

I'd quite like to sort of start thinking about going, so to speak.

6 *one*

In middle- and upper-class British speech, *one* is sometimes used instead of *I* or *we*. This makes a statement sound less personally assertive.

*'Hello, Charles. How's it going?' 'Oh, **one** can't complain.'*

For more information about requests, see 483.
For more about the different structures discussed here, consult the various entries elsewhere in the book (see Index for references).

162 do (1): introduction

Do has three main uses.

1 auxiliary verb

The auxiliary *do* is used with the infinitives of other verbs mainly to form emphatic, interrogative, negative and shortened verb forms. For details, see 163.

> *I **do** like your ear-rings.*   ***Did** you remember to post my letters?*
> *This **doesn't** taste very nice.*
> *'That carpet needs cleaning.' 'Yes, it certainly **does**.'*

2 general-purpose verb

Do is also an ordinary (non-auxiliary) verb. It can refer to almost any kind of activity, and is used when it is not necessary or not possible to be more precise. For details, and the difference between *do* and *make*, see 164.

> *What are you **doing**?*   *Don't just stand there. **Do** something.*
> *I've finished the phone calls, and I'll **do** the letters tomorrow.*
> *He would rather talk about things than **do** them.*
> *All I **did** was give him a little push.*

3 substitute verb

In British English, *do* can be used alone as a substitute for a main verb after an auxiliary. For details, see 165.

> *'Do you think Phil will **come**?' 'He might **do**.'* (US *'He might.'*)

Do so/it/that can be used as a substitute expression when we want to avoid repeating another verb and what follows. For details, see 166.

> *I am ready to **have a nervous breakdown**, and I shall **do so** as soon as*
>   *I can find time.*
> *He told me to **open the door**. I **did it** as quietly as I could.*

4 combined forms

Auxiliary *do* and non-auxiliary *do* can occur together.

> ***Do** you **do** much gardening?*   *How **do** you **do**?*
> *The company **didn't do** very well last year.*
> *She **doesn't do** much, but what she **does do**, she does very well.*

163 do (2): auxiliary verb

The auxiliary verb *do* is used in a number of ways.

1 questions

We use *do* to make questions with ordinary verbs, but not with other auxiliary verbs (see 461). Compare:

> ***Do** you **like** football?* (NOT *Like you football?*)
> ***Can** you **play** football?* (NOT *Do you can play football?*)

The auxiliary *do* can also be used to make questions with the ordinary verb *do*.

> *What **do** you **do** in the evenings?*   ▶

2 negatives

We use *do* to make negative clauses with ordinary verbs (including the ordinary verb *do*), but not with other auxiliary verbs (see 358). Compare:

> *I **don't like** football.* (NOT ~~I like not football.~~)
> *I **can't play** football.* (NOT ~~I don't can play football.~~)
> *I **don't do** much in the evenings.*   ***Don't** go.*

3 emphasis

We can use *do* in an affirmative clause for emotive or contrastive emphasis (see 189).

> ***Do** sit down.*   *You **do** look nice today!*
> *She thinks I don't love her, but I **do** love her.*
> *I don't take much exercise now, but I **did** play football a lot when I was younger.*

4 inversion

Do is used in some inversion (verb before subject) structures (see 298).

> *At no time **did he** lose his self-control.*

5 ellipsis

In cases where an auxiliary is used instead of a whole verb phrase (see 185), *do* is common in affirmative clauses as well as questions and negatives.

> *She doesn't like dancing, but I **do**.* (= ... *but I like dancing.*)
> *Ann thinks there's something wrong with Bill, and so **do** I.*
> *You saw Alan, **didn't** you?*
> *'That meat smells funny.' 'Yes, it **does, doesn't** it?'*

For *do* with *be*, see 89.
For weak pronunciations of *do* and *does*, see 588.
For *do* in short answers, see 493.

164 do (3): general-purpose verb; **do** and **make**

The general-purpose verb *do* has several uses, and can sometimes be confused with *make*.

1 *do* for indefinite activities

We use *do* when we do not say exactly what activity we are talking about – for example with words like *thing, something, nothing, anything, everything, what*.

> *Then he **did** a very strange thing.* (NOT ~~Then he made a very strange thing.~~)
> ***Do** something!*   *I like **doing** nothing.* (NOT ... ~~making nothing.~~)
> *What shall we **do**?*

2 *do* for work

We use *do* when we talk about work and jobs.

> *I'm not going to **do** any work today.*   *It's time to **do** the accounts.*
> *Could you **do** the shopping for me?*

I wouldn't like to **do** *your job.*
Has Ben **done** *his homework?*
Could you **do** *the ironing first, and then* **do** *the windows if you've got time?*

3 *do...ing*

We use *do* in the informal structure *do...ing*, to talk about activities that take a certain time, or are repeated (for example jobs and hobbies). There is usually a determiner (e.g. *the, my, some, much*) before the *-ing* form.

During the holidays I'm going to **do** *some* **walking**, *some* **swimming** *and a lot of* **reading**.
Let your fingers **do** *the* **walking**. (advertisement for telephone shopping)
Note that the verb after *do* cannot have an object in this structure.

I'm going to watch some TV. (NOT *~~I'm going to~~* **~~do some watching TV~~**.)
However, *do* is often followed by a compound noun that corresponds to **verb + object**.

I want to **do some bird-watching** *this weekend.*
It's time I **did some letter-writing**.

4 *make* for constructing, creating etc

We often use *make* to talk about constructing, building, creating etc.

I've just **made** *a cake.*
Let's **make** *a plan.*
My father and I once **made** *a boat.*

5 *do* instead of *make*

We sometimes use *do* in place of *make* in order to sound casual about a creative activity – as if we are not claiming to produce any very special results.

'What shall we eat?' 'Well, I could **do** *an omelette.'*

6 common fixed expressions

do *good, harm, business, one's best, a favour, sport, exercise, one's hair, one's teeth, one's duty, 50 mph*
make *a journey, an offer, arrangements, a suggestion, a decision, an attempt, an effort, an excuse, an exception, a mistake, a noise, a phone call, money, a profit, a fortune, love, peace, war, a bed, a fire, progress*

Note that we say *make a bed*, but we often talk about *doing the bed(s)* as part of housework. Compare:

He's old enough to **make** *his own bed now.*
I'll start on the vegetables as soon as I've **done** *the beds.*

We use *take*, not *make*, in *take a photo*, and *have*, not *make*, in *have an (interesting) experience*.

For more information about *make*, see 327.

165 **do** (4): substitute verb

auxiliary verb + *do*

In British English (but not American), *do* can be used alone as a substitute verb after an auxiliary verb.

> *'Come and stay with us.' 'I **may (do)**, if I have the time.'* (US *'I **may**, if …'*)
> *'He's supposed to have locked the safe.' 'He **has (done)**.'* (US *'He **has**.'*)
> *I found myself thinking of her as I **had** never **done** before.*
> *He didn't pass his exam, but he **could have (done)** if he'd tried harder.*
> *He smokes more than he **used to (do)**.*

Progressive forms are possible, but not very common.

> *'You should be getting dressed.' 'I **am (doing)**.'*

Note that the auxiliary verb is stressed in this structure.

> *'Close the door.' 'I **HAVE done**.'* (NOT *… 'I have DONE.'*)

For auxiliary *do* as substitute for a whole verb phrase, see 185.
For other kinds of substitution, see 542.

166 **do so / it / that**

1 *do so*

The expression *do so* can sometimes be used to avoid repeating a verb and its object or complement. It is usually rather formal.

> *'Put the car away, please.' 'I've already **done so**.'*
> *Eventually she divorced Stephen. It was a pity she had not **done so** earlier.*
> *He told me to get out, and I **did so** as quietly as possible.*

2 *do so* and *do it/that*

Do it and *do that* can be used instead of *do so*.

> *I promised to get the tickets, and I will **do so/it** as soon as possible.*
> *She rode a camel: she had never **done so/that** before.*

We use *do so* mainly to refer to the same action, with the same subject, that was mentioned before. In other cases we prefer *do it/that* or *do* alone.

> *I haven't got time to get the tickets. Who's going to **do it**?*
> (NOT *… Who's going to **do so**?*)
> *'I rode a camel in Morocco.' 'I'd love to **do that**.'* (NOT *… to **do so**.*)
> *I always eat peas with honey. My wife never **does**.*
> (NOT *… My wife never **does so**.*)

3 *do so/it/that*: deliberate actions

Do so/it/that are mainly used to refer to deliberate dynamic actions.
We do not usually use these expressions to replace verbs like *fall, lose, like, remember, think, own*, which refer to involuntary actions or states.

> *I **like** the saxophone, and I always have **(done)**.*
> (NOT *… and I have always **done so/it/that**.*)
> *She **lost** her money. I wasn't surprised that she **did**.*
> (NOT *… that she **did so/it/that**.*)
> *They **think** Jake's wrong, and I **do** too.* (NOT *… and I **do so/it/that** too.*)

4 other verbs

Note that *so, it* and *that* are not normally used in this way after auxiliary verbs. It is not possible in standard English to say *I can so, She was it* or *I have that.*

For the use of *so* after *think, believe, hope* and similar verbs, see 515.
For *so* after *say* and *tell*, see 514.
For *so do I, so am I* etc, see 516.
For auxiliary *do* as substitute for a whole verb phrase, see 185.
For other kinds of substitution, see 542.
For differences between *it* and *that*, see 566.

167 doubt

Clauses after the verb *doubt* can be introduced by *whether, if* or *that.*
> Economists **doubt whether** interest rates will fall in the near future.
> I **doubt if** she'll come this evening.
> The directors **doubt that** new machinery is really necessary.

In an informal style, some people use no conjunction.
> I **doubt** we'll have enough money for a holiday.

After negative forms of *doubt*, we use *that.*
> I **don't doubt that** there will be more problems.

For *no doubt* meaning 'probably', see 370.

168 dress

1 noun

The countable noun *dress* means an article of women's clothing (it goes from the shoulders to below the hips).
> This is the first time I've seen you wearing **a dress**.

There is also an uncountable noun *dress* (not used with the article *a/an*). It means 'clothing', 'clothes'. It is not very common in modern English, and is used mostly to talk about special kinds of clothing (for example *national **dress**, evening **dress**, battle**dress**).
> He looks good in **evening dress**. (NOT ... *in an evening dress.*)

2 verb: putting clothes on

The verb *dress* can be used to talk about putting clothes on oneself or somebody else. *Undress* is used for taking clothes off.
> It only takes me five minutes to **dress** in the morning.
> Could you **dress** the children for me?
> I'm going to **undress** in front of the fire.

In informal English, it is common to use *get dressed* to talk about dressing oneself.
> **Get dressed** and come downstairs at once!

Put on and *take off* are generally used when clothes are mentioned.
> I **put on** a sweater when I got up, but it was so warm that I had to **take** it **off** again.
> Can you **take** John's boots **off** for him? ▶

3 verb: wearing clothes

To say what somebody is / was wearing on a particular occasion, we can use the form *be dressed in* (note the preposition).

> *I didn't recognise him because he **was dressed in** a dark suit.*
> (NOT ... ~~*dressed with*~~ ... OR ... ~~*dressing in*~~ ...)
> *She **was dressed in** orange pyjamas.*

Be wearing is also very common in British English; *have on* is more usual in American English.

> *She **was wearing** orange pyjamas.* (GB)
> *She **had on** orange pajamas.* (US)

The active form *dress (in)* can be used to give the idea of repetition or habit.

> *She always **dresses in** green.*   *He **dresses** well.*

Note also the expression *well dressed.*

169 drown

In British English, both active and passive forms of *drown* can be used to talk about accidental drowning.

> *He **(was) drowned** while trying to swim across a river.*

In American English, only active forms are used to talk about accidental drowning. Compare:

> *He **drowned** while trying to swim across a river.*
> *The police believe he **was drowned** in a gangland revenge killing.*

170 due to and owing to

Due to and *owing to* both mean 'because of'. Phrases beginning *due/owing to* are often separated from the rest of their sentence by a comma.

> ***Due/Owing** to the bad weather(,) the match was cancelled.*
> *We have had to postpone the meeting(,) **due/owing** to the Chairwoman's illness.*

Some people believe it is incorrect to use *due to* at the beginning of a clause in this way, but the structure is common in educated usage.

Due to can also follow the verb *be*. *Owing to* is not usually used like this.

> *His success was **due to** his mother.* (NOT ... ~~*was **owing to** his mother.*~~)

For *because* and *because of*, see 93.

171 during and for

During is used to say *when* something happens; *for* is used to say *how long* it lasts. Compare:

> *My father was in hospital **during** the summer.*
> *My father was in hospital **for** six weeks.* (NOT ... ~~***during** six weeks.*~~)
> *It rained **during** the night **for** two or three hours.*
> *I'll call in and see you **for** a few minutes **during** the afternoon.*

For *during* and *in*, see 172.
For *for, since, in* and *from*, see 214.

172 **during** and **in**

We use both *during* and *in* to say that something happens inside a particular period of time.

*We'll be on holiday **during/in** August.*

*I woke up **during/in** the night.*

We prefer *during* when we stress that we are talking about the whole of the period.

*The shop's closed **during** the whole of August.*

(NOT ...~~in the whole of August.~~)

We often prefer *during* when we say that something happens between the beginning and end of an *event* or *activity* (not a period of time).

*He had some strange experiences **during** his military service.*

(NOT ...~~in his military service.~~)

*I'll try to phone you **during** the meeting.* (NOT ...~~in the meeting.~~)

*I met them **during** my stay in China.*

173 **each**

1 *each* + singular

Each is a determiner (see 157). We use it before a singular noun.

> *each* + singular noun

Each new day is different. (NOT ~~Each new days~~ ...)

*I enjoy **each moment**.*

2 *each of*

We use *each of* before a pronoun or a determiner (for example *the, my, these* – see 157). The pronoun or noun is plural.

> *each of us/you/them*
> *each of* + determiner + plural noun

Each of us sees the world differently.

*I write to **each of my children** once a week.*

A verb after *each of*... is usually singular, but it can be plural in an informal style.

*Each of them **has** problems.*

*Each of them **have** problems.* (more informal)

3 *each* in mid-position

When *each* refers to the subject, it can go with a verb in mid-position, like *all*, *both* and some adverbs (see 36, 110 and 22). In this case plural nouns, pronouns and verbs are used.

> auxiliary verb + *each*
> *are/were* + *each*

*They **have each** been told.*

*We **can each** apply for our own membership card.*

*You **are each** right in a different way.*

▶

each + other verb

*We **each think** the same.*
*The plans **each have** certain advantages and disadvantages.*

4 position with object

Each can follow an object (direct or indirect) as part of a longer structure.
*I want **them each to be happy**.*
*She kissed **them each on the forehead**.*
*I bought **the girls each an ice-cream**.*
*She sent **them each a present**.*
(BUT NOT ~~I helped them each~~ OR ~~I wrote to them each~~.)

5 *one each* etc

Each can follow a noun object in sentences that say how much / many of something each person gets.
*They got **£20,000 each** when their mother died.*
*I bought the girls **two ice-creams each**.*
A similar structure is used in giving prices.
*They cost **£3.50 each**.*

6 *each* without a noun

We can drop a noun and use *each* alone, if the noun has already been mentioned, but *each one* or *each of them* is more common in an informal style. Note that a following verb is normally singular.
*I've got five brothers, and **each (one/of them)** is quite different from the others.*

7 pronouns

When a pronoun or possessive is used later in a clause to refer back to **each + noun/pronoun**, the later word can be singular (more formal) or plural (less formal).
***Each girl** wore what **she** liked best.* (more formal)
***Each student** wore what **they** liked best.* (less formal)
***Each of them** explained it in **his/her/their** own way.*

For the difference between *each* and *every*, see 174.

174 **each** and **every**: the difference

1 *each* with two or more; *every* with three or more

Each and *every* are both normally used with singular nouns. *Each* can be used to talk about two or more people or things; *every* is normally used to talk about three or more.
*The business makes less money **each/every** year.* (NOT ...~~each/every years.~~)
*She had a child holding on to **each** hand.* (NOT ...~~every hand.~~)

For expressions like *every two years, every three steps,* see 509.8.

2 difference of meaning

In many cases, both *each* and *every* can be used without much difference of meaning.
> *You look more beautiful **each/every** time I see you.*

But we prefer *each* when we are thinking of people or things separately, one at a time. And *every* is more common when we are thinking of people or things together, in a group. (*Every* is closer to *all*.) Compare:
> ***Each** person in turn went to see the doctor.*
> *He gave **every** patient the same medicine.*

We do not use *each* with words and expressions like *almost, practically, nearly* or *without exception*, which stress the idea of a whole group.
> *She's lost **nearly every** friend she had.* (NOT *...~~nearly each friend~~...*)

For more information about *each*, see 173.
For more information about *every*, see 199.
For the difference between *every* and *all*, see 37.
For *each other*, see 175.

175 each other and one another

1 no difference

In modern English, most people normally use *each other* and *one another* in the same way. Perhaps *one another* is preferred (like *one*) when we are making very general statements, and not talking about particular people. Compare:
> *They sat for two hours without talking to **each other** / **one another**.*
> *The translation of 'se parler' is 'to talk to **one another**'.*
> (More natural than ... *to talk to each other*.)

2 not used as subject

Each other and *one another* are not normally used as subjects, though this occasionally happens in very informal speech.
> *They each listened carefully to what the other said.*
> (NOT USUALLY *They listened carefully to **what each other said**.*)

3 *each other's / one another's*

Both expressions have possessive forms.
> *They'll sit for hours looking into **each other's** / **one another's** eyes.*

4 *-selves* and *each other / one another*

Note the difference between *-selves* and *each other / one another*. Compare:
> *They talk to **themselves** a lot.* (Each of them talks to himself/herself.)
> *They talk to **each other** a lot.* (Each talks to the other.)

5 words used without *each other*

Note that we do not usually use *each other* after *meet, marry* and *similar*.
> *They **met** in 1992.*
> *They **married** in 1994.*
> *Their interests are very **similar**.*

176 **east** and **eastern**, **north** and **northern** etc

1 adjectives: the difference

We often prefer *eastern, northern* etc when we are talking about vague, rather indefinite areas, and *east, north* etc for more clearly defined places. Compare:

the **northern** part of the county   the **north** side of the house

However, there are a lot of exceptions to this rule, especially in place names (see below).

2 place names

In place names, the use of *East* or *Eastern, North* or *Northern* etc is often just a matter of custom, with no real reason for the difference. Compare:

- **North/South** Korea, **North/South** Africa, **West** Virginia, **East** Sussex, the **North** and **South** Poles
- **Northern** Ireland, **Eastern/Western** Europe, the **Northern/Southern** Hemisphere, **Northern** Territory (in Australia), **Western** Australia

Note the difference between **South** Africa (the country whose capital is Pretoria) and **Southern** Africa (the southern part of the African continent).

3 capital letters

Capital letters are used at the beginning of *East, Eastern, North, Northern* etc when these come in official or well-established place names.

North Carolina   *Western Australia*   *the Far East*
unemployment in the North (place name meaning 'the North of England')

In other cases, adjectives and nouns normally begin with small letters, as do adverbs.

We spent the winter in southern California.
I live in north London.   *The sun rises in the east.*
There's a strong north wind.   *By sunrise we were driving south.*

4 prepositions

Note the difference between **in** the north etc of... and **to** the north etc of...
I live in the west of Scotland.
Hawaii lies 5,500 km to the west of Mexico.

For *up* meaning 'north' and *down* meaning 'south', see 576.

177 **efficient** and **effective**

If somebody/something is *efficient*, he/she/it works in a well-organised way without wasting time or energy.

*He's not very **efficient**: he keeps filing letters in the wrong place, he works very slowly, and he keeps forgetting things.*
*The postal service is even less **efficient** than the telephone system.*

If something is *effective*, it has the right *effect*: it solves a problem or gets a result.

> *My headache's much better. Those tablets really are* **effective**.
> *I think a wide black belt would look very* **effective** *with that dress.*

178 **either**: determiner

1 *either* + **singular**

We use *either* before a singular noun to mean 'one or the other'.

> *either* + singular noun

> *Come on Tuesday or Thursday.* **Either** *day is OK.*

Sometimes *either* can mean *each*, especially in the expressions *on either side* and *at either end*.

> *There are roses* **on either side** *of the door.*

2 *either of*

We use *either of* before a pronoun or a determiner (for example *the, my, these* – see 157).

> *either of us/you/them*
> *either of* + determiner + plural noun

> *I don't like* **either of them**.
> *I don't like* **either of my maths teachers**.

A verb after *either of* is normally singular, but it can sometimes be plural in an informal style, especially in a negative statement.

> *Either of the children* **is** *quite capable of looking after the baby.*
> *I don't think either of them* **is/are** *at home.*

3 *either* without a noun

We can drop a noun that has already been mentioned and use *either* alone.

> *'Would you like tea or coffee?' 'I don't mind.* **Either**.'

4 **pronouns**

When a pronoun is used later in a clause to refer back to *either* + noun / pronoun, the later pronoun can be singular (more formal) or plural (more informal).

> *If* **either of the boys** *phones, tell* **him/them** *I'll be in this evening.*

5 **pronunciation**

Either is pronounced /ˈaɪðə(r)/ or /ˈiːðə(r)/ (in American English usually /ˈiːðər/).

For *either ... or*, see 179.
For *not ... either, neither* and *nor*, see 364.

179 either ... or

We use *either ... or* to talk about a choice between two possibilities (and sometimes more than two).

> *You can **either** have tea **or** coffee.*
> *I don't speak **either** French **or** German.*
> *You can **either** come with me now **or** walk home.*
> ***Either** you'll leave this house **or** I'll call the police.*
> *If you want ice-cream you can have **either** coffee, lemon **or** vanilla.*

For *either* as a determiner, see 178.
For pronunciation, see 178.5.
For *not ... either, neither* and *nor*, see 364.

180 elder and eldest

Elder and *eldest* can be used instead of *older* and *oldest* to talk about the order of birth of the members of a family. They are only used attributively (before nouns). Compare:

– *My **elder/older** brother has just got married.*
  *He's three years **older than** me.* (NOT *...~~elder than me.~~*)
– *His **eldest/oldest** daughter is a medical student.*
  *She's the **oldest** student in her year.*

Elder brother/sister are used when a person has only one brother/sister who is older; *eldest* is used when there are more. An *elder son/daughter* is the older of two; an *eldest son/daughter* is the oldest of two or more.

181 ellipsis (1): general

We often leave out words to avoid repetition, or in other cases when the meaning can be understood without them. This is called 'ellipsis'.

1 replies

In replies we usually avoid repeating information that has just been given.

> *'What time are you coming?' 'About ten.'*
>   (More natural than '***I'm coming** about ten.*')
> *'Who said that?' 'John.'*
>   (More natural than '*John **said that**.*')
> *'How many chairs do you need?' 'Three.'*
>   (More natural than '***I need** three **chairs**.*')
> *'She's out this evening?' 'Yes, working.'*
>   (More natural than '*Yes, **she's** working **this evening**.*')

For 'short answer' structures, see 493.

2 structures with *and, but* and *or*

Repeated words are often dropped in co-ordinate structures. For details, see 182.

> *a knife and fork* (= *a knife and **a** fork*)
> *She was poor but honest.* (= *... but **she was** honest.*)

3   at the beginning of a sentence

In informal speech, unstressed words are often dropped at the beginning of a sentence, if the meaning is clear. For details, see 183.

Seen Lucy? (= **Have you** *seen Lucy?)*
Doesn't know what she's talking about. (= **She** *doesn't . . .)*

4   at the end of a noun phrase

It is sometimes possible to drop nouns after adjectives, noun modifiers and / or determiners. For details, see 184.

'Do you want large eggs?' 'No, I'll have small.' (= '. . . small **eggs.** *')*
My car isn't working. I'll have to use Mary's. (= . . . Mary's **car.** *)*
We're going to hear the London Philharmonic tonight.
    (= . . . the London Philharmonic **Orchestra.** *)*
'Which shoes are you going to wear?' **'These.'**

For substitution with *one(s)*, see 391.

5   at the end of a verb phrase

Auxiliary verbs are often used alone instead of full verbs. For details, see 185.

'I haven't paid.' 'I **haven't** *either.'*
    (= . . . 'I **haven't paid** *either.')*
She said she'd phone, but she **didn't.** *(= . . .* **didn't phone.** *)*

This type of ellipsis can include words that follow the verb phrase.

I was planning to go to Paris next week, but I **can't.**
    (= . . . I **can't go to Paris next week.** *)*

The same structures are possible with non-auxiliary *be* and *have*.

I thought she would be angry, and she **was.**
He says he hasn't any friends, but I know he **has.**

For substitution with *do* and *do so*, see 165, 166.

6   infinitives

We can use *to* instead of repeating a whole infinitive. For details, see 186.

'Are you and Gillian getting married?' 'We hope **to.** *'*
    (= 'We hope to **get married.** *')*
I don't dance much now, but I used **to** *a lot.*

Sometimes a whole infinitive, including *to*, is left out.

Come when you want. (= . . . when you want **to come.** *)*
'Have a good time.' 'I'll try.' (= 'I'll try **to have a good time.** *')*

7   comparative structures with *as* and *than*

We can leave out words after *as* and *than*, if the meaning is clear.

The weather isn't as good **as** *last year. (= . . . as* **it was** *last year.)*
I found more blackberries **than** *you. (= . . . than you* **found.** *)*

For inversion after *as* and *than*, see 298.6.
For missing subject or object after *as* and *than*, see 557.3   ▶

8   question-word clauses

Clauses can be dropped after question words.

*Somebody's been stealing our flowers, but I don't know **who**.*
(=... *I don't know who**'s been stealing our flowers**.*)
*Become a successful writer. This book shows you **how**.*

9   *that* and relative pronouns

In an informal style, the conjunction *that* is often dropped. For details, see 560.

*I knew **(that)** she didn't want to help me.*
Object relative pronouns can also be dropped in an informal style.
For details, see 474–476.

*This is the restaurant **(which)** I was talking about.*

10   reduced relative structures

We can sometimes leave out a relative pronoun and the verb *be* before participles or adjectives such as *available, possible*. For details, see 477.6.

*Who's the girl **dancing** with your brother? (=... **who is dancing** ...)*
*Please let me have all the tickets **available**. (=... **that are available**.)*

11   *be* after conjunctions

Subject pronouns with forms of *be* can be left out after certain conjunctions, especially in a formal style.

*Start **when** ready. (=... when **you are** ready.)*
***Though** intelligent, he was very poorly educated.*
   *(= Though **he was** intelligent...)*
***When** ordering, please send £1.50 for postage and packing.*
*Phone me **if (it is)** necessary.*
*I'm enclosing my cheque for £50, **as (was)** agreed.*
*He had a small heart attack **while** asleep.*
*Leave in oven **until** cooked.*

12   prepositions

In an informal style, prepositions can be dropped in a few time expressions (see 439.2,5).

*See you **(on)** Monday night.*
*We're staying here **(for)** another three months.*
***What time** shall I come? (More natural than **At what time**...?)*

For cases like *We need a place to live **(in)***, see 427.

13   pronouns after prepositions

In British English, pronoun objects can sometimes be dropped after prepositions. This happens, for example, when *have* or *with* are used in descriptive structures.

*My socks have got holes **in (them)**.*
*I'd like a piece of toast with butter **on (it)**.*

14   abbreviated styles

In certain styles, many or all non-essential words can be dropped. For details, see 1.

Take 500g butter and place in small saucepan.
Essential fee agreed before contract signed
WOMAN WALKS ON MOON

182   ellipsis (2): with **and**, **but** and **or**

1   various kinds of word left out

When expressions are joined by *and, but* or *or*, we often leave out repeated words or phrases of various kinds.

*a knife and **(a)** fork   these men and **(these)** women*
*ripe apples and **(ripe)** pears   antique **(furniture)** or modern furniture*
*in France, **(in)** Germany or **(in)** Spain*
*She can read, but **(she)** can't write.*
*The Minister likes golf but **(the Minister)** hates fishing.*
*We drove **(across America)**, rode **(across America)**, flew **(across America)***
*   and walked across America.*
*She was poor but **(she was)** honest.*
*The food **(is ready)** and the drinks are ready.*
*Phil **(washed the dishes)** and Sally washed the dishes.*

2   word order

Note that when two verbs, objects etc are the same, it is not always the second that is left out. We leave out the first if that will produce a simpler word order and sentence structure.

*Cats **(catch mice)** and dogs catch mice. (*N O T *~~Cats catch mice and dogs.~~)*
*I can **(go)** and will go.*

In informal speech and writing, ellipsis does not usually interrupt the normal word order of a clause or sentence. Sentences like the following are typical of a more formal style.

Peter planned and Jane paid for the holiday.
Kevin likes dancing and Annie athletics.
The children will carry the small boxes and the adults the large ones.
Jane went to Greece and Alice to Rome.
You seem, and she certainly is, ill.

We can sometimes drop a verb that is repeated in a different form.

*I have always **paid** my bills and I always will **(pay ...)**.*

But this is not common if the dropped form comes first.

(N O T U S U A L L Y *I always have, and always will pay my bills.*)

3   singular and plural

When one verb follows two singular subjects connected by *and*, a plural verb form is of course used if necessary.

*My mother and father **smoke**. (*N O T *~~My mother and father smokes.~~)*

When two singular subjects are connected by *or*, the verb is singular.

*Either Jake or Steve **was** here this morning.*

For singular and plural verbs with *neither ... nor*, see 365.   ▶

4 other conjunctions

Ellipsis is not normally possible after other conjunctions besides *and, but* and *or*.

>*She didn't know where she was **when** she woke up.*
>(NOT ... ~~when woke up.~~)

However, ellipsis of subject pronouns with forms of *be* is possible in some cases (e.g. *if possible, when arriving*). See 261.10, 73.4, 406.6.

5 *(and) then*

In an informal style, ellipsis is sometimes possible after *then* even if *and* is dropped.

>*Peter started first, (and) then Colin **(started)**.*

183 ellipsis (3): at the beginning of a sentence

1 words that can be left out

In informal spoken English we often leave out unstressed words at the beginning of a sentence if the meaning is clear without them. Words that can be left out include articles (*the, a/an*), possessives (*my, your* etc), personal pronouns (*I, you* etc), auxiliary verbs (*am, have* etc) and the preparatory subject *there*.

>*Car's running badly.* (= ***The** car's ...*)
>*Wife's on holiday.* (= ***My** wife's ...*)
>*Couldn't understand a word.* (= ***I** couldn't ...*)
>*Must dash.* (= ***I** must dash.*)
>*Won't work, you know.* (= ***It** won't work ...*)
>*Seen Joe?* (= ***Have you** seen Joe?*)
>*Keeping well, I hope?* (= ***You're** keeping well ...*)
>*Nobody at home.* (= ***There's** nobody at home.*)
>*Careful what you say.* (= ***Be** careful ...*)
>*Be four pounds fifty.* (= ***That'll** be ...*)

2 unstressed forms of *be, will, would, have*

We do not usually drop words so as to begin sentences with unstressed forms of *be, will, would* or auxiliary *have* (though this sometimes happens in postcards, diary entries and other kinds of very informal writing).

>*I'm coming tomorrow.* OR *Coming tomorrow.*
>(BUT NOT ~~Am coming tomorrow.~~ *Am* is not stressed.)
>*I'll see you soon.* OR *See you soon.*
>(BUT NOT ~~Will see you soon.~~ *Will* is not stressed.)
>*Haven't seen him.* (BUT NOT ~~Have seen him.~~ *Have* is not stressed.)

3 *I* and *it*

Auxiliary verbs can be left out before personal pronouns except *I* and *it*.

>*You ready?* (= ***Are** you ready?*)
>*She want something?* (= ***Does** she want something?*)
>(BUT NOT ~~I late? It raining?~~)

4 tags

Ellipsis is very common in sentences that have some sort of tag (see 465–466, 472) on the end, especially in British English.

> *Can't swim, **myself**.*   *Like my pint, **I do**.*
> *Dutch, **aren't you**?*   *Getting in your way, **am I**?*
> *Going on holiday, **your kids**?*

184 ellipsis (4): in noun phrases

1 ellipsis after adjectives

A repeated noun can sometimes be dropped after an adjective, if the meaning is clear, especially when one is talking about common kinds of choice.

> *'What kind of potatoes would you like?' '**Boiled (potatoes)**, please.'*
> *We haven't got any large eggs. Only **small (eggs)**.*

This often happens after superlatives.

> *I think I'll buy the **cheapest**.*

Note that nouns are not normally dropped in other situations.

> *Poor little **boy**!* (NOT *Poor little!*)
> *The most important **thing** is to keep calm.*
>   (NOT *The most important is to...*)

For other structures in which adjectives are used without nouns, see 18.

2 ellipsis after determiners

Nouns can also be dropped after most determiners (see 157) and similar words, including numbers, nouns with possessive *'s, own* and *(an)other*.

> *Those are Helen's gloves, and **these (gloves)** are mine.*
> *I'm not sure how many packets I need, but I'll take **two (packets)** to start with.*
> *Our train's the **second (train)** from this platform.*
> *You take Pete's car, and I'll take **Susie's (car)**.*
> *'Can I borrow your pen?' 'No, find your **own (pen)**.'*
> *'That beer went down fast.' 'Have **another (beer)**.'*

For more information about the use of determiners without nouns, see 157. See also the entries for particular determiners.

3 well-known names

The last words of well-known names are often dropped.

> *She's playing **the Beethoven** with **the London Philharmonic** tomorrow*
>   *night.* (=... the Beethoven **violin concerto** with the London
>   Philharmonic **Orchestra**...)
> *He's staying at **the Hilton**.* (=... the Hilton **Hotel**.)
> *We're going to see 'Hamlet' at **the Mermaid**.* (=... the Mermaid **Theatre**.)

When we talk about people's houses and shops, the words *house* and *shop* are often dropped (see 432.4).

> *We spent the weekend at **John and Mary's**.*
> *Could you pick up some chops from the **butcher's**?*

For the substitute word *one(s)*, see 391.   ▶

185 ellipsis (5): after auxiliary verbs

1 auxiliary instead of complete verb phrase

We can avoid repetition by using an auxiliary verb instead of a complete verb phrase, if the meaning is clear. The auxiliary verb usually has a 'strong' pronunciation (see 588), and contractions (see 144) are not normally used except in negatives.

> *'Get up.' 'I **am** /æm/.'* (= *'I am **getting up**.'*) (N O T ~~*I'm.*~~)
> *He said he'd write, but he **hasn't**.* (= ... *hasn't **written**.*)
> *I'll come and see you when I **can**.* (= ... *can **come and see you**.*)
> *I **wouldn't** if I were you.*
>> (Said to somebody who is just going to do something stupid.)

Do can be used before ellipsis if there is no other auxiliary to repeat.

> *They hardly ever give a party, but when they **do**, they **do**.*
> *He **said** he would arrive before seven, and he **did**.*

2 ellipsis of verb + object, complement etc

Other words, as well as the rest of the verb phrase, can be left out after the auxiliary – for example an object, a complement, an adverbial, or even a whole clause.

> *I can't see you today, but I **can** tomorrow.* (= ... *I **can see you** ...*)
> *I've forgotten the address.' 'I **have** too.'*
> *'You're not trying very hard.' 'I **am**.'*
> *'You wouldn't have won if I hadn't helped you.' 'Yes, I **would**.'*

Ellipsis of an object, complement etc is also possible after forms of non-auxiliary *be* and *have*.

> *'I'm tired.' 'I **am** too.'*
> *'Who's the driver?' 'I **am**.'*
> *'Who has a dictionary?' 'I **have**.'*

3 more than one auxiliary

When there is more than one auxiliary verb, ellipsis most often happens after the first.

> *'You wouldn't have enjoyed the film.' 'Yes, I **would**.'*
>> (= ...*'I would **have enjoyed the film**.'*)

However, more auxiliaries can be included. The first is stressed.

> *'Could you have been dreaming?' 'I suppose I **could** / COULD **have** /*
>> *COULD **have been**.'*

We often include a second auxiliary verb if it has not appeared before in the same form.

> *'I think Mary **should be** told.' 'She **has been**.'*
>> (More natural than ... *'She has.'*)

And we normally include a second auxiliary verb after a change of modal auxiliary.

> *'Mary **should be** told.' 'She **must be**.'*
>> (More natural than ... *'She must.'*)

4 short answers etc

Ellipsis is used regularly in short answers (see 493), reply questions (see 463) and tags (see 465–466 and 472).

> *'Have you finished?' 'Yes, I* **have**.'
> *'I can whistle through my fingers.' '* **Can** *you, dear?'*
> *You don't want to buy a car,* **do** *you?*

5 *so am I* etc

Ellipsis also happens after *so* (see 516), *neither* and *nor* (see 364).

> *'I've forgotten the address.' '* **So have I**.'
> *She doesn't like olives, and* **neither do** *I.*

6 ellipted form before complete form

Ellipsis normally happens when an expression is used for a second time, after the complete form has already been used once (see above examples). However, it can sometimes happen the other way round. This is common in sentences beginning *If/When ... can/could ...* or *If you like/wish/want/prefer.*

> **If you can**, *send me a postcard when you arrive.*
> **If you could**, *I'd like you to help me this evening.*
> **If you prefer**, *we can go tomorrow instead.*

7 substitution with *do*

In British English, a main verb that is left out after an auxiliary can be replaced by *do*. For details, see 165.

> *'Do you think he'll phone?' 'He might* **do**.' *(US ... 'He might.')*

For more about substitution, see 542.
For *do so*, see 166.
For ellipsis of an infinitive after *to*, see 186.

186 ellipsis (6): infinitives

1 *to* used instead of whole infinitive

We can use *to* instead of the whole infinitive of a repeated verb (and a following complement), if the meaning is clear.

> *'Are you and Gillian getting married?' 'We hope* **to**.'
> *'Let's go for a walk.' 'I don't want* **to**.'
> *I don't dance much now, but I used* **to** *a lot.*
> *Sorry I shouted at you. I didn't mean* **to**.
> *'Somebody ought to clean up the bathroom.' 'I'll ask John* **to**.'

Be and stative *have* (see 241) are not usually dropped.

> *There are more flowers than there used* **to be**. (NOT *...~~than there used to.~~*)
> *She hasn't been promoted yet, but she ought* **to be**.
> (NOT *...~~but she ought to.~~*)
> *You've got more freckles than you used* **to have**.
> (NOT *~~You've got more freckles than you used to.~~*)

▶

2 ellipsis of whole infinitive

In some cases the whole infinitive can be left out. This happens after nouns and adjectives, and after verbs which can stand alone without a following infinitive.

> *He'll never leave home; he hasn't got the **courage (to)**.*
> *You can't force him to leave home if he's not **ready (to)**.*
> *'Can you start the car?' 'I'll **try (to)**.'*

3 *(would) like, want* etc

We cannot usually leave out *to* after *would like/love/hate/prefer, want* and *choose*.

> *'Are you interested in going to University?' '**I'd like to**.'* (NOT *'...I'd like.'*)
> *My parents encouraged me to study art, but I didn't **want to**.*
> (NOT *...I didn't want.*)

However, *to* is often dropped after *want*, and almost always after *like*, when these are used after certain conjunctions – for instance *when, if, what, as*.

> *Come **when** you **want (to)**.*
> *I'll do **what** I **like**.*
> *Stay as long **as** you **like**.*

187 else

1 use

We use *else* to mean 'other' or 'more' after:
somebody, someone, something, somewhere; anybody/one/thing/where; everybody/one/thing/where; nobody/one/thing/where; who, what, why, when, where, how; whatever, whenever etc; *little; much*

> *Would you like **anything else**?*
> *I'm sorry. I mistook you for **somebody else**.*
> *Why can't you wear a suit like **everybody else**?*
> *'Harry gave me some perfume for Christmas.' 'Oh, lovely. **What else** did you get?'*
> *Where else** did you go besides Madrid?*
> *Whatever else** he may be, he's not a mathematician.*
> *We know when Shakespeare was born and when he died, but we don't know **much else** about his life.*

In a very formal style, *else* is sometimes used after *all*.

> *When **all else** fails, read the instructions.*

2 word order

Note that *else* comes immediately after the word it modifies.

> *What else** would you like?* (NOT *What would you like else?*)

3 *else's*

Else has a possessive *else's*.

> *You're wearing somebody **else's** coat.*

4 singular only

There is no plural structure with *else*. The plural of *somebody else* is *(some) other people*.

5 *or else*

Or else means 'otherwise', 'if not'.
> Let's go, **or else** we'll miss the train.

Or else is sometimes used with no continuation, as a threat.
> You'd better stop hitting my little brother, **or else**!

6 *elsewhere*

This is a formal word for *somewhere else*.
> If you are not satisfied with my hospitality, go **elsewhere**.

188 embedding and comprehension problems

1 What is 'embedding'?

Sometimes a long phrase or clause is 'embedded' in another clause – fitted into the middle of it, interrupting the normal subject-verb-object sequence. Sentences that are constructed like this can be difficult for learners to understand.

2 descriptive expressions after subjects

When the subject of a sentence is followed by an embedded descriptive phrase or relative clause, the subject is separated from the verb, and this may make the sentence confusing and hard to sort out.
> That picture **of the children being talked to by the Prime Minister** is *wonderful*. (The sentence says that the picture is wonderful, not that the Prime Minister is wonderful.)

Here is a more complex example from a newspaper.
> A 24-year-old labourer **who was arrested in Trafalgar Square when he allegedly attempted to knife a traffic warden** is said to have injured three policemen.

The subject (*a 24-year-old labourer*) and the verb (*is said to have injured*) are separated by 15 other words; and the verb *is said* comes immediately after a noun (*a traffic warden*) which is not its subject. Both of these things can cause problems for the reader.

3 relative pronouns left out

When relative pronouns are left out at the beginning of embedded clauses, this can cause difficulty.
> The film **she was talking about at Celia's party** turned out to be very boring. (= ... the film **which** she was talking about ...)

> The manager of Brown's, the chemist's, has confirmed that bottles of shampoo **he took off the shelves after animal rights protesters claimed to have put bleach into them** did contain poisonous chemicals.
> (= ... bottles of shampoo **which** he took off ...)

▶

*Pictures of the baby **the judge ordered should not be identified by**
reporters appeared in a Sunday newspaper. (= . . . the baby **which** . . .)*

4 past participles that look like past tenses

Past participles (e.g. *arrested, accused*) are often used descriptively after
nouns, rather like reduced relative clauses (see 477.6). When these look the
same as past tenses, they can cause confusion. In the following examples,
arrested means 'who was arrested', *accused* means 'who is accused', and
asked means 'who were asked'.

*A court has heard that a young civil servant **arrested after shootings on**
Tyneside left one man dead is to be charged with murder.*

*A Karnak separatist **accused of leading an attack on a French police**
barracks in which four gendarmes died has been arrested.*

*A number of the children **asked for comments on the proposals to expel**
some immigrants told the police they disagreed.* (Who asked? Who said
they disagreed?)

5 adverbial clauses

Embedded adverbial clauses can also make sentences complicated and hard
to follow.

*One way of deciding what to do **when you have difficulty in choosing the**
best course of action is to toss a coin.*

*Arthur was not sure which way to go, **for he had been left alone by his**
friends, and, when an old man came along the road accompanied by
a little boy, he said 'Excuse me'.* (Who said 'Excuse me'?)

*The really important point is that **because he did not invite the one man**
he certainly should have asked his father was furious.* (Should he have
asked his father?)

*The rebel leader found out that **in spite of the precautions of the soldiers**
he had bought the guns from the police had planted an informer
among them.* (Had he bought the guns from the police?)

6 reporting expressions

Complicated structures can be produced when reporting expressions are put
into the middle of sentences.

*This is the man who **Ann said** will tell us all about the church.*
*He's gone **I don't know** how far.*

For combined relative and indirect speech structures, see 477.10–11.
For other problems with conjunctions and clauses, see 143.
For difficulties with relative clauses, see 477.

189 emphasis

1 emotive and contrastive emphasis

We often emphasise ('strengthen') a particular word or expression. There are
two main reasons for this. We may wish to show that we feel strongly about
what we are saying ('emotive emphasis').

*You **do** look nice today!   Your hair looks **so** good like that.*

Or we may wish to show a contrast between, for example, true and false, or present and past, or a rule and an exception ('contrastive emphasis').

> '*Why weren't you at the meeting?*' '*I **was** at the meeting.*'
>
> *I don't take much exercise now, but I **did** play a lot of football when I was younger.*
>
> *I don't have much contact with my family, but I **do** see my mother occasionally.*

We can also use emphasis to show that something expected actually happened.

> *I thought I'd pass the exam, and I **did** pass.*

2 pronunciation: stress

In speech, we can give words extra stress – make them sound 'stronger' – by pronouncing them louder and with a higher intonation. We may also make the vowel longer, and pause before a stressed word. Stress is reflected in printing by using *italics* or **bold type**, and in writing by using CAPITAL LETTERS or by <u>underlining</u>.

> This is the *last* opportunity.
>
> He lived in **France**, not Spain.
>
> Mary, I'm IN LOVE! Please don't tell <u>anybody</u>!

Changes in stress can affect the meaning of a sentence. Compare:

> ***Jane** phoned me yesterday.* (Not somebody else.)
>
> *Jane **phoned** me yesterday.* (She didn't come to see me.)
>
> *Jane phoned **me** yesterday.* (She didn't phone you.)
>
> *Jane phoned me **yesterday**.* (Not today.)

We often stress auxiliary verbs. This can make the whole sentence sound more emphatic, or can emphasise a contrast (see above). Most auxiliary verbs change their pronunciation when they are stressed (see 588).

> *It **was** a nice party!*   *You **have** grown!*
>
> *I **am** telling the truth – you **must** believe me!*

In emphatic sentences without auxiliary verbs we can add *do* to carry the stress.

> ***Do** sit down.*   *She **does** like you.*
>
> *If he **does** decide to come, let me know, will you?*

When auxiliary verbs are stressed the word order can change (see 23.12). Compare:

> *You have certainly grown.*   *You certainly **have** grown!*

For intonation and stress, see 540.

3 vocabulary: special words

Certain words, such as *so*, *such*, *really* and *just*, can be used to show emphasis.

> *Thank you **so** much. It was **such** a lovely party. I **really** enjoyed it.*
>
> *I **just** love the way she talks.*

Swearwords (see 550) are often used for emphasis in an informal style.

> *That's a **bloody** good idea.*

Question words can be emphasised by adding *ever* (see 595), *on earth* or *the hell* (very informal).

> ***Why ever** did he marry her?*   ***What on earth** is she doing here?*
>
> ***Where the hell** have you been?*

▶

4 structures

If we can move words to an unusual position, this usually gives them more importance. Words are often 'fronted' for this reason (see 217).

That film – what did you think of it?   *Asleep, then, were you?*

*I knew he was going to cause trouble, and **cause trouble** he did!*

'Cleft' structures with *it* and *what* can be used to focus on particular parts of a sentence and give them extra importance (see 131).

*It was **John** who paid for the drinks.*   *What I need is **a good rest**.*

Do can be used to emphasise an affirmative verb (see above).

*She **does** seem to be trying.*   ***Do** come in.*

Myself, yourself etc can be used to emphasise nouns (see 471).

*I got a letter from the **Managing Director himself**.*

Indeed can be used to emphasise *very* with an adjective or adverb (see 274).

*I was **very surprised indeed**.*

Very can emphasise superlatives, *next, last, first* and *same* (see 139.4).

*I'd like a bottle of your **very best** wine.*

*The letter arrived on the **very next** day.*

*We were born in the **very same** street in the **very same** year.*

Repetition can be used for emphasis.

*She looks **much, much** older than she used to.*

190 enable

Enable is normally used in the structure *enable somebody to do something*.

*He invented a machine to **enable people in wheelchairs to get up stairs**.*

*The gears on a mountain bike practically **enable you to ride up a wall**.*

It is less usual to use *enable* with a direct object and no following infinitive.

*The extra money will **make repairs possible**. OR ... will **enable us to carry out repairs**.* (More common than ... *will **enable repairs**.*)

*The new machinery will **make greater production possible**. OR ... will **enable us to produce more**.* (More common than ... *will **enable greater production**.*)

191 end and finish (verbs)

These verbs have similar meanings, but there are some differences, especially when they are followed by direct objects.

1 *finish* + object = 'complete'

When we talk about getting to the end of something or completing an activity, we usually prefer *finish*.

*He never lets me **finish** a sentence.*

*She's always starting something new, but she never **finishes** anything.*

*You'll never **finish** that hamburger – it's too big for you.*

*Have you **finished** cleaning the floor yet?*

Note that *finish* can be followed by an *-ing* form (see 293).

2   *end* + object = 'stop'

When we talk about stopping or breaking something off, we usually prefer *end*.

> *I decided it was time to **end** our affair.*
> *It's time to **end** the uncertainty – the Prime Minister must speak out.*

End cannot be followed by an *-ing* form.

> *I decided to **stop seeing** her.* (NOT *...to **end seeing** her.*)

3   *end* + object = 'bring to a close'

When we are talking about a special way of bringing something to a close or 'shaping' the end of something, we usually prefer *end*.

> *'How do you **end** a letter to somebody you don't know?'*
> *She **ended** her concert with three songs by Schubert.*
> *My father **ended** his days* (= 'died') *in a mental hospital.*

4   shape

When we are referring to the shape of things, rather than to time, we normally use *end*.

> *The road **ended** in a building site.* (NOT *The road **finished**...*)
> *Nouns that **end** in -s have plurals in -es.*

5   other cases

In other cases, there is often little or no difference of meaning.

> *What time does the concert **end/finish**?*   *Term **ends/finishes** on June 23.*

For *finished* meaning 'ready', see 211.

192   enjoy

> *enjoy* + noun / pronoun / *-ing*

Enjoy normally has an object. When we talk about having a good time, we can use *enjoy myself/yourself/* etc.

> *'Did you **enjoy the party**?' 'Yes, I **enjoyed it** very much.'*
> *I really **enjoyed myself** when I went to Rome.*
>   (NOT *I really **enjoyed when**...*)
> *'We're going to Paris for the weekend.' '**Enjoy yourself**!'*
>   ('*Enjoy!*' alone would be possible in very informal American English.)

Enjoy can be followed by *-ing*.

> *I don't **enjoy looking** after small children.* (NOT *...**enjoy to look**...*)

193   enough

1   adjective / adverb + *enough*

When *enough* modifies an adjective or adverb, it normally comes after the adjective / adverb.

> *Is it **warm enough** for you?* (NOT *...**enough warm**...*)
> *You're not driving **fast enough**.*

▶

*We haven't got a **big enough** house.*
*We'll go swimming if we get **warm enough** weather.*
*You could wear my shoes – you've got **big enough** feet.*

2 *enough* + noun

Enough can also be used before a noun phrase as a determiner.
We do not generally use *of* when there is no other determiner (e.g. article or possessive).

*Have you got **enough milk**?* (NOT ... ~~enough of milk?~~)
*There isn't **enough blue paint** left.*

However, *enough of* can be used without a following determiner in a few cases – for instance, before personal and geographical names.

*We haven't seen **enough of Ray and Barbara** recently.*
*I've **had enough of England** for a bit. I'm going home.*

Enough is occasionally used after a noun, but this is rare in modern English except in a few expressions.

*If only we had **time enough** ...*   *I was **fool enough** to believe him.*

3 position with adjective + noun

Enough follows an adjective which it modifies (see paragraph 1 above). But when *enough* modifies an adjective and noun together, it comes before the adjective. Compare:

*We haven't got **big enough** nails.*
  (= *We need bigger nails – enough modifies big.*)
*We haven't got **enough big nails**.*
  (= *We need more big nails – enough modifies big nails.*)

4 *enough of* + determiner / pronoun

Before determiners (e.g. *a, the, my, this*) and pronouns, we use *enough of*.
*I think my letter gave him **enough of** a shock, don't you?*
*The exam was bad. I couldn't answer **enough of the** questions.*
*Have we got **enough of those** new potatoes?*
*We didn't buy **enough of them**.*

5 *enough* + infinitive

We can use an infinitive structure after *enough*.
*She's **old enough to do** what she wants.*
*I haven't got **enough money to buy** a car.*

Infinitives can be introduced by *for* + **noun/pronoun**. Object forms of pronouns are used.
*It's late enough **for the staff to stop** work.*
*There was just enough light **for us to see** what we were doing.*

The subject of the sentence can be the object of the following infinitive. (For more about this structure, see 285.4.) Object pronouns are not normally used after the infinitive in this case.
*The radio's small enough **to put** in your pocket.*
  (NOT ... ~~to put it in your pocket.~~)
*Those tomatoes aren't ripe enough **to eat**.* (NOT ... ~~to eat them.~~)

However, object pronouns are possible in structures with *for*.
> *The radio was small enough **for me to put (it)** in my pocket.*
> *Those tomatoes aren't ripe enough **for the children to eat (them)**.*

For other examples of ***for* + object + infinitive**, see 280.

6 *enough* without a noun

Enough can be used alone without a noun, if the meaning is clear.
> ***Enough** is **enough**.*   *That's **enough**, thank you.*
> *Half a pound of carrots will be **enough**.*

Note that we prefer to use a structure with *there is* where possible.
> ***There's enough** meat.* (NOT ~~The meat is **enough**.~~)
> ***There weren't enough** chairs.* (NOT ~~The chairs weren't **enough**.~~)

7 *the* = *enough*; leaving out *enough*

The article *the* can be used to mean 'enough'.
> *I hardly had **the strength** to take my clothes off.*
> *I didn't quite have **the money** to pay for a meal.*

Time and *room* are often used alone to mean 'enough time' and 'enough room'.
> *Have you got **time** to look at this letter?*
> *There isn't **room** for everybody to sit down.*

For similar structures with *too* and *too much/many*, see 570–571.

194 especial(ly) and special(ly)

Especially and *specially* can often both be used with the same meaning.
> *It was not **(e)specially** cold.*

Especially is used to mean 'above all'.
> *I play a lot of tennis, **especially** on Sundays.*
> *It rains a lot, **especially** in the north.*
> *The children are very noisy, **especially** when we have visitors.*
> *I like all kinds of fruit, **especially** apples.*

Especially follows a subject.
> *All my family like music. **My father, especially**, goes to as many concerts as he can.* (NOT *...~~Especially my father goes~~...*)

Specially is used to mean 'for a particular purpose'.
> *These shoes were **specially** made for me.*

The adjective *especial* is rare. We normally use *special*.
> *He took **special** trouble over his work.*

195 even

1 meaning and position

We can use *even* to talk about surprising extremes – when people do more than we expect, or go too far, for example. *Even* most often goes in mid-position (see 22).

> auxiliary verb + *even*
> *be* + *even*

*She has broken all her toys. She **has even** broken her bike.*
    (NOT ~~*Even she has broken*~~...)
*He's rude to everybody. He**'s even** rude to the police.*

> *even* + other verb

*They do everything together. They **even brush** their teeth together.*
*He speaks lots of languages. He **even speaks** Esperanto.*

Even goes at the beginning of a clause when it refers just to the subject; and it can go just before other words and expressions that we want to emphasise.

*Anybody can do this. **Even a child** can do it.*
*He eats anything – **even raw potatoes**.*
*I work every day, **even on Sundays**.*

2 not even

We use *not even* to talk about a negative extreme – for example, to say that we are surprised because somebody does not manage a very small thing.

*He ca**n't even** write his own name.*
*I haven't written to anybody for months – **not even** my parents.*
*She did**n't even** offer me a cup of tea.*

3 even and also

Also is not used to talk about surprising extremes.

*Everybody helped with the packing – **even** the dog.* (NOT ...~~***also** the dog*.~~)

For *also, too* and *as well*, see 45.

4 even if and even though

Even is not used as a conjunction, but we can use *even* before *if* and *though*.

***Even if** I become a millionaire, I shall always be a socialist.*
    (NOT ...~~***Even** I become*~~...)
***Even though** I didn't know anybody at the party, I had a nice time.*

We sometimes use *if* in the sense of *even if*, when there is no possibility of confusion.

*I'll do it **if** it kills me.* (= ... ***even if** it kills me*.)

5 even so

Even so means 'however'.

*He seems nice. **Even so**, I don't really trust him.*
    (NOT ...~~***Even though**, I don't really trust him.*~~)

196 eventual(ly)

Eventual and *eventually* mean 'final(ly)', 'in the end', 'after all that'.
We use them when we say that something happens after a long time or after
a lot of effort.

>*The chess game lasted for three days. Androv was the **eventual** winner.*
>*The car didn't want to start, but **eventually** I got it going.*

Eventually is not used to give news.

>*Steve has found a job **at last**!* (NOT ~~Steve has **eventually** found a job!~~)

Note that *eventual* and *eventually* are 'false friends' for people who speak
some languages of European origin. They do not mean the same as, for
instance, *eventuel* or *eventuellement*, and are not used to express the idea of
possibility. For this meaning we use *possible, perhaps, if, may, might* etc.

>*In our new house I'd like to have a spare bedroom for **possible** visitors.*
>   (NOT ...~~**eventual** visitors.~~)
>*I'm not sure what I'll do next year. I **might** go to America if I can find a job.*
>   (NOT ...~~**Eventually** I'll go to America...~~)

For *finally, at last* and *in/at the end*, see 210.

197 ever

1 *ever* meaning 'at any time'

Ever generally means 'at any time', and is used mainly in questions (see
below). Compare:

>*Do you **ever** go to Ireland on holiday?* (= at any time)
>*We **always** go to Ireland on holiday.* (= every time)
>*We **never** have holidays in England.* (= at no time)

2 *ever* meaning 'always'

Ever is not normally used to mean 'always'.

>*I shall **always** remember you.* (NOT ~~I shall **ever** remember you.~~)

But *ever* is sometimes used to mean 'always' in compound expressions with
adjectives and participles.

>*his **ever-open** mouth*   *an **ever-increasing** debt*
>***evergreen** trees*   *his **ever-loving** wife*

Ever also means 'always' in *forever* (or *for ever*) and *ever since*, and in a few
other expressions like *ever after* and *Yours ever* (used at the end of letters).

>*I shall love you **forever**.*   *I've loved you **ever since** I met you.*

3 use

Ever is a 'non-assertive' word (see 374), and is used mostly in questions. It is
also possible in negative clauses, but *never* is more usual than *not ever*.

>*Do you **ever** go to pop concerts?*
>*I **don't ever** want to see you again.* (OR *I **never** want...*)

We also use *ever* after *if*, and with words that express a negative idea (like
nobody, hardly or *stop*).

>*Come and see us **if** you are **ever** in Manchester.*
>***Nobody ever** visits them.*   *I **hardly ever** see my sister.*
>*I'm going to **stop** her **ever** doing that again.*

▶

4 superlative + *ever*

Ever is used in affirmative clauses after superlatives and *only*.
> *What is the **best** book you've **ever** read?*
> *It's the **largest** picture **ever** painted.*
> *She's the **only** woman **ever** to have climbed Everest in winter.*

5 *ever* + perfect

When *ever* is used with a present perfect tense (see 418), it means 'at any time up to now'. Compare:
> ***Have** you **ever been** to Greece?*
> ***Did** you **ever go** to Naples when you lived in Italy?*
With a past perfect, *ever* means 'at any time up to then'.
> ***Had** you **ever thought** of getting married before you met June?*

6 *than ever*

After a comparative, we can use the expression *than ever*.
> *You're looking lovelier **than ever**.*

7 *ever, yet* and *already*

Ever is not used in the same way as *yet* and *already*. These two words are used for things that happen around the present. Compare:
> *Have you been to Belfast **yet**?* (A trip is planned.)
> *Good heavens. Have you been to Belfast **already**?* (The trip has taken place earlier than expected.)
> *Have you **ever** been to Belfast?* (at any time in the past)

8 *ever* and *before*

Ever and *before* can both be used to mean 'at any time in the past', but there is a slight difference. *Before* refers to a present event, and asks whether it has happened at another time; *ever* does not refer to a present event. Compare:
> *Have you been to Scotland **before**?* (The hearer is probably in Scotland.)
> *Have you **ever** been to Africa?* (The hearer is not in Africa.)
But note that *ever before* can refer to a present event.
> *What are you staring at? Haven't you **ever** seen somebody dancing **before**?*

For more information about *ever*, see a good dictionary.
For *who ever, what ever* etc, see 595.
For *whoever, whatever* etc, see 596.
For *already, yet* and *still*, see 539.
For *forever* with progressive forms, see 452.

198 ever so, ever such

These expressions are often used in very informal British English to mean 'very'. Some people consider them substandard.
> *She's **ever so** nice.*
> *It's **ever such** a good film.*
For the difference between *so* and *such*, see 544.

199   every (one)

1   *every* + singular

Every is a determiner (see 157). We normally use it before a singular noun (but see paragraph 5). If the noun is a subject, its verb is also singular.

> *every* + singular noun

> *I see her **every day**.* (NOT . . .~~every days.~~)
> ***Every room is** being used.* (NOT ~~Every room are~~ . . .)

2   *every one of*

We use *every one of* before a pronoun or a determiner (for example *the, my, these* – see 157). The pronoun or noun is plural, but a following verb is singular.

> *every one of us/you/them*
> *every one of* + determiner + plural noun

> *His books are wonderful. I've read **every one of them**.*
> ***Every one of** the children **was** crying.*

3   *every one* without a noun

We can drop a noun and use *every one* alone, if the noun has already been mentioned.

> *His books are great. **Every one**'s worth reading.*

4   negative structures

To negate *every*, we normally use *not every*.

> ***Not every** kind of bird can fly.* (More natural than ***Every** kind of bird* ***cannot** fly.*)

5   pronouns and possessives

When a pronoun or possessive is used later in a clause to refer back to *every (one)*, the later word can usually be either singular (more formal) or plural (less formal).

> ***Every** person made **his/her** own travel arrangements.*
> ***Every** person made **their** own travel arrangements.*
> *I told **every** single student what I thought of **him/her/them**.*

But if we are talking about something that concerns every member of a group at the same time, a plural word is necessary.

> *When **every** passenger's ticket had been checked, the door opened and **they** all got on.* (NOT . . .~~and he/she all got on.~~)

6   *every* + plural noun

Every is used before a plural noun in expressions that refer to intervals.

> *I see her **every few days**.*
> *There's a meeting **every six weeks**.*
> *She had to stop and rest **every two or three steps**.*   ▶

7 *everybody* etc

Everybody, everyone, everything and *everywhere* are used with singular verbs, like *every*.

> ***Everybody has*** *gone home.* (NOT ~~Everybody have~~...)
> ***Everything*** *I like **is** either illegal, immoral or fattening.*
> *I found that **everywhere was** booked up.*

When possessives and pronouns refer back to *everybody/one*, they can usually be either singular (more formal) or plural (less formal). Sometimes only a plural word makes sense. Compare:

> *Has **everybody** got **his or her** ticket?* (more formal)
> *Has **everybody** got **their** tickets?* (less formal)
> *When **everybody** had finished eating, the waiters took away **their plates**.*
> (NOT ...~~his or her plate~~.)

Note that *everyone* (= 'everybody') does not mean the same as *every one* (which can refer to things as well as people – see paragraph 2 above).

8 *everyday*

Everyday is an adjective meaning 'ordinary', 'usual', 'routine'. It is not the same as the adverbial expression *every day*. Compare:

> *In **everyday** life, you don't often find an elephant in a supermarket.*
> *You don't see elephants **every day**.*

9 common expressions

Note the following common expressions with *every*.

every single
> *She visits her mother **every single** day.*

every other
> *We meet **every other** Tuesday.* (= ... *every second Tuesday*.)

every so often; every now and then
> *We go out for a drink together **every so often / every now and then**.*

For the difference between *every* and *each*, see 174.
For *every* and *all*, see 37.
For *every* and *any*, see 55.
For more information about *everybody/everyone*, see 523.

200 except (for)

1 *except* with or without *for*

We use *except (for)* after general statements, especially after generalising words like *all, every, no, everything, anybody, nowhere, whole* etc.

> *He ate **everything** on his plate **except (for)** the beans.*
> *He ate the **whole** meal, **except (for)** the beans.*

2   *except for*

In other cases we usually use *except for*, not *except*. Compare:
- *I've cleaned **all** the rooms **except (for)** the bathroom.*
    (*Except* is possible after *all*.)
    *I've cleaned the house **except for** the bathroom.*
    (NOT . . . *except the bathroom*.)
- *Nobody came **except (for)** John and Mary*. (after *nobody*)
    ***Except for** John and Mary, **nobody** came.* (before *nobody*)
- *You couldn't hear **anything except (for)** the noise of Louise typing.*
    *The house was quiet **except for** the noise of Louise typing.*

3   *except*

We use *except*, not *except for*, before prepositions and conjunctions.
    *It's the same everywhere **except in** Scotland.*
        (NOT . . . *except for in Scotland*.)
    *He's good-looking **except when** he smiles.*

4   *except (for)* + pronoun

After *except (for)* we use object pronouns, not subject pronouns.
    *Everybody understands **except me**.*
    *We're all ready **except her**.*

5   *except* + verb

A verb form after *except* usually depends on what came before. Infinitives are normally without *to*.
    *He does nothing **except eat** all day.* (*does . . . eat*)
    *She's not interested in anything **except skiing**.* (*interested in . . . skiing*)

6   *except* and *without*

Except (for) is only used to talk about exceptions to generalisations. In other cases, *without* or *but for* may be preferable. Compare:
    *Nobody helped me **except** you.*
    ***Without / But for** your help, I would have failed.*
        (NOT *Except for your help, I would have failed*.)

For the use of *but* to mean 'except', see 116.
For the difference between *except*, *besides* and *apart from*, see 101.

201   exclamations: structures

Exclamations are often constructed with *how* and *what* or with *so* and *such*; negative question forms are also common.

1   exclamations with *how*

These are often felt to be a little formal or old-fashioned.

> *how* + adjective

*Strawberries! **How nice!***   ▶

how + adjective / adverb + subject + verb

How cold it is! (NOT ~~How it is cold!~~)
How beautifully you sing! (NOT ~~How you sing beautifully!~~)

how + subject + verb

How you've grown!

For the structure of expressions like *How strange a remark,* see 16.

2 exclamations with *what*

what a/an (+ adjective) + singular countable noun

What a rude man! (NOT ~~What rude man!~~)
What a nice dress! (NOT ~~What nice dress!~~)
What a surprise!

what (+ adjective) + uncountable / plural noun

What beautiful weather! (NOT ~~What a beautiful weather!~~)
What lovely flowers!
What fools!

3 exclamations with *so* and *such*

so + adjective

You're **so kind**!

such a/an (+ adjective) + singular countable noun

He's **such a** nice boy! (NOT ... ~~a such nice boy!~~)

such (+ adjective) + uncountable / plural noun

They talk **such** rubbish! (NOT ... ~~such a rubbish!~~)
They're **such** kind people! (NOT ... ~~so kind people!~~)

what + object + subject + verb (note word order)

What a beautiful smile **your sister has**! (NOT ... ~~has your sister.~~)

For more information about *such* and *so,* see 544.

4 negative question forms

Isn't the weather nice!   **Hasn't** she grown!
Americans and some British speakers may use ordinary (non-negative)
question forms in exclamations.

Boy, **am I** hungry!   Wow, **did she** make a mistake!
Was I furious!

For more information about negative questions, see 360.

202 expect, hope, wait and look forward

1 *expect* and *hope*: difference of meaning

Expecting is mental rather than emotional. If I *expect* something to happen,
I have a good reason to think it will in fact happen. *Hoping* is more
emotional. If I *hope for* something to happen, I would like it to happen, but
I do not know whether it will. Compare:
– *She's **expecting** a baby.* (= She's pregnant.)
  *She's **hoping** it will be a girl.*
– *I'm **expecting** John to phone at three o'clock.*
  *I **hope** he's got some good news.*
One can *expect* good or bad things to happen, but one only *hopes* for good
things.
  *I **expect** it will rain at the weekend. But I **hope** it won't.*

2 *expect* and *wait*: difference of meaning

One *waits* when somebody or something is late, when one is early for
something, or when one wants time to pass so that something will happen.
Compare:
– *I'm **expecting** a phone call from John at three o'clock.*
   (NOT ~~I'm **waiting** for a phone call from John at three o'clock.~~)
   *I hope he rings on time. I hate **waiting** for people to phone.*
   (NOT ~~I hate **expecting** people to phone.~~)
– *He **expects** to get a bike for his birthday.* (= He thinks he'll get one.)
   *It's hard to **wait** for things when you're five years old.*
– *I **expected** her at ten, but she didn't turn up.*
   *I **waited** for her till eleven, and then went home.*
Can't wait often expresses impatience.
   *I **can't wait** for the holidays!*

3 *expect, hope* and *wait*: structures

a direct object

Before a direct object, *hope* and *wait* have the preposition *for*. Compare:
   *We're **expecting** rain soon.*
   *We're **hoping for** a lot of rain – the garden's very dry.*
   *We've been **waiting for** rain for weeks.*

b infinitive

All three verbs can be used with a following infinitive.
   *We **expect to spend** the summer in France.*
   *We **hope to see** Annemarie while we're there.*
   *But we're still **waiting to hear** from her.*

c object + infinitive

An **object + infinitive** structure is possible.
   *I **expect him to arrive** about ten o'clock.*
   *We're **hoping for John to come up** with some new ideas.*
   *I'm still **waiting for Harry to pay** me back that money.*   ▶

To be cannot be left out in these structures.

> *She's quite short – I **expected her to be** taller.* (NOT *I expected her taller.*)

Expect is often used with **object + infinitive** to talk about people's duties. Passive versions of the structure are also common.

> *We **expect you to work** on the first Saturday of every month.*
> ***Staff are expected to start** work punctually at 8.30.*

d   *that*-clause

Expect and *hope* can be followed by *that*-clauses.

> *I **expect (that)** she'll be here soon.*
> *I **hope (that)** I'll recognise her.*
> BUT NOT *I'm waiting that she arrives.*

*I **expect (that)** ...* can be used to talk about the present or past, with the meaning of 'I suppose', 'I have good reason to think'.

> *I **expect** you're all tired after your journey.*
> *Sarah isn't here. I **expect** she was too tired to come.*

Hope is often followed by a present tense with a future meaning (see 252).

> *I **hope** she **doesn't** miss the train.*

e   *expect something of somebody*

This structure refers to people's feelings about how other people ought to behave.

> *My parents **expected too much of me** when I was at school – they were terribly upset when I failed my exams.*

f   progressive forms

Before a *that*-clause, simple and progressive forms of *hope* can often be used with little difference of meaning.

> *We **hope** / We'**re hoping** you can come and stay with us soon.*

Before a *that*-clause, progressive forms of *expect* are not normally used.

> *I **expect (that)** she'll be here soon.* (NOT *I'm expecting (that)...*)
> *I **expect (that)** you're wondering what this is all about.*
> (NOT *I'm expecting (that)...*)

Before an infinitive, simple and progressive forms of *hope* and *expect* can often be used with little difference of meaning.

> *We **hope** / We'**re hoping to get** to Scotland next weekend.*
> *We **expect** / We'**re expecting to hear** from Lucy today.*

4   *look forward*

Look forward means 'think about (something in the future) with pleasure'. One *looks forward* to something that is certain to happen, and that one is glad about.

> *He's **looking forward** to his birthday.*

Look forward can be followed by *to ...ing*, but not by an infinitive.

> *I **look forward to meeting** you.* (NOT *...to meet you.*)
> *I **look forward to hearing** from you.*
> (common formula at the end of a letter)

Simple and progressive forms can often be used with little difference of meaning.

>I **look forward** / I'm **looking forward** to the day when the children leave home.

For *hope* and *expect* in negative clauses, see 359.
For *not* and *so* after *hope* and *expect*, see 515.
For *and* after *wait*, see 52.
For the 'casual' use of progressive forms, see 161.
For *wish*, see 601.

203 experiment and experience

An *experiment* is a test which somebody does to see what the result will be, or to prove something. *Experiment* is generally used with the verb *do*. There is also a verb *to experiment*.

>We did an **experiment** in the chemistry lesson, to see if you could get chlorine gas from salt. (NOT *We did an* ~~experience~~...)
>I'm **experimenting** with a new perfume.

An *experience* is something that you live through; something that happens to you in life. *Experience* is generally used with the verb *have*. There is also a verb *to experience*.

>I had a lot of interesting **experiences** during my year in Africa.
>(NOT *I* ~~made a lot of interesting experiences~~...)
>Have you ever **experienced** the feeling that you were going mad?
>(NOT ~~Have you ever experimented the feeling...?~~)

The uncountable noun *experience* means 'the knowledge that you get from doing things'.

>Salesgirl wanted – **experience** unnecessary.

204 explain

After *explain*, we use *to* before an indirect object.

>I explained my problem **to her**. (NOT ~~I explained her my problem.~~)
>Can you explain **to me** how to get to your house?
>(NOT ~~Can you explain me...?~~)

205 fairly, quite, rather and pretty: adverbs of degree

1 *fairly*

Fairly generally modifies adjectives and adverbs. It does not suggest a very high degree: if you say that somebody is *fairly nice* or *fairly clever*, for example, he or she will not be very pleased.

>'How was the film?' '**Fairly** good. Not the best one I've seen this year.'
>I speak Russian **fairly** well – enough for everyday purposes.

►

2 *quite*

Quite (mainly British English) suggests a higher degree than *fairly*.
> '*How was the film?*' '***Quite** good. You ought to go.*'
> *It's **quite** a difficult book – I had trouble with it.*
> *He's lived in St Petersburg, so he speaks Russian **quite** well.*

Quite can modify verbs and nouns.
> *I **quite** enjoyed myself at your party.*   *The room was **quite** a mess.*

For word order rules, the use of *quite* to mean 'completely', and other details, see 467.

3 *rather*

Rather is stronger than *quite*. It can suggest 'more than is usual', 'more than was expected', 'more than was wanted', and similar ideas.
> '*How was the film?*' '***Rather** good – I was surprised.*'
> *Maurice speaks Russian **rather** well. People often think he is Russian.*
> *I think I'll put the heating on. It's **rather** cold.*
> *I've had **rather** a long day.*

Rather can modify verbs (especially verbs that refer to thoughts and feelings) and nouns.
> *I **rather think** we're going to lose.*   *She **rather likes** gardening.*
> *It was **rather** a disappointment.*

For word order rules and other details of the use of *rather*, see 468.

4 *pretty*

Pretty is similar to *rather*, but only modifies adjectives and adverbs. It is informal.
> '*How's things?*' '***Pretty** good. You OK?*'   *She's a **pretty** nice girl.*

Pretty well means 'almost'.
> *I've **pretty well** finished.*

5 intonation

Note that the exact meaning of these words may depend on the intonation used.

For more about structures expressing degree, see 153–156.

206 **far** and **a long way**

1 *far* in questions and negatives

Far is most common in questions and negative clauses.
> **How far** did you walk?   *The youth hostel is **not far** from here.*

2 *a long way* in affirmative clauses

In affirmative clauses we usually prefer *a long way*.
> *We walked **a long way**.* (NOT ~~We walked **far**.~~)
> *The station is **a long way** from here.*
> (More natural than *The station is **far** from here.*)

3 *far* in affirmative clauses

However, *far* is normal in affirmative clauses with *too, enough, as* and *so*.
> *'Have I gone **far enough**?' 'A bit **too far**.'*   *It's ready **as far** as I know.*
> *'Any problems?' 'OK **so far**.'*

Far is also used (in all kinds of clauses) to modify comparatives, superlatives and *too*.
> *She's **far older** than her husband.*   *This bike is **by far the best**.*
> *You're **far too** young to get married.*

4 attributive adjective

Far can be used as an adjective before a noun, meaning 'distant'. This is rather formal and old-fashioned.
> *Long ago, in a **far** country, there lived a woman who had seven sons.*

Much, many and *long* (for time) are also more common in questions and negative
sentences (see 348 and 323).

207 **farther** and **further**

1 distance

We use both *farther* and *further* to talk about distance. There is no difference of meaning.
> *Edinburgh is **farther/further** away than York.*

2 'additional'

We can use *further* (but not *farther*) to mean 'additional', 'extra', 'more advanced'.
> *For **further** information, see page 277.*

208 **feel**

Feel has several different meanings. Progressive forms can be used with some meanings, but not with others. *Feel* can be a 'copular verb' (see 147), followed by an adjective or noun complement. It can also be an ordinary verb, followed by a direct object.

1 copular verb: *I feel*

Feel can be used with a personal subject (*I, you* etc) to mean 'experience the condition of one's own mind or body'. Adjective or (in British English) noun complements are used.
> *I **feel fine**.*   *Do you **feel happy**?*   *Andrew was beginning to **feel cold**.*
> *I always **feel sleepy** on Mondays.*
> *When Louise realised what she had done, she **felt a complete idiot**.* (GB)

Note that in this sense *feel* is not normally used with reflexive pronouns (*myself* etc).
> *He always **felt** inferior when he was with her.*
> (More natural than *He always **felt himself** inferior ...*)   ▶

To talk about feelings that are going on at a particular moment, simple or progressive forms can be used. There is little difference of meaning.

>*I feel fine. / I'm feeling fine.*
>*How do you feel? / How are you feeling?*

2 reactions and opinions

Feel is often used to talk about reactions and opinions. Progressive forms are not usually used in this case.

>*I feel sure you're right.* (NOT *I'm feeling sure...*)
>*He says he feels doubtful about the new plan.*

That-clauses are common.

>*I feel (that) she's making a mistake.*

A structure with **object + to be + complement** is possible in a formal style, but it is not very often used.

>*I felt her to be unfriendly.* (More normal: *I felt that she was unfriendly.*)

When the object is an infinitive, preparatory *it* is used and *to be* is often dropped (especially before adjectives). The structure with **object + to be + complement** is rather more common in this case, though it is still formal.

>*I felt it (to be) my duty to call the police.*
>*We felt it necessary to call the police.*

3 copular verb: *it feels*

Feel can also be used, usually with a non-personal subject, to mean 'give somebody sensations'. Progressive forms are not used.

>*The glass felt cold against my lips.*
>*My head feels funny.*
>*That feels nice!*

4 copular verb: *feel like*; *feel as if/though*

Feel can be followed by *like* or *as if/though.*

>*My legs feel like cotton wool.*
>*Alice felt as if/though she was in a very nice dream.*
>>(*Alice felt like she was...* is also possible – see 74.)

Note that *feel like* can also mean 'want', 'would like'.

>*I feel like a drink. Have you got any beer?*

In this sense, *feel like* is often followed by an *-ing* form.

>*I felt like laughing, but I didn't dare.*

Compare:

>*I felt like swimming.* (= *I wanted to swim.*)
>*I felt like / as if I was swimming.* (= *It seemed as if I was swimming.*)

5 ordinary verb: 'receive physical sensations'

Feel can be used with a direct object to talk about the physical sensations that come to us through the sense of touch.

>*I suddenly felt an insect crawling up my leg.*

Progressive forms are not used, but we often use *can feel* to talk about a sensation that is going on at a particular moment.

>*I can feel something biting me!*

6 ordinary verb: 'touch'

Feel can be also used with a direct object to mean 'touch something deliberately in order to learn about it or experience it'. Progressive forms are possible.

> **Feel the car seat**. *It's wet.*
> *'What are you doing?' 'I'm feeling the shirts to see if they're dry.'*

209 female and feminine; male and masculine

Female and *male* are used to say what sex people, animals and plants belong to.

> *A **female** fox is called a vixen.*   *A **male** duck is called a drake.*

Feminine and *masculine* are used for qualities and behaviour that are felt to be typical of men or women.

> *She has a very **masculine** laugh.*   *It was a very **feminine** bathroom.*

Feminine and *masculine* are used for grammatical forms in some languages.

> *The word for 'moon' is **feminine** in French and **masculine** in German.*

210 finally, at last, in the end and at the end

1 *finally*

Finally can introduce the last element in a series.

> *We must increase productivity. We must reduce unemployment.*
>   *And **finally**, we must compete in world markets.*

Finally can also suggest that one has been waiting a long time for something. In this sense, it often goes in mid-position (with the verb – see 22).

> *After putting it off three times, we **finally** managed to have a holiday in Greece.*
> *Steve has **finally** found a job.*

2 *at last*

At last also suggests – very strongly – the idea of impatience or inconvenience resulting from a long wait or delay.

> *James has passed his exams **at last**.*
> *When **at last** they found him he was almost dead.*

At last can be used as an exclamation. (*Finally* cannot be used in this way.)

> ***At last!** Where the hell have you been?*

Note that *lastly* (introducing the last item in a series) is not the same as *at last*.

> *Firstly, we need to increase profits. Secondly, ... Thirdly, ... And **lastly**, we need to cut down administrative expenses.*
> (NOT ...*And **at last** we need to cut down*...)

3 *in the end*

In the end suggests that something happens after a lot of changes, problems or uncertainty.

> *We made eight different plans for our holiday, but **in the end** we went to Brighton again.*   ▶

*I left in the middle of the film. Did they get married **in the end**?*
*The tax man will get you **in the end**.*

4   *at the end*

At the end simply refers to position at the end of something. There is no sense of waiting or delay.

*A declarative sentence usually has a capital letter at the beginning and a full stop **at the end**.*
*I wish I was paid at the beginning of the week and not **at the end**.*

For other expressions with *end*, see a good dictionary.
For the verbs *end* and *finish*, see 191.
For *eventually*, see 196.

211   finished

Finished can be used as a normal past participle in perfect verb forms (e.g. *I've nearly finished*). It can also be used as an adjective after *be*, meaning 'ready' (e.g. *I'm nearly finished*). There is not much difference of meaning between *I* etc *am finished* (in this sense) and *I* etc *have finished*. The adjective construction (*be finished*) is common in an informal style.

*How soon will you **be/have finished**, dear?*
*Hang on – **I'm/I've** nearly **finished**.*
*I went to get the car from the garage, but they **weren't/hadn't finished**.*

212   fit and suit

These words do not mean exactly the same.

Fit refers to size and shape: if your clothes *fit* you, they are neither too big nor too small.

*These shoes don't **fit** me – have you got a larger size?*

Suit refers to style, colour etc.

*Red and black are colours that **suit** me very well.*
(NOT ... *colours that fit me very well.*)
*Do you think this style **suits** me?*

Suit can also be used to talk about whether arrangements and situations are convenient.

*Tuesday would **suit** me very well for a meeting.*

For other uses of these two words, see a good dictionary.

213   for: purpose and cause

1   people's purposes

For can be used to talk about somebody's purpose in doing something, but only when it is followed by a noun.

*We stopped at the pub **for a drink**.*
*I went to the college **for an interview** with Professor Taylor.*

For is not used before a verb in this sense. The infinitive alone is used to express a person's purpose (see 281).

> *We stopped at the pub **to have** a drink.* (NOT ...*for having a drink.*)
> *I went to the college **to see** Professor Taylor.*
> (NOT ...*for seeing Professor Taylor.*)

2   the purposes of things: *-ing* forms and infinitives

For can be used before the *-ing* form of a verb to express the 'purpose' of a thing – what it is used for – especially when the thing is the subject of the clause.

> *Is that cake **for eating** or just **for looking at**?*
> *An altimeter is used **for measuring** height above sea level.*

When the clause has a person as subject, it is more common to use an infinitive to express the purpose of a thing.

> *We use altimeters **to measure** height above sea level.*

3   causes of reactions

For ...ing can also be used after a description of a positive or negative reaction, to explain the behaviour that caused it.

> *We are grateful to you **for helping** us out.*
> *I'm angry with you **for waking me up**.*
> *They punished the child **for lying**.*
> *He was sent to prison **for stealing**.*

214   **for**, **in**, **from** and **since** (time)

1   *for*

We use *for* when we measure duration – when we say how long something lasts.

> *for* + period of time

> *I once studied the guitar **for three years**.*
> *That house has been empty **for six months**.*
> *We go away **for three weeks** every summer.*
> *My boss will be in Italy **for the next ten days**.*
> *I'm going to Canada **for the summer**.*

To measure duration up to the present, we use a present perfect tense (see 418 – 420), not a present tense.

> *I've known her for a long time.* (NOT *I know her for a long time.*)

A present tense with *for* refers to duration into the future. Compare:

> *How long **are you** here for?* (= *Until when ...?*)
> *How long **have you been** here for?* (= *Since when ...?*)

We can often leave out *for* in an informal style, especially with *How long ...?* And *for* is not usually used before *all*.

> ***How long** have you been waiting (for)?*
> *We've been here (for) six weeks.*
> *I've had a headache **all** day.*

▶

2   *in* after negatives and superlatives (US)

After negatives and superlatives, *in* can be used to talk about duration. This is especially common in American English.

> I **haven't** seen him **for/in** months.
> It was the **worst** storm **for/in** ten years.

3   *from* and *since*

From and *since* give the starting points of actions, events or states: they say when things begin or began.

> *from/since* + starting point

> I'll be here **from three o'clock** onwards.
> I work **from nine** to five.
> **From now** on, I'm going to go running every day.
> **From his earliest childhood** he loved music.
> I've been waiting **since six o'clock**.
> I've known her **since January**.

Since is used especially when we measure duration from the point of view of a particular present or past end-point. A present perfect or past perfect tense is normal. *From* is used in other cases. Compare:

– **I've been working since** six o'clock, and I'm getting tired.
  (NOT ~~I've been working from six o'clock~~...)
  I **had been working since** six o'clock, and I was getting tired.
– The shop was open **from** eight in the morning, but the boss didn't arrive till ten. (NOT ~~The shop was open since eight~~...)
  I'll be at home **from** Tuesday morning (on).
  (NOT ...~~since Tuesday morning.~~)

From is sometimes possible with a present perfect, especially in expressions that mean 'right from the start'.

> She**'s been** like that **from** her childhood. (OR ... **since** her childhood.)
> **From** the moment they were married, they**'ve quarrelled**.
> **From** the dawn of civilisation, people **have made** war.

For *from ... to* and *from ... until*, see 575.

4   *for* and *since*

For and *since* can both be used with perfect tenses (see 418.6). They are not the same. Compare:

> *for* + period

> I've known her **for three days**. (NOT ...~~since three days.~~)
> She's been working here **for a long time**. (NOT ...~~since a long time.~~)

> *since* + starting point

> I've known her **since Tuesday**.
> She's been working here **since July**.

For more about tenses with *since*, see 499.
For *since* meaning 'as' or 'because', see 72.

215 forget and leave

We can use *forget* to talk about accidentally leaving things behind.
> *Oh damn! I've **forgotten** my umbrella.*

However, we normally use *leave* if we mention the place.
> *Oh damn! I've **left** my umbrella at home.*
> (NOT ~~*I've **forgotten** my umbrella **at home.***~~)

For infinitives and *-ing* forms after *forget*, see 296.1.

216 formality and politeness

1 formal and informal language

Most people speak and write in different ways on different occasions. In some languages, for example, there are very complicated rules about how to speak to older or more important people. English does not have a system of this kind. However, there are some words and structures which are mostly used in *formal* situations – that is to say, situations when people are careful about how they express themselves, like report writing, business meetings, conferences or polite conversations with strangers. And some words and structures are mostly used in *informal* situations – for example conversations with friends, or letters to one's family. Writing is more often formal, and speech is more often informal, but informal writing and formal speech are used when the situation makes them necessary.

Most words and expressions are neither formal nor informal, but neutral – English speakers do not have to know two ways of saying everything.

2 grammar

Some grammatical structures have different formal and informal versions. For example, contracted auxiliary verbs and negatives (see 144) are common in informal speech and writing. Compare:

Formal: *It **has** gone. It **is not** possible.*
Informal: *It's gone. It **isn't** possible.*

Prepositions come at the end of certain structures in informal language (see 440). Compare:

Formal: *In which century did he live?*
Informal: *Which century did he live **in**?*

Some relative structures are different (see 474.5–6). Compare:

Formal: *The man **whom** she married . . .*
Informal: *The man she married . . .*

Some determiners are followed by singular verb forms in formal language, and plural forms in informal language (see 509.5). Compare:

Formal: ***Neither** of us **likes** him.*
Informal: ***Neither** of us **like** him.*

Some pronouns have different forms (see 425). Compare:

Formal: *It was **she who** first saw what to do.*
Informal: *It was **her that** first saw what to do.*
Formal: ***Whom** did they elect?*
Informal: ***Who** did they elect?*

▶

Ellipsis (leaving out words – see 181–186) is more common in informal language. Compare:

Formal:	***Have you seen*** *Mr Andrews?*
Informal:	***Seen*** *John?*
Formal:	*We think **that** it is possible.*
Informal:	*We think it's possible.*

3 vocabulary

Some words and expressions are used mainly in informal situations; in neutral or formal situations other words or expressions are used. Some examples:

Formal	Neutral	Informal
repair	*mend* (GB)	*fix*
commence	*begin/start*	*begin/start*
in order	*all right*	*OK*
Thank you	*Thank you*	*Thanks*
I beg your pardon?	*Pardon?/Sorry?*	*What?*

4 polite requests and questions

Formal language is of course used when one wishes to be polite – to show respect to important people or strangers. Requests and questions can be made more polite by making them less direct. A common way of making requests less direct is to use *yes/no* questions. These suggest that the hearer can choose whether to agree or not.

> ***Could you tell*** *me the time, please?*
> > (Much more polite than *Please tell me the time.*)

Another way of making requests and questions less direct is to use 'distancing' verb forms (e.g. past instead of present).

> *How much **did** you want to spend, sir?*

For more about polite requests, see 483.
For more about 'distancing', see 161.
For the language used in particular social situations, see 520.
For taboo language, see 550.
For slang, see 510.
For the use of out-of-date grammar and vocabulary in ceremonies and other situations, see 388.

217 fronting

1 normal order

Affirmative sentences most often begin with the grammatical subject.

> ***Jake*** *is a vegetarian.*

If we begin a sentence with something else, this is often to make it the *topic* – the thing we are talking about – even though it is not the grammatical subject.

> ***People like that*** *I just can't stand.*

We can also move things to the front for emphasis.

> *Crazy, that driver.*

Moving something to the beginning of a sentence in this way is called 'fronting'.

2 fronted objects and complements

It is possible to begin an affirmative clause with the object or complement, in order to make this the topic or give it more immediate importance. This kind of fronting is common in informal speech.

> *Very good lesson we had yesterday.*
> *Strange people they are!*

Fronting of the object is also possible in a more formal style.

> *This question we have already discussed at some length.*

In a few exclamatory expressions, a noun is fronted before *that*, but these are uncommon in modern English.

> *Fool that I was!*

Question-word clauses are often fronted.

> *What I'm going to do next I just don't know.*
> *How she got the gun through customs we never found out.*

For the use of passive structures to bring objects to the front, see 409.1.

3 detached fronted subjects and objects

In informal speech, it is common to detach a subject or object, announce it at the front of a sentence, and then repeat it with a pronoun.

> *This guy who rang up, he's an architect. Well, ...*
> *That couple we met in Berlin, we don't want to send them a card, do we?*
> *One of my brothers, his wife's a singer, he says ...*

This does not usually happen with pronoun subjects, but *me* and *myself* are occasionally detached and fronted.

> *Me, I don't care.*
> *Myself, I think you're making a big mistake.*

4 adverbs etc

Many adverbs and adverbial expressions can go at the beginning of a clause (see 22–23). This often happens when we are using the adverbs to structure a piece of narrative or a description.

> *Once upon a time there were three little pigs. One day ... Then ...*
> *Soon after that ... After dark, ...*
> *Inside the front door there is ... Opposite the living room is ...*
> *On the right you can see ... At the top of the stairs ...*

Adverb particles are often fronted when giving instructions to small children.

> *Off we go!*
> *Down you come!*

Another reason for fronting adverbs is for emphasis.

> *Now you tell me! (= Why didn't you tell me before?)*

▶

Inversion (see 298–299) is necessary after some emphatic fronted adverbs and adverbial expressions.

> *Under no circumstances **can we** accept cheques.*
> (NOT *Under no circumstances **we can**…*)
> *Round the corner **came Mrs Porter**.*

5 fronting with *as* or *though*

Fronted adjectives and adverbs are possible in a structure with *as* or *though* (see 71).

> *Young as I was*, I realised what was happening.
> *Tired though she was*, she went on working.
> *Fast though she drove*, she could not catch them.
> *Much as I respect his work*, I cannot agree with him.

6 ellipsis

In a very informal style, articles, pronouns and auxiliary verbs are often left out, bringing a more important word to the front of the clause. This is called 'ellipsis': for details, see 183.

> *Postman been?*
> *Seen John?*

Sometimes an elliptical structure is used to front a verb and / or complement, while the subject is put in a 'tag' (see 472) at the end.

> *Likes his beer*, Stephen does.
> *Funny*, your brother.
> *Nice day*, isn't it?

See also entries on information structure (289), emphasis (189) and cleft sentences (131).

218 fun and funny

These two words are sometimes confused. *Fun* is normally an uncountable noun. It often comes after *is* and other copular verbs (see 147), and can be used to say that things or people are enjoyable, entertaining etc. *Funny* is an adjective, and is used to say that something makes you laugh. Compare:

> *The party was **fun**, wasn't it?* (NOT *The party was **funny**.*)
> *Canoeing can be a lot of **fun**.*
> *Why are you wearing that **funny** hat?*

Note that *funny* has another meaning: 'strange', 'peculiar'.

> *'Celia's got a **funny** way of talking.' 'Do you mean **funny** ha-ha or **funny** peculiar?'*

In informal American English, *fun* is sometimes used as an adjective.

> *That was a real **fun** party.*

219 **future** (1): introduction

There are several ways to use verbs to talk about the future in English. This is a complicated area of grammar: the differences between the meanings and uses of the different structures are not easy to analyse and describe clearly. In many, but not all situations, two or more structures are possible with similar meanings.

1 **present tenses**

When we talk about future events which have already been planned or decided, or which we can see are on the way, we often use present tenses. The present progressive is common. For details, see 220.

> *I'm seeing John tomorrow.*
> *What are you doing this evening?*

The present progressive of *go* is often used as an auxiliary verb in sentences about the future. For details, see 220.

> *Sandra is going to have another baby.*
> *When are you going to get a job?*

The simple present can also be used to talk about the future, but only in certain situations. For details, see 223.

> *The train leaves at half past six tomorrow morning.*

2 *shall/will*

When we are simply giving information about the future, or predicting future events which are not already decided or obviously on the way, we usually use *shall/will* + **infinitive** (*shall* is rare in American English). For details, see 221.

> *I shall probably be home late tonight.*
> *Nobody will ever know what happened to her.*
> *I think Liverpool will win.*

Shall and *will* are also used to express our intentions and attitudes towards other people: they are common in offers, requests, threats, promises and announcements of decisions. For details, see 222.

> *Shall I carry your bag?*
> *I'll hit you if you do that again.*
> *I'll phone you tonight.*
> *'You can have it for £50.' 'OK. I'll buy it.'*

3 **other ways of talking about the future**

We can use the future perfect to say that something will be completed, finished or achieved by a certain time. For details, see 224.

> *By next Christmas we'll have been here for eight years.*

The future progressive can be used to say that something will be in progress at a particular time. For details, and other uses of this tense, see 225.

> *This time tomorrow I'll be lying on the beach.*

The structure *be about* + **infinitive** is used to say that a future event is very close. For details, see 5.

> *I think the plane's about to take off. Is your seat belt done up?*   ▶

Be + **infinitive** is used to talk about plans, arrangements and schedules, and to give instructions. For details, see 90.

> *The President **is to visit** Beijing in January.*
> *You**'re not to tell** anybody about this.*

4 'future in the past'

To say that something was still in the future at a certain past time, we can use a past form of one of the future structures. For details, see 226.

> *I knew she **would** arrive before long.*
> *Something **was going to happen** that **was to** change the world.*

5 subordinate clauses

In many subordinate clauses we refer to the future with present tenses instead of *shall/will* + *infinitive*. For details, see 556.

> *Phone me when you **have** time.* (NOT . . . ~~when you'll have time.~~)
> *I'll think of you when I**'m lying** on the beach next week.*
> (NOT . . . ~~when I'll be lying on the beach~~ . . .)
> *I'll follow him wherever he **goes**.* (NOT . . . ~~wherever he'll go.~~)
> *You can have anything I **find**.* (NOT . . . ~~anything I'll find.~~)

220 future (2): present progressive and be going to

1 When do we use these present tenses to talk about the future?

We use these two present tenses to talk about future actions and events that have some *present reality*. If we say that something in the future *is happening* or *is going to happen*, it is usually already planned or decided, or it is starting to happen, or we can see it coming now.

> *'What **are** you **doing** this evening?' 'I**'m washing** my hair.'*
> *Look at the sky. It**'s going to rain**.*

Note that the simple present is not often used to talk about the future. For details, see 223.

> (NOT ~~What **do** you **do** this evening?~~)

2 present progressive: arrangements and plans

The present progressive is used mostly to talk about personal arrangements and fixed plans, especially when the time and place have been decided.

> *We**'re going** to Mexico next summer.*
> *I**'m seeing** Larry on Saturday.*
> *Did you know I**'m getting** a new job?*
> *What **are** we **having** for dinner?*
> *My car**'s going** in for a service next week.*

We often use the present progressive with verbs of movement, to talk about actions which are just starting.

> *Are you **coming** to the pub?*
> *I**'m** just **popping** out to the post office. Back in a minute.*
> *Get your coat on! I**'m taking** you down to the doctor!*

3 *be going* + infinitive: plans

This structure, too, can be used to talk about plans, especially in an informal style. *Going to* often emphasises the idea of intention, of a decision that has already been made.

> We*'re going to get* a new car soon.
> John says he*'s going to call in* this evening.
> When *are* you *going to get* your hair cut?
> I*'m going to keep* asking her out until she says 'Yes'.
> I*'m going to stop* him reading my letters if it's the last thing I do.

4 *be going* + infinitive: things that are on the way

Another use of the *going to* structure is to predict the future on the basis of present evidence – to say that a future action or event is on the way, or starting to happen.

> Sandra*'s going to have* another baby in June.
> Look at the sky. It*'s going to rain*.
> Look out! We*'re going to crash!*

5 differences between the two structures

In many cases, both structures can be used to express the same idea. But there are some differences.

a fixed arrangement / intention

The present progressive can emphasise the idea of 'fixed arrangement'; *going to* can emphasise the idea of 'intention', or 'previous decision'. Compare:
– *Are* you *doing* anything this weekend?
    (asking about arrangements – more natural than *Are you going to do anything this weekend?*)
   Are you *going to do* anything about that letter from the tax people?
    (pressing to know what has been decided – more natural than *Are you doing anything about that letter ...*)
– *Who's cooking* lunch? (asking what has been arranged)
   Who's going to cook lunch? (asking about a decision)
– *I'm seeing* Phil tonight. (emphasis on arrangement)
   I'm really *going to tell* him what I think of him.
    (emphasis on intention – NOT *I'm really telling him*...)
– *I'm getting* a new job. (It's already arranged.)
   I'm going to get a new job. (I've decided to.)

b events outside people's control

The present progressive is not generally used to make predictions about events that are outside people's control.

> *Things are going to get* better soon. (NOT *Things are getting better soon.*)
> He*'s going to have* an accident one of these days.
>   (NOT *He's having an accident one of these days.*)
> It*'s going to snow* before long. (NOT *It's snowing before long.*) ▶

c   permanent states

The present progressive is used for actions and events, but not usually for permanent states. Compare:

> Our house **is getting / is going to get** new windows this winter.
> Their new house **is going to look** over the river.
>   (NOT ~~Their new house is looking over the river.~~)

6   commands and refusals

Both structures can be used to insist that people do things or do not do things.

> You**'re finishing / going to finish** that soup if you sit there all afternoon!
> She**'s taking / going to take** that medicine whether she likes it or not!
> You**'re not playing / going to play** football in my garden.
> You**'re not wearing / going to wear** that skirt to school.

The present progressive is common in emphatic refusals.

> I'm sorry, you**'re not taking** my car.
> I**'m not** bloody well **washing** your socks!

7   *gonna*

In informal speech, *going to* is often pronounced /gənə/. This is sometimes shown in writing as *gonna*, especially in American English.

> Nobody's **gonna** talk to me like that.

For *will* and *shall*, see 221 – 222.
For *was going to, has been going to* etc, see 226.

221   future (3): **shall / will** (information and prediction)

1   forms

> I shall/will ⎫
> you will   ⎪
> he/she/it will ⎬ + infinitive without *to*
> we shall/will ⎪
> they will   ⎭
>
> questions: *shall/will I? will you?* etc
> negatives: *I will/shall not, you will not* etc
> negative questions: *will/shall I not? will you not?* etc
>   OR *won't/shan't I? won't you?* etc
> contractions: *I'll, you'll* etc; *shan't* /ʃɑːnt/ (GB only), *won't* /wəʊnt/

British people use *I shall/ I will* and *we shall/ we will* with no difference of meaning in most situations. (For cases where there is a difference, see 222.) However, *shall* is becoming very much less common than *will*. *Shall* is not normally used in American English.

For second- and third-person uses of *shall*, see 222.6.
For strong and weak pronunciations of *shall* and *will*, see 588.
For information about all uses of *will*, see 600.

2   giving information about the future; predicting

The *shall/will* structure is used to give (or ask for) information about the
future, in cases where there is no reason to use a present progressive or *going
to* (see 220).

> We **shall need** the money on the 15th.
> It**'ll be** spring soon.
> All the family **will be** at the wedding.
> In another thirteen minutes the alarm **will go off**. This **will close** an
>   electrical contact, causing the explosive to detonate.
> She**'ll be here** in a couple of minutes.

We often use *shall/will* in predictions of future events – to say what we think,
guess or calculate will happen.

> Tomorrow **will be** warm, with some cloud in the afternoon.
> Who do you think **will win** on Saturday?
> I **shall be** rich one day.
> You**'ll** never **finish** that book.

Note that some questions beginning *Will you . . . ?* are used for giving orders,
not asking for information (see paragraph 8 below).

3   conditional use

The *shall/will* structure is often used to express conditional ideas, when we
say what *will happen* if something else happens.

> He**'ll have** an accident if he goes on driving like that.
> If it rains the match **will be cancelled**.
> Look out – you**'ll fall**! (If you're not more careful.)
> 'Come out for a drink.' 'No, I**'ll miss** the film on TV.'
> Don't leave me. I**'ll cry**!

4   'predicting' the present or past

We can use *will* to make a kind of prediction about the present or past – to
say what we think is probably the case, or has probably happened.

> Don't phone them now – they**'ll be having** dinner.
> 'There's somebody at the door.' 'That**'ll be** the postman.'
> As you **will have noticed**, there is a new secretary in the front office.
> It's no use expecting Barry to turn up. He**'ll have forgotten**.

5   predictions as orders

Predictions can be used as a way of giving orders – instead of telling
somebody to do something, the speaker just says firmly that it will happen.
This is common in military-style orders.

> The regiment **will attack** at dawn.
> You **will start** work at six o'clock sharp.

6   *shall/will* and present tenses: both used

Often *shall/will* and present-tense forms (especially the *going to* structure)
are possible with similar meanings. The choice depends on whether we want

to emphasise present ideas like intention / certainty (present tenses), or not
(*shall/will*). Compare:
– *What **will** you **do** next year?*
 *What **are** you **doing** next year?*
 *What **are** you **going to do** next year?*
– *All the family **will be** there.*
 *All the family **are going to be** there.*
– *If your mother comes, you'**ll have** to help with the cooking.*
 *If your mother comes, you'**re going to have** to help with the cooking.*
– *You **won't believe** this.*
 *You'**re not going to believe** this.*
– *Next year **will be** different.*
 *Next year **is going to be** different.*

7 differences

We prefer present tenses when we are talking about future events that have
some *present reality* (see 220). Compare:
> *I'**m seeing** Janet on Tuesday.* (The arrangement exists now.)
> *I wonder if she'**ll recognise** me.* (no present reference)

In predictions, we use *going to* when we have *outside evidence* for what we
say – for example a page in a diary, black clouds in the sky, a person who is
obviously about to fall. We prefer *will* for predictions when there is not such
obvious outside evidence – when we are talking more about what is inside
our heads: what we know, or believe, or have calculated. (When we use *will*,
we are not *showing* the listener something; we are asking him or her to
believe something.) Compare:
– *Look out – we'**re going to crash**!* (There is outside evidence.)
 *Don't lend him your car. He's a terrible driver – he'**ll crash** it.*
  (the speaker's knowledge)
– *I've just heard from the builder. That roof repair'**s going to cost** £7,000.*
  (outside evidence – the builder's letter)
 *I reckon it'**ll cost** about £3,000 to put in new lights.* (the speaker's opinion)
– *Alice **is going to have** a baby.* (outside evidence – she is pregnant now)
 *The baby **will** certainly **have** blue eyes, because both parents have.*
  (speaker's knowledge about genetics)

8 other uses of *shall* and *will*

Shall and *will* are not only used to give and ask for information about the
future. They can also be used to express 'interpersonal' meanings such as
requests, offers, orders, threats and promises. For details, see 222.
> ***Shall** I **open** a window?*
> ***Will** you **get** here at nine tomorrow, please?*
> *I'**ll break** his neck!*

9 *will you …?*

With a verb referring to a state, *will you … ?* asks for information.
> *How soon **will you know** your holiday dates?*
> ***Will you be** here next week?*

With a verb referring to an action, ***will you* + infinitive** usually introduces an order or request (see 222.5).

> ***Will you do** the shopping this afternoon, please?*

To ask for information about people's plans, we use a present tense (see 220) or the future progressive (see 225).

> ***Are you doing** the shopping this afternoon?*
> ***Will you be doing** the shopping . . . ?*

For *This is the last time I'll* . . . and similar structures, see 307.5.

222 future (4): shall and will (interpersonal uses)

1 differences between *shall* and *will*

Shall and *will* are not only used for giving information about the future. They are also common in offers, promises, orders and similar kinds of 'interpersonal' language use. In these cases, *will* (or *'ll*) generally expresses willingness, wishes or strong intentions (this is connected with an older use of *will* to mean 'wish' or 'want'). *Shall* expresses obligation (like a more direct form of *should*).

2 announcing decisions: *will*

We often use *will* when we tell people about a decision as we make it, for instance if we are agreeing to do something.

> *OK. We**'ll buy** the tickets if you**'ll buy** supper after the show.*
> *'The phone's ringing.' 'I**'ll answer** it.'* (NOT ~~'I'm going to answer it.'~~)
> *'Remember to phone Joe, **won't** you?' 'Yes, I **will**.'*

Shall is not used in this way.

> *'You can have it for £50.' 'OK. I**'ll buy** it.'* (NOT *'. . . I **shall buy** it.'*)

Note that the simple present is not normally used to announce decisions.

> *I think I**'ll go** to bed.* (NOT ~~I think I go to bed.~~)
> *'There's the doorbell.' 'I**'ll go**.'* (NOT *. . . ~~I go.~~'*)

To announce decisions that have already been made, we generally prefer the present progressive or *going to* (see 220).

> *Well, we've agreed on a price, and I**'m going to** buy it.*

Stressed *will* can express a strong intention.

> *I **will** stop smoking! I really **will**!*

3 refusals: *won't*

Will not or *won't* is used to refuse, or to talk about refusals.

> *I don't care what you say, I **won't do** it.*
> *The car **won't start**.*

I shan't (British only) is also sometimes used in refusals, but this is unusual in modern English.

▶

4 asking for instructions and decisions: *shall*

Questions with *shall I/we* are used (especially in British English) to ask for instructions or decisions, to offer services, and to make suggestions. *Will* is not used in this way.

>*Shall I open a window?* (NOT ~~Will I open a window?~~)
>*Shall I carry your bag?*
>*What time shall we come and see you?*
>*What on earth shall we do?*
>*Shall we go out for a meal?*
>*Let's go and see Lucy, shall we?*

5 giving instructions and orders: *will*

We can use *Will you . . . ?* to tell or ask people to do things. (In polite requests, *Would you . . . ?* is preferred – see 604.5.)

>*Will you get me a newspaper when you're out?*
>*Will you be quiet, please!*
>*Make me a cup of coffee, will you?*

6 threats and promises: *will*

We often use *will/'ll* in threats and promises. *Shall* is also possible in British English, especially after *I* and *we*, but it is less common than *will*.

>*I'll hit you if you do that again.*   *You'll suffer for this!*
>*I promise I won't smoke again.* (NOT ~~I promise I don't smoke~~...)
>*I shall give you a teddy bear for your birthday.*
>*I'll phone you tonight.* (NOT ~~I phone~~...)

In older English, *shall* was often used with second and third person subjects in threats and promises. This is now very unusual.

>*You shall have all you wish for.*   *He shall regret this.*

7 obligation: *shall*

In contracts and other legal documents, *shall* is often used with third-person subjects to refer to obligations and duties.

>*The hirer shall be responsible for maintenance of the vehicle.*

In other cases, we prefer *must* or *should* to express ideas of this kind.

For details of structures used in requests, see 483.
For reporting of interpersonal *will* and *shall* in indirect speech, see 481.7.

223 future (5): simple present

1 timetables etc

We can sometimes use the simple present to talk about the future. This is common when we are talking about events which are part of a timetable or something similar.

>*The summer term starts on April 10th.*
>*What time does the bus arrive in Seattle?*
>*My plane is at three o'clock.*
>*Are you on duty next weekend?*

2   subordinate clauses

The simple present is often used with a future meaning in subordinate clauses – for example after *what, where, when, until, if, than*. For details, see 556.

> *I'll tell you what I **find** out.* (NOT ...*what I'll find out.*)
> *She'll pay us back when she **gets** a job.* (NOT ...*when she'll get a job.*)

3   other cases

In other cases, we do not usually use the simple present to talk about the future.

> *Lucy **'s coming** for a drink this evening.* (NOT *Lucy comes...*)
> *I promise I**'ll phone** you this evening.*
>   (NOT *I promise I phone you this evening.*)
> *'There's the doorbell.' 'I**'ll go**.'* (NOT ...*'I go.'*)

Occasionally the simple present is used with a future meaning when giving and asking for instructions.

> *So when you get to London you **go** straight to Victoria Station, you **meet** up with the others, you **get** your ticket from Ramona and you **catch** the 17.15 train for Dover. OK?*
> *Well, what **do** we **do** now?   Where **do** I **pay**?*

224   **future** (6): future perfect

> *shall/will have* + past participle

We can use the future perfect to say that something will have been done, completed or achieved by a certain time in the future. (For the exact meaning of *by* in this case, see 118.)

> *By next Christmas we**'ll have been** here for eight years.*
> *The builders say they**'ll have finished** the roof by Tuesday.*

A progressive form can be used if we want to emphasise the continuity of a future achievement.

> *I**'ll have been teaching** for twenty years this summer.*
>   (OR *I'll have taught...*)

We can also use *will have...* to 'predict the present' (see 221.4) – to say what we think or guess has probably happened.

> *It's no use phoning – he**'ll have left** by now.*

For more about perfect forms, see 423.
For more about progressive forms, see 450.

225 **future** (7): future progressive

> *shall/will + be + …ing*

1 events in progress in the future

We can use the future progressive to say that something will be in progress
(going on) at a particular moment in the future.

> *This time tomorrow I'll **be lying** on the beach.*
> *Good luck with the exam. We'll **be thinking** of you.*

The future progressive is also used (without a progressive meaning) to refer
to future events which are fixed or decided, or which are expected to happen
in the normal course of events. It does not suggest the idea of personal
intention.

> *Professor Baxter **will be giving** another lecture on Roman glass-making at
> the same time next week.*
> *You'll **be hearing** from my solicitors.*
> *I'll **be seeing** you one of these days, I expect.*

2 'predicting the present'

This tense can also be used to 'predict the present' (see 221.4) – to say what
we think or guess is probably happening now.

> *Don't phone now – they'll **be having** lunch.*

3 polite enquiries

The future progressive can be used to make polite enquiries about people's
plans. (By using this tense to ask 'What have you already decided?', the
speaker shows that he / she does not want to influence the listener's
intentions.) Compare:

> ***Will** you **be staying** in this evening?*
> (very polite enquiry, suggesting 'I simply want to know your plans')
> ***Are** you **going to stay** in this evening? (pressing for a decision)*
> ***Will** you **stay** in this evening, please? (instruction or order)*

In older English, ***Shall you** + **infinitive*** was used to make polite enquiries in
this way.

4 progressive form with *going to*

A progressive form of the *going to* structure is also possible.

> *I'm **going to be working** all day tomorrow, so I won't have time to shop.*

For more about the use of progressive forms for polite 'distancing', see 161.
For progressive forms in general, see 450.

226 **future** (8): future in the past

Sometimes when we are talking about the past, we want to talk about
something which *was* in the future at that time – which had not yet
happened. To express this idea, we use the structures that are normally used
to talk about the future (see 219–225), but we make the verb forms past. For

example, instead of *is going to* we use *was going to*; instead of the present progressive we use the past progressive; instead of *will* we use *would*; instead of *is to* we use *was to*.

> Last time I saw you, you **were going to** start a new job.
> I didn't have much time to talk to her because I **was leaving** for Germany in two hours.
> In 1968 I arrived in the town where I **would** spend the next ten years of my life.
> I went to have a look at the room where I **was to** talk that afternoon.

Perfect forms of *be going to* are also possible.

> **I've been going to write** to you for ages, but I've only just found time.

For *was to* + perfect infinitive (e.g. *She **was to have taken** over my job, but she fell ill*), see 90.1.

227 **gender** (references to males and females)

English does not have many problems of grammatical gender. Usually, people are *he* or *she* and things are *it*. Note the following points.

1 animals, cars, ships and countries

People sometimes call animals *he* or *she*, especially when they are thought of as having personality, intelligence or feelings. This is common with pets and domestic animals like cats, dogs and horses.

> Once upon a time there was a rabbit called Joe. **He** lived …
> Go and find the cat and put **her** out.

He is sometimes used in cases where the sex of an animal is not known.

> Look at the little frog, darling. Isn't **he** sweet?

Some people use *she* for cars, motorbikes etc; sailors often use *she* for boats and ships (but most other people use *it*).

> 'How's your new car?' 'Terrific. **She's** running beautifully.'
> The ship's struck a rock. **She's** sinking!

We can use *she* for countries, but *it* is more common in modern English.

> France has decided to increase **its** trade with Romania.
> (OR … **her** trade …)

2 *he or she*

Traditionally, English has used *he* in cases where the sex of a person is not known, or in references that can apply to either men or women, especially in a formal style.

> If I ever find the person who did that, I'll kill **him**.
> If a student is ill, **he** must send **his** medical certificate to the College office.
> A doctor can't do a good job if **he** doesn't like people.

Many people now regard such usage as sexist and try to avoid it. The expression *he or she* is becoming increasingly common.

> If a student is ill, **he or she** must send a medical certificate to the College office.

▶

3 unisex *they*

In an informal style, we often use *they* to mean 'he or she', especially after indefinite words like *somebody, anybody, nobody, person*. This usage is sometimes considered 'incorrect', but it has been common in educated speech for centuries.

> *If anybody wants my ticket **they** can have it.*
> *'There's somebody at the door.' 'Tell **them** I'm out.'*
> *When a person gets married, **they** have to start thinking about **their** responsibilities.*
> *God send everyone **their** heart's desire.* (Shakespeare)

For more details of this structure, see 505.

4 *actor* and *actress* etc

A few jobs and positions have different words for men and women. Examples:

Man	Woman
actor	*actress*
(bride)groom	*bride*
duke	*duchess*
hero	*heroine*
host	*hostess*
monk	*nun*
policeman	*policewoman*
prince	*princess*
waiter	*waitress*
widower	*widow*

A *mayor* can be a man or a woman; in Britain a *mayoress* is the wife of a male mayor.

Some words ending in *-ess* (e.g. *authoress, poetess*) have gone out of use (*author* and *poet* are now used for both men and women). *Steward* and *stewardess* are being replaced by other terms such as *flight attendant*.

5 words ending in *-man*

Some words ending in *-man* do not have a common feminine equivalent (e.g. *chairman, fireman, spokesman*). As many women dislike being called, for example, 'chairman' or 'spokesman', these words are now often avoided in references to women or in general references to people of either sex. In many cases, *-person* is now used instead of *-man*.

> *Alice has just been elected **chairperson** (or **chair**) of our committee.*
> *A **spokesperson** said that the Minister does not intend to resign.*

In some cases, new words ending in *-woman* (e.g. *spokeswoman*) are coming into use. But there is also a move to choose words, even for men, which are not gender-marked (e.g. *supervisor* instead of *foreman, ambulance staff* instead of *ambulance men, firefighter* instead of *fireman*).

6 *man*

Man and *mankind* have traditionally been used to refer to the whole of the human race.

> *Why does **man** have more diseases than animals?*
> *That's one small step for a man, one giant leap for **mankind**.*
> (Neil Armstrong, on stepping onto the moon)

Some people find this usage sexist, and prefer to avoid it by using terms such as *people, humanity* or *the human race*. Note also the increasingly common use of *synthetic fibres* instead of *man-made fibres*.

7 titles

Ms (pronounced /mɪz/ or /məz/) is often used instead of *Mrs* or *Miss*. Like *Mr*, it does not show whether the person referred to is married or not.

For more information about names and titles, see 353.

228 get

Get is one of the commonest words in English, and is used in many different ways. It is sometimes avoided in a very formal style, but it is correct and natural in most kinds of speech and writing. The meaning of *get* depends on what kind of word comes after it. With a direct object, the basic meaning is 'come to have'; with other kinds of word, the basic meaning is 'come to be'.

1 *get* + noun/pronoun

With a direct object (noun or pronoun), *get* usually means 'receive', 'fetch', 'obtain', 'catch' or something similar.

> *I **got a letter** from Lucy this morning.*
> *Can you come and **get me** from the station when I arrive?*
> *If I listen to loud music I **get a headache**.*
> *If you **get a number 6 bus**, it stops right outside our house.*

Get can be used with two objects (see 583).

> *Let me **get you a drink**.*

Other meanings are sometimes possible.

> *I didn't **get the joke**. (= 'understand')*
> *I'll **get you** for this, you bastard. (= 'punish, make suffer')*

Could I get . . . ? is not generally used to order things. Compare:

> *Could I **have** a coffee? (= Please bring me one.)*
> *Could I **get** a coffee? (= Could I make/buy myself one?)*

***Get* + noun/pronoun** is not normally used to mean 'become'. *Get to be . . .* is common with this meaning (see paragraph 6, below).

> *Wayne's **getting to be** a lovely kid.* (NOT *Wayne's getting a lovely kid.*)

2 *get* + adjective

Before an adjective, *get* usually means 'become'.

> *As you **get old**, your memory **gets worse**.*
> *My feet are **getting** cold.*

▶

With **object + adjective**, the meaning is 'make something/somebody become'.

> *I can't **get my hands warm**.*
> *We must **get the house clean** before Mother arrives.*
> *It's time to **get the kids ready** for school.*

For **go + adjective** (*go green*, *go blind* etc), and the differences between *get*, *go*, *become*, *turn* etc, see 129.

3 *get* + adverb particle or preposition

Before an adverb particle (like *up*, *away*, *out*) or a preposition, *get* nearly always refers to a movement of some kind. (For the difference between *get* and *go*, see 229.)

> *I often **get up** at five o'clock.*
> *I went to see him, but he told me to **get out**.*
> *Would you mind **getting off** my foot?*

In some idioms the meaning is different – e.g. *get to a place* (= *arrive at . . .*); *get over something* (= *recover from*); *get on with somebody*.

With an object, the structure usually means 'make somebody/something move'.

> *You can't **get him out of** bed in the morning.*
> *Would you mind **getting your papers off** my desk?*
> *Have you ever tried to **get toothpaste back** into the tube?*
> *The car's OK – it **gets me from** A to B.*

4 *get* + past participle

Get can be used with a past participle. This structure often has a reflexive meaning, to talk about things that we 'do to ourselves'. Common expressions are *get washed*, *get dressed*, *get lost*, *get drowned*, *get engaged/married/divorced*.

> *You've got five minutes to **get dressed**.*
> *She's **getting married** in June.*

Get + past participle is also used to make passive structures, in the same way as **be + past participle**.

> *My watch **got broken** while I was playing with the children.*
> *He **got caught** by the police driving at 120 mph.*
> *I never **get invited** to parties.*

This structure is less often used to talk about longer, more deliberate, planned actions.

> *Our house **was built** in 1827.* (NOT *~~Our house got built in 1827.~~*)
> *Parliament **was opened** on Thursday.* (NOT *~~Parliament got opened . . .~~*)

5 *get* + object + past participle

This structure can be used to mean 'finish doing something'. The past participle has a passive meaning.

> *It will take me another hour to **get the washing done**.*
> *After you've **got the children dressed**, can you make the beds?*

Another meaning is 'arrange for something to be done by somebody else'.

> *I must **get my hair cut**.   You ought to **get your watch repaired**.*

We can also use the structure to talk about things that happen to us. In this case, *get* means 'experience'.

> *We **got our roof blown off** in the storm last week.*
> *I **got my car stolen** twice last year.*

For the use of *have* in a similar structure, see 242.

6 *get ...ing*; *get* + **infinitive**

Get ...ing is sometimes used informally to mean 'start ...ing', especially in the expressions *get moving, get going.*

> *We'd better **get moving** – it's late.*

With an object, the structure means 'make somebody/something start ...ing'.

> *Don't **get him talking** about his illnesses.*
> *Once we **got the heater going** the car started to warm up.*

With an infinitive, *get* can mean 'manage', 'have an opportunity' or 'be allowed'.

> *We didn't **get to see** her – she was too busy.*
> *When do I **get to see** your new baby?*

There is often an idea of gradual development.

> *He's nice when you **get to know** him.*
> *You'll **get to speak** English more easily as time goes by.*
> *Wayne's **getting to be** a lovely kid.*

With an object, the infinitive structure means 'make somebody/something do something' or 'persuade somebody/something to do something': there is often an idea of difficulty.

> *I can't **get that child to go** to bed.*   ***Get Penny to help*** *us if you can.*
> *See if you can **get the car to start**.*

For similar structures with ***have* + object + verb form**, see 242.

7 *got* and *gotten*

In American English the past participle of *get* is *gotten*, except in the structure *have got* (see 241).

229 **get** and **go** (movement)

Go is used to talk about a whole movement.
Get is used when we are thinking mainly about the end of a movement – the arrival. Compare:

– *I **go** to work by car and Lucy **goes** by train.*
   *I usually **get** there first.*
– *I **went** to a meeting in Bristol yesterday.*
   *I **got** to the meeting at about eight o'clock.*

We often use *get* to suggest that there is some difficulty in arriving.

> *It wasn't easy to **get** through the crowd.*
> *I don't know how we're going to **get** over the river.*
> *Can you tell me how to **get** to the police station?*

For other uses of *get*, see 228.
For *get* and *go* meaning 'become', see 129.

230 **give** with action-nouns

We often replace certain verbs by a structure with *give* and a noun. This happens, for example, with some verbs referring to sounds made by people (e.g. *cough, cry, scream, chuckle, laugh, shout*).

> He **gave a cough** to attract my attention.
> Suddenly she **gave a loud scream** and fell to the ground.

The structure can be used with an indirect object (e.g. *She gave **me** a smile*). This often happens in an informal style to replace transitive verbs like *push, kick, clean.*

> If the car won't start, we'll **give it a push**.
> If something doesn't work, I usually **give it a kick**.
> Could you **give the carpet a clean**?

Examples of other common expressions:

> 'Perhaps salt will make it taste better.' 'OK, let's **give it a try**.'
> I'll **give you a ring** if I hear anything. (GB)
> 'Are you coming to the film?' 'No, I'm tired. I'll **give it a miss**.' (GB)

For taboo expressions like *I don't give a damn*, see 550.
For other structures in which nouns replace verbs, see 573.
For more about structures with *give*, see 583.

231 go/come for a . . .

We can use the structure *go/come for a . . .* in some common fixed expressions referring to actions, mostly leisure activities. Using this structure makes the action sound casual and probably rather short. (Compare *go . . . ing* – see 232.) Common examples:

> *go/come for a walk/run/swim/ride/drive/sail/drink*

Note also the expressions *go for a bath/shower, go for a pee/piss/crap/shit* (taboo – see 550).

This structure is only used with particular action-nouns – we would probably not say, for example, *Come for a ski with us* or *I'm going for a read*.

For other structures in which nouns are used to refer to actions, see 573.

232 go/come . . . ing

1 *go . . . ing*

We use *go* with an *-ing* form in a number of common expressions, mostly referring to sporting and leisure activities.

> Let's **go climbing** next weekend.
> Did you **go dancing** last Saturday?

Common expressions:

> *go: climbing, dancing, fishing, hunting, riding, sailing, shooting, shopping, skating, skiing, swimming, walking*

2   *come...ing*

Come...ing is also possible in certain situations (for the difference between *come* and *go*, see 134).

Come swimming *with us tomorrow.*

3   **prepositions**

Note that prepositions of place, not direction, are used after *go/come...ing*.

*I went swimming **in** the river.* (NOT ~~I went swimming **to** the river.~~)
*She went shopping **at** Harrods.* (NOT ...~~**to** Harrods.~~)
*It's dangerous to go skating **on** the lake.* (NOT ...~~**to** the lake.~~)

For *go for a...*, see 231.

233   **gone** with **be**

Gone can be used like an adjective after *be*, to say that somebody is away, or that something has disappeared or that there is no more.

*She's **been gone** for three hours – what do you think she's doing?*
*You can go out shopping, but don't **be gone** too long.*
*When I came back my car **was gone**.*
*Is the butter all **gone**?*

For *be* with *finished*, see 211.
For *been* used as a past participle of *go* or *come*, see 94.

234   **had better**

1   **meaning**

We use *had better* to give strong advice, or to tell people what to do (including ourselves).

*You'**d better** turn that music down before your Dad gets angry.*
*It's seven o'clock. I'**d better** put the meat in the oven.*

Had better may suggest a threat. It is not used in polite requests. Compare:

Could you help me, if you've got time? (request)
*You'**d better** help me. If you don't, there'll be trouble.* (order / threat)

Had better refers to the immediate future. It is more urgent than *should* or *ought*. Compare:

*'I really **ought** to go and see Fred one of these days.' 'Well, you'**d better** do it soon – he's leaving for South Africa at the end of the month.'*

Note that *had better* does not usually suggest that the action recommended would be better than another one that is being considered – there is no idea of comparison. The structure means 'It would be good to ...', not 'It would be better to ...'.

▶

2 forms

Had better refers to the immediate future, but the form is always past
(*have better* is impossible). After *had better* we use the infinitive without *to*.

> *It's late – you **had better hurry** up.*
>> (NOT *...~~you **have better**~~...*)
>> (NOT *~~You had better **hurrying / to hurry**~~...*)

In British English, *better* can come before *had* for emphasis.

> *'I promise I'll pay you back.' 'You **better had**.'*

We normally make the negative with **had better not + infinitive**.

> *You**'d better not wake** me up when you come in.*
>> (*You hadn't better wake me...* is possible but very unusual.)

A negative interrogative form *Hadn't ... better ...?* is possible.

> ***Hadn't** we **better** tell him the truth?*

Normal unemphatic short answer forms are as follows:

> *'Shall I put my clothes away?' 'You**'d better**!'*
> *'He says he won't tell anybody.' 'He**'d better not**.'*

Had is sometimes dropped in very informal speech.

> *You **better** go now.*
> *I **better** try again later.*

235 half

1 *half (of)*

We can use *half* or *half of* before a noun with a determiner (article,
possessive or demonstrative). We do not normally put *a* or *the* before *half*
(but see below).

> *She spends **half (of)** her time travelling.* (NOT *~~She spends **a/the half**~~...*)
> *I gave him **half (of)** a cheese pie to keep him quiet.*

When *half (of)* is followed by a plural noun, the verb is plural.

> ***Half (of)** my friends **live** abroad.* (NOT *~~**Half of my friends lives**~~...*)

Of is not used in expressions of measurement and quantity.

> *I live **half a mile** from here.* (NOT *...~~**half of a mile**~~...*)
> *How much is **half a loaf** of bread?* (NOT *...~~**half of a loaf**~~...*)

We use *half of* before pronouns.

> *'Did you like the books?' 'I've only read **half of them**.'*
> ***Half of us** are free on Tuesdays, and the other half on Thursdays.*

2 no following noun

Half can be used without a following noun, if the meaning is clear.

> *I've bought some chocolate. You can have **half**.*
>> (NOT *...~~You can have **the half**~~.*)

3 *the half*

We use *the* before *half* if we talk about a particular half. In this case, *of* must
be used before a noun.

> *Would you like **the big half** or **the small half**?*
> *I didn't like **the second half** of the film.*

4 *half a* and *a half*

Half usually comes before the article *a/an*, but it is possible to put it after in expressions of measurement.

> *Could I have **half a pound** of grapes?* (OR *... **a half pound** ...*)

We usually say *a half bottle* to refer to a half-sized bottle of wine or spirits.

5 *one and a half*

The expression *one and a half* is plural. Compare:

> *I've been waiting for **one and a half hours**.* (NOT *... ~~one and a half hour~~.*)
> *I've been waiting for **an hour and a half**.*

For more information about numbers and counting expressions, see 385.
For *half two* (= 'half past two'), see 555.

236 happen

Happen can be used with a following infinitive to suggest that something happens unexpectedly or by chance.

> *If you **happen to see** Joan, ask her to phone me.*
> *One day I **happened to get** talking to a woman on a train, and she turned out to be a cousin of my mother's.*

In sentences with *if*, the idea of *by chance* can be emphasised by using *should* before *happen*.

> *Let me know **if** you **should happen to** need any help.*

237 hardly, scarcely and no sooner

These three expressions can be used (often with a past perfect tense) to suggest that one thing happened very soon after another. Note the sentence structure:

> *... hardly ... when/before ...*
> *... scarcely ... when/before ...*
> *... no sooner ... than ...*

> *I had **hardly/scarcely** closed my eyes **when** the phone rang.*
> *She was **hardly/scarcely** inside the house **before** the kids started screaming.*
> *I had **no sooner** closed the door **than** somebody knocked.*
> *We **no sooner** sat down in the train **than** I felt sick.*

In a formal or literary style, these structures are sometimes used with inverted word order (see 298).

> ***Hardly had I** closed my eyes when I began to imagine the most fantastic shapes.*
> ***No sooner had she** agreed to marry him than she started to have terrible doubts.*
> ***No sooner did Steve** start going out with Tracy than she fell in love with Jasper.*

For the difference between *hard* and *hardly*, see 21.
For *hardly any* etc, see 41.3.
For the use of the past perfect tenses, see 421.

238   have (1): introduction

Have is used in several different ways:

a   as an auxiliary verb
   Have *you heard about Peter and Corinne?*

b   to talk about possession, relationships and other states
   *They **have** three cars.*
   ***Have** you got any brothers or sisters?*
   *Do you often **have** headaches?*

c   to talk about actions and experiences
   *I'm going to **have** a bath.*
   *We're **having** a party next weekend.*

d   with an infinitive, to talk about obligation (like *must*)
   *I **had to work** last Saturday.*

e   with **object + verb form**, to talk about causing or experiencing actions and events
   *He soon **had everybody laughing**.*
   *I must **have my shoes repaired**.*
   *We **had our car stolen** last week.*

For details of the different structures and meanings, see the following sections.

For contractions (*I've, haven't* etc), see 144.
For weak forms, see 588.
For ***had better* + infinitive**, see 234.

239   have (2): auxiliary verb

have + past participle

1   perfect verb forms

We use *have* as an auxiliary verb with past participles, to make 'perfect' verb forms.
   *You**'ve heard** about Peter and Corinne?* (present perfect: see 418–420)
   *I realised that I **had met** him before.* (past perfect: see 421)
   *We**'ll have been living** here for two years next Sunday.*
      (future perfect: see 224)
   *I'd like **to have lived** in the eighteenth century.*
      (perfect infinitive: see 276)
   ***Having been** there before, he knew what to expect.*
      (perfect participle: see 403.1)

2 questions and negatives

Like all auxiliary verbs, *have* makes questions and negatives without *do*.

Have you heard the news? (NOT *Do you have heard . . . ?*)

I **haven't seen** them. (NOT *I don't have seen them.*)

3 progressive forms

There are no progressive forms of the auxiliary verb *have*.

I **haven't** seen her anywhere. (NOT *I'm not having seen her anywhere.*)

For contractions, see 144.
For weak forms, see 588.

240 **have** (3): actions

1 meaning and typical expressions

We often use **have + object** to talk about actions and experiences, especially in an informal style.

Let's **have a drink**.   I'm going to **have a bath**.

I'll **have a think** and let you know what I decide.   **Have** a good time.

In expressions like these, *have* can be the equivalent of 'eat', 'drink', 'enjoy', 'experience' or many other things – the exact meaning depends on the following noun. Common expressions:

have breakfast / lunch / supper / dinner / tea / coffee / a drink / a meal

have a bath / a wash / a shave / a shower

have a rest / a lie-down / a sleep / a dream

have a good time / a bad day / a nice evening / a day off / a holiday

have a good journey / flight / trip etc

have a talk / a chat / a word with somebody / a conversation /
    a disagreement / a row / a quarrel / a fight

have a swim / a walk / a ride / a dance / a game of tennis etc

have a try / a go

have a look

have a baby (= 'give birth')

have difficulty / trouble (in) . . .ing

have an accident / an operation / a nervous breakdown

(Note American English **take** a bath/shower/rest/swim/walk.)

Have can also be used to mean 'receive' (e.g. I've **had** a phone call from Sue). And *won't have* can mean *won't allow* (e.g. I **won't have** her boyfriend in my house).

2 grammar

In this structure, we make questions and negatives with *do*. *Got* is not used. Progressive forms are possible. Contractions and weak forms of *have* are not used.

Did you **have** a good holiday? (NOT *Had you a good holiday?*)

'What are you doing?' 'I'**m having** a bath.'

I **have** lunch at 12.30 most days. (NOT *I've lunch . . .*)

For other common structures in which nouns are used to talk about actions, see 573.

241 have (4): **have (got)** – possession, relationships and other states

1 meanings

We often use *have* to talk about states: possession, relationships, illnesses, the characteristics of people and things, and similar ideas.

*Her father **has** a flat in Westminster.*
*They hardly **have** enough money to live on.*
***Have** you any brothers or sisters?*
*The Prime Minister **has** a bad cold.*
*My grandmother didn't **have** a very nice personality.*
*The house **has** got a wonderful atmosphere.*

Sometimes *have* simply expresses the fact of being in a particular situation.

*She **has** a houseful of children this weekend.*
*I think we **have** mice.*

2 short and long forms

Instead of the short forms *I have, you have* etc, we can use longer forms made by adding *got*. The short question and negative forms *have I?* etc and *I have not* etc are often avoided (and are not normally used in American English); instead, we use longer forms with *got* or *do*. *Got*-forms are especially common in an informal style.

*I've **got** a new boyfriend.* (More natural than *I **have** a new boyfriend.*)
***Has** your sister **got** a car?* OR ***Does** your sister **have** a car?*
  (More natural than ***Has** your sister a car?*)
*I **haven't got** your keys.* (More natural than *I **haven't** your keys.*)
*The school **does not have** adequate sports facilities.* (More natural than
  *The school **has not** adequate sports facilities.*)

3 *have got* (details)

Note that *have got* means exactly the same as *have* in this case – it is a present tense of *have*, not the present perfect of *get*. *Got*-forms of *have* are informal, and are most common in the present. *Do* is not used in questions and negatives with *got*.

*I've **got** a new car.*
*My mother**'s got** two sisters.*
***Have** you **got** a headache?*
*It's a nice flat, but it **hasn't got** a proper bathroom.*
*I've **got** an appointment with Mr Lewis at ten o'clock.*

Got-forms of *have* are not used in short answers or tags.

*'Have you got a light?' 'No, I **haven't**.'*
*Anne's got a bike, **hasn't** she?*

Got-forms of *have* are less common in the past tense.

*I **had** flu last week.* (NOT *I had got flu...*)
***Did** you **have** good teachers when you were at school?*

Got is not generally used with infinitives, participles or *-ing* forms of *have*: you cannot usually say *to have got a headache* or *having got a brother*. *Got*-infinitives are sometimes possible after modal verbs (e.g. *She **must have got** a new boyfriend*).

4 repetition and habit

When we are talking about repeated states, *got*-forms of *have* are less often used; *do* is normally used in questions and negatives. Compare:
– *I've got* toothache.
   I often have toothache.
– *Have you got* time to go to London this weekend?
   Do you ever have time to go to London?
– *Sorry, I haven't got* any beer.
   We don't usually have beer in the house.

5 progressive forms, weak forms and contractions

Progressive forms of *have* are not used with these 'state' meanings.
   I have (got) a headache. (NOT ~~I am having a headache.~~)
Contractions and weak forms (see 588) are used before *got*. In British English, contractions are also possible before nouns with determiners like *a/an, some, any, no, every*.
   I've got a problem.
   We've some tickets for the opera, if you're interested. (GB)
   I've no idea. (GB)
   She's every chance of a gold medal. (GB)

6 British-American differences

Traditionally, *do*-forms of *have* have been used in British English mostly to express habit or repetition. Compare (GB):
   Do you often have meetings?
   Have you got a meeting today?
In American English, *do*-forms are not limited in this way. Compare (US):
   Do you often have meetings?
   Do you have a meeting today? (OR *Have you got a meeting today?*)
In modern British English (which is heavily influenced by American English), *do*-forms are common even when there is no idea of repetition.
   Do you have time to go to the beach this weekend? (US / modern GB)
In British English, short question and negative forms of *have* are possible, though these are often formal. They are not used in American English. Compare:
– *Have you an appointment?* (formal GB only)
   Do you have an appointment? (US / GB)
– *Birmingham has not the charm of York or Edinburgh.* (formal GB only)
   Birmingham does not have the charm . . . (US / GB)
Contracted short forms of *have* are used only in British English. Compare:
   We've a swimming pool in the village. (GB only)
   We have / We've got a swimming pool . . . (US / GB)
In very informal American speech, people may drop *'ve* (but not *'s*) before *got.*
   I('ve) got a problem.
Got- and *do*-forms may be mixed in American English, especially when short answers, reply questions and tags follow *got*-forms.
   'I've got a new apartment.' 'You do?'
   I don't think we've got any choice, do we?

242 have (5): + object + verb form

Have can be followed by **object + infinitive (without *to*)**, **object + -ing**, and **object + past participle**.

1 *have* + object + infinitive/-*ing* form

In this structure, *have* often means 'experience'. The usage is rather informal.

*I **had a very strange thing happen** to me when I was fourteen.*
*We **had a gipsy come** to the door yesterday.*
*It's lovely to **have children playing** in the garden again.*
*I looked up and found we **had water dripping** through the ceiling.*

Note the difference between the infinitive in the first two examples (for things that **happen(ed)**), and the *-ing* form in the last two (for things that **are/were happening**). This is like the difference between the simple and progressive past tenses (see 417).

Another meaning is 'cause somebody/something to do something'.

*He **had us laughing** all through the meal.*
*We'll soon **have your car going**.*

The infinitive structure is not common in British English with this meaning. It is used in American English to talk about giving instructions or orders.

*I'm ready to see Mr Smith. **Have him come in**, please.*
*The manager **had everybody fill out** a form.*

I won't have + **object** + *-ing* **form** can mean 'I won't allow ...'

*I **won't have you telling** me what to do.*

2 *have* + object + past participle

This structure can be used to talk about arranging for things to be done by other people. The past participle has a passive meaning.

*I must **have my watch repaired**. (= I want my watch **to be repaired**.)*
*If you don't get out of my house I'll **have you arrested**.*

Another meaning is 'experience'. Again, the past participle has a passive meaning.

*We **had our roof blown off** in the storm.*
*King Charles I **had his head cut off**.*

I won't have ... (= 'I won't allow ...') can be followed by **object + past participle**.

*I **won't have my house turned** into a hotel.*

For similar structures with *get*, see 228.5.

243 have (6): have (got) to

1 meaning

We can use *have (got)* + **infinitive** to talk about obligation. The meaning is quite similar to *must*; for the differences, see 352.

*Sorry, I've **got to go** now.*
*Do you often **have to travel** on business?*

Have (got) + **infinitive** can also be used, like *must*, to express certainty. (This used to be mainly an American English structure, but it is now becoming common in British English.)

> *I don't believe you. You **have (got) to be** joking.*
> *Only five o'clock! It's **got to be** later than that!*

2 grammar

In this structure, *have* can be used like an ordinary verb (with *do* in questions and negatives), or like an auxiliary verb (without *do*). *Got* is usually added to present-tense auxiliary-verb forms.

> *When **do you have to be** back?*
> *When **have you (got) to be** back?*

Have got to is not normally used to talk about repeated obligation.

> *I usually **have to get** to work at eight.* (NOT *I've usually got to . . .*)

Progressive forms are possible to talk about temporary continued obligation.

> *I'm **having to work** very hard at the moment.*

For more details of the use of *do*-forms and *got*-forms of *have*, see 241.

3 future obligation

To talk about the future, we can use *have (got) to* if an obligation exists now; we use *will have to* for a purely future obligation. Compare:

> *I've **got to get up** early tomorrow – we're going to Devon.*
> *One day everybody **will have to get** permission to buy a car.*

Will have to can be used to tell people what to do. It 'distances' the instructions, making them sound less direct than *must* (see 352).

> *You can borrow my car, but **you'll have to bring** it back before ten.*

For more about 'distancing', see 161.

4 pronunciation; *gotta*

Have to is often pronounced /ˈhæftə/.

> *He'll **have to** /ˈhæftə/ get a new passport soon.*

Note the spelling *gotta*, sometimes used in informal American English (for instance in strip cartoons) to show the conversational pronunciation of *got to*.

> *I **gotta** call home.*
> *A man's **gotta** do what a man's **gotta** do.*

244 hear and listen (to)

1 *hear*: meaning

Hear is the ordinary word to say that something 'comes to our ears'.

> *Suddenly I **heard** a strange noise.*
> (NOT *Suddenly I listened to a strange noise.*)
> *Can you **hear** me?*

2 *listen (to)*: meaning

Listen (to) is used to talk about **paying attention** to sounds that are **going on**, in progress. It emphasises the idea of concentrating, trying to hear as well as possible. You can *hear* something without wanting to, but you can only *listen to* something deliberately. Compare:

> I **heard** them talking in the next room, but I didn't really **listen to** what they were saying.
>
> '**Listen** very carefully, please.' 'Could you speak a bit louder? I can't **hear** you very well.'
>
> I didn't **hear** the phone because I was **listening to** the radio.

3 complete experiences: *hear*

Note that *listen (to)* is mostly used to talk about experiences that are going on, in progress. To talk about experiencing the whole of a performance, speech, piece of music, broadcast etc, we generally use *hear*. Compare:

– When she arrived, I was **listening to** a record of Brendel playing Beethoven. (NOT ...*I was hearing*...)

> I once **heard** Brendel play all the Beethoven concertos. (NOT *I once listened to Brendel play*...)

– I wish I had more time to **listen to** the radio. (NOT ...*to hear the radio.*)

> Did you **hear/listen to** the news yesterday?

4 *hear* not used in progressive forms

Hear is not usually used in progressive forms. To say that one hears something at the moment of speaking, *can hear* is often used, especially in British English (see 125).

> I **can hear** somebody coming. (NOT *I am hearing*...)

5 *listen* and *listen to*

When there is no object, *listen* is used without *to*. Compare:

> **Listen!** (NOT *Listen to!*)
>
> **Listen to** me! (NOT *Listen me!*)

There are similar differences between *see*, *look (at)* and *watch*. See 489.
For **hear + object + infinitive/-ing**, see 245.

245 hear, see etc + object + verb form

1 object + infinitive or -*ing* form

Hear, see, watch, notice and similar verbs of perception can be followed by **object + infinitive (without *to*)** or **object + -*ing*** form.

> I **heard him go** down the stairs.
>
> I **heard him going** down the stairs.
>
> (NOT *I heard him went down the stairs.*)

There is often a difference of meaning. We use an infinitive after these verbs to say that we hear or see the whole of an action or event, and we use an -*ing* form to suggest that we hear or see an action or event in progress, going on. Compare:

– I **saw her cross** the road. (= As I looked, she crossed it from one side to the other.)

> I **saw her crossing** the road. (= As I looked, she was crossing it – she was in the middle, on her way across.)

–   I once **heard him give a talk** on Japanese politics.
    As I walked past his room I **heard him talking** on the phone.
–   **Watch me jump** over the stream.
    I like to **watch people walking** in the street.
–   I **heard the bomb explode**. (NOT ~~I heard the bomb exploding.~~)
    I **saw the book lying** on the table. (NOT ~~I saw the book lie~~...)
A progressive form can suggest repetition.
    I saw her **throwing** stones at the other children.
After *can see/hear* (which refer to actions and events that are in progress –
see 125), only the -*ing* structure is used.
    I **could see John getting** on the bus. (NOT ~~I could see John get~~...)
These structures can be used after passive forms of *hear* and *see*. In this case,
the infinitive has *to*.
    He **was** never **heard to say** 'thank you' in his life.
        (NOT ~~He was never heard say~~...)
    Justice must not only be done; it must **be seen to be done**.
    She **was seen walking** away from the accident.
Passive forms of *watch* and *notice* are not used in this way.

2   possessives not used

After these verbs, possessives cannot be used with -*ing* forms.
    I saw **Mary** crossing the road. (NOT ~~I saw Mary's crossing the road.~~)

3   object + past participle

In this structure, the past participle has a passive meaning.
    I **heard my name repeated** several times. (= My name **was repeated**.)
    Have you ever **seen a television thrown** through a window?
The idea of 'action or event in progress' can be given by a progressive form
(*being* + past participle).
    As I **watched the tree being cut** down ...
    I woke up to **hear the bedroom door being opened slowly**.
These structures are not possible after passive forms of *hear* and *see*.

5   *look at*

Look at can be followed by **object + -*ing* form**, and in American English also
by **object + infinitive**.
    Look at him eating!
    Look at him eat! (US)

For more about verbs that can be followed by both infinitives and -*ing* forms, see 296.
For the difference between *hear* and *listen*, see 244.
For *see*, *look* and *watch*, see 489.

246   hear, see etc with that-clause

The present-tense forms *I hear (that)* ... and *I see (that)* ... are often used to
introduce pieces of news which one has heard, read or seen on television.
    I hear (that) Alice is expecting a baby.
    I see (that) the police are going on strike.

▶

Some other verbs can be used like this. Common examples are *understand* and *gather*. These are often used when the speaker or writer is checking information.

> '*I understand* you're moving to a new job.' 'Yes, that's right.'
> '*I gather* you didn't like the party.' 'What makes you say that?'

For cases when *that* can be left out, see 560.

247 help

After *help*, we can use **object + infinitive**.

> Can you **help me to find** my ring? (NOT ~~Can you **help me finding** my ring?~~)
> Thank you so much for **helping us to repair** the car.

We often use the infinitive without *to*; in British English, this is rather informal.

> Can you **help me find** my ring?　　**Help me get** him to bed.

Help can also be followed directly by an infinitive without an object.

> Would you like to **help wash up**?

For the expression *can't help . . . ing*, see 126.

248 here and there

We use *here* for the place where the speaker/writer is, and *there* for other places.

> (on the telephone) 'Hello, is Tom **there**?' 'No, I'm sorry, he's not **here**.'
>   (NOT . . . ~~he's not **there**.~~)
> Don't stay **there** in the corner by yourself. Come over **here** and talk to us.
> (in a letter) I hope you're enjoying yourself over **there** in the sun. But I wish
>   you were **here** with me.

Note that *here* and *there* cannot normally be used as nouns.

> **This place** is terrible.　　**It** is terrible **here**.
> BUT NOT ~~**Here** is terrible.~~
> Did you like **that place**?
> BUT NOT ~~Did you like **there**?~~

There are similar differences between *this* and *that* (see 565), *come* and *go* (see 134) and
  bring and *take* (see 112).
For *here's* and *there's* followed by plural nouns, see 509.4.
For inverted word order after *here* and *there*, see 444.6.
For *Here you are*, see 520.18.

249 high and tall

1 What kind of things are *tall*?

We use *tall* mostly for people, trees, buildings with many floors, and a few other things which are higher than they are wide (e.g. factory chimneys or electricity pylons).

> How **tall** are you? (NOT ~~How **high** are you?~~)
> There are some beautiful **tall** trees at the end of our garden.
> I'd like something cool to drink in a **tall** glass.

In other cases we usually prefer *high*.
>*Mount Elbruz is the **highest** mountain in Europe.*
>*The garden's got very **high** walls.*

2   measurements

In measurements, we use *tall* for people, but we often use *high* for things. Compare:
>*I'm six feet **tall**.*
>*That tree is about eighty feet **high/tall**.*

3   distance above the ground

We use *high*, not *tall*, to talk about distance above the ground. A child standing on a chair may be *higher* than her mother, although she is probably not *taller*.
>*That shelf is too **high** for me to reach.*
>*The clouds are very **high** today.*

4   parts of the body

Parts of the body can be *long*, but not *tall*.
>*Alex has got beautiful **long** legs.* (NOT ...~~tall legs.~~)

For *big*, *great* and *large*, see 105.

250   holiday and holidays

In British English, the plural *holidays* is often used for the 'big holiday' of the year. In other cases we normally use the singular *holiday*. Compare:
>*Where are you going for your summer **holiday(s)**?*
>*We get five days' Christmas **holiday** this year.*
>*Next Monday is a public **holiday**.*

The singular is used in the British expression *on holiday* (note the preposition).
>*I met Marianne **on holiday** in Norway.* (NOT ...~~on/in holidays~~...)

Americans normally use the word *vacation*. (In British English, *vacation* is mainly used for the periods when universities are not teaching.) *Holiday* is used in American English for a day of publicly observed celebration (such as Thanksgiving), whether or not people work on it.

251   home

1   articles and prepositions

No article is used in the expression *at home* (meaning 'in one's own place').
>*Is anybody **at home**?* (NOT ...~~at the home?~~)

At is often dropped, especially in American English.
>*Is anybody **home**?*

Home (without *to*) can be used as an adverb referring to direction.
>*I think I'll go **home**.* (NOT ...~~to home.~~)   ▶

There is no special preposition in English to express the idea of being at somebody else's home (like French *chez*, German *bei*, Danish / Swedish / Norwegian *hos* etc). One way of saying this is to use *at* with a possessive.

*We had a great evening **at Philip's**.*

*Ring up and see if Jacqueline is **at the Smiths'**, could you?*

Possessive pronouns cannot be used in this way, though.

*Come round to **my place** for a drink.* (NOT *...to **mine**...*)

2 *house* and *home*

House is an emotionally neutral word: it just refers to a particular type of building. *Home* is used mostly in more personal senses: it is the place that somebody lives in, and can express the idea of emotional attachment to a place. Compare:

*There are some horrible new **houses** in our village.*

*I lived there for six years, but I never really felt it was my **home**.*

252 hope

1 tenses after *hope*

After *I hope*, we often use a present tense with a future meaning.

*I hope she **likes** (= will like) the flowers.*   *I hope the bus **comes** soon.*

For a similar use of present tenses after *bet*, see 102.

2 negative sentences

In negative sentences, we usually put *not* with the verb that comes after *hope*.

*I **hope** she **doesn't wake up**.* (NOT *I **don't hope** she **wakes up.***)

For 'transferred negation' with *think, believe* etc, see 359.

3 special uses of past tenses

We can use *I was hoping...* to introduce a polite request.

*I **was hoping** you could lend me some money.*

I had hoped... is used to talk about hopes that were not realised – hopes for things that did not happen.

*I **had hoped** that Jennifer would become a doctor, but she wasn't good enough at science.*

For more about the use of past tenses in polite requests, see 483.
For *I hope so/not*, see 515.
For the differences between *hope, expect, wait* and *look forward*, see 202.

253 hopefully

One meaning of *hopefully* is 'full of hope', 'hoping'.

*She sat there waiting **hopefully** for the phone to ring.*

Another meaning is 'it is to be hoped that' or 'I hope'. This is a fairly recent use in British English, and some people consider it incorrect.

***Hopefully**, inflation will soon be under control.*

***Hopefully** I'm not disturbing you?*

254 how

1 use and word order

How is used to introduce questions or the answers to questions.
How *did you do it?*   *Tell me* **how** *you did it.*   *I know* **how** *he did it.*

We also use *how* in exclamations. The word order is not the same as in questions: the verb comes after the subject in exclamations. Compare:
- *How cold* **is it***?*
  How cold **it is***!*
- **How do you like** *my hair?*
  How I love *weekends!* (NOT ~~How do I love weekends!~~)
- **How have you** *been?*
  How you've *grown!* (NOT ~~How have you grown!~~)

When *how* is used in an exclamation with an adjective or adverb, this comes immediately after *how*.
    How beautiful *the trees are!* (NOT ~~How the trees are **beautiful**!~~)
    How well *she plays!* (NOT ~~How she plays **well**!~~)

For more information about exclamations, see 201.
For the difference between *how* and *what like*, see 255.

2 comparisons: *how* not used

In comparisons we use *as* or *like* (see 320) or *the way* (see below), not *how*.
    Hold it in both hands, **as / like / the way** *Mummy does.*
       (NOT *...* ~~**how Mummy does.**~~)

3 *how, what* and *why*

These three question words can sometimes be confused. Note particularly the following common structures.
    How *do you know?* (NOT ~~**Why do you know?**~~)
    What *do you call this?* (NOT ~~**How do you call this?**~~)
    What's *that school called?* (NOT ~~**How is that school called?**~~)
    What *do you think?* (NOT ~~**How do you think?**~~)
    What*?* **What** *did you say?* (NOT ~~**How? How did you say?**~~)
    Why *should I think that?* (NOT ~~**How should I think that?**~~)

Both *What about ...?* and *How about ...?* are used to make suggestions.
    What/How about *eating out this evening?*

What about ...? is used to bring up points that have been forgotten.
    What about *the kids? Who's going to look after them?*

In exclamations, *what* is used before noun phrases; *how* is used before adjectives (without nouns), adverbs and verb phrases.
    What *a marvellous house!*   **How** *marvellous!*   **How** *you've changed!*

4 other expressions beginning with *how* ...

Many interrogative expressions of two or more words begin with *how*. These are used to ask for measurements, quantities etc. Examples:
    How much *do you weigh?*   **How far** *is your house?*
    How many *people were there?*   **How often** *do you come to New York?*
    How old *are your parents?*   ▶

Note that English does not have a special expression to ask for ordinal numbers (*first, second* etc).

> *'It's our wedding anniversary.' 'Congratulations. **Which one**?'*
>> (NOT *'. . .~~the how-manyeth?~~'*)

5 *how*-clauses in sentences

In longer sentences, *how*-clauses are common as the objects of verbs like *ask, tell, wonder* or *know*, which can introduce indirect questions.

> *Don't ask me **how the journey was**.*
> *Tell us **how you did it**.*
> *I wonder **how animals talk to each other**.*
> *Does anybody know **how big the universe is**?*

How-clauses can also be used as subjects, complements or adverbials, especially in a more informal style.

> ***How you divide up the money** is your business.*
> *This is **how much I've done** since this morning.*
> *Son, spend your money **how you like**, only don't buy yourself anything that eats.*

Prepositions can sometimes be dropped before *how*-clauses, but not in all cases.

> *Have you got any idea **(of) how** she got away?*
> *I'm worried **about how** we're going to pay for the car.*
> *Let's look **(at) how** the sales figures are going.*

6 *the way*

The way can often be used instead of non-interrogative *how*. Note that *the way* and *how* are not used together.

> *Have you ever watched **the way** cats wash each other?*
>> (NOT *. . .~~the way how cats wash~~ . . .*)
> ***The way** you organise the work is for you to decide.*
>> (NOT *~~The way how you organise~~ . . .*)

For more about *the way*, see 587.
For more information about the use of prepositions before conjunctions, see 441.
For infinitives after *how*, see 288.
For *how* after *learn*, see 310.

255 how and **what . . . like?**

1 changes

We generally use *how* to ask about things that change – for example people's moods and health. We usually prefer *what . . . like?* to ask about things that do not change – for example people's character and appearance. Compare:

– *'**How**'s Ron?' 'He's very well.'*
  *'**What**'s Ron **like**?' 'He's quiet and a bit shy.'* (NOT *'~~How's Ron?~~' . . .*)
– *'**How** does she look today?' 'Tired.'*
  *'**What** does your sister look **like**?' 'Short and dark, pretty, very cheerful-looking.'*

2 reactions

We often use *how* to ask about people's reactions to their experiences.
> '*How* was the film?' 'Very good.'
> *How's* your steak?
> *How's* the new job?

In cases like these, *what ... like?* is usually also possible.

256 -ic and -ical

Many adjectives end in *-ic* or *-ical*. There is no general rule to tell you which form is correct in a particular case.

1 some adjectives ending in *-ic*

academic	dramatic	majestic	semantic
artistic	emphatic	neurotic	syntactic
athletic	energetic	pathetic	systematic
catholic	fantastic	phonetic	tragic
domestic	linguistic	public	

Some of these words ended in *-ical* in older English (e.g. *fantastical, majestical, tragical*).

New adjectives which come into the language generally end in *-ic*, except for those in *-logical*.

2 some adjectives ending in *-ical*

biological (and many other adjectives ending in *-logical*)

chemical	logical	musical	tactical
critical	mathematical	physical	topical
cynical	mechanical	radical	
grammatical	medical	surgical	

3 adjectives with both forms

A few adjectives can have both forms without any important difference of meaning. Examples are:
> *algebraic(al)*   *egoistic(al)*   *geometric(al)*
> *arithmetic(al)*   *fanatic(al)*   *strategic(al)*

4 differences of meaning

In some cases, both forms exist but with a difference of meaning.

a *classic* and *classical*

Classic usually refers to a famous or supreme example of its type.
> Vosne Romanée is a **classic** French wine.

Classical refers to the culture of ancient Greece and Rome, or to European works of art of the so-called 'classical' period in the 18th century. (*Classical music* often refers simply to any serious music, especially older music.)
> She's studying **classical** languages.
> It's hard to learn **classical** guitar.

▶

b *comic* and *comical*

Comic is the normal adjective for artistic comedy.
comic *verse*   *Shakespeare's* **comic** *technique*
comic *opera*
Comical is a rather old-fashioned word meaning 'funny'.
a **comical** *expression*

c *economic* and *economical*

Economic refers to the science of economics, or to the economy of a country,
state etc.
economic *theory*   **economic** *problems*
Economical means 'not wasting money'.
an **economical** *little car*   *an* **economical** *housekeeper*

d *electric* and *electrical*

Electric is used with the names of particular machines that work by
electricity.
an **electric** *motor*   **electric** *blankets*
Note also: *an* **electric** *shock; an* **electric** *atmosphere* (full of excitement).
Electrical is used before more general words.
electrical *appliances*   **electrical** *equipment*
electrical *components*   **electrical** *engineering*

e *historic* and *historical*

Historic is used in the sense of 'making history'.
1 January 1973 – the **historic** *date when Britain joined the European
Common Market.*
Historical means 'connected with history' or 'really existing in history'.
historical *research*   *a* **historical** *novel*
Was King Arthur a **historical** *figure?*

f *magic* and *magical*

Magic is the more common word, and is used in a number of fixed
expressions.
a **magic** *wand* (= *a magician's stick*)
the **magic** *word*   *a* **magic** *carpet*
Magical is sometimes used instead of *magic*, especially in metaphorical
senses like 'mysterious', 'wonderful' or 'exciting'.
It was a **magical** *experience.*

g *politic* and *political*

Politic is a rather unusual word for 'wise', 'prudent'.
I don't think it would be **politic** *to ask for a loan just now.*
Political means 'connected with politics'.
political *history*   *a* **political** *career*

5   adverbs

Note that whether the adjective ends in *-ic* or *-ical*, the adverb ends in *-ically* (pronounced /ɪkli/). The one common exception is *publicly* (NOT ~~publically~~).

6   nouns ending in *-ics*

Many nouns ending in *-ics* are singular (e.g. *physics, athletics*). Some can be either singular or plural (e.g. *mathematics, politics*). For details, see 501.3.

257   idioms and collocations

1   What are idioms?

An expression like *turn up* (meaning 'arrive'), *break even* (meaning 'make neither a profit nor a loss') or *a can of worms* (meaning 'a complicated problem') can be difficult to understand, because its meaning is different from the meanings of the separate words in the expression. (If you know *break* and *even*, this does not help you at all to understand *break even*.) Expressions like these are called 'idioms'. Idioms are usually special to one language and cannot be translated word for word (though related languages may share some idioms).

2   verbs with particles or prepositions

Common short verbs like *bring, come, do, get, give, go, have, keep, make, put*, and *take* are very often used with prepositions or adverb particles (e.g. *on, off, up, away*) to make two-word verbs. These are called 'prepositional verbs' or 'phrasal verbs', and many of them are idiomatic.

> *Can you **look after** the cats while I'm away?*
> *She just doesn't know how to **bring up** children.*
> *I **gave up** chemistry because I didn't like it.*

Many of these two-word verbs are especially common in informal speech and writing. Compare:

– *What time are you planning to **turn up**?* (informal)
  *Please let us know when you plan to **arrive**.* (more formal)
– *Just **keep on** till you get to the crossroads.* (informal)
  ***Continue** as far as the crossroads.* (formal)

For details of phrasal and prepositional verbs, see 582.
For the difference between prepositions and adverb particles, see 19.

3   collocations (conventional word combinations)

We can talk about a *burning desire* or a *blazing row*, but we don't say ~~a blazing desire~~ or ~~a burning row~~. Somebody can be a *heavy smoker* or a *devoted friend*, but not ~~a devoted smoker~~ or ~~a heavy friend~~. Expressions like these are also idiomatic, in a sense. They are easy to understand, but not so easy for a learner to produce correctly. One can think of many adjectives that might be used with *smoker* to say that somebody smokes a lot – for example *big, strong, hard, fierce, mad, devoted*. It just happens that English speakers have chosen to use *heavy*, and one has to know this in order to express the idea correctly. (A learner who uses the wrong words for an idea like this may be understood, but he or she will not sound natural.) These conventional combinations are called 'collocations', and all languages have large numbers of them. Some more English examples:

a crashing bore (BUT NOT ~~*a crashing nuisance*~~)
a golden opportunity (BUT NOT ~~*a golden chance*~~)
change one's mind (BUT NOT ~~*change one's thoughts*~~)
Thanks a lot. (BUT NOT ~~*Thank you a lot.*~~)
slightly annoyed (BUT NOT ~~*slightly interesting*~~)

4 situational language

The expressions that are used in typical everyday situations are often idiomatic in the same sense. With the help of a dictionary and a grammar, one could invent various possible ways of expressing a particular idea, but generally there are only one or two ways that happen to be used by English speakers, and one has to know what they are in order to speak or write naturally. Some examples:

Could you check the oil? (More natural than *Could you inspect the oil?* or *Could you see how much oil there is in the engine?*)
Is it a direct flight or do I have to change? (More natural than *Does the plane go straight there or do I have to get another one?*)
Sorry I kept you waiting. (More natural than *Sorry I made you wait.*)
Could I reserve a table for three for eight o'clock? (More natural than *Could you keep me a table for three persons for eight o'clock?*)

5 using idioms

Idioms are common in all kinds of English, formal and informal, spoken and written. However, informal spoken language is often very idiomatic.

Students should not worry because they do not know all the collocations and other idiomatic expressions that are commonly used by English speakers. If they use non-idiomatic ways of expressing ideas, they will normally be understood, and English speakers do not expect foreigners to speak perfectly idiomatically or correctly. It is therefore not necessary for students to make a special effort to learn and use idioms: they will learn the most common idiomatic expressions naturally along with the rest of their English. If they try consciously to fill their speech and writing with idioms the effect will probably be very strange.

Note that books of idioms often contain expressions which are slangy, rare or out of date, and which students should avoid unless they understand exactly how and when the expressions are used. This is particularly true of colourful idioms like *raining cats and dogs, hit the nail on the head, eat like a horse* or *as old as the hills.*

For more about formal and informal language, see 216.
For slang, see 510.

258 **if** (1): introduction

1 **uncertain events and situations**

In clauses after *if*, we usually talk about uncertain events and situations:
things which may or may not happen, which may or may not be true, etc.

*Ask John **if he's staying tonight**.* (He may or may not be staying.)
***If I see Annie** I'll give her your love.* (I may or may not see Annie.)

2 **conditions**

An *if*-clause often refers to a **condition** – something which must happen first,
so that something else can happen.

***If you get here before eight**, we can catch the early train.*
*Oil floats **if you pour it on water**.*

Clauses of this kind are often called 'conditional' clauses. Verb phrases with
would/should are also sometimes called 'conditional'.

3 *if ... then*

We sometimes construct sentences with *if ... then* to emphasise that one
thing depends on another. (Note that we do not use *if ... so* in this way.)

*If she can't come to us, **then** we'll have to go and see her.*
    (NOT ...*so we'll have to go and see her.*)

4 *if* meaning 'if it is true that'

Another common use of *if* is to mean 'if it is true that' or 'if it is the case that'.

***If you were in Boston**, why didn't you come and see us?*
***If it will help**, I'll lend you some money.*

5 **tenses**

The same tenses can be used after *if* as after other conjunctions (see 259 for
details). However, special tenses can also be used to give the idea that
something is unlikely, imaginary or untrue (see 260).

*If I **married** you, we would both be unhappy.*
    (past tense used to talk about an imaginary future situation)

6 **'first', 'second' and 'third' conditionals**

Some students' grammars concentrate on three common patterns with *if*,
which are often called the 'first', 'second' and 'third' conditionals.

'first conditional'

if + present	*will* + infinitive
If we play tennis	*I'll win.*

'second conditional'

if + past	*would* + infinitive
If we played tennis	*I would win.*

'third conditional'

if + past perfect	*would have* + past participle
If we had played tennis	*I would have won.*

▶

Although these are useful structures to practise, it is important to realise that there are many different structures with *if*, and that they do not really divide into three main kinds. As far as tenses are concerned, it is more accurate to distinguish two kinds of structure (see paragraph 2 above): (1) *if* with ordinary tenses (including the so-called 'first' conditional), and (2) *if* with 'special' tenses (including the so-called 'second' and 'third' conditionals).

For details of the use of *if*, see the following sections.
For *if* in indirect speech, see 481.6.
For more information about *would/should*, see 498.
For the difference between *if* and *when*, see 590.
For the difference between *if not* and *unless*, see 574.
For the difference between *if* and *in case*, see 271.

259 if (2): ordinary tense-use

1 the same tenses as with other conjunctions

When we do not want to suggest that a situation is unreal or imaginary, we use ordinary tenses with *if* – the same tenses as with other conjunctions. Present tenses are used to refer to the present, past tenses to the past, and so on.

> *If you **want** to learn a musical instrument, you **have to** practise.*
> *If you **didn't do** much maths at school, you'll **find** economics difficult to understand.*
> *If that **was** Mary, why **didn't** she **stop** and say hello?*

2 present tense with future meaning

In the *if*-clause, we normally use a present tense to talk about the future. (This happens after most conjunctions – see 556.)

> *If I **have** enough time tomorrow, I'll come and see you.*
>   (NOT *If I **will have** enough time*...)
> *I'll give her your love if I **see** her.* (NOT ...*if I **will see** her.*)
> *If it's fine tomorrow, I'm going to paint the windows.*

For *will* in conditional *if*-clauses, see next paragraph and 261.1.
For *if + will* in reported speech (e.g. *I don't know if I'll be here tomorrow*), see 481.

3 *if ... will/would*

We can use *if + will* in polite requests. In this case, *will* is not a future auxiliary; it means 'are willing to'.

> *If you **will** come this way, I'll take you to the manager's office.*
> *If your mother **will** fill in this form, I'll have her luggage taken up to her room.*

Would can be used to make a request even more polite.

> *If you **would** come this way ...*   *Wait over there, if you **would**.*
> *We would appreciate it if you **would** be so kind as to let us have your cheque by return.*

Stressed *will* can also be used after *if* when it expresses the idea of insistence.

> *If you **will** get drunk every night, it's not surprising you feel ill.*
> (= *If you insist on getting drunk . . .*)

For sentences like *If it **will** make you happy, I'll stop smoking,* see 261.1.
For more information about the 'distancing' use of *would* and other past forms, see 161.

4 position of *if*-clause

Note that an *if*-clause can come at the beginning or end of a sentence.
When an *if*-clause comes first, it is often separated by a comma. Compare:

> *If you **eat too much,** you get fat.*
> *You get fat **if you eat too much**.*

For *if not* and *unless*, see 574.
For *if* and *whether* in indirect speech, see 593.
For the use of special tenses with *if*, see 260–261.
For *some* and *any* with *if*, see 522.5.

260 if (3): special tense-use

1 unreal situations

We use 'special' tenses with *if* when we are talking about **unreal** situations –
things that will probably not happen, situations that are untrue or imaginary,
past events that did not happen, and similar ideas. In these cases, we use
would and past tenses to 'distance' our language from reality.

For more about 'distancing', see 161.

2 present and future situations

To talk about unreal or improbable situations now or in the future, we use a
past tense in the *if*-clause (even though the meaning is present or future),
and *would* + **infinitive** in the other part of the sentence.

> *If I **knew** her name, I **would tell** you.* (NOT *If I know . . .*)
>   (NOT *If I would know . . .*) (NOT *. . . I will tell you.*)
> *She **would be** perfectly happy if she **had** a car.*
> *What **would** you **do** if you **lost** your job?*

This structure can be used to make a suggestion sound less definite (for
example, if we want to be more polite).

> *It **would be** nice **if** you **helped** me a bit with the housework.*
> ***Would** it **be** all right **if** I **came** round about seven tomorrow?*

3 *would, should* and *'d*

After *I* and *we, should* can be used in British English with the same meaning
as *would* (see 498).

> *If I knew her name, I **should** tell you.*
> *If we had a map we **should** be able to get out of here.*

We use *'d* as a contraction (see 144).

> *I'**d** get up earlier if there was a good reason to.*

For *I should . . .* meaning 'I advise you to . . .', see 264.2.
For *would* in the *if*-clause, see 261.8.
For *should* in the *if*-clause, see 261.2.

4 *if I were* etc

We often use *were* instead of *was* after *if*. This is common in both formal and informal styles. In a formal style it is much more common than *was*, and many people consider it more correct, especially in American English. The grammatical name for this use of *were* is 'subjunctive' (see 541).

> *If I **were** rich, I would spend all my time travelling.*
> *If my nose **were** a little shorter I'd be quite pretty.*

Note that *were* is not normally used instead of *would be* in polite requests (see 259.3).

> *We should be grateful if you **would be** so kind as to let us have your cheque as soon as possible.* (NOT *...if you were so kind...*)

For the expression *If I were you...*, see 264.

5 special tense-use and ordinary tense-use compared

In conditional clauses, the difference between, for example, *if I **come*** and *if I **came*** is not a difference of time. They can both refer to the present or future; the past tense suggests that the situation is less probable, or impossible, or imaginary. Compare:

- *If I **become** President, I'll...* (said by a candidate in an election)
  *If I **became** President, I'd...* (said by a schoolboy)
- *If I **win** this race, I'll...* (said by the fastest runner)
  *If I **won** this race, I'd...* (said by the slowest runner)
- *Will it **be** all right **if I bring** a friend tonight?* (direct request)
  *Would it **be** all right **if I brought** a friend tonight?*
  (less direct, more polite request)

6 unreal past situations

To talk about past situations that did not happen, we use a past perfect tense (**had + past participle**) in the *if*-clause, and **would have + past participle** in the other part of the sentence.

> *If you **had asked** me, I **would have told** you.*
> (NOT *If you would have asked me...*)
> (NOT *If you asked me...*)
> (NOT *...I had told you.*)
> *If you **had worked** harder, you **would have passed** your exam.*
> *I'd **have** been in bad trouble **if** Jane **hadn't helped** me.*

7 unrealised present and future possibilities

The same structure can sometimes be used (especially in British English) to talk about present and future situations which are no longer possible because of the way things have turned out.

> *If my mother **had been** alive, she **would have been** 80 next year.*
> (OR *If my mother **were** alive, she **would be**...*)
> *It **would have been** nice to go to Australia this winter, but there's no way we can do it.* (OR *It **would be** nice...*)
> *If my mother hadn't knocked my father off his bicycle thirty years ago,*
> *I **wouldn't have been** here now.* (OR *...I **wouldn't be** here now.*)

8 *could* and *might*

In unreal conditional sentences, we can use *could* to mean 'would be able to' and *might* to mean 'would perhaps' or 'would possibly'.

*If I had another £500, I **could** buy a car.*

*If you asked me nicely, I **might** get you a drink.*

Could have . . . and *might have . . .* can be used in sentences about the past.

*If he'd run a bit faster, he **could have** won.*

*If I hadn't been so tired, I **might have** realised what was happening.*

For other cases where a past tense is used with a present or future meaning, see 422.
For *if only*, see 265.
For *if so* and *if not*, see 261.12.
For ordinary tenses with *if*, see 259.

261 **if** (4): other points

1 future in *if*-clauses

We normally use a present tense with *if* (and most other conjunctions) to refer to the future (see 556).

*I'll phone you if I **have** time.* (NOT . . . ~~if I will have time.~~)

But we use *if . . . will* when we are talking about later results rather than conditions (when *if* means 'if it is true that' – see 258.4). Compare:

*I'll give you £100 if you **stop** smoking.* (Stopping smoking is a **condition** of getting the money – it must happen first.)

*I'll give you £100 if it**'ll help** you to go on holiday.*
(The help is a **result** – it follows the gift of money.)

For *if* with non-future *will*, see 259.3.

2 *if . . . should; if . . . happen to*

We can suggest that something is unlikely, or not particularly probable, by using *should* (not *would*) in the *if*-clause.

*If you **should** run into Peter, tell him he owes me a letter.*

If . . . happen to has a similar meaning.

*If you **happen to** pass a supermarket, perhaps you could get some eggs.*

Should and *happen to* can be used together.

*If you **should happen to** finish early, give me a ring.*

Would is not common in the main clause in these structures.

*If he should be late, we**'ll** have to start without him.*
(NOT . . . ~~we'd have to start without him.~~)

3 *if . . . was/were to*

This is another way of talking about unreal or imaginary future events.

*If the boss **was/were to** come in now, we'd be in real trouble.*
(= *If the boss **came**. . .*)

*What would we do **if** I **was/were to** lose my job?* ▶

It can be used to make a suggestion sound less direct, and so more polite.

*If you **were to** move your chair a bit, we could all sit down.*

This structure is not used with state verbs.

*If I **knew** her name I would tell you.* (NOT ~~If I **were to know** her name~~...)

For the difference between *was* and *were* after *if,* see 260.4.

4 *if it was/were not for*

This structure is used to say that one particular event or situation changes everything.

*If it **wasn't/weren't for** his wife's money he'd never be a director.*
(= *Without his wife's money* ...)

*If it **wasn't/weren't for** the children, we wouldn't have anything to talk about.*

To talk about the past we use *If it had not been for.*

*If it **hadn't been for** your help, I don't know what I'd have done.*

But for can be used to mean 'if it were not for' or 'if it had not been for'.

But for your help, I don't know what I'd have done.

5 leaving out *if*: conversational

If is sometimes left out at the beginning of a sentence in a conversational style, especially when the speaker is making conditions or threats.

You want to get in, you pay like everybody else. (= *If you want* ...)

You touch me again, I'll kick your teeth in.

6 leaving out *if*: formal inversion-structures

In formal and literary styles, *if* can be dropped and an auxiliary verb put before the subject. This happens with *were*, *had* and *should*; very rarely with other auxiliary verbs.

Were she my daughter, ... (= *If she were my daughter* ...)

Had I realised what you intended, ... (= *If I had realised* ...)

Should you change your mind, ... (= *If you should change* ...)

Negatives are not contracted.

Had we not changed our reservations, we should all have been killed in the crash. (NOT ~~Hadn't we changed~~...)

For other uses of inverted word order, see 298–299.

7 extra negative

An extra *not* is sometimes put into *if*-clauses after expressions suggesting doubt or uncertainty.

*I wonder if we **shouldn't** ask the doctor to look at Mary.*
(= *I wonder if we should ask* ...)

*I wouldn't be surprised if she **didn't** get married soon.*
(= ... *if she got married soon.*)

For more details of double negative structures, see 361.

8 parallel structures: *would ... would*

Conditional *would* is sometimes used in both clauses of an *if*-sentence. This is very informal, and is not usually written. It is common in spoken American English.

> It **would** be better if they **would** tell everybody in advance.
> How **would** we feel if this **would** happen to our family?

For *I would be grateful if you would ...* etc, see 259.3.

9 parallel structures: *'d have ... 'd have*

In informal spoken English, *if*-clauses referring to the past are sometimes constructed with *'d have*. This is frequently considered incorrect, but happens quite often in educated people's speech. It is not normally written.

> If I**'d have** known, I'd have told you.
> It would have been funny if **she'd have** recognised him.

Instead of the contracted *'d*, full forms are sometimes used for emphasis or in negatives. Both *had* and *would* occur.

> I didn't know. But if I **had**'ve known ...
> We would never have met if he **hadn't** have crashed into my car.
> If you **wouldn't** have phoned her we'd never have found out what was happening.

10 elliptical structures

In a formal style, **subject + be** is sometimes left out after *if*.

> **If in doubt**, ask for help. (= If **you are** in doubt ...)
> **If about to go** on a long journey, try to have a good night's sleep.

For more details of elliptical structures, see 181–186.

11 *if any* etc

Note also the common rather formal use of *if* before non-assertive words (see 374) like *any, anything, ever* and *not*.

> There is little **if any** good evidence for flying saucers.
>   (= There is little evidence, if there is any at all, ...)
> I'm not angry. **If anything**, I feel a little surprised.
> He seldom **if ever** travels abroad.
> Usually, **if not** always, we write 'cannot' as one word.

12 *if so* and *if not*

After *if*, we can use *so* and *not* instead of repeating or negating a clause that has come before.

> Are you free this evening? **If so**, let's go out for a meal.
>   (= ... **If you are free** ...)
> I might see you tomorrow. **If not**, then it'll be Saturday.
>   (= ... **If I don't see you tomorrow** ...)

13 giving reasons with *if*

An *if*-clause can be used when somebody admits a fact and gives a reason for it.

> **If I'm a bit sleepy**, it's because I was up all night.   ▶

14   *if* meaning 'I'm saying this in case'

If-clauses are quite often used to explain the purpose of a remark – to suggest 'I'm saying this in case . . .'

> There's some steak in the fridge *if you're hungry*.
> *If you want to go home*, Anne's got your car keys.

262   **if** (5): other words with the same meaning

Many words and expressions can be used with a similar meaning to *if*, and often with similar structures. Some of the commonest are *imagine (that)*, *suppose (that)*, *supposing (that)* (used to talk about what might happen), and *providing (that)*, *provided (that)*, *as/so long as*, *on condition (that)* (used to make conditions).

> *Imagine* we could all fly. Wouldn't that be fun!
> *Supposing* you fell in love with your boss, what would you do?
> You can borrow my bike *providing/provided* you bring it back.
> I'll give you the day off *on condition that* you work on Saturday morning.
> You're welcome to stay with us *as/so long as* you share the expenses.

For suggestions with *suppose, supposing* and *what if*, see 546. For omission of *that*, see 560. For *when* and *if*, see 590.

263   **if** (6): meaning 'although'

In a formal style, *if* can be used with a similar meaning to *although*. This is common in the structure *if* + **adjective** (with no verb). *If* is not as definite as *although*; it can suggest that what is being talked about is a matter of opinion, or not very important.

> His style, *if simple*, is pleasant to read.
> The profits, *if a little lower* than last year's, are still extremely healthy.

The same kind of idea can be expressed with *may . . . but* (see 334).

> His style *may* be simple, *but* it is pleasant to read.

For *even if/though*, see 195.4.

264   **if I were you**

1   advice

We often use the structure *If I were you . . .* to give advice.

> *If I were you*, I'd get that car serviced.   I shouldn't worry *if I were you*.

If I was you . . . is also possible, but some people consider it incorrect (see 260.4).

2   *I should . . .*

Sometimes we leave out *If I were you*, and just use *I should . . .* to give advice. (*I would . . .* is normal in American English.)

> *I should* get that car serviced.   *I shouldn't* worry.

In this case, *I should* means more or less the same as *you should*.

265 **if only**

We can use *If only ...!* to say that we would like things to be different. It means the same as *I wish ...* (see 601), but is more emphatic. The clause with *if only* often stands alone, without a main clause. We use the same tenses after *If only ...!* as after *I wish*.

a   past to talk about the present

> ***If only** I **knew** more people!*   ***If only** I **was** better-looking!*

We can use *were* instead of *was* (see 260.4). This is considered more correct in a formal style.

> ***If only** I **were** better looking!*

b   *would* + infinitive to refer to the future

> ***If only** it **would stop** raining, we could go out.*
> ***If only** somebody **would smile!***

c   past perfect (***had* + past participle**) to refer to the past

> ***If only** she **hadn't told** the police, everything would have been all right.*

266 **ill** and **sick**

Ill is often used to mean 'unwell' in British English. (In American English *ill* is unusual except in a formal style.) *Ill* is most common in predicative position (after a verb).

> *George didn't come in last week because he was **ill**.*

In attributive position (before a noun), many British people prefer to use *sick*. *Sick* is also the normal informal American word for 'unwell'.

> *He spent twenty years looking after his **sick** father.*
> *The President is **sick**.*

Be sick can mean 'vomit' (= 'bring food up from the stomach').

> *I **was sick** three times in the night.*   *She's never **sea-sick**.*
> *I **feel sick**. Where's the bathroom?*
>   (US also *I feel sick to my stomach ...*)

267 **immediately, the moment** etc (conjunctions)

In British English, *immediately* and *directly* can be used as conjunctions, to mean 'as soon as'.

> *Tell me **immediately** you have any news.*
> *I knew something was wrong **immediately** I arrived.*
> ***Directly** I walked in the door I smelt smoke.*

The moment (that), the instant (that), the second (that) and *the minute (that)* can be used in the same way (in both British and American English).

> *Telephone me **the moment (that)** you get the results.*
> *I loved you **the instant (that)** I saw you.*

For information about when *that* can be left out, see 560.
For *once* and *now (that)* used as conjunctions, see 383, 390.

268 imperatives

1 forms and use

In sentences like *Come here, Be quiet, Have a drink* or *Don't worry about it,* the verb forms *come, be, have* and *don't worry* are called 'imperatives'. Affirmative imperatives have the same form as the infinitive without *to*; negative imperatives are constructed with ***do not (don't)* + infinitive**.

Imperatives are used, for example, to tell or ask people what to do, to make suggestions, to give advice or instructions, to encourage and offer, and to express wishes for people's welfare.

Look *in the mirror before you drive off.*　**Try** *again – you nearly did it.*
Please do not *lean out of the window.*　**Have** *some more tea.*
Tell *him you're not free this evening.*　**Enjoy** *your holiday.*

An imperative followed by *and* or *or* can have a similar meaning to an *if*-clause.

Walk *down our street any day* **and** *you'll see kids playing.*
　(= **If** *you walk* ...)
Shut up or *I'll lose my temper.* (= **If** *you don't shut up* ...)
Don't do *that again* **or** *you'll be in trouble.*

2 emphatic imperative

We can make an emphatic imperative with ***do* + infinitive**. This is common in polite requests, complaints and apologies.

Do sit *down.*　**Do be** *a bit more careful.*
Do forgive *me – I didn't mean to interrupt.*

3 passive imperative

To tell people to arrange for things to be done to them, we often use *get* + past participle.

Get vaccinated *as soon as you can.*

For more about *get* as passive auxiliary, see 228.4.

4 *do(n't) be*

Although *do* is not normally used as an auxiliary with *be, do* is used before *be* in negative and emphatic imperatives (see 89).

Don't be *silly!*　**Do be** *quiet!*

5 subject with imperative

The imperative does not usually have a subject, but we can use a noun or pronoun to make it clear who we are speaking to.

Mary come *here –* **everybody else stay** *where you are.*
Somebody answer *the phone.*　**Nobody move.**
Relax, everybody.

You before an imperative can suggest emphatic persuasion or anger.

You *just* **sit down** *and relax for a bit.*　**You take** *your hands off me!*

Note the word order in negative imperatives with pronoun subjects.

Don't you believe *it.* (NOT ~~**You don't believe it.**~~)
Don't anybody say *a word.* (NOT ~~**Anybody don't say** ...~~)

6   question tags

After imperatives, the normal question tags (see 465–466) are *will you? won't you? would you? can you? can't you?* and *could you?* After negative imperatives, *will you?* is used.

>*Give me a hand, **will you?***
>*Sit down, **won't you?***
>*Get me something to drink, **can you?***
>*Be quiet, **can't you?***
>*Don't tell anybody, **will you?***

7   word order

Always and *never* come before imperatives.

>***Always remember** what I told you.* (NOT *-Remember always...*)
>***Never speak** to me like that again.*

8   *let*

Some languages have a first person imperative form (used to suggest that 'I' or 'we' should do something). English does not have this, but there is a structure with ***let** + **infinitive*** that has a similar meaning. *Let us* is contracted to *let's* except in a very formal style.

>***Let me see.** Do I need to go shopping today?*
>***Let's go** home.   **Let us** pray.*

Let can also be used with third person nouns or pronouns.

>*'Mr Parker's in the waiting room.' '**Let him stay** there all day as far as I'm concerned.'*

For more details of this use of *let*, see 315.

269   **in** and **into**, **on** and **onto** (prepositions)

1   position and movement

We generally use *in* and *on* to talk about the positions of things – where they **are**; and *into* and *onto* to talk about directions and destinations – where things are ***going***. Compare:

– *A moment later the ball was **in** the goal.*
  *The ball rolled slowly **into** the goal.* (NOT *...rolled slowly **in** the goal.*)
– *She's **in** the bedroom getting dressed.*
  *She ran **into** the room carrying a paper.* (NOT *She walked **in** the room...*)
– *She was walking **in** the garden.*
  *Then she walked **into** the house.*
– *The cat's **on** the roof again.*
  *How does it get **onto** the roof?*

Note that *into* and *onto* are normally written as single words. *On to* is also possible in British English.

2   *in* and *on* for movement

After some verbs (e.g. *throw, jump, push, put*) we can use both *in* and *into*, or *on* and *onto*, to talk about directional movement. We prefer *into/onto*

when we think of the movement itself, and *in/on* when we think more of the end of the movement – the place where somebody or something will be. Compare:
- *The children keep **jumping into** the flowerbeds.*
  *Go and **jump in** the river.*
- *The experiment involved **putting** glowing magnesium **into** jars of pure oxygen.*
  *Could you **put** the ham **in** the fridge?*
- *He was trying to **throw** his hat **onto** the roof.*
  ***Throw** another log **on** the fire.*

We always use *in* and *on* after *sit down* and *arrive*.
> *He **sat down in** the armchair, and I **sat down on** the floor.*
> (NOT *He sat down into . . . and I sat down onto . . .*)
> *We arrive **in** Athens at midday.* (NOT *We arrive into Athens . . .*)

3 *into* for change

We normally use *into* after verbs suggesting change.
> *When she kissed the frog, it **changed into** a handsome prince.*
> (NOT *. . . changed in a handsome prince.*)
> *Can you **translate** this **into** Chinese?* (NOT *. . . translate this in Chinese?*)

Cut can be followed by *into* or *in*.
> ***Cut** the onion **in(to)** small pieces.*

And note the expression *in half*.
> *I broke it **in half**.* (NOT *. . . into half.*)

4 *in* and *on* as adverbs

In and *on* are used as adverbs for both position and movement.
> *I stayed **in** last night.*   *What have you got **on**?*
> *Come **in**!* (NOT *Come into!*)   *Put your coat **on**.*

For the difference between *in* and *to*, see 270.

270 in and to

1 *go to school in . . .* etc

After expressions like *go to school, go to work,* we use *in*, not *to*, to say where the school, work etc is located.
> *He went **to** school **in** Bristol.* (NOT *He went to school to Bristol.*)

At is also possible.
> *She went to university **at/in** Oxford.*

For the difference between *in* and *at*, see 80.

2 *arrive* etc

We use *in* (or *at*), not *to*, after *arrive* and *land*.
> *We **arrive in** Bangkok on Tuesday morning.*
> (NOT *We **arrive to** Bangkok . . .*)
> *What time do we **land at** Barcelona?* (NOT *. . . land to Barcelona?*)

271 **in case** and **if**

1 precautions

In case is mostly used to talk about precautions – things which we do in order to be ready for possible future situations.

> *I always take an umbrella **in case** it rains.* (= ... *because it might rain.*)

In clauses which refer to the future, *in case* is normally followed by a present tense (like most other conjunctions – see 556).

> *I've bought a chicken **in case** your mother **stays** to lunch.*
> (NOT ...*in case your mother will stay*...)

2 *in case ... should*

We often use *should* + infinitive (with a similar meaning to *might*) after *in case*. This adds the meaning 'by chance'.

> *I've bought a chicken in case your mother **should stay** to lunch.*

This structure is especially common in sentences about the past.

> *I wrote down her address in case I **should forget** it.*

The meaning 'by chance' can also be expressed by *(should) happen to*.

> *We took our swimming things in case we **happened to** find a pool.*
> (OR ... *in case we **should happen to** find a pool.*)

3 *in case* and *if*

In British English, *in case* and *if* are normally used in quite different ways.

'I do A **in case** B happens' usually means 'I do A first because B might happen later'. A is first.

'I do A **if** B happens' means 'I do A if B has already happened'. B is first.

Compare:
– *Let's buy a bottle of wine **in case** Roger comes.*
>   (= *Let's buy some wine now because Roger might come later.*)
>   *Let's buy a bottle of wine **if** Roger comes.* (= *We'll wait and see. If Roger comes, then we'll buy the wine. If he doesn't we won't.*)
– *I'm taking an umbrella **in case** it rains.*
   *I'll open the umbrella **if** it rains.*
>   (NOT *I'll open the umbrella in case it rains.*)
– *People insure their houses **in case** they catch fire.* (NOT ...*if they catch fire.*)
   *People telephone the fire brigade **if** their houses catch fire.*
>   (NOT ...*telephone*... *in case their houses catch fire.*)
In American English, *in case* can sometimes be used in the same way as *if*.
> ***In case** the house burns down, we'll get the insurance money.* (GB *If*...)

4 *in case of*

The prepositional phrase *in case of* has a wider meaning than the conjunction *in case*, and can be used in similar situations to *if*.

> ***In case of** fire, break glass.* (= ***If** there is a fire*...)

272 in front of, facing and opposite

We do not use *in front of* to mean 'across a road/river/room etc from'. This idea is usually expressed with *opposite* or *facing*. (US *across from*).

> *There's a garage opposite my house.* (NOT ...~~in front of my house.~~)
> *She sat facing me across the table.* (NOT ...~~in front of me...~~)

In front of is the opposite of *behind*. Compare:

> *There's a bus stop in front of the school.*
>> (The bus stop is on the same side of the road as the school.)
> *There's a bus stop opposite the school.*
>> (The bus stop is on the other side of the road from the school.)

For the difference between *before* and *in front of*, see 97.

273 in spite of

In spite of is used as a preposition. ***In spite of* + noun** means more or less the same as ***although* + clause**.

> *We went out in spite of the rain.* (= ... *although it was raining.*)
> *We understood him in spite of his accent.*
>> (= ... *although he had a strong accent.*)

In spite of is the opposite of *because of*. Compare:

> *She passed her exams in spite of her teacher.* (She had a bad teacher.)
> *She passed her exams because of her teacher.* (She had a good teacher.)

In spite of can be followed by an *-ing* form.

> ***In spite of having** a headache I enjoyed the film.*
> *She failed the exam **in spite of having** worked very hard.*

In more formal English, *despite* can be used in the same way as *in spite of*.

274 indeed

1 *very ... indeed*

Indeed is often used after an adjective or adverb, to strengthen the meaning of *very*.

> *Thank you **very** much **indeed**.*
> *I was **very** pleased **indeed** to hear from you.*
> *He was driving **very** fast **indeed**.*

Indeed is unusual in this sense without *very*, and is not normally used after *extremely* or *quite*.

> (NOT ~~He was driving fast indeed.~~)
> (NOT ~~He was driving quite/extremely fast indeed.~~)

2 *indeed* with verb

Indeed can also be used after *be* or an auxiliary verb in order to suggest confirmation or emphatic agreement. This is rather formal. It is common in short answers (see 493).

> *We are **indeed** interested in your offer, and would be glad to have prices as soon as possible.*

*'It's cold.' 'It is **indeed**.'*
*'Henry made a fool of himself.' 'He did **indeed**.'*

For other ways of using *indeed*, see a good dictionary.

275 **infinitives** (1) : introduction

Infinitives are forms like *(to) write, (to) stand*. Unlike verb tenses (e.g. *writes, stood*), infinitives do not usually show the actual times of actions or events. They usually refer to actions and events in a more general way, rather like *-ing* forms. (See 290–296).

Infinitives are generally used with the marker *to*; for cases when *to* is not used, see 277.

Besides simple infinitives like *(to) write*, there are also progressive infinitives (e.g. *(to) be writing*), perfect infinitives (e.g. *(to) have written*) and passive infinitives (e.g. *(to) be written*). For details of the various forms, see 276.

Infinitives have many functions. An infinitive can be used, for example:

a   after *do* or a modal auxiliary verb, as part of a verb phrase
　　　*Do you **think** she's ready?*　　　*We **must get** some more light bulbs.*

b   as the subject or complement of a clause (see 279)
　　　To watch him eating really gets on my nerves.
　　　*The main thing is **to stay** calm.*　　　*It's nice **to talk** to you.*

c   to express a person's purpose (see 281)
　　　*He came to London **to look** for work.*

d   as object or complement of a verb, adjective or noun (see 283–287)
　　　*I don't **want to go** to bed.*　　　*I'm **anxious to contact** your brother.*
　　　*You have **the right to remain** silent.*

For full details of these and other uses of infinitives, see the following sections.

276 **infinitives** (2): forms

Besides the ordinary infinitive (e.g. *(to) go, (to) work*), there are also progressive, perfect and passive forms.

1 **progressive infinitive: *(to) be ...ing***

Like other progressive forms (see 450), the progressive infinitive is used to suggest that actions and events are / were / will be continuing around the time we are talking about.
　　　*It's nice **to be sitting** here with you.*
　　　*I noticed that he seemed **to be smoking** a lot.*
　　　*This time tomorrow I'll **be lying** on the beach.*
　　　　　(future progressive tense: see 225)
　　　*Why's she so late? She can't still **be working**.*

　　　　　　　　　　　　　　　　　　　　　　　　　　　　　　　　　▶

2   perfect infinitive: *(to) have* + past participle

Perfect infinitives can have the same kind of meaning as perfect tenses (see 418–420) or past tenses (see 416–417).

> *It's nice **to have finished** work.* (= *It's nice that I **have finished**.*)
> *I'm sorry **not to have come** on Thursday.* (= ... *that I **didn't come** ...*)

We often use perfect infinitives to talk about 'unreal' past events: things that did not happen, or that may not have happened.

> *I meant **to have telephoned**, but I forgot.*
> *You should **have told** me you were coming.*

For details, see 278.

3   passive infinitive: *(to) be* + past participle

Passive infinitives have the same kind of meaning as other passive forms (see 407–414).

> *There's a lot of work **to be done**.*
> *She ought **to be told** about it.*
> *That window **must be repaired** before tonight.*

Sometimes active and passive infinitives can have similar meanings, especially after a noun or *be* (see 287).

> *There's a lot of work **to do** / **to be done**.*

4   combinations

Perfect progressive and perfect passive infinitives are common.

> *I'd like **to have been sitting** there when she walked in.*
> *They were lucky – they could **have been killed**.*

Progressive passive infinitives are possible but unusual.

> *'What would you like to be doing right now?' 'I'd like **to be being massaged**.'*

Progressive perfect passive infinitives (e.g. *It must **have been being built** at the time*) do not normally occur.

5   negative forms

Negative infinitives are normally made by putting *not* before the infinitive.

> *Try **not to be** late.* (NOT USUALLY *Try **to not be** late.*) (NOT *Try **to don't be** late.*)
> *You were silly **not to have locked** your car.*
> *He's very busy. I'm afraid he ca**n't be disturbed**.*

6   *to*

The marker *to* is normally used before infinitives (e.g. *He wanted **to go***). However, in some cases we use infinitives without *to* (e.g. *She let him **go***). See 277 for details. Note that this *to* is not a preposition; after the preposition *to* we use *-ing* forms (see 295.2).

7   split infinitive

A 'split infinitive' is a structure in which *to* is separated from the rest of the infinitive by an adverb.

> *I'd like **to really understand** philosophy.*
> *He began **to slowly get up** off the floor.*

Split infinitive structures are quite common in English, especially in an informal style. Some people consider them incorrect or careless, and avoid them if possible by putting the adverb in another position.

> He began **slowly to get up** off the floor.

For details of the use of infinitives, see the following sections.
For the use of *to* instead of a whole infinitive (e.g. *I'd like **to***), see 186.

277 infinitives (3): without **to**

We usually put the marker *to* before the infinitive (for example *I want **to know**, It's nice **to see** you*). But we use the infinitive without *to* in some cases.

1 after modal auxiliary verbs

After the modal auxiliary verbs *will, shall, would, should, can, could, may, might* and *must*, we use the infinitive without *to*.

> *I **must go** now.* (NOT ~~I must to go now.~~)
> ***Can** you **help** me?*   *I **would** rather **go** alone.*
> *Do you think she **might be joking**?*   *She **will** probably **be elected**.*
> *I **will have finished** by tomorrow morning.* (future perfect tense – see 224)
> *They **would have won** if they had played a bit harder.*

The infinitive without *to* can also be used after *need* and *dare* in some cases (see 357, 150), and after *had better* (see 234).

> ***Need** I **do** the washing up?*   *How **dare** you **call** me a liar?*
> *You'**d better see** what she wants.*

The *to*-infinitive is used after *ought* (see 398), *used* (see 577), *be* (see 90) and *have* (see 243).

2 after *let, make, hear* etc

Certain verbs are followed by **object + infinitive without *to***. They include *let, make, see, hear, feel, watch* and *notice*.

> *She **lets her children stay** up very late.* (NOT ~~She lets her children to stay~~ ...)
>   (NOT ~~She lets her children staying~~ ...)
> *I **made them give** me the money back.*   *I didn't **see you come** in.*
> *We both **heard him say** that I was leaving.*
> *Did you **feel the earth move**?*

Help can also be used in this way (see 247).

> *Could you **help me (to) unload** the car?*

This structure is also possible in certain cases with *have* (see 242) and *know* (see 306).

> ***Have Mrs Hansen come in**, please.* (mainly US)
> *I've never **known him (to) pay** for a drink.* (perfect tenses of *know* only)

In passive versions of these structures (with *make, see, hear, help* and *know*) the infinitive with *to* is used.

> *He **was made to pay** back the money.*
> *She **was heard to say** that she disagreed.*

For more information about structures with *let*, see 316. For *make*, see 327.
For more information about *see, hear, watch* etc + object + verb, see 245, 296.5.
For verbs that are followed by **object + *to*-**infinitive, see 284.   ▶

3 after *why (not)*

We can introduce questions and suggestions with ***why (not)*** + **infinitive without *to***. For more details, see 599.

> *Why pay more at other shops? We have the lowest prices.*
> *Why stand up if you can sit down? Why sit down if you can lie down?*
> *You're looking tired. Why not take a holiday?*

4 after *and, or, except, but, than, as* and *like*

When two infinitive structures are joined by *and, or, except, but, than, as* or *like*, the second is often without *to*.

> *I'd like **to lie down** and **go** to sleep.*
> *Do you want **to have** lunch now or **wait** till later?*
> *We had nothing **to do** except **look** at the cinema posters.*
> *I'm ready **to do** anything but **work** on a farm.*
> *It's easier **to do** it yourself than **explain** to somebody else how to do it.*
> *It's as easy **to smile** as **frown**.*
> *I have **to feed** the animals as well as **look** after the children.*
> *Why don't you **do** something useful like **clean** the flat?*

Rather than is usually followed by an infinitive without *to*.

> ***Rather than wait*** *any more, I decided to go home by taxi.*

For more information about leaving words out ('ellipsis') with *and, or* etc, see 182.

5 after *do*

Expressions like *All I did was, What I do is* etc can be followed by an infinitive without *to*.

> *All I did was **(to) give** him a little push.*
> *What a fire-door does is **(to) delay** the spread of a fire.*

278 infinitives (4): using perfect infinitives

1 perfect or past meaning

Perfect infinitives can have the same kind of meaning as perfect or past tenses.

> *I'm glad **to have left** school. (= I'm glad that I **have left** . . .)*
> *She was sorry **to have missed** Bill. (= . . . that she **had missed** Bill.)*
> *We hope **to have finished** the job by next Saturday.*
> (= . . . *that we **will have finished** . . .)*
> *You seem **to have annoyed** Anne yesterday.*
> (= *It seems that **you annoyed** Anne yesterday.)*

2 perfect infinitive for 'unreal' past

After some verbs (e.g. *mean, be, would like*) we can use perfect infinitives to refer to 'unreal' past situations that are the opposite of what really happened.

> *I **meant to have telephoned**, but I forgot. (The speaker did not telephone.)*
> *He **was to have been** the new ambassador, but he fell ill.*
> *I wish I'd been there – I **would like to have seen** Harry's face when Nan walked in.*

With *would like, would prefer* and one or two other verbs, a double perfect infinitive is sometimes used in informal speech; the extra perfect infinitive does not change the meaning.

> *I **would have liked to have seen** Harry's face.*

3 modals

After the modal verbs *could, might, ought, should, would* and *needn't*, we often use perfect infinitives to refer to unreal situations.

> *Did you see him fall? He **could have killed** himself.*
>> (He did not kill himself.)
> *You **should have written** – I was getting worried.*
>> (The person did not write.)
> *I **would have gone** to university if my parents had had more money.*
>> (The speaker did not go to university.)
> *She **needn't have sent** me flowers.*
>> (She did send flowers.)

Note that the structure **modal verb + perfect infinitive** does not always refer either to the past or to an 'unreal' situation. It can also be used, for instance, when we say how confident we are that something has happened.

> *She **could/should/ought to/may/will/must have arrived** by now.*

For more details, see the entries for the different modal verbs.

279 **infinitive clause** as subject, object or complement of sentence

1 infinitive clause as subject

In older English, an infinitive clause could easily be the subject of a sentence.

> ***To make mistakes** is easy.*
> ***To wait for people who were late** made him angry.*

In modern English, this is unusual in an informal style. We more often use *it* as a 'preparatory subject' and put the infinitive clause later (see 301 for details).

> *It's easy **to make** mistakes.*
> *It made him angry **to wait** for people who were late.*

When we are talking about an activity in general, we often use an *-ing* structure at the beginning of a sentence as the subject, rather than an infinitive clause (see 292).

> ***Selling insurance** is a pretty boring job.*
>> (More natural than ***To sell insurance** ...*)

For more information about *-ing* forms, see 290 – 296.

2 infinitive clause as complement

An infinitive clause can be used after *be* as a subject complement.

> *My ambition was **to retire at thirty**.*
> *Your task is **to get across the river without being seen**.*

Sentences like these can also be constructed with 'preparatory *it*' (see 301).

> *It was my ambition **to retire at thirty**.*
> *It is your task **to get across the river without being seen**.*

▶

3 infinitive as object

Many verbs can be followed by an infinitive clause in the place of the direct object. Compare:

– *I like **cornflakes** for breakfast.* (noun object)
*I like **to have cornflakes** for breakfast.* (infinitive clause as object)
– *She wants **some exercise**.* (noun object)
*She wants **to dance**.* (infinitive object)

For details of verbs that can be followed by an infinitive, see 283.

4 infinitive with its own subject

Sometimes it is necessary to make it clear who or what is the subject of an infinitive, especially if this is not the same as the subject of the sentence. The subject of the infinitive is normally introduced by *for*.

> ***For Ann to go** to France would make me very happy.*
> (NOT ~~**Ann to go to France would**...~~)

For details of this structure, see the next entry.
For the use of *it* as a 'preparatory object' in structures like *He made **it** difficult **to refuse***, see 302.

280 infinitive clause introduced by for + noun/pronoun

1 infinitive with its own subject

The structure *for + noun/pronoun + infinitive* is very common in English. It is used when an infinitive needs its own subject. Compare:

– *Ann will be happy **to help you**.* (Ann will help.)
*Ann will be happy **for the children to help you**.* (The children will help.)
– *My idea was **to learn Russian**.*
*My idea was **for her to learn Russian**.*
– ***To ask Joe** would be a big mistake.*
***For you to ask Joe** would be a big mistake.*
> (NOT ~~**You to ask Joe would be**...~~)

Note that the subject of the infinitive is the object of the preposition *for*. **Object** forms of pronouns are used.

> *Ann will be happy for **them** to help you.* (NOT ...~~for **they** to help you.~~)

2 use

The structure is often used when we are referring to possibility, necessity or frequency, when we are expressing wishes, suggestions or plans for the future, and when we are giving personal reactions to situations. Like other infinitive structures, it is used especially after adjectives, nouns and verbs; it can also act as the subject or object of a clause. It often has the same meaning as a *that*-clause. Compare:

> *It's important **for the meeting to start** on time.*
> *It's important **that the meeting should start** on time.*

3 after adjectives (wishes etc)

The structure *for* + **object** + **infinitive** can be used after certain adjectives which express wishes and other personal feelings about the importance or value of future events (e.g. *anxious, eager, delighted, willing, reluctant*).

adjective + *for* + object + infinitive

*I'm **anxious for the party to be** a success.*
*She's **eager for us to see** her work.*
*Robert says he'd be **delighted for Mary to come** and stay.*

4 with preparatory *it*

For-structures with preparatory *it* (see 301) are common with many adjectives expressing possibility, necessity, importance, urgency, frequency and value judgements.

(…) *it* (…) + adjective + *for* + object + infinitive

*It's **impossible for the job to be** finished in time.*
*Would **it** be **easy for you to phone** me tomorrow?*
*It's **important for the meeting to start** at eight.*
*It seems **unnecessary for him to start** work this week.*
*I consider **it essential for the school to be** properly heated.*
*Is **it usual for foxes to come** so close to the town?*
*I thought **it strange for her to be** out so late.*
*It's not **good for the oil tank to be** so close to the house.*

Other common adjectives that are used in this way include *vital, necessary, pointless, unimportant, common, normal, unusual, rare, right, wrong*. Note that *likely* and *probable* are not used like this.

***She's likely to arrive** this evening.*
    (NOT ~~It's likely for her to arrive this evening.~~)
***It's probable that she'll be** in a bad temper.* OR ***She'll probably be** …*
    (NOT ~~It's probable for her to be…~~)

5 after nouns

The structure can also be used after nouns in expressions with meanings similar to the adjectives listed above. Examples are: *time, a good/bad idea, plan, aim, need, request, mistake, shame.*

*It's **time for everybody to go** to bed.*
*His **idea** is **for us to travel** in separate cars.*
*There's a **plan for Jack to spend** a year in Japan.*
*Our **aim** is **for students to learn** as quickly as possible.*
*It was a big **mistake for them not to keep** John as manager.*
*It was a real **shame for them not to win** after all their work.*

6 after *something, anything, nothing* etc

Something, anything, nothing and similar words are often followed by *for* + **object** + **infinitive**.

*Have you got **something for me to do**?*
*There's **nothing for the cats to eat**.*
*Is there **anybody for Louise to play** with in the village?*
*I must find **somewhere for him to practise** the piano.*

▶

7 after verbs

For-structures are not normally used in object position after verbs.

I **need you to help** me. (NOT ~~I need for you to help me.~~)

However, verbs which are normally followed by *for* (e.g. *ask, hope, wait, look, pay, arrange*) can often be used with *for* + **object** + **infinitive**.

Anne **asked for the designs to be** ready by Friday.

I can't **wait for them to finish** talking.

Can you **arrange for the gold to be** delivered on Monday?

(NOT ...~~for the gold being delivered.~~)

A few other verbs can be used with this structure. Examples are *suit* and *take (time)* (see 551.6).

When will it **suit you for us to call**?

It **took** twenty minutes **for the smoke to clear**.

In informal American English, *like, hate, mean, intend* and some other verbs with similar meanings can be used with a *for*-structure. This is not usually possible in British English.

I **would like for you to stay** as long as you want.

She **hates for people to feel** sad.

Did you **mean for John to mail** those letters?

8 after *too* and *enough*

A *for*-structure is often used after *too* and *enough*.

This is much **too heavy for you to lift**.

There are **too** many people here **for me to talk** to all of them.

Do you think it's **warm enough for the snow to melt**?

I explained **enough for her to understand** what was happening.

9 as subject or object

The *for*-structure can be the subject of a clause.

For us to fail now would be a disaster.

For her to lose the election would make me very happy.

However, it is more common for a structure with preparatory *it* to be used (see paragraph 4 above).

It would make me very happy **for her to lose** the election.

Preparatory *it* is normal when the *for*-structure is the object of a clause.

He made **it** very difficult **for us to refuse**.

10 *for there to be*

The infinitive of *there is* (*there to be*) is common after *for*.

I'm anxious **for there to be** plenty of time for discussion.

It's important **for there to be** a fire escape at the back of the building.

11 *that*-clauses

Instead of the *for* + **object** + **infinitive** structure, a *that*-clause with *should* or a subjunctive is often possible, especially when we want to express wishes, recommendations, suggestions and plans for the future. A *that*-clause is usually more formal than a *for*-structure.

It is important **that there should be** a fire escape.

I'm anxious **that the party should be** a success.

*His idea is **that we should travel** in separate cars.*
*It is essential **that the meeting start** at eight.*

For the use of *should* or the subjunctive in *that*-clauses, see 541.4.
For more information about *too* and *enough*, see 570, 193.

281 infinitive clauses of purpose

We often use an infinitive to talk about a person's purpose – why he or she
does something.
    *I sat down **to rest**.* (NOT ~~*I sat down for resting / for to rest.*~~)
    *He went abroad **to forget**.*   *I'm going to Austria **to learn** German.*
    ***To switch on**, press red button.*
We can also use *in order to* (more formal) or *so as to*.
    *He got up early **in order to have time** to pack.*
    *I moved to a new flat **so as to be** near my work.*
In order to and *so as to* are normal before 'stative' verbs like *be, know* and *have*.
    *I watched him **in order to know** more about him.*
        (More natural than *I watched him **to know** more about him.*)
We normally use *in order / so as* before a negative infinitive.
    *I'm going to leave now, **so as not to be** late.*
        (NOT ~~*I'm going to leave now, **not to be** late.*~~)
A *for*-structure (see 280) can be used to talk about a purpose that involves
action by somebody else.
    *I left the door unlocked **for Harriet to get in**.*

For the use of *for* to talk about purposes and causes, see 213.
For ***and** + **verb*** instead of an infinitive after *go, come, try* etc, see 52.

282 infinitive clauses: other uses

1 *I came home to find ...*

Infinitive clauses can be used to say what somebody found out or learnt at
the end of a journey or task.
    *I arrived home **to find** that the house had been burgled.*
The idea of surprise or disappointment can be emphasised by using *only*
before the infinitive.
    *After driving all night we got to Amy's place, **only to discover** that she was*
        away.
    *He spent four years getting a degree, **only to learn** that there were no jobs*
        for graduates.

2 *to hear her talk, you'd think ...*

The infinitives of *see* and *hear* can be used to explain the reason for a false
impression. The infinitive structure is usually followed by *you'd think* or a
similar expression.
    ***To see them together, you'd think** they were an old married couple. But*
        they only met yesterday.
    ***To see him walk** down the street, **you'd never know** he was blind.*
    ***To hear her talk, you'd think** she was made of money.*

283 infinitive complements (1): after verbs

verbs that can be followed by infinitives

After many non-auxiliary verbs, we can use the infinitives of other verbs.
> It's **beginning to rain**.
> I don't **want to see** you again.
> She **seems to be crying**.
> I **expect to have finished** by tomorrow evening.
> The car **needs to be cleaned**.

Common verbs that can be followed by infinitives (for more detailed entries on some of these, see Index):

afford	begin	fail	intend	prefer	seem
agree	care	forget	learn	prepare	start
appear	choose	go on	like	pretend	swear
arrange	consent	happen	love	promise	trouble
ask	continue	hate	manage	propose	try
attempt	dare	help	mean	refuse	want
(can't) bear	decide	hesitate	neglect	regret	wish
beg	expect	hope	offer	remember	

Some of these verbs can be followed by **object + infinitive** (e.g. I **want her to be** happy). For details, see 284. A few verbs are followed by **verb + for + object + infinitive** (e.g. I **arranged for her to have** violin lessons). For details of these, see 280.7.

After some verbs we can use not only an infinitive but also an -ing form (sometimes with a difference of meaning). For details, see 296.

After some verbs, it is not possible to use an infinitive. Many of these can be followed by -ing forms.
> I **enjoy sailing**. (NOT ~~I enjoy to sail.~~)

For details of verbs that can be followed by -ing forms, see 293.

For infinitive clause objects with preparatory it (e.g. I'll leave **it** to you **to lock up**; I find **it** difficult **to run fast**), see 302.
For perfect infinitives after verbs, see 278.
For **have + infinitive** (e.g. I **have to go** now), see 243.
For **be + infinitive** (e.g. You **are to start** tomorrow), see 90.
For **be able + infinitive**, see 3.
For **go + infinitive** as future auxiliary, see 220.
For **and + verb** instead of an infinitive after try, come, go etc, see 52.
For general information about 'verb + verb' structures, see 579.
For information about the structures that are possible with a particular verb, see a good dictionary.

284 infinitive complements (2): after verb + object

1 verbs that can be followed by object + infinitive

Many verbs in English are followed by **object + infinitive**, rather than by a that-clause.
> She didn't **want me to go**. (NOT ~~She didn't want that I go.~~)
> They don't **allow people to smoke**.
> (NOT ~~They don't allow that people smoke.~~)

*I didn't **ask you to pay** for the meal.*
    (NOT ~~I didn't **ask that you pay** for the meal.~~)
Some common verbs that can be followed by **object + infinitive**:

advise	*hate*	*persuade*
allow	*help* (see also 247)	*prefer*
ask	*instruct*	*recommend*
(can't) bear	*intend*	*remind*
beg	*invite*	*request*
cause	*leave*	*teach*
command	*like*	*tell*
compel	*love*	*tempt*
encourage	*mean*	*trouble*
expect	*need*	*want*
forbid	*oblige*	*warn*
force	*order*	*wish* (see also 601)
get (see also 228)	*permit*	

Some verbs (e.g. *let, make, see, hear, feel, watch, notice, have,* and sometimes *know* and *help*), are followed by **object + infinitive without *to***.
    *Why won't you **let me explain**?*
    *I **heard her open** the door and go out.*
For details, see 277.

Many of the verbs listed above can also be followed by other constructions such as an *-ing* form or a *that*-clause.

Some verbs cannot be followed by **object + infinitive**; for example *suggest*.
    *I **suggested that she should go** home.* (NOT ~~I **suggested her to go** home.~~)

For verbs that are followed by *for* + **object + infinitive** (e.g. *I **arranged for her to go** early*), see 295.3.

2 passive structures

Many of the verbs listed in paragraph 1 can be used in passive structures with infinitives. The normal structure is **subject + passive verb + infinitive**.
    *We **were advised to come** early.*
    *You **are expected to start** work at 8.00 every morning.*
However, some verbs can be used with infinitives in active structures but not passives – for example *like, dislike, love, hate, prefer, wish* and verbs with similar meanings.
    *She **likes people to be** happy.*
        (BUT NOT ~~**People are liked to be** happy by her.~~)
    *I **prefer you to call** me by my first name.*
        (BUT NOT ~~**You are preferred to call** ...~~)

For general information about passive structures, see 407–414.
For **object + *to be* + complement** after verbs of thinking and feeling (e.g. *I **considered him to be** an excellent choice*), see 580.
For structures with *take* (e.g. *The ferry took two hours to unload*), see 551.
For detailed information about the structures that are possible with a particular verb, see a good dictionary.

285 infinitive complements (3): after adjectives

1 reactions and feelings

Infinitives are often used after adjectives which describe people's reactions and feelings.

> *I'm **pleased to see** you.*   *John was **surprised to get** Ann's letter.*
> *She's **anxious to go** home.*   *We're **happy to be** here.*
> *I was **shocked to see** how ill he was.*
> *Most people are **afraid to hear** the truth about themselves.*

Not all adjectives of this kind are followed by the infinitives of other verbs; some are followed by **preposition + -ing** form (see 294), or by *that*-clauses (see 12). Some adjectives (e.g. *afraid, sure*) can be followed by either an infinitive or an *-ing* form, often with a difference of meaning: for details, see 296.

For structures with *for* (e.g. *She's **anxious for the children to go** home*), see 280.

2 other adjectives

Besides adjectives referring to reactions and feelings, many other common adjectives can be followed by infinitives. Examples are *right, wrong, stupid, certain* (see 296.15), *welcome, careful, due, fit, able* (see 3), *likely* (see 321), *lucky*.

> *We were **right to start** early.*   *I was **stupid to believe** him.*
> *She's **certain to win**.*   *You're **welcome to stay** as long as you like.*
> *Be **careful not to** wake the children.*   *It's very **likely to rain**.*
> *You were **lucky not to be killed**.*

For structures with preparatory *it* (e.g. *It is important (for the children) to get to bed early*), see 301.

3 superlatives etc

Superlatives can be followed by an infinitive structure. The meaning is similar to an identifying relative clause (see 474).

> *He's the **oldest** athlete ever **to win** an Olympic gold medal.*
>   (= *... who has ever won ...*)

This structure is also common with *first, second, third* etc, *next, last* and *only*.

> *Who was the **first** person **to climb** Everest without oxygen?*
> *The **next to arrive** was a big black snake.*
> *She's the **only** scientist **to have won** three Nobel prizes.*

Note that this structure is only possible when the noun with the superlative has a subject relationship with the following verb. In other cases, an infinitive cannot be used.

> *Is this the first time that you have stayed here?*
>   (NOT *... the first time for you to stay here.*)

4 subject of clause = object of infinitive

Some adjectives can be used with infinitives in a special structure, in which the subject of the clause is really the object of the infinitive. Examples are *easy, difficult, impossible, good, ready,* and adjectives after *enough* and *too*.

> *He's **easy to amuse**.*
>   (= *To amuse him is easy.* OR *It is easy to amuse him.*)

*Japanese is **difficult** for Europeans **to learn**.*
    (= *It is difficult for Europeans **to learn Japanese**.*)
*His theory is **impossible to understand**.*
    (= *It is impossible **to understand his theory**.*)
*Are these berries **good to eat**?*   *The letters are **ready to sign**.*
*The apples were **ripe enough to pick**.*   *The box was **too heavy to lift**.*
But note that *easy, difficult* and *impossible* cannot be used in this structure
when the subject of the clause is the **subject** of the infinitive. Other
structures have to be used.
Iron rusts easily. (NOT ~~*Iron is **easy to rust**.*~~)
She has difficulty learning maths. (NOT ~~*She is **difficult to learn** maths.*~~)
This material can't possibly catch fire.
    (NOT ~~*This material is **impossible to catch fire**.*~~)
The structure often ends with a preposition.
*She's nice to talk **to**.*   *He's very easy to get on **with**.*
*It's not a bad place to live **in**.*
Note that we do not put an object pronoun after the infinitive or preposition
in these cases.
*Cricket is not very **interesting to watch**.*
    (NOT ~~*Cricket is not very **interesting to watch it**.*~~)
*She's **nice to talk to**.* (NOT ~~*She's **nice to talk to her**.*~~)
When the adjective is used before a noun, the infinitive usually comes after
the noun.
*It's a **good wine to keep**.* (NOT ~~*It's a **good to keep wine**.*~~)

For more about ***enough/ too** + adjective + infinitive*, see 193, 570.
For ***so** + adjective + infinitive* (e.g. *Would you be **so kind as to** hold this for a moment?*),
    see 513.6.
For information about the structures that are possible with a particular adjective, see a good
    dictionary.

286 infinitive complements (4):
after nouns and pronouns

1 nouns related to verbs

We can use infinitives after some nouns which are related to verbs that can
be followed by infinitives (e.g. *wish, decide, need*).
*I have no **wish to change**.* (= *I do not **wish to change**.*)
*I told her about my **decision to leave**.*
    (= *I told her that I had **decided to leave**.*)
*Is there any **need to ask** Joyce?* (= *Do we **need to ask** Joyce?*)
Not all nouns can be followed by infinitives in this way.
*I hate **the thought of getting** old.* (NOT ... ~~***the thought to get old**.*~~)
And note that not all related verbs and nouns are followed by the same
structures. Compare:
– *I **hope to arrive**.*
  *There's no **hope of arriving**.*
– *She **prefers to live** alone.*
  *I understand her **preference for living** alone.*   ▶

– *I do not **intend to return**.*
*I have no **intention of returning**.*

2 nouns related to adjectives

We can also use infinitives after some nouns which are related to adjectives,
or which have an adjectival sense.

*You were **a fool to agree**. (= You were **foolish** to agree.)*
*What a **nuisance to have** to go! (= How **annoying** to have to go!)*
*It's a **pleasure to see** you again. (= It's **pleasant** to see you again.)*
*The car's **a pig to start**. (= ... **difficult** to start.)*

3 purpose

An infinitive can be used after a noun, or an indefinite pronoun such as
something, anything, to explain the purpose or intended effect of a particular
thing: what it does, or what somebody does with it. The noun or pronoun
can be the subject or object of the infinitive.

Subjects
*Have you got **a key to open** this door?*
*It was **a war to end** all wars.*
*I'd like **something to stop** my toothache.*

Objects
*I need some more **books to read**.*
*Is there any **milk to put** on the cornflakes?*
*Did you tell her which **bus to take**?*
*Is there **anything to drink**?*

Some/any/nowhere can also be followed by infinitives.
*The kids want **somewhere to practise** their music.*
If the noun or pronoun is the object of the infinitive, we do not add an object
pronoun after the infinitive.
*I gave her **a paper to read**. (NOT ...~~a paper to read it~~.)*
*He needs **a place to live in**. (NOT ...~~a place to live in it~~.)*

4 quantifiers

Quantifiers like *enough, too much/many/little/few, plenty* etc are often
followed by **noun + infinitive**.
*There was **enough light to see** what I was doing.*
*There's **too much snow** (for us) **to be able** to drive.*
*We've got **plenty of time to see** the British Museum.*
Enough is often dropped before *room* and *time*.
*There's hardly **(enough) room to breathe** in here.*
*Do you think we'll have **(enough) time to do** some shopping?*

5 infinitive with preposition

When a noun is followed by **infinitive + preposition**, another structure is
possible: **noun + preposition + whom/which + infinitive**. This is very formal.
*Mary needs **a friend to play with**.*
     OR *Mary needs **a friend with whom to play**.*
*He's looking for **a place to live in**.*
     OR *He's looking for **a place in which to live**.*

This is not possible when there is no preposition. One cannot say, for example, ~~I need a book which to read.~~

6   *the life to come* etc

In expressions like *the life to come* (= 'life after death'), *the world to come*, *his wife to be* (= 'his future wife'), the infinitive has the same meaning as a relative clause with *be* (= *the life/world **that is to come**, his wife **that is to be**).

For infinitives used to talk about people's purposes, see 281.
For passive infinitives (e.g. *There's work **to be done***), see 287.
For structures with ***for + object + infinitive*** (e.g. *Is there any **need for Peter to ask** Joyce?*), see 280.5.
For infinitives after ***first**, **next**, **last** or superlative + noun* (e.g. *the first* woman ***to climb** Everest*), see 285.3.
For *for + -ing* referring to purpose (e.g. *stuff **for cleaning silver***), see 294.
For detailed information about the structures that are possible with a particular noun, see a good dictionary.

287   infinitive complements (5): active and passive infinitive with similar meaning

1   obligation

The structure **noun + infinitive** can express the idea of obligation. Active and passive infinitives are both possible.

> *I've got **letters to write**.*   *The **carpets to be cleaned** are in the garage.*

If the subject of the clause is the person who has to do the action, active infinitives are used.

> *I've got work **to do**.* (NOT ~~I've got work **to be done**.~~)

If the subject is the person or thing that the action is done to, passive infinitives are normally used after *be*.

> *These sheets **are to be washed**.* (NOT ~~These sheets **are to wash**.~~)
> *This form **is to be filled in** in ink.* (NOT ~~This form **is to fill in**...~~)
> *The cleaning **is to be finished** by midday.* (NOT ~~...**is to finish**...~~)

Active infinitives are possible in a structure with *for* (see 280).

> *This form is **for you to fill in**.*

In other cases, active and passive infinitives are often both possible with the same meaning.

> *There's a lot of work **to do** / **to be done**.*
> *There are six letters **to post** / **to be posted**.*
> *Give me the names of the people **to contact** / **to be contacted**.*
> *The people **to interview** / **to be interviewed** are in the next room.*

2   *to be seen/found/congratulated* etc

The passive infinitives of *see* and *find* are normal after *be*.

> *He was nowhere **to be seen/found**.* (NOT ~~He was nowhere **to see/find**.~~)

We can use a similar structure to express value judgements with verbs like *congratulate, encourage, avoid.*

> *You are **to be congratulated**.* (NOT ~~...**to congratulate**.~~)
> *This behaviour is **to be encouraged**.*   ▶

But note the common expression *to blame,* meaning 'responsible' (for some unfortunate event).

> *Nobody was **to blame** for the accident.*

3 *nothing to do* and *nothing to be done* etc

Note the difference between *There's nothing to do* and *There's nothing to be done.*

> *I'm bored – there's **nothing to do**. (= There are no entertainments.)*
> *There's **nothing to be done** – we'll have to buy a new one.*
> > *(= There's no way of putting it right.)*

For structures like *She's easy to amuse,* see 285.4.
For structures with *take* (e.g. *The ferry took two hours to unload*), see 551.
For more about *be* + infinitive, see 90.

288 infinitive complements (6): after **who**, **what**, **how** etc

1 indirect questions

In indirect speech (see 481), we can use an infinitive after the question words *who, what, where* etc (but not usually *why*). This structure expresses ideas such as obligation and possibility.

> *I wonder **who to invite**. (=... who I **should** invite.)*
> *Show me **what to do**.*
> *Can you tell me **how to get** to the station?*
> > *(=... how I **can** get to the station?)*
> *I don't know **where to put** the car.*
> *Tell me **when to pay**.*
> *I can't decide **whether to answer** her letter.*
> *(BUT NOT ~~I can't understand why to do it.~~)*

2 direct questions

We do not usually begin a direct question with *How to...? What to...?* etc. After question words, we often use *shall* and *should.*

> ***How shall** I tell her?* (NOT ~~How to tell her?~~)
> ***What shall** we do?* (NOT ~~What to do?~~)
> ***Who should** I pay?* (NOT ~~Who to pay?~~)

3 titles

How to..., *What to...* etc are often found as titles for instructions, information leaflets, books etc.

> ***HOW TO IMPROVE** YOUR PRONUNCIATION*
> ***WHAT TO DO** IF FIRE BREAKS OUT*

For questions beginning *Why (not)* + infinitive, see 599.
For more information about question words, see 460.

289   information structure

1   different ways of organising information

When we talk about a situation, we can usually organise the information in various ways – for example, by choosing different elements of the situation as the subject of a clause or sentence.

The storm blew Margaret's roof off.
Margaret's roof was blown off in the storm.
Margaret had her roof blown off in the storm.

The way we choose to organise information in a clause or sentence can depend on what has been said before, on what the listener already knows, or on what we want to emphasise. This is a complicated area of English grammar, and it is still not very well understood. Some guidelines are given below.

2   normal order: important new information last

Most often, a clause or sentence moves from 'known' to 'new': from low to high information value. So we often choose as the subject a person or thing that is already being talked about or that has already been mentioned, or something that speaker and hearer are both familiar with, or even some new information that is not the main point of the message. The important new information generally comes at the end of a clause or sentence.

'How's Joe these days?' 'Oh, fine. He's just got married to a very nice girl.'
  (More natural than '. . . A very nice girl's just got married to him.')
My father was bitten by a dog last week.
  (More natural than *A dog bit my father last week.*)
Our dog bit the postman this morning.
  (More natural than *The postman was bitten by our dog this morning.*)
'I can't find my clothes.' 'Well, your trousers are under my coat.'
  (More natural than '. . . My coat's on your trousers.')

To avoid beginning a clause with a completely new element, we can use the *there is* structure. For details, see 563.

There's a cat on the roof.
  (More natural than *A cat's on the roof.*)

For 'known' and 'new' information with *as, since* and *because*, see 72.

3   getting the right subject: actives, passives, etc

In many situations, there is an *agent* (the person or thing who *does* something) and a *recipient* (the person or thing that something is done to). If we want to make the agent the subject, we can usually do this by choosing an active verb form (see 10).

The storm blew Margaret's roof off.
Somebody's stuck chewing gum all over the carpet.

If we want to make the recipient the subject, we can usually do this by choosing a passive verb form (see 407).

Margaret's roof was blown off in the storm.
Chewing gum's been stuck all over the carpet.   ▶

If we want to make something else the subject, we can often do this by using a structure with ***have + object + past participle*** (see 242.2).

> *Margaret **had** her roof **blown off** in the storm.*
> *The carpet's **had** chewing gum **stuck** all over it.*

Other structures with *have* can be used to 'personalise' a situation by making a person the subject. Compare:

> *The house is full of children.*   ***There** are children all over the house.*
> ***I've got** the house full of children.*

We can often get the subject we want by choosing the right verb. Compare:

- *The biscuit factory **employs** 7,000 people.*
  *7,000 people **work for** the biscuit factory.*
- *He **led** the children through the silent streets.*
  *The children **followed** him through the silent streets.*

Some verbs (called 'ergative verbs') can have both agent and recipient subjects. For details, see 579.3.

> *She **opened** the door.*   *The door **opened**.*

4 end-weight

Longer and heavier structures usually come last in a clause or sentence. (These usually have the highest 'information-value' in any case.)

> *Children are sometimes discouraged by **the length of time it takes to learn a musical instrument**. (More natural than **The length of time it takes to learn a musical instrument** sometimes discourages children.)*

Because of this, we often use a structure with 'preparatory *it*' in order to move a clause or infinitive subject or object to the end of a sentence. For details, see 301.

> ***It** worried me **that she hadn't been in touch for so long**.*
> (More natural than ***That she hadn't been in touch for so long** worried me.*)
> ***It's** important **to tell us everything you know**.*
> (More natural than ***To tell us everything you know** is important.*)
> *He made **it** clear **that he was not in the least interested**.*
> (More natural than *He made **that he was not in the least interested** clear.*)

Adverbs do not normally separate the verb from the object in an English clause (see 22.1). However, a very long and heavy object may come after a shorter adverb. Compare:

> *She plays **the violin very well**. (NOT ~~She plays very well the violin.~~)*
> *She plays **very well almost any instrument that you can think of, and several that you can't**.*

End-weight can also affect the word order of indirect questions. Compare:

> *I'm not sure what **the point is**.*
> *I'm not sure what **is the point of spending hours and hours discussing this**.*

5 emphatic structures

There are various ways of giving extra emphasis to one part of a sentence. One way is to use a 'cleft sentence' with *it* or *what*: this emphasises one idea by putting everything else into a subordinate clause. For details, see 131.

*It was **my mother** who finally called the police.*

*What I need is **a hot bath and a drink.***

If we move to the beginning of a sentence something that does not normally go there, this gives it extra emphasis. This kind of structure ('fronting') is common in speech, where intonation can make the information structure clear. For details, see 217.

The other plans we'll look at next week.　　*Nice man, your uncle.*

For more information about emphasis, see 189.

290 **-ing forms** ('gerunds' and 'participles'): introduction

1 uses and terminology

We can use *-ing* forms (e.g. *smoking, walking*) not only as verbs, but also like adjectives, adverbs or nouns. Compare:

*You're **smoking** too much these days.* (part of present progressive verb)

*There was a **smoking** cigarette end in the ashtray.*
　　(adjective describing *cigarette end*)

*She walked out of the room **smoking**.* (similar to an adverb)

***Smoking** is bad for you.* (noun: subject of sentence)

When *-ing* forms are used as verbs, adjectives or adverbs, they are often called 'present participles'. (This is not a very suitable name, because these forms can refer to the past, present or future.) When they are used more like nouns, they are often called 'gerunds'. In fact, the distinction is not really as simple as this, and some grammarians prefer to avoid the terms 'participle' and 'gerund'. For a detailed discussion of this point, see Section 17.54 of *A Comprehensive Grammar of the English Language*, by Quirk, Greenbaum, Leech and Svartvik (Longman 1985).

In *Practical English Usage* the expression '*-ing* form' is used except when there is a good reason to use one of the other terms. Noun-like uses of *-ing* forms are discussed in sections 292–296. Ways of using *-ing* forms like adjectives and adverbs are discussed in sections 403–406, together with similar uses of 'past participles' (e.g. *invited, broken*).

2 perfect, passive and negative *-ing* forms

Note the structure of perfect, passive and negative *-ing* forms.

***Having slept** for twelve hours, I felt marvellous.* (perfect)

*She loves **being looked at.*** (passive)

***Not knowing** what to do, I went home.* (negative)

*She's angry about **not having been invited**.* (negative perfect passive)　　▶

3 *-ing* clauses

We can combine *-ing* forms with other words into clause-like structures.
> *She went **running out of the room.***
> ***Collecting stamps** is a hobby of his.*
> ***Having lost all my money**, I went home.*
> *Who's the man **sitting in the corner**?*

For spelling rules, see 533–535.

291 -ing forms used as modifiers

-ing forms can be used as modifiers before nouns. This can happen both with
noun-like *-ing* forms ('gerunds') and adjective-like *-ing* forms ('participles').
The two structures do not have quite the same kind of meaning. Compare:
– *a **waiting** room* (= *a room **for waiting*** – *waiting* is a gerund, used rather
  like a noun)
  *a **waiting** train* (= *a train **that is waiting*** – *waiting* is a participle, used
  rather like an adjective)
– *a **sleeping** pill* (*sleeping* is a gerund)
  *a **sleeping** child* (*sleeping* is a participle)
– ***working** conditions* (gerund)
  ***working** men and women* (participle)

For more about the difference between participles and gerunds, see 290.
For **noun + noun** structures, see 378–382.
For participle structures, see 403–406.

292 -ing forms used like nouns (1): subject, object or complement

1 subject, object or complement

An *-ing* form can be the subject, object or complement of a verb.
> ***Smoking** is bad for you.* (subject)   *I hate **packing**.* (object)
> *My favourite activity is **reading**.* (complement)

2 *-ing* form with its own object

The *-ing* form subject, object or complement is still a verb, and can have its
own object.
> ***Smoking cigarettes** is bad for you.*   *I hate **packing suitcases**.*
> *My favourite activity is **reading poetry**.*

3 determiners and possessives with *-ing* forms

We can often use determiners (for example *the, my, this*) with *-ing* forms.
> ***the opening** of Parliament*   *I don't mind **your going** without me.*
> *Does **my smoking** annoy you?*   *I hate all **this** useless **arguing**.*
Possessive *'s* forms are also possible.
> ***John's going** to sleep during the wedding was rather embarrassing.*
> *She was angry at **Lina's trying** to lie to her.*

Note that possessives and pronouns are not used before *-ing* forms if it is already clear who is being talked about.

> *Thank you for **waiting**.* (NOT *Thank you for **your waiting**.*)

When an *-ing* form is used with an article, it cannot usually have a direct object. Instead, we can use an *of-*structure.

> ***the smoking of** cigarettes* (NOT *the smoking cigarettes*)

No is often used with an *-ing* form to say that something is not allowed, or is impossible. The structure often occurs alone in notices; it can also follow *there is.*

> *NO SMOKING   NO PARKING   NO WAITING*
>
> *Sorry – **there's no smoking** in the waiting room.*
>
> *She's made up her mind; **there's no arguing** with her.*

4 object pronouns before *-ing* forms

In an informal style it is more common to use object forms (like *me, John*) instead of possessives (*my, John's*) with *-ing* forms, especially when these come after a verb or preposition.

> *I don't **mind you going** without me.*
>
> *She was angry **at Lina trying** to lie to her.*

Some verbs (e.g. *see, hear, watch, feel*) are normally followed by **object + *-ing* form**.

> *I **saw him getting** out of the car.* (NOT *I saw **his getting**…*)

5 *it . . . -ing*

We can use *it* as a preparatory subject or object for an *-ing* form (see 301–302).

> ***It's** nice **being** with you.*
>
> *I thought **it** pointless **starting** before eight o'clock.*

This is common with *any/no good, any/no use* and *(not) worth* (see 603).

> ***It's no good talking** to him – he never listens.*
>
> *Is **it any use expecting** them to be on time?*
>
> *I didn't think **it worth complaining** about the meal.*

Possessives or object pronouns (but not subject pronouns) can be used before the *-ing* forms in these structures.

> *It's no use **his/him** apologising – I shall never forgive him.*
>
> (NOT *It's no use **he apologising**…*)

6 nouns and *-ing* forms

When there is a noun which has a similar meaning to an *-ing* form, the noun is usually preferred.

> *We're all excited about **his arrival**.* (NOT *…about **his arriving**.*)

293 -ing forms used like nouns (2): after verbs

1 verbs that can be followed by *-ing* forms

After some verbs we can use an *-ing* form, but not normally an infinitive.

> *I **enjoy travelling**.* (NOT *I enjoy to travel.*)
>
> *He's **finished mending** the car.* (NOT *He's finished to mend…*)
>
> *She's **given up smoking**.* (NOT *…given up to smoke.*)
>
> *The doctor **suggested taking** a long holiday.*
>
> (NOT *The doctor suggested (me) to take…*)

▶

Some common verbs that are normally followed by *-ing* forms:

admit	dislike	give up	postpone
appreciate	endure	(can't) help	practise
avoid	enjoy	imagine	put off
burst out	escape	involve	resent
(crying/laughing)	excuse	keep (on)	resist
consider	face	leave off	risk
contemplate	fancy	mention	(can't) stand
delay	feel like	mind	suggest
deny	finish	miss	understand
detest	forgive		

Some verbs can be followed by both *-ing* forms and infinitives – see paragraph 4 below.

2 verb + object + *-ing* form

Some of the verbs listed above, and some others, can be followed by **object + *-ing* form.**

> I **dislike people telling** me what to think.
> I can't **imagine him working** in an office.
> Nobody can **stop him doing** what he wants to.
> Would you rather **spend time gardening** or **spend money paying**
>   somebody to do it for you?
> Did you **see her talking** to the postman?

Stop (in an informal style) and *prevent* are often followed by **object + *from* + *-ing* form.**

> Try to **stop/prevent them (from) finding** out.

Note that after many verbs we can use **possessive + *-ing* form** rather than **object + *-ing* form**, especially in a formal style. (See 292.3 for details.)

3 *-ing* form with passive meaning

After *deserve*, *need* and *require*, the *-ing* form has a passive sense. This structure is more common in British English.

> I don't think his article **deserves reading**. (= ... **deserves to be read**.)
> Your hair **needs cutting**. (= ... **needs to be cut**.)

In informal British English, *want* can also be used like this.

> The car **wants servicing**. (= ... **needs to be serviced**.)

4 *-ing* form or infinitive

After some verbs, either an *-ing* form or an infinitive can be used. These include:

advise	forbid	hear	prefer	start
allow	forget	intend	propose	stop
can't bear	go	like	regret	try
begin	go on	love	remember	watch
continue	hate	permit	see	

In some cases there is a difference of meaning between the two structures: see 296 for details.

For details of the structures used after a particular verb, see a good dictionary.

294 -ing forms used like nouns (3): after nouns and adjectives

1 noun/adjective + -*ing* form: examples

Some nouns and adjectives can be followed by -*ing* forms. A preposition is normally used to connect the noun/adjective to the -*ing* form. Nouns/adjectives that are followed by -*ing* forms cannot usually be followed by infinitives (see paragraph 3 for some exceptions).

> *I hate the **idea of getting** old.* (NOT *...the idea to get old.*)
> *The **thought of failing** never entered his head.*
> (NOT *The thought to fail*...)
> *I'm **tired of listening** to this.* (NOT *I'm tired to listen*...)
> *She's very **good at solving** problems.* (NOT *...good to solve*...)

2 purpose

*For + -**ing** form* can be used after a noun, or after an indefinite pronoun such as *something* or *anything*, to explain the purpose of an object or material – what it is for.

> *A strimmer is a **machine for cutting** grass and weeds.*
> *I need **something for killing** flies.*
> *Have you got any **stuff for cleaning** silver?*

This structure is mostly used to talk in general about types of object and material. When we talk about an individual's purpose in using a particular object, we are more likely to use an infinitive after the noun or pronoun (see 213.2).

> *I must find **something to kill** that fly.*

3 -*ing* form or infinitive

After some nouns and adjectives, we can use either an -*ing* form or an infinitive. Normally there is little or no difference of meaning.

> *We have a good chance **of making / to make** a profit.*
> *I'm proud **of having won / to have won**.*

For *be used to ...ing*, see 578.
For infinitives after nouns and adjectives, see 285–286.
For information about the structures that are possible after a particular noun or adjective, see a good dictionary.

295 -ing forms used like nouns (4): after prepositions

1 after all prepositions

When we put a verb after a preposition, we normally use an -*ing* form, not an infinitive.

> *You can't make an omelette **without breaking** eggs.*
> (NOT *...without to break eggs.*)
> *Always check the oil **before starting** the car.*
> (NOT *...before to start the car.*)

▶

*We got the job finished **by working** sixteen hours a day.*
*He's talking **about moving** to the country.*
*They painted the house **instead of going** on holiday.*
(NOT ...~~instead to go~~...)
*I look forward **to hearing** from you.* (NOT ...~~to hear from you.~~)

2   *to* as a preposition

To is actually two different words. It can be an infinitive marker, used to
show that the next word is an infinitive (e.g. ***to** swim, **to** laugh*). It can also be
a preposition, followed for example by a noun (e.g. *She's gone **to** the park,*
*I look forward **to** Christmas*).

When *to* is a preposition, it can be followed by the *-ing* form of a verb, but
not normally by the infinitive. Common expressions in which this happens
are *look forward to, object to, be used to, prefer (doing one thing **to doing***
another), get round to, in addition to.

In the following examples, note how the preposition *to* can be followed by
either a noun or an *-ing* form.
– *I look forward **to your next letter**.*
   *I look forward **to hearing** from you.* (a common way of closing a letter)
– *Do you object **to Sunday work**?*
   *Do you object **to working** on Sundays?*
– *I'm not used **to London traffic**.*
   *I'm not used **to driving** in London.*
– *I prefer the seaside **to the mountains**.*
   *I prefer swimming **to walking**.*
– *I'll get round **to the washing up** sooner or later.*
   *I'll get round **to doing** the washing up sooner or later.*
A few verbs and adjectives are used with *to* before nouns, but are followed by
the infinitives of verbs. Examples are *agree, consent, entitled, inclined, prone.*
*She **agreed to our plan** / She **agreed to do** what we wanted.*
*He's **inclined to anger** / He's **inclined to lose** his temper.*
Accustomed can be followed by *to* + *-ing* form or an infinitive (see 296.11).

3   object + infinitive after *for*

Note that some verbs are followed by ***for* + object + infinitive**. An *-ing* form
is not usually possible in these cases.
*We're still **waiting for her to arrive**.* (NOT ...~~waiting for her arriving.~~)
*Can you **arrange for us to get** tickets?* (NOT ...~~for our getting tickets?~~)

For the difference between ***used to* + infinitive** and ***be used to* + *-ing*** form, see 577–578.
For *-ing* forms after conjunctions (e.g. ***When planning** a holiday...*), see 406.6.
For time clauses with ***on* + *-ing*** form, see 406.6.

296 -ing forms used like nouns (5): -ing form or infinitive?

Some verbs and adjectives can be followed by either an *-ing* form or an infinitive.

> I **started playing** / **to play** the violin when I was 10.
> She was **proud of having won** / **to have won**.

In some cases, there is a difference of meaning.

1 *remember* and *forget*

Remember/forget + -ing form refers back to the past – to things that one did. **Forget ...ing** is used mostly in the phrase *I'll never forget ...ing*, and expressions with similar meanings.

> I still **remember buying** my first bicycle.
> I'll never **forget meeting** the Queen.

Remember/forget + infinitive refers forward in time – to things that one still has or still had to do at the moment of remembering or forgetting.

> You must **remember to fetch** Mr Lewis from the station tomorrow.
> I **forgot to buy** the soap.

2 *go on*

Go on + -ing form means 'continue'.

> She **went on talking** about her illnesses until we all went to sleep.

Go on + infinitive refers to a change of activity.

> She stopped talking about her illnesses and **went on to tell** us about all her other problems.

3 *regret*

Regret + -ing form refers back to the past – something that one is sorry one did.

> I **regret leaving** school at 14 – it was a big mistake.

Regret + infinitive is used mostly in announcements of bad news.

> We **regret to inform** passengers that the 14.50 train for Cardiff will leave approximately 37 minutes late.
> We **regret to say** that we are unable to help you.

4 *advise, allow, permit* and *forbid*

In active clauses after these verbs, we use an *-ing* form if there is no object. If there is an object we use an infinitive. Compare:

– I wouldn't **advise taking** the car – there's nowhere to park.
 I wouldn't **advise you to take** the car ...
– We don't **allow/permit smoking** in the lecture room.
 We don't **allow/permit people to smoke** in the lecture room.
– The headmistress has **forbidden singing** in the corridors.
 The headmistress has **forbidden children to sing** ...

Note the corresponding passive structures.

– **Smoking** is not allowed/permitted in the lecture room.
 People are not allowed/permitted **to smoke** in the lecture room. ▶

– *Singing is forbidden.*
  Children are forbidden to sing.
– *Early booking is advised.*
  Passengers are advised to book early.

5 see, watch and hear

After these verbs, the difference between **object + -*ing* form** and **object + infinitive** is like the difference between progressive and simple tenses. With *-ing* forms the verbs suggest that one pays attention to events or actions that are already going on; infinitives usually refer to complete events/actions which are seen/heard from beginning to end. (Note that these verbs are followed by the infinitive without *to*.) Compare:

– *I looked out of the window and saw Mary crossing the road.*
  I saw Mary step off the pavement, cross the road and disappear into the post office.
– *As I passed his house I heard him practising the piano.*
  I once heard Brendel play all the Beethoven concertos.

For more details, see 245.
For differences between *see* and *watch*, see 489.

6 try

To talk about making an experiment – doing something to see what will happen – we use *try + -ing*.

  I tried sending her flowers, writing her letters, giving her presents, but she still wouldn't speak to me.

To talk about making an effort to do something difficult, we can use either *try + infinitive* or *try + -ing*.

  I tried to change the wheel, but my hands were too cold.
  (OR *I tried changing the wheel...*)

7 mean

Mean in the sense of 'involve', 'have as a result' (see 339) can be followed by an *-ing* form.

  If you want to pass the exam it will mean studying hard.

In the sense of 'intend', *mean* is followed by an infinitive.

  I don't think she means to get married for the moment.

8 learn and teach

These verbs (and others with similar meanings) are followed by *-ing* forms when we are referring to lessons or subjects of study.

  She goes to college twice a week to learn typing.
  Mr Garland teaches skiing in the winter and rock-climbing in the summer.

Infinitives are used when we talk about the result of the study – about successfully learning a skill.

  She learnt to read German at school, but she learnt to speak it in Germany.
  I taught myself to type.

9 *like, love, hate* **and** *prefer*

After these four verbs, both infinitives and -*ing* forms can generally be used without a great difference of meaning.

> I **hate working / to work** at weekends.
> I don't get up on Sundays. I **prefer staying / to stay** in bed.

In British English, **like + -ing** is used mostly to talk about enjoyment, and **like + infinitive** mostly to talk about choices and habits. In American English, **like + infinitive** is common in both senses. Compare:

> I **like climbing** mountains. (more typically GB)
> I **like to climb** mountains. (more typically US)
> When I'm pouring tea I **like to put** the milk in first. (GB / US)

After *would like, would prefer, would hate* and *would love*, infinitives are most often used.

> **I'd like to tell** you something. (NOT ~~I'd like telling you something.~~)
> 'Can I give you a lift?' 'No thanks, **I'd prefer to walk.**'
>   (NOT ... ~~I'd prefer walking.~~)

Compare:

> **Do** you **like dancing?** (= Do you enjoy dancing?)
> **Would** you **like to dance?** (= Do you want to dance now?)

For more about *like*, see 319.
For details of structures with *prefer*, see 435.

10 *begin* **and** *start*

Begin and *start* can be followed by infinitives or -*ing* forms. Usually there is no important difference.

> She **began playing / to play** the guitar when she was six.
> He **started talking / to talk** about golf, but everybody went out of the room.

After progressive forms of *begin* and *start*, infinitives are preferred.

> I'm **beginning to learn** karate. (NOT ~~I'm beginning learning karate.~~)

Infinitives are also preferred with stative verbs like *understand, realise, know*.

> I slowly **began to understand** how she felt.
>   (NOT ... ~~began understanding~~ ...)
> He **started to realise** that if you wanted to eat you had to work.
>   (NOT ... ~~started realising~~ ...)

11 *attempt, intend, continue, can't bear, be accustomed to,*
be committed to

After these words and expressions we can generally use either an -*ing* form or an infinitive without much difference of meaning.

> I **intend telling / to tell** her what I think.
> I'm not **accustomed to giving/give** personal information about myself to strangers.

For details of structures with *to + -ing*, see 295.2.

12 *-ing* **form or infinitive of purpose:** *stop*

Some verbs that are followed by -*ing* forms can also be followed by an infinitive of purpose (see 281). A common example is *stop*.

> I **stopped running.** (NOT ... ~~I stopped to run.~~)
> I **stopped to rest.** (= ... in order to rest.)

►

13 *afraid*

To talk about fear of things that happen accidentally, we prefer
afraid of + *-ing*.

> *I don't like to drive fast because I'm **afraid of crashing**.*
> *'Why are you so quiet?' 'I'm **afraid of waking** the children.'*

In other cases we can use *afraid of* + *-ing* or *afraid* + **infinitive** with no
difference of meaning.

> *I'm not **afraid of telling / to tell** her the truth.*

14 *sorry*

Sorry for/about + *-ing* is used to refer to past things that one regrets. (*That*-
clauses are also very common in an informal style.)

> *I'm **sorry for/about** losing my temper this morning.*
> > (OR *I'm sorry **that** I lost my temper.*)

Sorry + **perfect infinitive** can be used with the same meaning. This is rather
formal.

> *I'm **sorry to have woken** you up.* (OR *I'm **sorry that I woke** you up.*)

Sorry + **infinitive** is used to apologise for current situations – things that one
is doing or going to do, or that one has just done.

> ***Sorry to disturb** you – could I speak to you for a moment?*
> *I'm **sorry to tell you** that you failed the exam.*
> ***Sorry to keep** you waiting – we can start now.*

15 *certain* and *sure*

Certain/sure of + *-ing* are used to refer to the feelings of the person one is
talking about.

> *Before the game she felt **certain of winning**, but after a few minutes she
>   realised it wasn't going to be so easy.*
> *You seem very **sure of passing** the exam. I hope you're right.*

Certain/sure + **infinitive** refer to the speaker's or writer's own feelings.

> *The repairs are **certain to cost** more than you think.*
> > (NOT ~~The repairs are **certain of costing**...~~)
> *'Kroftova's **sure to win** – the other girl hasn't got a chance.'*

Note that *He is sure to succeed* means '**I** am sure that he will succeed'.

16 *interested*

To talk about reactions to things one learns, *interested* + **infinitive** is
commonly used.

> *I was **interested to read** in the paper that scientists have found out how to
>   talk to whales.*
> *I'm **interested to see** that Alice and Jake are going out together.*
> *I shall be **interested to see** how long it lasts.*

To talk about a wish to find out something, both *interested* + *-ing* and
interested + **infinitive** are common.

> *I'm **interested in finding out / to find out** what she did with all that money.*
> *Aren't you **interested in knowing / to know** whether I'm pregnant?*

To talk about a wish to do something, we usually use *interested* with an *-ing* form.

> *I'm **interested in working** in Switzerland. Do you know anybody who could help me?* (NOT ~~*I'm **interested to work** in Switzerland*~~...)

For the difference between **used to** + **infinitive** and **be used to** + **-ing**, see 577–578.
For **object** + **-ing** form or infinitive after *get* and *have*, see 228.5–6 and 242.

297 instead (of)

1 preposition: *instead of*

Instead is not used alone as a preposition; we use the two words *instead of*.

> *I'll have tea **instead of coffee**, please.* (NOT ...~~*instead coffee*~~...)
> *Can you work with Sally **instead of me** today, please?*

Instead of is not usually followed by an infinitive.

> *I stayed in bed all day **instead of going** to work.*
> (NOT ...~~*instead (of) to go to work.*~~)

2 *instead of* and *without*

These are sometimes confused. We use *instead of* when one person, thing or action **replaces** another. We use *without* to say that a person, thing or action is not **together with** another. Compare:

– *Ruth was invited to the reception, but she was ill, so Lou went **instead of** her.* (Lou replaced Ruth.) (NOT ...~~*Lou went **without** her.*~~)
  *Max and Jake were invited, but Max was ill, so Jake went **without** him.* (Normally they would have gone together.)
– *She often goes swimming **instead of** going to school.* (Swimming replaces school.) (NOT ~~*She often goes swimming **without** going to school.*~~)
  *She often goes swimming **without** telling her mother.* (Swimming and telling her mother should go together.)
  (NOT ~~*She often goes swimming **instead of** telling her mother.*~~)

3 adverb: *instead*

Instead (without *of*) is an adverb. It most often comes at the beginning or end of a clause.

> *She didn't go to Greece after all. **Instead**, she went to America.*
> *Don't marry Phil. Marry me **instead**.*

298 inversion (1): auxiliary verb etc before subject

> auxiliary verb + subject + main verb
> *have/be* + subject + main verb

We put an auxiliary verb (and non-auxiliary *have* and *be*) before the subject of a clause in several different structures.

1 questions

> ***Have your father and mother** arrived?*
> (NOT ~~***Have arrived** your father and mother?*~~) ▶

*Where **is the concert** taking place?*
    (N O T ~~*Where is taking place the concert?*~~)
    (N O T ~~*Where the concert is taking place?*~~)
Note that spoken questions do not always have this word order (see 462).
    You're coming tomorrow?
Indirect questions do not usually have this order (see 481.6).
    *I wondered what time **the film was** starting.*
    (N O T ...~~*what time was the film starting.*~~)
    (N O T ...~~*what time was starting the film.*~~)
However, in formal writing inversion is sometimes used with *be* in indirect questions after *how*, especially when the subject is long.
    *I wondered **how** reliable **was the information** I had been given.*

For more information about questions, see 461–466.

2   exclamations

Exclamations often have the same structure as negative questions (see 360).
    ***Isn't it** cold?*   ***Hasn't she** got lovely eyes?*
In spoken American English, exclamations often have the same form as ordinary (non-negative) questions.
    ***Have you** got a surprise coming!*   ***Am I** mad!*
In a rather old-fashioned literary style, inversion is sometimes found in exclamations after *how* and *what*.
    *How beautiful **are the flowers!***   *What a peaceful place **is Skegness!***

For more information about the grammar of exclamations, see 201.

3   with *may*

May can come before the subject in wishes.
    ***May all your wishes** come true!*
    ***May he** rot in hell!*

4   after *so, neither, nor*

In 'short answers' and similar structures, these words are followed by **auxiliary verb + subject**.
    *'I'm hungry.' 'So **am I**.'*   *'I don't like opera.' 'Neither/Nor **do I**.'*

For more details of these structures, see 516 and 364.

5   after negative and restrictive expressions

If a negative adverb or adverbial expression is put at the beginning of a clause for emphasis, it is usually followed by **auxiliary verb + subject**. These structures are mostly rather formal.
    ***Under no circumstances can we** cash cheques.*
    ***At no time was the President** aware of what was happening.*
    ***Not until much later did she learn** who her real father was.*
The same structure is possible after a complete clause beginning *not until* ...
    ***Not until he received her letter did he** fully understand the depth of her feelings.*

Inversion is also used after restrictive words like *hardly, seldom, rarely, little* and *never*, and after expressions containing *only*. These structures, too, are formal or literary.

> **Hardly had I** arrived when trouble started.
> **Seldom have I** seen such a remarkable creature.
> **Little did he** realise the danger he faced.
> **Never ... was so much** owed by so many to so few. (Churchill)
> **Only then did I** understand what she meant.
> **Only after her death was I** able to appreciate her.
> **Not only did we** lose our money, but we were nearly killed.

Inversion is not used after non-emphatic adverbial expressions of place and time.

> **Not far from here you can** see foxes.
> (NOT ~~Not far from here can you~~...)

Inversion is used when **not + object** is put at the beginning of a sentence for emphasis.

> **Not a single word did she** say.

6   after *as, than* and *so*

Inversion sometimes happens after *as, than* and emphasising *so* in a literary style.

> She was very religious, **as were most of her friends**.
> City dwellers have a higher death rate **than do country people**.
> **So** ridiculous **did she** look that everybody burst out laughing.

7   conditional clauses

In formal and literary conditional clauses, an auxiliary verb can be put before the subject instead of using *if*.

> **Were she** my daughter ... (= If she were my daughter ...)
> **Had I** realised what you intended ... (= If I had realised ...)

Negatives are not contracted in this case.

> **Had we not** spent all our money already, ... (NOT ~~Hadn't we spent~~...)

For more details of this structure, see 261.6.
For more about fronting, see 217.

299   **inversion** (2): whole verb before subject

1   after adverbial expressions of place

When an adverbial expression of place or direction comes at the beginning of a clause, intransitive verbs are often put before their subjects. This happens especially when a new indefinite subject is being introduced. The structure is most common in literary and descriptive writing.

> Under a tree **was lying one of the biggest men** I had ever seen.
> On the grass **sat an enormous frog**.
> Directly in front of them **stood a great castle**.
> Along the road **came a strange procession**.

This structure is often used in speech with *here, there* and other short adverbs and adverb particles.   ▶

Here **comes Freddy!** (NOT ~~*Here* **Freddy comes.**~~)
There **goes your brother.**
I stopped the car, and up **walked a policeman.**
If the subject is a pronoun, it goes before the verb.
Here **she comes.** (NOT ~~*Here* **comes she.**~~)
Off **we go!**

2 reporting

In story-telling, the subject often comes after reporting verbs like *said, asked, suggested* etc when these follow direct speech.
'What do you mean?' **asked Henry.** (OR *... Henry asked.*)
'I love you,' **whispered Jan.**
If the subject is a pronoun, it usually comes before the verb.
'What do you mean?' **he asked.**

300 irregular verbs

1 common irregular verbs

This is a list of the more common irregular verbs. Students should check that they know all of them. For a complete list of English irregular verbs, see a good dictionary.

Infinitive	Simple past	Past participle
arise	arose	arisen
awake	awoke	awoken
be	was, were	been
bet	bet, betted	bet, betted
beat	beat	beaten
become	became	become
begin	began	begun
bend	bent	bent
bind	bound	bound
bite	bit	bitten
bleed	bled	bled
blow	blew	blown
break	broke	broken
bring	brought	brought
build	built	built
burn	burnt/burned	burnt/burned
buy	bought	bought
catch	caught	caught
choose	chose	chosen
come	came	come
cost	cost	cost
cut	cut	cut

Infinitive	Simple past	Past participle
deal	dealt /delt/	dealt /delt/
dig	dug	dug
do	did	done
draw	drew	drawn
dream	dreamt /dremt/	dreamt /dremt/
	dreamed /driːmd/	dreamed /driːmd/
drink	drank	drunk
drive	drove	driven
eat	ate /et/	eaten /ˈiːtn/
fall	fell	fallen
feed	fed	fed
feel	felt	felt
fight	fought	fought
find	found	found
fly	flew	flown
forget	forgot	forgotten
forgive	forgave	forgiven
freeze	froze	frozen
get	got	got
give	gave	given
go	went	gone / been
grow	grew	grown
hang	hung	hung
have	had	had
hear	heard /hɜːd/	heard /hɜːd/
hide	hid	hidden
hit	hit	hit
hold	held	held
hurt	hurt	hurt
keep	kept	kept
know	knew	known
lay	laid	laid
lead	led	led
lean	leant / leaned	leant / leaned
learn	learnt / learned	learnt / learned
leave	left	left
lend	lent	lent
let	let	let
lie	lay	lain
light	lit / lighted	lit / lighted
lose	lost	lost
make	made	made
mean	meant /ment/	meant /ment/
meet	met	met

▶

Infinitive	Simple past	Past participle
pay	paid	paid
put	put	put
read /riːd/	read /red/	read /red/
ride	rode	ridden
ring	rang	rung
rise	rose	risen
run	ran	run
say	said /sed/	said /sed/
see	saw	seen
sell	sold	sold
send	sent	sent
set	set	set
shake	shook	shaken
shine	shone /ʃɒn/	shone /ʃɒn/
shoot	shot	shot
show	showed	shown
shut	shut	shut
sing	sang	sung
sink	sank	sunk
sit	sat	sat
sleep	slept	slept
smell	smelt / smelled	smelt / smelled
speak	spoke	spoken
speed	sped	sped
spell	spelt / spelled	spelt / spelled
spend	spent	spent
spill	spilt / spilled	spilt / spilled
spin	span / spun	spun
spit	spat	spat
split	split	split
spoil	spoilt / spoiled	spoilt / spoiled
stand	stood	stood
steal	stole	stolen
stick	stuck	stuck
strike	struck	struck
swing	swung	swung
swim	swam	swum
take	took	taken
teach	taught	taught
tear	tore	torn
tell	told	told
think	thought	thought
throw	threw	thrown
understand	understood	understood

Infinitive	Simple past	Past participle
wake	woke	woken
wear	wore	worn
win	won	won
wind /waɪnd/	wound /waʊnd/	wound /waʊnd/
write	wrote	written

Note that the old past participle *drunken* is still used as an adjective in some expressions (e.g. *drunken driving*).
Speed can also have regular forms.
Says is pronounced /sez/.

2 verbs that are easily confused

Infinitive	Simple past	Past participle
fall	fell	fallen
feel	felt	felt
fill	filled	filled

find	found	found
(= 'get back something lost')		
found	founded	founded
(= 'start up an organisation or institution')		

flow	flowed	flowed
(of a liquid = 'move')		
fly	flew	flown
(= 'move in the air')		

lay	laid	laid
(= 'put down flat')		
lie	lay	lain
(= 'be down')		
lie	lied	lied
(= 'say things that are not true')		

For more details of these three verbs, see 309.

Infinitive	Simple past	Past participle
leave	left	left
live	lived	lived

raise	raised	raised
(= 'put up')		
rise	rose	risen
(= 'go / get up')		

strike	struck	struck
(= 'hit')		
stroke	stroked	stroked
(= 'pass the hand gently over')		

wind /waɪnd/	wound /waʊnd/	wound /waʊnd/
(= 'turn, tighten a spring etc')		
wound /wuːnd/	wounded	wounded
(= 'injure in a battle')		

▶

3 **American English**

Note the following differences between British and American English.

a *burn, dream, lean, learn, smell, spell, spill* and *spoil* are all regular in American English. In British English, irregular past tenses and participles with -*t* are more common (see list in paragraph 1), but regular forms also occur; there may sometimes be a difference of usage.

b *Wake* can be regular in American English.

c *Spit* has both *spit* and *spat* as past tense and participle in American English.

d *Quit* and *wet* are regular in British English, but irregular in American; *fit* is also usually irregular in American English.

    fit   fit   fit
    quit quit quit
    wet wet wet

e *Dive* is regular in British English, but can be irregular in American.

    dive dived/dove (/doʊv/) *dived*

f The American past participle of *get* is either *got* or *gotten* (see 228.7).

g Note the standard American pronunciations of *ate* (/eɪt/) and *shone* (usually /ʃoʊn/).

301 **it** (1): preparatory subject

1 **infinitive subjects**

When the subject of a clause is an infinitive expression, this does not normally come at the beginning. We usually prefer to start with the 'preparatory subject' *it*, and to put the infinitive expression later (long or complicated items are often put towards the end of a sentence – see 289). Preparatory *it* is common before **be + adjective/noun complement**.

    *It's nice **to talk** to you.*
        (More natural than *To talk to you is nice.*)
    *It's important **to book** in advance.*
    *It's my ambition **to run** a three-hour marathon.*
    *It upsets me **to hear** people arguing all the time.*
    *It was good of you **to phone**.*

It can also be used as a preparatory subject for the ***for* + infinitive** structure (see 280).

    *It will suit me best **for you to arrive** at about ten o'clock.*
    *It's essential **for the papers to be ready** before Thursday.*

2 **clause subjects**

We also normally use preparatory *it* when the subject of a clause is itself another clause.

    *It's probable **that we'll be a little late**.*
    *It doesn't interest me **what you think**.*
    *It's surprising **how many unhappy marriages there are**.*

It's exciting **when a baby starts talking**.
It seems **that he forgot to buy the tickets**.
It is said **that only three people in the world can understand his theory**.
It's essential **that she should be told immediately**.

For more details of structures with *should*, see 497.
For the use of subjunctives in sentences about necessity and importance, see 541.

3   *-ing* form subjects

It can be a preparatory subject for an *-ing* form. This is usually rather informal.

It was nice **seeing you**.
It's crazy **her going off like that**.
It's worth **going to Wales** if you have the time.
It's no use **trying to explain** – I'm not interested.
It surprised me **your not remembering my name**.

For more information about structures with *worth*, see 603.
For *there* as a preparatory subject with *any/no use*, see 563.2.

4   *it takes …* + infinitive

We can use this structure to talk about the time necessary for things to happen (see 551).

It **took** me months **to get** to know her.
How long does **it take to get** to London from here?

5   *if, as if* and *as though*

It is used to introduce some clauses with *if, as if* and *as though*.

It looks **as if** we're going to have trouble with Ann again.
It's not **as if** this was the first time she's been difficult.
It will be a pity **if** we have to ask her to leave.
But *it* looks **as though** we may have to.

6   emphasis: 'cleft sentences'

It can be used in 'cleft sentences' with *who-* and *that*-clauses to emphasise one part of a sentence.

It was my aunt **who took** Peter to London yesterday, not my mother.
   (emphasising *my aunt*)
It was Peter **that my aunt took** to London yesterday, not Lucy.
   (emphasising *Peter*)
For more details of cleft sentences, see 131.

For 'impersonal' *it* in sentences like *It's raining*, see 424.7.
For passive structures with *it* as a preparatory subject, see 411.
For *it* as 'preparatory object', see next section.

302 it (2): preparatory object

1 infinitive or clause object + complement

We can sometimes use *it* as a preparatory object. This happens when the object of a verb is an infinitive expression or a clause with an adjective or noun complement.

> subject + verb + *it* + complement + infinitive / clause

*I find **it difficult to talk** to you.*
*My blister made **it a problem to walk**.*
*I thought **it strange that she hadn't written**.*
*George made **it clear what he wanted**.*

Note that this structure is not normally used when there is no adjective or noun complement after the verb.

I cannot bear to see people crying.
   (NOT ~~I cannot bear it to see people crying.~~)
I remember that we were very happy. (NOT ~~I remember it that...~~)

But note the structure *I like/love/hate it when ...*

*I **love it when** you sing.*

Note also the idiom *I take it that ...* (= 'I assume that ...').

*I **take it that** you won't be working tomorrow.*

2 *-ing* form object + complement

This structure is also possible with *-ing* form objects.

*I find **it interesting talking** to you.*

3 *if*-clauses

It is used as a preparatory object for an *if*-clause after *would appreciate*.

*I would appreciate **it** if you would keep me informed.*
   (NOT ~~I would appreciate if you would...~~)

4 *owe* and *leave*

Note the structures *owe it to somebody to ...* and *leave it to somebody to ...*

*We **owe it** to society **to make our country a better place**.*
*I'll **leave it** to you **to decide**.*

For *it* as a preparatory subject, see 301.

303 its and it's

These two words are often confused by native speakers of English as well as by foreign learners.

Its is a possessive word (like *my*, *your*).

*Every country has **its** traditions.* (NOT ~~...it's traditions.~~)

It's is the contracted form of *it is* or *it has*.
> *It's* raining again. (N O T ~~*Its raining again.*~~)
> *Have you seen my camera?* *It's* disappeared. (N O T . . . ~~*Its disappeared.*~~)

There is a similar difference between *whose* and *who's* – see 598.
For more about contractions, see 144.

304 it's time

1 followed by infinitive

It's time (or *it is time*) can be followed by an infinitive.
> *It's* **time to buy** a new car.

When it is necessary to express the subject of the infinitive, the **for + object + infinitive** structure (see 280) can be used.
> *It's time* **for her to go** to bed.

2 followed by past tense with present meaning

It's time can also be followed by a subject with a past tense verb. The meaning is present.
> *It's* **time she went** to bed.   *It's* **time you washed** those trousers.
> *I'm getting tired.* *It's* **time we went** home.

For other structures in which a past tense has a present or future meaning, see 422.

305 just

1 meanings

Just has several meanings.

a time

Just often emphasises the idea of 'at the present' or 'close to the present'.
> *I'll be down in a minute – I'm* **just** *changing my shirt.* (= 'right now')
> *Alice has* **just** *phoned.* (= 'a short time ago')
> *'Where's my tea?' 'I'm* **just going to** *make it.'* (= 'immediately')
> *'What's happened to Keith? He seems to have disappeared.' 'No, he's around. I saw him* **just last week**.*'* (= 'as recently as')

Note that *just now* can mean either 'at this moment' or 'a few moments ago', depending on the tense. Compare:
> *She's not in* **just now**. *Can I take a message?*
> *I saw Phil* **just now**. *He wanted to talk to you.*

In expressions like *just after*, *just before* and *just when*, *just* suggests closeness to the time in question.
> *I saw him* **just after** *lunch.* (= . . . **very soon after** *lunch.*)

b 'only', 'scarcely'

Just can mean 'only', 'nothing more than'.
> *Complete set of garden tools for* **just** *£15.99!*
> *I* **just** *want somebody to love me – that's all.*
> *I'm* **just** *a poor boy.*

▶

In some contexts, the meaning is more like 'scarcely', 'with nothing to spare', 'with nothing in reserve'.

> We **just** caught the train.   I've got **just** enough money for a cup of coffee.

This meaning can be emphasised by *only*.

> I'd **only just** got into the bath when she phoned.
> There was **only just** enough light to read by.

Just can be used as a 'softener', to make a request seem less demanding, and therefore more polite.

> Could I **just** use your phone for a moment?   **Just** sign here.
> **Just** a moment.

c 'exactly'

Just often means 'exactly'.

> 'What's the time?' 'It's **just** four o'clock.'
> Thanks. That's **just** what I wanted.
> **Just** then, the door opened and Graham came in.
> I got home **just** as the sun was setting.

Just as ... as means 'no less than'.

> She's **just as** bad-tempered **as** her father.

d emphasiser

Just can emphasise other words and expressions. It means 'simply', 'there's no other word for it'.

> You're **just** beautiful.   I **just** love your dress.
> It **just** breaks my heart to see her so unhappy.

2 **tenses**

When *just* means 'a moment ago', a present perfect tense is most common in British English.

> 'Where's Eric?' 'He**'s just gone** out.'   I've **just had** a call from Sarah.

In American English a past tense is common in this case.

> 'Where's Eric?' 'He **just went** out.'   I **just had** a call from Sarah.

When *just now* means 'a moment ago', it is used with a past tense in both British and American English.

> **Did** you **hear** a strange noise **just now**?

For the position of *just* as a focusing adverb, see 23.3.

306 know

1 *know how* + **infinitive**

Know cannot be followed directly by an infinitive. We use the structure *know how to*.

> I **know how to** make Spanish omelettes. (NOT ~~I know to make...~~)

For more information about the use of infinitives after *how, what, whether* etc, see 288.

2 **object + infinitive**

In a formal style, *know* is occasionally followed by **object + infinitive**.

> They **knew him to be** a dangerous criminal.

However, this is unusual; *that*-clauses are generally more natural.

> They **knew that he was** a dangerous criminal.

The passive equivalent of **know** + **object** + **infinitive** is more common, at least in a formal style.

> He **was known to be** a dangerous criminal.

Know is used to mean 'experience' in the common structure *I've never* **known** + **object** + **infinitive**; an infinitive without *to* is sometimes used in British English.

> I've never known it **(to) rain** like this. (GB)

3 tenses

Know is one of the verbs that cannot usually be used in progressive forms (see 451).

> I **know** exactly what you mean. (NOT ~~I am knowing~~...)

Note that a present perfect tense is used to say how long one has known somebody or something. (See 418.6 for more details.)

> We**'ve known** each other since 1974. (NOT ~~We know each other since 1974.~~)

4 *know* and *know about/of*

Know + **object** is used mainly to talk about knowledge that comes from direct personal experience. In other cases, we normally use *know about/of*, *have heard of* or another structure. Compare:

– 'You don't **know** my mother, do you?' 'No, I've never met her.'
  We all **know about** Abraham Lincoln.
  > (NOT ~~We all know Abraham Lincoln.~~)
– **I know** your home town. (= I've been there.)
  I've heard of your home town (but I haven't been there).
  I know where you come from.
  > (= I know the answer to the question 'Where do you come from?').

5 *know* and *find out* etc

Know is not normally used to talk about the process of finding something out: to know something is **to have learnt** it, not **to learn** it. To talk about getting knowledge we can use for example *find out, get to know, learn, hear, can tell*.

> 'She's married.' 'Where did you **find** that **out**?'
> (NOT ...~~'Where did you know that?'~~)
> I want to travel round the world and **get to know** people from different countries. (NOT ...~~and know people~~...)
> He's from Liverpool, as you **can tell** from his accent.
> (NOT ...~~as you can know from his accent.~~)

6 *I know* and *I know it*

Note the difference between these two short answers.

I know refers to facts – it could be completed by a *that*-clause.

> 'You're late.' '**I know.**' (= I know **that I'm late**.) (NOT ...~~'I know it.'~~)

I know it generally refers to things – *it* replaces a noun.

> 'I went to a nice restaurant called The Elizabeth last night.' '**I know it.**'

307 last and the last

1 *last week, month* etc

Last (without *the*) contrasts with *this* and *next*. *Last week, last month* etc is the week, month etc just before the one in which the words are said or written. (On 20 July 1994, for example, *last month* is June 1994.) Note that these time expressions are normally used with past tenses, without articles, and without prepositions.

> *I had a cold **last week**.*
>> (NOT ~~*I have had a cold last week.*~~)
>> (NOT ~~*I had a cold **the** last week.*~~)
>> (NOT *...**in** last week.*)
> *Were you at the meeting **last Tuesday**?*
> *We bought this house **last year**.*

2 *the last week, month* etc

The last week, the last month etc can mean the period of seven / thirty / etc days up to the moment of speaking or writing. (On 20 July 1994, for example, *the last month* is the period from 20 June to 20 July 1994.) Note that these time expressions are normally used with perfect tenses and with prepositions.

> *I've had a cold for **the last week**.* (for the seven days up to now)
> *We've lived here **for the last year**.* (since twelve months ago)

The last week etc can also be used to refer to a period up until a particular past moment. A past perfect tense is normally used.

> *I decided to see the doctor, because I'd been feeling ill during **the last two months**.*

Note the word order in expressions like *the last three weeks* etc.

> *I've been busy for **the last three months**.*
>> (NOT *...**for the three last months**.*)

We generally say *the last few days/weeks* etc, not *the last days/weeks* etc.

> ***The last few days** have been very wet.*
>> (NOT ~~*The last days have been very wet.*~~)

3 the last in a series

The last can also refer to the last item in a series (with no relation to present time).

> *In **the last** week of the holiday something funny happened.*
> *This is going to be **the last** Christmas I'll spend at home.*

4 *last* and *latest*

In talking about events, actions and productions, we use *latest*, not *last*, to refer to new or very recent things. *Last* can mean 'before this'. Compare:

- *She says her **latest** book's being published next week.* (her **most recent** book) (NOT ~~*She says her **last** book's being published next week.*~~)
  *She thinks it's much better than her **last** one.* (her **previous** one)
- *He's enjoying his **latest** job.* (NOT ~~*He's enjoying his **last** job.*~~)
  *But it doesn't pay as much as his **last** one.*

Latest suggests there may be more to come; *last* can mean 'final' (see paragraph 3 above). Compare:

> Have you seen Bill's **latest** car? He seems to buy a new one every week.
> This is the **last** car we buy. I'm afraid I'm getting too old to drive.

5   tenses with *This is the last . . .*

Present and future tenses are both possible with *This is the last . . .*, and similar structures with *last*.

> This is the last time I**'m paying** for you.
>   (OR *This is the last time I**'ll pay** for you.*)
> That's the last letter he **gets** from me.
>   (OR *That's the last letter he**'ll get** from me.*)

The difference between *next* and *the next* is like the difference between *last* and *the last*. See 367.

For tenses with *this is the first/second . . .* etc, see 419.7.

308   later and in

With a time expression, *later* generally means 'after that time'.

> She was so happy when she got married. But **six months later** she was divorced.
> So you and Penny will come on the Monday, and Colin will arrive about **a week later**.

With a time expression, we usually use *in*, not *later*, to say 'after now'.

> I'll see you **in a few days**. (NOT ~~I'll see you a few days later.~~)

But without a time expression, *later* can be used to mean 'after now'.

> Bye! See you **later**!

309   lay and lie

There are three similar verbs that can be confused: *lay* (regular except for spelling), *lie* (irregular) and *lie* (regular).

1   *lay*

Lay is a regular verb except for its spelling. Its forms are:

- infinitive: *(to) lay*
- *-ing* form: *laying*
- past: *laid*
- past participle: *laid*

Lay means 'put down carefully' or 'put down flat'. It has an object.

> I **laid** the papers on the table. (NOT ~~I lay . . .~~)
> **Lay** the tent down on the grass and I'll see how to put it up.

Note the expressions *lay a table* (= put plates, knives etc on a table) and *lay an egg* (a bird's way of having a baby).

▶

2 *lie* (irregular)

The forms of the irregular verb *lie* are:
- infinitive: *(to) lie*
- *-ing* form: *lying*
- past: *lay*
- past participle: *lain* (used mostly in a formal / literary style)

Lie (irregular) means 'be down', 'be / become horizontal'. It has no object.

*Don't **lie** in bed all day. Get up and do some work.*
  (NOT *Don't lay in bed...*)
*I **lay** down and closed my eyes.* (NOT *I laid down...*)

3 *lie* (regular)

The regular verb *lie* (*lied*) means 'say things that are not true'.

*You **lied** to me when you said you loved me.*

4 dialect forms

In many British and American dialects, different forms of *lay* and irregular *lie* are used. *Lay* is often used in cases where standard English has *lie*.

*I'm going to **lay** down for a few minutes.* (Standard English ... ***lie** down ...*)

For more information about irregular verbs, see 300.

310 learn

1 structures before a verb

Learn can be followed by ***how* + infinitive** or by an infinitive alone. There is not usually much difference of meaning: *learn (how)* can be used to talk both about the process of learning and its result.

*She enjoyed **learning (how)** to look after young animals.*
*Last year I **learnt (how)** to water-ski.*
*It takes a long time to **learn (how)** to drive in city traffic.*
*He soon **learnt (how)** to help his wife in her work.*

How is common especially in cases where there is a method or technique to be learnt. In other cases it is not generally used. Compare:

*It's time you **learnt (how)** to change the oil in the car.*
*In the new job, I soon **learnt** to keep my mouth shut.*
  (More natural than ... *I soon **learnt how** to keep my mouth shut.*)

2 forms

Learn is usually irregular in British English (*learn/learnt*) and regular in American English (*learn/learned*). For other verbs like this, see 300.3.

For the adjective *learned* (/ˈlɜːnɪd/), see 13.

311 least and fewest

1 *the least* as determiner: superlative of *little*

The least is used before uncountable nouns as a determiner referring to quantity (see 157); it is the superlative of *little* (= 'not much'), and the opposite of *most*.

> In a 'slow bicycle race', the winner is the person who travels **the least distance** in one minute without falling off or turning round.
> I think I probably do **the least work** in this office.

The least can be used without a noun if the meaning is clear from what comes before.

> Jan earns the most money in our family; Pete earns **the least**.
> 'Thanks for your help.' 'Oh, it was **the least** I could do.'

Note also the expression *the least of* (= 'the smallest of'), used before plural abstract nouns.

> 'What will your mother think?' 'That's **the least of my worries**.'

2 *any ... at all*

The least can have a similar meaning to 'any ... at all'. This happens mostly before singular abstract nouns in 'non-assertive' contexts (see 374): for instance in questions, negative clauses and *if*-clauses.

> Do you think there's **the least chance** of Labour winning the election?
> 'What's the time?' 'I haven't got **the least idea**.'
> If you have **the least difficulty** with the arrangements for the conference, phone me at once.
> She's not **the least bit** afraid of horses.

For countable and uncountable uses of words like *chance, idea* and *difficulty*, see 148.5.

3 *the fewest* as determiner: superlative of *few*

The fewest is used before plural nouns as the superlative of *few*.

> The translation with **the fewest mistakes** isn't always the best.

Least is often used instead of *fewest* before plural nouns (... *the least mistakes*), especially in an informal style. Some people feel this is incorrect.

4 *(the) least* with adjectives: the opposite of *(the) most* or *(the) ...est*

(The) least is used before adjectives in the same way as *(the) most* or *(the) ...est* (see 136), but with the opposite meaning.

> **The least expensive** holidays are often the most interesting.
> Don't give the job to Keith: he's **the least experienced**.
> I'm **least happy** when I have to work at weekends.

For the use of *the* with superlatives, see 65.4, 138.12.

5 *least* as adverb

Least can be used as an adverb (the opposite of *most*).

> She always arrives when you **least** expect it.
> I don't much like housework, and I like cooking **least** of all.

▶

6 *at least*

At least means 'not less than (but perhaps more than)'.
> *'How old do you think he is?' '**At least** thirty.'*
> *He's been in love **at least** eight times this year.*

We can also use *at least* as a discourse marker (see 159) to suggest that one thing is certain or all right, even if everything else is unsatisfactory.
> *We lost everything in the fire. But **at least** nobody was hurt.*

7 *not in the least*

We can use *not in the least* in a formal style to mean 'not at all', especially when talking about personal feelings and reactions.
> *I was **not in the least upset** by her bad temper.*
> *She did **not** mind working late **in the least**.*

For *little* and *few*, see 322.
For *less* and *fewer*, see 313.

312 left

The past participle of *leave*, *left*, can be used in a special way, to mean 'remaining', 'not used', 'still there'.
> *What did you do with the money that was **left**?*
> *After the explosion, only two people were **left** alive.*

Left is very common in the following structures:

$$
\left.\begin{matrix} there\ is \\ have\ got \end{matrix}\right\} \left\{\begin{matrix} \text{noun} \\ \text{something / anything / nothing} \\ \text{somebody / anybody / nobody} \\ \text{someone / anyone / no one} \end{matrix}\right\} \ left
$$

Note the position of *left*: at the end of the structure.
> *There are **two eggs left**, if you're hungry.*
> *There's **nothing left** in the fridge.*
> *I **haven't got any money left**: can you get the tickets?*
> *Now that her friends have moved to London she **hasn't got anybody left** to play bridge with.*

313 less and fewer

1 the difference

Less is the comparative of *little* (used especially before uncountable nouns).
Fewer is the comparative of *few* (used before plural nouns). Compare:
> *I earn **less money** than a postman.*
> *I've got **fewer problems** than I used to have.*

Less is quite common before plural nouns, as well as uncountables, especially in an informal style. Some people consider this incorrect.
> *I've got **less problems** than I used to have.*

2   *less/fewer* **with and without** *of*

Less of and *fewer of* are used before determiners (like *the*, *my* or *this*) and pronouns.

> *I'd like to spend **less of my time** answering letters.*
> *At the college reunions, there are **fewer of us** each year.*

Before nouns without determiners, *of* is not used.

> *If you want to lose weight, eat **less food**.* (NOT ... ~~less of food~~.)
> ***Fewer people** make their own bread these days.* (NOT ~~Fewer of people~~ ...)

3   *less* **and** *fewer* **without nouns**

Nouns that have already been mentioned can be dropped after *less* and *fewer*, if the meaning is clear.

> *Some people in our village still go to church, but **less/fewer** than*
>   *20 years ago.*

Less can be used as an adverb (the opposite of the adverb *more*).

> *I worry **less** than I used to.*

4   *lesser*

Lesser is used in a few expressions (in a rather formal style) to mean 'smaller' or 'not so much'.

> *the **lesser** of two evils   a **lesser**-known writer*

For *little* and *few*, see 322.
For *least* and *fewest*, see 311.
For the use of *much, far, a lot* etc with *fewer* and *less*, see 139.

314   lest

Lest has a similar meaning to *in case* (see 271) or *so that ... not* (see 519). It is very rare in modern British English, and is found mostly in older literature and in ceremonial language. It is a little more common in formal American English.

> *They kept watch all night **lest** robbers should come.*
> *We must take care **lest** evil thoughts enter our hearts.*

Lest can be followed by a subjunctive verb (see 541).

> *The government must take immediate action, **lest** the problem of child*
>   *poverty **grow** worse.*

For fear that is used in a similar way, and is also unusual in modern English.

> *He hid in the woods **for fear that** the soldiers would find him.*

For more about older English, see 388.

315   **let** introducing imperatives

Let can be used to introduce suggestions and orders, when these are not addressed to the hearer/reader (or not only to the hearer/reader). This structure can be considered a kind of imperative (see 268).   ▶

1   first-person plural imperative

We can use *let us* (formal) or *let's* (informal) to make suggestions or to give orders to a group that includes the speaker.

> **Let us** *pray.*
> **Let's have** *a drink.*
> *OK,* **let's all get** *moving.*

Shall we? is used as a question tag (see 465–466) in British English; *let's* is used as a short answer.

> '*Let's go for a walk,* **shall we?**' '*Yes,* **let's.**'

There are two possible negatives, with *let us not* and *do not let us* (informal *let's not* / *don't let's*).

> **Let us not** *despair.* (formal)
> **Let's not** *get angry.* (informal)
> **Do not let us** *forget those who came before us.* (formal)
> **Don't let's** *stay up too late tonight.* (informal)

Forms with *don't let's* (and *let's don't* in American English) are very informal.

2   first-person singular imperative

Let me is used to 'give instructions to oneself'; the expressions *Let me see* and *Let me think* are very common.

> '*What time do you want to have breakfast?*' '**Let me think.** *Yes, I reckon eight o'clock will be early enough.*'
> *Now what's the best way to get to Manchester?* **Let me see** – *suppose I take the M6 from Birmingham . . .*
> **Let me** *just get my coat and I'll be with you.*

In a very informal style, *let's* is often used to mean *let me* (see 424.9).

> **Let's see.** *Suppose I take the M6 from Birmingham . . .*

3   third-person imperative

Let can also introduce a suggestion or order for someone or something else, not the speaker or hearer. This is common in formal and ceremonial language, but informal uses are also possible.

> **Let** *the prayers begin.*
> **Let** *our enemies understand that we will not hesitate to defend our territory and our interests, wherever they may be.*
> '*Your boyfriend's going out with another girl.*' '**Let** *him. I don't care.*'

Note the structure with **let + the infinitive of there is.**

> **Let there be** *no doubt in your minds about our intentions.*

316   let: structures

1   followed by infinitive without *to*

Let is followed by **object + infinitive without to.**

> *We usually* **let the children stay** *up late on Saturdays.*
> (NOT . . . ~~let the children **to stay** / **staying**~~ . . .)
> *She didn't* **let me see** *what she was doing.* (NOT . . . ~~let me **saw**~~ . . .)
> '*We'll take you to London.*' '*Well,* **let us pay** *for the petrol.*'

Note also the expressions *let ... know* (= 'tell', 'inform') and *let ... have* (= 'send', 'give').

> I'll **let you know** my holiday dates next week.
> Could you **let me have** the bill for the car repair?

Let go of means 'release'.

> Don't **let go of** Mummy's hand.

2 not used in passives

Let is unusual in passive forms; we prefer *allow*.

> After questioning he **was allowed to go** home.

3 with object + preposition / adverb particle

Let can be followed by an object and a prepositional phrase or adverb particle expressing movement.

> You'd better **let the dog out of the car**.
> **Let him in**, could you?   Those kids **let my tyres down**.

For more about infinitives without *to*, see 277.
For *let* in first- and third-person imperatives, see 315.

317 letters

Each culture has its own way of organising a letter and arranging it on a page. English-speaking people generally observe the following rules.

1   Put your own address at the top on the right. Addresses generally follow the rule of 'smallest first': house number, then street, then town. Postcode and telephone number come last. Don't put your name with the address.

2   Put the date directly under the address. A common way to write the date is to put the number of the day, followed by the month and year (e.g. *17 May 1992*). For other ways (and differences between British and American customs) see 151.

3   In formal letters and business letters, put the name and address of the person you are writing to on the left side of the page, starting on the same level as the date or slightly below.

4   Different styles are common in formal letters on paper which has the address ready-printed at the top of the page. For example, the date may be put on the left, and the address of the person written to may come at the end of the letter or of the first page.

5   Begin the letter (*Dear X*) on the left. Common ways of addressing people are:
    □ by first name (informal): *Dear Penny*
    □ by title and surname (more formal): *Dear Ms Hopkins*
    □ *Dear Sir(s), Dear Sir or Madam, Dear Madam* (especially to somebody whose name is not known)
    Some people like to use the first name and surname (*Dear Penny Hopkins*) when writing to strangers or people that they do not know well.

    Do not use a title like *Mr* together with a first name
    (NOT *Dear Mr James Carter*).   ▶

6 After 'Dear X', put a comma or nothing at all, not an exclamation mark (!). (In American English, a comma is preferred in personal letters, and a colon (:) in business letters.) **Either** leave an empty line after 'Dear X' and start again on the left, **or** start again on the next line, a few spaces from the left. Do the same for each new paragraph. (The first method is now the most common in Britain.)

7 Letters which begin *Dear Sir(s)* or *Dear Madam* usually finish *Yours faithfully*. Formal letters which begin with the person's name (e.g. *Dear Miss Hawkins, Dear Peter Lewis*) usually finish *Yours sincerely*. Informal letters may finish, for example, *Yours, See you* or *Love*. (*Love* is not usually used by one man to another.) In formal letters, many people put a closing formula before *Yours . . .*, especially when writing to people they know: common expressions are *With best wishes* and *With kind regards*.

8 Sign with your first name (informal) or your full name (formal), but without writing any title (*Mr/Ms/Dr/* etc). Ways of writing one's full name: *Alan Forbes, A Forbes, A J Forbes*.

In a formal typewritten letter, add your full typewritten name after your handwritten signature. Friendly business letters are often signed with the first name only above the full typewritten name:

Yours sincerely

A lan

Alan Forbes

9 In informal letters, afterthoughts that are added after the signature are usually introduced by *P S* (Latin *post scriptum* = 'written afterwards').

10 On the envelope, put the first name before the surname. People usually write a title (*Mr, Mrs* etc) before the name. You can write the first name in full (*Mrs Angela Brookes*), or you can write one or more initials (*Mrs A E Brookes*). It was once common to put the abbreviated title *Esq* (= *Esquire*) after a man's name; this is now very unusual.

11 British people now usually write abbreviated titles, initials, addresses, dates, and opening and closing formulae without commas or full stops.

12 American usage is different from British in some ways:
   - Commas are sometimes used at the ends of lines in addresses; full stops may be used at the ends of addresses; full stops are used after abbreviated titles. After the opening salutation, Americans may put a colon, especially in business letters (*Dear Mr. Hawkes:*), or a comma.
   - *Gentlemen* is used instead of *Dear Sirs*.
   - Dates are written differently (month before day) – see 151.
   - *Yours faithfully* is not used; common endings are *Sincerely, Sincerely yours* or *Yours truly*, followed by a comma.
   - Americans are often addressed (and sign their names) with the first name in full, followed by the initial of a middle name (*Alan J. Parker*). This is less usual in Britain.

13   Letters to strangers often begin with an explanation of the reason for writing.
      Dear X
      I am writing to ask ...

One does not normally begin a letter to a stranger with an enquiry about
health.
      (NOT ~~Dear X~~
            ~~How are you getting on?~~)

For more information about names and titles, see 353.
For more information about the use of commas and full stops, see 455, 457.
For more information about paragraphing, see 401.
For the use of polite enquiries about health etc (*How are you getting on?*), see 520.1.

Examples of letters and envelopes

Formal

                                              14 Plowden Road
                                              Torquay
                                              Devon
                                              TQ6 1RS
                                              Tel 0742 06538

The Secretary   16 June 1995
Hall School of Design
39 Beaumont Street
London
W4 4LJ

Dear Sir or Madam

I should be grateful if you would send me
information about the regulations for admission
to the Hall School of Design. Could you also tell
me whether the School arranges accommodation for
students?

Yours faithfully

Keith Parker

Keith Parker

The Secretary
Hall School of Design
39 Beaumont Street
London
W4 4LJ

▶

Informal

22 Green Street
London
WIB 6DH
Phone 071 066 429

19 March

Dear Keith and Ann

Thanks a lot for a great weekend. We really enjoyed ourselves.

Bill and I were talking about the holidays. We thought it might be nice to go camping in Scotland for a couple of weeks. Are you interested? Let me know if you are, and we can talk about dates etc.

See you soon, I hope. Thanks again.

Love
Cathy

P S Did I leave a pair of jeans behind in the bedroom? If so, do you think you could send them on?

Keith and Ann Sharp
14 West Way House
Bothey Road
Oxford
OX3 5JP

318 **life**: countable or uncountable noun

When *life* refers to the whole of a particular person's life, it is normally countable.
*My grandmother had **a hard life**.* (NOT *...had **hard life.***)
*My mother's parents lived interesting **lives**.*
When *life* refers to a particular way of living, it is normally uncountable.
*I think I would enjoy **city life**.* (NOT *...**a city life.***)

When *life* means 'the situation someone is living in', it is normally uncountable if used alone. However, *a/an* is common if there is an adjective or other defining expression. Compare:

> She enjoys **life**.
> She has **a wonderful life**.

For more about countable and uncountable nouns, see 148.

319 like (verb)

1 not used in progressive forms

Like is one of those verbs which are not usually used in progressive forms (see 451), even when we are talking about temporary present events.

> *'What do you think of the soup?' 'I **like** it.'* (NOT ... *I'm liking it.*)

2 not used without an object

Like cannot normally be used without an object.

> *'How do you feel about ballet?' 'I **like** it.'* (NOT ... *I like.*)
> *'Do you like music?' 'Yes, I do.'* (NOT ... *Yes, I like.*)

3 position of adverbs

Note that *very much* does not come between *like* and its object.

> *I like you and your sister **very much**.*
> OR *I **very much** like you and your sister.*
> (NOT *I like very much you and your sister.*)
> *I **very much** like going to parties and meeting people.*
> (NOT *I like very much going...*)

For more information about adverb position, see 22–23.

4 *like* + verb

In British English, *like* + *-ing* form is used mostly to talk about enjoyment, and *like* + infinitive mostly to talk about choices and habits. In American English, *like* + infinitive is common in both senses. Compare:

– *I **like climbing** mountains.* (more typically GB)
> *I **like to climb** mountains.* (more typically US)

– *When I'm pouring tea I **like to put** the milk in first.* (GB / US)

Not like to can mean 'think it better not to'.

> *'Why didn't you tell me before?' 'I **didn't like to disturb** you while you were having breakfast.'*

Like can be followed by **object + verb form**.

> *I don't **like people phoning** me in the middle of the night.*
> *She **likes people to feel** at home when they stay with her.*

5 *would like*

The conditional *would like* (+ infinitive) is often used as a polite way of saying 'want', especially in requests and offers.

> *I'd **like** two kilos of tomatoes, please.*
> *'Would you **like to dance**?' 'Yes, OK.'* (NOT *Would you like dancing?...*) ▶

Do you like . . . ? is not used in this way.
  (NOT ~~*Do you like some more coffee?*~~)
To can be used instead of repeating a whole infinitive (see 186).
  *'How about playing tennis?' 'I'd like **to**.'*
Polite requests often begin *If you would like . . .* ; the following clause is
sometimes dropped.
  ***If you would like** to take a seat, I'll see if Mr Smithers is free.*
  ***If you would like** to come this way.*
Would is sometimes dropped in this structure.
  ***If you like** to come this way.*

For more about the 'distancing' use of conditionals and past tenses, see 161.
For *would like* with a perfect infinitive (e.g. *I **would like to have seen** that*), see 278.

6   *if you like* etc

In subordinate clauses after *if, any, as soon as, who(ever), what(ever),
when(ever), where, where(ever)* and *how(ever)*, we often use *like* to mean
'want (to)'. Note that *to* is not used.
  *'Can I go now?' '**If you like**.'* (NOT ~~*If you like to.*~~)
  *Do it **any** way you **like**.*   *Come **when** you **like**.*
  *You can sit **wherever** you **like**.*

320   **like** and **as** (similarity, function)

We can use *like* or *as* to say that things are similar.

1   similarity: *like* (preposition)

Like is similar to a preposition. We use it before a noun or pronoun.

> *like* + noun/pronoun

  *You look **like your sister**. (NOT . . . ~~as your sister.~~)*
  *He ran **like the wind**.   **Like his brother**, he is a vegetarian.*
  *She's dressed just **like me**.*
We can use *very, quite* and other adverbs of degree (see 153) to modify *like*.
  *He's **very like** his father.   She looks **a bit like** Queen Victoria.*
We can use *like* to give examples.
  *She's good at scientific subjects, **like mathematics**.*
    (NOT . . . ~~as mathematics.~~)
  *In mountainous countries, **like Peru**, . . .*

2   similarity: *as* (conjunction)

As is a conjunction. We use it before a clause, and before an expression
beginning with a preposition.

> *as* + clause
> *as* + preposition phrase

  *Nobody knows her **as I do**.*
  *We often drink tea with the meal, **as they do** in China.*
  *In 1939, **as in 1914**, everybody seemed to want war.*
  *On Friday, **as on Tuesday**, the meeting will be at 8.30.*

3   informal use of *like*

In informal English *like* is often used as a conjunction instead of *as*. This is very common in American English. It is not generally considered correct in a formal style.

> *Nobody loves you **like I do**.*
> *You look exactly **like your mother did** when she was 20.*

4   *as* with inverted word order

In a very formal style, *as* is sometimes followed by **auxiliary verb + subject** (note the inverted word order – see 298).

> *She was a Catholic, **as were** most of her friends.*
> *He believed, **as did** all his family, that the king was their supreme lord.*

And *as* can sometimes replace *it* as the subject of a clause (rather like the relative pronoun *which*), especially before *happen* and verbs with similar meanings.

> *An earthquake can destroy one part of a city while leaving other parts*
> *untouched, **as happened** in Mexico in 1986.* (NOT ...~~as it happened~~...)

5   *as you know* etc

Some expressions beginning with *as* are used to introduce facts which are 'common ground' – known to both speaker/writer and listener/reader. Examples are *as you know, as we agreed, as you suggested*.

> ***As you know**, next Tuesday's meeting has been cancelled.*
> *I am sending you the bill for the repairs, **as we agreed**.*

There are some passive expressions of this kind – for example *as is well known*; *as was agreed*. Note that there is no subject *it* after *as* in these expressions.

> ***As is well known**, more people get colds in wet weather.*
> (NOT ~~As it is well known~~...)
> *I am sending you the bill, **as was agreed**.* (NOT ...~~as it was agreed~~.)

6   comparison with *as* and *like* after negatives

After a negative clause, a comparison with *as* or *like* usually refers only to the positive part.

> *I don't smoke, **like Jane**.* (Jane smokes.)
> *I am not a Conservative, **like Joe**.* (Joe is a Conservative.)
> *I am no orator, **as Brutus is**.* (Shakespeare, *Julius Caesar*)

Before a negative clause, the comparison refers to the whole clause.

> ***Like Mary**, I don't smoke.* (Mary doesn't smoke.)

7   function or role: *as* used as a preposition

Another use of *as* is to say what function or role a person or thing has – what jobs people do, what purposes things are used for, what category they belong to, etc. In this case, *as* is used like a preposition, before a noun.

> *He worked **as a waiter** for two years.* (NOT ...~~like a waiter~~.)
> *Please don't use that knife **as a screwdriver**.*
> *A crocodile starts life **as an egg**.*   ▶

Compare this use of *as* with *like*.
> **As your brother**, *I must warn you to be careful*. (I am your brother.)
> **Like your brother**, *I must warn you to be careful*.
>> (I am not your brother, but he and I have similar attitudes.)

Note that *as* is usually pronounced /əz/ (see 588).
For *like* used instead of *as if*, see 74.
For *What . . . like?*, see 255.
For *alike*, see 32.
For comparisons with *as . . . as*, see 70.
For *the same as*, see 486.
For *such as*, see 543.9.
For *like* used to join two infinitive structures, see 277.4.

321 likely

1 meaning

Likely is an adjective with a similar meaning to *probable*.
> *I don't think a Labour victory is **likely**.*
> *What's a **likely** date for the election?*
Note also the informal adverb phrases *very/most likely*.
> *I think she'll **very/most** likely be late.*

2 *it is likely* + *that*-clause

When a *that*-clause is the subject of *is likely*, we usually use *it* as a 'preparatory subject' (see 301).
> *It's likely **that the meeting will go on late**.*
It can also be used as a 'preparatory object' with *likely* (see 302).
> *I didn't think **it** likely **that she would come back**.*

3 infinitive after *be likely*

Be + *likely* is often followed by an infinitive. (*Probable* cannot be used in this way.)
> *I'**m likely to be** busy tomorrow.*
> *Are you **likely to be staying** in this evening?*
> *Do you think it'**s likely to rain**?*
> *He'**s unlikely to agree**.*
It is not used as a preparatory subject in this structure.
> *He's likely to succeed.* (NOT *It's likely for him to succeed.*)

322 (a) little and (a) few

1 uncountable and plural

We use *(a) little* with singular (usually uncountable) words, and *(a) few* with plurals. Compare:
> *I have **little interest** in politics.*
> ***Few politicians** are really honest.*
> *We've got **a little bacon** and **a few eggs**.*

2 *of* after *(a) little* and *(a) few*

We use *(a) little of* and *(a) few of* before a pronoun or determiner (for example *the, my, these* – see 157).

> *(a) little of it/this/yours* etc
> *(a) few of us/you/them/these/mine* etc
> *(a) little/few of* + determiner + noun

Compare:
– ***Few people*** can say that they always tell the truth.
Few of us can say that we always tell the truth.
– Could I try ***a little wine*?**
Could I try ***a little of your*** wine?
– Only ***a few children*** like maths.
Only ***a few of the children*** in this class like maths.

3 use of *a/an*

There is a difference between *little* and *a little*, and between *few* and *a few*.

Without articles, *little* and *few* usually have rather negative meanings. They may suggest 'not as much / many as one would like', 'not as much / many as expected', and similar ideas.
*The average MP has **little** real power.*
***Few** people can speak a foreign language perfectly.*
A little and *a few* are more positive: their meaning is generally closer to *some*. They can often suggest ideas like 'better than nothing' or 'more than expected'.
*Would you like **a little** soup?*
*You don't need to go shopping. We've got **a few** potatoes and some steak.*
Compare:
– *Cactuses need **little** water.* (not much water)
*Give the roses **a little** water every day.* (not a lot, but some)
– *His ideas are difficult, and **few** people understand them.*
*His ideas are difficult, but **a few** people understand them.*
Quite a few (informal) means 'a considerable number'.
*We've got **quite a few** friends in the village.*

4 formal and informal language

Little and *few* (with no article) are rather formal. In an informal style (e.g. ordinary conversation), we generally prefer *not much/many*, or *only a little/few*.
*Come on! We haven't got **much** time!*
***Only a few** people speak a foreign language perfectly.*

5 *little* and *few* without nouns

We can drop a noun and use *little/few* alone, if the noun has already been mentioned.
*'Some more soup?' 'Just **a little**, please.'* ▶

6 complements

Note that *(a) little* and *(a) few* are quantifiers, and are normally used before nouns. They can be used alone if a noun has been dropped (see above), but they can rarely be used alone as complements after *be* when a noun has not been dropped.

> They had **little hope**. (BUT NOT ~~Their hope was little.~~)

7 *(a) little* as a modifier

(A) little can modify comparatives.

> *'How are you?' '**A little better**, thanks.'*
> *The new model is **little faster** than the old one.*

Little is not normally used to modify other adjectives or adverbs.

> *It's not very interesting.* (NOT ~~It's **little interesting**.~~)

A little can be used, like *a bit* (see 106), before adjectives and adverbs with a critical or negative meaning.

> *It's **a little inconvenient**.*
> *You must forgive her – she's **a little confused**.*
> *They arrived **a little late**.*

The negative form *not a little* (e.g. *She was **not a little** shaken by her experience*) is rare and literary.

Note also the expression *little known*.

> *He's studying the work of a **little known** German novelist.*

For *less* and *fewer*, see 313.
For the adjective *little*, see 511.

323 long and (for) a long time

1 *long* in questions and negatives

Long (meaning '(for) a long time') is most common in questions and negative clauses, and with restrictive words like *hardly, seldom*.

> *Have you been waiting **long**?*
> *It doesn't take **long** to get to her house.*
> *She **seldom** stays **long**.*

2 *(for) a long time* in affirmative clauses

In affirmative clauses we usually prefer *(for) a long time*.

> *I waited **(for) a long time**, but she didn't arrive.* (NOT ~~I waited **long**...~~)
> *It takes **a long time** to get to her house.* (NOT ~~It takes **long**...~~)

3 *long* in affirmative clauses

However, *long* is normal even in affirmative clauses with *too, enough, as* and *so*.

> *The meeting went on much **too long**.*
> *I've been working here **long enough**. Time to get a new job.*
> *You can stay **as long** as you want.*
> *Sorry I took **so long**.*

Long is also used in affirmative clauses to modify adverbs and conjunctions, and in a few other common expressions.

*We used to live in Paris, but that was **long before** you were born.*
***Long after** the accident he used to dream that he was dying.*
***Long ago**, in a distant country, there lived a beautiful princess.*
(rather formal)
*This is a problem that has **long** been recognised.*
(pre-verb use – rather formal)
*She sits dreaming **all day long**.* (also *all night/week/year long*)
*I'll be back **before long**.*

4 *for a long time* in negative clauses

When *for a long time* is used in a negative clause, it sometimes has a different meaning from *for long*. Compare:
– *She didn't speak **for long**.* (= *She only spoke for a short time.*)
  *She didn't speak **for a long time**.* (= *She was silent for a long time.*)
– *He didn't work **for long**.* (= *He soon stopped working.*)
  *He didn't work **for a long time**.* (= *He was unemployed for a long time.*)
The reason for the difference is to do with the 'scope of negation': in the first and third sentences, *not* goes with *for long*, but in the second and fourth *for a long time* is outside the influence of *not* (it could go at the beginning of the clause).

5 *How long are you here for?*

Note that the question *How long are you here for?* refers to (or includes) the future. Compare:
  'How long are you here for?' 'Until the end of next week.'
  'How long have you been here for?' 'Since last Monday.'

6 comparative

The comparative of *for a long time* is *(for) longer*.
  *I hope you'll stay **longer** next time.* (NOT ... *for a longer time.*)

For *no longer*, see 372.
Much, many and *far* are also more common in questions and negative clauses (see 348 and 206).

324 look

1 copular verb (= 'seem')

Look can mean 'seem' or 'appear'. In this case it is a copular verb (see 147) and can be followed by adjectives.
  *You **look angry** – what's the matter?* (NOT *You look angrily ...*)
A few noun phrases can be used after *look* in the same way as adjectives.
  *I **looked a real fool** when I fell in the river.*
  *The garden **looks a mess**.*
To talk about a temporary appearance, we can use simple or progressive forms; there is not much difference of meaning.
  *You **look** / You're **looking** very unhappy. What's the matter?*

▶

Look can be followed by *like* or *as if.* (Progressive forms are not usually used in this case.)

> *She **looks like** her mother.*
> *It **looks as if** it's going to rain.* (NOT ~~It's looking as if...~~)
> *She **looks as if** she's dreaming.*
> *She **looks like** she's dreaming.* (informal) (NOT ~~She looks like dreaming.~~)

Look like being... is occasionally used informally in British English with future reference.

> *It **looks like being** a wet night.* (= *It looks as if it will be...*)

For more about *as if,* and the use of *like* for *as if,* see 74.

2 ordinary verb (= 'direct one's eyes')

When *look* means 'direct one's eyes', it is used with adverbs, not adjectives. Before an object, a preposition is necessary (usually *at*). A preposition is not used when there is no object.

> *The boss **looked at me angrily**.* (NOT ~~The boss looked at me angry.~~)
> ***Look carefully*** *– it's changing colour.*
> (NOT ~~Look careful...~~)
> (NOT ~~Look at carefully...~~)

3 not followed by *if*

We do not normally use *if* or *whether* after *look.* Instead, we use *see* or *look to see.*

> *Could you **see if** Ann's in the kitchen?*
> (NOT ~~Could you look if Ann's in the kitchen?~~)
> *'What are you doing?' 'I'm **looking to see** whether these batteries are OK.'*
> (NOT ~~I'm looking whether...~~)

4 *look after* and *look for*

Note the difference between these two prepositional verbs. *Look after* means 'take care of'; *look for* means 'try to find'. Compare:

> *Could you **look after** the kids while I go shopping?*
> *I spent ages **looking for** her before I found her.*

Look for is not used to talk about going to get people or things if one knows where they are.

> *I'm going to the station at three o'clock to **fetch** Daniel.*
> (NOT ...~~to look for Daniel.~~)

For other phrasal and prepositional verbs with *look,* see a good dictionary.
For the difference between *look (at), watch* and *see,* see 489.
For *Look!* and *Look here!* used as discourse markers, see 159.19.

325 lose and loose

Lose (pronounced /luːz/) is an irregular verb (*lose – lost – lost*). *Loose* (pronounced /luːs/) is an adjective (the opposite of *tight*).

> *I must be **losing** weight – my clothes all feel **loose**.*
> (NOT ~~I must be loosing weight...~~)

326 a lot, lots, plenty, a great deal, a large number, the majority

1 introduction; use of *of*

These expressions have similar meanings to the determiners *much*, *many* and *most*, but the grammar is not quite the same. In particular, *of* is used after these expressions even before nouns with no determiner. Compare:
- *There's not **a lot of** meat left.* (NOT ~~There's not **a lot** meat left.~~)
  *There's not **much** meat left.* (NOT ~~There's not **much of** meat left.~~)
- ***Plenty of** shops open on Sunday mornings.* (NOT ~~**Plenty shops**...~~)
  ***Many** shops open on Sunday mornings.* (NOT ~~**Many of shops**...~~)

For *much*, *many* and *most* with and without *of*, and other details of their use, see 348 and 347.

2 *a lot of* and *lots of*

These are rather informal. In a more formal style, we prefer *a great deal of*, *a large number of*, *much* or *many*. (*Much* and *many* are used mostly in questions and negative clauses – see 348.)

There is not much difference between *a lot of* and *lots of*: they are both used mainly before singular uncountable and plural nouns, and before pronouns. It is the subject, and not the form *lot/lots*, that makes a following verb singular or plural. So when *a lot of* is used before a plural subject, the verb is plural; when *lots of* is used before a singular subject, the verb is singular.

> ***A lot of time is** needed to learn a language.*
> ***Lots of patience is** needed, too.* (NOT ~~**Lots of patience are needed, too.**~~)
> ***A lot of my friends want** to emigrate.* (NOT ~~**A lot of my friends wants**...~~)
> ***Lots of us think** it's time for an election.*

3 *plenty of*

Plenty of is usually rather informal. It is used mostly before singular uncountables and plurals. It suggests 'enough and more'.

> *Don't rush. There's **plenty of time**.* **Plenty of shops** take cheques.*

4 *a large amount of*, *a great deal of* and *a large number of*

These are used in similar ways to *a lot of* and *lots of*, but are more formal. *A large amount of* and *a great deal of* are generally used with uncountable nouns.

> *I've thrown out **a large amount of old clothing**.*
> *Mr Lucas has spent **a great deal of time** in the Far East.*

A large number of is used before plurals, and a following verb is plural.

> ***A large number of problems** still **have** to be solved.* (More natural than
> ***A large amount** of problems ... OR **A great deal** of problems ...)

For articles after *the number/amount of*, see 69.8.

5 *the majority of*

The majority of (= 'most' or 'most of') is mostly used with plural nouns and verbs.

> ***The majority of criminals are** non-violent.* ▶

6 measurement nouns

These expressions are not generally used before words for units of measure, like *pounds, years* or *miles*. Other words have to be used.

    *It cost **several** pounds.* (NOT ~~It cost **a lot of pounds**.~~)

    *They lived **many** miles from the town.*

        (NOT ~~They lived **plenty of** miles from the town.~~)

7 use without following nouns

These expressions can be used without nouns if the meaning is clear. In this case, *of* is not used.

    *'How much did it cost?' '**A lot**.'* (= *'A lot of money.'*)

    *We should be all right for cheese – I've bought **plenty**.*

    *He stays silent for long periods, but when he does speak he says **a
    great deal**.*

8 use as adverbs

A lot and *a great deal* can be used as adverbs.

    *On holiday we walk and swim **a lot**.*

        (BUT NOT ~~...we walk **plenty**~~ OR ~~...swim **lots**~~.)

    *The government seems to change its mind **a great deal**.*

327 make

1 object + infinitive

When ***make* + object** is followed by another verb, we use the infinitive without *to*.

    *I **made her cry**.*

        (NOT ~~I **made her to cry**.~~)

        (NOT ~~I **made her crying**.~~)

Note that the infinitive must follow the object.

    *I can't **make the washing machine work**.*

        (NOT ~~I can't **make work the washing machine**.~~)

In passive structures the infinitive with *to* is used.

    *She **was made to repeat** the whole story.*

For information about other verbs which are used in similar structures, see 277.

2 reflexive object + past participle

In a few cases *make* can be followed by *myself, yourself* etc and a past participle. The structure is common with *understood, heard* and *liked/disliked/hated*.

    *I don't speak good French, but I can **make myself understood**.*

        (NOT ~~...**make myself understand**.~~)

    *She had to shout to **make herself heard**.*

    *In his three months in the job he **made himself** thoroughly **disliked**.*

3 with two objects

Make (meaning 'prepare', 'manufacture' etc) can be used in a structure with two objects.
> *Can you **make me a birthday cake** by Friday?*

For more information about verbs with two objects, see 583.

4 with object + object complement

Make can be followed by an object, with an adjective or noun referring to a change in the object. Note the word order.
> *The rain **made the grass wet**.* (NOT ~~The rain **made wet the grass**.~~)
> *You have **made me a very happy man**.*

For more information about verbs with object complements, see 580.

5 with subject complement

Make is sometimes followed by a subject complement – a noun phrase saying what somebody or something becomes, or what job he/she/it does. This is most common in the expression *make a good . . .*
> *That wood will **make a good hiding place**.*
> *Terriers **make good hunting dogs**.*
An indirect object can be put into this structure.
> *He made **her** a good husband.* (= *He was a good husband **to her**.*)

For the difference between *make* and *do*, see 164.
For prepositions after *make*, see 328.

328 make: prepositions

We usually say *made of* when we are identifying the material used to make something.
> *Most things seem to be **made of** plastic these days.*
> *What are your loudspeakers **made of**?*
When we are thinking about the process of manufacture, *out of* is more often used.
> *They **made** all the furniture **out of** oak.* (More natural than . . . *of oak*.)
When a material is changed into a completely different form to make something, we often use *make from*.
> *Paper is **made from** wood.* (NOT ~~Paper is **made of wood**.~~)
> *My mother **makes** wine **from** blackberries.*
To mention just one of the materials that something is made of, we use *make with*.
> *'The soup's good.' 'Yes, I **make** it **with** lots of garlic.'*

For sentence structures with *make*, see 327.

329 **marry** and **divorce**

1 *get married/divorced*

When there is no object, *get married* and *get divorced* are more common than *marry* and *divorce* in an informal style.

> *Lulu and Joe **got married** last week.*
>> (*Lulu and Joe **married**...* is more formal.)
> *When are you going to **get married?***
> *The Robinsons are **getting divorced.***

In a more formal style, *marry* and *divorce* are preferred.

> *Although she had many lovers, she never **married**.*
> *After three very unhappy years they **divorced**.*

2 **no preposition before object**

Before a direct object, *marry* and *divorce* are used without prepositions.

> *She **married** a builder.* (NOT ~~She married **with a builder**.~~)
> *Will you **marry** me?*
> *Andrew's going to **divorce** Carola.*

3 *get/be married to*

We can also use *get/be married to* with an object.

> *She **got married to** her childhood sweetheart.*
> *I've **been married to** you for sixteen years and I still don't understand you.*

330 **may** and **might** (1): introduction

1 **grammar**

May and *might* are modal auxiliary verbs (see 344–345).

a   There is no *-s* in the third person singular.

> *She **may** be here tomorrow.* (NOT ~~She **mays**...~~)
> *It **might** rain this afternoon.*

b   Questions and negatives are made without *do*.

> ***May** I help you?* (NOT ~~**Do I may**...~~)
> *We **might not** be home before midnight.*

c   After *may* and *might* we use the infinitive without *to* of other verbs.

> *You **may be** right.* (NOT ~~You **may to be right**.~~)
> *She **might not want** to come with us.*

Progressive, perfect and passive infinitives are also possible (see 276).

> *'Why hasn't Laurie come?' 'He **might be working** late.'*
> *'She didn't say hello.' 'She **may not have recognised** you.'*
> *Do you think we **might be asked** for our opinion?*

d   *May* and *might* do not have infinitives or participles (~~to may, maying, mighted~~ do not exist). When necessary, we use other words.

> *She wants **to be allowed** to open a bank account.* (NOT ...~~to **may open**...~~)

e   *Might* does not normally have a past meaning. It is used in the same way as
     may, to talk about the present and future. The difference is that *might*
     usually refers to situations which are less probable or less definite (see 331.2
     and 332.1). *Might* also replaces *may* in past indirect speech (see 481).

f   However, certain past ideas can be expressed by *may* or *might* followed by a
     perfect infinitive (**have** + **past participle**).
     *She's late. I think she **may have missed** the train.*
     *Why did you do that? You **might have killed** yourself.*

g   *Might* has a contracted negative *mightn't*. *Mayn't* is very unusual.

     For more information about contractions, see 144.

2   meanings

May and *might* are used mainly to talk about possibility (especially the
chances of something happening), and to ask for and give permission
(especially in a more formal style).
    *I **may** see you tomorrow.*
    *Do you think I **might** borrow your typewriter?*

For more details of the use of *may* and *might*, see the following sections.
For *may* and *might* after *so that* and *in order that*, see 519.

331   **may** and **might** (2): possibility

1   chances

We often use *may* and *might* to say that there is a chance that something is
true, or that there is a possibility of it happening.
    *'I think Labour are going to win.' 'You **may** be right.'*
        (= '*It is **possible** that you are right.*')
    *We **may** go climbing in the Alps next summer.*
    *'Where's Emma?' 'I don't know. She **may** be out shopping.'*
    *Peter **might** phone. If he does, ask him to ring later.*
    *'I **might** get a job soon.' 'Yes, and pigs **might** fly.' (= 'It's very unlikely.')*
    *You **might** be needed at the office on Saturday.*
May well can be used to suggest a strong possibility.
    *'I think it's going to rain.' 'You **may well** be right – the sky's really black.'*

2   *may* and *might*: the difference

Might is not used as a past form of *may*: both *may* and *might* are used to talk
about the present or future. *Might* is mostly used as a less definite or more
hesitant form of *may*, suggesting a smaller chance – it is used when people
think something is possible but not very likely. Compare:
    *I **may** go to London tomorrow.* (perhaps a 50% chance)
    *Joe **might** come with me.* (perhaps a 30% chance)

For the 'distancing' use of past forms to express uncertainty, hesitation etc, see 161.   ▶

3 typical occurrences: *may*

May can be used to talk about typical occurrences – things that can happen in certain situations. This is common in scientific and academic language. *Might* is only used in this way to talk about the past.

> *After having a baby, a woman **may** suffer from depression for several months.*
>
> *The flowers **may** have five or six petals; colour **may** range from light pink to dark red.*
>
> *Children of divorced parents **may** have difficulty in forming stable relationships themselves.*
>
> *In those days, a man **might** be hanged for stealing a sheep.*

Can is used in a similar way, especially in a less formal style. See 123.1.

4 questions

May is not normally used in direct questions about probability.

> *Are you likely to go camping this summer?*
> (N O T -*May you go camping* . . . ?)
> *Do you think Emma's gone shopping?*
> (N O T -*May Emma have gone shopping?*)

But *may* is possible in negative questions about probability.

> ***May we not** be making a big mistake?* (very formal)

And *may* is possible in indirect questions (for example after *Do you think*).

> *Do you think **you may** go camping this summer?*

5 negatives

Note the difference between *may/might not* and *cannot/can't*.
May/might not means 'It is possible that . . . not . . .'
Cannot/can't means 'It is not possible that . . .' Compare:

> *It **may/might not** be true. (= **It is possible that** it is **not** true.)*
> *It **can't** be true. (= **It is not possible** that it is true.)*

6 conditional: *might* meaning 'would perhaps'

Might (but not *may*) can have a conditional meaning (= 'would perhaps').

> *If you went to bed for an hour you **might** feel better.*
> (= . . . **perhaps** you **would** feel better.)
> *Don't play with knives. You **might** get hurt. (= **Perhaps** you **would** get hurt if you did.)*

7 indirect speech: *might*

Might is used as the indirect speech equivalent of both *may* and *might* after a past reporting verb. Compare:

> *'What are you doing at the weekend, Anne?' 'Oh, I **may** go to Scotland – or I just **might** stay at home.'*
>
> *Anne **said** that she **might** go to Scotland at the weekend, or she **might** stay at home.*

8 past

May and *might* cannot normally be used to say that something was possible in the past. Other words have to be used.

> *I couldn't think clearly, and I felt hot. Perhaps I was ill.*
>   (NOT ... ~~I might be ill.~~)

However, *might* can refer to the past in indirect speech (see paragraph 7 above). For the use of ***may/might*** + **perfect infinitive**, see next paragraph.

9 *may/might* + **perfect infinitive**

To say that it is possible that something happened or was true in the past, a special structure can be used: ***may/might*** + **perfect infinitive (*have* + past participle)**.

> *'Polly's very late.' 'She **may have missed** her train.'*
>   (= *'It is **possible** that she missed . . .'*)
> *'What was that noise?' 'It **might have been** a cat.'*

We can use the same structure (especially with *might*) to say that something was possible but did not happen.

> *You were stupid to try climbing up there. You **might have killed** yourself.*
> *If she hadn't been so bad-tempered, I **might have married** her.*

May is occasionally used in the same way in British English, but many people feel that this is incorrect.

> *You were stupid to try climbing up there. You **may have killed** yourself.*

May/might + **perfect infinitive** can also refer to the present or future (like present perfect and future perfect tenses).

> *I'll try phoning him, but he **may have gone out** by now.*
> *By the end of this year I **might have saved** some money.*

For the use of ***could have*** + **past participle** in similar senses, see 123.6.
For more information about perfect infinitives, see 278.

10 *may, might* and *can*

Can is not used in affirmative clauses to talk about the chances that something actually will happen or is happening (= 'It is possible that . . .'). To express this meaning, we use *may/might/could*. We use *can* to talk about a more general or theoretical kind of possibility (= 'It is possible to . . .'). Compare:

– *There **may/might** be a strike next week.*
>   (= ***It is possible that** there will be . . .*)
>   (NOT ~~*There **can** be a strike next week.*~~)
> *Strikes **can** happen at any time.* (= ***It is possible** for strikes to happen . . .*)
– *I **may** fly to Amsterdam on Tuesday.*
> *One **can** travel to Holland by boat or by air.*

However, in questions and negative clauses *can* is sometimes used to talk about present possibilities, especially the question of whether something is logically possible. (This is not quite the same as the use of *may* and *might* to talk about the chance of something happening.)

> ***Can** that be Mike? I thought he was in Greece.*
> *Jake's getting married? You **can't** mean it.*

▶

11 *may, might* and *could*

Could is often used in similar ways to *may* and *might*, to talk about the chance of something happening or being true.

> War **could** break out any day. (OR War **might**...)
> You **could** be right. (OR You **may**...)

For more about the use of *can* and *could* to talk about possibility, see 123.
For basic grammatical information about *may* and *might*, see 330.
For the use of *may* and *might* to refer to permission, see 332.
For other uses of *may* and *might*, see 333–336.

332 **may** and **might** (3): permission

1 asking for permission

May and *might* can both be used to ask for permission. They are more formal than *can* and *could*. *Might* is very polite and formal; it is not common, and is mostly used in indirect question structures.

> **May** I put the TV on?
> I wonder if I **might** have a little more cheese.
> (Very formal; more natural than **Might I have**...?)

For the use of past forms to express politeness and hesitation, see 161.

2 giving and refusing permission

May is used to give permission; *may not* is used to refuse permission and to forbid.

> 'May I put the TV on?' 'Yes, of course you **may**.'
> 'May I borrow the car?' 'No, I'm afraid you **may not**.'
> Students **may not** use the staff car park.

These are rather formal. In an informal style *can* and *cannot/can't* are more common (see 124).

Must not is also used to forbid (see 351.3). It is a little stronger or more emphatic than *may not*.

> Students **must not** use the staff car park.

3 talking about permission

We do not usually use *may* and *might* to talk about permission which has already been given or refused, about freedom which people already have, or about rules and laws. Instead, we use *can, could* or *be allowed*.

> These days, children **can / are allowed to** do what they like.
> (NOT ...~~children may do what they like.~~)
> I **could / was allowed to** read what I liked when I was a child.
> (NOT ~~I might read what I liked~~...)
> **Can you / Are you allowed to** park on both sides of the road here?
> (More natural than **May you park**...?)

4 indirect speech

However, *may* and *might* can be used in indirect speech to report the giving of permission. *May* is used after present reporting verbs and *might* after past verbs.

> The Manager says that we **may** leave our coats in the downstairs toilet.
> 'What are you doing here?' 'Peter said that I **might** look round.'
> (very formal)

333 may and might (4): may in wishes and hopes

May (but not *might*) is used in formal expressions of wishes and hopes.

> I hope that the young couple **may** enjoy many years of happiness together.
> Let us pray that peace **may** soon return to our troubled land.

May often comes at the beginning of the sentence.

> **May** you both be very happy!
> **May** the New Year bring you all your heart desires.
> **May** God be with you.
> **May** she rest in peace. (prayer for a dead person)

For more information about inverted word order (auxiliary verb before subject), see 298.

334 may and might (5): may/might ... but

May (and sometimes *might*) can be used in a discussion rather like *although*: to introduce a fact, when one is going to say that the fact makes no difference to the main argument. They are often followed by *but*.

> It **may** be a comfortable car, **but** it uses a lot of petrol.
> (= **Although** it is a comfortable car, it uses ...)
> He **may** be clever, **but** he hasn't got much common sense.
> You **might** have plenty of money, **but** that doesn't mean you're better
> than me.
> She **may** have had a lovely voice when she was younger, **but** ...

Note that in this structure, *may* is often used to talk about things that are definitely true, not just possible. *It **may** be a comfortable car, but ...* means 'I agree that it is comfortable, but ...', not 'There's a chance that it is comfortable ...'

In indirect speech, *might* is used after a past reporting verb.

> I **said** that he **might** be clever, but that he hadn't got much common sense.

335 may and might (6): may/might as well

This expression is used in an informal style to suggest that one should do something because there is nothing better, nothing more interesting or nothing more useful to do. *May as well* is perhaps a little more definite than *might as well*.

> There's nobody interesting to talk to. We **may as well** go home.
> 'Shall we go and see Fred?' 'OK, **might as well**.'

▶

Note the difference between *may/might as well* and *had better* (see 234). Compare:
> We *may as well* have something to eat.
>> (= There is nothing more interesting to do.)
> We'*d better* have something to eat.
>> (= We ought to eat; there is a good reason to eat now.)

Might as well is also used to compare one unpleasant situation with another.
> This holiday isn't much fun. We *might* just *as well* be back home.
>> (= Things wouldn't be any different if we were at home.)
> You never listen – I *might as well* talk to a brick wall.

336 **may** and **might** (7): **might** (requests, suggestions and criticisms)

Might is often used in affirmative clauses to make requests and suggestions.
> You *might* see if John's free this evening.
> You *might* try asking your uncle for a job.

The structure can be used to criticise. **Might have + past participle** is used to talk about the past.
> You *might* ask before you borrow my car.
> She *might have told* me she was going to stay out all night.

For the use of *could* in similar senses, see 124.

337 **maybe** and **perhaps**

These two words mean the same. In British English both are common: *maybe* is used mostly in an informal style. Compare:
> *Maybe/Perhaps* it'll stop raining soon.
> *Julius Caesar* is *perhaps* the greatest of Shakespeare's early plays.

Perhaps is often pronounced 'praps' by British people.

In American English *perhaps* is less common, and is rather formal.

338 **meals**

Not everybody uses the same names for meals: there are quite wide regional and social differences.

1 British usage

a midday: *dinner* or *lunch*

The midday meal is called *dinner* by many people, especially if it is the main meal of the day. Middle and upper class people usually call it *lunch*.

b afternoon: *tea*

Some people have a light meal of tea and biscuits or cakes, called *tea*, at four or five o'clock in the afternoon. However, this is no longer very common.

c   early evening: *(high) tea* or *supper*

Many people have a cooked meal around five or six o'clock. This is often
called *tea* or *high tea*; some people call it *supper*.

d   later evening: *supper* or *dinner*

A meal later in the evening is often called *supper* (and some people use the
same word for a bedtime snack). Some people use *dinner* for the evening
meal if it is the main meal of the day. A more formal evening meal with
guests, or in a restaurant, is usually called *dinner*, especially by middle and
upper class people.

2   American usage

Americans generally use *lunch* for the midday meal and *dinner* for the
evening meal. Celebration meals at Christmas and Thanksgiving are called
Christmas/Thanksgiving dinner, even if they are eaten at midday.

339   mean

1   questions

Note the structure of questions with *mean*.
>   Excuse me. **What does** *'hermetic'* **mean**? (NOT *What means 'hermetic'?*)

Note also the preposition in *What do you mean* **by** *'hermetic'?* (= *In what
sense are you using the word?*)

2   *mean* and *think, meaning* and *opinion*

Mean and *meaning* are 'false friends' for speakers of some European
languages. They are not usually used to mean 'think' or 'opinion' (but see
paragraph 4 below).
>   I **think** that Labour will win the next election.
>   (NOT *I mean that Labour will win…*)
>   What's your **opinion**? (NOT *What's your meaning?*)

3   structures

Mean (in the sense of 'intend', 'plan') can be followed by **(object) +
infinitive**.
>   I **mean to find out** what's going on.
>   Sorry – I didn't **mean to interrupt** you.
>   Did you **mean John to post** those letters?

In the sense of 'involve', 'have as a result', *mean* can be followed by a noun
or an *-ing* form.
>   The Fantasians have invaded Utopia. This **means war**!
>   If you want to pass the exam it will **mean studying** hard.

4   *I mean*

I mean is used informally as a 'discourse marker' (see 159) to introduce
explanations or additional details. In this use, it is separated from what
follows by a pause.
>   He's funny – **I mean**, he's really strange.

▶

*It was a terrible evening. **I mean**, they all sat round and talked politics the
whole time.*
*Would you like to come out tonight? **I mean**, only if you want to, of course.*
I mean, used before a pause in this way, can also introduce expressions of
opinion. In this case, it is close to *I think* or *I feel*.
*A hundred pounds for a thirty hour week. **I mean**, it's not right, is it? It's
not right.* (BUT NOT ~~I mean that it's not right~~...)
Another use is to introduce corrections.
*She lives in Southport – **I mean** Southampton.*
In informal speech, *I mean* is also very common as a general-purpose
connector or 'filler', with little real meaning.
*Let's go and see Phil on Saturday. **I mean**, we could make an early start ...*

5 *What do you mean ...?*

What do you mean ...? can express anger or protest.
***What do you mean**, I can't sing?*
***What do you mean** by waking me up at this time of night?*

6 **no progressive form**

Mean is not normally used in progressive forms when it refers to meanings.
*What **does** that strange smile **mean**?*
(NOT ~~What is that strange smile meaning?~~)
But progressive forms can be used to refer to intentions.
*I'**ve been meaning** to phone you for weeks.*

340 means

1 **singular and plural ending in -*s***

Both the singular and the plural of *means* end in *-s*.
*In the 19th century a new **means** of communication was developed –
the railway.* (NOT *...~~a new mean of communication~~...*)
*There are several **means** of transport on the island.*

For other words with singular forms ending in *-s*, see 501.3.

2 *by all/any/no means*

By all means is not the same as *by all possible means*. It is used to give
permission or to encourage somebody to do something, and means 'of
course' or 'it is all right to ...' Compare:
– *'Can I borrow your sweater?' '**By all means**.'*
***By all means** get a new coat, but don't spend more than £80.*
*If there isn't a bus, then **by all means** take a taxi.*
– *We must help her **by all possible means**.*
(NOT ~~We must help her by all means.~~)
By no means (or *not by any means*) is not the opposite of *by all means*. It is
similar to *definitely not*, or *not by a long way*.
*'Is that all you've got to say?' '**By no means**.'*
*Galileo was **by no means** the first person to use a telescope.*
*Schumann is **not by any means** my favourite composer.*

341 measurements: 'marked' and 'unmarked' forms

Many adjectives that are used in measurements come in pairs (e.g. *tall/short, old/young, heavy/light, fast/slow*). The word that is used for the 'top' end of the measurement scale can usually be used in another sense, to talk about the quality in general. For instance, one can ask how *long* something is even if it is relatively short. Grammarians call these uses of words 'unmarked'. Compare:

– *She's very **tall** and he's very **short**.* (marked)
 *Exactly how **tall** are they both?* (unmarked)
  (NOT *Exactly how **short** are they both?*)
– *He's very **young** for the job.* (marked)
 *I don't really know how **old** he is.* (unmarked)
  (NOT *...how **young** he is.*)
 *He's only twenty-three years **old**.* (unmarked)
  (NOT *...twenty-three years **young**.*)
– *Lead is one of the **heaviest** metals.* (marked)
 *Scales are used to measure how **heavy** things are.* (unmarked)
  (NOT *...how **light** things are.*)

Some nouns are used in similar 'unmarked' ways. Compare:
– ***Age** brings wisdom but I'd rather have **youth** and stupidity.* (marked)
 *What is her exact **age**?* (unmarked) (NOT *What is her exact **youth**?*)
– *The worst thing about the film was its **length**.* (marked)
 *What's the **length** of a football field?* (unmarked)
  (NOT *What's the **shortness**...?*)

342 mind

Mind can mean 'dislike', 'be annoyed by', 'object to'. We use *mind* mostly in questions and negative clauses.
 *I **don't mind** you coming in late if you don't wake me up.*
 *'**Do you mind** the smell of tobacco?' 'Not at all.'*
Would you mind...? and *Do you mind...?* are often used to ask people to do things, or to ask for permission. We can use *-ing* forms or *if*-clauses.

 Would/Do you mind ...ing?

 ***Would/Do you mind opening** the window?* (= *Please open ...*)
 ***Would/Do you mind my opening** the window?* (= *Can I open ...?*)

 Would/Do you mind if...?

 ***Would you mind if** I opened the window?*
 ***Do you mind if** I smoke?*
To ask general questions about people's feelings, we can use *Do you mind...?* but not usually *Would you mind...?*
 ***Do you mind** people smoking in your house?*
 ***Do you mind** if people smoke in your house?*
  (BUT NOT ***Would you mind** people smoking in your house?*) ▶

Note that the answer *No* or *Not at all* is used to *give* permission after *Would/Do you mind . . . ?* (but we usually add more words to make the meaning quite clear).

> **'Do you mind** *if I look at your paper?'* **'No,** *please do.'*

In subordinate clauses after *mind*, a present tense is usually used if we want to express a future meaning (see 556).

> *I don't mind what you **do** after you leave school.*
>   (NOT ~~I don't mind what you **will do** . . .~~)

343 miss

1 'fail to contact', 'be late for'

Miss often expresses the idea of failing to contact somebody/something, or being late for somebody/something.

> *She threw a plate at me, but **missed**.*
> *How could he **miss** an easy goal like that?*
> *If you don't hurry we'll **miss** the train.* (NOT . . .~~lose the train.~~)
> *You've just **missed** her – she went home five minutes ago.*
> *The station's about five minutes' walk, straight ahead. You can't **miss** it.*

An *-ing* form can be used after *miss*.

> *I got in too late and **missed seeing** the news on TV.*

2 'be sorry to be without'

We can use *miss* to say that we are sorry because we are no longer with somebody, or no longer have something.

> *Will you **miss** me when I'm away?*
> *He doesn't like going to the country – he **misses** the noise and the bright lights.*

An *-ing* form is possible.

> *I **miss** living in the mountains.*

Note that *regret* is not used in the same way. Compare:

> *I'll always **miss** being with you.*
>   (= *I'll always be sorry I'm not with you any more.*)
> *I'll always **regret** being with you.* (= *I'll always be sorry I was with you.*)

3 'notice the absence of'

Another meaning of *miss* is 'notice that somebody/something is not there'.

> *The child ran away yesterday morning, but nobody **missed** her till lunchtime.*

4 *miss* not used

Miss is not used simply to say that somebody has not got something.

> *In some of the villages they **haven't got** electricity.*
>   (NOT . . .~~they **miss** electricity.~~)

In a formal style, the verb or noun *lack* can be used to express this idea.

> *. . . they **lack** electricity.*
> *I am sorry that **lack** of time prevents me from replying at greater length to your enquiry.*

5 *missing*

Missing is often used as an adjective, meaning 'lost'.
> *When did you realise that the money was **missing**?*
> *The **missing** children were found at their aunt's house.*

We can use *missing* after a noun. This often happens in clauses beginning with *there is*.
> *There's a page **missing** from this book.*

In an informal style, a structure with *have . . . missing* is also possible.
> *We**'ve got** some plates **missing** – do you think Alan's borrowed them?*
> *He **had** several teeth **missing**.*

344 **modal auxiliary verbs**: introduction

1 **What are modal auxiliary verbs?**

The verbs *can, could, may, might, will, would, shall* (mainly British English), *should, must* and *ought* are called 'modal auxiliary verbs'. They are used before the infinitives of other verbs, and add certain kinds of meaning connected with certainty or with obligation and freedom to act (see next section). *Need* (see 357) and *dare* (see 150) can sometimes be used like modal auxiliary verbs, and the expression *had better* (see 234) is also used like a modal auxiliary.

2 **grammar**

a Modal verbs have no *-s* in the third person singular.
> *She **may** know his address.* (NOT ~~She **mays**...~~)

b Questions, negatives, tags and short answers are made without *do*.
> ***Can you** swim?* (NOT ~~**Do you can** swim?~~)
> *He **shouldn't** be doing that, **should he**?* (NOT ~~He **doesn't should**...~~)

c After modal auxiliary verbs, we use the infinitive without *to* of other verbs. *Ought* is an exception – see 398.
> *I **must water** the flowers.* (NOT ~~I **must to water**...~~)

Progressive, perfect and passive infinitives are also possible (see 276).
> *I **may not be working** tomorrow.*
> *She was so angry she **could have killed** him.*
> *The kitchen **ought to be painted** one of these days.*

d Modal verbs do not have infinitives or participles (~~to may, maying, mayed~~ do not exist), and they do not normally have past forms (though *would, could, should* and *might* can sometimes be used as past tenses of *will, can, shall* and *may*). Other expressions are used when necessary.
> *I'd like **to be able to** skate.* (NOT ~~...**to can** skate.~~)
> *People really **had to** work hard in those days.*
> (NOT ~~People really **musted** work...~~)

For more about infinitives without *to*, see 277. ▶

e   However, certain past ideas can be expressed by a modal verb followed by a perfect infinitive (***have* + past participle**).

>   *You **should have told** me you were coming.*
>   *I think I **may have annoyed** Aunt Mary.*

For details of these uses, see the entries on particular modal verbs.

f   Modal verbs have contracted negative forms (*can't, won't* etc) which are used in an informal style. (*Shan't* and *mayn't* are only used in British English; *mayn't* is very rare.) *Will* and *would* also have contracted affirmative forms (*'ll, 'd*). For details, see 144. Some modals have both 'strong' and 'weak' pronunciations. For details, see 588.

g   *There* is quite often used as a preparatory subject with modal verbs, especially when these are followed by *be* (see 562).

>   ***There may be** rain later today.*

3   meanings

We do not normally use modal verbs to say that situations definitely exist or that particular events have definitely happened. We use them, for example, to talk about things which we expect, which are or are not possible, which we think are necessary, which we want to happen, which we are not sure about, which tend to happen, or which have not happened.

>   *He **may arrive** any time.*
>   *She **could be** in London or Paris or Tokyo – nobody knows.*
>   *I **can't swim**.*
>   *I think you **ought to see** a lawyer.*
>   *We really **must tidy up** the garden.*
>   *What **would** you **do** if you had a free year?*
>   *Edinburgh **can be** very cold in winter.*
>   *I think they **should have consulted** a doctor earlier.*
>   *You **might have told me** Frances was ill.*

For further general information about the meanings of modal auxiliary verbs, see next section. For more detailed information, see the sections for each verb.

345   modal auxiliary verbs: meanings

1   two kinds of meaning

Most of the meanings of modal verbs can be divided into two groups. One is to do with *degrees of certainty*: modal verbs can be used to say for instance that a situation is certain, probable, possible or impossible. The other is to do with *obligation, freedom to act* and similar ideas: modal verbs can be used to say that somebody is obliged to do something, that he / she is able to do something, that there is nothing to stop something happening, that it would be better if something happened (or did not), or that something is permitted or forbidden.

2 degrees of certainty

Modal verbs can express various degrees of certainty about a fact or an event.

a complete certainty (positive or negative)

I **shall be** away tomorrow.	It **won't rain** this evening.
I **shan't be** late on Tuesday.	You **must be** tired.
There's the phone. That**'ll be** Tony.	That **can't be** John – he's in Dublin.
Things **will be** all right.	I knew it **couldn't be** John.

They knelt in front of the child who **would** one day **rule** all England.
I told you you **wouldn't be** ready in time.

b probability / possibility

She **should / ought to be** here soon.
It **shouldn't / oughtn't to be** difficult to get there.
We **may be buying** a new house.
The water **may not be** warm enough to swim.

c weak probability

I **might see** you again – who knows?
Things **might not be** as bad as they seem.
We **could** all **be** millionaires one day.

d theoretical or habitual possibility

How many people **can get** into a telephone box?
New England **can be** very warm in September.
Small children **may have** difficulty in understanding abstract ideas.

e conditional certainty or possibility

If we had enough time, things **would be** easy.
I **wouldn't do** this if I didn't have to.
If John came we **could** all **go** home.
I **couldn't do** anything without your help.
If you stopped criticising I **might get** some work done.
It **mightn't be** a bad thing if we took a short holiday.

3 obligation and freedom to act

Modal verbs can express various aspects of obligation and freedom. These uses of modal verbs are very important in the polite expression of requests, suggestions, invitations and instructions.

a strong obligation

Students **must register** at the tutorial office in the first week of term.
All sales staff **will arrive** for work by 8.40 a.m.
Need I get a visa for Hungary?

b prohibition

Students **must not use** the staff car park.
Books **may not be taken** out of the library.
You **can't come** in here.

▶

c   weak obligation; recommendation

> *You **should** try to work harder.*   *She really **ought to** wash her hair.*
> *That child **had better start** saying thank-you for things.*
> *You **might** see what John thinks.*   *What **shall** we **do**?*

d   willingness, volunteering, resolving, insisting and offering

> *If you **will come** this way . . .*
> *I should be grateful if you **would let** me know your decision as soon*
>   *as possible.*
> *I'll **pay** for the drinks.*   *I'll definitely **work** harder next term.*
> *She **will keep** interrupting people.*   ***Shall** I **give** you a hand?*

e   permission

> ***Can** I **borrow** your keys?*   ***May** we **use** the phone?*
> *Do you think I **might take** a break now?*

f   absence of obligation

> *You **needn't work** this Saturday.*

g   ability

> *She **can speak** six languages.*

Note that obligation, permission etc are usually seen from the *speaker's*
point of view in statements and the *hearer's* in questions. Compare:
–   *You **must** go and see Ann.* (***I** think it is necessary.*)
    ***Must** you go and see Ann?* (*Do **you** think it is necessary?*)
–   *You **can** borrow my car.* (***I** give permission.*)
    ***Can** I borrow your car?* (*Will **you** give permission?*)

4   other meanings

Besides the meanings discussed in paragraphs 2 and 3, *will* and *would* are
used to talk about habitual behaviour (see 600, 604).
> *Most evenings he'll just **sit** in front of the TV and go to sleep.*
> *When we were kids, my mum **would take** us out on bikes all round*
>   *the countryside.*
***Used to** +* **infinitive** (see 577) is similar to a modal verb structure in some
ways. It is used to talk about habitual behaviour and (unlike *would*) habitual
states.
> *I **used to** play a lot of tennis when I was younger.*
> *The grass **used to** look greener when I was a child.*
>   (N O T *~~The grass **would** look greener when I was a child.~~*)

5   subject-independence

An interesting, rather complicated point about modal verbs is that their
meaning usually 'spreads over' a whole clause. This means that one can
change a modal structure from active to passive, for example, without
affecting the meaning very much. Compare:
–   *A child **could understand** his theory.*
    *His theory **could be understood** by a child.*

– *You **mustn't put** adverbs between the verb and the object.*
*Adverbs **mustn't be put** between the verb and the object.*
– *Dogs **may chase** cats.*
*Cats **may get chased** by dogs.*

With most other verbs that are followed by infinitives, their meaning is attached to the subject, so that a change from active to passive changes the sense of the sentence completely. Compare:

– *Dogs **like to chase** cats.*
*Cats **like to be chased** by dogs.* (different and – of course – untrue)
– *Pete **wants to phone** Ann.*
*Ann **wants to be phoned** by Pete.* (not the same meaning)

For more details of the use of the various modal verbs, see the entries for each verb.

346 more

1 *more* + noun

We can use *more* before a noun phrase as a determiner (see 157). We do not generally use *of* when there is no other determiner (e.g. article or possessive).

*We need **more time**.* (NOT *...~~more of time~~.*)
*Could I have some **more pie**?* (NOT *...~~more of pie~~.*)
***More university students** are having to borrow money these days.*
    (NOT *~~More of university students~~...*)

However, *more of* can be used without a following determiner in a few cases – for instance, before personal and geographical names.

*It would be nice to see **more of Ray and Barbara**.*
*Five hundred years ago, much **more of Britain** was covered with trees.*

2 *more of* + determiner / pronoun

Before determiners (e.g. *a, the, my, this*) and pronouns, we use *more of*.

*He's **more of a** fool than I thought.*
*Three **more of the** missing climbers have been found.*
*Could I have some **more of that** smoked fish?*
*I don't think any **more of them** want to come.*

3 *more* without a noun

We can drop a noun after *more* if the meaning is clear.

*I'd like some **more**, please.*

4 *one more* etc

Note the structure *one more, two more* etc + noun phrase.

*There's just **one more river** to cross.*

For *another* used in a similar way, see 53.

5 *more* as an adverb

More can also be used as an adverb.

*I hate this job **more** every day.*   ►

6 comparative structures

More is used to make the comparative forms of longer adjectives and most adverbs (see 136 and 137).

> *As you get older you get **more tolerant**.*
> *Please drive **more slowly**.*

For *no more*, *not any more/longer*, see 372.
For *far more*, *much more*, *many more* etc, see 139.

347 most

1 *most* + noun

We can use *most* before a noun phrase as a determiner (see 157). We do not generally use *of* when there is no other determiner (e.g. article or possessive).

> ***Most cheese*** *is made from cow's milk.* (NOT ~~*Most of cheese*~~...)
> ***Most Swiss people*** *understand French.* (NOT ~~*Most of Swiss people*~~...)

However, *most of* can be used without a following determiner in a few cases – for instance, before personal and geographical names.

> ***Most of George*** *seemed to be covered with hair.*
> *The Romans conquered **most of England**.*

2 *most of* + determiner / pronoun

Before determiners (e.g. *a*, *the*, *my*, *this*) and pronouns, we use *most of*.

> *He's eaten two pizzas and **most of a** cold chicken.*
> *You've got **most of the** bed, as usual.*
> ***Most of the** people here know each other.*
> ***Most of my** friends live abroad.* (NOT ~~*Most my friends*~~...)
> *She's eaten **most of that** cake.*
> ***Most of us** thought he was wrong.*

3 *most* without a noun

We can drop a noun after *most* if the meaning is clear.

> *Some people had difficulty with the lecture, but **most** understood.*
> *Ann and Robby found a lot of blackberries, but Susan found **the most**.*

4 *the most* with nouns

In comparisons (when *most* has a superlative meaning) it is normally used with *the*, though this is sometimes dropped in an informal style in British English.

> *Susan found **(the) most** blackberries.*
> *Which country produces **(the) most** wine?*

However, *the* is not used when there is no comparison, and *most* simply means 'the majority of'.

> ***Most** children like ice-cream.* (NOT ~~*The most children*~~...)

5 *(the) most* as an adverb

(The) most can also be used as an adverb. *The* is often dropped in an informal style.

> *They all talk a lot, but your little girl talks **(the) most**.*
> *The truth hurts **most**.*

6 superlative adjectives and adverbs

(The) most is used to make the superlative forms of longer adjectives and most adverbs (see 136 and 137).

> *I wasn't as clever as the others, but I was **the most beautiful**.*
> *Which car goes **fastest**?*

7 *most* meaning 'very'

Most can be used before adjectives to mean 'very' in evaluating expressions, especially in a formal style.

> *That is **most kind** of you.*
> *Thank you for a **most interesting** afternoon.*
> *The experience was **most distressing**.*

348 much and many

1 the difference

Much is used with singular nouns; *many* is used with plurals.

> *I haven't got **much time**.*
> ***How much** of the roof needs repairing?*
> *You can have as **much** of the **milk** as you like.*
> *I don't know **many** of your **friends**.*
> *She didn't stay for as **many days** as she had intended.*

2 *much/many* + noun

We can use *much* and *many* before noun phrases as determiners. We do not generally use *of* when there is no other determiner (e.g. article or possessive).

> *She didn't eat **much breakfast**.* (NOT *...~~much of breakfast~~.*)
> *There aren't **many large glasses** left.* (NOT *...~~many of large glasses left~~.*)

However, *much of* can be used without a following determiner in a few cases – for instance, before personal and geographical names.

> *I've seen too **much of Howard** recently.*
> *Not **much of Denmark** is hilly.*

3 *much/many of* + determiner + noun

Before determiners (e.g. *a, the, my, this*) and pronouns, we use *much of* and *many of*.

> *You can't see **much of a country** in a week.*
> *How **much of the** house do you want to paint this year?*
> *I won't pass the exam: I've missed too **many of my** lessons.*
> *You didn't eat **much of it**.*
> *How **many of you** are there?*

▶

4 *much/many* without a noun

We can drop a noun after *much* or *many*, if the meaning is clear.

*You haven't eaten **much**.*

*'Did you find any mushrooms?' 'Not **many**.'*

Note that *much* and *many* are only used like this when a noun has been dropped. They are not used as the complements of nouns: other structures are used. Compare:

*There wasn't **much (food)**.*

*That's too **much (food)**.*

BUT NOT ~~The food wasn't **much**~~.

(Because you couldn't say ~~The food wasn't much food.~~)

Many is not usually used alone to mean 'many people'.

***Many people** think it's time for a change.* (NOT ~~**Many think**...~~)

5 not used in affirmative clauses

In an informal style, we use *much* and *many* mostly in questions and negative clauses. They are unusual in affirmative clauses except after *so, as* and *too*; other words and expressions are used. Compare:

*'How **much** money have you got?' 'I've got **plenty**.'* (NOT ~~I've got **much**.~~)

*He's got **lots of** men friends, but he doesn't know **many** women.*

(More natural than *He's got **many** men friends.*)

*There was **so much** traffic that it took me an hour to get home. And there was **a lot of** bad driving on the road.*

(More natural than ... *there was **much** bad driving...*)

*You make **too many** mistakes – **lots of** spelling mistakes, for example.*

(More natural than ... *many* spelling mistakes ...)

Very much is common in affirmative clauses as an adverb, but not as a determiner. Compare:

*I liked it **very much**.*

*Thank you **very much**.*

*There's **a whole lot of** water coming under the door.*

(NOT ~~There's **very much** water coming...~~)

In a formal style, *much* and *many* are not so unnatural in affirmative clauses.

***Much** has been written about the causes of unemployment. In the opinion of **many** economists, ...*

Far and *long* (= 'a long time') are also used mostly in questions and negative clauses. See 206 and 323.

6 *much* as adverb

We can use *much* as an adverb.

*I don't travel **much** these days.*

Much can come before some verbs expressing enjoyment, preference and similar ideas, especially in a formal style.

*I **much appreciate** your help.*

*We **much prefer** the country to the town.*

*Janet **much enjoyed** her stay with your family.*

Before some other verbs (e.g. *like, dislike*), this is only possible in negative structures and after *very*. Compare:

*I **very much like** your brother.*
*I **don't much like** your sister.*
*I like your parents **a lot**.* (NOT ~~I **much like your parents**.~~)

For more information about *a lot (of), lots (of), plenty (of)* etc, see 326.
For *much* and *many* modifying comparatives (e.g. *much older, many more*), see 139.
For *much* and *very* as modifiers before past participles (e.g. *much/very amused*), see 405.4.

349 **must** (1): introduction

1 grammar

Must is a modal auxiliary verb (see 344–345).

a There is no *-s* in the third person singular.
*He **must** start coming on time.* (NOT ~~He **musts**...~~)

b Questions and negatives are made without *do*.
***Must you** go?* (NOT ~~Do you **must** go?~~)
*You **mustn't** worry.* (NOT ~~You **don't must** worry.~~)

c After *must*, we use the infinitive without *to* of other verbs (see 277).
*I **must write** to my mother.* (NOT ~~I **must to write**...~~)
Progressive, perfect and passive infinitives are also possible (see 276).
*You **must be joking**.*
*It **must have been** terrible to live during the war.*
*Dogs **must be kept** on a lead.*

d *Must* has no infinitive or participles (~~to must, musting, musted~~ do not exist), and it has no past tense. When necessary, we use other words, for example forms of *have to* (see 243).
*It's annoying **to have to** get up early on Sundays.*
        (NOT ...~~to must get up~~...)
*He'll **have to** start coming on time.* (NOT ~~He'll **must**...~~)
*She's always **had to** work hard.* (NOT ~~She's always **musted**...~~)
*We **had to** cut short our holiday because my mother was ill.*
        (NOT ~~We **musted**...~~)

e However, ideas about the past can be expressed by *must* followed by a perfect infinitive (***have** + **past participle***). See 350.4.
*I can't find my keys. I **must have left** them at home.*
Must can also be used with a past sense in indirect speech.
*Everybody told me I **must** stop worrying.*

f There is a contracted negative *mustn't* (/ˈmʌsnt/).
Must has two pronunciations: a 'strong' pronunciation /mʌst/ and a 'weak' pronunciation /m(ə)st/. The weak pronunciation is used in most cases (see 588). ▶

2 meanings

Must is used mostly to express the conclusion that something is certain
(see 350), and (less often in American English) to talk about necessity and
obligation (see 351).

> You **must** be Anna's sister – you look just like her.
> You really **must** get your hair cut.

For the difference between *must* and *have to*, see 352.
For the difference between *must* and *should*, see 496.

350 must (2): concluding that something is certain

1 statements

Must can be used to express the conclusion that something is certain or
highly probable – to suggest that there are excellent arguments for believing
something.

> If A is bigger than B, and B is bigger than C, then A **must** be bigger than C.
> Mary **must** have a problem – she keeps crying.
> 'I'm in love.' 'That **must** be nice, dear.'
> There's the doorbell. It **must** be Roger.

2 questions and negatives: *can*

Must is not often used to express certainty in questions and negative clauses.
In questions we use *can*.

> There's somebody at the door. Who **can** it be? (NOT ... ~~Who **must** it be?~~)

In negative clauses we generally use *cannot/can't* to say that something is
certainly not the case.

> It **can't** be the postman at the door. It's only seven o'clock.
>> (NOT ~~It **mustn't** be the postman~~ ...)

However, *must not/mustn't* is occasionally used in this sense, especially in
American English.

> I haven't heard Molly moving about. She **mustn't** be awake yet. Her alarm
> **mustn't** have gone off.
>> (OR ... She **can't** be awake yet. Her alarm **can't** have gone off.)

And *mustn't* is normal in this sense in British English in question tags (see
465–466) after *must*, and in negative questions.

> It **must** be nice to be a cat, **mustn't it**? (NOT ... ~~**can't it**?~~)
> **Mustn't** it have been strange to live in the Middle Ages?

3 *need not*

Need not is used in British English to say that something is not necessarily so;
does not have to can also be used. *Must not* is not used in this sense.

> 'Look at those tracks. That must be a dog.' 'It **needn't** be – it could be a fox.'
>> (OR ... 'It **doesn't have to** be ...')
>> (NOT ... ~~It **mustn't** be~~ ...)

4 conclusions about the past

We can use *must* with a perfect infinitive (***have* + past participle**) to express conclusions about the past.

> *'We went to Rome last month.'* *'That **must have been** nice.'*
> *'A woman phoned while you were out.'* *'It **must have been** Kate.'*

Can is used in questions and negatives.

> *Where **can** John **have put** the matches? He **can't have thrown** them away.*

5 indirect speech

Must can be used after a past reporting verb as if it were a past tense.

> *I felt there **must** be something wrong.*

6 *must* and *should*

Should can be used as a weaker form of *must*. Compare:

> *Ann **must be** at home by now.* (= *I think she's certainly at home.*)
> *Ann **should be** at home by now.* (= *I think she's very probably at home.*)

For more about the difference between *must* and *should*, see 496.

351 must (3): necessity and obligation

1 statements: the speaker's point of view

In affirmative statements, we can use *must* to say what is necessary, and to give strong advice and orders to ourselves or other people. This is especially common in British English; in American English *have to* is generally preferred, particularly in speech.

> *Plants **must** get enough light and water if they are to grow properly.*
> *British industry **must** improve its productivity.*
> *I really **must** stop smoking.*
> *You **must** be here before eight o'clock tomorrow.*

Must is common in emphatic invitations.

> *You really **must** come and see us soon.*

In statements about obligation with *must* the obligation normally comes from the speaker. To talk about an obligation that comes from 'outside' (for instance a regulation, or an order from somebody else), we usually prefer *have to* (see 352).

> *I **have to** work from nine to five.*
> (More natural than *I **must** work from nine to five.*)
> *In my job I **have to** travel a lot.*
> (More natural than *In my job I **must** travel a lot.*)

2 questions: the hearer's point of view

In questions, British people can use *must* to ask about what the hearer thinks is necessary. (Americans generally prefer *have to*.)

> ***Must** I clean all the rooms?* (US *Do I **have to** ...?*)
> *Why **must** you always leave the door open?*

▶

3 negatives: prohibitions

British people can use *must not* / *mustn't* to say that things should not be done, or tell people not to do things. *Can't* is also possible, and is normal in American English.

> *The government really **mustn't/can't** expect people to work hard for no money.*
> *You **mustn't/can't** open this parcel until Christmas Day.*

Note that *must not* / *mustn't* is not used to say that things are unnecessary. This idea is expressed by *do not need to* or *do not have to*.

> *You **don't need to** get a visa to go to Scotland.*
> (NOT ~~You **mustn't** get a visa to go to Scotland.~~)

In British English, we can give permission not to do things with *need not*.

> *You **needn't** work tomorrow if you don't want to.*
> (US *You **don't have to** work* ...)

4 past necessity and obligation

Must is not normally used to talk about past obligation (except in indirect speech – see below). This is because *must* is used mainly for giving orders and advice and for making recommendations, and one cannot do these things in the past. *Had to* is used to talk about 'outside' obligation in the past.

> *I **had to** cycle three miles to school when I was a child.*

For *must* + **perfect infinitive** expressing conclusions about the past, see 350.4.

5 indirect speech

Must can be used (especially in British English) after a past reporting verb as if it were a past tense.

> *The doctor said that I **must** stop smoking.*

Obligation can also be reported with *had to* and *would have to*.

> *The doctor said that I **had to** / **would have to** stop smoking.*

6 *must* and *should*

Should can be used as a weaker form of *must*. Compare:

> *That carpet **must** be cleaned.* (= It is absolutely necessary.)
> *That carpet **should** be cleaned.* (= It would be a good idea.)

For more about the difference between *must* and *should*, see 496.
For more information about *have (got) to*, see 243; for more about the difference between *must* and *have to*, see 352.

352 must (4): must and have (got) to

There are some differences between *must* and *have to*.

1 concluding that something is certain

Both *must* and *have (got) to* can be used to express the conclusion that something is certain. *Must* is unusual in this sense in American English, especially in speech. *Have (got) to* used to be unusual in British English in this sense, but it is now becoming common.

*This **must be** the worst job in the world.* (GB)

(OR *This **has (got) to** be the worst job . . .*)

*You **must** be joking.* (GB) (OR *You **have (got) to** be joking.*)

Negative conclusions are not usually expressed with *must not*.

*That **can't** be his mother – she's not old enough.*

(NOT in British English *That **mustn't** be his mother . . .*)

Does not have to is used to say that something is not necessarily true.

*'A dog's been killing our chickens.' 'It **doesn't have to** be a dog – it could be a fox.'*

Conclusions about the past are usually expressed with *must* followed by the perfect infinitive (**have + past participle**).

*I hear you've been to Patagonia. That **must have been** interesting.*

(NOT *That **has to have been** interesting.*)

2 necessity and obligation

Must and *have (got) to* can both be used in British English to talk about necessity. In American English, *have to* is more common, especially in speech.

*Plants **must / have to** get enough light and water if they are to grow properly.*

Both verbs can be used in British English to talk about obligation. (In American English, *have to* is the normal form.) British English often makes a distinction as follows. *Must* is used mostly to talk about the feelings and wishes of the speaker and hearer – for example, to give or ask for orders. *Have (got) to* is used mostly to talk about obligations that come from 'outside' – for example from laws, regulations, agreements and other people's orders. Compare:

– *I **must** stop smoking.* (I want to.)

*I've **got to** stop smoking. Doctor's orders.*

– *This is a terrible party. We really **must** go home.*

*This is a lovely party, but we've **got to** go home because of the baby-sitter.*

– *I've got bad toothache. I **must** make an appointment with the dentist.*

*I can't come to work tomorrow morning because I've **got to** see the dentist at ten o'clock.*

– *You really **must** go to church next Sunday – you haven't been for ages.*

(I am telling you to.)

*Catholics **have to** go to church on Sundays.* (Their religion tells them to.)

– ***Must** you wear dirty old jeans all the time?*

(Is it personally important for you?)

*Do you **have to** wear a tie at work?* (Is there a regulation?)

Opinions about what people should do can be expressed with *must* or *should*, but not usually with *have to* in British English.

*People **must/should** understand that the world is changing.*

3 future obligation: *will have to, have (got) to* and *must*

Will have to is used to talk about future obligation, but *have (got) to* is preferred when arrangements for the future have already been made. Compare:

*When you leave school you'**ll have to** find a job.*

*I've **got to** go for a job interview tomorrow.* ▶

Must can be used to give orders or instructions for the future.
>*You can borrow my car, but you **must** bring it back before ten.*

Will have to can be used to 'distance' the instructions, making them sound less like direct orders from the speaker.
>*You can borrow my car, but you**'ll have to** bring it back before ten.*

Will need to can be used in the same way (see 357.3).

4   talking about the past: *had to ...* and *must have ...*

Had to is used to talk about past obligation. *Must* is used with the perfect infinitive (***have* + past participle**) to express certainty about the past (see paragraph 1, above). Compare:
>*Edna isn't in her office. She **had to go** home.*
>>(= *It was necessary for her to go home.*)
>
>*Edna isn't in her office. She **must have gone** home.*
>>(= *It seems certain that she has gone home.*)

5   negative forms

The negative forms *must not* and *do not have to / have not got to* have quite different meanings. *Must not* is used to prohibit (to tell people not to do things) and to refer to prohibitions; *do not have to / have not got to* is used to say that there is no obligation. Compare:

– *You **mustn't** tell George.* (= *Don't tell George.*)
  *You **don't have to** tell George.* (= *You can if you like but it isn't necessary.*)
– *You **mustn't** park on double yellow lines in England.*
  *You **don't have to** carry identity papers in England.*

For more about *have (got) to*, see 243.
For more about the use of *must* to express conclusions about certainty, see 350.
For more about the use of *must* to express necessity and obligation, see 351.
For *needn't* and *don't need to*, see 357.

353   names and titles

Names and titles are used both when talking about people and when talking to them. There are some differences.

1   talking about people

When we talk about people we can name them in four ways.

a   first name

This is informal. We use first names mostly to talk about relatives, friends and children.
>*Where's **Peter**? He said he'd be here at three.*
>*How's **Maud** getting on at school?*

b   first name + surname

This is neutral – neither particularly formal nor particularly informal.
>*Isn't that **Peter Connolly** the actor?*
>*We're going on holiday with **Mary** and **Daniel Sinclair**.*

c title (*Mr, Mrs* etc) + surname

This is more formal. We talk like this about people we do not know, or when we want to show respect or be polite.

*Can I speak to **Mr Lewis**, please?*
*We've got a new teacher called **Mrs Campbell**.*
*Ask **Miss Andrews** to come in, please.*
*There's a **Ms Sanders** on the phone.*

Note that it is less usual to talk about people by using title + first name + surname (e.g. *Mr John Parker*).

d surname only

We often use just the surname to talk about public figures – politicians, sportsmen and sportswomen, writers and so on.

*Do you think **Roberts** would make a good President?*
*The women's 5,000 metres was won by **Jones**.*
*I don't think **Eliot** is a very good dramatist.*

Surnames alone are sometimes used for employees (especially male employees), and by members of groups (especially all-male groups like soldiers, schoolboys, team members) when they refer to each other.

*Tell **Patterson** to come and see me at once.*
*Let's put **Billows** in goal and move **Carter** up.*

2 talking to people

When we talk to people we generally name them in one of two ways.

a first name

This is informal, used for example to relatives, friends and children.

*Hello, **Pamela**. How are you?*

b title + surname

This is more formal or respectful.

*Good morning, **Miss Williamson**.*

Note that we do not usually use both the first name and the surname of a person that we are talking to. It would be unusual to say '*Hello, **Peter Matthews**'*, for example.

Members of all-male groups sometimes address each other by their surnames alone, but this is unusual in modern English.

Mr, Mrs and *Ms* are not generally used alone.

Excuse me. Can you tell me the time?

(NOT *Excuse me, **Mr*** or *Excuse me, **Mrs**.*)

Doctor can be used alone to talk to medical doctors whom one is consulting, but not usually in other cases.

***Doctor**, I've got this pain in my elbow.*

Sir and *madam* are used in Britain mostly by people in service occupations (e.g. shop assistants). Some employees call their male employers *sir*, and some schoolchildren call their teachers *sir* or *miss*. *Dear Sir* and *Dear Madam* are common ways of beginning letters to strangers (see 317) – note the capital

letters. In other situations *sir* and *madam* are unusual in British English.
> *Excuse me. Can you tell me the time?* (NOT ~~*Excuse me, sir*~~...)

In American English, *sir* and *ma'am* are less formal than in British English, and are quite often used (especially in the South and West) when addressing people.

3 notes on titles

Note the pronunciations of the titles *Mr, Mrs* and *Ms* (used before names):
> *Mr* /'mɪstə(r)/   *Mrs* /'mɪsɪz/   *Ms* /mɪz/

Mr (= *Mister*) is not normally written in full, and the other two cannot be.

Like *Mr, Ms* does not show whether somebody is married or not. It is often used, especially in writing, to talk about or address women when one does not know (or has no reason to say) whether they are married. Many women also choose to use *Ms* before their own names in preference to *Mrs* or *Miss*. *Ms* is a relatively new title: it has been in common use in Britain since the 1970s, and a little longer in the United States.

Dr (= *Doctor*) is used as a title for medical and other doctors (but see paragraph 2 for its use.)

Professor does not mean 'teacher'; it is used only for certain very senior university teachers.

Note that we do not normally combine two titles such as *Prof Dr* or *Mrs Dr*.

For ways of addressing people in letters, see 317.
For ways of introducing people, see 520.1.
For full stops with abbreviated titles and initials, see 2.

354 nationalities, countries and regions

1 introduction

In order to refer to a nation or region and its affairs it is usually necessary to know four words:
- the name of the country or region
  Denmark, Japan, France, Catalonia
- the adjective
  Danish, Japanese, French, Catalan
- the singular noun used for a person from the country
  a Dane, a Japanese, a Frenchman/woman, a Catalan
- the plural expression *the*... used for the population as a whole
  the Danes, the Japanese, the French, the Catalans

Usually the singular noun is the same as the adjective (e.g. *Japanese, Mexican*), and the plural expression is the same as the adjective + *-s* (e.g. *the Mexicans*). See paragraph 2 below for more examples. However, there are a number of exceptions (see paragraph 3).

All words of this kind (including adjectives) begin with capital letters.
> *American literature* (NOT ~~*american literature*~~)

The name of a national language is often the same as the national adjective.
> *Danish is difficult to pronounce.   Do you speak Japanese?*

2 examples

Country/region	Adjective	Person	Population
America (The United States)	American	an American	the Americans
Belgium	Belgian	a Belgian	the Belgians
Brazil	Brazilian	a Brazilian	the Brazilians
Europe	European	a European	the Europeans
Italy	Italian	an Italian	the Italians
Kenya	Kenyan	a Kenyan	the Kenyans
Morocco	Moroccan	a Moroccan	the Moroccans
Norway	Norwegian	a Norwegian	the Norwegians
Tyrol	Tyrolean	a Tyrolean	the Tyroleans
Greece	Greek	a Greek	the Greeks
Iraq	Iraqi	an Iraqi	the Iraqis
Israel	Israeli	an Israeli	the Israelis
Thailand	Thai	a Thai	the Thais
China	Chinese	a Chinese	the Chinese
Congo	Congolese	a Congolese	the Congolese
Portugal	Portuguese	a Portuguese	the Portuguese
Switzerland	Swiss	a Swiss	the Swiss

3 exceptions

Country/region	Adjective	Person	Population
Britain	British	a British person (Briton)	the British
England	English	an English-woman/man	the English
France	French	a Frenchman/woman	the French
Ireland	Irish	an Irishwoman/man	the Irish
Spain	Spanish	a Spaniard	the Spanish
The Netherlands/Holland	Dutch	a Dutchwoman/man	the Dutch
Wales	Welsh	a Welshman/woman	the Welsh
Denmark	Danish	a Dane	the Danes
Finland	Finnish	a Finn	the Finns
Poland	Polish	a Pole	the Poles
Scotland	Scottish, Scotch	a Scot	the Scots
Sweden	Swedish	a Swede	the Swedes
Turkey	Turkish	a Turk	the Turks

▶

Notes

a   The Scots prefer the adjective *Scottish*, but other people often use *Scotch*.

b   The word *Briton* is unusual except in newspaper headlines – for example *TWO **BRITONS** KILLED IN AIR CRASH*. *Brit* is sometimes used informally. (But most British people call themselves *Scottish, Welsh, Irish* or *English*.)

c   *English* is not the same as *British*, and is not used for Scottish, Welsh or Irish people (see 114).

d   Although *American* is the normal English word for United States citizens and affairs, people from other parts of the American continent may object to this use, and some people avoid it for this reason.

e   *Arabic* is used for the language spoken in Arab countries; in other cases, the normal adjective is *Arab*. *Arabian* is used in a few fixed expressions and place names (e.g. *Saudi **Arabian**, the **Arabian** Sea*).

f   Note the pronunciation of words like *Irishman/men, Dutchman/men*: the singular is the same as the plural (/'aɪrɪʃmən, 'dʌtʃmən/).

355   near (to)

The adjective *near* can be used like a preposition, with or without *to*. *To* is not normally used when we are talking about physical closeness.

>   *We live **near** the station.*

When we are not talking about physical closeness, *near to* is often preferred.

>   *I came very **near to** hitting him.*

Nearer and *nearest* are generally used with *to*, though *to* can be dropped in an informal style.

>   *Come and sit **nearer (to)** me.*   *Who's the girl sitting **nearest (to)** the door?*

For the difference between *nearest* and *next*, see 356.

356   nearest and next

1   place and time

Nearest is used for place – it means 'most near in space'.

>   *Excuse me. Where's the **nearest** tube station?* (NOT . . . ~~the next tube station.~~)
>   *If you want to find Alan, just look in the **nearest** pub.*

Next is used to talk about time or series – it means 'nearest in the future' or 'after this/that one'.

>   *We get off at the **next** station.* (= the station that we will come to first.)
>   *I'm looking forward to her **next** visit.*
>   *As soon as he had finished one trip, he started planning the **next**.*

2   exceptions: *next* used for place

We use *next* in a few fixed expressions to mean 'nearest in space'. The most common are *next door* and *next to*.

>   *My girl-friend lives **next door**.*   *Come and sit **next to me**.*

For *next* and *the next*, see 367.

357 need

When *need* is followed by another verb, it can have the forms either of an ordinary verb or (in British English) of a modal auxiliary verb.

1 ordinary verb

Need most often has the same forms as ordinary verbs: the third person singular has *-s*, and questions and negatives are made with *do*. *Need* is usually followed by an infinitive with *to*.

*Everybody **needs to rest** sometimes.*
***Do** we **need to reserve** seats on the train?*

2 modal auxiliary verb

In British English, *need* can also have the same present-tense forms as modal auxiliary verbs: the third person singular has no *-s*, and questions and negatives are made without *do*. In this case, *need* is normally followed by an infinitive without *to*.

*We **needn't reserve** seats – there'll be plenty of room.*

These modal forms are used mainly in negative sentences, but they are also possible in questions, after *if*, and in other 'non-assertive' structures (see 374).

*You **needn't fill in** a form.   **Need I fill in** a form?*
*I wonder **if I need fill in** a form.   This is the **only** form you **need fill in**.*
(BUT NOT ~~You **need fill in** a form.~~)

Modal forms of *need* normally refer to immediate necessity. They are often used to ask for or give permission – usually permission not to do something. Modal verb forms are not used to talk about habitual, general necessity. Compare:

*It's OK – You **needn't pay** for that phone call.*
    (OR ... *You **don't need to pay** for that phone call.*)
*You **don't need to pay** for emergency calls in most countries.*
    (NOT ~~You **needn't pay** ... in most countries.~~)

Modal forms of *need* are rare in American English.

3 talking about the future

Present tense forms of *need* are used when making decisions about the future.

***Need I come** in tomorrow?   Tell her she **doesn't need to** work tonight.*

Will need to ... can be used to talk about future obligation, and give advice for the future. It can make orders and instructions sound less direct.

*We**'ll need to repair** the roof next year.*
*You**'ll need to start** work soon if you want to pass your exams.*
*You**'ll need to fill in** this form before you see the Inspector.*

For similar uses of *have to*, see 243.3.

4 *need ... ing*

After *need* an *-ing* form can be used in British English, with the same meaning as a passive infinitive.

*That sofa **needs cleaning** again. (= ... needs to be cleaned ...)*

A structure with **object + ...** *ing* is also possible in some cases.

*You **need your head examining**. (OR ... examined.)*   ▶

5   *need not* + **perfect infinitive**

If we say that somebody *need not have done something* (GB), we mean that
he or she did it, but that it was unnecessary – a waste of time.
> *You **needn't have woken** me up. I don't have to go to work today.*
> *I **needn't have cooked** so much food. Nobody was hungry.*

On the other hand, if we say that somebody *did not need to do something*, we
are simply saying that it was not necessary (whether or not it was done).
Compare:
> *I **needn't have watered** the flowers. Just after I finished it started raining.*
> *It started raining, so I **didn't need to water** the flowers.*

6   *need not* and *must not*

Need not (GB) is used to say that there is no obligation; *must not* is used to
say that there is an obligation not to do something. Compare:
> *You **needn't** tell Jennifer – she already knows.*
> *You **mustn't tell** Margaret – I don't want her to know.*

Need not is also sometimes used to say that something is not necessarily true.
> *'She looks quite ill. I'm sure it's flu.' 'It **needn't** be – maybe she's just over-tired.'*

For *there is no need to . . .*, see 563.2.
For more about verbs followed by perfect infinitives, see 278.
For more about modal auxiliary verbs, see 344–345.

358   **negative structures** (1): basic rules

1   **negative verb forms**

We make negative verb forms by putting *not* after an auxiliary verb.
> *We **have not** forgotten you.*   *It **was not** raining.*   *She **can't** swim.*

Do is normally used if there is no other auxiliary verb.
> *I like the salad, but I **don't** like the soup.* (NOT *I like not the soup.*)

Do is followed by the infinitive without *to*.
> *I **didn't** think.*
> (NOT *I didn't to think*, *I didn't thinking* OR *I didn't thought.*)

Do is not used with another auxiliary verb.
> *You **mustn't** worry.* (NOT *You **don't must** worry.*)

Do is not normally used with *be* (even when *be* is the main verb).
> *The supper **isn't** ready.* (NOT *The supper **doesn't be** ready.*)

Do is not used with negative subjunctives (these are mainly US – see 541),
infinitives or *-ing* forms.
> *It is important that she **not realise** what is happening.*
> *Remind me **not to come** here again.* (NOT *. . . to do not come . . .*)

For negative forms of *have*, *dare*, *need* and *used* with and without *do*, see the entries on
these verbs.
For the dialect form *ain't*, see 144.4.
For negatives without *do* in older English (e.g. *I like him not*), see 388.

2   **imperatives**

Negative imperatives are made with ***do not/don't*** + **infinitive** (see 268).
> ***Do not expect*** *quick results when you start learning a language.*
> (NOT *Expect not . . .*)

Don't worry – *I'll look after you.* (NOT ~~*Worry not*~~...)
Do not/don't is also used to make the negative imperative of *be*.
Don't be *rude.*

3   infinitives and -*ing* forms

We put *not* before infinitives and -*ing* forms. *Do* is not used.
*It's important **not to worry***. (NOT ...~~*to don't worry.*~~)
*The best thing about a holiday is **not working**.*

4   other parts of a clause

We can put *not* with other parts of a clause, not only a verb.
*Ask Jake, **not his wife**.*   *Come early, but **not before six**.*
*It's working, but **not properly**.*
We do not usually put *not* with the subject. Instead, we use a structure with *it*.
It was not George *that came, but his brother.* (NOT ~~*Not George came*~~...)

For the difference between *not* and *no* with nouns, see 375.

5   other negative words

Other words besides *not* can make a clause negative. Compare:
*He's **not** at home.*
*He's **never** at home.*
*He's **seldom / rarely / hardly ever** at home.*
We do not normally use the auxiliary *do* with these other words. Compare:
*He **doesn't work**.*
*He never **works**.* (NOT ~~*He does never work.*~~)
*He seldom / rarely / hardly ever **works**.*
However, *do* can be used after one of these negative words for emphasis or contrast.
*I **never did** like her.*

6   question tags

Affirmative question tags are used after negative clauses.
*You **don't** work on Sundays, **do you**?*
*You **seldom** work on Saturdays, **do you**?*
    (NOT ~~*You seldom work on Saturdays, don't you?*~~)
Clauses with *little* and *few* (see 322) also have a negative sense, and are followed by affirmative question tags.
*There's **little** point in doing anything about it, **is there**?* (NOT ...~~*isn't there?*~~)
*He has **few** reasons for staying, **has he**?*

For more information about question tags, see 465–466.

7   'non-assertive words' (*any* etc)

We do not usually use *some, somebody, something* etc in negative clauses.
Instead, we use the 'non-assertive' words *any, anybody, anything* etc.
Compare:
*I've found **some** mushrooms.*
*I haven't found **any** mushrooms.*

▶

Some other words (e.g. *ever, yet*) are 'non-assertive', and found mostly in questions and negative clauses. See 374 for more details.

For transferred negation (e.g. *I **don't think** he's coming*), see 359.
For negative questions, see 360.
For double negatives, see 361.

359 negative structures (2): transferred negation

1 *think, believe* etc

When we introduce negative ideas with *think, believe, suppose, imagine* and words with similar meanings, we usually make the first verb (*think* etc) negative, not the second.

*I **don't think** you've met my wife.*
> (More natural than *I think you haven't met my wife.*)
*I **don't believe** she's at home.*
> (More natural than *I believe she isn't at home.*)

However, surprise is often expressed with *I **thought** +* **negative**.

*'Would you like a drink?' '**I thought** you'd **never** ask.'*
*Hello! **I thought** you **weren't** coming.*

2 *hope*

Transferred negation is not used with *hope*.

*I **hope** it **doesn't** rain.* (NOT ~~I don't hope it rains.~~)

3 short answers

In short answers, *think, believe, hope* etc can be followed by *not* (see 515).

*'Are we going to see Alan again?' 'I **believe/suppose/hope not**.'*

Another possible short answer construction is *I don't ... so* (see 515). (*Hope* is not used in this structure.)

*'Do you think there'll be snow tomorrow?' 'I **don't believe/suppose/think so**.'*
> (BUT *'I **hope not**.'*)

I don't think so is more common than *I think not*, which is rather formal.

4 verbs followed by infinitives

Many verbs can be followed by infinitives (see 283). In an informal style we often prefer to make the first verb negative rather than the infinitive, although this may not change the meaning at all. This happens, for example, with *appear, seem, expect* and *happen*.

*Sibyl **doesn't seem** to like you.*
> (Less formal than *Sibyl seems **not to like** you.*)
*I **don't expect** to see you before Monday.*
> (More natural than *I expect **not to see** you ...*)
*Angela and I were at the same university, but we **never happened** to meet.*
> (Less formal than *... we happened **never to meet**.*)

With *intend* and *want* + infinitive, we almost always put *not/never* with the first verb.

*I **don't want** to fail this exam.* (NOT ~~I want **not to fail**...~~)
*After I've finished this contract I **never intend** to teach again.*

5 *always, almost*

We usually use *never ... any* and *hardly ... any/ever*, rather than *always ... no* and *almost ... no/never*.

> She **never** gives people **anything**. (NOT ~~She **always gives people nothing**.~~)
> **Hardly anyone** turned up. (More natural than **Almost no one** turned up.)

360 **negative structures** (3): negative questions

1 structure

Contracted and uncontracted negative questions have different word order. (Uncontracted negative questions are usually formal.)

> auxiliary verb + *n't* + subject

> **Doesn't she** understand?   **Why haven't you** booked your holiday yet?

> auxiliary verb + subject + *not*

> **Does she not** understand?   **Why have you not** booked your holiday yet?

Non-auxiliary *have* (British English) and non-auxiliary *be* go in the same position as auxiliary verbs.

> **Hasn't she** any friends to help her? (GB – see 241)
> **Have they not** at least a room to stay in? (GB)
> **Aren't you** ready?   **Is Mrs Allen not** at home?

2 two meanings

Negative questions can have two different kinds of meaning. It is usually clear from the situation and context which kind of question is being asked.

a **'Isn't it true that ... ?'** A negative question can ask for confirmation of a positive belief. In this case the question expects the answer *Yes*, and means 'Isn't it true that ... ?'

> **Didn't you go** and see Helen yesterday? How is she?
>   (= I believe you went and saw Helen yesterday ...)

Expressions of opinion can be made less definite by expressing them as negative questions.

> **Wouldn't it be** better to switch the lights on?

Negative questions of this kind are common in exclamations (see 201) and rhetorical questions (see 464).

> **Isn't it** a lovely day!
> 'She's growing up to be a lovely person.' 'Yes, **isn't she**!'
> **Isn't the answer** obvious? (= Of course the answer is obvious.)

b **'Is it true that ... not ... ?'** A negative question can also ask for confirmation of a negative belief. In this case the question expects the answer *No*, and means 'Is it true that ... not ... ?'

> **Don't you feel** well? (= Am I right in thinking you don't feel well?)
> Oh, dear. **Can't they come** this evening?

This kind of negative question can show that the speaker is surprised that something has not happened or is not happening.

> **Hasn't the postman come** yet?
> **Didn't the alarm go** off? I wonder what's wrong with it.

▶

3 polite requests, invitations, offers, complaints and criticisms

Pressing invitations and offers often begin *Won't you . . . ? Wouldn't you . . . ?*
or *Why don't you . . . ?*

> ***Won't you*** *come in for a few minutes?*
> ***Wouldn't you*** *like something to drink?*
> ***Why don't you*** *come and spend the weekend with us?*

But in other cases we do not usually use negative questions to ask people to
do things. This is done with ordinary questions, or with **negative statement
+ question tag**.

> ***Excuse me, can you help*** *me for a moment?*
>> (ordinary question, used as a request)
> *You **can't help** me for a moment, **can you**?*
>> (negative statement + question tag, common in informal requests)
> BUT NOT ~~*Can't you help me for a moment?*~~

Negative questions may be understood as complaints or criticisms.

> ***Can't you lend*** *me your pen for a minute?* (Meaning something like
>> *Are you too selfish to lend me . . . ?*)
> ***Don't you*** *ever **listen** to what I say?*

4 *yes* and *no*

In a reply to a negative question, *Yes* suggests an affirmative verb, and *No*
suggests a negative verb. Compare:

– *'Haven't you written to Mary?' '**Yes**.'* (= *'I have written to her.'*)
  *'Haven't you told her about us?' '**No**.'* (= *'I haven't told her about us.'*)
– *'Didn't the postman come this morning?' '**Yes**, he did.'*
  *'Didn't he bring anything for me?' '**No**, he didn't.'*

361 **negative structures** (4): double negatives

1 English and other languages

In some languages, a negative word like *nobody, nothing* or *never* has to be
used with a negative verb. In standard English, *nobody, nothing, never* etc
are themselves enough to give a negative meaning, and *not* is unnecessary.

> *I opened the door, but I **could see nobody**.* (NOT ~~*I couldn't see nobody.*~~)
> ***Nothing matters*** *now – everything's finished.*
>> (NOT ~~*Nothing doesn't matter . . .*~~)
> *I've **never understood** what she wants.*
>> (NOT ~~*I haven't never understood . . .*~~)

2 *nobody* and *not anybody*, etc

Nobody, nothing, never etc are rather emphatic. We often prefer to use *not
anybody, not anything, not ever* etc. Note that *anybody, anything, ever* etc
are not themselves negative words – they have to be used with *not* to give a
negative meaning.

> *I opened the door, but I **couldn't see anybody**.*
>> (NOT *. . . ~~but I could see anybody.~~*)
> *I'm sorry, I **can't** tell you **anything**.*

At the beginning of a clause, only *nobody, nothing* etc are used.
> *Nothing matters.* (NOT ~~Not anything matters.~~)
> *Nowhere is safe.*

For more information about 'non-assertive' words like *any, anybody, anything, ever* etc, see 374.

3 double and multiple negatives and their meaning

Double negatives are possible in standard English, but then both words normally have their full meaning. Compare:
> *Say **nothing**.* (= *Be silent.*)
> *Don't just say **nothing**. Tell us what the problem is.* (= *Don't be silent...*)

Multiple negatives are sometimes used instead of simple positive structures for special stylistic effects. This is rather literary; in spoken English it can seem unnatural or old-fashioned.
> ***Not** a day passes when I **don't** regret **not** having studied music in my youth.* (More natural: *Every day I regret not having studied music when I was younger.* OR *I wish I had studied music when I was younger.*)

4 dialects

In many British, American and other dialects, two or more negatives can be used with a single negative meaning.
> *I **ain't** seen **nobody**.* (Dialect for *I **haven't** seen **anybody**.*)
> *I **ain't never** done **nothing** to **nobody**, and I **ain't never** got **nothing** from **nobody no** time.* (American song by Bert Williams)

For more information about *ain't*, see 144.4.

5 extra negative in expressions of doubt

In informal standard spoken English, a negative verb (without a negative meaning) is sometimes used after expressions of doubt or uncertainty.
> *I shouldn't be surprised if they **didn't get** married soon.*
>   (= *... if they **got** married soon.*)
> *I wonder whether I **oughtn't to go** and see a doctor – I'm feeling a bit funny.* (= *... whether I **ought to** ...*)

6 *... I don't think* etc

In informal speech, expressions like *I don't think* or *I don't suppose* are often added after negative statements. In this case, the extra negative makes no difference to the meaning of the statement.
> *She has**n't** got much chance of passing the exam, **I don't think**.*
> *We wo**n't** be back before midnight, **I don't suppose**.*

362 negative structures (5): ambiguous sentences

In a negative structure, *not* can refer to different parts of a sentence. Compare:
> *Arthur did**n't** **write** to Sue yesterday – he phoned her.*
> *Arthur did**n't** write to **Sue** yesterday – he wrote to Ann.*
> *Arthur did**n't** write to Sue **yesterday** – he wrote this morning.*   ▶

The exact meaning is shown in speech by stress and intonation, and even in writing it is usually clear from the context and situation. However, confusions sometimes arise. They can usually be avoided by reorganising the sentence. Compare:

The car crash didn't kill him. (Did he live, or did something else kill him?)
It wasn't the car crash that killed him. (Only one possible meaning.)

Negative sentences with *because*-clauses are often ambiguous.

*I didn't sing **because Pam was there**.*

This sentence could mean 'My reason for not singing was that Pam was there' or 'My reason for singing was not that Pam was there'. The first meaning could be shown clearly by putting the *because*-clause at the beginning.

***Because Pam was there**, I didn't sing.*

363 neither (of): determiner

1 *neither* + singular noun

We use *neither* before a singular noun to mean 'not one and not the other (of two)'.

*'Can you come on Monday or Tuesday?' 'I'm afraid **neither day** is possible.'*

2 *neither of* + plural

We use *neither of* before a determiner (for example *the, my, these*), and before a pronoun. The noun or pronoun is plural.

***Neither of my brothers** can sing.* (NOT ~~*Neither my brothers can sing.*~~)
***Neither of us** saw it happen.*

After *neither of* + noun / pronoun, we use a singular verb in a formal style.

*Neither of my sisters **is** married.*

In an informal style, a plural verb is possible.

*Neither of my sisters **are** married.*

3 *neither* used alone

We can use *neither* alone, without a noun or pronoun.

*'Which one do you want?' '**Neither**.'*

4 pronunciation

In British English, *neither* can be pronounced both /'naɪðə(r)/ and /'niːðə(r)/. In American English, the usual pronunciation is /'niːðər/.

364 neither, nor and not … either

1 *neither* and *nor*

We can use *neither* and *nor* as adverbs to mean 'also not'. *Neither* and *nor* come at the beginning of a clause, and are followed by inverted word order: **auxiliary verb + subject**. (In American English, *nor* is not used after *and*.)

> *neither/nor* + auxiliary verb + subject

*'I can't swim.' '**Neither** can I.'* (NOT ~~*I also can't.*~~)
*Ruth didn't turn up, and **nor** did Kate.* (GB) (NOT *… ~~and Kate didn't too.~~*)

2   *not either*

We can also use *not ... either* with the same meaning and normal word order.
> *'I can't swim.' 'I can't either.'*
> *Ruth didn't turn up, and Kate didn't either.*

In very informal speech, *me neither* (and occasionally *me either*) can be used instead of *I ... n't either*.
> *'I can't swim.' 'Me neither.'*

3   *not ... nor*

Nor can follow *not*, especially after a pause; it is more emphatic than *or*.
> *She didn't phone that day, nor the next day.* (More emphatic than *... that day or the next day*.) (NOT *... ~~neither the next day~~*.)
> *Our main need is not food, nor money. It is education.*

For the pronunciation of *neither*, see 363.
For other uses of *either*, see 178–179.
For *so am I, so do I* etc, see 516.
For the difference between *too/also* and *either* in negative sentences, see 46.
For more about inverted word order, see 298–299.

365   neither ... nor

This structure is used to join two negative ideas. (It is the opposite of *both ... and*.) It is usually rather formal.
> *I neither smoke nor drink.* (less formal: *I don't smoke or drink*.)
> *The film was neither well made nor well acted.*

Sometimes more than two ideas are connected by *neither ... nor*.
> *He neither smiled, spoke, nor looked at me.*

When singular subjects are connected by *neither ... nor*, the verb is normally singular, but it can be plural in a less careful style.
> *Neither James nor Virginia was at home.* (normal)
> *Neither James nor Virginia were at home.* (less careful)

See also *both ... and ...* (111) and *either ... or* (179).

366   newspaper headlines

1   special language

Headlines are the short titles above newspaper reports (e.g. RUSSIAN WOMAN LANDS ON MOON). The headlines in English-language newspapers can be very difficult to understand. One reason for this is that newspaper headlines are often written in a special style, which is very different from ordinary English. In this style there are some special rules of grammar, and words are often used in unusual ways.   ▶

2 grammar

a Headlines are not always complete sentences. Many headlines consist of noun phrases with no verb.

MORE WAGE CUTS

HOLIDAY HOTEL DEATH

EXETER MAN'S DOUBLE MARRIAGE BID

b Headlines often contain strings of three, four or more nouns; nouns earlier in the string modify those that follow.

FURNITURE FACTORY PAY CUT ROW

Headlines like these can be difficult to understand. It sometimes helps to read them backwards. *FURNITURE FACTORY PAY CUT ROW* refers to a ROW (disagreement) about a CUT (reduction) in PAY at a FACTORY that makes FURNITURE.

c Headlines often leave out articles and the verb *be*.

SHAKESPEARE PLAY IMMORAL, SAYS HEADMASTER

WOMAN WALKS ON MOON

d In headlines, simple tenses are often used instead of progressive or perfect forms. The simple present is used for both present and past events.

*BLIND GIRL **CLIMBS** EVEREST* (= ... *has climbed* ...)

*STUDENTS **FIGHT** FOR COURSE CHANGES* (= ... *are fighting* ...)

The present progressive can be used, especially to talk about changes. *Be* is usually dropped.

*BRITAIN **GETTING** WARMER, SAY SCIENTISTS*

*TRADE FIGURES **IMPROVING***

e Many headline words are used as both nouns and verbs, and nouns are often used to modify other nouns (see paragraph 2b). So it is not always easy to work out the structure of a sentence. Compare:

*US **CUTS AID** TO THIRD WORLD*

(= *The US reduces its help* ... *CUTS is a verb, AID is a noun.*)

*AID **CUTS** ROW* (= *There has been a disagreement about the reduction in aid. AID and CUTS are both nouns.*)

CUTS AID REBELS (= *The reduction is helping the revolutionaries. CUTS is a noun, AID is a verb.*)

f Headlines often use infinitives to refer to the future.

*PM **TO VISIT** AUSTRALIA*

*HOSPITALS **TO TAKE** FEWER PATIENTS*

For is also used to refer to future movements or plans.

*TROOPS **FOR** GLASGOW?* (= *Are soldiers going to be sent to Glasgow?*)

g Auxiliary verbs are usually dropped from passive structures, leaving past participles.

*MURDER HUNT: MAN **HELD*** (= ... *a man **is being held** by police.*)

*SIX **KILLED** IN EXPLOSION* (= *Six people **have been killed** ...*)

Note that forms like *held, attacked* are usually past participles with passive meanings, not past tenses (which are rare in newspaper headlines). Compare:

– *AID ROW: PRESIDENT **ATTACKED*** (= ... *the President **has been attacked**.*)

*AID ROW: PRESIDENT **ATTACKS** CRITICS*

(= ... *the President **has attacked** her critics.*)

- *BOY **FOUND** SAFE* (= *The missing boy **has been found** safe.*)
  *BOY **FINDS** SAFE* (= *A boy **has found** a safe.*)

h   A colon (:) is often used to separate the subject of a headline from what is said about it.

> *STRIKES: PM TO ACT*
> *MOTORWAY CRASH: DEATH TOLL RISES*

Quotation marks ('...') are used to show that words were said by somebody else, and that the newspaper does not necessarily claim that they are true.

> *CRASH DRIVER 'HAD BEEN DRINKING'*

A question mark (?) is often used when something is not certain.

> *CRISIS OVER BY SEPTEMBER?*

For other styles with special grammar, see 1.

3   vocabulary

Short words save space, and so they are very common in newspaper headlines. Some of the short words in headlines are unusual in ordinary language (e.g. *curb*, meaning 'restrict' or 'restriction'), and some are used in special senses which they do not often have in ordinary language (e.g. *bid*, meaning 'attempt'). Other words are chosen not because they are short, but because they sound dramatic (e.g. *blaze*, which means 'big fire', and is used in headlines to refer to any fire). The following is a list of common headline vocabulary.

act take action; do something
> *FOOD CRISIS: GOVERNMENT TO **ACT***

aid military or financial help; to help
> *MORE **AID** FOR POOR COUNTRIES*
> *UNIONS **AID** HOSPITAL STRIKERS*

alert alarm, warning
> *FLOOD **ALERT** ON EAST COAST*

allege make an accusation
> *WOMAN **ALLEGES** UNFAIR TREATMENT*

appear appear in court accused of a crime
> *MP TO **APPEAR** ON DRUGS CHARGES*

axe abolish, close down; abolition, closure
> *COUNTRY BUS SERVICES **AXED***
> *SMALL SCHOOLS FACE **AXE***

BA British Airways
> *BA MAKES RECORD LOSS*

back support
> *AMERICA **BACKS** BRITISH PEACE MOVE*

ban forbid, refuse to allow something; prohibition
> *CHINA **BANS** US IMPORTS*
> *NEW **BAN** ON DEMONSTRATIONS*

bar refuse/refusal to allow entry
> *HOTEL **BARS** FOOTBALL FANS*
> *NEW **BAR** ON IMMIGRANTS*

bid attempt
> *JAPANESE WOMEN IN NEW EVEREST **BID***

▶

blast explosion; criticise violently
> *BLAST AT PALACE*
> *PM BLASTS OPPOSITION*

blaze fire
> *SIX DIE IN HOTEL BLAZE*

block stop, delay
> *TORIES BLOCK TEACHERS' PAY DEAL*

blow bad news; discouragement; unfortunate happening
> *SMITH ILL: BLOW TO WORLD CUP HOPES*

bolster give support / encouragement to
> *EXPORT FIGURES BOLSTER CITY CONFIDENCE*

bond political / business association
> *INDIA CUTS TRADE BONDS WITH PAKISTAN*

boom big increase; prosperous period
> *SPENDING BOOM OVER, SAYS MINISTER*

boost encourage(ment); to increase; an increase
> *GOVERNMENT PLAN TO BOOST EXPORTS*

brink edge (of disaster)
> *WORLD ON BRINK OF WAR*

call (for) demand / appeal (for)
> *CALL FOR STRIKE TALKS*
> *HOSPITAL ROW: MP CALLS FOR ENQUIRY*

campaign organised effort to achieve social or political result
> *MP LAUNCHES CAMPAIGN FOR PRISON REFORM*

cash money
> *MORE CASH NEEDED FOR SCHOOLS*

charge accusation (by police)
> *THREE MEN HELD ON BOMB CHARGE*

chop abolition, closure
> *300 BANK BRANCHES FACE CHOP*

City London's financial institutions
> *NEW TRADE FIGURES PLEASE CITY*

claim (make) a statement that something is true (especially when there may be disagreement); **pay claim** demand for higher wages
> *SCIENTIST CLAIMS CANCER BREAKTHROUGH*
> *RACISM CLAIM IN NAVY*
> *TEACHERS' PAY CLAIM REJECTED*

clamp down on deal firmly with (usually something illegal)
> *POLICE TO CLAMP DOWN ON SPEEDING*

clash quarrel, fight (noun or verb)
> *STUDENTS CLASH WITH POLICE*

clear find innocent
> *DOCTOR CLEARED OF DRUGS CHARGE*

Commons the House of Commons (in Parliament)
> *MINISTERS IN COMMONS CLASH OVER HOUSING*

con swindle
> *TEENAGERS CON WIDOW OUT OF LIFE SAVINGS*

crackdown firm application of the law
GOVERNMENT PROMISES **CRACKDOWN** ON DRUGS DEALERS
crash financial failure
BANK **CRASH** THREATENS TO BRING DOWN GOVERNMENT
curb restrict; restriction
NEW PRICE **CURBS**
cut reduce; reduction
BRITAIN **CUTS** OVERSEAS AID
NEW HEALTH SERVICE **CUTS**
cutback reduction (usually financial)
TEACHERS SLAM SCHOOL **CUTBACKS**

dash (make) quick journey
PM IN **DASH** TO BLAST HOSPITAL
deadlock disagreement that cannot be solved
DEADLOCK IN PEACE TALKS
deal agreement, bargain
TEACHERS REJECT NEW PAY **DEAL**
demo demonstration
30 ARRESTED IN ANTI-TAX **DEMO**
dole unemployment pay
DOLE QUEUES LENGTHEN
drama dramatic event; tense situation
PRINCE IN AIRPORT **DRAMA**
drive united effort
DRIVE TO SAVE WATER
drop give up, get rid of; fall (noun)
GOVERNMENT TO **DROP** CHILD LABOUR PLAN
BIG **DROP** IN INDUSTRIAL INVESTMENT
due expected to arrive
QUEEN **DUE** IN BERLIN TODAY

edge move gradually
WORLD **EDGES** TOWARDS WAR
envoy ambassador
FRENCH **ENVOY** DISAPPEARS

face be threatened by
HOSPITALS **FACE** MORE CUTS
STRIKERS **FACE** SACK
feud long-lasting quarrel or dispute
FAMILY **FEUD** EXPLODES INTO VIOLENCE: SIX HELD
find something that is found
BEACH **FIND** MAY BE BONES OF UNKNOWN DINOSAUR
firm determined not to change
PM **FIRM** ON TAX LEVELS
flak heavy criticism
GOVERNMENT FACES **FLAK** OVER VAT
flare begin violently
RIOTS **FLARE** IN ULSTER

▶

foil prevent somebody from succeeding
*TWELVE-YEAR-OLD **FOILS** BANK RAIDERS*
fraud swindle, deceit
*JAIL FOR TICKET **FRAUD** MEN*
freeze keep(ing) prices etc at their present level; block(ing) a bank account
*MINISTER WANTS TWO-YEAR PAY **FREEZE***
*DRUG PROFITS **FROZEN***

gag censor(ship), prevent(ion) from speaking
*AFRICAN PRESIDENT ACTS TO **GAG** PRESS*
gaol older British spelling for *jail*
gems jewels
*£2M **GEMS** STOLEN*
go resign; be lost, disappear
*PM TO **GO**?*
*4,000 JOBS TO **GO** IN NORTH*
go for be sold for
*PICASSO DRAWING **GOES FOR** £5M*
go-ahead approval
*SCOTTISH ROAD PLAN GETS **GO-AHEAD***
grab take violently
*GERMANS **GRAB** SHARES IN BRITISH COMPANIES*
grip control; hold tightly
*REBELS TIGHTEN **GRIP** ON SOUTH*
*COLD WAVE **GRIPS** COUNTRY*
gun down shoot
*TERRORISTS **GUN DOWN** PRIEST*

hail welcome, praise
*PM **HAILS** PEACE PLAN*
halt stop
*CAR PLANT TO **HALT** PRODUCTION*
haul amount stolen in robbery, or seized by police or customs
*TRAIN ROBBERY: BIG GOLD **HAUL***
*RECORD DRUGS **HAUL** AT AIRPORT*
head lead; leader
*PM TO **HEAD** TRADE MISSION*
*COMMONWEALTH **HEADS** TO MEET IN OTTAWA*
head for move towards
*ECONOMY **HEADING FOR** DISASTER, EXPERTS WARN*
hike (US) rise in costs, prices etc
*INTEREST **HIKE** WILL HIT BUSINESS*
hit affect badly
*SNOWSTORMS **HIT** TRANSPORT*
hit out at attack (with words)
*PM **HITS OUT AT** CRITICS*
hitch problem that causes delay
*LAST-MINUTE **HITCH** DELAYS SATELLITE LAUNCH*
hold arrest; keep under arrest
*POLICE **HOLD** TERROR SUSPECT*
*MAN **HELD** AFTER STATION BLAST*

in (the) red in debt; making a financial loss
BRITISH STEEL IN RED
IRA Irish Republican Army
IRA LEADER MAKES STATEMENT

jail prison
JAIL FOR PEACE MARCHERS
jobless unemployed (people)
THREE MILLION JOBLESS BY APRIL?

key important, vital
KEY WITNESS VANISHES

landslide victory by large majority in election
LANDSLIDE FOR SCOTTISH NATIONALISTS
lash criticise violently
BISHOP LASHES TV SEX AND VIOLENCE
launch send (satellite etc) into space; begin (campaign etc); put (new product) on market
SPACE TELESCOPE LAUNCH DELAYED
ENVIRONMENT MINISTER LAUNCHES CAMPAIGN FOR CLEANER BEACHES
BRITISH FIRM LAUNCHES THROW-AWAY CHAIRS
lead clue (in police enquiry)
NEW LEAD IN PHONEBOX MURDER CASE
leak unofficial publication of secret information
PM FURIOUS OVER TAX PLAN LEAKS
leap big increase
LEAP IN IMPORTS
life imprisonment 'for life'
LIFE FOR AXE MURDERER
link connection, contact
NEW TRADE LINKS WITH PERU
loom threaten to happen
VAT ON FOOD: NEW ROW LOOMS
Lords the House of Lords (in Parliament)
LORDS VOTE ON DOG REGISTRATION

mar spoil
CROWD VIOLENCE MARS CUP FINAL
mercy intended to save lives
DOCTOR IN MERCY DASH TO EVEREST
mission delegation (official group sent to conference etc)
SHOTS FIRED AT UN MISSION
mob angry crowd; organised crime / Mafia (US)
MOBS RAMPAGE THROUGH CITY STREETS
MOB LEADERS HELD
move step towards a particular result (often political)
MOVE TO BOOST TRADE LINKS WITH JAPAN
MP Member of Parliament
MP DENIES DRUGS CHARGE   ▶

nail force somebody to admit the truth
*MP **NAILS** MINISTER ON PIT CLOSURE PLANS*
net win, capture
*TWO SISTERS **NET** £3M IN POOLS WIN*

odds chances, probability
*JONES RE-ELECTED AGAINST THE **ODDS***
on about, on the subject of, concerning
*NEW MOVE **ON** PENSIONS*
opt (for) choose
*WALES **OPTS FOR** INDEPENDENCE*
oust drive out, replace
*MODERATES **OUSTED** IN UNION ELECTIONS*
out to intending to
*SCOTS NATIONALISTS **OUT TO** CAPTURE MASS VOTE*
over about, on the subject of, because of
*ROW **OVER** AID CUTS*

pact agreement
*DEFENCE **PACT** RUNS INTO TROUBLE*
pay wages
*TRANSPORT **PAY** TALKS BREAK DOWN*
PC police constable
PC SHOT IN BANK RAID
peak high point
*BANK LENDING HITS NEW **PEAK***
peer lord; Member of the House of Lords
***PEERS** REJECT GOVERNMENT WAGE-FREEZE PLAN*
peg hold (prices etc) at present level
*BANKS **PEG** INTEREST RATES*
peril danger
*FLOOD **PERIL** IN THAMES VALLEY*
pit coal mine
*THREAT OF MORE **PIT** CLOSURES*
plant factory
*STEEL **PLANT** BLAZE*
plea call for help
*BIG RESPONSE TO **PLEA** FOR FLOOD AID*
pledge promise
*GOVERNMENT GIVES **PLEDGE** ON JOBLESS*
PM Prime Minister
*EGG THROWN AT **PM***
poll election; public opinion survey
*TORIES AHEAD IN **POLLS***
pools football pools: a form of gambling in which people guess the results of football matches
*SISTERS SHARE BIG **POOLS** WIN*
premier head of government
*GREEK **PREMIER** TO VISIT UK*
press the newspapers
*BID TO GAG **PRESS** OVER DEFENCE SPENDING*

press (for) urge, encourage, ask for urgently
*MINISTER **PRESSED** TO ACT ON HOUSING*
*OPPOSITION **PRESS** FOR ENQUIRY ON AIR CRASHES*
probe investigation; investigate
*CALL FOR STUDENT DRUGS **PROBE***
*POLICE **PROBE** RACING SCANDAL*
pull out withdraw; **pull-out** withdrawal
*US **PULLS OUT** OF ARMS TALKS*
*CHURCH CALLS FOR BRITISH **PULL-OUT** FROM ULSTER*
push (for) ask for, encourage
*SCHOOLS **PUSH FOR** MORE CASH*

quake earthquake
*HOUSES DAMAGED IN WELSH **QUAKE***
quit resign, leave
*CHURCH LEADER **QUITS***
*MINISTER TO **QUIT** GOVERNMENT*
quiz question (verb)
*POLICE **QUIZ** MILLIONAIRE SUPERMARKET BOSS*

raid enter and search; attack (noun and verb), rob, robbery
*POLICE **RAID** DUCHESS'S FLAT*
*BIG GEMS **RAID***
rampage riot
*FOOTBALL FANS **RAMPAGE** THROUGH SEASIDE TOWNS*
rap criticise
*DOCTORS **RAP** NEW MINISTRY PLANS*
record bigger than ever before
***RECORD** LOSS BY INSURANCE FIRM*
riddle mystery
*MISSING ENVOY **RIDDLE**: WOMAN HELD*
rift division, disagreement
*LABOUR **RIFT** OVER DEFENCE POLICY*
rock shock, shake
*BANK SEX SCANDAL **ROCKS** CITY*
*IRELAND **ROCKED** BY QUAKE*
row noisy disagreement, quarrel
*NEW **ROW** OVER PENSION CUTS*
rule out reject the possibility of
*PM **RULES OUT** AUTUMN ELECTION*

sack dismiss(al) from job
*STRIKING POSTMEN FACE **SACK***
saga long-running news story
*NEW REVELATIONS IN BANK SEX **SAGA***
scare public alarm, alarming rumour
*TYPHOID **SCARE** IN SOUTHWEST*
scrap throw out (as useless)
*GOVERNMENT **SCRAPS** NEW ROAD PLANS*
seek look for
*POLICE **SEEK** WITNESS TO KILLING*

▶

seize take (especially in police and customs searches)
>*POLICE **SEIZE** ARMS AFTER CAR CHASE*
>*£3M DRUGS **SEIZED** AT AIRPORT*

set to ready to; about to
>*INTEREST RATES **SET TO** RISE*

shed get rid of
>*BRITISH RAIL TO **SHED** 5,000 JOBS*

slam criticise violently
>*BISHOP **SLAMS** DEFENCE POLICY*

slash cut, reduce drastically
>*GOVERNMENT TO **SLASH** HEALTH EXPENDITURE*

slate criticise
>*PM **SLATES** BISHOP*

slay (US) murder
>*FREEWAY KILLER **SLAYS** SIX*

slump fall (economic)
>*EXPORTS **SLUMP***
>*CITY FEARS NEW **SLUMP***

snatch rob, robbery
>*BIG WAGES **SNATCH** IN WEST END*

soar rise dramatically
>*IMPORTS **SOAR** FOR THIRD MONTH*

spark cause to start
>*REFEREE'S DECISION **SPARKS** RIOT*

split disagree(ment)
>*CABINET **SPLIT** ON PRICES POLICY*

spree wild spending expedition
>*BUS DRIVER SPENDS £30,000 IN THREE-DAY CREDIT CARD **SPREE***

stake financial interest
>*JAPANESE BUY **STAKE** IN BRITISH AIRWAYS*

storm angry public disagreement
>***STORM** OVER NEW STRIKE LAW*

storm out of leave angrily
>*TEACHERS' LEADERS **STORM OUT OF** MEETING*

stun surprise, shock
>*JOBLESS FIGURES **STUN** CITY*

surge sudden increase; rise suddenly
>***SURGE** IN JOBLESS FIGURES*

swap exchange
>*HEART **SWAP** BOY BETTER*

sway persuade
>*HOSPITAL PROTEST **SWAYS** MINISTERS*

switch to change; a change
>*DEFENCE POLICY **SWITCH***

swoop to raid; a police raid
>*POLICE IN DAWN **SWOOP** ON DRUGS GANG*

threat danger
>*TEACHERS' STRIKE **THREAT***

toll number killed
>*QUAKE **TOLL** MAY BE 5,000*

top (adj) senior, most important
TOP BANKER KIDNAPPED
top (verb) exceed
IMPORTS TOP LAST YEAR'S FIGURES
Tory Conservative
VICTORY FOR TORY MODERATES
trio three people
JAILBREAK TRIO RECAPTURED
troops soldiers
MORE TROOPS FOR BORDER AREA

UK The United Kingdom (of Great Britain and Northern Ireland)
EC CRITICISES UK JAIL CONDITIONS
Ulster Northern Ireland
PM IN SECRET TRIP TO ULSTER
UN The United Nations
UN IN RED: CANNOT BALANCE BUDGET
urge encourage
GOVERNMENT URGED TO ACT ON POLLUTION
US The United States of America
US URGED TO PULL OUT OF ARMS DEAL

VAT value added tax
NEXT, VAT ON BABYFOOD?
vow promise
EXILED PRESIDENT VOWS TO RETURN

walk out leave in protest
CAR WORKERS WALK OUT OVER WAGE FREEZE
wed marry
BISHOP TO WED ACTRESS

367 **next** and **the next**

1 *next*

Next week, next month etc is the week or month just after this one. If I am speaking in July, *next month* is August; if I am speaking in the year 2006, *next year* is 2007.

> *Goodbye – see you **next week**.* (NOT *...see you the next week.*)
> *I'm spending **next Christmas** with my family.*
> (NOT *I'm spending the next Christmas...*)
> ***Next year** will be difficult.* (the year starting next January)

Prepositions are not generally used before these time expressions.

2 *next Sunday* etc

When *next* is used with the names of days or months, it is not always clear exactly what is meant.

> *'See you **next Sunday**.' 'Do you mean this coming Sunday or the one after?'*

The closer the day/month referred to, the more likely people are to understand *next* as meaning 'the one in next week/year'; the further away it is, the more likely they are to interpret *next* as meaning 'the one in this week/year'; the dividing line (where confusion is greatest) is probably somewhere about three days/months before the time referred to. But not everybody uses *next* in exactly the same way in this situation. To avoid misunderstanding, one can say for example (1) *on Sunday, this Sunday, the/this Sunday coming, the/this coming Sunday* or *(on) Sunday this week*, and (2) *on Sunday week, a week on Sunday* or *(on) Sunday next week.*

3   *the next*

One meaning of *the next* is 'counting forward from this moment'. *The next week, the next month* etc can mean the period of seven days, thirty days etc starting at the moment of speaking. On July 15th, 1992, *the next month* is the period from July 15th to August 15th; *the next year* is the period from July 1992 to July 1993.

> *I'm going to be very busy for **the next week**.*
> > (= *the seven days starting today*)
> ***The next year** will be difficult.* (= *the twelve months starting now*)

Note the word order in *the next six weeks* etc. When there is no number we generally say *the next few days*, not *the next days*.

> *I'll be at college for **the next three years**.* (NOT ... ~~the three next years~~.)
> ***The next few days** are going to be wet.*
> > (NOT ~~The next days are going to be wet.~~)

For other uses of *the next*, and the difference between *the next* and *the nearest*, see 356. For *last* and *the last*, see 307.

368   no and none

1   the difference

We use *no* (= 'not a', 'not any') immediately before a singular or plural noun.

> ***No aeroplane** is 100% safe.*
> *We've got **no plans** for the summer.*
> *There is **no time** to talk about it now.*

Before a determiner (e.g. *the, my, this*) we use *none of*. We also use *none of* before a pronoun.

> ***None of the** keys would open the door.*
> ***None of my** brothers remembered my birthday.*
> ***None of this** cheese is any good.*
> ***None of it** is worth keeping.*
> ***None of us** speaks French.*

When we use *none of* with a plural noun or pronoun, the verb can be singular (more formal) or plural (more informal).

> *None of my friends **is** interested.* (formal)
> *None of my friends **are** interested.* (informal)

2   *none* without a noun

We can use *none* alone, without a noun, if the meaning is clear from what comes before.

> *'How many of the books have you read?' '**None**.'*

3 not used to talk about two

We use *neither of,* not *none of,* to talk about two people or things.
> **Neither of my parents** *could be there.* (NOT ~~*None of my parents*~~...)

For the difference between *no/none* and *not a/any,* see 369.
For *no* and *not,* see 375.
For *none* and *no one,* see 373.
For *no* as a modifying adverb (e.g. *no better*), see 56.
For more information about *neither,* see 363.

369 no/none and not a/any

1 emphatic

No can be used instead of *not a* or *not any* when we want to emphasise the negative idea.
> *Would you believe it? There's **no wardrobe** in the bedroom!*
>> (More emphatic than ... *There isn't a wardrobe* ...)
> *Sorry I can't stop. I've got **no time**.*
>> (More emphatic than ... *I haven't got **any** time.*)
> *There were **no letters** for you this morning, I'm afraid.*
>> (More emphatic than *There weren't **any** letters* ...)

None of can be used instead of *not any of.*
> *She's done **none of the work** I told her to do.*
>> (More emphatic than *She hasn't done **any*** ...)

After *no,* countable nouns are usually plural unless the sense makes a singular noun necessary. Compare:
> *He's got **no children**.* (More natural than *He's got **no child**.*)
> *He's got **no wife**.* (More normal than *He's got **no wives**.*)

We prefer *not a/any* in objects and complements when the sense is not emphatic. Compare:
> *He's **no fool**.* (= *He's not a fool at all.* – emphatic negative)
> *A spider is **not an** insect.*
>> (NOT ~~*A spider is **no** insect*~~ – the sense is not emphatic.)

2 subjects

Not any cannot normally be used with subjects. *No* and *none of* are used instead.
> ***No** brand of cigarette is completely harmless.* (NOT ~~***Not any** brand*~~...)
> ***No** tourists ever came to our village.* (NOT ~~***Not any** tourists*~~...)
> ***None of** my friends lives near me.* (NOT ~~***Not any of** my friends*~~...)

3 *nobody* etc

Nobody, nothing, no one and *nowhere* are used in similar ways to *no.*
> *I saw **nobody**.* (More emphatic than *I didn't see **anybody**.*)
> ***Nobody** spoke.* (NOT ~~***Not anybody** spoke.*~~)

For the difference between *no* and *none,* see 368.
For more about the difference between *no* and *not,* see 375.
For more about *no one,* see 373.
For more about *any,* see 54.

370 no doubt

No doubt is often used to mean 'probably' or 'I suppose'.
> **No doubt** *it'll rain soon.*
> *You're tired,* **no doubt**. *I'll make you a cup of tea.*

No doubt is not used alone to say that something is certain. Possible expressions are *there is no doubt that* (formal), *without any doubt* (formal), *certainly, definitely.*
> **There is no doubt that** *the world is getting warmer.*
> (NOT ~~**No doubt** the world is getting warmer.~~)
> *Cycling is* **certainly** *healthier than driving.*
> (NOT ~~**No doubt** cycling is healthier than driving.~~)

Note that *doubtless* is similar to *no doubt* (but more formal), while *undoubtedly* is similar to *there is no doubt that.*

For structures with the verb *doubt*, see 167.

371 no matter

1 conjunction

No matter can be used with *who, whose, what, which, where, when* and *how.* These expressions are conjunctions, used to join clauses together. The meaning is similar to 'it doesn't matter who/what/etc'.
> *I'll love you* **no matter what** *you do.*
> **No matter where** *you go, I'll follow you.*

Note the use of a present tense with a future meaning after *no matter* (see 556).
> *No matter who* **telephones**, *say I'm out.*
> *No matter where you* **go**, *you'll find Coca-Cola.*
> *You'll be welcome no matter when you* **come**.

2 *no matter who* etc and *whoever* etc

The conjunctions *no matter who/what* etc are used rather like *whoever, whatever* etc (see 596). Compare:
– **No matter what** *you say, I won't believe you.*
  Whatever *you say, I won't believe you.*
– *Phone me when you arrive,* **no matter how** *late it is.*
  Phone me when you arrive, **however** *late it is.*

However, clauses with *whoever, whatever* and *whichever* can be used as the subjects or objects of other clauses. Clauses with *no matter who/what/which* cannot be used in this way.
> *I'll believe* **whatever you say.**
> (BUT NOT ~~I'll believe **no matter what you say.**~~)

3 use without a verb

Sometimes *no matter who/what* etc can be used at the end of a clause, without a following verb.
> *I'll always love you,* **no matter what**. (= ... *no matter what happens.*)

4 *no matter* and *it doesn't matter*

It doesn't matter is not a conjunction, and can be used to introduce a
sentence that has only one clause. *No matter* cannot be used in this way.
> *It doesn't matter* what you think. (BUT NOT ~~*No matter what you think.*~~)
Note that the verb *matter* is not used in progressive forms (see 451).
> *Your opinions don't matter.* (NOT ~~*Your opinions aren't mattering.*~~)

For more about the use of preparatory *it* (as in *It doesn't matter what* . . .), see 301–302.

372 no more, not any more, no longer, not any longer

We use *no more* with nouns, to talk about quantity or degree – to say
how much.
> *There's **no more** bread.*   *She's **no more** a great singer than I am.*
We do not use *no more* in standard modern English as an adverb to express
the idea of actions and situations stopping. Instead, we use *no longer*
(usually before the verb), *not . . . any longer* or *not . . . any more* (informal).
> *I **no longer** support the Conservative party.* (NOT ~~*I no more support* . . .~~)
> *This ca**n't** go on **any longer**.*   *Annie does**n't** live here **any more**.*
Anymore may be written as one word, especially in American English.
> *She felt that he did not love her **anymore**.*

373 no one and none

1 *no one*

No one (also written *no-one* in British English) means the same as *nobody*.
It cannot be followed by *of*.
> *No one* wished me a happy birthday. (NOT ~~*No one of my friends* . . .~~)
> *I stayed in all evening waiting, but **no one** came.*

2 *none*

To express the idea 'not a single one (of)', we can use *none (of)*, *not any (of)*
or *not one (of)* (more emphatic). *No one* is not used in this way.
> ***None of** my friends wished me a happy birthday.*
> *I have**n't** read **any** of his books.*
> ***Not one of** my shirts is clean.* (NOT ~~*No one of my shirts* . . .~~)
> *'Have you found any blackberries?' '**Not one.**'*

For more about *none*, see 368.

374 non-assertive words

1 What are assertive and non-assertive words?

There are some words that are used mainly in affirmative sentences.
Examples are *some* (and *somebody, someone, something* and *somewhere*),
once, sometimes and *already*. These are called 'assertive', because they

are mainly used when we *assert* – that is, when we say that something is true. In questions and negatives we more often use other words like *any*, *anybody* etc, *ever* and *yet*. These are not generally used when we assert things, and are called 'non-assertive'. Compare:

– **Somebody** *telephoned.* (assertive)
  *Did **anybody** telephone?* (non-assertive)
– *I've bought you **something**.* (assertive)
  *I haven't bought you **anything**.* (non-assertive)
– *I met the Prime Minister **once**.* (assertive)
  *Have you **ever** met the Prime Minister?* (non-assertive)
– *I **sometimes** go to the theatre.* (assertive)
  *Do you **ever** go to the theatre?* (non-assertive)
– *She's **already** here.* (assertive)
  *Is she here **yet**?* (non-assertive)

2 Where are they used?

Non-assertive words are used in questions and negative sentences, in *if*-clauses, in comparisons, and together with adverbs, verbs, prepositions, adjectives and determiners that have a negative kind of meaning.

> *Let me know **if** you have **any** trouble.*
> *I wonder **if** she found **anything**.*
> *She writes **better** than **anybody** I know.*
> *He **seldom** says **anything**.*
> *I've **hardly** been **anywhere** since Christmas.*
> *He **denied** that he had **ever** seen her.*
> *Please **forget** that I **ever** told you **anything** about it.*
> *I'd rather do it **without anybody's** help.*
> *It's **difficult** to understand **anything** he says.*
> ***Few** people have **ever** seen her laugh.*

3 assertive words in questions etc

Assertive words can be used in questions, *if*-clauses etc in order to give a more positive feeling to a sentence.

> *Did you say **something**?* (Suggests 'I think you said something'.)
> *Would you like **some** more chips?* (invitation to have some more)
> *If you've **already** finished, let's go.* (The person seems to have finished.)

For information about particular non-assertive words, see the entries for the words in question.
For assertive uses of *any*, see 54

375 not and no

To make a word, expression or clause negative, we use *not*.

> **Not surprisingly**, *we missed the train.* (NOT ~~No surprisingly~~...)
> *The students went on strike, but **not the teachers**.*
>   (NOT ...~~but no the teachers.~~)
> *I can see you tomorrow, but **not on Thursday**.*
> *I **have not received** his answer.*

We can use *no* with a noun or *-ing* form to mean 'not any', or 'not a / an'.

> **No teachers** *went on strike.* (= *There were***n't** *any teachers on strike.*)
>
> *I've got* **no Thursdays** *free this term.* (= *I have***n't** *got* **any** *Thursdays* ...)
>
> *I telephoned, but there was* **no answer***.* (= *There was***n't an** *answer.*)
>
> *NO SMOKING*

Sometimes sentences constructed with **verb + *not*** and ***no* + noun** have similar meanings. The structure with *no* is usually more emphatic.

> *There* **wasn't** *an answer.* / *There was* **no answer***.*

For *no* ... *ing,* see 292.3.
For more information about *no,* see 368.

376 not only

In the rather formal structure *not only* ... *but also, not only* and *but also* can go immediately before the words or expressions that they modify.

> *We go there* **not only** *in winter,* **but also** *in summer.*
>
> **Not only** *the bathroom was flooded,* **but also** *the rest of the house.*
>
> *The place was* **not only** *cold,* **but also** *damp.*

Mid-position with the verb (see 15) is also possible. In this case, *not only* is generally used without *do.*

> *She* **not only sings** *like an angel, but also dances divinely.*
>
> *She* **not only plays** *the piano, but also the violin.*

Not only can be moved to the beginning of a clause for emphasis. It is then followed by **auxiliary verb + subject**; *do* is used if there is no other auxiliary (for more about this word order, see 298). *But* can be left out in this case.

> **Not only has she been** *late three times; she has also done no work.*
>
> **Not only do they need** *clothing, but they are also short of water.*

Note that in informal English *not only* ... *but also* is not very common; other structures are generally preferred.

> *We don't only go there in winter. We go in summer too.*

377 noun complementation

Many nouns, especially abstract nouns, can be followed by 'complements' – other words and expressions that 'complete' their meaning. These complements can be prepositional phrases, infinitive expressions or clauses (with or without prepositions).

> *Alan's* **criticism of the plan** *made him very unpopular.*
>
> *I hate the* **thought of leaving** *you.*
>
> *Does she understand the* **need to keep** *everything secret?*
>
> *I admire your* **belief that you are always right***.*
>
> *There's still the* **question of whether we're going to pay her***.*

Many nouns can be followed by more than one kind of complement.

> *He didn't give any* **reason for the changes***.*
>
> *You've no* **reason to get** *angry.*
>
> *The main* **reason why I don't believe her** *is this.*

Not all nouns can be followed by all kinds of complement.

> – *the idea* **of marriage**
>
>   *the idea* **that I might get married**
>
>   BUT NOT *the idea to get married*

▶

– *freedom **to choose***
*freedom **of choice***
BUT NOT ~~*freedom **of choosing***~~

Note that a related noun and verb may have different kinds of complement.

*I have no **intention of resigning**.*

*I do not **intend to resign**.*

To find out what complement structures are possible with a particular noun, it is necessary to consult a good dictionary.

For complementation in general, see 140.
For more information about *-ing* forms after nouns, see 294.
For infinitives after nouns, see 286.
For *should* in clauses after nouns, see 497.
For subjunctives in clauses after nouns, see 541.
For the prepositions that are used after some common nouns, see 437.
For prepositions before clauses, see 441.
For structures with preparatory *it* (e.g. *It's a pity that we can't see him*), see 301–302.

378 noun modifiers

It is common in English to use nouns in a similar way to adjectives, to modify other nouns. Noun modifiers are especially common in attributive position (before other nouns); for details of this structure, see 379.

*We need some new **garden** chairs.*

*That **shoe** shop's closed down.*

*He's a **Birmingham** man.*

Some nouns can also be used as modifiers in predicative position (after *be* and sometimes after other copular verbs). This happens especially with nouns which refer to material or origin.

*It's not **leather**, you know; it's **plastic**.*

*He doesn't sound **Birmingham**; I think he's **Liverpool**.*

Noun modifiers can be modified themselves.

*That **sports shoe** shop's closed down.*

*It's not **real leather**, you know.*

*My family were all **working class**.*

379 nouns in groups (1): introduction and general rules

1 three structures

There are three main ways in which we can put nouns together so that one modifies another.

a noun + noun

*a **bicycle factory**   a **war film**   the **table leg**   **coffee beans***

b noun + *'s* + noun

*my **sister's car**   a **bird's nest**   **cow's milk***
*the **prisoner's complaint***

c   noun + preposition + noun

> the **top of the page**   a **man from Birmingham**
> a **feeling of disappointment**   a **book on modern music**

2   choice of structures

A particular idea is normally expressed in only one of these ways, though
sometimes there are two possibilities.

> a table leg (NOT ~~a table's leg~~ or ~~a leg of a table~~)
> cow's milk (NOT ~~cow milk~~ or ~~milk of a cow~~)
> the top of the page (NOT ~~the page('s) top~~)
> the earth's gravity OR the gravity of the earth (NOT ~~the earth gravity~~)
> a Birmingham man OR a man from Birmingham
>   (NOT ~~a Birmingham's man~~)

Unfortunately the exact differences between the three structures are
complicated and difficult to analyse – this is one of the most difficult areas of
English grammar. The following paragraphs give general information about
the three structures; sections 380–382 give more details and some
information about the differences. Note that the 'rules' given in these
sections only describe tendencies, and there are quite a number of
exceptions. In order to be certain which structure is used to express a
particular idea, it is necessary to consult a good dictionary.

3   noun + noun

In the **noun + noun** structure, the first noun modifies or describes the
second, a little like an adjective.

> a horse race (a kind of race)   milk chocolate (a kind of chocolate)
> a race horse (a kind of horse)   chocolate milk (a kind of milk)
>
> a book case (a kind of case)   mineral water (a kind of water)

Noun + noun expressions can often be changed into structures where the
second noun becomes a subject and the first an object.

> an oil well (= a **well** that produces **oil**)
> a sheepdog (= a **dog** that looks after **sheep**)
> a Birmingham man (= a **man** who comes from **Birmingham**)
> the airport bus (= the **bus** that goes to the **airport**)

Note that the first noun is usually singular in form, even if it has a plural
meaning. (For exceptions, see 508.)

> a **shoe** shop (= a shop that sells **shoes**)   a **horse** race (= a race for **horses**)
> a **tooth**brush (= a brush for **teeth**)   **trouser** pockets (= pockets in **trousers**)
> a **ticket** office (= an office that sells **tickets**)

Articles belonging to the first (modifying) noun are dropped in **noun + noun**
combinations. Compare:

> Officers in **the army** are well paid.
> **Army officers** are well paid. (NOT ~~The army officers are well paid.~~)

More than two nouns can be put together. A group of two nouns can modify
a third noun, these can modify a fourth, and so on.

> oil production costs   road accident research centre

This kind of structure is very common in newspaper headlines (see 366)
because it saves space.

> FURNITURE FACTORY PAY CUT ROW   ▶

4   noun + *'s* + noun

In the **noun + *'s* + noun** structure, too, the first noun modifies or describes the second.

  *my **mother's** car* (a particular car)   *a **child's** bicycle* (a kind of bicycle)

These expressions often correspond to structures in which the **first** noun is a subject and the **second** is a verb or object (the opposite of the **noun + noun** structure).

  *my **mother's** car* (my **mother** has a **car**)
  *the **committee's** report* (the **committee** made a **report**)
  *a **child's** bicycle* (a **child** rides this kind of **bicycle**)
  ***goat's** milk* (**goats** give this kind of **milk**)
  *the **train's** arrival* (the **train arrived**)

For more information about the grammar of possessive *'s* structures, see 432.

5   noun + preposition + noun

Sometimes the **noun + noun** or the **noun + *'s* + noun** structure is not possible, and it is necessary to use a structure with *of* or another preposition.

  *a feeling **of** disappointment* (NOT ~~a disappointment('s) feeling~~)
  *letters **from** home* (NOT ~~home('s) letters~~)

6   pronunciation

Most **noun + noun** combinations have the main stress on the first noun.

  a'bicycle factory   *'coffee beans*   *a'fruit drink*   *'ski boots*

However, there are quite a number of exceptions.

  a garden'chair   *a fruit'pie*

The difference between noun modifiers and adjectival modifiers is sometimes shown by stress. Compare:

  a'French teacher (noun modifier: *a person who teaches French*)
  a French'teacher (adjective modifier: *a teacher who is French*)

Noun + *'s* + noun combinations have the main stress on the first noun mostly in classifying expressions (see 380), which name a certain kind of thing. Compare:

– *a'doll's house* (a kind of house)
  my brother's'house (not a kind of house)
– *'goat's milk* (a kind of milk)
  the goat's'tail (not a kind of tail)

Here, too, there are exceptions.

  a child's'bicycle (a kind of bicycle)

To be sure of the stress on a particular combination, it is necessary to check in a good dictionary.

For the stressing of road and street names, see 485.

7   spelling

Some short, common **noun + noun** combinations are generally written together like single words.

  bathroom   *lampshade*   *seaside*   BUT NOT ~~railwaystation~~

Others may be written with a hyphen (e.g. *girl-friend*) or separately (e.g. *furniture shop*). In many cases usage varies, and some combinations can be found written in all three ways (e.g. *skiboots, ski-boots* or *ski boots*; *headmaster, head-master* or *head master*). Hyphens are becoming less common in modern English, and (except with very common short combinations like *bathroom*) it is usually acceptable to write the two words separately. For information about the spelling of particular combinations, see a good dictionary.

380 nouns in groups (2): classifying expressions

1 noun + noun

The **noun + noun** structure is mostly used to make 'classifying' expressions, which name a particular kind of thing.

> *a sheep dog* (a particular kind of dog)
> *mountain plants* (a special group of plants)
> *mineral water* (a sort of water)

We use the **noun + noun** structure especially to talk about things that belong to common well-known classes (so that the two nouns really describe a single idea). In other cases we prefer a preposition structure. Compare:

> *the postman, the milkman, the insurance man* (all well-known kinds of people who may call regularly at a British home)
> *a man from the health department* (not a regular kind of visitor)

More examples:

– *He was reading a **history book**.* (a common class of book)
  *He was reading a **book about the moon**.* (NOT *a moon book*)
– *She was sitting at a **corner table** in the restaurant.*
  (Restaurants often have corner tables.)
  *Who's the **girl in the corner**?* (NOT *Who's the corner girl?*)
– *What does that **road sign** say?*
  *She was showing **signs of tiredness**.* (NOT *... tiredness signs.*)

2 noun + 's + noun

The *'s* structure is also used with a classifying meaning in certain expressions. These expressions usually refer to something that is **used by** or **produced by or from** a person or animal; the first noun refers to the person or animal. Generally, either both nouns are singular or both are plural.

> *a child's toy*   *children's clothes*   *a man's sweater*
> *a pair of women's jeans*   *cow's milk*   *birds' nests*
> BUT *a **women's** magazine*

See 382.3–4 for more details.

381 nouns in groups (3): the 's structure and the of structure

1 meanings of the 's structure

We can use the possessive *'s* to talk about several different sorts of ideas: for example possession, relationship, physical features and characteristics, non-physical qualities and measurement. The *'s* structure often corresponds to a sentence in which the first noun becomes the subject of *have* or some other verb.

*That's my **father's** house. (**My father has** that house.)*
*Mary's brother is a lawyer. (**Mary has** a brother who is a lawyer.)*
*Pete's eyes are like yours. (**Pete has** eyes like yours.)*
*the **plan's** importance (the importance that **the plan has**)*
*I didn't believe the **girl's** story. (**The girl told** a story.)*
*Have you read **John's** letter? (**John wrote** a letter.)*
*the **government's** decision (**The Government made** a decision.)*
*the **train's** arrival (**The train arrived**.)*

In some cases, the first noun may correspond to the object of a verb.

*the **prisoner's** release (Somebody **released the prisoner**.)*

2 possessive *'s* and *of*

We express these ideas with the possessive *'s* structure most often when the first noun refers to a person or animal, or to a country, organisation or other group of living creatures, especially if the relationship between the two nouns could be expressed with *have*.

*my **father's** name (NOT ~~the name of my father~~)*
Ann's back (NOT ~~the back of Ann~~)
*a **bird's** nest (NOT ~~a nest of a bird~~)*
America's gold reserves

In other cases, we more often use a structure with *of*.

*the name **of** the street (NOT ~~the street's name~~)*
*the back **of** the room (NOT ~~the room's back~~)*

Sometimes both structures are possible.

*the **earth's** gravity OR the gravity **of** the earth*
*the **Queen's** arrival OR the arrival **of** the Queen*
*the **plan's** importance OR the importance **of** the plan*
*Algeria's history OR the history **of** Algeria*
*the **concerto's** final movement OR the final movement **of** the concerto*

In place names like *Cologne Cathedral* or *Birmingham Airport*, the **noun + noun** structure is normal. (For *the* in place names, see 69.18.)

For the use of the *'s* structure in expressions of time, see 382.8.
For details of the grammar of the possessive *'s* structure, see 432.

382 nouns in groups (4): special cases

1 parts

We use the *'s* structure to talk about parts of people's and animals' bodies.

*a **man's** leg   an **elephant's** trunk   a **sheep's** heart*

But to talk about parts of non-living things, we usually use the **noun + noun** structure or the *of* structure.

*a **table** leg (NOT ~~a table's leg~~)*
*the **car** door (NOT ~~the car's door~~)*
*the roof **of** a house*

With words like *top, bottom, front, back, side, edge, inside, outside, beginning, middle, end, part*, we usually prefer the *of* structure.

the **top of** the page (NOT ~~the **page top**~~)
the **back of** the bus (NOT ~~the **bus back**~~)
the **bottom of** the glass (NOT ~~the **glass bottom**~~)
the **end** of the film

There are a number of common exceptions – for example *the water's edge, the seaside, the roadside, a mountain top*.

2   units, selections and collections

We also prefer the *of* structure with words that refer to units, selections and collections, like *piece, slice, lump* (of sugar), *bunch* (of flowers), *blade* (of grass), *pack* (of cards), *herd, flock, group* and so on.

a **piece of** paper (NOT ~~a **paper piece**~~)
a **bunch** of flowers (NOT ~~a **flower bunch**~~)

3   'used by'

The *'s* structure can refer to something that is used by a person or animal: the first noun refers to the user.

children's clothes   **women's** magazines   a **bird's** nest

There are some exceptions.

baby clothes   a **bird**cage

British and American usage sometimes differ. Compare:

a **baby's** bottle (GB)   a **doll's** house (GB)   a **baby's** pram (GB)
a **baby** bottle (US)   a **doll** house (US)   a **baby** carriage (US)

4   'produced by/from'

The *'s* structure is often used for products from living animals.

cow's milk   **lamb's** wool   **sheep's** wool
a **bird's** egg   a **hen's** egg
BUT **camel** hair, **horse**hair

When the animal is killed to provide something, we usually use **noun + noun**.

calf skin   **chamois** leather   **fox** fur
chicken soup   a **lamb** chop   **tortoise** shell

5   containers

The **noun + noun** structure is used for particular kinds of container.

a **matchbox**   a **paint** tin   a **coffee** cup

But we use the *of* structure to talk about a container together with its contents.

a **box of** matches   a **tin of** paint   a **cup of** coffee

6   'made of'

The **noun + noun** structure is normally used to say what things are made of.

a **silk** dress   a **stone** bridge   an **iron** rod   a **gold** ring

In older English, the *of* structure was more common in this case (e.g. *a dress **of silk**, a bridge **of stone***), and it is still used in some metaphorical expressions.

▶

*He rules his family with a **rod of iron**.*
*The flowers were like a **carpet of gold**.*

A few pairs of nouns and adjectives (e.g. *gold, golden*) are used as modifiers with different meanings. Generally the noun simply names the material something is made of, while the adjective has a more metaphorical meaning.

*a **gold** watch – **golden** memories*
silk *stockings – **silken** skin*
*a **lead** pipe – a **leaden** sky* (grey and depressing)
*a **stone** roof – a **stony** silence*

But *wooden* and *woollen* just mean 'made of wood / wool'.

7 measurement

The **noun + noun** structure is used in measurements, with a number before the first noun. The number is usually joined to the first noun by a hyphen (-). Note that the first noun is normally singular in form in these cases.

*a **five-litre** can   a **ten-pound** note*
    (NOT ~~a five-litres can~~, ~~a ten-pounds note~~)
*a **six-pound** chicken   a **three-mile** walk   a **five-day** course*
*a **two-person** tent   ten **two-hour** lessons*

The number *one* is often left out.

*a **pint** mug*

In fractions, the plural *-s* is not dropped.

*a **two-thirds** share* (NOT ~~a two-third share~~)

Note the use of the *'s* structure before *worth*.

*a **pound's** worth of walnuts*
*three **dollars'** worth of popcorn*

8 measurement of time

The *'s* structure (or the plural with *s'*) is often used to say how long things last.

*a **day's** journey   three **hours'** journey   twenty **minutes'** delay*

The second noun's article is sometimes included, and the apostrophe (') is sometimes dropped, but this is not generally considered correct.

***a** three hours(') journey* (= ***a** journey of three hours*)

Noun + noun structures are also possible.

*a **three-hour** journey   a **twenty-minute** delay*

9 other expressions of time

We use the **noun + noun** structure for the names of things that happen or appear regularly.

*the **evening** news   a **Sunday** paper*

But we prefer the *'s* structure to talk about particular moments and events.

***yesterday's** news   last **Sunday's** match*

383 now (that)

Now (that) can be used as a conjunction. In an informal style, *that* is often dropped (see 560).

> **Now that** *Andrew is married, he has become much more responsible.*
> **Now** *the exams are over I can enjoy myself.*

For *now* as a discourse marker used to structure talk, see 159.8.
For the use of *once* as a conjunction, see 390.
For conjunctions in general, see 142–143.

384 nowadays

Nowadays is an adverb meaning 'these days', 'at the present time'.

> *People seem to be very depressed* **nowadays***.*
> **Nowadays** *we think nothing of space travel.*

Nowadays cannot be used as an adjective or possessive.

> *I don't like* **modern** *fashions.* (NOT ~~*I don't like the* **nowadays** *fashions.*~~)

385 numbers

1 fractions and decimals

We say simple fractions like this:

> $^1/_8$ *one eighth*
> $^3/_7$ *three sevenths*
> $^2/_5$ *two fifths*
> $^{11}/_{16}$ *eleven sixteenths*
> $^3/_4$ hour *three quarters of an hour*
> $^7/_{10}$ mile *seven tenths of a mile*

More complex fractions can be expressed by using the word *over.*

> $^{317}/_{509}$ *three hundred and seventeen* **over** *five hundred and nine*

We write and say decimals like this:

> *0.375 nought point three seven five* (US *zero point three . . .*)
> (NOT ~~*0,375 nought comma three seven five*~~)
> (NOT ~~*nought point three hundred and seventy-five*~~)
> *4.7 four point seven*

2 singular and plural with fractions and decimals

With fractions below 1, we normally use ***of a* + singular noun**. The same structure is common with decimals below 1.

> *three quarters* ***of a ton***
> *0.1625 cm nought point one six two five* ***of a centimetre***

However, decimals below 1 can also be followed directly by a plural noun.

> *nought point one six two five* **centimetres**

Fractions and decimals over 1 are normally followed directly by a plural noun.

> *one and a half* **hours** (NOT ~~*one and a half* **hour**~~)
> *1.3 millimetres* (NOT ~~*1.3* **millimetre**~~)

Note also the structure *a . . . and a half.*

> *I've been waiting for* **an hour and a half***.*

▶

Singular verbs are normally used after fractions and other expressions referring to amounts (for more details, see 504).

> *Three quarters of a ton* **is** *too much.* (N O T ~~*Three quarters of a ton are*~~ ...)
> *3.6 kilometres* **is** *about 2 miles.*

3   *nought, zero, nil* etc

The figure 0 is usually called *nought* in British English, and *zero* in American English. When we say numbers one figure at a time, 0 is often called *oh* (like the letter O).

> *My account number is four one three* **oh** *six.*

In measurements of temperature, 0 is called *zero* in both British and American English. *Zero* is followed by a plural noun.

> **Zero** *degrees Celsius is thirty-two degrees Fahrenheit.*

Zero scores in team games are called *nil* (American *zero* or *nothing*). In tennis and similar games, the word *love* is used (originally from French *l'oeuf*, meaning 'the egg' – the figure 0 is egg-shaped).

> *And the score at half-time is: Scotland three, England* **nil**.
> *Forty-***love***; Andrews to serve.*

4   telephone numbers

We say each figure separately, pausing after groups of three or four (not two). When the same figure comes twice, British people usually say *double*.

> *307 4922 three oh seven, four nine* **double** *two*
>   (US *three zero seven, four nine* **two two**)

5   Roman numbers

Roman numbers (*I, II, III, IV* etc) are not common in modern English, but they are still used in a few cases – for example the names of kings and queens, page numbers in the introductions to some books, the numbers of paragraphs in some documents, the numbers of questions in some examinations, the figures on some clock faces, and occasionally the names of centuries.

> *It was built in the time of* **Henry V**.
> *For details, see Introduction* **page ix**.
> *Do* **question (vi)** *or* **question (vii)**, *but not both.*
> *a fine* **XVIII** *Century English walnut chest of drawers*

The Roman numbers normally used are as follows:

1	*I*	*i*	10	*X*	*x*	40	*XL*	*xl*
2	*II*	*ii*	11	*XI*	*xi*	45	*XLV*	*xlv*
3	*III*	*iii*	12	*XII*	*xii*	50	*L*	*l*
4	*IV*	*iv*	13	*XIII*	*xiii*	60	*LX*	*lx*
5	*V*	*v*	14	*XIV*	*xiv*	90	*XC*	*xc*
6	*VI*	*vi*	19	*XIX*	*xix*	100	*C*	*c*
7	*VII*	*vii*	20	*XX*	*xx*	500	*D*	
8	*VIII*	*viii*	21	*XXI*	*xxi*	1000	*M*	
9	*IX*	*ix*	30	*XXX*	*xxx*	1995	*MCMXCV*	

6   cardinal and ordinal numbers: books, chapters etc; kings and queens

After a noun we usually use a cardinal number instead of an ordinal number. This structure is common in titles. Compare:

> the **fourth** book – Book **Four**
> the **third** act – Act **Three**
> Mozart's **thirty-ninth** symphony – Symphony No. **39**, by Mozart
> the **third** day of the course – Timetable for Day **Three**

However, the names of kings and queens are said with ordinal numbers.

> Henry VIII: Henry **the Eighth** (N O T ~~Henry Eight~~)
> Louis XIV: Louis **the Fourteenth**
> Elizabeth II: Elizabeth **the Second**

7   centuries

Note how the names of centuries relate to the years in them. The period from 1701 – 1800 is called the **18**th century (not the **17**th); 1801 – 1900 is the **19**th century, etc.

8   floors

The *ground floor* of a British house is the *first floor* of an American house; the British *first floor* is the American *second floor*, etc.

9   *and*; punctuation

In British English we always use *and* before the tens in a number.
In American English, *and* can be dropped.

> *310 three hundred **and** ten* (US also *three hundred ten*)
> *5,642 five thousand, six hundred **and** forty-two*

In measurements containing two different units, *and* is possible before the smaller, but is usually left out.

> *two hours **(and)** ten minutes*
> *two metres **(and)** thirty centimetres*

In writing we generally use commas (,) to divide large numbers into groups of three figures, by separating off the thousands and the millions. Full stops (.) are not used in this way.

> *3,127* (N O T ~~3.127~~)   *5,466,243*

We do not always use commas in four-figure numbers, and they are not used in dates.

> *4,126* O R *4126*
> *the year **1648***

Spaces are also possible in British English.

> *There are **1,000** (*O R *1 000*) *millimetres in a metre.*

10   *a* and *one*

We can say *a hundred* or *one hundred, a thousand* or *one thousand, a million* or *one million. One* is more formal.

> *I want to live for **a** hundred years.* (N O T *... ~~for hundred years.~~*)
> *Pay Mr J Baron **one** thousand pounds.* (on a cheque)   ▶

A can only be used at the beginning of a number. Compare:
> *a/one hundred*
> *three thousand **one** hundred*
> (NOT ~~three thousand **a** hundred~~)

A thousand can be used alone, and before *and*, but not usually before a number of hundreds. Compare:
> *a/one thousand*
> *a/one thousand and forty-nine*
> ***one** thousand, six hundred and two*
> (More natural than *a thousand, six hundred and two.*)

We can use *a* or *one* with measurement words. The rules are similar.
> *a/one kilometre* (BUT ***one** kilometre, six hundred metres*)
> *an/one hour and seventeen minutes* (BUT ***one** hour, seventeen minutes*)
> *a/one pound* (BUT ***one** pound twenty-five*)

11   numbers with determiners

Numbers can be used after determiners. Before determiners, a structure with *of* is necessary.
> *You're **my one** hope.*
> ***One of my friends** gave me this.* (NOT ~~One my friend...~~)

12   *eleven hundred* etc

In an informal style we often use *eleven hundred, twelve hundred* etc instead of *one thousand, one hundred* etc. This is most common with round numbers between 1,100 and 1,900.
> *We only got **fifteen hundred** pounds for the car.*

This form is used in historical dates (see 151).
> *He was born in **thirteen hundred**.*
> *It was built in **fifteen (hundred** and) twenty-nine.*

13   billion

In American English, a *billion* is a thousand million. This is now generally true in British English, but a British *billion* used to be a million million, and this still occasionally causes misunderstandings among British speakers.

14   singular forms with plural meanings

After a number, *dozen, hundred, thousand, million* and *billion* have no final -*s*, and *of* is not used. This also happens after *several* and *a few*. Compare:
-   *five **hundred** pounds*
    ***hundreds** of pounds*
-   *several **thousand** times*
    *It cost **thousands**.*
-   *a few **million** years*
    ***millions** of years*

Singular forms are used as modifiers before nouns in plural measuring expressions.

*a five-**pound** note   a three-**mile** walk*
*six two-**hour** lessons   a three-**month**-old baby*
*a four-**foot** deep hole   a six-**foot** tall man*

In an informal style, we often use *foot* instead of *feet* in other structures, especially when we talk about people's heights.

*My father's just over six **foot** two.*

For the use of *be* in measurements, see 91.
For the use of possessive forms in expressions of time (e.g. *ten **minutes'** walk*; *four **days'** journey*), see 382.8.
For *of* after *half,* see 235.
For singular verbs after expressions referring to amounts and quantities, see 504.

15 British money

There are 100 *pence* in a *pound.* Sums of money are named as follows:

1 p   one penny (informal *one p* (/piː/) OR *a penny*)
5 p   five pence (informal *five p*)
£3.75   three pounds seventy-five (pence) OR *three pounds **and** seventy-five pence* (more formal)

Some people now use the plural *pence* as a singular in informal speech; *pound* is sometimes used informally as a plural.

*That's two pounds and one **pence**, please.*
*It cost me eight **pound** fifty.*

Singular forms are used in expressions like *a five-**pound** note* (see above). However, *pence* is often used instead of *penny* (*a five **pence** stamp*).

16 American money

There are 100 *cents* (¢) in a *dollar* ($). Sums of money are named very much as in British English. Some coins have special names: one-cent coins are called *pennies*; five-cent coins are *nickels*; ten-cent coins are *dimes*; a twenty-five cent coin is a *quarter.*

17 non-metric measures

In recent years, Britain has adopted some metric measurement units, but non-metric measures are still quite widely used. America uses mainly non-metric units. Approximate values are as follows:

1 inch (1 in) = 2.5 cm
12 inches = 1 foot (30 cm)
3 feet (3 ft) = 1 yard (90 cm)
5,280 feet / 1,760 yards = 1 mile (1.6 km)
5 miles = 8 km

1 ounce (1 oz) = 28 gm
16 ounces = 1 pound (455 gm)
2.2 pounds (2.2 lb) = 1 kg
14 pounds (14 lb) = 1 stone (6.4 kg) (British only)

▶

1 British pint = 56.8 cl
1 US pint = 47.3 cl
8 pints (8 pt) = 1 gallon
1 British gallon = 4.55 litres
1 US gallon = 3.78 litres

1 acre = 4,840 square yards = 0.4 hectares
1 square mile = 640 acres = 259 ha

British people usually measure their weight in *stones* and *pounds*; Americans just use *pounds*. Height is measured in *feet*; distance can also be measured in *feet*, but longer distances are often measured in *yards*.

> *I weigh eight **stone** six.* (NOT *...eight **stones** six*)
> *We are now flying at an altitude of 28,000 **feet**.*
> *The car park's straight on, about 500 **yards** on the right.*

18 areas

We say, for example, that a room is *twelve feet **by** fifteen feet*, or that a garden is *thirty metres **by** forty-eight metres*.

A room *twelve feet by twelve feet* can be called *twelve **feet square***; the total area is *144 **square feet***.

19 *a* and *per*

When we relate two different measures, we usually use *a/an*; *per* is often used in formal writing.

> *It costs two pounds **a** week.* (... *£2 **per** week*.)
> *We're doing seventy miles **an** hour.* (... *70 miles **per** hour / mph*.)

20 numbers as complements

Numbers are used as subjects or objects, but not usually as complements after *be*.

> *I've got three sisters.* (NOT *My sisters are three.*)
> *There are twelve of us in my family.*
>   (More natural than *We are twelve...*)

21 spoken calculations

Common ways of saying calculations in British English are:

2 + 2 = 4	*Two and two is/are four.* (informal)
	Two plus two equals/is four. (formal)
7 – 4 = 3	*Four from seven is/leaves three.* (informal)
	Seven take away four is/leaves three. (informal)
	Seven minus four equals/is three. (formal)
3 × 4 = 12	*Three fours are twelve.* (informal)
	Three times four is twelve. (informal)
	Three multiplied by four equals/is twelve. (formal)
9 ÷ 3 = 3	*Three(s) into nine goes three (times).* (informal)
	Nine divided by three equals/is three. (formal)

page 388

22   example of a spoken calculation

Here, for interest, is a multiplication (146 × 281) together with all its steps, in the words that a British English speaker might have used as he/she was working it out on paper before the days of pocket calculators.

$$
\begin{array}{r}
146 \\
\times\ 281 \\
\hline
29200 \\
11680 \\
146 \\
\hline
41026 \\
\hline
\end{array}
$$

A hundred and forty-six times two hundred and eighty-one.

beginning:	*Put down two noughts. Two sixes are twelve; put down two and carry one; two fours are eight and one are nine; two ones are two.*
next line:	*Put down one nought. Eight sixes are forty-eight; put down eight and carry four; eight fours are thirty-two and four is thirty-six; put down six and carry three; eight ones are eight and three is eleven.*
next line:	*One times 146 is 146.*
the addition:	*Six and nought and nought is six; eight and four and nought is twelve; put down two and carry one; six and two are eight and one is nine and one is ten; put down nought and carry one; nine and one are ten and one is eleven; put down one and carry one; two and one are three and one are four.*
total:	*forty-one thousand and twenty-six.*

Note how *is* and *are* can often be used interchangeably.

For ways of saying and writing dates, see 151.
For ways of telling the time, see 555.

386   of course

We use *of course* to mean something like 'as everybody knows' or 'as is obvious'.

> *It looks as if the sun goes round the earth, but **of course** the earth really goes round the sun.*

> *We'll leave at eight o'clock. Granny won't be coming, **of course**.*

This means that *of course* is not a very polite reply to a statement of fact. Compare:

> *'Could you help me?' '**Of course**.'*

> *'It's cold.' 'It certainly is.'* (*'**Of course** it is'* would be quite rude, because it would suggest that the first speaker had said something too obvious to be worth mentioning.)

For another way of using *of course*, see 159.5.

387   often

Often is used to mean 'frequently on different occasions'. If we want to say 'frequently on the same occasion', we generally use a different expression (e.g. *a lot of times, several times, frequently*), or the structure *keep...ing.* Compare:

>I **often** fell in love when I was younger.
>I fell **several times** yesterday when I was skiing.
>>(OR I **kept falling** yesterday...) (NOT ~~I often fell yesterday~~...)

Note that **often** *has two common pronunciations:* /'ɒfən/ and /'ɒftən/.

For the position of *often* and other adverbs of indefinite frequency, see 23.2.

388   older English verb forms

The English that was used a few hundred years ago was different in very many ways from modern English – grammar, vocabulary, pronunciation and spelling have all changed greatly since Shakespeare's time. Some of the most striking differences are in the way verbs are used. For example, older English had distinct second-person singular verb forms ending in *-st*, with a corresponding second-person singular pronoun *thou* (object form *thee*, possessives *thy, thine*). There were also third-person singular verb forms ending in *-th*, and *ye* could be used as a second-person plural pronoun.

>Tell me what **thou knowest**.
>How can I help **thee**?
>Where **thy** master **goeth**, there **goest thou** also.
>Oh come, all **ye** faithful.

Older forms of *be* included *art* and *wert*.

>I fear **thou art** sick.
>**Wert thou** at work today?

Questions and negatives were originally made without *do*; at a later stage, forms with and without *do* (including affirmative forms with *do*) were both quite common.

>**Came you** by sea or by land?
>They **know not** what they do.
>**Be not** afraid.
>Then he **did take** my hand and kiss it.

Simple tenses were often used in cases where modern English has progressive forms.

>We **go not out** today, for **it raineth**.

Subjunctives (see 541) were more widely used than in modern English.

>If she **be** here, then tell her I wait her pleasure.

Inversion (see 298–299) was more common, and infinitives and past participles could come later in a clause than in modern English.

>Now **are we** lost indeed.
>Hamlet, thou hast thy father much **offended**. (Shakespeare)
>And she **me caught** in her arms long and small
>>and therewithal so sweetly **did me kiss**
>>and softly said 'Dear heart, how **like you** this?' (Wyatt)

These forms were not only common in older literature; some of them continued to be used by 19th-century and early 20th-century writers (particularly in poetry) long after they had died out of normal usage. Modern writers of historical novels, films or plays often make their characters use some of these older forms in order to give a 'period' flavour to the language. And the forms also survive in certain special contexts where tradition is especially valued – for example the language of religious services, public ceremonies and the law. Some dialects, too, preserve forms which have disappeared from the rest of the language – second-person pronouns (*thou* etc) are still used by many people in Yorkshire.

389 once (adverb)

When the adverb *once* has the indefinite meaning 'at some time', we use it to talk about the past but not the future. To refer to an indefinite time in the future, we can use *sometime* or *one day*. Compare:
- *I met her **once** in Venezuela.*
  ***Once** upon a time there were three baby rabbits.*
- *Come up and see me **sometime**.* (NOT *Come up and see me **once**.*)
- *We must have a drink together **one day**.*
  (NOT *We must have a drink together **once**.*)

When *once* has the more precise meaning of 'one time (not twice or three times)', it can be used to talk about any time, including the future.
*I'm only going to say this **once**.*

390 once (conjunction)

Once can be used as a conjunction, meaning 'after', 'as soon as'. It often suggests that something is finished or completed, and is most often used with a perfect tense.
Once *you've passed your test I'll let you drive my car.*
*I'd like to go for a walk **once** the rain's stopped.*
Once *he had found somewhere to live he started looking for work.*
Once *you know how to ride a bike you never forget it.*

Note that we do not use *that* after *once* (NOT *...**once that** the rain's stopped*).

For present perfect instead of future perfect after conjunctions, see 556.
For the use of *now (that)* as a conjunction, see 383.

391 one: substitute word

1 use

We often use *one* instead of repeating a singular countable noun.
*'Which is your **boy**?' 'The **one** in the blue coat.'*
*I'd like a **cake**. A big **one** with lots of cream.*
*'Can you lend me a **pen**?' 'Sorry, I haven't got **one**.'*

▶

2   *a ... one*

We drop *a* if there is no adjective. Compare:

> *I'm looking for a flat. I'd like **a small one** with a garden.*
> *I'd like **one** with a garden.* (NOT ...~~a one with a garden.~~)

3   *ones*

One has a plural *ones*.

> *'I'd like to try on those shoes.' 'Which **ones**?' 'The **ones** at the front of the window.'*
> *Green apples often taste better than red **ones**.*
> *'What sort of sweets do you like?' '**Ones** with chocolate inside.'*

4   leaving out *one(s)*

One(s) can be left out immediately after superlatives, *this, that, these, those, either, neither, another* and some other determiners.

> *I think my dog's the **fastest (one)**.*
> *'**Which (one)** would you like?' '**That (one)** looks the nicest.'*
> ***Either (one)** will suit me.*
> *She looked at **each (one)** very carefully before she chose.*
> *Let's have **another (one)**.*

In American English, *ones* is not generally possible immediately after *these* and *those* (and it is unusual in British English).

> *I don't think much of **these**.* (GB ... *these ones* also possible)

We do not use *one(s)* immediately after *my, your* etc, *some, any, both* or a number.

> *Take your coat and pass me **mine**.* (NOT ...~~pass me my one.~~)
> *'Are there any grapes?' 'Yes, I bought **some** today.'*
>   (NOT ...~~I bought some ones today.~~)
> *I need some matches. Have you got **any**?* (NOT ...~~any ones?~~)
> *I'll take **both**.* (NOT ...~~both ones.~~)
> *She bought **six**.* (NOT ...~~six ones.~~)

But *one(s)* is used in all these cases if there is an adjective.

> *I'd like **that green one**.* (NOT ...~~that green.~~)
> *I don't think much of **those new ones**.* (NOT ...~~those new.~~)
> *I bought **some sweet ones** today.* (NOT ~~I bought some sweet today.~~)
> *'Has the cat had her kittens?' 'Yes, she had **four white ones**.'*
>   (NOT ...~~four white.~~)

5   uncountable and abstract nouns

We do not use *one(s)* for uncountable nouns. Compare:

> *If you haven't got a fresh **chicken** I'll take a frozen **one**.*
> *If you haven't got fresh **cream** I'll take tinned (cream).*
>   (NOT ...~~tinned one.~~)

And it is unusual to use *one* for abstract nouns.

> *The Dutch grammatical system is very similar to the English **system**.*
>   (More natural than ... *to the English **one**.*)

6 noun modifers

One(s) is not generally used after noun modifiers, except those which refer to materials.

Do you need coffee (cups) or tea cups? (NOT *...~~or tea ones.~~*)
BUT *We can lend you plastic chairs or **metal ones**.*

7 *one(s)* always refers back

We use *one(s)* to avoid repeating a noun which has been mentioned before. It cannot normally be used in other cases.

*Then I saw a round **thing** in the sky with flashing lights.*
    (NOT *...~~a round one with flashing lights.~~*)
*Let's go and ask the old **man** for advice.* (NOT *...~~ask the old one~~...*)

8 *that of*

One(s) is not normally used after a noun with possessive *'s*. Instead, we can either just drop *one(s)*, or use a structure with *that/those of* (more formal).

A grandparent's job is easier than a parent's. (NOT *...~~than a parent's one.~~*)
*A grandparent's job is easier than **that of** a parent.*
    (NOT *...~~than the one of a parent.~~*)
*Trollope's novels are more entertaining than **those of** Dickens.*
    (NOT *...~~than Dickens' ones / the ones of Dickens.~~*)

9 *one* and *it*

To refer to one particular thing that has already been clearly identified, we use *it*, not *one*. Compare:

*'Can you lend me **a pen**?' 'Sorry, I haven't got **one**.'*
    (NOT *~~'Sorry, I haven't got it.'~~*)
*'Can I borrow **your pen**?' 'Sorry, I need **it**.'* (NOT *~~'Sorry, I need one.'~~*)

For substitution in general, see 542.
For repetition and avoidance of repetition in general, see 479.

392 one, you and they: indefinite personal pronouns

1 *one* and *you*: meaning

We can use *one* or *you* to talk about people in general, including the speaker and hearer.

***One** always thinks other people's lives are more interesting.*
    (OR ***~~You always think~~**...*)
***One/You** can't learn a language in six weeks.*
***One/You** should never give people advice.*

2 *one* and *you*: formality and class

One is rather more formal than *you*. Compare:
– *If **you** want to make people angry, **you** just have to tell them the truth.*
    *If **one** wishes to make **oneself** thoroughly unpopular, **one** has merely
        to tell people the truth.*

▶

– *'How do **you** get to Newbury?' 'Go straight down the A34.'*
> *There are three principal routes by which **one** can drive to North Wales.*

One is often considered typical of more upper-class and intellectual usage, and is avoided by many people for this reason; it is rare in informal American English.

3   *one* and *you*: only used in generalisations

One and *you* are only used in this way in very general statements, when we are talking about 'anyone, at any time'. Compare:

– *   **One/You** can usually find people who speak English in Sweden.*
    *English **is spoken** in this shop.* OR ***They** speak English in this shop.*
    > (NOT ~~*One speaks English*~~... – the meaning is not 'people in general'.)

– *   **One/You** should knock before going into somebody's room.*
    ***Somebody**'s knocking at the door.* (NOT ~~*One is knocking*~~...)

– *   It can take **you/one** ages to get served in this pub.*
    *Thanks, **I'm being served**.* (NOT ~~*Thanks, one is serving me.*~~)

One generally has a singular meaning (= 'any individual'); it is not used to refer to groups.

> ***We** speak a strange dialect where I come from.*
> > (NOT ~~*One speaks a strange dialect where I come from.*~~)

4   people including the speaker/hearer

One is not used to generalise about people who could not include the speaker; *you* is not used to generalise about people who could not include the hearer. Compare:

> ***One/You** must believe in something.*
> *In the sixteenth century **people** believed in witches.*
> > (NOT ... ~~*one/you believed in witches*~~ – this could not include the speaker or hearer.)

5   *one/you* as subject, object etc

One can be a subject or object; there is a possessive *one's* and a reflexive pronoun *oneself.*

> *He talks to **one** like a teacher.*
> ***One's** family can be very difficult.*
> ***One** should always give **oneself** plenty of time to pack.*

You/your/yourself can be used in similar ways.

6   pronouns referring back: American English

When *one* is used in American English, *he, him* and *his* are generally used later in a sentence to refer back to *one*. This is not normal in British English.

> ***One** cannot succeed at this unless **he** tries hard.*
> > (GB ... *unless **one** tries hard.*)

> ***One** should always be polite to **his** bank manager.*
> > (GB ... *to **one's** bank manager.*)

7 *they*

They has a rather different, less general kind of meaning than *one* and *you*. It usually refers to a particular but rather vague group (for example the neighbours, the people around, the authorities).

> ***They*** *don't like strangers round here.*
> ***They****'re going to widen the road soon.*
> *I bet **they** put taxes up next year.*

Note also the common expression *they say* (= *people say*).

> ***They say*** *her husband's been seeing that Mrs Hastings again.*
> (NOT ~~*One says*~~...)

393 one of ...

One of is followed by a determiner and a noun phrase (usually plural), or by a plural pronoun. *Of* cannot be dropped in this structure.

> *one of my **friends***
> (NOT ~~*one of my friend*~~)
> (NOT ~~*one my friend*~~)
> *one of **them***

After *one of*, a noun phrase must have a determiner.

> *one of **the/my/those** horses* (BUT NOT ~~*one of horses*~~)

Occasionally *one of* is used with a singular noun referring to a group.

> *Why don't you ask one of the **crew**?*

When *one of* ... is a subject, the verb is singular.

> *One of my friends **is** a pilot.* (NOT ~~*One of my friends **are** a pilot.*~~)
> *One of our cats **has** disappeared.* (NOT ~~*One of our cats **have** disappeared.*~~)

For sentences like *She's one of the only women who have/has climbed Everest*, see 506.

394 only (focusing adverb)

Only can be used as a 'focusing adverb' (see 23.3). It can refer to different parts of a sentence.

1 referring to the subject

Only normally comes before a subject that it refers to.

> ***Only you*** *could do a thing like that.*
> ***Only my mother*** *really understands me.*

2 referring to other parts of a sentence

When *only* refers to another part of a sentence, it often goes in 'mid-position' with the verb (see 23.10 for details).

> *She **only** reads **biographies**.*
> *I **only** like swimming **in the sea**.*
> *She is **only** on duty **on Tuesdays**.*
> *She was **only** talking like that **because she was nervous**.*
> *I've **only** been to India **once**.*

▶

3   ambiguous sentences

Sometimes sentences with *only* are ambiguous (they can be understood in more than one way).

> I **only** kissed your sister last night.

(The sense can be 'only kissed', 'only your sister' or 'only last night'.)
In speech, the meaning is usually clear because the speaker stresses the part of the sentence that *only* refers to. Even in writing, the context generally stops sentences like these from being really ambiguous. However, if necessary *only* can be put directly before the object, complement or adverbial expression that it refers to. This is rather formal. Compare:

> They **only play** poker on Saturday nights. (could be ambiguous)
> They play **only poker** on Saturday nights.
> They play poker **only on Saturday nights**.

Another way of making the meaning more precise is to split the sentence by using a relative structure.

> Poker is **the only game they play** on Saturday nights.
> Saturday nights are **the only time they play poker**.

4   *only today* etc

Only with a time expression can mean 'as recently as', 'not before'.

> I saw her **only today** – she looks much better.
> My shoes will **only** be ready **on Friday**.
> **Only last week** you said you would never smoke again. That didn't last long, did it?
> **Only then** did she realise what she had agreed to.

For inverted word order after *only*, as in the last example above, see 298.

395   open

1   *open* and *opened*

We normally use *open*, not *opened*, as an adjective.

> I can read you like an **open** book. (NOT *...an **opened** book.*)
> Are the banks **open** this afternoon? (NOT *Are the banks **opened**...?*)

Opened is used as the past tense and past participle of the verb *open*, to talk about the action of opening.

> She **opened** her eyes and sat up.
> The safe was **opened** with dynamite.

2   when *open* is not used

Note that *open* is not the most normal word to refer to the fastenings of clothes, or to switches or taps.

> I can't **untie/undo** this shoelace. (NOT *I can't **open** this shoelace.*)
> How do you **unfasten** this belt?
> Could you **turn/switch** the radio **on**? (NOT *...**open** the radio?*)
> Who left the taps **turned on**? (NOT *Who left the taps **open**?*)

For *closed* and *shut*, see 132.

396 **opportunity** and **possibility**

We often say that somebody *has the opportunity to do / of doing* something.
> *I **have the opportunity to go** to Denmark next year.* (= *I **can** go . . .*)

Possibility is not often used in this structure. We more often say that *there is a possibility of something happening.*
> *There's **a possibility of my going** to Denmark next year.* (= *I **may** go . . .*)
> (NOT *~~I have the possibility to go~~ to ~~Denmark~~ . . .*)

397 **opposite**: position

We put the adjective *opposite* before a noun when we are talking about one of a pair of things that naturally face or contrast with each other.
> *I think the picture would look better on the **opposite wall**.*
> *She went off in the **opposite direction**.*
> *I've got exactly the **opposite opinion** to yours.*
> *His brother was fighting on the **opposite side**.*

We put *opposite* after the noun when it means 'facing the speaker or listener' or 'facing a person or place that has already been mentioned'.
> *I noticed that the **man opposite** was staring at me.*
> (NOT *. . . ~~the opposite man was staring at me.~~*)
> *The man you're looking for is in the **shop directly opposite**.*
> *The people in the **house opposite** never draw their curtains.*

In American English, this idea is usually expressed by using *across (from)*.
> *the man sitting **across from** me*
> *the house **across the street***

For *opposite* and *in front of*, see 272.
For *opposite* and *contrary*, see 145.

398 **ought**

1 forms

Ought is a modal auxiliary verb (see 344–345). The third person singular has no *-s*.
> *She **ought** to understand.* (NOT *~~She oughts~~ . . .*)

Questions and negatives are made without *do*.
> ***Ought we** to go now?* (NOT *~~Do we ought~~ . . . ?*)
> *It **oughtn't** to rain today.*

After *ought*, we use the infinitive with *to*. (This makes *ought* different from other modal auxiliary verbs.)
> *You **ought to see** a dentist.*

To is not used in question tags (see 465).
> *We ought to wake Helen, **oughtn't we**?* (NOT *. . . ~~oughtn't we to?~~*)

In American English, interrogative and contracted negative forms of *ought to* are rare; *should* is generally used instead.
> *He **ought to** be here soon, **shouldn't** he?* ▶

2   obligation

We can use *ought* to advise people (including ourselves) to do things; to tell people that they have a duty to do things; to ask about our duty. The meaning is very similar to that of *should*; it is not so strong as *must* (see 496).

> What time **ought** I to arrive?
> I really **ought** to phone Mother.
> People **ought** not to drive like that.
> He **ought to be given** a medal for living with her.
> There **ought to be** traffic lights at this crossroads.

3   deduction

We can use *ought* to say that we guess or conclude that something is probable (because it is logical or normal).

> Henry **ought** to be here soon – he left home at six.
> 'We're spending the winter in Miami.' 'That **ought** to be nice.'
> The weather **ought to improve** after the weekend.

4   questions and negatives

Some people feel that the normal question and negative forms of *ought* are rather formal. In an informal style, it is common to avoid them by using a structure with *think … ought* or by using *should*.

> Do you **think we ought** to go now? (Less formal than **Ought we to …?**)
> **Should** we go now?
> I don't **think** people **ought** to drive like that.

In some dialects, questions and negatives are made with *did* (e.g. *She **didn't** ought to do that*), but this structure is not used in standard English.

5   *ought to have …*

Ought has no past form, but we can use **ought to have + past participle** to express certain ideas about the past. This structure can be used to talk about things which were supposed to happen but did not, or to make guesses or draw conclusions about things which are not certain to have happened.

> I **ought to have phoned** Ed this morning, but I forgot.
>   (NOT ~~I ought to phone Ed this morning, but I forgot.~~)
> The Parkers **ought to have got** back from holiday yesterday. Has anybody
>   seen them?

It is also possible to talk about things that *ought to have happened* by now, or by a future time.

> Ten o'clock. She **ought to have arrived** at her office by now.
> We **ought to have finished** painting the house by the end of next week.

6   word order

'Mid-position' adverbs like *always, never, really* (see 23.10) can go before or after *ought* in a verb phrase. The position before *ought* is less formal.

> You **always ought** to carry some spare money. (less formal)
> You **ought always** to carry some spare money. (more formal)

In negative clauses, *not* comes before *to*.

> You **ought not** to go. / You **oughtn't to** go. (NOT ~~You ought to not go.~~)

399 out of

1 movement

The opposite of the preposition *into* is *out of.*
> She ran **out of** the room.
>> (NOT ~~She ran **out** the room.~~)
>> (NOT ~~She ran **out from** the room.~~)
> I took Harry's letter **out of** my pocket.

Note that *out of* can be used not only when we mention the place that somebody / something leaves, but also when we mention the opening through which somebody / something passes.
> I walked **out of** the front door without looking back.
> Why did you throw the paper **out of** the window?
> He sat staring **out of** the window.

In informal American English, *out* can be used without *of* in this case.
> She turned and went **out** the back door.

2 position

Out of can also be used to talk about position – the opposite of *in.*
> I'm afraid Mr Pallery is **out of** the country at the moment. He should be back next week.

For *into* and *in*, see 269.
For other ways of using *out of*, see a good dictionary.

400 own

1 after possessives

We only use *own* after a possessive word. It cannot directly follow an article.
> It's nice if a child can have **his or her own** room. (NOT ... ~~**an own** room.~~)
> Car hire is expensive. It's cheaper to take **one's own car**.
>> (NOT ... ~~**the own car**.~~)
> I'm **my own** boss.
> She likes to have things **her own** way.
> It was my **mother's very own** engagement ring.

2 *a/some ... of one's own*

This structure makes it possible to include *a/an*, *some* or another determiner in the phrase.
> I'd like to have **a car of my own**.
> It's time you found **some friends of your own**.
> He's got **no ideas of his own**.

For the structure *a ... of mine* etc, see 434.

3 *own* with no following noun

We cannot use *mine*, *yours* etc with *own*, but we can drop a noun after *my own*, *your own* etc if the meaning is clear.
> 'Would you like to use my pen?' 'No, thanks. I can only write with **my own**.' (NOT ... ~~**mine own**.~~)

▶

4   *own* and *-self*

The emphatic and reflexive pronouns *myself, yourself* etc (see 471) do not have possessive forms. *My own* etc is used instead.

> *I'll do it **myself**, and I'll do it in **my own** way.* (NOT ...~~in **myself's way**~~.)
> *She can wash **herself** and brush **her own** hair now.*
> (NOT ...~~brush **herself's hair**~~.)

5   *on one's own*

Note the two meanings of *on one's own*.

> *My mother lives **on her own**.* (without company)
> *Don't help him. Let him do it **on his own**.* (without help)

For *by oneself* used in similar ways, see 471.6.

401   paragraphs

Written English text is usually divided into blocks called 'paragraphs' in order to make it easier to read. The divisions between paragraphs break the material up into easily 'digestible' sections, providing places where it is easy for the reader to pause and think for a moment if necessary. And in addition, a good writer can show the structure of his / her text by making the paragraph divisions in suitable places.

A paragraph division is usually shown, as in the passage below, by starting the text on a new line and 'indenting' (leaving a space at the beginning of the line).

> *Bill decided that it was too late to start slimming, and put some more sugar in his coffee. The way things were, he needed all the help he could get. Everything was going wrong at work, everything had already gone wrong at home, and the weather in Edinburgh in November was lousy. The only remaining question was: should he commit suicide now or wait till after payday and get drunk first?*
> *Three months ago everything had seemed so perfect. His boss had ...*

Another practice, common in typed letters and documents, and used in this book, is to leave a blank line without indenting.

> *Dear Sirs*
>
> *Three months ago I sent you an order for one of your 'Bouncewipe' inflatable doormats, together with my cheque for £35. You wrote acknowledging my order, and said that the doormat would be dispatched within 15 days. Since then I have heard nothing, and repeated phone calls to your offices have had no result beyond vague promises to 'look into the matter'.*
>
> *I am afraid that my patience is now at an end. If ...*

402 part

A is usually dropped before *part* if there is no adjective.

Part *of the roof was missing.* (BUT ***A large part*** *of the roof was missing.*)
Part *of the trouble is that I can't see very well.*
    (More natural than ***A part*** *of the trouble ...*)
Jan was in Australia **part** *of last year.*

403 participles (-ing and -ed forms) (1): introduction

1 names

When *-ing* forms are used in certain ways (see below) they are called 'present participles'. Forms like *broken, gone, opened, started* are called 'past participles'. These are not very suitable names: both forms can be used to talk about the past, present or future.

She was **crying** *when I saw her.*   *Who's the man* **talking** *to Elizabeth?*
This time tomorrow I'll be **lying** *on the beach.*
It was **broken** *in the storm.*   *You're* **fired**.
The new school is going to be **opened** *next week.*

Present and past participles can be put together to make progressive and perfect forms (e.g. *being employed, having arrived, having been invited*).

For the spelling of participles, see 533–535.

2 use

a verb forms

Participles are used with the auxiliary verbs *be* and *have* to make progressive, perfect and passive verb forms.

It **was raining** *when I got home.*   *I've* **forgotten** *your name.*
You'll **be told** *as soon as possible.*

b adjectives

Participles can be used like adjectives.

I love the noise of **falling** *rain.*   *She says she's got a* **broken** *heart.*
John has become very **boring**.   *The house looked* **abandoned**.

c adverbs

Sometimes participles are used like adverbs.

She ran **screaming** *out of the room.*

d clauses

Participles can combine with other words into clause-like structures.

Who's the fat man **sitting in the corner**?
Having lost all my money, *I went home.*
Most of the people **invited to the party** *didn't turn up.*
Rejected by all his friends, *he decided to become a monk.*

For details of these uses, see the following sections.
For *-ing* forms used like nouns ('gerunds'), see 292–296.

404 participles (2): active and passive

1 active present participles, passive past participles

When -*ing* forms are used like adjectives or adverbs, they have similar meanings to active verbs.

falling leaves (= leaves that *fall*)
a meat-*eating* animal (= an animal that *eats* meat)
She walked out *smiling*. (= She *was smiling*.)

Most past participles have passive meanings when they are used like adjectives or adverbs.

a *broken* heart (= a heart that *has been broken*)
He lived alone, *forgotten* by everybody.
    (= He *had been forgotten* by everybody.)

2 *interested* and *interesting* etc

The past participles *interested, bored, excited* etc are used to say how people feel.

I was very *interested* in the lesson.
    (NOT ~~I was very *interesting* in the lesson.~~)
I didn't enjoy the party because I was *bored*.
    (NOT ... ~~because I was *boring*.~~)
The children always get terribly *excited* when Granny comes.
    (NOT ~~The children always get terribly *exciting* ...~~)
His explanation made me very *confused*.
    (NOT ... ~~made me very *confusing*.~~)

The present participles *interesting, boring* etc describe the people or things that cause the feelings. Compare:

She's an *interesting* writer, and I'm very *interested* in the subjects that she writes about.
Boring teachers make *bored* students.

3 exceptions: active past participles

A few intransitive verbs have past participles that can be used as adjectives with active meanings, especially before nouns. Examples:

a *fallen* leaf (= a leaf that *has fallen*)
advanced students (= students who *have advanced* to a high level,
    NOT ~~students who *have been advanced* ...~~)

developed countries	a *grown-up* daughter
increased activity	an *escaped* prisoner
vanished civilisations	*faded* colours
a *retired* general	*swollen* ankles

Rescuers are still working in the ruins of the *collapsed* hotel.

Some more past participles can only be used in this way in phrases with adverbs. Examples:

a *well-read* person (BUT NOT ~~a *read* person~~)
a *much-travelled* man
recently-arrived immigrants
The train *just arrived* at platform six is the delayed 13.15 from Hereford.

Some active past participles can also be used after *be*. Examples:

*She **is retired** now.*

*My family **are** all **grown up** now – except my husband, of course.*

*Those curtains **are** badly **faded**.   This class **is** the most **advanced**.*

Recovered, camped, stopped, finished (see 211) and *gone* (see 233) are used in this way after *be*, but not before nouns.

*Why **are** all those cars **stopped** at the crossroads?*

> (BUT NOT ... ~~a stopped car~~...)

*I hope you're fully **recovered** from your operation.*

*We're **camped** in the field across the stream.*

*I'll **be finished** in a few minutes.   Those days **are gone** now.*

*He **has been gone** for hours – where do you think he is?*

Note that *worry* can be used both actively and passively with similar meanings.

*I **worry** about you.   **I'm worried** about you.*

405 **participles** (3): details

1 used as adjectives

Participles can often be used as adjectives before nouns, or after *be* and other copular verbs.

> an **interesting book**   a **lost** dog
>
> a **falling** leaf   The upstairs toilet window is **broken**.
>
> **screaming** children   His idea seems **exciting**.

An *-ing* form with an object can be used as an adjective. Note the word order.

> **English-speaking** Canadians. (NOT ~~speaking-English Canadians.~~)
>
> a **fox-hunting** man   Is that watch **self-winding**?

Other compound structures with participles are also common before nouns.

> **quick-growing** trees   **government-inspired** rumours
>
> **home-made** cake   the **above-mentioned** point
>
> a **recently-built** house

Not all participles can be used as adjectives before nouns – for example, we can say *a lost dog*, but not *a found dog*. It is not possible to give clear rules for this – it is a complicated area of English grammar which has not yet been completely analysed.

2 after nouns

We often use participles after nouns in order to define or identify the nouns, in the same way as we use identifying relative clauses (see 474).

*We couldn't agree on any of the **problems discussed**.*

> (= ... the **problems that were discussed**.)
>
> (NOT ... the ~~discussed problems~~.)

*The **people questioned** gave very different opinions.*

> (= The **people who were questioned** ...)
>
> (NOT ~~The questioned people~~...)

*I watched the match because I knew some of the **people playing**.*

> (NOT ... the ~~playing people~~.)

*I got the only **ticket left**. (NOT ... ~~the only left ticket~~.)*   ▶

Those is often used with a participle to mean 'the ones who are/were'.
> *Most of **those questioned** refused to answer.*
> ***Those selected** will begin training on Monday.*

3 differences of meaning

A few participles change their meaning according to their position.
Compare:
- *a **concerned** expression* (= *a **worried** expression*)
  *the people **concerned*** (= *the people who are/were **affected***)
- *an **involved** explanation* (= *a **complicated** explanation*)
  *the people **involved*** (= the same as *the people **concerned***)
- *an **adopted** child* (= *a child who is brought up by people who are not his/her biological parents*)
  *the solution **adopted*** (= *the solution that is/was **chosen***)

4 *very* with past participles

When a past participle is used as a gradable adjective, it can usually be modified by *very*. This is common with words referring to mental states, feelings and reactions.
> *a **very frightened** animal* (NOT ~~*a **much** frightened animal*~~)
> *a **very shocked** expression*
> *The children were **very bored**.*   *She looked **very surprised**.*

Common exceptions:
> *That's Alice, unless I'm **(very) much mistaken**.*
>   (NOT ... ~~*unless I'm **very** mistaken.*~~)
> *He's **well known** in the art world.* (NOT ... ~~***very known**...*~~)

When a past participle is part of a passive verb, *much* or *very much* is normal.
> *He's **very much** admired by his students.* (NOT ... ~~***very admired**...*~~)
> *Britain's trade position has been **(very) much weakened** by inflation.*
>   (NOT ... ~~***very weakened**...*~~)

With some words referring to emotional states and reactions, usage is divided.
> *I was **very amused** / **much amused** / **very much amused** by Miranda's performance.*

To be sure whether a particular participle is used with *very* or *much*, it is necessary to look in a good dictionary.

5 *by* with past participles

By is used after passive verbs to introduce the agent (the person or thing that does the action – see 408).
> *Most of the damage was caused **by your sister**.*

After past participles that are used like adjectives, we prefer other prepositions. Compare:
- *She was **frightened by** a mouse that ran into the room.*
  (*Frightened* is part of a verb referring to an action.)
  *She's always been terribly **frightened of** dying.*
  (*Frightened* is an adjective referring to a state of mind.)
- *The kids were so **excited by** the noise that they couldn't get to sleep.*
  *Joe's **excited about** the possibility of going to the States.*

>   – I was **annoyed by** the way she spoke to me.
>   I'm **annoyed with** you.
>   – The burglar was **surprised by** the family coming home unexpectedly.
>   I'm **surprised at/by** your attitude.
>   – He was badly **shocked by** his fall.
>   We were **shocked at/by** the prices in London.

Other examples:

>   His whereabouts are **known to** the police.
>   The hills are **covered in** snow.
>   The room was **filled with** thick smoke.

6 special past participle forms

A few older forms of past participles are still used as adjectives before nouns in certain expressions.

>   **drunken** driving/laughter/singing etc
>   a **shrunken** head
>   a **sunken** wreck/ship etc
>   **rotten** fruit/vegetables etc

406 participles (4): clauses

1 structures

Participles can combine with other words into participle clauses.

>   There's a woman **crying her eyes out** over there.
>   Most of the people **invited to the reception** were old friends.
>   **Not knowing what to do**, I telephoned the police.
>   **Served with milk and sugar**, it makes a delicious breakfast.

2 after nouns; reduced relative clauses

Participle clauses can be used after nouns.

>   We can offer you a **job cleaning cars**.
>   In came the first **runner, closely followed by the second**.

Participle clauses are often very like relative clauses (see 473–474), except that they have participles instead of complete verbs.

>   Who's the girl **dancing with your brother**?
>   (= ... the girl **who is dancing** ...)
>   Anyone **touching that wire** will get a shock. (= Anyone **who touches** ...)
>   There's Neville, **eating as usual**.
>   Half of the **people invited to the party** didn't turn up.
>   I found him sitting at a **table covered with papers**.

Perfect participles are not often used in this way.

>   Do you know anybody **who's lost** a cat?
>   (NOT ~~Do you know anybody **having lost a cat?**~~)

3 adverbial clauses

Participle clauses can also be used in similar ways to full adverbial clauses, expressing condition, reason, time relations, result etc. (This can only happen, of course, when the idea of condition, reason etc is so clear that no conjunction is needed to signal it.) Adverbial participle clauses are usually rather formal.

> **Used economically**, one tin will last for six weeks. (= **If** it is used . . .)
> **Having failed my medical exams**, I took up teaching. (= **As** I had failed . . .)
> **Putting down my newspaper**, I walked over to the window.
> (= **After** I had put down my newspaper, . . .)
> It rained for two weeks on end, **completely ruining our holiday**.
> (= . . . **so that** it completely ruined our holiday.)

Note that -ing clauses can be made with verbs like be, have, wish and know, which are not normally used in progressive tenses (see 451). In these cases, the participle clause usually expresses reason or cause.

> **Being** unable to help in any other way, I gave her some money.
> Not **wishing** to continue my studies, I decided to become a dress designer.
> **Knowing** her pretty well, I realised something was wrong.

4 subjects; misrelated participles

Normally the subject of an adverbial participle clause is the same as the subject of the main clause in a sentence.

> **My wife** had a long talk with Sally, **explaining** why she didn't want the children to play together. (*My wife* is the subject of *explaining*.)

It is often considered a mistake to make sentences in which an adverb clause has a different subject from the main clause. The following sentence, with its 'misrelated participle' (also called 'hanging' or 'dangling' participle), would be considered incorrect by many people.

> **Looking** out of the window of our hotel room, there was a wonderful range of mountains. (This could sound as if the mountains were looking out of the window.)

However, sentences with 'misrelated participles' are common and often seem quite natural, particularly when the main clause has preparatory *it* or *there* as a subject.

> **Being French**, **it**'s surprising that she's such a terrible cook.
> **Having so little time**, **there** was not much that I could do.

'Misrelated participles' are normal in some expressions referring to the speaker's attitude. Examples:

> **Generally speaking**, **men** can run faster than women.
> **Broadly speaking**, **dogs** are more faithful than cats.
> **Judging from** his expression, **he**'s in a bad mood.
> **Considering everything**, **it** wasn't a bad holiday.
> **Supposing** there was a war, what would **you** do?
> **Taking everything into consideration**, **they** ought to get another chance.

5 participle clauses with their own subjects

A participle clause can have its own subject. This happens most often in a rather formal style.

> **Nobody having** any more to say, the meeting was closed.
> **All the money having been spent**, we started looking for work.
> A little girl walked past, **her doll dragging** behind her on the pavement.
> **Hands held** high, the dancers circle to the right.

The subject is often introduced by *with* when the clause expresses accompanying circumstances.

> *A car roared past **with smoke pouring** from the exhaust.*
> ***With Peter working** in Birmingham, and **Lucy travelling** most of the week, the house seems pretty empty.*

6 participle clauses after conjunctions and prepositions

Participle clauses can be used after many conjunctions and prepositions, such as *after, before, since, when, while, whenever, once, until, on, without, instead of, in spite of* and *as*. Note that *-ing* forms after prepositions can often be considered as either participles or gerunds – the dividing line is not clear (see 290).

> ***After talking** to you I always feel better.*
> ***After having annoyed** everybody he went home.*
> *Depress clutch **before changing** gear.*
> *She's been quite different **since coming** back from America.*
> ***When telephoning** from abroad, dial 865, not 0865.*
> ***Once deprived of oxygen**, the brain dies.*
> *Leave in oven **until cooked** to a light brown colour.*
> ***On being introduced**, British people often shake hands.*
> *They left **without saying** goodbye.*
> *She struck me **as being** a very nervy kind of person.*

For clauses like *when ready*, see 73.4.
For other (more noun-like) uses of *-ing* forms after prepositions, see 295.

7 object complements

The structure **object + participle (clause)** is used after verbs of sensation (e.g. *see, hear, feel, watch, notice, smell*) and some other verbs (e.g. *find, get, have, make*).

> *I **saw a small girl standing** in the goldfish pond.*
> *Have you ever **heard a nightingale singing**?*
> *I **found her drinking** my whisky.*
> *We'll have to **get the car repaired** before Tuesday.*
> *Do you think you can **get the radio working**?*
> *We'll soon **have you walking** again.*
> *I can **make myself understood** pretty well in English.*

For more about structures with *see*, see 245. For *hear*, see 245. For *get*, see 228. For *have*, see 241. For *make*, see 327.

407 **passives** (1): passive structures and verb forms

1 active and passive structures

Compare:
– *They **built** this house in 1486.* (active)
  *This house **was built** in 1486.* (passive)
– *Channel Islanders **speak** French and English.* (active)
  *French **is spoken** in France, Belgium, Switzerland, the Channel Islands . . .*
    (passive)   ▶

– *A friend of ours **is repairing** the roof.* (active)
  *The roof **is being repaired** by a friend of ours.* (passive)
– *This book **will change** your life.* (active)
  *Your life **will be changed** by this book.* (passive)

When we say what people and things *do*, we use active verb forms like *built, speak, is repairing, will change.* When we say what *happens* to people and things – what *is done* to them – we often use passive verb forms like *was built, is spoken, is being repaired, will be changed.*

The object of an active verb corresponds to the subject of a passive verb.

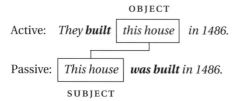

OBJECT

Active: *They **built** | this house | in 1486.*

Passive: | *This house* | ***was built** in 1486.*

SUBJECT

In most cases, the subject of an active verb is not expressed in the corresponding passive sentence. If it does have to be expressed, this usually happens in an expression with *by*; the noun is called the 'agent' (see 408).
  *This house was built in 1486 **by Sir John Latton.***

2   passive verb forms

We normally make passive forms of a verb by using tenses of the auxiliary *be* followed by the past participle (= pp) of the verb. (For *get* as a passive auxiliary, see 228.4.) Here is a list of all the passive forms of an ordinary English verb, with their names.

Tense	Structure	Example
simple present	*am/are/is* + pp	*English **is spoken** here.*
present progressive	*am/are/is being* + pp	*Excuse the mess; the house **is being painted**.*
simple past	*was/were* + pp	*I **wasn't invited**, but I went anyway.*
past progressive	*was/were being* + pp	*I felt as if I **was being watched**.*
present perfect	*have/has been* + pp	***Has** Mary **been told**?*
past perfect	*had been* + pp	*I knew why I **had been chosen**.*
will future	*will be* + pp	*You'**ll be told** when the time comes.*
future perfect	*will have been* + pp	*Everything **will have been done** by Tuesday.*
going to future	*am/are/is going to be* + pp	*Who'**s going to be invited**?*

Future progressive passives (*will be being* + pp) and perfect progressive passives (e.g. *has been being* + pp) are unusual.
Examples of passive infinitives: *(to) be taken; (to) have been invited.*
Examples of passive *-ing* forms: *being watched; having been invited.*

Note that verbs made up of more than one word (see 582) can have passive forms if they are transitive.

>*The furniture **was broken up** for firewood.*
>*She likes **being looked at**.*
>*I need **to be taken care of**.*
>*He hates **being made a fool of**.*

For the rules for the use of the different passive forms, see the entries on the various tenses etc.

3 verbs not used in the passive

Not all verbs can have passive forms. Passive structures are impossible with intransitive verbs like *die* or *arrive*, which cannot have objects, because there is nothing to become the subject of a passive sentence. Some transitive verbs, too, are seldom used in the passive. Most of these are 'stative verbs' (verbs which refer to states, not actions). Examples are *fit, have, lack, resemble, suit.*

>*They **have** a nice house.* (BUT NOT ~~A nice house **is had** by them.~~)
>*My shoes **don't fit** me.* (BUT NOT ~~I'm not fitted by my shoes.~~)
>*Sylvia **resembles** a Greek goddess.*
> (BUT NOT ~~A Greek goddess **is resembled** by Sylvia.~~)
>*Your mother **lacks** tact.* (BUT NOT ~~Tact **is lacked** . . .~~)
>*She **was having** a bath.* (BUT NOT ~~A bath **was being had** by her.~~)

Some prepositional verbs are mainly used in the active.

>*Everybody **agreed with** me.* (BUT NOT ~~I was agreed with by everybody.~~)
>*We **walked into** the room.* (BUT NOT ~~The room **was walked into**.~~)

There are no clear rules about this, and students have to learn by experience which verbs cannot be used in the passive.

4 confusing forms

Students often confuse active and passive verb forms in English. Typical mistakes:

>~~I was very **interesting** in the lesson.~~
>~~We were **questioning** by the immigration officer.~~
>~~She **has** put in prison for life.~~

Mistakes like these are not surprising, because:
(1) *Be* is used to make both passive verb forms and active progressive tenses.
(2) Past participles are used to make both passive verb forms and active perfect tenses.

Compare:

>*He **was** calling.* (active – past progressive)
>*He **was called**.* (passive – simple past)
>*He has **called**.* (active – present perfect simple)

For more about transitive and intransitive verbs, see 579.2.
For the position of prepositions in passive clauses, see 440.
For active verb forms, see 10.

408 **passives** (2): agent

In a passive clause, we usually use a phrase beginning with *by* if we want to mention the *agent* – the person or thing that does the action, or that causes what happens. (Note, however, that agents are mentioned in only about 20 per cent of passive clauses.)

> *All the trouble was caused **by your mother**.*
> *I was shocked **by your attitude**.*
> *These carpets are made **by children who work twelve hours a day**.*

After the past participles of some stative verbs, including some which are used like adjectives, other prepositions can be used instead of *by* (see 405.5).

> *We were **worried about/by** her silence.*
> *Are you **frightened of** spiders?*

With is used when we talk about an instrument which is used by an agent to do an action.

> *He was shot (by the policeman) **with a rifle**.*

For more about *with* and *by*, see 117.

409 **passives** (3): choice of passive structures

1 **active or passive?**

We often choose to use passive structures when we want to talk about an action, but are not interested in saying who or what does/did it. Passives without 'agents' (see 408) are common in academic and scientific writing for this reason.

> *The positive hydrogen atoms **are attracted** to the negative oxygen atoms.*
> *Those pyramids **were built** around 400 AD.*
> *Too many books **have been written** about the Second World War.*

We often prefer to begin a sentence with something that is already known, or that we are already talking about, and to put the 'news' at the end. This is another common reason for choosing passive structures – often including agents. Compare:

> *John**'s painting** my portrait.* (active verb so that the 'news' – the portrait – can go at the end)
> *'Nice picture.' 'Yes, it **was painted** by my grandmother.'* (passive verb so that the 'news' – the painter – can go at the end)

Longer and heavier expressions often go at the end of a clause, and this can also be a reason for choosing a passive structure.

> *I **was annoyed** by Mary wanting to tell everybody what to do.*
> (More natural than *Mary wanting to tell everybody what to do annoyed me* – the phrase *Mary . . . do* would make a very long subject.)

2 **meaning and grammar**

Meaning and grammar do not always go together. Not all active verbs have 'active' meanings; for instance, if you say that somebody *receives* something or *suffers*, you are really saying that something is done to him/her. Some English active verbs might be translated by passive or reflexive verbs in certain other languages (e.g. *My shoes **are wearing out***; *She **is sitting***;

*Suddenly the door **opened**). And some English passives might be translated by active or reflexive verbs (e.g. *I **was born** in 1956; English **is spoken** here*). Some verbs can be used in both active and passive forms with similar meanings: for example *to worry / to be worried; to drown / to be drowned* (see 169). Sometimes active and passive infinitives can be used with very similar meanings: for example *There's a lot of work **to do / to be done*** (for details, see 287).

For more about verbs like *open* ('ergative verbs'), see 579.3.
For more about reflexive verbs, see 471.
For active and passive past participles, see 404.3.
For *-ing* forms with passive meanings after *need* and *want* (e.g. *My watch **needs cleaning***), see 293.3.
For more about the way information is organised in sentences, see 289.

410 **passives** (4): verbs with two objects

Many verbs, such as *give, send, show, lend,* can be followed by two objects, an 'indirect object' and a 'direct object'. These usually refer to a person (indirect object) and a thing (direct object). Two structures are possible.

A. verb + indirect object + direct object

She gave her sister the car.
I had already shown the policewoman Sam's photo.

B. verb + direct object + preposition + indirect object

She gave the car to her sister.
I had already shown Sam's photo to the policewoman.

Both of these structures can be made passive.

A. indirect object becomes subject of passive verb

*Her sister **was given** the car.*
*The policewoman **had** already **been shown** Sam's photo.*

B. direct object becomes subject of passive verb

*The car **was given** to her sister.*
*Sam's photo **had** already **been shown** to the policewoman.*

The choice between the two passive structures may depend on what has been said before, or on what needs to be put last in the sentence (see 289 for more about 'information structure'). Structure A (e.g. *Her sister was given the car*) is probably the more common of the two. More examples:
I've just been sent a whole lot of information.
You were lent ten thousand pounds last year.
The visitors were shown a collection of old manuscripts.
The headmaster was sent an invitation.

In structure B (e.g. *The car was given to her sister*), prepositions are sometimes dropped before indirect object pronouns.
*This watch was given **(to) me** by my father.*

Other common verbs used in these structures include *pay, promise, refuse, tell, offer.* Note that *explain* and *suggest* cannot be used in structure A (see 204, 545).

> *The problem was explained to the children.*
> (BUT NOT ~~The children were explained the problem.~~)
> *A meeting place was suggested to us.*
> (BUT NOT ~~We were suggested a meeting place.~~)

For more details of verbs with two objects, see 583.

411 passives (5): sentences with infinitive and clause objects

Some sentences have infinitives or clauses as their objects. These cannot normally become the subjects of passive sentences.

> *John hoped **to meet her**.*
> (BUT NOT ~~To meet her was hoped by John.~~)
> *They all thought **that she was a spy**.*
> (BUT NOT ~~That she was a spy was thought by them all.~~)
> *We felt **that he was the right man for the job**.*
> (BUT NOT ~~That he was . . . was felt.~~)
> *The newspapers say **that his company is in trouble**.*
> (BUT NOT ~~That his company is in trouble is said . . .~~)

However, passive structures are often possible if *it* is used as a preparatory subject for a clause (see 301).

> *It **was thought** that she was a spy.*
> *It **was felt** that he was the right man for the job.*
> *It **is said** that his company is in trouble.*

For passive versions of **object + infinitive** structures (e.g. *They thought her to be a spy / She was thought to be a spy*), see next section.

412 passives (6): verbs with object + infinitive

1 passive structures with following infinitive

Many verbs can be followed by **object + infinitive** (see 284).

> *He **asked me to send** a stamped addressed envelope.*
> *They **believe him to be** dangerous.*
> *We **chose Felicity to be** the Carnival Queen.*

In most cases, these structures can be made passive.

> *I **was asked to send** a stamped addressed envelope.*
> *He **is believed to be** dangerous.*
> *Felicity **was chosen to be** the Carnival Queen.*
> *We **were told not to come** back.*
> *They **are allowed to visit** Harry once a week.*
> *He **is known to be** a criminal.*
> *Moriarty **is thought to be** violent.*

Note that with *say* the infinitive structure is only possible in the passive.
> *His company **is said to be** in trouble.*
> (BUT NOT ~~They say his company to be in trouble.~~)

In some other cases, the infinitive structure is more common in the passive than in the active (see 580.3).

2 infinitives without *to*

Hear, see, make and *help* can be followed, in active structures, by **object + infinitive without *to*** (see 277). In passive structures *to*-infinitives are used. Compare:

– *I **saw him come** out of the house.*
  *He **was seen to come** out of the house.*
– *They **made him tell** them everything.*
  *He **was made to tell** them everything.*

3 preparatory *there*

With some verbs (e.g. *say, think, feel, report, presume, understand*), the passive structure is possible with *there* as a 'preparatory subject'.
> ***There are thought to be** more than 3,000 different languages in the world.*
> (= *It is thought that **there are** ...*)
> ***There was said to be** disagreement between the Prime Minister and the Home Secretary.*

4 perfect, progressive and passive infinitives

A passive verb can be followed by a perfect, progressive or passive infinitive.
> *He is believed **to have crossed** the frontier last night.*
> *I was told **to be waiting** outside the station at 6 o'clock.*
> *The hostages are expected **to be released** today.*

5 exceptions: wanting and liking

Verbs that refer to wanting, liking and similar ideas cannot usually be used in passive structures with following infinitives.
> *Everybody **wanted Doris to be** the manager.*
> (BUT NOT ~~Doris was wanted to be the manager.~~)
> *We **like our staff to say** what they think.*
> (BUT NOT ~~Our staff are liked to say what they think.~~)

413 **passives** (7): object complements

After some verbs the direct object can be followed by an 'object complement' – a noun or adjective which describes or classifies the object.
> *Queen Victoria considered him **a genius**.*
> *They elected Mrs Sanderson **President**.*
> *We all regarded Kathy as **an expert**.*
> *Most people saw him as **a sort of clown**.*
> *The other children called her **stupid**.*
> *You've made the house **beautiful**.*

In passive clauses these are subject complements; they come after the verb.

*He was considered **a genius** by Queen Victoria.*
*Mrs Sanderson was elected **President**.*
*Kathy was regarded as **an expert**.*
*He was seen as **a sort of clown**.*
*She was called **stupid** by the other children.*
*The house has been made **beautiful**.*

For more about object complements, see 580.

414 **passives** (8): finished-result verbs

Some verbs refer to actions that produce a finished result. Examples are *cut, build, pack, close*. Other verbs do not: for example *push, live, speak, hit, carry*. The past participles of finished-result verbs, and some of their passive tenses, can have two meanings. They can refer to the action, or they can describe the result (rather like adjectives). Compare:

*The theatre **was closed** by the police on the orders of the mayor.*
      (refers to the action of closing)
*When I got there I found that the theatre **was closed**.*
      (refers to the state of being shut – the result of the action)
Because of this, for example, present passive forms can have similar meanings to present perfect passives.

*The vegetables **are** all **cut up** – what shall I do now?*
      (= *The vegetables **have** all **been cut up** ...*)
*I got caught in the rain and my suit's **ruined**.*
      (= ... **has been ruined**.)
*I think your ankle **is broken**.*
      (= ... **has been broken**.)

415 **past time** (1): talking about the past in English

1 six different tenses

In English, six different tenses are used to talk about the past:

- ☐ the simple past (*I worked*)
- ☐ the past progressive (*I was working*)
- ☐ the simple present perfect (*I have worked*)
- ☐ the present perfect progressive (*I have been working*)
- ☐ the simple past perfect (*I had worked*)
- ☐ the past perfect progressive (*I had been working*)

The differences between these tenses are quite complicated. Some English tenses express meanings (e.g. completion, continuation, present importance) which are not expressed by verb forms in all other languages, and this can make the use of tenses difficult for students to learn. The most important rules for past and perfect tenses are given in the following sections.

2 progressive forms

Progressive forms (also called 'continuous' forms) are used especially when we describe a past event as going on or continuing (perhaps at a particular time, or up to a particular time).

> *When you phoned I **was working** in the garage.*
> *I was tired because I **had been working** all day.*

For general information about progressive verb forms, see 450. For details of the use of particular progressive forms to talk about the past, see the following sections.

3 perfect forms

Perfect forms are used especially when we want to suggest a connection between a past event and the present, or between an earlier and a later past event.

> *I **have worked** with children before, so I know what to expect in my new job.*
> *After I **had worked** with Jake for a few weeks, I felt I knew him pretty well.*

Perfect forms can also suggest completion.

> *I**'ve done** the shopping. What shall I do now?*

For general information about perfect verb forms, see 423.
For details of the use of present and past perfect tenses, see the following sections.
For a list of all active verb forms, see 10.
For passive verb forms, see 407.

416 **past time** (2): the simple past tense

1 forms (regular verbs)

Affirmative	Question	Negative
I worked	did I work?	I did not work
you worked	did you work?	you did not work
he/she/it worked	did he/she/it work?	he/she/it did not work
etc	etc	etc

Contracted negatives (see 144): *I didn't work, you didn't work* etc.
Negative questions (see 360): *did I not work?* or *didn't I work?* etc.
For the affirmative past forms of common irregular verbs, see 300.
Questions and negatives of irregular verbs are made in the same way as those of regular verbs (with ***did* + infinitive**).

For detailed information about question structures, see 461–466.
For negatives, see 358–362.
For passive forms (e.g. *Work **was done***), see 407.   ▶

2 pronunciation of -*ed*

The regular past ending -*ed* is pronounced as follows:
- /d/ after vowels and voiced consonants
  (except /d/): /ð/, /b/, /v/, /z/, /ʒ/, /dʒ/, /g/, /m/, /n/, /ŋ/, /l/
  tried /traɪd/   *clothed* /kləʊðd/
  used /juːzd/   *failed* /feɪld/
- /t/ after unvoiced consonants
  (except /t/): /θ/, /p/, /f/, /s/, /ʃ/, /tʃ/, /k/
  stopped /stɒpt/   *laughed* /lɑːft/   *worked* /wɜːkt/
  passed /pɑːst/   *watched* /wɒtʃt/
- /ɪd/ after /d/ and /t/
  ended /'endɪd/   *started* /'stɑːtɪd/

3 spelling of regular affirmative past tense forms

Most regular verbs: add -*ed*	work → work**ed** help → help**ed** start → start**ed** rain → rain**ed** stay → stay**ed** show → show**ed** wonder → wonder**ed** visit → visit**ed** gallop → gallop**ed**
Verbs ending in -*e*: add -*d*	hope → hope**d** decide → decide**d**
Verbs ending in one stressed vowel + one consonant (except *w* or *y*): double the consonant and add -*ed*	shop → shop**ped** plan → plan**ned** refer → refer**red** regret → regret**ted**
Verbs ending in consonant + -*y*: change *y* to *i* and add -*ed*	hurry → hurr**ied** cry → cr**ied** study → stud**ied**

Verbs ending in -*c* have *ck* in the past (e.g. *picnic* → *picnicked*).
In British English, -*l* is doubled in the past after a short vowel even if the
vowel is not stressed: *travel* → *travelled*.

4 use

We use the simple past tense to talk about many kinds of past events: short,
quickly finished actions and happenings, longer situations, and repeated
events.
*Peter **broke** a window last night.*
*I **spent** all my childhood in Scotland.*
*Regularly every summer, Janet **fell** in love.*

The simple past is common in story-telling and when we are telling people about past events.

> *One day the Princess **decided** that she **didn't like** staying at home all day, so she **told** her father that she **wanted** to get a job...*

The simple past is often used with references to finished periods and moments of time.

> *I **saw** John **yesterday morning**. He **told** me...*

In general, the simple past tense is the 'normal' one for talking about the past; we use it if we do not have a special reason for using one of the other tenses.

For the use of the simple past with a present or future meaning, see 422.
For special uses in subordinate clauses, see 556.

417 **past time** (3): the past progressive tense

1 forms

Affirmative	Question	Negative
I was working	was I working?	I was not working
you were working	were you working?	you were not working
etc	etc	etc

For passive forms (e.g. *Work **was being** done*), see 407.

2 use

We use the past progressive to say that something was in progress (going on) around a particular past time.

> *'What **were** you **doing** at eight o'clock yesterday evening?' 'I **was watching** TV.'* (NOT *'What **did you do**...?' 'I **watched** TV.'*)
> *When I got up this morning the sun **was shining**, the birds **were** singing,...* (NOT *...the sun **shone**, the birds **sang**...*)

Another use of the past progressive is to stress that an activity was in progress at every moment during a period of time.

> *I **was painting** all day yesterday.*
> *They **were quarrelling** the whole time they were together.*

Some verbs are not used in progressive forms (see 451).

> *I tried a bit of the cake to see how it **tasted**.* (NOT *...how it **was tasting**.*)

3 past progressive and simple past: 'background' events

We often use the past progressive together with a simple past tense. The past progressive refers to a longer 'background' action or situation; the simple past refers to a shorter action or event that happened in the middle of the longer action, or that interrupted it.

> *As I **was walking** down the road, I **saw** Bill.*
> *The phone **rang** while I **was having** dinner.*
> *Mozart **died** while he **was composing** the Requiem.*
> *The Presidential motorcade **was moving** slowly through the Central Square. The crowds **were cheering**. Photographers **were jostling** each other for the best positions. Suddenly a woman **screamed**...*

▶

4 past progressive and simple past: temporary and permanent

The past progressive, like other progressive forms (see 450), is used for temporary actions and situations. When we talk about longer, more permanent situations we use the simple past. Compare:
- *It happened while I **was living** in Eastbourne last year.*
  *I **lived** in London for ten years while I was a child.*
- *When I got home, I found that water **was running** down the kitchen walls.*
  *Explorers believed that the river **ran** into the Atlantic.*

5 past progressive and simple past: repeated actions

The past progressive is not the normal tense for talking about repeated or habitual past actions. The simple past is usually used with this meaning.
> *I **rang** the bell six times.* (NOT ~~I was ringing the bell six times.~~)
> *When I was a child we **made** our own amusements.*
> (NOT *... we **were making** our own amusements.*)

However, the past progressive is possible if the repeated actions form a 'background' for the main action.
> *At the time when it happened, I **was seeing** a lot of Belinda, and I **was** also **going** to the opera a lot.*

See also 'special uses', below.

6 special uses

Because we often use the past progressive to talk about something that is a 'background', not the main 'news', we can make something seem less important by using this tense.
> *I **was talking** to the President last night, and she said ...* (as if there was nothing special for the speaker about talking to the President)

The past progressive can be used with *always, continually* and similar words to talk about things that happened repeatedly and unexpectedly, or in an unplanned way.
> *Aunt Lucy **was always turning up** without warning and **bringing** us presents.*
> *I didn't like him – he **was continually borrowing** money.*

For more about this use of progressive forms with *always* etc, see 452.
For the 'distancing' use of past progressives (e.g. *I **was wondering** whether you'd like to come out with me this evening*), see 161.

418 past time (4): the simple present perfect tense

1 forms

Affirmative	Question	Negative
I have worked	have I worked?	I have not worked
you have worked	have you worked?	you have not worked
etc	etc	etc

In older English, some present perfect forms were made with *be*, not *have* (e.g. *Winter **is** come*). This does not normally happen in modern English.

For passive forms (e.g. *The work **has been done***), see 407.
For sentences like *The potatoes **are** all **gone***, see 233.
For sentences like *Are you **finished** yet*, see 211.
For other active uses of *be* + past participle, see 404.

2 other languages

In some other languages there are tenses which are constructed like the English present perfect (compare English *I have worked*, French *j'ai travaillé*, German *ich habe gearbeitet*, Italian *ho lavorato*, Spanish *he trabajado*). Note that the English present perfect is used rather differently from most of these similar tenses in other languages.

3 finished events connected with the present

We can use the simple present perfect to say that a finished action or event is connected with the present in some way. If we say that something *has happened*, we are thinking about the past and the present at the same time.

> *I can't go on holiday because I **have broken** my leg.*
> (NOT *~~I can't go on holiday because I broke my leg.~~*)

We could often change a simple present perfect sentence into a present sentence with a similar meaning.

> *I've **broken** my leg.* (→ *My leg **is** broken now.*)
> ***Have** you **read** the Bible?* (→ ***Do** you **know** the Bible?*)
> *Some fool **has let** the cat in.* (→ *The cat **is** in.*)
> *Utopia **has invaded** Fantasia.* (→ *Utopia **is** at war with Fantasia.*)
> *Mary **has had** a baby.* (→ *Mary now **has** a baby.*)
> *Our dog **has died**.* (→ *Our dog **is** dead.*)
> *All the wars in history **have taught** us nothing.* (→ *We **know** nothing.*)
> *My experience at school, all those years ago, **has given** me a permanent hatred of authority.* (→ *I **hate** authority.*)

The present perfect is often used to express the idea of completion or achievement.

> *At last! I've **finished**!*
> ***Have** you **done** all the housework?*

We do not use the present perfect if we are not thinking principally about the present. Compare:

– *I've **travelled** in Africa a lot.* (I know Africa.)
> *Some people think that Shakespeare **travelled** a lot in Germany.*
> (NOT *~~Some people think that Shakespeare has travelled~~* ...)
– *We've **learnt** enough to pass the exam.* (The exam is still to come.)
> *We **learnt** enough to pass the exam.* (The exam is over.)
– *Look what John's **given** me!* (focus on the gift)
> *Who **gave** you that?* (focus on the past action of giving)

We do not use the present perfect in story-telling.

> *Once upon a time there **was** a beautiful princess who **lived** ...* ▶

4 finished events: news

The simple present perfect is the most normal tense for giving news of recent events.

> *And here are the main points of the news again. The pound **has fallen** against the dollar. The Prime Minister **has said** that the government's economic policies are working. The number of unemployed **has reached** five million. There **has been** a fire ...*

The present perfect is not often used to talk about a finished event, if we say when it happened (see below). Compare:

– *There **has been** an explosion at Edinburgh Castle.*
  *There **was** an explosion at Edinburgh Castle **last night**.*
  (NOT *There **has been** ... last night.*)
– *I've **had** a word with the boss, and he says it's OK.*
  *I **had** a word with the boss **today**, and he says it's OK.*

Note that after using the present perfect to announce a piece of news, we usually change to simple or progressive past tenses to give the details.

> *There **has been** a plane crash near Bristol. Witnesses say that there **was** an explosion as the aircraft **was taking off**, ...*
> *The Prime Minister **has had** talks with President Kumani. During a three-hour meeting, they **discussed** the economic situation, and **agreed** on the need for closer trade links between the two countries.*

For more further details, exceptions and notes on American usage, see 419.5.

5 finished events with expressions of 'time up to now'

We often use the simple present perfect for past events when we are thinking of a period of time continuing up to the present – for example when we use indefinite time adverbs that mean 'at some / any time up to now', like *ever, before, never, yet, already.*

> ***Have** you **ever seen** a ghost?*
> *You've **only ever called** me 'darling' once.*
> *I'm sure we've **met before**.*
> *She's **never apologised** for anything in her life.*
> *'**Has** Ben **come yet**?' 'Yes, and he's **already started** to make trouble.'*

If we use a more definite expression of 'time up to now' (e.g. *today, this week*), we usually prefer a simple past tense in affirmative clauses. Compare:

– *I've **already spoken** to the boss about my holiday.*
  *I **spoke** to the boss **today** about my holiday.*
    (More natural than *I've **spoken** to the boss today ...*)
– ***Have** you **seen** John **this week**?*
  *I **haven't seen** John **this week**.*
  *I **saw** John this week, and he says ...*
    (More natural than *I've **seen** John this week ...*)

And with adverbs of finished time (e.g. *yesterday, last weekend*) the present perfect is very unusual (see paragraph 7 below).

For the present perfect progressive with 'time up to now', see 420.3.
For other tenses with *ever*, see 197.

6 repetition and continuation to now

We can use the simple present perfect to say that something has happened several times up to the present.

I've written six letters since lunchtime.
How often have you been in love in your life?

We often use the simple present perfect to talk about how long present situations have lasted. Note that present tenses are not used in this way.

I've studied hard for years. (NOT *I study hard for years.*)
We've known each other since 1960. (NOT *We know each other since 1960.*)
I've never liked you.
How long have you been a doctor? (NOT *How long are you a doctor?*) –
We've always lived here.

We can also use the present perfect progressive in this way. For the difference, see 420.4–6.

In an informal style, simple past tenses are sometimes possible with *always*, *ever* and *never* when they refer to 'time up to now'.

I always knew I could trust you. (OR *I've always known . . .*)
Did you ever see anything like that before? (OR *Have you ever seen . . . ?*)

For the difference between *for* and *since*, see 214. For tenses with *since*, see 499.
For sentences like *This is the first time I have been here*, see 419.7.

7 expressions of finished time: present perfect not used

We do not often use the present perfect with expressions that refer to a completely finished period of time, like *yesterday, last week, then, when, three years ago, in 1970*. This is because the present perfect focuses on the present, and time-expressions like these focus on the past, so they contradict each other.

I saw Lucy yesterday. (NOT *I have seen Lucy yesterday.*)
Tom was ill last week. (NOT *Tom has been ill last week.*)
What did you do then? (NOT *What have you done then?*)
She died three years ago. (NOT *She has died three years ago.*)
He was born in 1970. (NOT *He has been born in 1970.*)

For tenses with *just* and *just now*, see 305.

8 time not mentioned

We use the present perfect when we are thinking of a period of 'time up to now', even if we do not mention it. On the other hand, we do not use the present perfect when we are thinking of a particular finished time, even if we do not mention it. Compare:

– *Have you seen 'Romeo and Juliet'?*
    (*Have you ever seen it?* OR *Have you seen the current production?*)
  Did you see 'Romeo and Juliet'?
    (Did you see the production on TV **last night**?)
– *You've done a lot for me.* (. . . **up to now**)
  My grandfather did a lot for me. (. . . **when he was alive**)

▶

In some cases, there is little difference between the two points of view, and past and perfect tenses are both possible.

*Welcome home! I(**'ve**) **missed** you.*
*We (**have**) **heard** that you have rooms to let.*

For present perfect tenses in clauses referring to the future (e.g. *I'll take a rest when I've* **finished** *cleaning the kitchen*), see 556.

419 past time (5): simple present perfect and simple past (advanced points)

1 origins

We normally use the simple present perfect when we are thinking about past events together with their present results (see 418.3).

*I can't come to your party because I've **broken** my leg.*

However, we usually prefer a simple past tense when we identify the person, thing or circumstances responsible for a present situation (because we are focusing on the past cause, not the present result). Compare:

– *Some fool **has let** the cat in.*
*Who **let** that cat in?* (NOT *Who **has let** that cat in?*)
– *Look what John **has given** me!*
*Who **gave** you that watch?* (NOT *Who**'s given** you that watch?*)

Other examples:

*'Why are you crying?' 'Granny **hit** me.'* (NOT *...'Granny **has hit** me.'*)
*The Chinese **invented** paper.* (NOT *The Chinese **have invented** paper.*)
*That's a nice picture. **Did** you **paint** it yourself?*
*Some people think that 'Pericles' **was** not **written** by Shakespeare.*
*I'm glad you **were** born.*   *How **did** you **get** that bruise?*

2 expectation and reality

We use a past tense to refer to a belief that has just been shown to be true or false.

*It's not as big as I **expected**.* (NOT *...as I **have expected**.*)
*You're older than I **thought**.* (NOT *...than I **have thought**.*)
*But you **promised** ...!* (NOT *But you **have promised** ...!*)

3 present perfect with past time adverbs

Grammars usually say that the present perfect tenses cannot be used together with expressions of finished time – we can say *I **have seen** him* or *I **saw** him yesterday*, but not *I **have seen** him yesterday*. In fact, such structures are unusual but not impossible (though learners should avoid them). Here are some real examples taken from news broadcasts, newspaper articles, advertisements, letters and conversations.

*France **has detonated** a Hiroshima-sized nuclear bomb on Mururoa Atoll in the South Pacific **at 17.02 GMT on Wednesday**.*
*Police **have arrested** more than 900 suspected drugs traffickers in raids throughout the country **on Friday and Saturday**.*
*... a runner who**'s beaten** Linford Christie **earlier this year**.*

*A 24-year-old soldier **has been killed** in a road accident **while on patrol last night**.*

*A lot of the drivers will be thinking about the circuit, because **we've had** some rain **earlier today**.*

*The horse's trainer **has had** a winner here **yesterday**.*

*... indicating that the geological activity **has taken place a very long time ago**.*

*Perhaps what **has helped** us to win eight major awards **last year alone** ...*

*I **have stocked** the infirmary cupboard **only yesterday**.*

*I am pleased to confirm that Lloyds Bank ... **has opened** a Home Loan account for you **on 19th May 1982**.*

4 simple past for news

Recently, some British newspapers have started regularly using the simple past for smaller news announcements – probably to save space. Some authentic examples from the front page of one newspaper:

*The Swedish prosecutor leading the Olaf Palme murder hunt **resigned** after accusing police chiefs of serious negligence.*

*An unnamed Ulster businessman **was shot** dead by terrorists ...*

*Driving wind and rain **forced** 600 out of 2,500 teenagers to abandon the annual 'Ten Tor' trek across Dartmoor.*

5 American English

In American English the simple past is often used to give news.

***Did** you **hear**? Switzerland **declared / has declared** war on Mongolia!*
   (GB ***Have** you **heard**? Switzerland **has declared** war ...*)

*Uh, honey, I **lost / I've lost** the keys.* (GB *...**I've lost** ...*)

*Lucy **just** called.* (GB *Lucy **has** just **called**.*)

In American English, it is also possible to use the simple past with indefinite past-time adverbs like *already, yet, ever* and *before.*

***Did** you **eat already**?* (OR ***Have** you **eaten** ...?*)
   (GB ***Have** you **eaten already**?*)

*I **didn't call** Bobby **yet**.* (OR *I **haven't called** ...*)
   (GB *I **haven't called** ...*)

For more about tenses with *just*, see 305.
For more about British-American differences, see 50.

6 bad rules

Grammars sometimes say that the present perfect is not used with expressions referring to 'definite time'. This is confusing – the present perfect is not often used with *finished* time expressions, but it actually is very common with *definite* time expressions. Compare:

*I've **lived** here for **exactly three years, seven months and two days**.*
   (present perfect with very definite time-reference)

***Once upon a time** a little girl **lived** with her mother in a lonely house in a dark forest.* (simple past with very indefinite time-reference)

Note also that the choice between simple present perfect and simple past does not depend on whether we are talking about *finished actions*, as learners' grammars sometimes suggest (though it has a lot to do with whether we are talking about *finished time periods*). Compare:

*That cat **has eaten** your supper.* (finished action – present perfect)

*I **ate** the last of the eggs this morning.* (finished action – simple past)

The choice also does not depend directly on whether events are recent (though recent events are more likely to be 'news', and we are more likely to be concerned about their present results, so many present perfect sentences are in fact about recent events). Compare:

*The French revolution **has influenced** every popular radical movement in Europe since 1800.* (200-year-old event – present perfect)

*Ann **phoned** five minutes ago.* (very recent event – simple past)

7 *this is the first time* etc

We use a simple present perfect tense in sentences constructed with *this/it/that is the first/second/third/only/best/worst/* etc.

*This is the first time that I**'ve heard** her sing.*

(NOT ~~This is the first time that I **hear** her sing.~~)

*This is the fifth time you**'ve asked** me the same question.*

(NOT ~~This is the fifth time you **ask**...~~)

*That's the third cake you**'ve eaten** this morning.*

*It's one of the most interesting books I**'ve** ever **read**.*

When we talk about the past, we use past perfect tenses in these structures.

*It was the third time he **had been** in love that year.*

(NOT ... ~~the third time he **was in love**...~~)

For tenses with *since*, see 499.

For present perfect and simple present passives with similar meanings (e.g. *The shop **has been** / **is** closed*), see 414.

420 **past time** (6): the present perfect progressive tense

1 **forms**

Affirmative	Question	Negative
I have been working you have been working etc	have I been working? have you been working? etc	I have not been working you have not been working etc

2 **use: general**

We use the present perfect progressive, in general, to talk about situations which started in the past and are still going on, or which have just stopped and have present results.

*I**'ve been keeping** the bread in the top cupboard – is that OK?*

*Sorry I'm late. **Have** you **been waiting** long?*

*'You look hot.' 'Yes, I**'ve been running**.'*

We cannot use the present perfect progressive with expressions that refer to a finished period of time.

> *'You look tired.' 'Yes. I **was cycling** non-stop **until five o'clock**.'*
> (NOT . . . ~~*I've been cycling non-stop until five o'clock.*~~)

3 present perfect progressive and present

Both the present perfect progressive and the present (simple or progressive) can be used to talk about situations which started in the past and are still going on. The difference is that the present perfect progressive has an 'up to now' focus. It is common when we are talking about situations which are just coming to an end or may change, or when we are talking about how long a situation has lasted. Compare:

- *I **have** violin lessons every two weeks.*
  *I**'ve been having** violin lessons every two weeks, but I think I'll make it every week from now on.*
- *Who **is** she **talking** to?*
  *'Sorry I'm late, darling.' 'That's all right. I**'ve been talking** to this nice boy.'*
- *It**'s raining** again.*
  *It**'s been raining** since Christmas.* (NOT ~~*It's raining since Christmas.*~~)
- *Are you **learning** English?*
  *How long **have** you **been learning** English?*
  (NOT ~~*How long **are** you **learning** English?*~~)
- *'I hear you**'re working** at Smiths.'*
  *'Yes, I**'ve been working** there for about three months.'*
  (NOT . . . ~~*I'm working there for about three months.*~~)

For the difference between *since* and *for* in this situation, see 214.

4 progressive and simple: continuation / completion

Both the present perfect tenses (simple and progressive) can be used to talk about recent actions and situations that have present results. There is an important difference. The present perfect progressive focuses on the action / situation itself, looking at it as a continuous, extended activity (not necessarily finished). The simple present perfect, on the other hand, looks more at the ideas of completion and present result. Compare:

- *I must have a bath. I**'ve been gardening** all afternoon.*
  (focus on continuous activity)
  *I**'ve planted** a lot of new rose bushes.* (focus on result)
- *I**'ve been reading** your book.* (focus on continuous activity)
  *I**'ve read** your book.* (focus on completion)
- *I**'ve been learning** irregular verbs all afternoon.*
  (focus on continuous activity)
  *I**'ve learnt** all my irregular verbs.* (focus on completion)
- *Sorry about the mess – I**'ve been painting** the house.*
  (focus on continuous activity)
  *I**'ve painted** two rooms since lunchtime.* (focus on completion)
- *Who**'s been sleeping** in my bed?* (emphasis on continuous activity – makes the action sound longer and more annoying)
  *I think she**'s slept** enough – I'll wake her up.*

▶

5 progressive and simple: repeated actions

We can use the present perfect progressive to talk about repeated actions and events, but not if we say how often they have happened (because this stresses the idea of completion – see above). Compare:

*I've **been playing** a lot of tennis recently.*
*I've **played** tennis three times this week.*

6 progressive and simple: temporary and permanent

We often prefer the present perfect progressive to talk about more temporary actions and situations; when we talk about longer-lasting or permanent situations we often prefer the simple present perfect. Compare:

- *That man **has been standing** on the corner all day.*
  *For 900 years the castle **has stood** on the hill above the village.*
- *I **haven't been working** very well recently.*
  *He **hasn't worked** for years.*
- *I've **been living** in Sue's flat for the last month.*
  *My parents **have lived** in Bristol all their lives.*

Generally, however, both progressive and simple tenses are possible in cases like these, with a slight difference of emphasis.

*It's **been raining** / It's **rained** steadily since last Saturday.*
*Harry **has been working** / **has worked** in the same job for thirty years.*

We generally use the progressive to talk about continuous change or development, even if this is permanent.

*Scientists believe that the universe **has been expanding** steadily since the beginning of time.*

7 non-progressive verbs

Some verbs are not used in progressive forms (see 451), even if the meaning is one for which a progressive form is more suitable.

*I've only **known** her for two days.* (NOT *I've only been knowing her...*)
*She's **had** a cold since Monday.* (NOT *She's been having a cold...*)

421 past time (7): the past perfect tenses

1 forms

simple past perfect

Affirmative	Question	Negative
I had worked	had I worked?	I had not worked
you had worked	had you worked?	you had not worked
etc	etc	etc

past perfect progressive

Affirmative	Question	Negative
I had been working	had I been working?	I had not been working
you had been	had you been	you had not been
working	working?	working
etc	etc	etc

For passives (e.g. *The work **had been done***), see 407.

2   simple past perfect: use

The basic meanings of the simple past perfect are 'earlier past' and 'completed in the past'. A common use is to 'go back' when we are already talking about the past, so as to make it clear that something had already happened at the time we are talking about.

*I realised that we **had met** before.* (NOT *I realised that we **met** before.*)
    (NOT *I realised that we **have met** before.*)
*When I arrived at the party, Lucy **had** already **gone** home.*
    (NOT ... *Lucy already **went** home.*)
    (NOT ... *Lucy **has** already **gone** home.*)

The past perfect is common after past verbs of saying and thinking, to talk about things that had happened before the saying or thinking took place.

*I **told** her that I **had finished**.* (NOT ... *that I **(have) finished**.*)
*I **wondered** who **had left** the door open.*
*I **thought** I **had sent** the cheque a week before.*

For sentences like *I arrived before she **had finished** unpacking* (where a past perfect refers to a time later than the time of the main verb), see 96.3.
For more about tenses in indirect speech, see 481.

3   past perfect progressive: use

We use the past perfect progressive to talk about longer actions or situations which had continued up to the past moment that we are thinking about, or shortly before it.

*At that time we **had been living** in the caravan for about six months.*
*When I **found** Mary, I could see that she **had been crying**.*

4   progressive and simple: differences

Progressive tenses are often used to talk about more temporary actions and situations; when we talk about longer-lasting or permanent situations we prefer simple tenses (though both forms are often possible in the same situation, with a slight difference of emphasis). Compare:

*My legs were stiff because I **had been standing** still for a long time.*
*They lived in a castle which **had stood** on a hill above the village for 800 years.*

Progressive forms generally emphasise the continuation of an activity; we use simple tenses to emphasise the idea of completion. Compare:

*I **had been reading** science fiction, and my mind was full of strange images.*
*I **had read** all my magazines, and was beginning to get bored.*   ▶

Some verbs are not normally used in progressive forms (see 451), even if the meaning is one for which a progressive form would be more suitable.

*I **hadn't known** her for very long when we got married.*
(NOT *I ~~hadn't been knowing her~~...*)

5 time conjunctions

We can use time conjunctions to talk about two actions or events that happen one after the other. Usually the past perfect is not necessary in these cases, though it can often be used.

*After he **(had) finished** his exams he went to Paris for a month.*
*She didn't feel the same **after** her dog **(had) died**.*
*As soon as I **(had) put** the phone down it rang again.*

The past perfect can help to mark the first action as separate, independent of the second, completed before the second started. In contrast, the simple past can suggest that the first action 'leads into' the other, or that there is a cause-and-effect link between them. Compare:

– *When I **had opened** the windows I sat down and had a cup of tea.*
   (NOT *~~When I opened the windows I sat down~~...*)
   *When I **opened** the window the cat jumped out.*
   (More natural than *When I **had opened** the windows...*)
– *When I **had written** my letters I did some gardening.*
   (NOT *~~When I wrote my letters I did some gardening.~~*)
   *When I **wrote** to her she came at once.*

The past perfect is rather more common with *when* than with other time conjunctions (*when* has several meanings, so the exact time relations may have to be shown by the verb tense).

6 unrealised hopes and wishes; things that did not happen

The past perfect can be used to express an unrealised hope, wish etc.

*I **had hoped** we would be able to leave tomorrow, but it's beginning to look difficult.*
*He **had intended** to make a cake, but he ran out of time.*

After *if*, *wish* and *would rather*, the past perfect can be used to talk about past events that did not happen.

*If I **had gone** to university I would have studied medicine.*
*I wish you **had told** me the truth.*
*I'd rather she **had asked** me before borrowing the car.*

7 past perfect not used

Past perfect tenses are normally only used as described above. The past perfect is not used simply to say that something happened some time ago, or to give a past reason for a present situation.

*General Cary, who **commanded** a parachute regiment for many years, is now living in retirement.* (NOT *~~General Cary, who had commanded~~...*)
*I **left** some photos to be developed. Are they ready yet?*
(NOT *~~I had left some photos~~...*)

422 **past verb form** with present or future meaning

A past tense does not always have a past meaning. In some kinds of sentence we can use verbs like *I had, you went* or *I was wondering* to talk about the present or future.

1 after *if, unless, supposing* etc

After *if, unless* and words with similar meanings, we often use past forms to refer to the present or future.

*If I **had** the money now I'd buy a car.*
*If you **caught** the ten o'clock train tomorrow you **could** be in Edinburgh by supper-time, unless the train **was** delayed, of course.*
*You look as if you **were** just about to scream.*
*Supposing we **didn't go** on holiday next year?*

For more about structures with *if*, see 258–264.
For *supposing* etc, see 546.
For *unless*, see 574.
For *as if*, see 74.

2 after *it's time, would rather* and *wish*

After these expressions, too, past forms can have present or future meanings.

*Ten o'clock – it's time you **went** home.*
*Don't come and see me today – I'd rather you **came** tomorrow.*
*I wish I **had** a better memory.*

For structures with *it's time*, see 304.
For *would rather*, see 469.2–3.
For *wish*, see 601.

3 distancing in questions, requests etc

We can make questions, requests and offers less direct (and so more polite) by using past tenses. (For more about 'distancing' of this kind, see 161.) Common formulae are *I wondered, I thought, I hoped, did you want*. Past progressive forms (*I was wondering* etc) make sentences even less direct.

*I **wondered** if you were free this evening.*
*I **thought** you might like some flowers.*
***Did you want** cream with your coffee, sir?*
*I **was hoping** we **could** have dinner together.*

4 'past' modals

The 'past' modal forms *could, might, would* and *should* usually have present or future reference; they are used as less direct, 'distanced' forms of *can, may, will* and *shall*.

***Could** you help me for a moment?*
*I think it **might** rain soon.*
***Would** you come this way, please?*
*Alice **should** be here soon.*

▶

5 past focus on continuing situations

If we are talking about the past, we usually use past tenses even for things which are still true and situations which still exist.

*Are you deaf? I asked how old you **were**.*
*I'm sorry we left Liverpool. It **was** such a nice place.*
*Do you remember that nice couple we met on holiday? They **were** German, **weren't** they?*
*I got this job because I **was** a good driver.*
*Bill applied to join the police last week, but he **wasn't** tall enough.*

For indirect speech examples, see 482.
For past tenses with conditional meanings, see 556.

423 perfect verb forms

1 construction

Perfect verb forms are made with *have* + past participle.

*She **has lost** her memory.* (simple present perfect tense)
*They **have been living** in France for the last year.*
    (present perfect progressive tense)
*I told him that I **had** never **heard** of the place.* (simple past perfect tense)
*When I got there the house **had been pulled** down.*
    (simple past perfect passive tense)
*We **will have finished** by tomorrow afternoon.*
    (simple future perfect tense)
*I'm sorry **to have disturbed** you.* (perfect infinitive)
***Having seen** the film, I don't want to read the book.* (perfect -*ing* form)

2 terminology and use

A perfect verb form generally shows the time of an event as being earlier than some other time (past, present or future). But a perfect form does not only show the time of an event. It also shows how the speaker sees the event – perhaps as being connected to a later event, or as being completed by a certain time. Because of this, grammars often talk about 'perfect aspect' rather than 'perfect tenses'.

For details of the use of the various perfect verb forms, see the individual entries in the book.

424 personal pronouns (1): general

1 terminology and use

The words *I, me, you, he, him, she, her, it, we, us, they* and *them* are usually called 'personal pronouns'. (This is a misleading name: *it, they* and *them* are used to refer to things as well as people.) *One* is also used as a personal pronoun (see 392). *Who* is an interrogative personal pronoun (see 594).

Personal pronouns are used when it is not necessary to use or repeat more exact noun phrases.

> *John's broken his leg. **He**'ll be in hospital for a few days.*
> (NOT ~~John's broken his leg. **John**'ll be in hospital~~...)
> *Tell Mary I miss **her**.* (NOT ~~Tell Mary I miss **Mary**.~~)

2   *you*: dialect forms

Although standard modern English uses *you* for both singular and plural, separate forms exist in certain dialects. Some speakers in Yorkshire use *thu* or *tha* as a singular subject form and *thee* as a singular object form; Irish dialects have a separate plural form *ye*, *youse* or *yiz*. Many Americans use *you guys* (to both men and women) as an informal second-person plural. In southern US speech there is a familiar second-person plural form *you all* (pronounced *y'all*), used instead of *you* when people wish to sound friendly or intimate; there is also a possessive written *you all's* or (informally) *y'all's*.

> *Hi, everybody. How're **you all** doing? What are **you all's** plans for Thanksgiving?*

For the older English forms *thee* and *thou*, see 388.
For the use of *he* and *she* to refer to animals, ships etc, see 227.
For *they, them, their* with singular reference, see 505.

3   modification of *you*

You can be modified by adjectives in a few informal British expressions such as *Poor/Clever/Lucky (old) you!* (This occasionally happens also with *me*.)

Note also the expressions *you people, you lot, you guys, you two/three/* etc.
> *What are **you guys** doing tonight?*

4   subject and object forms

I, he, she, we and *they* are used mainly as subjects before verbs. *Me, him, her, us* and *them* are used as objects and (especially in an informal style) in most other cases. (See 425 for details.)

I need help.	*It's **me** that needs help.*
*Can you help **me**?*	*You don't need help as much as **me**.*
*'Who needs help?' '**Me**.'*	*She's taller than **him**.*

For pronoun-verb agreement in sentences like *It's **me** that **needs** help*, see 425.7.

5   *it* used to identify

We use *it* to refer to a person when we are identifying him or her.
> *'Who's that over there?' '**It's** John Cook.'* (NOT ~~He's John Cook.~~)
> *'Is that our waiter?' 'No, **it** isn't.'* (NOT ~~No, he isn't.~~)
> On the phone: *Hello. **It's** Alan Williams.* (NOT ...~~I'm Alan Williams.~~)
> ***It's** your sister who plays the piano, isn't it?*

6   *it* referring to *nothing* etc

It not only refers to the names of things. We can also use *it* to refer to *nothing, everything* and *all*.

> ***Nothing** happened, did **it**?*   ***Everything**'s all right, isn't **it**?*
> *I did **all** I could, but **it** wasn't enough.*   ▶

7 *it* as 'empty' subject

We use *it* as a meaningless subject with expressions that refer to time,
weather, temperature, distances, or just the current situation.
> *It's ten o'clock.*
> *It's Monday again.*
> *It rained for three days.*
> *It's thirty degrees.*
> *It's ten miles to the nearest petrol station.*
> *It's terrible – everybody's got colds, and the central heating isn't working.*
> *Wasn't **it** lovely there!*

8 inclusive and exclusive *we*

We and *us* can include or exclude the listener or reader. Compare:
> *Shall **we** go and have a drink?* (*We* includes the listener.)
> ***We**'re going for a drink. Would you like to come with **us**?*
> (*We* and *us* exclude the listener.)

9 *us* meaning 'me'

In very informal British speech, *us* is quite often used instead of *me*
(especially as an indirect object).
> *Give **us** a kiss, love.*

10 'general' uses of pronouns

We can refer to people in general, including the speaker and hearer.
> ***We** must love one another or die.*

One can refer to people in general, including the speaker (see 392).
> ***One** should never take advice.*

You can refer to people in general, including the hearer (see 392).
> *If **you** want adventure, romance and excitement, don't live in*
> *Lower Barton.*

They can mean 'the people around' or 'the authorities' (see 392).
> ***They** say she's pregnant again.*
> *Why don't **they** pay nurses enough?*

11 politeness

It is considered polite to use names or noun phrases, rather than *he, she* or
they, to refer to people who are present.
> *'**Dad** said I could go out.' 'No, I didn't.'*
> (More polite than *'**He** said I could go out.'.*..)
> ***This lady** needs an ambulance.*

However, pronouns need to be used to avoid repetition (see 479).
> *Dad said **he** didn't mind* ... (NOT ~~*Dad said **Dad** didn't mind*~~...)

People usually mention themselves last in phrases like *you and I, she and I.*
> *Why don't **you and I** go away for the weekend?*
> (NOT ~~*Why don't **I and you** ...?*~~)
> *The invitation was for **Tracy and me**.*
> (More polite than ... *for **me and Tracy**.*)

12 personal pronouns cannot normally be left out

We cannot normally leave out personal pronouns, even if the meaning is clear without them (for some exceptions, see below).

It's raining. (NOT ~~Is raining.~~)

*She loved the picture because **it** reminded her of home.*
    (NOT ... ~~because reminded her of home.~~)

*They arrested Alex and put **him** in prison.* (NOT ... ~~and put in prison.~~)

*'Have some chocolate.' 'No, I don't like **it**.'* (NOT '... ~~I don't like.~~')

However, in informal speech, subject pronouns and / or auxiliary verbs are sometimes left out at the beginning of a sentence. For details of this, see 183.

Can't help you, I'm afraid. (= **I** can't ...)

Seen Paul? (= **Have you** seen Paul?)

Note that we seldom put *it* after *know*. See 306 for details.

*'It's getting late.' '**I know**.'* (NOT ~~I know it.~~)

After certain verbs (e.g. *believe, think, suppose*), we use *so* rather than *it*. (For details, see 515.)

*'Is that the manager?' 'I believe **so**.'* (NOT ... ~~'I believe (it).'~~)

In British English, personal pronouns can be dropped after prepositions in descriptive structures with *have* and *with*.

*All the trees **have** got blossom **on (them)**.*

*He was carrying a box **with** cups **in (it)**.*

13 infinitive clauses

Object pronouns are not normally used in infinitive clauses if the object of the infinitive has just been mentioned. (See 285.4 for details and exceptions.)

*She's easy **to please**.* (NOT ~~She's easy to please her.~~)

*The pie looked too nice **to eat**.* (NOT ... ~~too nice to eat it.~~)

*The bridge wasn't strong enough to **drive over**.* (NOT ... ~~to drive over it.~~)

*This dish takes two hours to **prepare**.*

14 one subject is enough

One subject is enough. We do not usually use a personal pronoun to repeat a subject that comes in the same clause.

My car is parked outside. (NOT ~~My car it is parked outside.~~)

The boss really gets on my nerves.
    (NOT ~~The boss he really gets on my nerves.~~)

The situation is terrible. (NOT ~~It is terrible the situation.~~)

However, structures like this are sometimes possible in very informal speech.

***That woman**, I'll be glad when **she** goes back home.*

*It's terrible, **the unemployment** down there.*

*He's not a bad bloke, **Jeff**.*

*It's a horrible place, **London**.*

For more about 'reinforcement tags', see 472.
For *it* as a 'preparatory subject' for an infinitive or a clause, see 301.
For *it* as a 'preparatory object', see 302.

▶

15 personal and relative pronouns

We do not use personal pronouns to repeat the meaning of relative
pronouns (see 473.5).

> *That's the girl **who** lives in the flat upstairs.* (NOT *...~~who she lives~~...*)
> *Here's the money **(that)** you lent me.*
>> (NOT *~~Here's the money (that) you lent me it.~~*)

In modern English, the structure *he/she who*... (meaning 'the person who')
is very unusual.

> ***The person who** leaves last should put the lights out.*
>> (OR ***Whoever** leaves last...*) (NOT *~~He/She who leaves last~~...*)

425 personal pronouns (2): subject and object forms

1 pronouns with two forms

Six English pronouns have one form when they are used as subjects, and a
different form for other uses – for example, when they are the objects of
verbs or prepositions.

Subject	Object
I	me
he	him
she	her
we	us
they	them
who	whom

Compare:
- ***I** like dogs.*
  *Dogs don't like **me**.*
- ***We** sent **her** some flowers.*
  ***She** sent **us** some flowers.*
- *This is Mr Perkins, **who** works with me.*
  *This is Mr Perkins, with **whom** I am working at the moment.*

Whomever is not normally used in modern English.

2 informal use of object forms

In informal English, we use object forms not only as the objects of verbs and
prepositions, but also in most other cases where the words do not come
before verbs as their subjects. Object forms are common, for example, in
one-word answers and after *be*.

> *'Who said that?' '(It was) **him**.'*   *'Who's that?' '(It's) **me**.'*

In a more formal style, we often prefer to use **subject form + verb** where
possible.

> *'Who said that?' '**He did**.'* (BUT NOT *~~He.~~'*)

It is possible to use a subject form after *be*, but this is extremely formal, and is usually considered over-correct (especially in British English).

>*It is **I**.*   *It was **he**.*

Object forms are sometimes used in co-ordinated subjects with *and* in informal speech; this is considered incorrect in more formal usage.

>***John and me** are going skiing this weekend.*
>   (More correct: *John and I*...)

3   *I* in objects

I is often used informally in co-ordinated objects; this is also considered incorrect in more formal usage.

>*Between **you and I**, I think his marriage is in trouble.*
>   (More correct: *Between **you and me**...*)
>*That's a matter for **Peter and I**.* (More correct: *... for **Peter and me**.*)

Some people use forms like *you and I* as objects because they have been corrected at school for using *you and me* as a subject, and consequently have a vague sense that *you and me* is always wrong.

4   *who(m)* in questions

Whom is not often used in informal English. We prefer to use *who* as an object, especially in questions.

>***Who** did they arrest?*
>***Who** did you go with?*

We use *whom* in a more formal style; and we must use *whom* after a preposition.

>***Whom** did they arrest?* (formal)
>*With **whom** did you go?* (very formal)

5   *who(m)* in relative clauses

In identifying relative clauses, (see 474), *whom* is unusual. Either we leave out the object pronoun, or we use *that* or *who* (see 473–474 for details).

>*There's the man **(that)/(who)** we met in the pub last night.*

In non-identifying relative clauses (see 474), we usually use *whom* as an object when necessary (but these clauses are not very common in informal English).

>*This is John Perkins, **whom** you met at the sales conference.*
>*I have a number of American relatives, most of **whom** live in Texas.*

6   *who(m) he thought* etc

In a sentence like *He was trying to find an old school friend, **who(m)** he thought was living in New Zealand*, people are often unsure whether to use *whom* (because it seems to be the object of the first following verb) or *who* (because it is the subject of the second verb). *Who* is considered more correct, but *whom* is quite often used. Another example:

>*There is a child in this class **who(m)** I believe is a musical genius.*

In cases with a following infinitive, usage is mixed, but *whom* is considered more correct.

>*There is a child in the class **who(m)** I believe to be a musical genius.*   ▶

7 *It is/was me/I* + relative clause

When a relative clause comes after an expression like *It is/was me/I*, there are two possibilities:

> object form + *that* (very informal)

*It's **me that** needs your help.*
*It was **him that** told the police.*

> subject form + *who* (very formal)

*It is **I who** need your help.*
*It was **he who** told the police.*

We can avoid being too formal or too informal by using a different structure.
*He was **the person/the one who** told the police.*

8 mixed subject and object

Sometimes a pronoun is the object of a verb or preposition, but the subject of a following infinitive or clause. Normally an object form is used in this case.

*It's for **him** to decide.* (NOT ~~It's for **he** to decide.~~)
*I think it's a good idea for **you and me** to meet soon.*
> (Considered more correct than ... *for you and **I** to meet soon*.)

*Everything comes to **him** who waits.*
> (Considered more correct than ... *to **he** who waits*.)

9 *as, than, but* and *except*

After *as* and *than*, object forms are generally used in an informal style, especially in British English.

*My sister's nearly as tall **as me**.*
*I can run faster **than her**.*

In a more formal style, subject forms are used; they are usually followed by verbs.

*My sister's nearly as tall **as I am**.*
*I can run faster **than she can**.*

But and *except* are followed by object forms (see 116 and 200).

*Everybody **but me** knew what was happening.*
*Everybody **except him** can come.*

426 piece- and group-words

1 pieces

To talk about a limited quantity of something we can use a word for a piece or unit, together with *of*, before an uncountable noun. The most general words of this kind are *piece* and *bit*. *Bit* is informal, and usually suggests a small quantity.

*a **piece/bit** of cake/bread*
*some **pieces/bits** of paper/wood*
*a **piece/bit** of news/information*

Other words are less general, and are used before particular nouns. Some common examples:

> *a **bar** of chocolate/soap*
> *a **blade** of grass*
> *a **block** of ice*
> *a **drop** of water/oil/vinegar*
> *a **grain** of sand/salt/rice/corn*
> *an **item** of information/news/clothing/furniture*
> *a **length** of material*
> *a **loaf** of bread*
> *a **lump** of sugar/coal*
> *a **slice** of bread/cake/meat*
> *a **speck** of dust*
> *a **sheet** of paper/metal/plastic/stamps*
> *a **stick** of dynamite/chalk/celery*
> *a **strip** of cloth/tape/land/water*
> *a **suit** of clothes/armour*

2   *not a ... of ...*

Some of these 'piece' words can be used in a negative structure meaning 'no ... at all'.

> *There's **not a grain of truth** in what he says.*
> *There hasn't been **a breath of air** all day.*
> *We haven't got **a scrap (of food)** to eat.*
> *He came downstairs **without a stitch of clothing** on.*

3   pairs

Pair is used for many things that normally go in twos, and with plural nouns that refer to some two-part objects (see 501.7).

> *a **pair** of shoes/socks/ear-rings*   *a **pair** of glasses/binoculars*
> *a **pair** of trousers/jeans/pyjamas*   *a **pair** of scissors/pliers*

4   collections

Special words are used before certain nouns to talk about groups or collections.

> *a **bunch** of flowers*   *a **crowd** of people*
> *a **flock** of sheep/birds*   *a **herd** of cattle/goats*
> *a **pack** of cards* (US *a **deck** of cards*)

Set is used before many uncountable and plural nouns referring to groups which contain a fixed number of things.

> *a **set** of cutlery/napkins/dishes/tyres/sparking plugs/spanners*

For *a bit* as a modifier before adjectives and adverbs, see 106.
For *a bit of a ...*, see 154.
For *an amount, a lot, a large number* etc, see 326.
For *sort, type, kind* etc, see 526.

427 place

In an informal style, *place* can often be followed directly by an infinitive or relative clause, with no connecting relative word or preposition. This is particularly common in American English.

*I'm looking for a **place to live**.*
(More formal: ... *a place to live **in*** OR ... *a place **in which** to live*.)
*There's no **place to sit** in this room.*
*You remember **the place we had lunch**?*
(More formal: ... *the place we had lunch **at**?* OR ... *the place **at which / where** we had lunch?*)
*I went back to **the place I bought the scarf**, but it was closed.*

Note also the informal expression *go places*, meaning 'become very successful in life'.

*They always said I'd **go places**, but they never told me how boring the places would be.*

For similar structures with *way, time* and *reason*, see 477.3.

428 play and game

1 nouns

A *play* is a piece of dramatic literature, written for the theatre, radio or television.

*'Julius Caesar' is one of Shakespeare's early **plays**.*

A *game* is an activity like, for example, chess, football or bridge.

*Chess is a very slow **game**.* (NOT ...*a very slow play*.)

The uncountable noun *play* can be used to mean 'playing' in general.

*Children learn a great deal through **play**.*

2 verbs

People *act* in plays or films, and *play* games or musical instruments.

*My daughter is **acting** in her school play this year.*
*Have you ever **played** rugby football?*

Play can be used with the same meaning as *act* before the name of a character in a play or film.

*I'll never forget seeing Olivier **play Othello**.*

429 please and thank you

1 requests

We use *please* to make a request more polite.

*Could I have some more rice, **please**?*
*'Would you like some help?' 'Yes, **please**.'*

Note that *please* does not change an order into a request. Compare:

Stand over there. (order)
***Please** stand over there.* (more polite order)
*Could you stand over there, **please**?* (polite request)

Please do is a rather formal answer to a request for permission.
> '*Do you mind if I open the window?*' '***Please do.***'

For more about requests, see 483.

2 when *please* is not used

We do not use *please* to ask people what they have said.
> '*I've got a bit of a headache.*' '**I beg your pardon?**'
> (NOT . . . '~~Please?~~')

We do not use *please* when we give things to people.
> '*Have you got a pen I could use?*' '*Yes,* **here you are.**'
> (NOT . . . '~~Please.~~')

Please is not used as an answer to *Thank you* (see below).
> '*Thanks a lot.*' '**That's OK.**' (NOT . . . '~~Please.~~')

3 *thank you* and *thanks*

Thanks is more informal than *thank you*.
> *Thank you.* (NOT ~~Thanks you.~~) *Thank you very much.*
> *Thanks very much.* *Thanks a lot.* (BUT NOT ~~Thank you a lot.~~)
> *Thank God it's Friday.* (NOT ~~Thanks God~~ . . .)

Indeed can be used to strengthen *very much*.
> *Thank you very much* **indeed.** (BUT NOT normally ~~Thank you indeed.~~)

Thank you for / *Thanks for* can be followed by an *-ing* form. Possessives are unnecessary and are not used.
> '*Thank you* **for coming.**' '*Not at all. Thank you* **for having** *me.*'
> (NOT '~~Thank you for your coming.~~' . . .)

4 accepting and refusing

We often use *Thank you* / *Thanks* like *Yes, please,* to accept offers.
> '*Would you like some potatoes?*' '**Thank you.**' '*How many?*'

To make it clear that one wishes to refuse something, it is normal to say *No, thank you* / *No, thanks.*
> '*Another cake?*' '**No, thanks.** *I've eaten too many already.*'

Note that *Yes, thanks* is not used to accept offers, but to confirm that things are all right.
> '*Have you got enough potatoes?*' '**Yes, thanks.**'

5 replies to thanks

In English, there is not an automatic answer to *Thank you*; British people, especially, do not usually answer when they are thanked for small things. If a reply is necessary, we can say *Not at all* (rather formal), *You're welcome, Don't mention it, That's (quite) all right* or *That's OK* (informal British). Compare:
> '*Could you pass the salt?*' '*Here you are.*' '**Thanks.**' (no answer)
> '*Here's your coat.*' '**Thanks.**' (no answer)
> '**Thanks so much** *for looking after the children.*' '**That's all right**. *Any time.*'
> (answer necessary)

For more about the language of common social situations, see 520.

430 point of view

From somebody's point of view is not quite the same as *in somebody's view/opinion*. It usually means something more like 'from somebody's position in life' (for example as a student, as a woman, as a Greek or as a Catholic), and is used to talk about how somebody is affected by what happens. Compare:
– ***In my opinion**, war is always wrong.*
    (NOT *From my point of view, war is always wrong.*)
    *He wrote about the war **from the point of view** of the ordinary soldier.*
– ***In my view**, it's a pretty good school.*
    *You have to judge a school **from the child's point of view**.*
– ***In Professor Lucas's opinion**, everybody should work a 20-hour week.*
    ***From the employers' point of view**, a 20-hour week would cause a lot of problems.*

431 politics and policy

Politics (usually singular but always with *-s* – see 501.3) is used to talk about the theory and practice of government, the profession of government, conflicts between governing groups, and related ideas.
>   *I don't know much about **politics**, but I always support the Radical Conservative Centre Coalition Party.*
>   *You talk beautifully – you should be in **politics**.*

Policy means a 'political line' or a rule of behaviour (not necessarily connected with politics).
>   *After the war, British foreign **policy** was rather confused.*
>   (NOT *...British foreign **politics**...*)
>   *It's not my **policy** to believe everything I hear.*
>   *It's the firm's **policy** to employ a certain number of handicapped people.*

432 possessive 's: forms and grammar

1 spelling

singular noun + *'s*	*my father's car*
plural noun + *'*	*my parents' house*
irregular plural + *'s*	*the children's room*

We sometimes just add an apostrophe (') to a singular noun ending in *-s*, especially older and foreign names.
>   *Socrates' ideas.*

But *'s* is more common.
>   *Denis's terrible wife   Tess's family*
>   *Dickens's novels   Mr Lewis's dog*

We can add *'s* or *'* to a whole phrase.
>   *the man next door's wife*
>   *Paul and Mary's dog*
>   *Henry the Eighth's six wives*

2 pronunciation

The ending *'s* is pronounced just like a plural ending (see 502).

> *doctor's* /'dɒktəz/   *dog's* /dɒgz/   *president's* /'prezɪdənts/
> *Jack's* /dʒæks/   *Madge's* /'mædʒɪz/   *Alice's* /'ælɪsɪz/
> *James's* /'dʒeɪmzɪz/

The apostrophe in a word like *parents'* does not change the pronunciation at all. But with singular classical (ancient Greek and Roman) names ending in *s'*, we sometimes pronounce a possessive *'s* even when it is not written.

> *Oedipus' little problem* /'iːdɪpəs(ɪz)/

3 possessive *'s* and other determiners

A noun cannot normally have an article or other determiner with it as well as a possessive word (see 157). Definite articles are usually dropped when possessives are used.

> *the car that is **John's** = **John's** car* (NOT ~~the John's car~~ or ~~John's the car~~)

But a possessive word may of course have its own article.

> *the car that is **the boss's** = **the boss's** car*

Compound nouns beginning with possessive words ('classifying genitives') are treated differently. Articles belonging to the possessive word are dropped.

> *He works as **a Queen's Messenger**.* (NOT *...~~a the Queen's Messenger.~~*)

When we want to use a noun with *a/an* or *this/that* etc as well as a possessive, we usually use the *'of mine'* construction (see 434).

> *She's **a** cousin **of John's**.* (NOT *...~~a John's cousin.~~*)
> *I saw **that** stupid boyfriend **of Angie's** yesterday.*
> (NOT *...~~that Angie's stupid boyfriend...~~*)

4 possessive without a noun

We can use a possessive without a following noun, if the meaning is clear.

> *'Whose is that?' '**Peter's**.'*

We often talk about people's houses, shops, firms and churches in this way. The apostrophe is often dropped in the names of shops and firms.

> *We had a nice time at **John and Susan's** last night.*
> *I bought it at **Smiths**.*
> *She got married at **St Joseph's**.*

In modern English, expressions like *the doctor, the dentist, the hairdresser, the butcher* are often used without *'s*.

> *Alice is at the **hairdresser('s)**.*

For the meanings and use of possessive *'s* forms, see 379, 381.
For double possessive structures like *a friend of John's*, see 434.

433 possessives: my, mine etc

1 determiners: *my, your* etc

My, your, his, her, its, our and *their* are determiners (see 157), and are used at the beginning of noun phrases. They are not adjectives (although they are sometimes called 'possessive adjectives' in grammars and dictionaries).

> *Have you seen **my** new coat?*   ▶

One's is used in the same way.

> *It's easy to lose **one's** temper when one is criticised.*

Note the spelling of the possessive *its*. The contraction *it's* is not a possessive: it means *it is* or *it has* (see 303). Compare:

> *The dog's in a good mood. **It's** just had **its** breakfast.*
> (NOT ...~~it's breakfast.~~)

2 possessives and other determiners

My, your etc already have a 'definite' meaning, and so do not need to be used with *the*.

> *She's lost **her** keys.* (NOT ...~~the her keys.~~)

Other determiners like *a, this, that* cannot be used together with *my* etc. Instead, we use the '... *of mine*' structure (see 434).

> ***A friend of mine** has just invited me to Italy.* (NOT ~~A my friend~~...)
> *How's **that brother of yours**?* (NOT ...~~that your brother?~~)

3 pronouns: *mine, yours* etc

Mine, yours, his, hers, ours and *theirs* are pronouns, used without following nouns.

> *That coat is **mine**.*
> *Which car is **yours**?*

We do not use articles with *mine* etc.

> *Can I borrow your keys? I can't find **mine**.* (NOT ~~I can't find the mine.~~)

Its and *one's* cannot be used as pronouns, but *one's own* can be.

> *Other people's jobs always seem more interesting than **one's own**.*
> (NOT ...~~than one's.~~)

4 *whose*

Whose is used both as a determiner and as a pronoun.

> ***Whose** bag is that?* (determiner)
> ***Whose** is that bag?* (pronoun)

Note the difference between *whose* (possessive) and *who's* (= *who is* or *who has*).

5 distributive use

After a plural possessive, we do not normally use a singular noun in the sense of 'one each'. (For details, see 507.)

> *The teacher told the children to open their **books**.* (NOT ...~~their book.~~)

6 articles and possessives

We sometimes use articles instead of *my, your* etc. This happens in prepositional phrases which refer to the subject or object, mostly when we are talking about blows, pains and other things that happen to parts of people's bodies. Compare:

> *I patted her **on the shoulder**.*
> *She's got a pain **in the shoulder**.*
> *She's got a parrot **on her shoulder**.*
> (NOT ~~She's got a parrot on the shoulder.~~)

In other cases we do not normally use articles instead of possessives.
> *Katy broke **her** arm mountain climbing.* (NOT ~~Katy broke **the arm**...~~)
> *He stood there, **his** eyes closed and **his** hands in **his** pockets, looking half*
> *asleep.* (NOT ...~~**the** eyes closed and **the** hands in **the** pockets~~...)

7 *my own* etc

My own, your own etc act as the possessive forms of the reflexive / emphatic pronouns *myself, yourself* etc. Compare:
> *I'll do it **myself**.*   *I'll do it in **my own** way.* (NOT ...~~in **myself's** way.~~)

For southern US *you all's*, see 424.2.
For the older English forms *thy* and *thine*, see 388.
For details of *myself* etc, see 471. For *own*, see 400.
For possessive forms of nouns (e.g. *John's, the government's*), see 432.

434 **possessives** with **of** (**a friend of mine** etc)

We cannot usually put a possessive before another determiner and a noun. We can say *my friend, **Ann's** friend, a friend* or *that friend*, but not *a my friend* or *that Ann's friend*. Instead, we use a structure with *of* + **possessive**.

> determiner + noun + *of* + possessive

> *That policeman is **a friend of mine**.*   *How's **that brother of yours**?*
> *I met **another boyfriend of Lucy's** yesterday.*
> *He's **a cousin of the Queen's**.*   *She's **a friend of my father's**.*
> *Have you heard **this new idea of the boss's**?*
> *He watched **each gesture of hers** as if she was a stranger.*
> *My work is **no business of yours**.*

The structure has a variant in which the noun does not have possessive *'s*: this is sometimes used when talking about relationships.
> *He's a cousin **of the Queen**.*   *She's a friend **of my father**.*

The word *own* is used in a similar structure (see 400).
> *I wish I had **a room of my own**.*

435 **prefer**

When we say that we prefer one activity to another, two *-ing* forms can be used. The second can be introduced by *to* or *rather than* (more formal).
> *I prefer **riding** to **walking**.* (NOT ~~I prefer riding to **walk**.~~)
> *She prefers **making** toys for her children **rather than buying** them in*
> *the shops.*

Prefer can also be followed by an infinitive (this is normal after *would prefer*). The structure can be continued by *rather than* with an infinitive or an *-ing* form.
> *I would prefer **to spend** the weekend at home **rather than***
> ***drive/driving** all the way to your mother's.*

For more about *to* with *-ing* forms, see 295.2.

436 prepositions (1): introduction

1 vocabulary problems

It is difficult to learn to use prepositions correctly in a foreign language. Most English prepositions have several different functions (for instance, one well-known dictionary lists eighteen main uses of *at*), and these may correspond to several different prepositions in another language. At the same time, different prepositions can have very similar uses (*in the morning, on Monday morning, at night*). Many nouns, verbs and adjectives are normally used with particular prepositions: we say *the reason for, arrive at, angry with somebody, on a bus*. Often the correct preposition cannot be guessed, and one has to learn the expression as a whole. In some expressions English has no preposition where one may be used in another language; in other expressions the opposite is true. For details of some difficult cases of prepositional usage, see 437–442.

2 word order

In English, prepositions can come at the end of clauses in certain structures, especially in an informal style. For details, see 440.

> *What are you thinking about?*   *You're just the person I was looking for.*
> *She's not very easy to talk to.*   *I hate being shouted at.*

3 -*ing* forms

When we use verbs after prepositions, we use -*ing* forms, not infinitives. For details, see 295, 442.

> *She saved money by giving up cigarettes.*

When *to* is a preposition, it is also followed by -*ing* forms. For details, see 295.2.

> *I look forward to seeing you soon.*

4 prepositions before conjunctions

Prepositions are sometimes dropped before conjunctions and sometimes not. For details, see 441.

> *I'm not certain (of) what I'm supposed to do.*
> *The question (of) whether they should turn back was never discussed.*

5 prepositions and adverb particles

Words like *on, off, up, down* can function both as prepositions and as adverb particles. For the difference, see 19. For verbs with prepositions and particles, see 582.

> *She ran up the stairs.* (preposition)   *She rang me up.* (adverb particle)

437 prepositions (2): after particular words and expressions

It is not always easy to know which preposition to use after a particular noun, verb or adjective. Here are some of the most common combinations, including a number which cause difficulty to students of English. Note that alternatives are sometimes possible, and that American and British usage sometimes differ. There is only room for very brief notes here; for more complete information about usage with a particular word, consult a good dictionary.

accuse somebody **of** something (NOT ~~for~~)
*She accused me **of** poisoning her dog.*
afraid of (NOT ~~by~~)
*Are you **afraid of** spiders?*
agree with a person, opinon or policy
*I entirely **agree with** you.*
*He left the firm because he didn't **agree with** their sales policy.*
agree about a subject of discussion
*We **agree about** most things.*
agree on a matter for decision
*Let's try to **agree on** a date.*
agree to a suggestion
*I'll **agree to** your suggestion if you lower the price.*
angry with (sometimes **at**) a person **for** doing something.
*I'm **angry with** her **for** lying to me.*
angry about (sometimes **at**) something
*What are you so **angry about**?*
anxious about (= worried about)
*I'm getting **anxious about** money.*
anxious for (= eager to have)
*We're all **anxious for** an end to this misunderstanding.*
anxious + infinitive (= eager, wanting)
*She's **anxious to find** a better job.*
apologise to somebody **for** something
*I think we should **apologise to** the Smiths.*
*I must **apologise for** disturbing you.*
arrive at or **in** (NOT ~~to~~)
*What time do we **arrive at** Cardiff?*
*When did you **arrive in** England?*
ask : see 78.

bad at (NOT ~~in~~)
*I'm not **bad at** tennis.*
believe a person or something that is said (= accept as truthful / true) (no preposition)
*Don't **believe** her.*
*I don't **believe** a word she says.*
believe in God, Father Christmas etc (= believe that ... exists; trust)
*I half **believe in** life after death.*
*If you **believe in** me I can do anything.*
belong in/on/etc (= go, fit, have its place in/on/etc)
*Those glasses **belong on** the top shelf.*
belong to (= be a member of)
*I **belong to** a local athletics club.*
blue with cold, **red with** anger etc
*My hands were **blue with cold** when I got home.*
borrow: see 108.

▶

care: see 127.

clever at (NOT ~~in~~)
*I'm not very **clever at** cooking.*

congratulate/congratulations on something (US also **for**)
*I must **congratulate** you **on** your exam results.*
***Congratulations on** your new job!*

congratulate/congratulations on/for doing something
*He **congratulated** the team **on/for** having won all their games.*

crash into (NOT USUALLY ~~against~~)
*I wasn't concentrating, and I **crashed into** the car in front.*

depend/dependent on (NOT ~~from~~ or ~~of~~)
*We may play football – it **depends on** the weather.*
*He doesn't want to be **dependent on** his parents.*
But: **independent of**

details of
*Write now for **details of** our special offer.*

die of or **from**
*More people **died of** flu in 1919 than were killed in the First World War.*
*A week after the accident he **died from** his injuries.*

different : see 158.

difficulty with something, (**in**) doing something (NOT ~~difficulties to~~ ...)
*I'm having **difficulty with** my travel arrangements.*
*You won't have much **difficulty (in) getting** to know people in Italy.*

disappointed with somebody
*My father never showed if he was **disappointed with** me.*

disappointed with/at/about something
*You must be pretty **disappointed with/at/about** your exam results.*

(a) discussion about something
*We had a long **discussion about** politics.*

(to) discuss something (no preposition)
*We'd better **discuss** your travel plans.*

divide into (NOT ~~in~~)
*The book is **divided into** three parts.*

dream of (= think of, imagine)
*I often **dreamed of** being famous when I was younger.*

dream about/of (while asleep)
*What does it mean if you **dream about/of** mountains?*

dress(ed) in (NOT ~~with~~)
*Who's the woman **dressed in** green?*

drive into (NOT ~~against~~)
*Granny **drove into** a tree again yesterday.*

enter into an agreement, a discussion etc
*We've just **entered into** an agreement with Carsons Ltd.*

enter a place (no preposition)
*When I **entered** the room everybody stopped talking.*

example of (NOT ~~for~~)
*Sherry is an **example of** a fortified wine.*

explain something **to** somebody (NOT ~~explain somebody something~~)
*Could you **explain** this rule **to** me?*

fight, struggle etc **with**
*I've spent the last two weeks **fighting with** the tax office.*
frightened of or **by**: see 405.5.

get in(to) and **out of** a car, taxi or small boat
*When I **got into** my car, I found the radio had been stolen.*
get on(to) and **off** a train, plane, bus, ship, (motor)bike or horse
***We'll be getting off** the train in ten minutes.*
good at (NOT ~~in~~)
*Are you any **good at** tennis?*

(the) idea of . . .ing (NOT ~~the idea to~~ . . .)
*I don't like **the idea of getting** married yet.*
ill with
*The boss has been **ill with** flu this week.*
impressed with/by
*I'm very **impressed with/by** your work.*
increase in activity, output etc (NOT ~~of~~)
*I'd like to see a big **increase in** productivity.*
independent of or sometimes **from**; **independence from**
*She got a job so that she could be **independent of** her parents.*
*When did India get its **independence from** Britain?*
insist on (NOT ~~to~~)
*George's father **insisted on** paying.*
interest/interested in (NOT ~~for~~)
*When did your **interest in** social work begin?*
*Not many people are **interested in** grammar.*

kind to (NOT ~~with~~)
*People have always been very **kind to** me.*

(a) lack of
***Lack of time** prevented me from writing.*
(to) lack (no preposition)
*Your mother **lacks** tact.*
(to) be lacking in
*She **is lacking** in tact.*
laugh at
*I hate being **laughed at**.*
laugh about
*We'll **laugh about** this one day.*
listen to
*If you don't **listen to** people, they won't **listen to** you.*
look at (= 'point one's eyes at')
*Stop **looking at** me like that.*
look after (= take care of)
*Thanks for **looking after** me when I was ill.*
look for (= try to find)
*Can you help me **look for** my keys?*

make, made of/from: see 328.

marriage to; get/be married to (NOT ~~with~~)
*Her **marriage to** Philip didn't last very long.*
*How long have you been **married to** Sheila?*
marry somebody (no preposition)
*She **married** her childhood sweetheart.*

near (to): see 355.
nice to (NOT ~~with~~)
*You weren't very **nice to** me last night.*

operate on a patient
*They **operated on** her yesterday evening.*

pay for something that is bought (NOT ~~pay something~~)
*Excuse me, sir. You haven't **paid for** your drink.*
pleased with somebody
*The boss is very **pleased with** you.*
pleased with/about/at something
*I wasn't very **pleased with/about/at** my exam results.*
polite to (NOT ~~with~~)
*Try to be **polite to** Uncle Richard for once.*
prevent . . . from . . .ing (NOT ~~to~~)
*The noise from downstairs **prevented** me **from sleeping**.*
proof of (NOT ~~for~~)
*I want **proof of** your love. Lend me some money.*

reason for (NOT ~~of~~)
*Nobody knows the **reason for** the accident.*
remind of (and see 478)
*She **reminds** me **of** a girl I was at school with.*
responsible/responsibility for
*Who's **responsible for** the shopping this week?*
rude to (NOT ~~with~~)
*Peggy was pretty **rude to** my family last weekend.*
run into (= meet)
*I **ran into** Philip at Victoria Station this morning.*

search (without preposition) (= look through; look everywhere in/on)
*They **searched** everybody's luggage.*
*They **searched** the man in front of me from head to foot.*
search for (= look for)
*The customs were **searching for** drugs at the airport.*
shocked at/by
*I was terribly **shocked at/by** the news of Peter's accident.*
shout at (aggressive)
*If you don't stop **shouting at** me I'll come and hit you.*
shout to (= call to)
*Mary **shouted to** us to come in and swim.*
smile at
*If you **smile at** me like that I'll give you anything you want.*
sorry about something that has happened
*I'm **sorry about** your exam results.*

sorry for/about something that one has done
*I'm **sorry for/about** breaking your window.*
sorry for a person.
*I feel really **sorry for** her children.*
speak to; speak with (especially US)
*Could I **speak to/with** your father for a moment?*
suffer from
*My wife is **suffering from** hepatitis.*
surprised at / by
*Everybody was **surprised at/by** the weather.*

take part in (NOT ~~at~~)
*I don't want to **take part in** any more conferences.*
think of/about (NOT ~~think to~~)
*I'm **thinking of** studying medicine.*
*I've also **thought about** studying dentistry.*
the thought of (NOT ~~the thought to~~)
*I hate **the thought of** going back to work.*
throw . . . at (aggressive)
*Stop **throwing** stones **at** the cars.*
throw . . . to (in a game etc)
*If you get the ball, **throw** it **to** me.*
translate into (NOT ~~in~~)
*Could you **translate** this **into** Greek for me?*
trip over
*He **tripped over** the cat and fell downstairs.*
typical of (NOT ~~for~~)
*The wine's **typical of** the region.*

write: see 583.
wrong with
*What's **wrong with** Rachel today?*

For *of* after determiners, see 157.
For *by* and other prepositions with *frightened, surprised, shocked* and similar words,
see 405.5.
For more on complementation of nouns, see 377. For complementation of verbs, see 579.
For complementation of adjectives, see 12.
For more details of the use of the words listed here, and for prepositions used after words
not listed here, see a good dictionary.

438 **prepositions** (3): before particular words and expressions

This is a list of a few expressions which often cause problems. For information about other **preposition + noun** combinations, see a good dictionary.

at the cinema; **at** the theatre; **at** a party; **at** university
*What's on **at** the cinema this week?*

a book (written) **by** Joyce; a concerto (composed) **by** Mozart; a film (directed) **by** Fassbinder (NOT ~~of~~ or ~~from~~)
*I've never read anything **by** Dickens.*
by car/bike/bus/train/boat/plane/land/sea/air; **on** foot (but **in** the car, **on** a bus etc)
*Let's take our time and go **by** boat.*

for . . . reason
*My sister decided to go to America **for** several reasons.*

from . . . point of view (NOT ~~according to~~ or ~~after~~)
*Try to see it **from** my point of view.*

in . . . opinion (NOT ~~according to~~ or ~~after~~ – see 8)
In my opinion, she should have resigned earlier.
in the end = finally, after a long time
In the end, I got a visa for Russia.
at the end = at the point where something stops
*I think the film's a bit weak **at** the end.*
in pen, pencil, ink etc
*Please fill in the form **in** ink.*
in a picture, photo etc (NOT ~~on~~)
*She looks much younger **in** this photo.*
in the rain, snow etc
*I like walking **in** the rain.*
in a suit, raincoat, shirt, skirt, hat etc
*Who's the man **in** the funny hat over there?*
in a . . . voice
*Stop talking to me **in** that stupid voice.*

on page 120 etc (NOT ~~in/at~~)
*There's a mistake **on** page 120.*
on the radio; **on** TV; **on** the phone
*Is there anything good **on** TV tonight?*
*It's Mrs Ellis **on** the phone: she says it's urgent.*
on time = at the planned time; neither late nor early
*Peter wants the meeting to start exactly **on** time.*
in time = with enough time to spare; before the last moment
*He would have died if they hadn't got him to the hospital **in** time.*

439 prepositions (4): expressions without prepositions

This is a list of some common expressions in which we do not use prepositions, or can leave them out.

1 *discuss, enter, marry, lack, resemble* and *approach*

These verbs are normally followed by direct objects without prepositions.
> *We must **discuss** your plans.* (NOT *...discuss **about** your plans.*)
> *Conversation stopped as we **entered** the church.*
> (NOT *...entered **in(to)** the church.*)
> *She **married** a friend of her sister's.* (NOT *...married **with**...*)
> *He's clever, but he **lacks** experience.* (NOT *...lacks **of**...*)
> *The child does not **resemble** either of its parents.* (NOT *...resemble **to**...*)
> *The train is now **approaching** London Paddington.*
> (NOT *...approaching **to**...*)

2 *next, last* etc

Prepositions are not used before a number of common expressions of time beginning *next, last, this, that* (sometimes), *one, every, each, some, any* (in an informal style), *all*.
> *See you **next Monday**.* (NOT *...**on** next Monday.*)
> *The meeting's **this Thursday**.*
> *I'll never forget meeting you **that afternoon**.*
> *We met **one Tuesday** in August.*
> *Come **any day** you like.*
> *The party lasted **all night**.*

Note also *tomorrow morning, yesterday afternoon* etc.

3 days of the week

In an informal style, we sometimes leave out *on* before the names of the days of the week. This is very common in American English.
> *Why don't you come for a drink **(on) Monday** evening?*

4 *a* meaning 'each'

No preposition is used in expressions like *three times **a** day, sixty miles **an** hour, eighty pence **a** kilo*.
> *Private lessons cost £20 **an hour**.*

For *per* in expressions like these, see 385.19.

5 *What time...?* etc

We usually leave out *at* before *what time*.
> ***What time** does Granny's train arrive?*
> (More natural than ***At** what time...?*)

In an informal style, we can also leave out *on* before *what/which day(s)*.
> ***What day** is your hair appointment?*
> ***Which day** do you have your music lesson?*

▶

6 *about*

In an informal style, *at* is often dropped before ***about*** + **time expression**.
> *I'll see you **(at) about** 3 o'clock.*

7 **duration**

In an informal style, *for* is often left out in expressions that say how long something lasts.
> *I've been here **(for) three weeks** now.*
> ***How long** are you staying **(for)**?*

8 **measurement expressions etc after *be***

Expressions containing words like *height, weight, length, size, shape, age, colour* are usually connected to the subject of the clause by the verb *be*, without a preposition.
> ***What colour** are her eyes?* (NOT *~~Of what colour~~...?*)
> *He is just **the right height** to be a policeman.*
> *She's **the same age** as me.*
> *His head's **a funny shape**.*
> *I'm **the same weight** as I was twenty years ago.*
> ***What shoe size** are you?*

9 *(in) this way* etc

We often leave out *in* (especially in informal speech) in expressions like *(in) this way, (in) the same way, (in) another way* etc.
> *They plant corn **(in) the same way** their ancestors used to 500 years ago.*

10 *home*

We do not use *to* before *home* (see 251).
> *I'm going **home**.*

In informal English (especially American), *at* can be left out before *home*.
> *Is anybody **home**?*

11 *place*

In an informal style, *to* can be dropped in some expressions with the word *place*. This is normal in American English.
> *Let's go **(to) some place** where it's quiet.*
> *I always said you'd **go places**.* (= *become successful*)

12 **infinitive structures**

In an informal style, prepositions can be dropped in the structure **noun + infinitive + preposition** (see 286.5).
> *She has no money to buy food **(with)**.*
> *We have an hour to do it **(in)**.*

This is particularly common with the noun *place*.
> *We need a **place** to live **(in)**.*
> *She had no **place** to go **(to)**.*

For the use of prepositions after *near*, see 355.

440 **prepositions** (5): at the ends of clauses

1 **introduction**

A preposition often connects two things: (1) a noun, adjective or verb that comes before it, and (2) a 'prepositional object' – a noun phrase or pronoun that comes after the preposition.

*This is a **present for you**.*   *He's **looking at her**.*
*I'm really **angry with Joe**.*   *They **live in a small village**.*

In some structures we may put the prepositional object at or near the beginning of a clause. In this case, the preposition does not always go with it – it may stay together with 'its' verb, adjective or noun at the end of the clause. This happens especially in four cases:

wh-questions: *Who's the **present for?***
relative structures: *It's **Joe** that I'm really **angry with**.*
passives: ***She** likes to be **looked at**.*
infinitive structures: ***The village** is pleasant **to live in**.*

2 *wh*-**questions**

When a question word is the object of a preposition, the preposition most often comes at the end of the clause, especially in informal usage.

Who's** the present **for**?* (For whom** is the present?* is extremely formal.)
***What** are you looking **at**?*   ***Who** did you go **with**?*
***Where** did she buy it **from**?*   ***Which** flight is the general travelling **on**?*
***What** kind of films are you interested **in**?*

This also happens in indirect *wh*-questions, and in *what*-clauses which are not questions.

*Tell me **what** you're worried **about**.*   ***What** a lot of trouble I'm **in**!*

Some questions consist simply of **question word + preposition**.

***What with**?*   ***Who for**?*

However, this structure is unusual when there is a noun with the question word.

*With **what money**?* (NOT ~~**What money with**?~~)

For more information about question structures, see 461–466.

3 **relative clauses**

When a relative pronoun is the object of a preposition, the preposition also often goes at the end of the clause, especially in informal usage.

*This is the house **(that)** I told you **about**.*
      (Less formal than ... ***about which** I told you*.)
*You remember the boy **(who)** I was going out **with**?*
*She's the only woman **(who)** I've ever really been in love **with**.*
*That's **what** I'm afraid **of**.*

Because *whom* is unusual in an informal style, it is very rare in clauses that end with prepositions (see 474.7).

For more information about relatives, see 473–477.   ▶

4 passives

In passive structures, prepositions go with their verbs.

*I don't know where he is – his bed hasn't been **slept in**.*
*Carol **was operated on** last night.*
*I hate **being laughed at**.*

For more information about passives, see 407–414.

5 infinitive structures

Infinitive complements (see 285–286) can have prepositions with them.

*She needs other children **to play with**.*
*Can you get me a chair **to stand on**?*
*I've got lots of tapes **to listen to**.*
*It's a boring place **to live in**.*
*Their house isn't easy **to get to**.*

6 exceptions

Many common adverbial expressions consist of **preposition + noun phrase**
(e.g. *with great patience, in a temper*). In these cases, the preposition is
closely connected with the noun, and is kept as near as possible to it; it
cannot usually be moved to the end of a clause.

*I admired the **patience with** which she spoke.*
   (NOT *...the patience she spoke **with**.*)

During and *since* are not normally put at the ends of clauses.

***During** which period did it happen?*
   (NOT *Which period did it happen **during**?*)
***Since** when have you been working for her?*
   (NOT *When have you been working for her **since**?*)

7 formal structures

In a more formal style, a preposition is often put earlier in questions and
relative structures, before the question word or relative pronoun.

***With whom** did she go?*
*It was the house **about which** he had told them.*
*She was the only woman **with whom** he had ever been in love.*

This can also happen in infinitive complements, in a very formal style.
A relative pronoun is used.

*She needs other children **with whom to play**.*
*It is a boring place **in which to live**.*

Note that after prepositions *which* and *whom* can be used, but not normally
who and *that*.

Even in a very formal style, prepositions are not often put at the beginning of
questions which have *be* as the main verb.

*Who **is** it **for**, madam?* (NOT *For whom is it?*)

And the structures *where ... to, what ... like* and *what ... for* have a fixed order.

***Where** shall I send it **to**?* (BUT NOT *To where shall I send it?*)
***What** does she look **like**?* (BUT NOT *Like what does she look?*)
***What** did you buy that **for**?* (BUT NOT *For what did you buy that?*)

Prepositions cannot be moved away from passive verbs even in a formal style.

> *In my family, money was never **spoken about**.*
> (NOT *...**about** money was never **spoken**.*)

For more information about formal and informal language, see 216.
For sentences like *It's got a hole in (it); I like cakes with cream on (them)*, see 181.13.
For structures with *worth*, see 603.

441 prepositions (6): before conjunctions

Prepositions can be followed by conjunctions in some cases but not in others.

1 indirect speech; words for emotional reactions: prepositions not used before *that*

Prepositions are not used directly before the conjunction *that*. In indirect speech – after words that refer to saying, writing, thinking etc – prepositions are usually dropped before *that*-clauses. Compare:

– *I **knew about** his problems.*
  *I **knew that** he had problems.*
    (NOT *I **knew about that** he had problems.*)
– *She had no **idea of** my state of mind.*
  *She had no **idea that** I was unhappy.*
    (NOT *She had no **idea of that** I was unhappy.*)
– *I wasn't **aware of** the time.*
  *I wasn't **aware that** it was so late.*
    (NOT *I wasn't **aware of that** it was so late.*)

Prepositions are also dropped before *that* after many common words that refer to emotional reactions. Compare:

– *We are **sorry about** the delay.*
  *We are **sorry that** the train is late.*
    (NOT *...**sorry about that** the train is late.*)
– *I was **surprised at** her strength.*
  *I was **surprised that** she was so strong.*

2 *the fact that*

In other cases (not involving indirect speech or words referring to emotional reactions) prepositions cannot so often be dropped before *that*-clauses. Instead, the expression *the fact* is generally put between the preposition and *that*.

> *The judge paid a lot of attention **to the fact that** the child was unhappy at home.*
> (NOT *The judge paid a lot of attention **to that** the child...*)
> (NOT *The judge paid a lot of attention **that** the child...*)
> *He said the parents were responsible **for the fact that** the child had run away.*
> (NOT *...**responsible for that** the child had run away.*)
> (NOT *...**responsible that** the child had run away.*)

For more about *the fact that*, see 559.3.

▶

3 question words

After some very common words like *tell, ask, depend, sure, idea, look,* prepositions can be dropped before *who, which, what* and other question words. This is especially common in indirect questions. Compare:

– **Tell** me **about** your trip.
  Tell me **(about) where** you went.
– I **asked** her **about** her religious beliefs.
  I **asked** her **whether** she believed in God.
    (More natural than I **asked** her **about whether** she believed in God.)
– We may be late – it **depends on** the traffic.
  We may be late – it **depends (on) how** much traffic there is.
– I'm not **sure of** his method.
  I'm not **sure how** he does it.
    (More natural than I'm not **sure of** how he does it.)
– **Look at** this.
  Look (at) what I've got.

In other cases it is unusual or impossible to leave out the preposition.

  I'm **worried about where** she is. (NOT ~~I'm worried where she is.~~)
  The police **questioned** me **about what** I'd seen.
    (NOT ~~The police questioned me what I'd seen.~~)
  There's the **question of who**'s going to pay.
    (More natural than . . . the **question who**'s going to pay.)
  People's chances of getting jobs vary **according to whether** they live in the
    North or the South. (NOT . . . ~~according whether~~ . . .)

If does not follow prepositions; we use *whether* instead.

  I'm worried **about whether** you're happy.
    (NOT ~~I'm worried about if you're happy.~~)

For the structures (with and without preposition) that are possible after a particular verb, noun or adjective, see a good dictionary.
For more about *if* and *whether,* see 593.

442 prepositions (7): -ing forms and infinitives

Prepositions are not normally used before infinitives in English. After
verb/noun/adjective + preposition, we usually use the *-ing* form of
a following verb.

  He **insisted on being** paid at once. (NOT ~~He insisted on to be paid~~ . . .)
  I don't like the **idea of getting** married. (NOT . . . ~~the idea of to get married.~~)
  I'm not very **good at cooking**. (NOT . . . ~~good at to cook.~~)

In some cases we drop the preposition and use an infinitive. Compare:

– He **asked for** a loan.
  He **asked to borrow** some money.
– She was **surprised at** his mistake.
  She was **surprised to see** what he had done.
– We're travelling **for pleasure**.
  We're travelling **to enjoy** ourselves.

Sometimes two structures are possible. There is often a difference of meaning or use. For more details, see 296.

I'm **interested in learning** more about my family.
I was **interested to learn** that my grandfather was Jewish.

For details of the structures that are possible after a particular verb, noun or adjective, see a
good dictionary.

443 present tenses (1): introduction

1 the two present tenses

Most English verbs have two 'present' tenses. Forms like *I wait, she thinks*
are called 'simple present' or 'present simple'; forms like *I am waiting* or
she's thinking are called 'present progressive' or 'present continuous'. Modal
verbs like *can* or *must* (see 344–345) do not have progressive forms, and
some other verbs such as *know* or *contain* are rarely used in progressive
forms (see 451). The two 'present' tenses are used to refer to several different
kinds of time.

2 general time: simple present

When we talk about permanent situations, or about things that happen
regularly or all the time (not just around now), we usually use the simple
present (see 444 for details).

My parents **live** near Dover.   Water **freezes** at 0° Celsius.
I **go** to London about three times a week.

3 around now: present progressive

When we talk about temporary continuing actions and events that are going on
around now, we usually use a present progressive tense (see 445 for details).

'What **are** you **doing**?' '**I'm reading**.'
I'm going to a lot of parties these days.

4 series of events: simple present

When we talk about series of actions and events that are completed as we
speak, we usually use simple present tenses (see 446 for details).

Watch carefully. First I **take** a bowl and **break** two eggs into it. Next …
Taylor **shoots** – and it's a goal!

5 future time

In subordinate clauses, we often use present tenses to refer to the future
(see 556 for details).

I'll go wherever you **go**.
Come and see us next week if you'**re passing** through London.

6 duration

Note that we use a perfect tense, not a present tense, to say how long a
present action or situation has been going on. (See 418 and 420 for details.)

I'**ve known** her since 1960. (NOT ~~I know her since 1960.~~)
I'**ve been learning** English for three years.
      (NOT ~~I'm learning English for three years.~~)

444 **present tenses** (2): the simple present tense

1 forms

Affirmative	Question	Negative
I work	do I work?	I do not work
you work	do you work?	you do not work
he/she/it works	does he/she/it work?	he/she/it does not work
we work	do we work?	we do not work
they work	do they work?	they do not work

For passives (e.g. *The work **is done***), see 407.

2 spelling of third person singular forms

Most verbs: add -*s* to infinitive	work→works sit→sits stay→stays
Verbs ending in consonant + *y*: change *y* to *i* and add -*es*	**cry**→cri**es** **hurry**→hurri**es** **reply**→repli**es**
Verbs ending in -*s*, -*z*, -*ch*, -*sh* or -*x*: add -*es* to infinitive	miss→miss**es** buzz→buzz**es** watch→watch**es** push→push**es** fix→fix**es**
Exceptions:	have→**has** go→goes do→does

3 pronunciation of third person singular forms

The pronunciation of the -*(e)s* ending depends on the sound that comes before it. The rules are exactly the same as for the pronunciation of the plural -*(e)s* ending – see 502 for details.

Note the irregular pronunciation of *says* (/sez/, not /seɪz/) and *does* (/dʌz/, not /duːz/).

4 use: general time

We often use the simple present to talk about permanent situations, or about things that happen regularly, repeatedly or all the time.

*What **do** frogs **eat**?* (NOT ~~What **are** frogs **eating**?~~)
*Water **boils** at 100° Celsius.* (NOT ~~Water **is boiling** at 100° Celsius.~~)
*I **play** tennis every Wednesday.*
*Alice **works** for an insurance company.*

5   present time: series of events

When we talk about completed actions and events that happen as we speak or write, we usually use the simple present. This happens, for example, in demonstrations and commentaries (see 446 for more details).

> First I **take** a bowl and **break** two eggs into it. Next . . .
> (NOT ~~First I am taking a bowl~~ . . .)
> Lydiard **passes** to Taylor. Taylor to Morrison, Morrison back to Taylor . . .
> and Taylor **shoots** – and it's a goal!

6   *here comes . . .* etc

Note the structures *here comes . . .* and *there goes . . .*

> **Here comes** your husband. (NOT ~~Here is coming~~ . . .)
> **There goes** our bus – we'll have to wait for the next one.

7   promises etc

Sometimes we do things by saying special words (e.g. promising, swearing). We usually use the simple present in these cases.

> I **promise** never to smoke again. (NOT ~~I'm promising~~ . . .)
> I **swear** that I will tell the truth . . .
> I **agree**. (NOT ~~I am agreeing~~.)
> He **denies** the charge. (NOT ~~He is denying~~ . . .)

8   formal correspondence

Some fixed phrases that are used in letter-writing can be expressed either in the simple present (more formal) or in the present progressive (less formal).

> We **write** to advise you . . . (Less formal: We **are writing** to let you know . . .)
> I **enclose** my cheque for £200. (Less formal: I **am enclosing** . . .)
> I **look** forward to hearing from you.
>   (Less formal: I'm **looking** forward to hearing . . .)

9   instructions

The simple present is often used when we ask for and give directions and instructions (see 446.3 for more details).

> 'How **do** I **get** to the station?' 'You **go** straight on to the traffic lights, then you **turn** left, . . .'

10   stories

The simple present is common in informal narrative and in summaries of plays, stories etc (see 446 for more details).

> In Act I, Hamlet **meets** the ghost of his father.

11   temporary situations: non-progressive verbs

We do not usually use the simple present to talk about temporary situations or actions that are only going on around the present.

> The kettle**'s boiling** – shall I make tea? (NOT ~~The kettle boils~~ . . .)

However, the simple present is used with verbs that cannot normally be used in progressive forms (see 451).

> I **like** this wine very much. (NOT ~~I'm liking~~ . . .)
> I **believe** you. (NOT ~~I'm believing you~~.)

▶

12   talking about the future

We do not normally use the simple present to talk about the future.
>   *I promise I **won't smoke** any more.*
>   (NOT *I promise I **don't smoke** any more.*)
>   *We're going to the theatre this evening.*
>   (NOT *We go to the theatre this evening.*)
>   *'There's the doorbell.' 'I'll get it.'* (NOT *I get it.'*)

However, the simple present is used to refer to future events which are timetabled (see 223).
>   *His train **arrives** at 11.46.   I **start** my new job tomorrow.*

And the simple present is often used instead of *will* . . . in subordinate clauses that refer to the future. (For details, see 556).
>   *I'll kill anybody who **touches** my possessions.* (NOT *. . . who **will touch** . . .*)
>   *I'll phone you when I **get** home.* (NOT *. . . when I'll get home.*)

Note also the use of the simple present in suggestions with *Why don't you . . . ?*
>   *Why **don't** you **take** a day off tomorrow?*

13   *I hear* etc

The simple present is used with a perfect or past meaning in introductory expressions like *I hear, I see, I gather, I understand* (see 246).
>   *I **hear** you're getting married.*
>   *I **see** there's been trouble down at the factory.*
>   *I **gather** Peter's looking for a job.*

Quotations are often introduced with . . . *says*.
>   *No doubt you all remember what Hamlet **says** about suicide.*
>   *It **says** in the paper that petrol's going up again.*

For simple and progressive tenses in older English, see 388.

445   present tenses (3): the present progressive tense

1   forms

Affirmative	Question	Negative
I am working	am I working?	I am not working
you are working	are you working?	you are not working
etc	etc	etc

For passive forms (e.g. *The work **is being done***), see 407.

2   use: 'around now'

We use the present progressive to talk about temporary actions and situations that are going on 'around now': before, during and after the moment of speaking.
>   *Hurry up! We're all **waiting** for you!* (NOT *We all **wait** . . .*)
>   *'What **are** you **doing**?' 'I'm **writing** letters.'* (NOT *. . . 'I **write** letters'.*)

*Why **are** you **crying**? Is something wrong?* (NOT ~~Why **do you cry**?~~ ...)
*He**'s working** in Saudi Arabia at the moment.*

We can also use the present progressive to talk about what is going on around a particular time that we are thinking of.

*At seven, when the post comes, I**'m** usually **having** breakfast.*
*She doesn't like to be disturbed if she**'s working**.*
*You look lovely when you**'re smiling**.*

3 changes

We also use the present progressive to talk about developing and changing situations, even if these are very long-lasting.

*That child**'s getting** bigger every day.*
*The climate **is getting** warmer.* (NOT ~~The climate **gets** warmer.~~)
*The universe **is expanding**, and has been since its beginning.*

4 talking about the future

We often use the present progressive to talk about the future. For details, see 220.

*What **are** you **doing** tomorrow evening?*
*Come and see us next week if you**'re passing** through London.*

5 present progressive and simple present: permanent situations

We do not usually use the present progressive to talk about more long-lasting or permanent situations. Compare:
– *My sister**'s living** at home for the moment.*
  *You **live** in North London, don't you?*
– *Why **is** that girl **standing** on the table?*
  *Chetford Castle **stands** on a hill outside the town.*

6 present progressive and simple present: repeated actions

The present progressive can refer to repeated actions and events, if these are happening around the moment of speaking.

*Why **is** he **hitting** the dog?*
*Jake**'s seeing** a lot of Felicity these days.*

But we do not normally use the present progressive to talk about repeated actions and events which are not closely connected to the moment of speaking.

*I **go** to the mountains about twice a year.*
  (NOT ~~I**'m going** to the mountains about twice a year.~~)
*Water **boils** at 100° Celsius.* (NOT ~~Water **is boiling** at 100° Celsius.~~)

7 physical feelings

Verbs that refer to physical feelings (e.g. *feel, hurt, ache*) can often be used in simple or progressive tenses without much difference of meaning.

*How **do** you **feel**?* OR *How **are** you **feeling**?*
*My head **aches**.* OR *My head **is aching**.*

▶

8   verbs not used in progressive forms

Some verbs are not normally used in progressive forms. For details, see 451.

*I **like** this wine.* (NOT ~~*I'm liking this wine.*~~)

***Do** you **believe** what he says?* (NOT ~~*Are you **believing**...?*~~)

*The tank **contains** about 7,000 litres at the moment.*
(NOT ~~*The tank **is containing**...*~~)

For progressive forms with *always* and similar words (e.g. *She's **always** losing her keys*),
see 452.
For progressive forms in general, see 450.
For present-tense story-telling, see 446.
For tense simplification in subordinate clauses, see 556.
For the 'distancing' use of progressive forms, see 161.

446   **present tenses** (4): stories, commentaries and instructions

1   stories

Present tenses are often used to tell stories, especially in an informal style.
The simple present is used for the events – the things that happen one after
another. The present progressive is used for 'background' – things that are
already happening when the story starts, or that continue through the story.
(This is like the difference between the simple past and past progressive:
see 417.)

*So I **open** the door, and I **look** out into the garden, and I **see** this man.*
*He**'s wearing** a pink skirt and a policeman's helmet. 'Good morning,'*
*he **says** ...*

*There's this Scotsman, you see, and he**'s walking** through the jungle when*
*he **meets** a gorilla. And the gorilla**'s eating** a snake sandwich. So the*
*Scotsman **goes** up to the gorilla ...*

The simple present is common in summaries of plays, stories, etc.

*In Act I, Hamlet **meets** the ghost of his father. The ghost **tells** him ...*

*Chapter 2: Postman Pat **goes** to Scotland and **makes** friends with a sheep.*

2   commentaries

In commentaries, the use of tenses is similar. The simple present is used for
the quicker actions and events (which are finished before the sentences that
describe them); the present progressive is used for longer actions and
situations. There are more simple and fewer progressive tenses in a football
commentary, for instance, than in a commentary on a boat race.

*Smith **passes** to Devaney, Devaney to Barnes, Barnes to Lucas – and Harris*
***intercepts** ... Harris to Simms, nice ball – and Simms **shoots**!*

*Oxford **are drawing** slightly ahead of Cambridge now; they**'re rowing** with*
*a beautiful rhythm; Cambridge **are looking** a little disorganised ...*

3 instructions and demonstrations

We often use present tenses in a similar way to give instructions, demonstrations and directions.

> OK, let's go over it again. You **wait** outside the bank until the manager **arrives**. Then you **radio** Louie, who**'s waiting** round the corner, and he **drives** round to the front entrance. You and Louie **grab** the manager . . .
> First I **put** a lump of butter into a frying pan and **light** the gas; then while the butter**'s melting** I **break** three eggs into a bowl, like this . . .
> 'How **do** I **get** to the station?' 'You **go** straight on to the traffic lights, then you **turn** left . . .'

447 presently

Presently is often used in British English to mean 'not now, later', 'in a minute'.

> 'Mummy, can I have an ice-cream?' '**Presently**, dear.'
> He's having a rest now. He'll be down **presently**.

In American English, the usual meaning of *presently* is 'now', 'at present'. This is becoming very common in British English too.

> Professor Holloway is **presently** working on plant diseases.

448 price and prize

The *price* is what you pay if you buy something. A *prize* is what you are given if you have done something exceptional, or if you win a competition.

> What's the **price** of the green dress? (NOT . . . ~~the **prize** of the green dress?~~)
> She received the Nobel **prize** for physics. (NOT . . . ~~the Nobel **price** . . .~~)

449 principal and principle

These two words have the same pronunciation. The adjective *principal* means 'main', 'most important'.

> What's your **principal** reason for wanting to be a doctor?
> (NOT . . . ~~your **principle** reason . . .~~)

The noun *principal* means 'headmaster' or 'headmistress' (especially, in Britain, of a school for adults).

> If you want to leave early you'll have to ask the **Principal**.

A *principle* is a scientific law or a moral rule.

> Newton discovered the **principle** of universal gravitation.
> (NOT . . . ~~the **principal** of universal gravitation.~~)
> She's a girl with very strong **principles**.

450 progressive verb forms (1): general

1 construction

Progressive verb forms (also called 'continuous' forms) are made with *be* + *-ing*.

> I **am waiting** for the shops to open. (present progressive tense)
> Your suit **is being cleaned**. (present progressive passive tense)

▶

*She phoned while I **was cooking**.* (past progressive tense)
*I didn't know how long she **had been sitting** there.*
    (past perfect progressive tense)
***Will** you **be going** out this evening?* (future progressive tense)
*I'd like **to be lying** on the beach now.* (progressive infinitive)

2 terminology and use

A progressive form does not simply show the time of an event. It also shows how the speaker sees the event – generally as ongoing and temporary, rather than completed or permanent. (Because of this, grammars often talk about 'progressive aspect' rather than 'progressive tenses'.) Compare:

- *I**'ve read** your letter.* (completed action)
  *I**'ve been reading** a lot of thrillers recently.* (not necessarily completed)
- *The Rhine **runs** into the North Sea.* (permanent)
  *We'll have to phone the plumber – water**'s running** down the kitchen wall.*
      (temporary)

When a progressive is used to refer to a short momentary action, it often suggests repetition.

    *Why **are** you **jumping** up and down?*   *The door **was banging** in the wind.*
For more details of the use of progressives, see the individual entries on the various forms.

451 progressive verb forms (2): non-progressive verbs

1 verbs not used in progressive forms

Some verbs are never or hardly ever used in progressive forms.
    *I **like** this music.* (NOT ~~*I'm liking this music.*~~)
    *I rang her up because I **needed** to talk.*
        (NOT *... ~~because I was needing to talk.~~*)
Some other verbs are not used in progressive forms when they have certain meanings. Compare:
    *I**'m seeing** the doctor at ten o'clock.*
    *I **see** what you mean.* (NOT ~~*I'm seeing what you mean.*~~)
Many of these non-progressive verbs refer to states rather than actions. Some refer to mental states (e.g. *know, think, believe*); some others refer to the use of the senses (e.g. *smell, taste*).

2 common non-progressive verbs

Here is a list of some common verbs which are not often used in progressive forms (or which are not used in progressive forms with certain meanings).

mental and emotional states

believe	*love*	*see* (= 'understand')
doubt	*hate*	*suppose*
feel (= 'have an opinion')	*prefer*	*think* (= 'have an opinion')
imagine	*realise*	*understand*
know	*recognise*	*want*
(dis)like	*remember*	*wish*

use of the senses

appear	look (= 'seem')	seem	sound
hear	see	smell	taste

communicating and causing reactions

agree	deny	impress	please	satisfy
astonish	disagree	mean	promise	surprise

other

be	deserve	measure (= 'have length etc')
belong	fit	need
concern	include	owe
consist	involve	own
contain	lack	possess
depend	matter	weigh (= 'have weight')

More details of the use of some of these verbs are given in other entries in the book. See the Index for references.

3 progressive and non-progressive uses

Compare the progressive and non-progressive uses of some of the verbs listed above.

- *I'm feeling fine.* (OR *I feel fine.* – see 445.7)
  I feel we shouldn't do it. (NOT *I'm feeling we shouldn't do it.*)
- *What are you thinking about?*
  What do you think of the government?
    (NOT *What are you thinking of the government?*)
- *I'm seeing Leslie tomorrow.*
  I see what you mean. (NOT *I'm seeing what you mean.*)
- *Why are you smelling the meat? Is it bad?*
  Does the meat smell bad? (NOT *Is the meat smelling bad?*)
- *I'm just tasting the cake to see if it's OK.*
  The cake tastes wonderful. (NOT *The cake's tasting wonderful.*)
- *The scales broke when I was weighing myself this morning.*
  I weighed 68 kilos three months ago – and look at me now!
    (NOT *I was weighing 68 kilos...*)

Note also that many 'non-progressive' verbs are occasionally used in progressive forms in order to emphasise the idea of change or development.

These days, more and more people are preferring to take early retirement.
The water's tasting better today.

4 *can see* etc

Can is often used with *see, hear, feel, taste, smell, understand* and *remember* to give a kind of progressive meaning, especially in British English. For details, see 125.

I can see Sue coming down the road.
Can you smell something burning? ▶

5 *-ing* forms

Even verbs which are never used in progressive tenses have *-ing* forms which can be used in other kinds of structure.

> **Knowing** her tastes, I bought her a large box of chocolates.
> I don't like to go to a country without **knowing** something of the language.

452 **progressive verb forms** (3): with **always** etc

We can use *always, continually* and similar words with a progressive form to mean 'very often'.

> I**'m always losing** my keys.
> Granny's nice. She**'s always giving** people little presents.
> I**'m continually running** into Paul these days.
> That cat**'s forever getting** shut in the bathroom.

This structure is used to talk about things which happen very often (perhaps more often than expected), but which are unexpected or unplanned. Compare:

– When Alice comes to see me, I **always meet** her at the station.
  (a regular, planned arrangement)
  I**'m always meeting** Mrs Bailiff in the supermarket.
  (accidental, unplanned meetings)
– When I was a child, we **always** had picnics on Saturdays in the summer.
  (regular, planned)
  Her mother **was always arranging** little surprise picnics and outings.
  (unexpected, not regular)

453 **punctuation** (1): apostrophe (/əˈpɒstrəfi/)

We use apostrophes (') for three main reasons.

1 missing letters

Apostrophes show where we have left letters out of a contracted form (see 144).

> can't (= cannot)   it's (= it is/has)   I'd (= I would/had)
> who's (= who is/has)

2 possessives

We use apostrophes before or after the possessive *-s* ending of nouns (see 432).

> the **girl's** father   **Charles's** wife   three **miles'** walk

Possessive determiners and pronouns do not have apostrophes.

> Has the cat had **its** food yet? (NOT ...*it's food*...)
> This is **yours**. (NOT ...*your's*.)   **Whose** is that coat? (NOT *Who's*...)

3 special plurals

Words which do not usually have plurals sometimes have an apostrophe when a plural form is written.

> It's a nice idea, but there are a lot of **if's**.

Apostrophes are used in the plurals of letters, and often of numbers and abbreviations.

> *He writes **b's** instead of **d's**.*
> *It was in the early **1960's**.* (OR ... *1960s.*)
> *I know two **MP's** personally.* (OR ... *MPs.*)

It is not correct to put apostrophes in normal plurals.

> *JEANS – HALF PRICE* (NOT ~~*JEAN'S*~~...)

454 **punctuation** (2): colon

1 **explanations**

Colons (:) are often used before explanations.

> *We decided not to go on holiday: we had too little money.*
> *Mother may have to go into hospital: she's got kidney trouble.*

2 **direct speech**

A colon is used when direct speech is introduced by a name or short phrase (as in the text of a play, or when famous sayings are quoted).

> ***POLONIUS:*** *What do you read, my lord?*
> ***HAMLET:*** *Words, words, words.*

> ***In the words of Murphy's Law:*** *'Anything that can go wrong will go wrong.'*

In other cases, direct speech is generally introduced by a comma (see 455.6).

> ***Stewart opened his eyes and said,*** *'Who's your beautiful friend?'*

But a long passage of direct speech may be introduced by a colon:

> *Introducing his report for the year, **the Chairman said:** 'A number of factors have contributed to the firm's very gratifying results. First of all, ...'*

3 **lists**

A colon can introduce a list.

> *The main points are as follows: (1) ..., (2) ..., (3) ....*
> *We need three kinds of support: economic, moral and political.*

4 **subdivisions**

A colon can introduce a subdivision of a subject – for instance, in a title or heading.

> **punctuation**: colon

5 **capitals**

In British English, it is unusual for a capital letter to follow a colon (except at the beginning of a quotation). However, this can happen if a colon is followed by several complete sentences.

> *My main objections are as follows:*
> *First of all, no proper budget has been drawn up.*
> *Secondly, there is no guarantee that ...*

In American English, colons are more often followed by capital letters. ▶

6 letters

Americans usually put a colon after the opening salutation (*Dear...*) in a business letter.

Dear Mr. Callan:
I am writing to ...

British usage prefers a comma or no punctuation mark at all in this case.

455 **punctuation** (3): comma

Commas (,) generally reflect pauses in speech.

1 lists

We use commas to separate items in a series or list. In British English, a comma is not usually used with *and* between the last two items unless these are long. Compare:

I went to Spain, Italy, Switzerland, Austria and Germany.
(US: ... *Austria, and Germany.*)
You had a holiday at Christmas, at New Year and at Easter.
I spent yesterday playing cricket, listening to jazz records, and talking
about the meaning of life.

2 adjectives

In predicative position (see 15), commas are always used between adjectives.

*The cowboy was **tall, dark** and handsome.*

Before a noun, we generally use commas between adjectives which give similar kinds of information.

*This is an **expensive, ill-planned, wasteful** project.*

Commas are sometimes dropped between short adjectives.

*a **tall(,) dark(,) handsome** cowboy*

Commas cannot be dropped when modifiers refer to different parts of something.

*a **green, red** and gold carpet* (NOT *a green red...*)
***concrete, glass** and plastic buildings*

Commas are not normally used between adjectives that give different kinds of information.

*Have you met our **handsome new financial** director?*
(NOT ...*our **handsome, new, financial** director?*)

3 word order

If words or expressions are put in unusual places or interrupt the normal progression of a sentence, we usually separate them off by commas.

*My father, **however,** did not agree.*
*Jane had, **surprisingly,** paid for everything.*
*We were, **believe it or not,** in love with each other.*
*Andrew Carpenter, **the deputy sales manager,** was sick.*

Two commas are necessary in these cases.

(NOT *Andrew Carpenter **the deputy sales manager,** was sick...*)

4   identifying expressions

When nouns are followed by identifying expressions which show exactly who or what is being talked about, commas are not used. Compare:

> *The driver **in the Ferrari** was cornering superbly.*
>> (The phrase *in the Ferrari* identifies the driver.)
>> (NOT ~~*The driver, in the Ferrari, was cornering superbly*~~ OR ~~*The driver in the Ferrari, was cornering superbly.*~~)
>
> *Stephens, **in the Ferrari**, was cornering superbly.*
>> (The phrase *in the Ferrari* does not identify the driver; he is already identified by his name, Stephens.)
>
> *The woman **who was sitting behind the reception desk** gave Parker a big smile.*
>
> *Mrs Grange, **who was sitting behind the reception desk**, gave Parker a big smile.*

For more about identifying and non-identifying relative clauses, see 474.

5   co-ordinate clauses

Clauses connected with *and, but* or *or* are usually separated by commas unless they are very short. Compare:

- *Jane decided to try the home-made steak pie, and Andrew ordered Dover sole with boiled potatoes.*
  Jane had pie and Andrew had fish.
- *She had very little to live on, but she would never have dreamed of taking what was not hers.*
  She was poor but she was honest.

6   direct speech

A comma is generally used between a reporting expression and a piece of direct speech.

> *Looking straight at her, **he said,** 'There's no way we can help him, is there?'*

If a reporting expression follows a piece of direct speech, we usually put a comma instead of a full stop before the closing quotation mark.

> *'I don't like this one bit,' **said Julia.***

7   subordinate clauses

When subordinate clauses begin sentences, they are often separated by commas. Compare:

> *****If you are ever in London,** come and see me.*
> *Come and see me **if you are ever in London**.*

Commas are not used before *that*-clauses.

> *It is quite **natural that** you should want to meet your father.*
>> (NOT ~~*It is quite **natural, that**...*~~)

8   indirect speech: no comma before *that* etc

We do not put commas before *that, what, where* etc in indirect speech structures.

> *Everybody **realised that** I was a foreigner.*
>> (NOT ~~*Everybody **realised, that**...*~~)

▶

*They quickly **explained what** to do.*
   (NOT ~~They quickly **explained, what**~~...)
*I didn't **know where** I should go.* (NOT ~~I didn't **know, where**~~...)

9 grammatically separate sentences

We do not usually put commas between grammatically separate sentences (in places where a full stop or a semi-colon would be possible – see 457 and 459).
   The blue dress was warmer. On the other hand, the purple one was prettier.
   (OR *The blue dress was warmer; on the other hand*...)
   (NOT ~~The blue dress was warmer, on the other hand~~...)

10 numbers

Commas are used to divide large numbers into groups of three figures, by separating off the thousands and millions.
   6,435 (NOT ~~6.435~~)   *7,456,189*
We do not always use commas in four-figure numbers, and they are never used in dates.
   3,164 OR *3164*   *the year **1946***
Spaces are sometimes used instead of commas.
   There are 1 000 millimetres in one metre.
We do not use commas in decimals (see 385.1).
   3.5 = three point five OR *three and a half* (NOT ~~3,5~~ ~~three comma five~~)

456 punctuation (4): dash

Dashes (–) are especially common in informal writing. They can be used in the same way as colons, semi-colons or brackets.
   There are three things I can never remember – names, faces, and
      I've forgotten the other.
   We had a great time in Greece – the kids really loved it.
   My mother – who rarely gets angry – really lost her temper.
A dash can introduce an afterthought, or something unexpected and surprising.
   We'll be arriving on Monday morning – at least, I think so.
   And then we met Bob – with Lisa, believe it or not!

For the use of hyphens (as in *hard-working* or *co-operative*), see 532.

457 punctuation (5): full stop, question mark and exclamation mark

1 sentence division

Full stops, question marks and exclamation marks are used to close sentences. A new sentence that follows one of these has a capital letter.
   I looked out of the window. It was snowing again.
   Why do we try to reach the stars? What is it all for?
   They have no right to be in our country! They must leave at once!

We do not normally put full stops, question or exclamation marks before or after grammatically incomplete sentences.

She phoned me as soon as she arrived.

(NOT ~~She phoned me.~~ ***As soon as she arrived.***)

In his job he has to deal with different kinds of people.

(NOT ***In his job.*** ~~He has to deal with different kinds of people.~~)

Did you understand why I was upset?

(NOT ~~Did you understand?~~ ***Why I was upset?***)

However, sometimes we can emphasise a clause or phrase by separating it with a full stop and capital letter.

*People are sleeping out on the streets. **In Britain. In the 1990s. Because there are not enough houses.***

2 abbreviations

Full stops can be used after abbreviations (see 2). This is becoming less common in British English.

Dr. Andrew C. Burke, M.A. OR *Dr Andrew C Burke, M A*

3 indirect questions

We do not use question marks after indirect questions (see 481.6).

I asked her what time it was. (NOT *...* ~~*what time it was?*~~)

458 punctuation (6): quotation marks

Quotation marks ('...' "...") are also called 'inverted commas' in British English.

1 special use of words

We often put quotation marks round words which are used in special ways – for example when we talk about them, when we use them as titles, or when we give them special meanings.

*Quotation marks are also called **'inverted commas'**.*

*People disagree about how to use the word **'disinterested'**.*

*His next book was **'Heart of Darkness'**.*

*A textbook can be a **'wall'** between teacher and class.*

2 direct speech

We use quotation marks when we quote direct speech. Single quotation marks ('...') are more common in British English, and double quotation marks ("...") in American English. For quotations inside quotations, we use double quotation marks inside single (or single inside double).

'His last words,' said Albert, 'were "Close that bloody window".'

For commas in quotations, see 455. For colons, see 454.

459 **punctuation** (7): semi-colon

1 **instead of full stops**

Semi-colons (;) are sometimes used instead of full stops, in cases where sentences are grammatically independent but the meaning is closely connected. Semi-colons are not nearly as common as full stops or commas.

Some people work best in the mornings; others do better in the evenings.
It is a fine idea; let us hope that it is going to work.

Commas are not usually possible in cases like these (see 455).

2 **in lists**

Semi-colons are also used to separate items in a list, particularly when these are grammatically complex.

You may use the sports facilities on condition that your subscription is paid
regularly; that you arrange for all necessary cleaning to be carried out;
that you undertake to make good any damage; . . .

460 **question words**

1 **interrogative use**

The words *who, whom, whose, which, what, when, where, why* and *how* are used in questions to show what kind of information is wanted.

***Who** said that?* (asking for a personal subject)
***What** did she want?* (asking for a non-personal object)
***When** will it be ready?* (asking for a time expression)
***Why** are you laughing?* (asking for a reason)

Who and *whom* are pronouns, and act as subject or object in their clauses. *When, where, why* and *how* act as adverbs. *What, which* and *whose* can be pronouns or determiners. Compare:

– ***What** do you want?* (pronoun)
***What** sort do you want?* (determiner)
– ***Which** is mine?* (pronoun)
***Which** coat is mine?* (determiner)
– ***Whose** is the red car?* (pronoun)
***Whose coat** is this?* (determiner)

2 **word order and structure**

Question words normally come at the beginning of their clauses. When a question word is the subject (or included in the subject), it comes before the verb, and *do* cannot normally be used (see 461.6). Compare:

Who (subject) ***said** that?* (NOT ~~Who **did say** that?~~)
Who (object) ***did you invite**?*

For more details of word order in questions, see 461–462.
For the position of prepositions with question words, see 440.

3 longer interrogative expressions

English does not have a single question word for every situation. In order to find out some kinds of information, we need to use expressions of two or more words.

What time is the meeting?   **How much** did you pay?
What's her new boyfriend **like**?   **How many** people are coming?
What sort of music do you like?   **How far** do you travel to work?

English has no special word to ask for an ordinal number.

'It's our wedding anniversary.' 'Congratulations. **Which one?**'
(NOT '...~~the **how-manyeth?**~~')

4 asking for a verb

Question words and expressions can be used to ask for most kinds of word – for example a subject (*who, what*), an object (*who(m), what*), a determiner (*what, which, whose*), an adjective (*what ... like*) or an adverbial expression (*when, where, why, how*). But there is no simple word or expression that can be used to ask for a verb. For this purpose we normally make a sentence using *what* with *do*.

'**What** are you **doing** next weekend?' 'Resting.'

The answer to *what ... do* can include a verb together with what follows it.

'**What's** Helen **doing?**' 'Getting all the rubbish out of the car.'

To ask for a transitive verb when the subject and object are both mentioned, we use *what ... do to/with*.

'**What have** you **done to** your leg?' 'Broken it.'
What are you **doing with** my camera?

To ask for complete information about an event, we use *what ... happen*.

What's happening in the office these days?

When the object is mentioned, we use *what ... happen to*.

'**What happened to** that chair?' 'Stan tried to dance on it.'

5 question-word clauses

Clauses beginning with question words can refer both to questions and to the answers to questions. They often act as the objects of verbs – for example, when questions and their answers are reported (see 481).

I asked **who wanted to come**.
She wondered **why he wasn't wearing a coat**.
We need to decide **where Ann's going to sleep**.
He told me **when he was arriving**, but I've forgotten.
She explained **what the problem was**.
Mary hasn't said **why she doesn't want to come**.

Question-word clauses can act not only as objects, but also as subjects, complements or adverbials. This structure is often rather informal (especially with *how*-clauses – see 254).

Who you invite is your business.   **Where we stay** doesn't matter.
A hot bath is **what I need**.   This is **how much I've done**.
I'm surprised at **how fast she can run**.
You can eat it **how you like**. (very informal)

The 'preparatory *it*' structure is often used with subject clauses (see 301).

It's your business **who you invite**.   It doesn't matter **where we stay**.   ▶

Question-word clauses can give more information about nouns. In this case they are called 'relative clauses' (see 473–477 for details).

> *There's that man **who threw stones at your dog**.*
> *The place **where Mary works** has just had a fire.*

Whether is a question word that is only used in indirect questions.

> *We need to know **whether he's coming tomorrow**.*

For more about *whether*, see 592–593.
For details of indirect question constructions, see 480–482.
For more information about particular question words and expressions, see the separate
    entries for the various words.
For singular and plural verbs with *who, what* and *which*, see 594.
For differences between *how, what* and *why*, see 254.3.
For *who ever, what ever* etc, see 595.
For *whoever, whatever* etc, see 596.
For *who else, what else* etc, see 187.
For question words after prepositions, in sentences like *I'm not sure **(of) where** we are*,
    see 441.
For infinitives after question words (e.g. ***How to succeed** in business*), see 288.

461 questions (1): basic rules

These rules apply to almost all written questions and most spoken questions. For 'declarative questions' (in which the subject comes before the verb), see the next section.

1 auxiliary verb before subject

In a question, an auxiliary verb normally comes before the subject.

> ***Have you*** *received my letter of June 17?* (NOT ~~*You have received . . . ?*~~)
> *Why **are you** laughing?* (NOT ~~*Why **you are** laughing?*~~)
> *What **are all those people** looking at?*
>   (NOT ~~*What **all those people are** looking at?*~~)
> *How much **does the room** cost?* (NOT ~~*How much **the room costs**?*~~)

2 *do*

If there is no other auxiliary verb, we use *do, does* or *did* to form a question.

> ***Do you*** *like Mozart?* (NOT ~~***Like you** Mozart?*~~)
> *What **does 'periphrastic'** mean?* (NOT ~~*What **means** 'periphrastic'?*~~)
> ***Did you*** *like the concert?*

3 *do* not used with other auxiliaries

Do is not used together with other auxiliary verbs or with *be*.

> ***Can you*** *tell me the time?* (NOT ~~***Do you can** tell me the time?*~~)
> ***Have you*** *seen John?* (NOT ~~***Do you have** seen John?*~~)
> ***Are you*** *ready?*

4 infinitive without *to*

After *do*, we use the infinitive without *to*.

> *What **does the boss want**?* (NOT ~~*What does the boss **wants**?*~~)
> ***Did you go*** *climbing last weekend?* (NOT ~~***Did you went** . . . ?*~~)
>   (NOT ~~***Did you to go** . . . ?*~~)

5 only auxiliary verb before subject

Only the auxiliary verb goes before the subject, not the whole of the verb.

Is your mother coming tomorrow?
(NOT *Is coming your mother tomorrow?*)
When was your reservation made?
(NOT *When was made your reservation?*)

This happens even if the subject is very long.

Where are the President and his family staying?
(NOT *Where are staying the President...?*)

6 word order with question word as subject

When *who, which, what* or *whose* is the subject (or part of the subject), the question word comes before the verb, and *do* cannot normally be used.

Who left the door open? (NOT *Who did leave...?*)
Which costs more – the blue one or the grey one?
(NOT *Which does cost more...?*)
Which type of battery lasts longest?
(NOT *Which type of battery does last longest?*)
What happened? (NOT *What did happen?*)
How many people work in your office?
(NOT *How many people do work...?*)

But *do* can be used after a subject question word for emphasis, to insist on an answer.

Well, tell us – what did happen when your father found you?
So who did marry the Princess in the end?

When a question word is the object, *do* is used.

Who do you want to speak to?
Which type of battery do you use?
What do you think?

For singular and plural verbs with *who* and *what*, see 594.

7 indirect questions

In an indirect question, we do not put an auxiliary before the subject, and we do not use a question mark. For details, see 481.6.

Tell me when you are going on holiday.
(NOT *Tell me when are you going on holiday?*)

8 questions about *that*-clauses

A *wh*-question usually refers to the words in the main clause which starts with the question word. However, questions can also refer to subordinate *that*-clauses after verbs like *wish, think* or *say.*

Who do you wish (that) you'd married, then?
How long do you think (that) we should wait?
What did you say (that) you wanted for Christmas?

▶

That is usually dropped; it must be dropped when the question word refers to the subject of the subordinate clause.

Who *do you think is outside?* (NOT ~~Who do you think **that** is outside?~~)
What *do you suppose will happen now?*
(NOT ~~What do you suppose **that** will happen now?~~)

For negative questions, see 360.
For more about question words, see 460.
For ellipsis in questions (e.g. *Seen John? Coming tonight?*), see 183.

462 questions (2): declarative questions

In spoken questions, we do not always use 'interrogative' word order.
You're *working late tonight?*
These 'declarative questions' can be used when the speaker thinks he / she knows or has understood something, but wants to make sure or express surprise. A rising intonation is common.

This is *your car?* (= *I suppose this is your car, isn't it?*)
That's *the boss? I thought he was the cleaner.*
*'We're going to Hull for our holidays.' '***You're** *going to Hull?'*
This word order is not normally possible after a question word.
Where **are you** *going?* (NOT ~~Where **you are** going?~~)

463 questions (3): reply questions

1 short questions

We often answer a statement by asking for more information. In informal speech, questions of this kind may have a very simple structure – perhaps just a question word, or a short phrase beginning with a question word.

*'Anne's leaving her job.' '***When?***'*
*'I'm going out.' '***Who with?***'*
*'The boss wants to see you.' '***What for?***'*
*'Can you talk to Tom this afternoon?' '***Why me?***'*
*'The buses aren't running.' '***Why not?***'*

2 echo questions

To question what has been said, a speaker may simply repeat ('echo') what he / she has heard. A rising intonation is common.
*'I'm getting married.' '***You're getting married?***'*
To question one part of a sentence, we can repeat the rest of the sentence, and put a stressed question word in place of the part we are asking about.
'Just take a look at that.' 'Take a look at **what?***'*
'She's invited thirteen people to dinner.' 'She's invited **how many?***'*
'We're going to Tierra del Fuego on holiday.' 'You're going **where?***'*
'I've broken the fettle gauge.' 'You've broken the **what?***'*
To question a verb, or the part of a sentence beginning with the verb, *do what* is used.
'She set fire to the garage.' 'She **did what** *(to the garage)?'*

A speaker may question a question, by repeating it with a rising intonation. Note that we use normal question structures with inverted word order, not indirect question structures, in this case.

*'Where are you going?' **'Where am I going?** Home.'*
(NOT ... *~~'Where I'm going?~~ ...'*)
*'What does he want?' **'What does he want?** Money, as usual.'*
(NOT ... *~~'What he wants?~~ ...'*)
*'Are you tired?' **'Am I tired?** Of course not.'*
(NOT ... *~~'Whether I'm tired?~~ ...'*)
*'Do squirrels eat insects?' **'Do squirrels eat insects?** I'm not sure.'*
(NOT ... *~~'Whether squirrels eat insects?~~ ...'*)

3 attention signals

Short questions are often used in conversation to show that the listener is paying attention and interested. Common attention signals are *Oh, yes? Really?* and a 'question tag' structure (see 465), consisting of **auxiliary verb + pronoun**.

*'It was a terrible party.' **'Was it?** 'Yes ...'*

Note that these questions do not ask for information – they simply show that the listener is reacting to what has been said. More examples:

*'We had a lovely holiday.' **'Did you?** 'Yes, we went ...'*
*'I've got a headache.' **'Have you,** dear? I'll get you an aspirin.'*
*'John likes that girl next door.' 'Oh, **does he?'***
*'I don't understand.' **'Don't you?** I'm sorry.'*

Negative questions in reply to affirmative statements express emphatic agreement (like negative-question exclamations – see 201.4).

*'It was a lovely concert.' 'Yes, **wasn't it?** I did enjoy it.'*
*'She's put on a lot of weight.' 'Yes, **hasn't she?'***

For similar structures, see 493 (short answers) and 465–466 (question tags).

464 questions (4): rhetorical questions

1 questions that do not expect an answer

Questions do not always ask for information. In many languages, including English, a question with an obvious answer can be used simply as a way of drawing attention to something. Questions of this kind are called 'rhetorical questions'.

Do you know what time it is? (= You're late.)
Who's a lovely baby? (= You're a lovely baby.)
'I can't find my coat.' 'What's this, then?' (= 'Here it is, stupid.')

Very often, a rhetorical question draws attention to a negative situation – to the fact that the answer is obviously 'No', or that there is no answer to the question.

What's the use of asking her? (= It's no use asking her.)
How do you expect me to find milk on a Sunday night? Where am I going to find a shop open?
(= You can't reasonably expect ... There aren't any shops open.) ▶

Where's my money? (= You haven't paid me.)
'I can run faster than you.' 'Who cares?' (= 'Nobody cares.')
Are we going to let them do this to us? (= We aren't...)
Have you lost your tongue? (= Why don't you say anything?)
What do you think you're doing? (= You can't justify what you're doing.)
Who do you think you are?
  (= You aren't as important as your behaviour suggests.)
Why don't you take a taxi? (= There's no reason not to.)

2   *why/how should...?*

Why should...? can be used aggressively to reject suggestions, requests and instructions.
  *'Ann's very unhappy.' '**Why should** I care?'*
  *'Could your wife help us in the office tomorrow?' '**Why should** she? She doesn't work for you.'*
How should I know? (American also *How would...?*) is an aggressive reply to a question.
  *'What time does the film start?' '**How should I know?**'*

3   negative *yes/no* questions

Negative *yes/no* questions often suggest a positive situation.
  Haven't I done enough for you? (= I have done enough for you.)
  Didn't I tell you it would rain? (= I told you...)
  'Don't touch that!' 'Why shouldn't I?' (= 'I have a perfect right to.')

For more about negative questions, see 360.

465   **questions** (5): question tags (basic information)

1   **What are question tags?**

'Question tags' are the small questions that often come at the ends of sentences in speech, and sometimes in informal writing.
  *Not a very good film, **was it?***
Negatives are usually contracted, but full forms are possible in formal speech.
  *That's the postman, **isn't it?***
  *You do take sugar in tea, **don't you?***
  *They promised to repay us within six months, **did they not?*** (formal)
Question tags can be used to check whether something is true, or to ask for agreement.

2   **negative after affirmative, and vice versa**

Question tags are used after affirmative and negative sentences, but not after questions.
  *You**'re** the new secretary, **aren't you?***
  *You**'re not** the new secretary, **are you?***
    (BUT NOT *~~Are you the new secretary, aren't you?~~*)

To check information or ask for agreement, we most often put negative tags after affirmative sentences, and non-negative tags after negative sentences.

+	–

*It's cold, **isn't** it?*

–	+

*It's **not** warm, is it?*

For 'same-way' tags, see 466.8.

3 auxiliaries

If the main sentence has an auxiliary verb (or non-auxiliary *be*), this is repeated in the question tag.

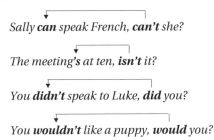

Sally **can** speak French, **can't** she?

The meeting**'s** at ten, **isn't** it?

You **didn't** speak to Luke, **did** you?

You **wouldn't** like a puppy, **would** you?

If the main sentence has no auxiliary, the question tag has *do*.

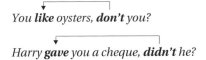

You **like** oysters, **don't** you?

Harry **gave** you a cheque, **didn't** he?

4 meaning and intonation

In speech, we can show the exact meaning of a question tag by the intonation. If the tag is a real question – if we really want to know something and are not sure of the answer – we use a rising intonation: the voice goes up.

*The meeting's at four o'clock, **isn't it?***

If the tag is not a real question – if we are sure of the answer – we use a falling intonation: the voice goes down.

*It's a beautiful day, **isn't it?***

In writing, the exact meaning of a question tag is normally clear from the context.

5 requests

We often ask for help or information by using the structure **negative statement + question tag.**

*You couldn't lend me a pound, **could you?***
*You haven't seen my watch anywhere, **have you?***

For more information about requests, see 483.
For details of other kinds of tags, see 472.

466 questions (6): question tags (advanced points)

1 *aren't I?*

The question tag for *I am* is *aren't I?*
> *I'm late,* ***aren't I?***

2 imperatives

After imperatives, *won't you?* is often used to invite people to do things (especially in British English), and *will/would/can/can't/could you?* to tell or ask people to do things.
> *Give me a hand,* ***will you?***
> *Do sit down,* ***won't you?*** (GB)
> *Open a window,* ***would you?***
> *Shut up,* ***can't you?***

After a negative imperative, we use *will you?*
> *Don't forget,* ***will you?***

3 *let's*

After *let's . . .* , we use *shall we?*
> ***Let's*** *have a party,* ***shall we?***

4 *there*

There can be a subject in question tags.
> *There's something wrong, isn't* ***there****?*
> *There weren't any problems, were* ***there****?*

5 negative words

Non-negative tags are used after sentences containing negative words like *never, no, nobody, hardly, scarcely* and *little*.
> *You* ***never*** *say what you're thinking,* ***do you?*** (NOT *. . .~~don't you?~~*)
> *It's* ***no*** *good,* ***is it?*** (NOT *. . . ~~isn't it?~~*)
> *It's* ***hardly*** *rained at all this summer,* ***has it?***
> *There's* ***little*** *we can do about it,* ***is there?***

6 *nothing, nobody, somebody* etc

We use *it* in question tags to refer to *nothing* and *everything*.
> ***Nothing*** *can happen, can* ***it****?*

We use *they* to refer to *nobody, somebody* and *everybody* (and *no one* etc).
> ***Nobody*** *phoned, did* ***they****?*
> ***Somebody*** *wanted a drink, didn't* ***they****? Who was it?*

For more about this use of *they*, see 505.

7 non-auxiliary *have*

After non-auxiliary *have* (referring to states), question tags with *have* and *do* are often both possible in British English. (*Do* is normal in American English.)
> *Your father* ***has*** *a bad back,* ***hasn't/doesn't*** *he?*

For more about the use of *do* with *have*, see 240–243.

8 'same-way' question tags

Non-negative question tags are quite common after affirmative sentences.
These are often used as responses to something that has been said, like
'attention signals' (see 463.3): the speaker repeats what he / she has just heard
or learnt, and uses the tag to express interest, surprise, concern or some
other reaction.

> So you're getting married, **are you?** How nice!
> So she thinks she's going to become a doctor, **does she?** Well, well.
> You think you're funny, **do you?**

'Same-way' tags can also be used to ask questions. In this structure, we use
the main sentence to make a guess, and then ask (in the tag) if it was correct.

> Your mother's at home, **is she?**
> This is the last bus, **is it?**
> You can eat shellfish, **can you?**

Negative 'same-way' tags are occasionally heard in British English; they
usually sound aggressive.

> I see. You don't like my cooking, **don't you?**

9 ellipsis

In sentences with question tags, it is quite common to leave out pronoun
subjects and auxiliary verbs. (This is called 'ellipsis'. For details, see 183.)

> (**It's a**) nice day, **isn't it?**
> (**She was**) talking to my husband, **was she?**

In very informal speech, a question tag can sometimes be used after a
question with ellipsis.

> Have a good time, **did you?**
> Your mother at home, **is she?**
> John be here tomorrow, **will he?**

For details of other kinds of tags, see 472.

467 quite

1 two meanings

Quite has two meanings in British English. Compare:

> It's **quite** good, but it could be better.
> It's **quite** impossible. (= It's completely impossible.)

Good is a 'gradable' adjective: things can be more or less good. With gradable
adjectives and adverbs, *quite* is used in British English affirmative sentences
to mean something like 'fairly' or 'rather' (for the differences, see 205).
Impossible is non-gradable: things are either impossible or they aren't, but
they cannot be more or less impossible. With non-gradable adjectives and
adverbs, *quite* means 'completely'. Compare:

- I'm **quite tired**, but I can walk a bit further.
  I'm **quite exhausted** – I couldn't walk another step.
- It's **quite surprising**. (similar to *fairly surprising*)
  It's **quite amazing**. (= *absolutely amazing*)
- He speaks French **quite well**, but he's got a strong English accent.
  He speaks French **quite perfectly**.

▶

Note that some adjectives and adverbs can have both gradable and non-gradable uses; with these, *quite* has two possible meanings in British English.

In American English *quite* generally means something like 'very', not 'fairly/rather'.

2 with verbs

Quite can be used to modify verbs, especially in British English. The meaning depends on whether the verb is gradable or not.

> I **quite like** her, but she's not one of my closest friends.
> Have you **quite finished**? (= Have you completely finished?)

3 word order with nouns

Quite can be used with *a/an* + **noun**. It normally comes before *a/an* if there is a gradable adjective or no adjective.

> It's **quite a nice** day.   We watched **quite an interesting** film last night.
> She's **quite a** woman!   The party was **quite a success**.

With non-gradable adjectives, *quite* normally comes after *a/an*.

> It was **a quite perfect** day. (NOT *It was quite a perfect day.*)

In British English, *quite* is sometimes used before *the*.

> You're **quite the** most exciting man I've ever known.
> He's going **quite the** wrong way.

4 comparisons

Quite is not used directly before comparatives.

> She's **rather/much/a bit** older than me.
>   (BUT NOT *She's quite older than me.*)

But note the expression *quite better*, meaning 'completely recovered' (from an illness).

Quite similar means (in British English) 'fairly/rather similar'; *quite different* means 'completely different'.

5 *quite a bit/few/lot* etc

Quite a bit and *quite a few* (informal) have fairly positive meanings – they are almost the same as *quite a lot*.

> We're having **quite a bit** of trouble with the kids just now.
> We thought the place would be empty, but actually there were **quite a few** people there.

6 *not quite*

Not quite means 'not completely' or 'not exactly'. It can be used before adjectives, adverbs, verbs and nouns, including nouns with *the*.

> I'm **not quite** ready – won't be a minute.
> She didn't run **quite** fast enough for a record.
> I don't think you're **quite** right, I'm afraid.
> I don't **quite** agree.   That's **not quite** the colour I wanted.

For the differences between *quite*, *fairly*, *rather* and *pretty*, see 205.
For other structures used to express degree, see 153–156.

468 **rather** (1): adverb of degree

1 **meaning**

In British English, *rather* can be used as an adverb of degree. The meaning is similar to 'quite' or 'fairly', but more emphatic. *Rather* is not often used in this way in American English.

2 **with adjectives and adverbs**

With adjectives and adverbs, *rather* often suggests 'more than is usual', 'more than was expected', 'more than was wanted' and similar ideas.
> *'How was the film?' '**Rather good** – I was surprised.'*
> *She sings **rather well** – people often think she's a professional.*
> *It's **rather warm** in here. Let's open a window.*

3 **with nouns**

Rather can modify noun phrases, with or without adjectives. It generally comes before articles, but can also come after *a/an* if there is an adjective.
> *He's **rather a fool**.*   *That's **rather the impression** I wanted to give.*
> *Jane's had **rather a good idea**.* (OR *Jane's had **a rather good idea**.*)
Rather is not normally used before a plural noun with no adjective.
> (NOT *They're **rather fools**.*)

4 **with verbs**

Rather can modify verbs (especially verbs that refer to thoughts and feelings).
> *I **rather think** we're going to lose.*   *She **rather enjoys** doing nothing.*
> *Some people **rather like** being miserable.*
> *We **were rather hoping** you could stay to supper.*

5 **with comparatives and *too***

Rather can modify comparatives and *too*.
> *It's **rather later** than I thought.*   *He talks **rather too** much.*

For the difference between *rather, fairly, quite* and *pretty*, see 205.
For other uses of *rather*, see 469.
For other structures used to express degree, see 153–156.

469 **rather** (2): preference

1 *rather than*

This expression is normally used in 'parallel' structures: for example with two adjectives, adverbials, nouns, infinitives or *-ing* forms.
> *I'd call her hair **chestnut rather than brown**.*
> *I'd prefer to go **in August rather than in July**.*
> *It ought to be **you rather than me** that signs the letter.*
> *We ought to invest in **machinery rather than buildings**.*
> *I always prefer **starting early rather than leaving** everything to the last
>   minute.*

▶

When the main clause has a *to*-infinitive, *rather than* is usually followed by an infinitive without *to*. An *-ing* form is also possible, especially at the beginning of a sentence.

> *I decided **to write rather than phone/phoning**.*
> *It's important to invest in new machinery **rather than increase** wages.*
> (OR ... ***rather than increasing** wages.*)
> ***Rather than using/use** the last of my cash, I decided to write a cheque.*

2 *would rather*

This expression means 'would prefer to', and is followed by the infinitive without *to*. We often use the contraction *'d rather*.

> ***Would** you **rather** stay here or go home?*
> *'How about a drink?' '**I'd rather** have something to eat.'*

Note that *would rather like* does not mean 'would prefer'; in this expression, *rather* means 'quite', and does not suggest preference. Compare:

> *'**I'd rather like** a cup of coffee.' (= 'I'd **quite** like ...')*
> *'Oh, would you? **I'd rather have** a glass of beer.' (= ... 'I'd **prefer** ...')*

3 *would rather*: past tense with present or future meaning

We can use *would rather* to say that one person would prefer another or others to do something. We use a special structure with a past tense.

> would rather + subject + past tense

> ***I'd rather you went** home now.*
> *Tomorrow's difficult. **I'd rather you came** next weekend.*
> *My wife **would rather we didn't see** each other any more.*
> *'Shall I open a window?' '**I'd rather you didn't**.'*

A present tense is sometimes used in this structure (e.g. *I'd rather you **go** home now*), but this is unusual.

To talk about past actions, a past perfect tense is possible.

> *I'd rather you **hadn't** done that.*

However, it is more common to express this kind of idea with *I wish* (see 601).

> ***I wish** you hadn't done that.*

In older English, *had rather* was used in the same way as *would rather*. This structure is still found in grammars, but it is not normally used in modern British English.

For other structures where a past tense has a present or future meaning, see 422.

4 *or rather*

People often use *or rather* to correct themselves.

> *He's a psychologist – **or rather**, a psychoanalyst.*
> (NOT ... ~~or **better**, a psychoanalyst.~~)

For *rather* as an adverb of degree, see 468.

470 reason

Reason can be followed by *why* ... or *that* ...

 The **reason why** *I came here was to be with my family.*
 The main **reason why** *he lost his job was that he drank.*
 Do you know the **reason that** *they're closing the factory?*

In an informal style, *why/that* is often left out.

 The **reason** *she doesn't like me is that I make her nervous.*
 The **reason** *I'm asking is that I'm short of money.*

The normal preposition after *reason* is *for*.

 What's the real **reason for** *your depression?*
  (NOT ... ~~*reason of your depression?*~~)

Some people consider it incorrect to use a *because*-clause as complement after *reason* (as in *Sorry I'm late – the* **reason** *is* **because I overslept**.)

471 reflexive pronouns

1 What are reflexive pronouns?

Reflexive pronouns are *myself, yourself, himself, herself, itself, oneself, ourselves, yourselves, themselves.*

2 use

A common use of reflexive pronouns is to talk about actions where the subject and object are the same person.

 I cut **myself** *shaving this morning.* (NOT ~~*I cut me* ...~~)
 We got out of the water and dried **ourselves**. (NOT ... ~~*dried us.*~~)
 I'm going to the shops to get **myself** *some tennis shoes.*
 Talking to **oneself** *is the first sign of madness.*

A reflexive pronoun can refer to other things besides the subject of a clause.

 His *letters are all about* **himself**.
 I'm going to tell **her** *a few facts about* **herself**.
 I love **you** *for* **yourself**, *not for your money.*

3 after prepositions

After prepositions of place, we often use a personal pronoun (*me, you* etc) instead of a reflexive to refer back to a previous noun or pronoun, in cases when only a reflexive meaning makes sense. Compare:

 She took her dog **with her**. (NOT ... ~~*with herself.*~~)
  (She could hardly take her dog with somebody else.)
 She's very pleased **with herself**.
  (She could be pleased with somebody else.)

4 emphatic use

We can use reflexives as subject or object emphasisers, to mean 'that person / thing and nobody / nothing else'.

 It's quicker if you do it **yourself**.
 The manageress spoke to me **herself**.
 The house **itself** *is nice, but the garden's very small.*
 I'll go and see the President **himself** *if I have to.*

▶

5   reflexives used instead of personal pronouns

Reflexives are often used instead of personal pronouns after *as, like, but (for)* and *except (for)*.

> *These shoes are specially designed for heavy runners **like yourself.***
>   (OR ... ***like you.***)
> *Everybody was early except **myself.*** (OR ... ***except me.***)

Reflexives can also be used instead of personal pronouns in co-ordinated noun phrases.

> *There will be four of us at dinner: Robert, Alison, Jenny and **myself.***
>   (OR ... ***and I/me.***)

6   *by oneself*

By myself/yourself etc can mean either 'alone, without company' or 'without help'.

> *I often like to spend time **by myself.***
> *'Do you need help?' 'No, thanks. I can do it **by myself.'***

7   *-selves* and *each other/one another*

Note the difference between *-selves* and *each other / one another* (see 175).

> *They talk to **themselves** a lot.* (Each of them talks to him / herself.)
> *They talk to **each other** a lot.* (Each of them talks to the other.)

8   *own*

There are no possessive reflexives. Instead, we use *my own, your own* etc (see 400).

> *I always type **my own** letters.* (NOT ... ~~*myself's letters.*~~)

9   reflexives not used

Certain verbs which are reflexive in some other languages are not used with reflexive pronouns in English. For example, we do not normally use reflexive pronouns with *wash, dress* or *shave*.

> *Do you **shave** on Sundays?* (NOT ~~*Do you shave **yourself** on Sundays?*~~)

However, reflexives can be used if it is necessary to make it clear who does the action.

> *She's old enough to **dress herself** now.*
> *The barber shaves all the people in the town who don't **shave themselves**.*
>   *So does he **shave himself** or not?*

A few other examples of verbs which are not normally reflexive in English:

> *Suddenly the door **opened**.* (NOT ~~*Suddenly the door **opened itself.***~~)
> *His book's **selling** well.* (NOT ~~*His book's **selling itself** well.*~~)
> *Try to **concentrate**.* (NOT ~~*Try to **concentrate yourself.***~~)
> *I **feel** strange.* (NOT ~~*I **feel myself** strange.*~~)
> ***Hurry!*** (NOT ~~***Hurry yourself!***~~)

For more about structures like *The door opened* and *His book's selling well*, see 579.3.

472 reinforcement tags

1 repeated subject and auxiliary verb

In informal spoken English (especially British English), a sentence sometimes ends with a 'tag' which repeats the subject and auxiliary verb.

*You've gone mad, **you have**.*

*I'm getting fed up, **I am**.*

If the main clause has no auxiliary verb, *do* is used in the tag.

*He likes his beer, **he does**.*

2 use

One reason for using a reinforcement tag is simply to emphasise the idea of the main clause by repeating it.

*You're really clever, **you are**.*

A tag can also move the subject to the end of the sentence, so that the verb comes earlier and gets more immediate attention. (This is called 'fronting'; for details, see 217.)

*Getting in my way, **you are**.*

*Likes his beer, **John does**.*

It is possible to 'announce' the subject with a pronoun, and put the full subject in a tag.

***He** hasn't a chance, **Fred hasn't**.*

***She** really got on my nerves, **Sylvia did**.*

3 subject-only tags

It is possible to have reinforcement tags without verbs. Ellipsis (see 183) of the subject and verb is possible.

*(You're) living in the clouds, **you lot**.*

*(They're) very polite, **your children**.*

Pronouns are not usually used alone in tags, except for reflexives.

*Don't think much of the party, **myself**.*

For similar structures, see 465–466 (question tags), 463 (reply questions) and 493 (short answers).

473 relatives (1): relative clauses and pronouns (introduction)

1 relative clauses

Clauses beginning with question words (e.g. *who, which, where*) are often used to modify nouns and some pronouns – to identify people and things, or to give more information about them. Clauses used like this are called 'relative clauses'.

*Have you ever spoken to the people **who live next door**?*

*Those **who have not yet registered** should do so at once.*

*There's a programme on tonight **which you might like**.*

*He's got a job in a new firm, **where they don't work such long hours**.*

Relative clauses can also be introduced by *that*.

*Here's the book **that** you were looking for.* ▶

2 relative pronouns

When *who, whom* etc are used to introduce relative clauses, they are called 'relative pronouns'. *Who, which* and *that* can be the subjects of verbs in relative clauses. *Who* refers to people and *which* to things; *that* can refer to both people and things.

> *What's the name of the tall man **who** just came in?*
> (NOT *...the tall man which*...)
> *It's a book **which** will interest children of all ages.* (NOT *...a book who*...)
> *The people **that** live next door keep having all-night parties.*
> *These are the keys **that** open the front and back door.*

Who, whom, which and *that* can also be used as the objects of verbs in relative clauses. *Who* is informal as an object; in a more formal style, *whom* is used, especially in certain kinds of relative clause (for details, see 474).

> *He's married somebody **who** I really don't like.* (informal)
> *He has married somebody **whom** I really do not like.* (formal)
> *I gave him an envelope, **which** he put in his pocket at once.*
> *Here are the papers **that** you were looking for.*

3 relative *when, where* and *why*

When and *where* can introduce relative clauses after nouns referring to time and place. They are used in the same way as **preposition + *which***.

> *I'll never forget the **day when** I first met you.*
> (= *... the day **on which**...*)
> *Do you know a **shop where** I can find sandals?*
> (= *... a shop **at which**...*)

Why is used in a similar way after *reason*.

> *Do you know the **reason why** she doesn't like me?*
> (= *... the reason **for which**...*)

4 leaving out object pronouns

In some kinds of relative clause (see 474), object pronouns can be left out.

> *She's somebody **I really can't stand**.* (= *... somebody **that**...*)
> *Here are the papers **you were looking for**.* (= *... the papers **that**...*)

5 double use of relative pronouns

Relative pronouns have a double use: they act as subjects or objects inside relative clauses, and at the same time they connect relative clauses to nouns or pronouns in other clauses – rather like conjunctions. As subjects or objects they replace words like *she* or *him*: one subject or object in a relative clause is enough. Compare:

> – *He's got a new girl-friend. **She** works in a garage.*
> *He's got a new girl-friend **who** works in a garage.*
> (NOT *...who she works in a garage.*)
> – *This is Mr Rogers. You met **him** last year.*
> *This is Mr Rogers, **whom** you met last year.*
> (NOT *...whom you met him last year.*)
> – *Here's an article. **It** might interest you.*
> *Here's an article **which** might interest you.*
> (NOT *...which it might interest you.*)

– *I've found the car keys. You were looking for **them**.*
*I've found the car keys **which** you were looking for.*
(NOT *...~~which you were looking for **them**.~~*)

6 *whose*

Whose is a possessive relative word, used as a determiner before nouns.
It replaces *his/her/its*. For more details, see 475.
*I saw a girl **whose hair** came down to her waist.*
(NOT *...~~whose her hair came down~~...*)

7 *which* referring to a whole clause

Which can refer not only to a noun, but also to the whole of a previous
clause. Note that *what, that* and *how* cannot be used in this way.
*He got married again a year later, **which** surprised everybody.*
(NOT *..., ~~what/that surprised everybody.~~*)
*She cycled from London to Glasgow, **which** is pretty good for a woman of 75.*
(NOT *~~She cycled..., what/that is pretty good~~...*)
*I was impressed by the way **in which** she did it.*
(NOT *~~I was impressed by the way **how** she did it.~~*)

8 separating a noun from its relative pronoun

Relative pronouns usually follow their nouns directly.
*The **idea which** she put forward was interesting.*
(NOT *~~The **idea** was interesting **which** she put forward.~~*)
*I rang up **Mrs Spencer, who** did our accounts.*
(NOT *~~I rang Mrs Spencer **up**, who did our accounts.~~*)
However, a descriptive phrase can sometimes separate a noun from its
relative pronoun.
*I rang up Mrs Spencer, **the Manager's secretary,** who did our accounts.*

For the use of *what* and *how* in nominal relative clauses, see 476.
For more about relative clauses and pronouns, see the following sections.
For other ways of using question-word clauses, see 460.5.

474 **relatives** (2): identifying and non-identifying clauses

1 two kinds of relative clause

Some relative clauses identify or classify nouns: they tell us which person or
thing, or which kind of person or thing, is meant. (In grammars, these are
called 'identifying', 'defining' or 'restrictive' relative clauses.)
*What's the name of the tall man **who just came in**?*
*Is that your car **that's parked outside**?*
*Paris is a city **I've always wanted to visit**.*
*People **who take physical exercise** live longer.*
*Have you got something **that will get ink out of a carpet**?*
Other relative clauses do not identify or classify; they simply tell us more
about a person or thing that is already identified. (In grammars, these are

called 'non-identifying', 'non-defining' or 'non-restrictive' relative clauses.)
> *This is Ms Rogers, **who's joining the firm next week**.*
> *In 1908 Ford developed his Model T car, **which sold for $500**.*

There are several grammatical differences between the two kinds of relative clause. There are also stylistic differences: non-identifying clauses are generally more formal, and are less frequent in informal speech.

2 **pronunciation and punctuation**

Identifying relative clauses usually follow immediately after the nouns that they modify, without a break: they are not separated by pauses or intonation movements in speech, or by commas in writing. (This is because the noun would be incomplete without the relative clause, and the sentence would make no sense or have a different meaning.) Non-identifying clauses are normally separated by pauses and / or intonation breaks and commas. Compare:

– *The woman **who does my hair** has moved to another hairdresser's.*
  *Dorothy, **who does my hair**, has moved to another hairdresser's.*
– *She married a man **that she met on a bus**.*
  *She married a very nice young architect from Belfast, **whom she met on a bus**.*

Note how the identifying clauses cannot easily be left out.
> *The woman has moved to another hairdresser's.* (Which woman?)
> *She married a man.* (!)

When a non-identifying clause does not come at the end of a sentence, two commas are necessary.
> *Dorothy, **who does my hair**, has moved . . .*
> (NOT *Dorothy, ~~who does my hair has moved~~ . . .*)

3 **use of *that***

That is common as a relative pronoun in identifying clauses. It can refer to things, and in an informal style to people. In non-identifying clauses, *that* is unusual. Compare:

– *Have you got a book **that's** really easy to read?* (OR . . . ***which is*** . . .)
  *I lent him 'The Old Man and the Sea', **which** is really easy to read.*
    (NOT *~~I lent him 'The Old Man and the Sea', that is really easy to read.~~*)
– *Where's the girl **that** sells the tickets?* (OR . . . ***who sells*** . . .)
  *This is Naomi, **who** sells the tickets.*
    (NOT *~~This is Naomi, that sells the tickets.~~*)

4 ***all that, only . . . that* etc**

That is especially common after quantifiers like *all, every(thing), some(thing), any(thing), no(thing), none, little, few, much, only*, and after superlatives.
> *Is this **all that's** left?* (More natural than . . . *all **which** is left?*)
> *Have you got **anything that** belongs to me?*
>   (More natural than . . . *anything **which*** . . .)
> *The **only** thing **that** matters is to find our way home.*
> *I hope the **little that** I've done has been useful.*
> *It's the **best** film **that's** ever been made about madness.*

Note that *what* (see 476) cannot be used in these cases.
> **All *that*** *you say is certainly true.* (NOT ~~*All **what** you say* . . .~~)

5 *who* and *whom*

Who can be used as an object in identifying clauses in an informal style.
Whom is more formal.
> *The woman **who** I marry will have a good sense of humour.*
> (More formal: *The woman **whom** I marry* . . .)

In non-identifying clauses, *who* is less common as an object, though it is
sometimes used in an informal style.
> *In that year he met Rachel, **whom** he was later to marry.*
> (OR . . . *Rachel, **who** he was later to marry.* – informal)

6 leaving out object pronouns

In identifying relative clauses, we often leave out object pronouns, especially
in an informal style. In non-identifying clauses this is not possible. Compare:
– *I feel sorry for the man **she married**.*
   *She went to work with my brother, **whom she later married**.*
   (NOT ~~*She went to work with my brother, she later married.*~~)
– *What did you think of the wine **we drank last night**?*
   *I poured him a glass of wine, **which he drank at once**.*
   (NOT ~~*I poured him a glass of wine, he drank at once.*~~)

For omission of *when, where* and *why*, see 477.3.

7 position of prepositions

Prepositions can come either before relative pronouns (more formal) or at
the end of relative clauses (more informal). Compare:
– *He was respected by the people **with whom** he worked.* (formal)
   *He was respected by the people **(that)** he worked **with**.* (informal)
– *This is the room **in which** I was born.* (formal)
   *This is the room **(that)** I was born **in**.* (informal)

Who and *that* are not used after prepositions.
> . . . *the people **with whom** he worked.*
> (NOT . . . ~~*the people **with who/that** he worked.*~~)

For more about prepositions at the end of clauses, see 440.
For tenses in identifying clauses, see 556.

475 relatives (3): **whose**

1 relative possessive

Whose is a relative possessive word, used as a determiner before nouns in the
same way as *his, her, its* or *their*. It can refer back to people or things. In a
relative clause, ***whose* + noun** can be the subject, the object of a verb or the
object of a preposition.
> *I saw a girl **whose beauty** took my breath away.* (subject)
> *It was a meeting **whose purpose** I did not understand.* (object) ▶

*Michel Croz, **with whose help** Whymper climbed the Matterhorn, was one
of the first professional guides.* (object of preposition)
*I went to see my friends the Forrests, **whose children** I used to look **after**
when they were small.* (object of preposition)

Whose can be used in both identifying and non-identifying clauses.

2 *of which; that ... of*

Instead of *whose*, we can use *of which* or *that ... of* (less formal) to refer to
things, and these are sometimes preferred. The most common word order is
noun + *of which* or ***that ... of***, but ***of which ... + noun*** is also possible.
Compare the following four ways of expressing the same idea.

*He's written a book **whose name** I've forgotten.*
*He's written a book **the name of which** I've forgotten.*
*He's written a book **that** I've forgotten the **name of**.*
*He's written a book **of which** I've forgotten **the name**.*

We do not normally use **noun + *of whom*** in a possessive sense.

3 only used as a determiner

Relative *whose* is only used as a possessive determiner, before a noun. In
other cases we use *of which/whom* or *that ... of*.

*He's married to a singer **of whom** you may have heard.*
OR ... ***that** you may have heard **of**.*
(NOT ... ~~a singer **whose** you may have heard.~~)

4 formality

Sentences with *whose* are generally felt to be rather heavy and formal; in an
informal style other structures are often preferred. *With* (see 602) is a
common way of expressing possessive ideas, and is usually more natural
than *whose* in descriptions.

*I've got some friends **with** a house that looks over a river.*
(Less formal than ... ***whose** house looks over a river.*)
*You know that girl **with** a brother who drives lorries?*
(Less formal than ... ***whose** brother drives lorries?*)
*She's married to the man over there **with** the enormous ears.*
(More natural than ... *the man over there **whose** ears are enormous.*)

For *whose* in questions, see 597.

476 relatives (4): **what** and other nominal relative pronouns

1 *what*: meaning and use

What does not refer to a noun that comes before it. It acts as **noun + relative
pronoun** together, and means 'the thing(s) which'.

***What** she said made me angry.*
*I hope you're going to give me **what** I need.*

Clauses beginning with *what* act as subjects or objects, and are called
'nominal relative clauses'.

For singular and plural verbs after *what* (e.g. *What we need most **is/are** books*), see 506.

2 *what* not used

What is only used as a nominal relative, meaning 'the thing(s) which'. It cannot be used as an ordinary relative pronoun after a noun or pronoun.

> *We haven't got **everything that** you ordered.* (NOT *...~~everything what~~...*)
> ***The only thing that** keeps me awake is coffee.*
>   (NOT *~~The only thing what~~...*)

We use *which*, not *what*, to refer to a whole clause that comes before.

> ***Sally married George, which** made Paul very unhappy.*
>   (NOT *...~~what made Paul very unhappy.~~*)

3 *what* as a determiner

What can be used as a determiner with a noun in a nominal relative clause.

> ***What money** he has comes from his family.*
> *I'll give you **what help** I can.* (=... ***any help that** I can.*)

4 other nominal relatives

Other words that are used as nominal relatives include *whatever, whoever, whichever, where, wherever, when, whenever* and *how*.

> *Take **whatever** you want.* (=... ***anything that** you want.*)
> *I often think about **where** I met you.* (=... ***the place where**...*)
> *We've bought a cottage in the country for **when** we retire.*
>   (=... ***the time when**...*)
> ***Whenever** you want to come is fine with me.* (= ***Any day that**...*)
> *Look at **how** he treats me.* (=... ***the way in which**...*)

For details of the use of *whoever, whatever* and other words ending in *-ever*, see 596. For more about *how*-clauses, see 254.

5 older English: *who* and *that which*

In older English, *who* could be used as a nominal relative, meaning 'whoever', 'anybody who' or 'the person(s) who'. In modern English, this is very unusual.

> ***Who** steals my purse steals trash.* (Shakespeare, *Othello*)
>   (Modern English: ***Whoever / Anybody who**...*)

That which used to be used in the same way as *what*. This, too, is very unusual in modern English.

> *We have **that which** we need.* (Modern English: *We have **what** we need.*)

For other uses of question-word clauses, see 460.5.

477 relatives (5): advanced points

1 *some of whom, none of which* etc

In non-identifying clauses, quantifying determiners (e.g. *some, any, none, all, both, several, enough, many* and *few*) can be used with *of whom, of which* and *of whose*. The determiner most often comes before *of which/whom/whose*, but can sometimes come after it in a very formal style.

> *They picked up five boat-loads of refugees, **some of whom** had been at sea for several months.* (OR *... **of whom some**...*)

▶

*We've tested three hundred types of boot, **none of which** is completely
    waterproof.* (OR *... **of which none** ...*)
*They've got eight children, **all of whom** are studying music.*
    (OR *... **of whom all** are studying...*)
*She had a teddy-bear, **both of whose** eyes were missing.*
This structure is also possible with other expressions of quantity, with
superlatives, with *first, second* etc, and with *last.*

a number of whom   three of which   half of which
the majority of whom   the youngest of whom

2   *which* as determiner

Which can be used as a determiner in relative clauses, with a general noun
which repeats the meaning of what came before. This structure is rather
formal, and is mainly used after prepositions, especially in some fixed
phrases like *in which case* and *at which point.*

*She may be late, **in which case** we ought to wait for her.*
*He lost his temper, **at which point** I decided to go home.*
*He was appointed Lord Chancellor, **in which post** he spent the rest of
    his life.*
*He spoke in Greek, **which language** I could only follow with difficulty.*

3   *when, where* etc replaced by *that* or dropped

After common nouns referring to time, *when* is often replaced by *that* or
dropped in an informal style.

*Come and see us any **time (that)** you're in town.*
*I'll never forget the **day (that)** we met.*
*That was the **year (that)** I first went abroad.*
The same thing happens with *where* after *somewhere, anywhere, everywhere,
nowhere* and *place* (but not after other words).

*Have you got **somewhere (that)** I can lie down for an hour?*
*We need a **place (that)** we can stay for a few days.*
    (BUT NOT ~~We need a **house** we can stay for a few days.~~)
After *way, in which* can be replaced by *that* or dropped in an informal style.

*I didn't like the **way (that)** she spoke to me.*
*Do you know a **way (that)** you can earn money without working?*
The same thing happens with *why* after *reason.*

*The **reason (that)** you're so bad-tempered is that you're hungry.*

For more about *place,* see 427. For *way,* see 587. For *reason,* see 470.

4   relative + infinitive

When a noun or pronoun is the object of a following infinitive, a relative
pronoun is not normally used.

*I can't think of **anybody to invite**.* (NOT *...~~anybody **whom** to invite.~~*)
However, relative pronouns are possible with preposition structures.

*We moved to the country so that the children would have **a garden in
    which to play**.*
*He was miserable unless he had **neighbours with whom to quarrel**.*

This structure is rather formal, and it is more common to use **infinitive + preposition** without a relative pronoun.

> *... so that the children would have **a garden to play in**.*
> (NOT *...~~which to play in.~~*)
> *... unless he had **neighbours to quarrel with**.*
> (NOT *...~~whom to quarrel with.~~*)

5 agreement of person

Most relative clauses have third-person reference; *I who ..., you who ...* and *we who ...* are unusual, though they sometimes occur in a very formal style.

> **You who** *pass by, tell them of us and say*
> *For their tomorrow we gave our today.*
> (Allied war memorial at Kohima)

A different kind of first- and second-person reference is common in the relative clauses of cleft sentences (see 131). However, the verb is usually third-person, especially in an informal style.

> *It's me that's responsible for the organisation.*
> (More formal: *It is **I** who **am** responsible ...*)
> *You're the one that **knows** where to go.* (NOT *...~~the one that know~~ ...*)

6 reduced relative clauses

A participle can often be used instead of a relative pronoun and full verb.

> *Who's the girl **dancing** with your brother?*
> (= *... **who is dancing** with your brother?*)
> *Anyone **touching** that wire will get a shock.*
> (= *... **who touches** ...*)
> *Half of the people **invited** to the party didn't turn up.*
> (= *... **who were invited** ...*)
> *I found him sitting at a table **covered with papers**.*
> (= *... **which was covered** with papers.*)

Reduced structures are also used with the adjectives *available* and *possible*.

> *Please send me all the tickets **available**.* (= *... that are available.*)
> *Tuesday's the only date **possible**.*

7 omission of subject

In a very informal style, a subject relative pronoun is sometimes dropped after *there is*.

> ***There's** a man at the door wants to talk to you.*

8 relative clauses after indefinite noun phrases

The distinction between identifying and non-identifying clauses (see 474) is most clear when they modify **definite** noun phrases like *the car, this house, my father, Mrs Lewis*. After **indefinite** noun phrases like *a car, some nurses* or *friends*, the distinction is less clear, and both kinds of clause are often possible with slight differences of emphasis.

> *He's got **a new car that goes like a bomb**.*
> OR *He's got **a new car, which goes like a bomb**.*
> *We became friendly with **some nurses that John had met in Paris**.*
> OR *We became friendly with **some nurses, whom John had met in Paris**.*

▶

In general, 'identifying' clauses are used when the information they give is felt to be centrally important to the overall message. When this is not so, non-identifying clauses are preferred.

9 relative pronouns as general-purpose connectors

In non-identifying clauses, the pronouns *who* and *which* sometimes act as general-purpose connecting words, rather like ***and* + pronoun**.

> *She passed the letter to Moriarty, **who** passed it on to me.*
> (= . . . ***and he** passed it on . . .*)
> *I dropped the saucepan, **which** knocked over the eggs, **which** went all over the floor.* (= . . . ***and it** knocked . . . **and they** went . . .*)
> *I do a lot of walking, **which** keeps me fit.* (= . . . ***and this** keeps me fit.*)

10 relative clauses with indirect statement etc

It is often possible to combine relative clauses with indirect statements and similar structures, e.g. *I know/said/feel/hope/wish (that)* . . . , especially in an informal style. Expressions like *I know, I said* etc come after the position of the relative pronoun.

> *We're going to meet somebody **(who/that) I know (that) you'll like**.*
> *It's a house **(which/that) we feel (that) we might want to buy**.*
> *That's the man **(who/that) I wish (that) I'd married**.*

Note that the conjunction (the second *that*) is usually dropped in this structure; it must be dropped if the relative pronoun is a subject.

> *This is the woman **(who/that) Ann said could show us the church**.*
> (NOT ~~*This is the woman (who/that) Ann said **that** could show us*~~ . . .)

In this structure, people sometimes use *whom* as a subject pronoun. This is not generally considered correct.

> *This is a letter from my father, **whom** we hope will be out of hospital soon.*
> (More correct: . . . ***who** we hope will be out* . . .)

Relative clauses can also be combined with *if*-clauses in sentences like the following.

> *I am enclosing an application form, **which** I should be grateful **if you would sign and return**.*

11 *a car that I didn't know how fast it could go*, etc

We do not usually combine a relative clause with an indirect question structure. However, this sometimes happens in informal speech.

> *I've just been to see an old friend that **I'm not sure when I'm going to see again**.*
> *There's a pile of washing-up in the kitchen that **I just don't know how I'm going to do**.*

There is no grammatically correct way of doing this when the relative pronoun is the subject of the relative clause. However, sentences like the following (with added pronouns) are also sometimes heard in informal British speech.

> *I was driving a car **that I didn't know how fast it could go**.*
> *It's ridiculous to sing songs **that you don't know what they mean**.*
> *There's a control at the back **that I don't understand how it works**.*
> *There's still one kid **that I must find out whether she's coming to the party or not**.*

12 double object

Occasionally a relative pronoun acts as the object of two verbs. This happens especially when a relative clause is followed by *before ... ing, after ... ing* or *without ... ing*.

*We have water **that** it's best not to drink **before boiling**.* (OR *... boiling **it**.)*

*I'm sending you a letter **that** I want you to destroy **after reading**.*

(OR *... after reading **it**.)*

*He was somebody **that** you could like **without admiring**.*

(OR *... admiring **him**.)*

478 remind

1 *remind* + object + infinitive; *remind* + *that*-clause

The infinitive structure refers to **actions**: you *remind somebody to do* something that he/she might forget.

*Please **remind me to go** to the post office.*

(NOT ~~Please remind me of going~~ ...)

The structure with a *that*-clause refers to **facts**.

*I **reminded him that** we hadn't got any petrol left.*

This kind of idea can also sometimes be expressed with *remind ... about*.

*I **reminded** her **about** her dental appointment.*

(= *... that she had to go to the dentist.*)

2 *remind ... of ...*

We use *remind ... of* to say that something makes us remember the past, or makes us think about things that have been forgotten.

*The smell of hay always **reminds me of** our old house in the country.*

(NOT *... ~~reminds me our old house~~ ...*)

***Remind me of** your phone number.*

We can also use *remind ... of* to talk about similarities.

*She **reminds me of** her mother.* (= *She is like her mother.*)

3 *remind* and *remember*

These two verbs are not the same. *Reminding* somebody means 'making somebody remember'. Compare:

– ***Remind** me to pay the milkman.* (NOT ~~Remember me to pay~~ ...)

*I'm afraid I won't **remember** to pay the milkman.*

– *This sort of weather **reminds** me of my home.*

(NOT ~~This sort of weather **remembers me**~~ ...)

*This sort of weather makes me **remember** my home.*

But note the idiomatic use of *remember* in ***Remember** me to your parents* and similar sentences.

479 repetition

1 avoidance of repetition

In English, unnecessary repetition is usually considered to be a bad thing. Careful writers generally try not to use the same words and structures in successive clauses and sentences without a good reason; when expressions are repeated, it is often for deliberate emphasis or other stylistic purposes. Casual repetition is more common in informal language, but even in conversation people often sound monotonous or clumsy if they do not vary their sentence structure and vocabulary. Some kinds of repetition are actually ungrammatical in both writing and speech.

2 unnatural/ungrammatical repetition

When we want to refer again to a person or thing that has already been mentioned, we normally have to use a pronoun instead of repeating the noun phrase that was first used. When the reference is very close to the original mention, repetition (unless there is a special reason for it) is usually so unnatural as to be ungrammatical.

> *'What's **Rachel** doing here?' '**She** wants to talk to you.'*
>> (NOT ... *'**Rachel** wants to talk to you.'*)
> *We got **that cat** because the children wanted **it**.*
>> (NOT *We got that cat because the children wanted **that cat**.*)
> ***Dad's** just cut **himself** shaving.* (NOT *Dad's just cut **Dad** shaving.*)
> ***Barbara** got **her** handbag stolen on the bus.*
>> (NOT *Barbara got **Barbara's** handbag stolen...*)

This kind of thing happens with other words besides nouns.

> *'I don't **smoke**.' '**I do**.'* (NOT ... *'**I smoke**.'*)
> *'My mother **has decided to retire**'. '**Oh, has** she?'*
>> (NOT *'Oh, has she **decided to retire**?'*)
> *'Do you know if **the bank's open**?' 'I think **so**.'*
>> (NOT *'I think **the bank's open**.'*)
> *She's staying at the Royal Hotel, so we said we'd meet her **there**.*
>> (NOT ... *so we said we'd meet her at **the Royal Hotel**.*)

Note, however, that repetition is quite normal when alternatives are discussed.

> *'Shall we dance or **go for a walk**?' 'Let's **go for a walk**.'*
> *'Would you rather have potatoes or **rice**?' '**Rice**, please.'*

For more about structures used for avoiding repetition, see 181–186 (ellipsis) and 542 (substitution).

3 duplicated subjects and objects

It is unusual in English to use both a noun and a pronoun as subjects or objects with the same verb.

> *That wall needs painting.*
>> (More normal than ***That wall, it** needs painting.*)
> *I saw my uncle yesterday.*
>> (More normal than ***My uncle, I** saw **him** yesterday.*)

However, this kind of structure is sometimes possible in very informal speech, especially with long subjects or fronted objects and / or with tags.

> *That friend of your mother's – **he**'s on the phone.*
> *Those bicycle wheels – I think we ought to put **them** in the garden shed.*
> ***She***'s a clever girl, your **Anne**.

4 related verbs and nouns

We usually avoid putting related verbs and nouns together.

– *He's made a wonderful **plan**.*
  OR *He's **planned** something wonderful.*
  BUT NOT ~~*He's **planned** a wonderful plan.*~~
– *She **wrote** an interesting paper.*
  OR *She did an interesting piece of **writing**.*
  BUT NOT ~~*She **wrote** an interesting piece of **writing**.*~~

There are some fixed expressions which are exceptions (e.g. *to sing a song, to live a good life, to die a violent death*).

5 *Wonderful, isn't it?* etc

There is a common kind of conversational exchange in which one speaker gives his / her opinion of something, and the other speaker agrees by saying the same thing in other words which are at least as emphatic. Repetition is carefully avoided.

> '***Glorious*** *day.*' '***Wonderful**, isn't it?*' (NOT ... '~~***Glorious**, isn't it?*~~')
> '***Terrible*** *weather.*' '***Dreadful**.*'
> '*Manchester did**n't** play **very well**, then.*' '*Bloody **rubbish**.*'

6 clumsy style

In writing, repetition is often considered clumsy even when it is not ungrammatical. Most of the repetitions in the following text would be avoided by a careful writer, by varying the structure and by careful use of synonyms (e.g. *tried/attempted, summarise/describe briefly, forecast/predict*).

> *In this report, I have tried to forecast likely developments over the next three years. In the first section, I have tried to summarise the results of the last two years, and I have tried to summarise the present situation. In the second section, I have tried to forecast the likely consequences of the present situation, and the consequences of the present financial policy.*

7 deliberate repetition

Speakers and writers can of course repeat vocabulary and structures deliberately. This may be done for emphasis.

> *I'm **very, very** sorry.*
> *I want **every** room cleaned – **every** single room.*

Structural repetition can show how ideas are similar or related (by using the same structure for the same kind of item).

> *First of all, I **want to** congratulate you all on the splendid results. Secondly, I **want to** give you some interesting news. And finally, I **want to** thank you all ...*　▶

8 literary examples

Here are two contrasting examples of repetition used deliberately for literary purposes. In the first, by John Steinbeck, structures and key vocabulary (nouns and verbs) are repeated and rhythmically balanced in order to create an impressive (or mock-impressive) effect – to make the story and characters sound striking and important.

> *This is the story of Danny and of Danny's friends and of Danny's house. It is a story of how these three became one thing, so that in Tortilla flat if you speak of Danny's house you do not mean a structure of wood flaked with old white-wash, overgrown with an ancient untrimmed rose of Castile. No, when you speak of Danny's house you are understood to mean a unit of which the parts are men, from which came sweetness and joy, philanthropy, and, in the end, a mystic sorrow. For Danny's house was not unlike the Round Table, and Danny's friends were not unlike the knights of it. And this is the story of how the group came into being, of how it flourished and grew to be an organisation beautiful and wise. This story deals with the adventuring of Danny's friends, with the good they did, with their thoughts and their endeavors. In the end, this story tells how the talisman was lost and how the group disintegrated.*
>
> (John Steinbeck, *Tortilla Flat*)

In contrast, the following text, by Ernest Hemingway, uses a kind of style which 'good' writers would normally avoid, repeating pronouns and simple structures in an apparently monotonous way. Hemingway's purpose is to show the simplicity of his hero, an uneducated old fisherman, by using a style that is supposed to reflect the way he thinks and speaks.

> *He did not remember when he had first started to talk aloud when he was by himself. He had sung when he was by himself in the old days and he had sung at night sometimes when he was alone steering on his watch in the smacks or in the turtle boats. He had probably started to talk aloud, when alone, when the boy had left. But he did not remember.*
>
> (Ernest Hemingway, *The Old Man and the Sea*)

480 reporting (1): introduction

There are two main ways of reporting people's words, thoughts, beliefs etc.

1 'direct speech'

We can give the exact words (more or less) that were said, or that we imagine were thought. This kind of structure is called 'direct speech'.

> *So he said, **'I want to go home,'** and just walked out.*
> *Did she say, **'What do you want?'***
> *And then I thought, **'Well, does he really mean it?'***

For the use of quotation marks with direct speech, see 458. For commas before and after direct speech, see 455.

2 'indirect speech'

We can make a speaker's words or thoughts part of our own sentence, using conjunctions (e.g. *that*), and changing pronouns, tenses and other words where necessary. This kind of structure is called 'indirect speech' or 'reported speech'.

> *So he said that **he wanted to go home**, and just walked out.*
> *Did she just ask **what I wanted**?*
> *And then I wondered **whether he really meant it**.*

3 mixing structures

These two structures cannot normally be mixed (but see 482).

> *She said to me **'I have got no money'** and asked me for help.*
> O R *She said to me **that she had got no money** and asked me for help.*
> B U T N O T ~~She said to me **that I have got no money** and asked me for help.~~

For details of direct and indirect speech, see the following sections.

481 reporting (2): basic rules for indirect speech

1 change of situation

Words that are spoken or thought in one place by one person may be reported in another place at a different time, and perhaps by another person. Because of this, there are often grammatical differences between direct and indirect speech. These changes are mostly natural and logical, and it is not necessary to learn complicated rules about indirect speech in English.

> B I L L (on Saturday evening): ***I don't** like **this** party. **I want** to go home **now**.*
> P E T E R (on Sunday morning): *Bill said that **he didn't** like **the** party, and **he wanted** to go home **right away**.*

2 pronouns

A change of speaker may mean a change of pronoun. In the example above, Bill says *I* to refer to himself. Peter, talking about what Bill said, naturally uses *he*.

> *Bill said that **he** didn't like the party ...*
> (N O T ~~Bill said that **I** didn't like the party ...~~)

3 'here and now' words

A change of place and time may mean changing words like *here, this, now, today*. Peter, reporting what Bill said, does not use *this* and *now* because he is no longer at the party.

> *Bill said that he didn't like **the** party ...*
> (N O T ~~Bill said that he didn't like **this** party ...~~)

Note that *next* and *last* are also 'here and now' words.

Original words	Reported words
*I'll be back **next** week.*	*She said she'd be back **the next** week, but I never saw her again.*
*I got my licence **last** Tuesday.*	*He said he'd got his licence **the Tuesday before**.*

▶

4   tenses

A change of time may mean a change of tense: the person reporting uses tenses that relate to the time when he/she is making the report, not to the time when the original words were used.

Bill **said** that he **didn't** like the party . . .
> (NOT ~~Bill said that he **doesn't** like the party~~ . . .)

So after past reporting verbs, the verbs of the original speech are usually 'backshifted' – made more past. Compare:

Original words	Reported words
Will you marry me?	I asked him if he **would** marry me.
	(NOT . . . ~~if he **will** marry me.~~)
You **look** nice.	I told her she **looked** nice.
	(NOT ~~I told her she **looks** nice.~~)
I **can't** swim.	He pretended he **couldn't** swim.
	(NOT ~~He pretended he **can't** swim.~~)
I'm learning French.	She said she **was learning** French.
	(NOT ~~She said she **is learning** French.~~)
I've forgotten.	He said he **had forgotten**.
	(NOT ~~He said he **has forgotten.**~~)
John **phoned**.	She told me that John **(had) phoned**.

Sometimes this means that past verbs are used to talk about the present or the future.

I knew you **were** American.

Sorry, I **didn't realise** this **was** your seat.

After present, future and present perfect reporting verbs, tenses are usually the same as in the original (because there is no important change of time).

He **says** he **doesn't** want to play any more.

I'**ll tell** her your idea **is** great.

The government **has announced** that taxes **will be raised**.

5   dropping *that*

The conjunction *that* is often dropped, especially after common reporting verbs (e.g. *say, think*) in informal speech.

She said **(that)** she'd had enough.

I think **(that)** you're probably right.

That cannot be dropped after certain verbs (e.g. *reply, telegraph, shout*), and it is not usually dropped after nouns.

I **replied that** I did not intend to stand for election.
> (NOT ~~I replied I did not intend~~ . . .)

She **shouted that** she was busy. (NOT ~~She shouted she was busy.~~)

He disagreed with Copernicus's **view that** the earth went round the sun.
> (NOT . . . ~~Copernicus's view the earth went~~ . . .)

For more about omission of *that*, see 461.8, 560.

6   questions and answers

In reported questions the subject normally comes before the verb in standard English, and auxiliary *do* is not used (except in negative questions – see 482.7). The same structure is used for reporting the answers to questions, and in other uses of question-word clauses.

*He wanted to know when **I was** leaving.* (NOT *...when **was I leaving**.*)
*I asked where **the President and his wife were** staying.*
    (NOT *I asked where **were**...*)
*I knew how **they felt**.* (NOT *...how **did they feel**.*)
*Nobody told me why **I had** to sign the paper.*
    (NOT *...why **did I have to sign**...*)
*How **you get** there is your problem.* (NOT *How **do you get there**...*)

Question marks are not used in reported questions.

We asked where the money was. (NOT *...where the money was?*)

Yes/no questions are reported with *if* or *whether* (for the difference, see 593).

*The driver asked **if/whether** I wanted the town centre.*
*I don't know **if/whether** I can help you.*

Say and *tell* are not used to report questions.

    NOT *The driver **said** whether I wanted the town centre.*

But *say* and *tell* can introduce the answers to questions.

*Please **say** whether you want the town centre.*
*He never **says** where he's going.*   *I **told** her what time it was.*

For the difference between *say* and *tell*, see 487.
For more about question-word clauses, see 460.5.

7   actions: promises, orders, requests, advice etc

Speech relating to actions (e.g. promises, agreements, orders, offers, requests, advice and suggestions) is often reported with infinitives, or **object + infinitive**.

*He promised **to write**.   She agreed **to wait** for me.*
*I told **Andrew to be** careful.*
*The lady downstairs has asked **us to be** quiet after nine o'clock.*
*Ann has offered **to baby-sit** tonight.*
*I advise **you to think** again before you decide.*
*The policeman told **me not to park** there.*

The structure **question word + infinitive** is common (see 288).

*He asked her **how to make** a white sauce.   Don't tell me **what to do**.*

We do not use infinitive structures after *suggest* or (usually) after *say*. However, after these and many other verbs, instructions etc can be reported with *that*-clauses, usually with modal verbs (see 344) or subjunctives (see 541).

*He suggested **that I try the main car park**.*
    (NOT *He suggested **me to try**...*)
*The policeman said **that I mustn't park there**.*
    (NOT *The policeman said **me not to park there**.*)
*I told Andrew **that he ought to be careful**.*

For *ought, must* and other modal verbs in indirect speech, see 482.5.
For *suggest*, see 545.
For the structures that are possible after particular verbs, see a good dictionary.

482 reporting (3): advanced points

1 direct speech: word order with reporting verbs

In informal spoken reports, *say* and *think* are the normal reporting verbs. They can go before sentences or at other natural breaks (e.g. between clauses or after discourse markers).

> *So I **said** 'What are you doing in our bedroom?' 'I'm sorry', he **said**, 'I thought it was my room.' Well, I **thought**, that's funny, he's got my handbag open. 'If that's the case,' I **said**, 'what are you doing with my handbag?'*

In novels, short stories etc, a much wider variety of reporting verbs are used: for example *ask, exclaim, suggest, reply, cry, reflect, suppose, grunt, snarl, hiss, whisper*. And inversion (see 299) is often used.

> *'Is this Mr Rochester's house?' **asked Emma**.*
>
> *'Great Heavens!' **cried Celia**. 'Is there no end to your wickedness? I implore you – leave me alone!' 'Never,' **hissed the Duke** . . .*

Inversion is not normal with pronoun subjects.

> *'You monster!' **she screamed**.* (NOT *. . . ~~screamed she~~.*)

In literary writing, reporting expressions often interrupt the normal flow of the sentences quoted.

> *'Your information,' **I replied**, 'is out of date.'*

For more about inversion, see 298, 299.

2 indirect speech: word order with *what, who* and *which*

When we report questions constructed with ***who/what/which* + *be* + complement**, *be* can be put before or after the complement.

- Direct: *Who's the best player here?*
  Indirect: *She asked me **who was the best player**.*
             *She asked me **who the best player was**.*
- Direct: *What's the matter?*
  Indirect: *I asked **what was the matter**.*
             *I asked **what the matter was**.*
- Direct: *Which is my seat?*
  Indirect: *She wondered **which was her seat**.*
             *She wondered **which her seat was**.*

3 indirect speech: reporting past tenses

In indirect speech, a speaker's present perfect and past tenses are often reported using past perfect tenses (because the events he / she spoke about had happened before he / she spoke, and because the reporter's point of view is not the same as the original speaker's point of view).

- Direct: *I**'ve just written** to John.*
  Indirect: *She told me she **had just written** to John.*
- Direct: *I **saw** Penny at the theatre a couple of days ago.*
  Indirect: *In his letter, he said he**'d seen** Penny at the theatre a couple of days before.*

However, it is often unnecessary to show the time relationship between the events spoken about and the original speech. When this is so – when the reporter sees the past events from the same point of view as the original speaker – past perfect tenses are not used.

> *This man on TV said that dinosaurs **were** around for 250 million years.*
>> (NOT ...~~that dinosaurs **had been** around~~...)
> *I told you John **phoned** this morning, didn't I?*
> *We were glad to hear you **enjoyed** your trip to Denmark.*

4   indirect speech: reporting present and future tenses

If somebody talked about a situation that has still not changed – that is to say, if the original speaker's present and future are still present and future – a reporter can often choose whether to keep the original speaker's tenses or change them. Both structures are common.

– Direct: *The earth **goes** round the sun.*
 Indirect: *He proved that the earth **goes/went** round the sun.*
– Direct: *How old **are** you?*
 Indirect: *Are you deaf? I asked how old you **are/were**.*
– Direct: *Where **does** she work?*
 Indirect: *I've often wondered where she **works/worked**.*
– Direct: *It **will** be windy tomorrow.*
 Indirect: *The forecast said it **will/would** be windy tomorrow.*

We do not keep the original speaker's tenses if we do not agree with what he / she said, if we are not certain of its truth, or if we wish to make it clear that the information comes from the original speaker, not from ourselves.

> *The Greeks thought that the sun **went** round the earth.*
>> (NOT ...~~that the sun **goes** round the earth.~~)
> *Did you hear that? She just said she **was** fourteen!*
> *He announced that profits **were** higher than forecast.*

5   modal verbs in indirect speech

The modals *would, should, could, might, ought* and *must* are usually unchanged after past reporting verbs in indirect speech. This is also true of modal *need* (see 357) and *had better* (see 234).

– Direct: *It **would** be nice if I **could** see you again.*
 Indirect: *He said it **would** be nice if he **could** see me again.*
– Direct: *It **might** be too late.*
 Indirect: *I was afraid that it **might** be too late.*
– Direct: *It **must** be pretty late. I really **must** go.*
 Indirect: *She said it **must** be pretty late and she really **must** go.*
– Direct: *You **needn't** pretend to be sorry.*
 Indirect: *I said he **needn't** pretend ...*

First-person *shall* and conditional *should* may be reported as *would* in indirect speech (because of the change of person).

Direct: *We **shall/should** be delighted to come.*
Indirect: *They said they **would** be delighted to come.*

▶

Note the different ways of reporting questions beginning *Shall I . . .?*
(depending on whether the speaker is asking for information or making an
offer).

– Direct: ***Shall I*** *be needed tomorrow?*
   Indirect: *He wants to know if he **will** be needed tomorrow.*
– Direct: ***Shall I*** *carry your bag?*
   Indirect: *He wants to know if he **should/can** carry your bag.*

6   conditionals

After past reporting verbs, conditional sentences referring to 'unreal'
situations are often reported with past conditionals.

Direct: *If I **had** any money I**'d buy** you a drink.*
Indirect: *She said if she **had had** any money she **would have bought** me a*
             drink. (OR *She said if she **had** any money she **would** buy . . .*)

(Compare the first example in paragraph 5, which does not refer to an
'unreal' situation.)

For details of conditional structures, see 258–264.
For *had to* as a past of *must*, see 349, 351.

7   negative questions

Do can be used in indirect negative questions, as a negative auxiliary.

Direct: *'Why **don**'t you work harder?'*
Indirect: *She asked why he **did**n't work harder.*

Note that negative questions often express emotions such as surprise or
enthusiasm (see 360), and these are usually reported in special ways.

Direct: *Don't the children like ice-cream?*
Indirect: *She **was surprised that** the children didn't like ice-cream.*
             (NOT ~~She **asked if** the children didn't like ice-cream.~~)
Direct: *Isn't she lovely!*
Indirect: *I **remarked how** lovely she was.*
             (NOT ~~I **asked if** she wasn't lovely.~~)

8   embedded reporting expressions

Complicated structures can be produced in informal speech when reporting
expressions are put into sentences with question-word clauses or relatives.

*She's written **I don't know** how many books.*
*He's gone **I don't know** where.*
*This is the man who **Ann said** would tell us about the church.*

For more about relative structures of this kind, see 477.10–11.
For more about embedding in general, see 188.

9   indirect speech without reporting verbs

In British newspaper, radio and TV reports, reports of parliamentary
debates, records of conferences, minutes of meetings etc, the indirect speech

construction is often used with very few reporting verbs. The use of tenses is enough to make it clear that a text is a report.

*The Managing Director began his address to the shareholders by summarising the results for the year. Profits on the whole **had been** high, though one or two areas **had been** disappointing. It **was**, however, important to maintain a high level of investment, and he **was** sure that the shareholders **would** appreciate . . .*

In literary narrative, similar structures are common. The reported speech may be made more vivid by using direct question structures and 'here and now' words.

At breakfast, Peter refused to go to school. Why should he spend all his time sitting listening to idiots? What use was all that stuff anyway? If he stayed at home he could read books. He might even learn something useful. His father, as usual, was unsympathetic. Peter had to go to school, by damn, and he had better get moving now, or there'd be trouble.

483 requests

1 *yes/no* questions

We usually ask people to do things for us by making *yes/no* questions. (This is because a *yes/no* question appears to leave people free to refuse.) Some typical structures used in requests:

__Could you possibly__ help me for a few minutes? (very polite)
__Would you mind__ helping me for a few minutes?
__Would you like__ to help me for a few minutes?
__Could you__ help me for a few minutes? (more informal)
__You couldn't__ help me for a few minutes, __could you?__ (informal)

Indirect *yes/no* questions are also used in polite requests.

__I wonder if__ you could (possibly) help me for a few minutes.

2 other structures: telling people to do things

If we use other structures (for example imperatives, *should, had better*), we are not *asking* people to do things, but *telling* or advising them to do things. These structures can therefore seem rude if we use them in requests, especially in conversation with strangers or people we do not know well. *Please* makes an order or instruction a little more polite, but does not turn it into a request. The following structures can be used perfectly correctly to give orders, instructions or advice, but they are not polite ways of requesting people to do things.

Please help me for a few minutes.
Help me, would you?
Carry this for me, please.
Please answer by return of post.
Please type your letter.
You ought to tell me your plans.
You should shut the door.
You had better help me.
You are kindly requested not to smoke.

For the use of imperatives to give advice, make suggestions etc, see 268. ▶

3 shops, restaurants etc

Typical structures used in shops, restaurants etc are:

Can I have one of those, please?
Could I have a look at the red ones?
I'd like to see the wine list, please.
I would prefer a small one.

In places where only a few kinds of thing are sold and not much needs to be said, it is enough just to say what is wanted and add *please.*

'The Times', please.
Pint of bitter, please.
Two cheeseburgers, please.
Second-class return to Lancaster, please.

4 negative questions

Negative questions are not used in polite requests.

Could you give me a light?
(NOT *Couldn't you give me a light?* – this sounds like a complaint.)

But negative *statements* with question tags are used in informal requests.

You couldn't give me a light, *could you?*
I don't suppose you could give me a light, *could you?* (very polite)

For more about negative questions, see 360.
For *(I should be grateful) if you would . . .*, see 259.3.
For other rules of 'social language', see 520.
For formality and politeness, see 216.

484 (the) rest

The rest means 'what is left'. It is always singular in form, and *the* is always used.

We only use three rooms. **The rest** of the house is empty.

To talk about what is left after something has been used up, eaten, destroyed etc, we often use other words.

There were **remains** of the meal all over the floor. (NOT *There were rests . . .*)
Supper tonight is **leftovers** from lunch. (NOT *. . . rests . . .*)

When *the rest* refers to a plural noun, it has a plural verb.

There are four chocolates for Penny, four for Joe and **the rest are** mine.
(NOT *. . . the rest is mine.*)

485 road and street

1 the difference

A *street* is a road with houses on either side. We use *street* for roads in towns or villages, but not for country roads.

Cars can park on both sides of the **street** here.
Our village has only got one **street.**

Road is used for both town and country.

Cars can park on both sides of our **road.**
The **road** out of our village goes up a steep hill.
(NOT *The street out of our village . . .*)

2 street names: stress

In street names we normally stress the word *Road*, but the word before *Street*.
>   *Marylebone*'***Road***   '***Oxford*** *Street*

486 (the) same

We normally use *the* before *same*.
>   *Give me **the same** again, please.* (NOT ~~*Give me **same** again, please.*~~)

Before a noun or pronoun, we use *the same as*.
>   *I want a shirt that's **the same as the one** in the window.*
>   (NOT ~~*I want **a same** shirt like*~~ . . .)
>   *You've got **the same idea as** me.* (NOT . . . ~~*my same idea.*~~)
>   *Her hair's **the same colour as her mother's**.*

Before a clause, *the same . . . that* or *the same . . . who* can be used.
>   *That's **the same man that/who** asked me for money yesterday.*

As is also possible before a clause, especially with a noun that is the object of the following verb. There is no difference of meaning between *the same . . . that* and *the same . . . as* in this case.
>   *He was wearing **the same shirt that/as** he'd had on the day before.*

As/who/that can be left out when they refer to the object of the following verb.
>   *He was wearing the same shirt he'd had on the day before.*

Note also the expression *do the same*.
>   *Why do you always try to **do the same** as your brother?*
>   *Joe and Carol went on a camping holiday, and I think we're going to **do the***
>   ***same**.*

For *do that* and *do so*, see 166.
For other uses of *the same*, see a good dictionary.

487 **say** and **tell**

1 meaning and use

Both *say* and *tell* are used with direct and indirect speech. (*Say* is more common than *tell* with direct speech.) *Say* refers to any kind of speech; *tell* is only used to mean 'instruct' or 'inform'.
- *'Turn right,' I **said**.*
>   OR *'Turn right,' I **told** him.*
- *She **said** that it was my last chance.*
>   OR *She **told** me that it was my last chance.*
- *He **said**, 'Good morning.'*
>   (BUT NOT ~~*He **told** them, 'Good morning.'*~~)
- *Mary **said**, 'What a nice idea.'*
>   (BUT NOT ~~*Mary **told** us, 'What a nice idea.'*~~)
- *'What's your problem?' I **said**.*
>   (BUT NOT ~~*'What's your problem?' I **told** her.*~~)   ▶

2 objects

After *tell*, we usually say who is told.

*She **told me** that she would be late.* (NOT ~~She **told** that~~...)

Say is most often used without a personal object.

*She **said** that she would be late.* (NOT ~~She **said** me~~...)

If we want to put a personal object after *say*, we use *to*.

*And I **say to all the people** of this great country*...

Tell is not used before objects like *a word, a name, a sentence, a phrase.*

*Alice **said** a naughty word this morning.* (NOT ~~Alice **told**~~...)

We do not usually use *it* after *tell* to refer to a fact.

'What time's the meeting?' 'I'll tell you tomorrow.'

(NOT ~~'I'll tell you it tomorrow.'~~)

3 infinitives

Tell can be used before **object + infinitive**, in the sense of 'order' or 'instruct'. *Say* cannot be used like this.

*I **told the children to go away**.* (NOT ~~I **said** the children to go away.~~)

4 *tell* without a personal object

Tell is used without a personal object in a few expressions. Common examples: *tell the truth, tell a lie, tell a story/joke.*

*I don't think she's **telling the truth**.* (NOT ...~~**saying the truth**.~~)

Note also the use of *tell* to mean 'distinguish', 'understand', as in *tell the difference, tell the time.*

5 indirect questions

Neither *tell* nor *say* can introduce indirect questions.

*Bill **asked** whether I wanted to see a film.*

(NOT ~~Bill **said** whether I wanted to see a film.~~)

(NOT ~~Bill **told** me whether~~...)

But *say* and *tell* can introduce the answers to questions.

*Has she **said who's coming**?*

*He only **told** one person **where the money was**.*

For indirect speech, see 480–482.
For *so* after *say* and *tell*, see 514.

488 see

1 progressive forms not used

When *see* means 'perceive with one's eyes', progressive forms are not normally used. To talk about seeing something at the moment of speaking, *can see* is often used in British English (see 125).

*I **can see** an aeroplane.* (US also *I **see** an airplane.*)

(NOT ~~I am seeing an aeroplane.~~)

But we can say that somebody *is seeing things* if we mean that he/she is imagining things that are not there.

'Look! A camel!' 'You're seeing things.'

When *see* means 'understand' or 'have heard' (see 246), progressive forms are not normally used.

> *'We've got a problem.' 'I **see**.'*
> *I **see** they're talking about putting up taxes again.*

Note that we say ***have** a dream*, not ***see** a dream*.

2 changes

Progressive forms are occasionally used to talk about changes in people's ability to see.

> *I**'m seeing** much better since I got those new glasses.*
> *I'm reading 'War and Peace' again, and I**'m seeing** a lot of things that I missed the first time.*

3 'consider', 'think', 'find out'

See is used to mean 'consider' or 'think' in some expressions, like *I'll see* and *let me see*. Note that a preposition is necessary before the object in these cases.

> *We**'ll see about that** tomorrow.* (NOT ~~We'll **see that** tomorrow.~~)
> *You'd better **see about that** with Jim.* (NOT ~~You'd better **see that** with Jim.~~)

See can be used with *if/whether* to mean 'find out'.

> *Can you look out of the window and **see if** it's still snowing?*
> *I think I'll go round and **see whether** Janet's at home.*

See if ... can often means 'try to'.

> ***See if** you can get him to stop talking.*

4 'meet', 'arrange' etc

When *see* means 'meet', 'interview', 'talk to', 'go out with' or 'arrange', 'supervise', progressive forms are possible.

> *I**'m seeing** the dentist tomorrow.*
> ***Are** you still **seeing** that Henderson woman?*
> *John's down at the docks. He**'s seeing** that our stuff gets loaded properly.*

For *see* + object + infinitive/*-ing* form, see 245.
For the difference between *see*, *look* and *watch*, see 489.
For *see above* and *see over*, see 6.6.

489 see, look (at) and watch

1 see

See is the ordinary verb to say that something 'comes to our eyes', whether or not we are paying attention.

> *Suddenly I **saw** something strange.*
> (NOT ~~Suddenly I **looked at** something strange.~~)
> *Did you **see** the article about the strike in today's paper?*

Progressive forms of *see* are not normally used with this meaning.

> *I **(can) see** a light.* (NOT ~~I**'m seeing** a light.~~)

▶

2 *look (at)*

We use *look* to talk about concentrating, paying attention, trying to see what is there. You can *see* something without wanting to, but you can only *look at* something deliberately. Compare:

> I **looked** at the photo, but I didn't **see** anybody I knew.
> 'Do you **see** the man in the raincoat?' 'Yes.' '**Look** again.' 'Good heavens! It's Moriarty!'
> He **looked** at her with his eyes full of love.

When *look* has an object it is followed by a preposition. When there is no object there is no preposition. Compare:

> **Look at** me! (NOT ~~Look me!~~)   **Look!** (NOT ~~Look at!~~)

Note that *at* is often dropped before a *wh*-clause.

> **Look (at) what** you've done!   **Look who's** here!
> **Look where** you're going.

3 *watch*

Watch is like *look at*, but suggests that something is happening or going to happen. We *watch* things that change, move or develop.

> **Watch** that man – I want to know everything he does.
> I usually **watch** a football match on Saturday afternoon.
> The police **have been watching** the house for three days.

4 **complete experiences:** *see*

Watch is typically used to talk about experiences that are going on, in progress. We often prefer *see* to talk about the whole of a performance, play, cinema film, match etc. Compare:

> He got into a fight yesterday afternoon while he **was watching** a football match. (NOT ... ~~while he was seeing a football match.~~)
> Have you ever **seen** Chaplin's 'The Great Dictator'?
> (NOT ~~Have you ever watched Chaplin's 'The Great Dictator'?~~)

5 *watch TV*

Watch is normally used with *TV*; *watch* and *see* are both used to talk about TV programmes and films.

> You spend too much time **watching TV**.
> We **watched/saw** a great film on TV last night.
> Did you **watch/see** 'Top of the Pops' on Thursday?

6 *see if/whether*

See can be followed by *if/whether*, in the sense of 'find out'. *Look* and *watch* are not normally used in this way.

> **See if** that suit still fits you. (NOT ~~Look if that suit...~~)
> I'm looking to **see whether** there's any food left.
> (NOT ~~I'm looking whether there's...~~)
> Ring up and **see whether** she's in.

There are similar differences between *hear* and *listen (to)*. See 244.
For infinitives and *-ing* forms after these verbs, see 245.
For other meanings of *see* (and progressive uses), see 246, 451.2.
For other meanings of *look*, see 159.19.
For *if* and *whether*, see 593.

490 seem

1 copular verb: used with adjectives

Seem is a 'copular verb' (see 147); it is followed by adjectives, not adverbs.
> You **seem angry** about something. (NOT ~~You seem **angrily**...~~)

2 *seem* and *seem to be*

Seem is often followed by *to be*. In general, *seem to be* is preferred when we are talking about objective facts – things that seem definitely to be true; *seem* is used without *to be* when we are talking about subjective impressions. (The difference is not always clear-cut, and in many cases both are possible.) Compare:
- *The milk **seems to be** sterilised.*
  *She **seems** excited.*
- *The doctors have done all the tests, and he definitely **seems to be** insane.*
  *It **seems insane**, but I think I'm in love with the postman.*
    (NOT ~~It **seems to be** insane~~...)
- *According to the experts, the north side of the castle **seems to be** about 100 years older than the rest.*
  *He **seems** older than he is.*
    (NOT ~~He **seems to be** older than he is~~ – this would suggest that he might actually be older than he is.)
- *She doesn't **seem to be** ready yet.*
  *She **seems** (to be) very sleepy today.*

3 with nouns

Seem to be is normal before noun phrases.
> *I looked through the binoculars: it **seemed to be** some sort of large rat.*
>   (NOT ...~~it **seemed** some sort of large rat.~~)
> *I spoke to a man who **seemed to be** the boss.*
>   (NOT ...~~who **seemed** the boss.~~)

However, *to be* can be dropped before noun phrases which express more subjective feelings, especially in British English.
> *She **seems (to be)** a nice girl.*
> *The cup **seemed** almost doll's size in his hands.*
> *It **seems** a pity, but I can't see you this weekend.*
>   (NOT ~~It **seems to be** a pity~~...)

4 other infinitives

Seem can be followed by the infinitives of other verbs besides *be*.
> *Ann **seems to need** a lot of attention.*

Perfect infinitives (see 276) are possible.
> *The tax people **seem to have made** a mistake.*

To express a negative idea, we most often use a negative form of *seem*; but in a more formal style *not* can go with the following infinitive. Compare:
> *He **doesn't seem** to be at home.*
> *He **seems not** to be at home.* (formal)

▶

Note the structure *can't seem to . . .*
>*I **can't seem** to get anything right.*
>>(More formal: *I **seem not to be able** to get anything right.*)

For other examples of 'transferred negation', see 359.

5 *seem like*

We can use *like*, but not *as*, after *seem*.
>*North Wales **seems (like)** a good place for a holiday.*
>>(NOT . . . ~~*seems as a good place*~~ . . .)

6 *it seems*

It can be used as a preparatory subject for *that*-clauses and *as if*-clauses after *seem*.
>*It **seems that** Bill and Alice have had a row.*
>*It **seemed as if** the night was never going to end.*

7 *there seems*

There can be used as a preparatory subject for *seem to be*.
>*There **seems to be** some mistake.*

For *like* and *as*, see 320.
For *it* as a preparatory subject, see 301.
For *there* as a preparatory subject, see 562.
For *appear*, see 58.

491 **sensible** and **sensitive**

A *sensible* person has 'common sense', and does not make stupid decisions.
>*'I want to buy that dress.' 'Be **sensible**, dear. You haven't got that much money.'*

A *sensitive* person feels things easily or deeply, and may be easily hurt.
>*Don't shout at her – she's very **sensitive**.* (NOT . . . ~~*very **sensible**.*~~)
>*Have you got a sun cream for **sensitive** skin?* (NOT . . . ~~*for **sensible** skin?*~~)

Note that *sensible* is a 'false friend' – similar words in some languages mean 'sensitive'.

492 **shade** and **shadow**

Shade is protection from the sun.
>*I'm hot. Let's find some **shade** to sit in.*
>*The temperature's 30 degrees in the **shade**.*

We say *shadow* when we are thinking of the 'picture' made by an unlighted area.
>*In the evening your **shadow** is longer than you are.*
>*There's an old story about a man without a **shadow**.*

493 short answers

Answers are often grammatically incomplete, because they do not need to repeat words that have just been said. A typical 'short answer' pattern is **subject + auxiliary verb**, together with whatever other words are really necessary.

> *'Can he swim?' 'Yes, **he can**.'*
>> (More natural than *'Yes, **he can swim**.'*)
> *'Has it stopped raining?' 'No, **it hasn't**.'*
> *'Are you enjoying yourself?' '**I** certainly **am**.'*
> *'You'll be on holiday soon.' 'Yes, **I will**.'*
> *'Don't forget to telephone.' '**I won't**.'*
> *'You didn't phone Debbie last night.' 'No, but **I did** this morning.'*

Non-auxiliary *be* and *have* are also used in short answers.

> *'Is she happy?' 'I think **she is**.'*   *'Have you a light?' 'Yes, **I have**.'*

We use *do* and *did* in answers to sentences that have neither an auxiliary verb nor non-auxiliary *be* or *have*.

> *'She **likes** cakes.' '**She** really **does**.'*   *'That surprised you.' '**It** certainly **did**.'*

Short answers can be followed by tags (see 465–466).

> *'Nice day.' 'Yes, it is, **isn't it?**'*

Note that stressed, non-contracted forms are used in short answers.

> *Yes, I **am**.* (NOT ~~*Yes, I'm.*~~)

For similar structures, see 463 (reply questions), 465–466 (question tags) and 185 (ellipsis).
For *So am I* etc, see 516.1.
For *So I am* etc, see 516.2.

494 should (1): the difference between should and would

There are really three different verbs: *should*, *would*, and the mixed verb *should/would*.

1 *should*

This verb (*I should, you should, he/she/it should* etc) is used to talk about obligation, and in some other ways. For details, see 495–497.

> *Everybody **should wear** car seat belts.*   *She **should** be back tomorrow.*

2 *would*

This verb (*I would, you would, he/she/it would* etc) can be used to talk about past habits. For details, see 604.

> *When we were kids we **would** spend hours kicking a ball about, dreaming of being soccer internationals.*

3 *should/would*

This verb – often considered as a 'conditional auxiliary' – has mixed forms: *I should/would, you would, he/she/it would, we should/would, they would*. In general, *should/would* is used as a past form, or less definite form, of *shall/will.* It is common in requests, offers and sentences with *if.* For more details, see 498.

> *I told them we **should/would** probably be late.*
> *I **should/would** be grateful for an early reply.*
> ***Would** you like some help?*
> *If they could sing in tune it **wouldn't** be so bad.*
> *If you **would** come this way, madam.*

495 should (2): obligation, deduction etc

1 forms

Should is a modal auxiliary verb (see 344–345). It has no *-s* in the third person singular.

> *The postman **should** be here soon.* (NOT *The postman **shoulds**...*)

Questions and negatives are made without *do.*

> ***Should we** tell Judy?* (NOT *Do we should...?*)

Should is followed by an infinitive without *to.*

> *Should I **go**?* (NOT *Should I to go?*)   *She **should be told** the truth.*

There is a contracted negative *shouldn't.*

> *The meeting **shouldn't** take long.*

Should has a weak pronunciation /ʃ(ə)d/, often used when *should* is not stressed (see 588).

2 obligation

We often use *should* to talk about obligation, duty and similar ideas. It is less strong than *must.*

> *People **should** drive more carefully.*
> *You **shouldn't** say things like that to Granny.*
> *Applications **should** be sent before December 30th.*
>   (More polite than *Applications **must** be sent...*)

In questions, *should* is used to ask for advice or instructions, like a less definite form of *shall* (see 222).

> ***Should** I go and see the police, do you think?*   *What **should we** do?*

Should can also act as a past form of *shall* in indirect speech.

> Direct speech: *What **shall** we do?*
> Indirect speech: *They asked what they **should** do.*

For the differences between *should, ought to* and *must,* see 496.
For the difference between *should* and *had better,* see 234.

3 deduction

We can use *should* to say that something is probable (because it is logical or normal).

> *Henry **should** get here soon – he left home at six.*
> *'We're spending the winter in Florida.' 'That **should** be nice.'*

4 past uses

Should + infinitive can be used to talk about the past in indirect speech (see 482.5).

> *I knew that I **should write** to Jane, but it seemed too difficult.*

In other cases, ***should*** **+ infinitive** is not normally used to talk about the past. Instead, we can use for example *was/were supposed to . . .* (see 547).

>*It was going to be a long day. I **was supposed to clean** up all the stables,*
>>*and then start on the garden.* (NOT ...~~I should clean up~~...)
>*She **was supposed to be** in her office, but she wasn't.*
>(NOT ~~She should be in her office, but she wasn't.~~)

5 *should have . . .*

Should can be used with a perfect infinitive to talk about past events which did not happen, or which may or may not have happened.

>*I **should have phoned** Ed this morning, but I forgot.*
>*Ten o'clock: she **should have arrived** in the office by now.*

Should not have . . . refers to unwanted things that happened, or to negative probabilities.

>*You **shouldn't have called** him a fool – it really upset him.*
>*Nine o'clock: they **shouldn't have left** home yet – I'll phone them.*

For *should* in *if*-clauses, see 261.2.
For *should* after *in case*, see 271.2.
For *should* after *so that* and *in order that*, see 519.
For *How should . . .?* and *Why should . . .?*, see 464.2.
For special uses of *should* in other subordinate clauses, see 497.

496 should (3): **should**, **ought** and **must**

1 *should* and *ought*

Should and *ought* are very similar, and can often replace each other.

>*They **ought** to be more sensible, **shouldn't** they?*

They are both used to talk about obligation and duty, to give advice, and to say what we think it is right for people to do or have done. *Should* is much more frequent than *ought*.

>*You **should / ought to** see 'Daughter of the Moon' – it's a great film.*
>*You **should / ought to** have seen his face!*

Should and *ought* are not used in polite requests.

>***Could you move** your head a bit? I can't see.*
>(NOT ~~You should / ought to move your head a bit~~...)

Should and *ought* are both also used to talk about logical probability.

>*I've bought three loaves – that **should / ought to** be enough.*
>*That **should / ought to** be Janet coming upstairs now.*

Note that *should* is followed by the infinitive without *to*, and *ought* by the *to*-infinitive.

2 *must* and *should/ought*

Must has similar meanings to *should* and *ought*, but is stronger or more definite. It expresses great confidence that something will happen, or that something is true; *should* and *ought* express less confidence. Compare:

– *The doctor said I **must** give up smoking.*
>(an order which is likely to be obeyed)
*You really **ought to** give up smoking.*
>(a piece of advice which may or may not be followed) ▶

– *Rob **must** be home by now. (= I'm sure he is home.)*
*Rob **should** be home by now. (= I think he is probably home.)*

Should can be used instead of *must* to make orders and instructions sound more polite.

*This form **should** be filled in in ink.*
*Applications **should** be sent by 31 January.*

Should and *ought* can be used for predictions. *Must* is not used in this way.

*It **should** be fine tomorrow.* (BUT NOT ~~It **must** be fine tomorrow.~~)

Should and *ought* can be used with perfect infinitives to talk about unfulfilled obligation in the past. *Must* is not used like this.

*You **should have been** nicer to Annie.*
(BUT NOT ~~You **must have been** nicer to Annie.~~)

For more about *should*, see 494–495.
For details of the use of *must*, see 349–352.
For the difference between *should/ought* and *had better*, see 234.

497 should (4): in subordinate clauses

1 importance

In formal British English, *should* can be used in *that*-clauses after adjectives and nouns expressing the importance of an action (e.g. *important, necessary, vital, essential, eager, anxious, concerned, wish*).

*It's **important that** she **should** talk to me when she gets here.*
*Is it **necessary that** my uncle **should** be informed?*
*I'm **anxious that** nobody **should** be hurt.*
*It is his **wish that** the money **should** be given to charity.*

This also happens after verbs expressing similar ideas, especially in sentences about the past.

*He **insisted that** the contract **should** be read aloud.*
*I **recommended that** she **should** reduce her expenditure.*

In a less formal style, *should* is less often used and other structures are preferred.

*It's important that she **talks** to me when she gets here.*
*Was it necessary **to tell my uncle**?*

In American English, this use of *should* is unusual; subjunctives may be used (see 541).

*It's important that she **talk** to me when she gets here.*
*Was it necessary that my uncle **be** informed?*
*I recommend that she **reduce** her expenditure.*

2 reactions

Should is also used in subordinate clauses after words expressing personal judgements and reactions, especially to facts which are already known or have already been mentioned. (This use, too, is more common in British than American English.)

*It's **astonishing** that she **should** say that sort of thing to you.*
*I was **shocked** that she **shouldn't** have invited Phyllis.*
*I'm **sorry** you **should** think I did it on purpose.*
*Do you **think** it's **normal** that the child **should** be so tired?*

In American English, *would* is usual in this kind of case.

> *It was natural that they **would** want him to go to a good school.*
> (GB ... *that they **should** ...*)

Sentences like these can also be constructed without *should*. Subjunctives cannot be used.

> *It's astonishing that she **says/said** that sort of thing to you.*
> (BUT NOT ~~It's astonishing that she **say** ...~~)
> *I was shocked that she **didn't** invite Phyllis.*

3 other cases

Should can be used in *if*-clauses (see 261.2 for details), after *in case* (see 271.2), after *for fear that* and *lest* (see 314) and after *so that* and *in order that* (see 519).

> *If you **should** see Caroline, tell her I've got the tickets.*
> *I'll get a chicken out of the freezer **in case** Aunt Mary **should** come.*
> *He turned the radio down **so that** he **shouldn't** disturb the old lady downstairs.*

498 should (5): should/would

1 mixed forms

This modal auxiliary verb has the following forms:

> I should/would
> you would
> he/she/it would
> we should/would
> they would

After *I* and *we*, both *should* and *would* can be used with the same meaning. However, first-person *should* is rare in American English, and is becoming less common in British English.

In an informal style the contraction *'d* is often used instead of *should/would*, especially after pronouns.

2 past / less definite form of *shall/will*

Should/would can be used like a past or less definite form of the future auxiliary *shall/will*. This happens, for example, in indirect speech and in 'future in the past' constructions (see 226). Compare:

- *I **shall/will** be home soon.*
  *I knew that I **should/would** be home soon.*
- *That's the college where Sue **will** be studying in October.*
  *Sue looked at the college where she **would** be studying in October.*
- ***Will** you be able to baby-sit tomorrow night?* (definite enquiry)
  ***Would** you be able to baby-sit tomorrow night?*
  (less definite, more hesitant enquiry)

Should/would is commonly used in polite offers and requests with the verbs *like*, *love* and *prefer*.

> *'**Would** you **like** some tea?' 'I'**d prefer** coffee, if you don't mind.'*   ▶

3 conditional sentences

Because of its less definite meaning, *should/would* is used in some conditional structures (see 260), and is often called a 'conditional auxiliary'.

*If I had a free weekend, I **should/would** go and see Liz.*
  (NOT ~~If I had..., I shall/will...~~)
*If your father were alive now, he **would** be shocked to see how you're living.*
*Supposing war broke out, what **would** you do?*

4 *should/would have ...*

Should/would can be used with a perfect infinitive to talk about situations that are different from what actually happened.

*I **should/would** have liked to study medicine, but it wasn't possible.*
*If we'd known you were coming we **should/would have taken** the day off.*
*He **would not have succeeded** without his parents' help.*

Note the structure *I should/would have thought ...*, used in British English to express surprise.

*It's funny that she doesn't like him. **I should have thought** they'd get on terribly well.*

5 subordinate clauses

Should/would is most common in main clauses. In most kinds of subordinate clauses, the same meanings are expressed with past tenses (see 556).

*In a situation like that, I **would scream** until somebody **came** to help me.*
  (NOT *...~~until somebody would come...~~*)

For more about the 'indirect' use of past forms ('distancing'), see 161.
For *I should* meaning 'If I were you, I should ...', see 264.

499 since: tenses

1 tenses in the main clause

In sentences with *since*, we normally use present perfect and past perfect tenses in the main clause.

*They**'ve known** each other **since** 1980.*
  (NOT ~~They know each other since...~~)
*We **haven't seen** Jamie **since** Christmas.*
*I was sorry when Jacky moved to America; we **had been** good friends **since** university days.*

However, present and past tenses are also occasionally found, especially in sentences about changes.

*You**'re looking** much better **since** your operation.*
*She **doesn't come** round to see us so much **since** her marriage.*
***Since** last Sunday I **can't** stop thinking about you.*
***Since** he went on that course he **thinks** he knows everything.*
*Things **weren't going** so well **since** Father had lost his job.*

This often happens in the structure *It is/was ... since ...*

*It**'s (been)** a **long time since** the last meeting.*
*It **was ages since** our last game of tennis.* (OR *It **had been** ages since ...*)

2 tenses in *since*-clauses

In the examples above, *since* is used as a preposition. But *since* can also be used as a conjunction of time, introducing its own clause. The tense in the *since*-clause can be perfect or past, depending on the meaning. Compare:

– *I've known her **since we were** at school together.*
*I've known her **since I've lived** in this street.*
– *We visit my parents every week **since we bought** the car.*
*We visit my parents every week **since we've had** the car.*
– *You've drunk about ten cups of tea **since you arrived**.*
*You've drunk about ten cups of tea **since you've been sitting** here.*
– *They had been close friends **since Alice was** small.*
*They hadn't seen much of each other **since Polly (had) moved** away.*

Sometimes a present perfect tense is used in a *since*-clause, exceptionally, to refer to a finished point of time.

*It is now a year since we **have** last **discussed** your future.*
(More normal: *... since we last **discussed** ...*)

For more about present perfect tenses, including American usage, see 418–420.
For past perfect tenses, see 421.
For the difference between *since* and *for*, see 214.
For the difference between *since* and *from*, see 214.
For *since* meaning 'as' or 'because', see 72.

500 singular and plural (1): regular plurals

The plural of most nouns is made by just adding -*s* to the singular. But there are some special cases.

1 plural of nouns ending in consonant + *y*

If the singular ends in **consonant + *y*** (for example -*by*, -*dy*, -*ry*, -*ty*), the plural is normally made by changing *y* to *i* and adding -*es*.

Singular	Plural
... consonant + *y*	... consonant + *ies*
baby	*babies*
lady	*ladies*
ferry	*ferries*
party	*parties*

If the singular ends in **vowel + *y*** (e.g. *day, boy, guy, donkey*), the plural is made by adding -*s* (*days, boys, guys, donkeys*).

Proper names ending in **consonant + *y*** usually have plurals in -*ys*.

*Do you know the **Kennedys**?*
*I hate **Februarys**.*

▶

2 plural of nouns ending in *sh, ch, s, x* or *z*

If the singular ends in *-sh, -ch, -s, -x* or *-z*, the plural is made by adding *-es*.

Singular	Plural
...*ch/sh/s/x/z*	...*ches/shes/ses/xes/zes*
chur*ch*	chur*ches*
cra*sh*	cra*shes*
bu*s*	bu*ses*
bo*x*	bo*xes*
bu*zz*	bu*zzes*

Nouns ending in a single *-z* have plurals in *-zzes*: *quiz/quizzes, fez/fezzes*.

3 plural of nouns ending in *o*

Some nouns ending in *-o* have plurals in *-es*. The most common:

Singular	Plural	Singular	Plural
echo	echoes	potato	potatoes
hero	heroes	tomato	tomatoes
negro	negroes		

Nouns ending in **vowel + o** have plurals in *-s* (e.g. *radios, zoos*). So do the following, and most new words that come into the language:

Singular	Plural	Singular	Plural
commando	commandos	photo	photos
concerto	concertos	piano	pianos
Eskimo	Eskimos	solo	solos
kilo	kilos	soprano	sopranos
logo	logos		

A few common words ending in *-o* can have plurals in *-s* or *-es*.

Singular	Plural	Singular	Plural
buffalo	buffalo(e)s	tornado	tornado(e)s
mosquito	mosquito(e)s	volcano	volcano(e)s

501 singular and plural (2): irregular and special plurals

1 irregular plurals in *-ves*

The following nouns ending in *-f(e)* have plurals in *-ves*.

Singular	Plural	Singular	Plural
calf	calves	self	selves
elf	elves	sheaf	sheaves
half	halves	shelf	shelves
knife	knives	thief	thieves
leaf	leaves	wife	wives
life	lives	wolf	wolves
loaf	loaves		

Dwarf, hoof, scarf and *wharf* can have plurals in either *-fs* or *-ves*. Other words ending in *-f(e)* are regular.

2 other irregular plurals

Singular	Plural	Singular	Plural
child	child**ren**	ox	ox**en**
foot	feet	penny	pence
goose	geese	person	people
louse	lice	tooth	teeth
man	men	woman	women
mouse	mice		

The regular plural *pennies* can be used to talk about separate penny coins (and one-cent coins in the USA); *pence* is used to talk about prices and sums of money. Some British people now use *pence* as a singular (e.g. *That'll be three pounds and one **pence**, please*).

Persons is sometimes used as a plural of *person* in official language. There is also a singular noun *people* (plural *peoples*) meaning 'nation'.

3 plural same as singular

Some words ending in *-s* do not change in the plural. Common examples:

Singular	Plural	Singular	Plural
barracks	barracks	series	series
crossroads	crossroads	species	species
headquarters	headquarters	works (= factory)	works
means	means	Swiss	Swiss

Note that some singular uncountable nouns end in *-s*. These have no plurals. Examples are *news, billiards, draughts* (and some other names of games ending in *-s*), *measles* (and some other illnesses).

Most words ending in *-ics* (e.g. *mathematics, physics, athletics, politics*) are normally singular uncountable and have no plural use.

> Too **much mathematics is** *usually taught in schools.*
> (NOT ~~*Too **many** mathematics **are**...*~~)

Some words ending in *-ics* (e.g. *politics, statistics*) can also have plural uses.

> **Politics is** *a complicated business.* (BUT *What **are** your **politics**?*)
> *Statistics **is** useful in language testing.*
> (BUT *The unemployment statistics **are** disturbing.*)

Other nouns which do not change in the plural are *craft* (meaning 'vehicle'), *aircraft, hovercraft, spacecraft, Chinese, Japanese* (and other nationality nouns ending in *-ese*), *sheep, fish, deer*, and the names of some other living creatures (especially those that are hunted or used for food).

Dozen, hundred, thousand, million, stone (= *14 pounds*) and *foot* (= *12 inches*) have plurals without *-s* in some kinds of expressions. For details, see 385.14.

Dice (used in board games) is originally the plural of *die*, which is not now often used in this sense; in modern English *dice* is generally used as both singular and plural. *Data* is originally the plural of *datum*, which is not now used; in modern English *data* is used as both singular and plural.   ▶

4   foreign plurals

Some words which come from foreign languages have special plurals.
Examples:

Singular	Plural
analysis	*analyses* (Latin)
appendix	*appendices* (Latin) or *appendixes*
bacterium	*bacteria* (Latin)
basis	*bases* (Greek)
cactus	*cacti* (Latin) or *cactuses*
crisis	*crises* (Greek)
criterion	*criteria* (Greek)
diagnosis	*diagnoses* (Greek)
formula	*formulae* (Latin) or *formulas*
fungus	*fungi* (Latin) or *funguses*
hypothesis	*hypotheses* (Greek)
kibbutz	*kibbutzim* (Hebrew)
medium	*media* (Latin) or *mediums*
nucleus	*nuclei* (Latin) or *nucleuses*
oasis	*oases* (Greek)
phenomenon	*phenomena* (Greek)
radius	*radii* (Latin) or *radiuses*
stimulus	*stimuli* (Latin)
vertebra	*vertebrae* (Latin) or *vertebras*

Note that some foreign plurals (e.g. *agenda, spaghetti*) are singular in English
(see 148.2).

5   plurals in *'s*

An apostrophe (') is used before the -*'s* in the plurals of letters of the
alphabet, and sometimes in the plurals of dates and abbreviations.
>*She spelt 'necessary' with two **c's**.*
>*I loved the **1960's**.* (OR ... *the **1960s**.*)
>*Do you think **MP's** do a good job?* (OR ... ***MPs**...*)
It is not correct to use -*'s* in other plurals (e.g. ~~jean's~~).

6   compound nouns

In **noun + adverb** combinations, the plural -*s* is usually added to the noun.

Singular	Plural
passer-by	***passers**-by*
runner-up	***runners**-up*

The plural of *mother-in-law* and similar words is generally ***mothers**-in-law*
etc, but some people use *mother-in-laws* etc; the plural of *court martial*
(= 'military court') is either ***courts** martial* (more formal) or *court **martials***
(less formal).

In **noun + noun** combinations, the first noun is usually singular in form even
if the meaning is plural (e.g. ***shoe** shop*). There are some exceptions. For
details, see 508.

7 plurals with no singular forms

Cattle is a plural word used to talk collectively about bulls, cows and calves; it has no singular, and cannot be used for counting individual animals (one cannot say, for instance, *three cattle*).

> ***Many cattle are** suffering from a disease called BSE.*
> (NOT ~~*Much cattle is*~~...)

Police is normally used as a plural.

> *The **police are** looking for a fair-haired man in his twenties.*
> (NOT ~~*The police is looking*~~...)

Trousers, jeans, pyjamas (US *pajamas*), *pants, scales, scissors, glasses, binoculars, pliers,* and the names of many similar divided objects are plural, and have no singular forms. (The equivalent words in some other languages are singular.)

> *Your **jeans are** too tight.* (NOT ~~*Your jean is*~~...)
> *'Where **are** my **glasses**?' '**They're** on your nose.'*

Other common words which are normally plural include:

> *clothes* (see 133), *congratulations, contents, customs* (at a frontier), *funds* (= *money*), *goods, manners* (= social behaviour), *the Middle Ages* (a period in history), *oats* (but *corn, wheat* and *barley* are singular uncountable), *odds* (= *chances*), *outskirts, premises* (= *building*), *regards, remains, savings, stairs* (= *a flight of stairs*), *steps* (= *a flight of steps*), *surroundings, thanks*

For more information about 'plural uncountable' nouns, see 148.7.
For cases where plural nouns are used with singular verbs and pronouns (and the opposite), see 503–504.

502 singular and plural (3): pronunciation of regular plurals

1 nouns ending in /s/, /z/ and other sibilants

After one of the sibilant sounds /s/, /z/, /ʃ/, /ʒ/, /tʃ/ and /dʒ/, the plural ending *-es* is pronounced /ɪz/.

buses /ˈbʌsɪz/	*crashes* /ˈkræʃɪz/	*watches* /ˈwɒtʃɪz/
quizzes /ˈkwɪzɪz/	*garages* /ˈgærɑːʒɪz/	*bridges* /ˈbrɪdʒɪz/

2 nouns ending in other unvoiced sounds

After any other unvoiced sound (/p/, /f/, /θ/, /t/ or /k/), the plural ending *-(e)s* is pronounced /s/.

cups /kʌps/	*cloths* /klɒθs/	*books* /bʊks/
beliefs /bɪˈliːfs/	*plates* /pleɪts/	▶

3 nouns ending in other voiced sounds

After vowels, and all voiced consonants except /z/, /ʒ/ and /dʒ/, the plural ending -(e)s is pronounced /z/.

days /deɪz/   *clothes* /kləʊðz/   *legs* /legz/
boys /bɔɪz/   *ends* /endz/   *dreams* /driːmz/
trees /triːz/   *hills* /hɪlz/   *songs* /sɒŋz/
knives /naɪvz/

4 plurals with irregular pronunciation

Singular	Plural
bath /bɑːθ/	*baths* /bɑːðz/ OR /bɑːθs/
house /haʊs/	*houses* /ˈhaʊzɪz/
mouth /maʊθ/	*mouths* /maʊðz/ OR /maʊθs/
path /pɑːθ/	*paths* /pɑːðz/ OR /pɑːθs/
roof /ruːf/	*roofs* /ruːfs/ OR /ruːvz/
truth /truːθ/	*truths* /truːðz/ OR /truːθs/
wreath /riːθ/	*wreaths* /riːðz/ OR /riːθs/
youth /juːθ/	*youths* /juːðz/ OR /juːθs/

Third person singular forms (e.g. *catches, wants, runs*) and possessive forms (e.g. *George's, Mark's, Joe's*) follow the same pronunciation rules as regular plurals.

503 singular and plural (4): singular nouns with plural verbs

1 groups of people

In British English, singular words like *family, team, government*, which refer to groups of people, can be used with either singular or plural verbs and pronouns.

*This team **is/are** going to lose.*

Plural forms are common when the group is considered as a collection of people doing personal things like deciding, hoping or wanting; and in these cases we use *who*, not *which*, as a relative pronoun. Singular forms (with *which* as a relative pronoun) are more common when the group is seen as an impersonal unit. Compare:

– *My **family have** decided to move to Nottingham. **They think** it's a better place to live.*
*The average British **family has** 3.6 members. **It is** smaller and richer than 50 years ago.*
– *The **government, who are** hoping to ease export restrictions soon, . . .*
*The **government, which is** elected by a simple majority, . . .*
– *My **firm are** wonderful. **They** do all **they** can for me.*
*My **firm was** founded in the 18th century.*

When a group noun is used with a singular determiner (e.g. *a/an, each, every, this, that*), singular verbs and pronouns are normal. Compare:

*The **team are** full of enthusiasm.*
*A **team which is** full of enthusiasm **has** a better chance of winning.*
(More natural than *A **team who are** full . . .*)

Sometimes singular and plural forms are mixed.

> *The group gave **its** first concert in June and **they are** already booked up for the next six months.*

Examples of group nouns which can be used with both singular and plural verbs in British English:

bank	family	party
the BBC	firm	public
choir	government	school
class	jury	staff
club	ministry	team
committee	orchestra	union
England (the football team)		

In American English singular verbs are normally used with most of these nouns in all cases (though *family* can have a plural verb). Plural pronouns can be used.

> *The **team is** in Detroit this weekend. **They** have a good chance of winning.*

2 quantifying expressions

Many singular quantifying expressions can be used with plural nouns and pronouns; plural verbs are normally used in this case.

> *A **number of people have** tried to find the treasure, but **they** have all failed.*
> (More natural than *A number of people **has** tried . . .*)
> *A **group of us are** going to take a boat through the French canals.*
> *A **couple of my friends are** going to open a travel agency.*
> (NOT *A couple of my friends **is** . . .*)
> *A **lot of social problems are** caused by unemployment.*
> (NOT *A lot of social problems **is caused** . . .*)
> *The **majority of criminals are** non-violent.*
> *Some of these people are friends of mine and **the rest are** people from the office.*
> ***Half of his students don't** understand a word he says.*
> (NOT *Half of his students **doesn't** . . .*)

For more about *a lot* and *lots*, see 326. For *the rest*, see 484. For *(a) few*, see 322.
For singular and plural nouns with fractions, see 509.9.

504 singular and plural (5): plural expressions with singular verbs

1 amounts and quantities

When we talk about amounts and quantities we usually use singular determiners, verbs and pronouns, even if the noun is plural.

> *Where **is that** five pounds I lent you?*
> (NOT *Where **are those** five pounds . . .?*)
> *Twenty miles **is** a long way to walk.*
> *'We've only got five litres of petrol left.' **'That isn't** enough.'*

▶

2 calculations

Singular verbs are often possible after plural number subjects in spoken calculations.

> *Two and two **is/are** four.*
> *Ten times five **is** fifty.* (OR *Ten fives **are** fifty.*)

For more about spoken calculations, see 385.21–22.

3 more than one

The expression *more than one* is generally used with a singular noun and verb.

> *If things don't get better, **more than one person is** going to have to find a new job.*

4 *one of...*

Expressions beginning *one of* normally have a plural noun and a singular verb.

> ***One of my friends is** going to Honolulu next week.*

For singular and plural verbs in relative clauses after *one of . . .* , see 506.1.

5 *and*

Some expressions joined by *and* have singular determiners, verbs and pronouns. This happens when the two nouns are used together so often that we think of them as a single idea.

> ***This gin and tonic isn't** very strong, **is it?***
> ***'War and Peace' is** the longest book I've ever read.*

6 countries and organisations

Plural names of countries usually have singular verbs and pronouns.

> ***The United States is** anxious to improve **its** image in Latin America.*

Plural names of organisations may also have singular verbs and pronouns.

> ***Consolidated Fruitgrowers has** just taken over Universal Foodstores.*

For singular and plural verbs with nouns referring to groups, see 503.1.
For singular verbs after ***none of** +* **plural noun**, see 509.5.

505 singular and plural (6): **they** with singular reference

1 singular indefinite person

They/them/their is often used to refer to a singular indefinite person who has already been mentioned. This structure is common after *a person, anybody/one, somebody/one, nobody/one, whoever, each, every, either, neither* and *no*.

> *If **a person** doesn't want to go on living, **they are** often very difficult to help.*
> *If **anybody** calls, take **their** name and address and tell **them** to call again later.*
> ***Somebody** left **their** umbrella behind yesterday. Would **they** please collect it from the office?*

*Nobody was late, were **they**?*
*Whoever comes, tell **them** to go away.*
*Tell **each person** to help **themselves** to what **they** want.*
Everybody thinks they're different from everybody else.

This use of *they/them/their* is convenient when the person referred to could be male or female (as in most of the examples above). *He or she, him or her* and *his or her* are clumsy, especially when repeated, and many people dislike the traditional use of *he/him/his* to refer to people who may be male or female (see 227).

They/them/their is not only used when the person's sex is unknown.
*I swear more when I'm talking to **a boy**, because I'm not afraid of shocking **them***.
*No girl should have to wear school uniform, because it makes **them** look like a sack of potatoes.*

2 other uses

They/them/their is occasionally used to refer to a particular person who has been mentioned but not identified.
*I had **a friend** in Paris, and **they** had to go to hospital for a month, ...*

3 correctness

This use of *they/them/their* has been normal in English for centuries, and is perfectly correct. It is most common in an informal style, but can also be found in formal written English. Here is an example from a British passport application form.
*Dual nationality: if the child possesses the nationality or citizenship of another country **they** may lose this when **they** get a British Passport.*

506 singular and plural (7): mixed structures

In some complex structures, the same verb seems to belong with two different expressions, one singular and the other plural.

1 *one of the ...* + relative clause

In sentences like *She's one of the few women who have climbed Everest*, the verb *have* is plural, because its subject (*who*) has a plural reference (*the few women*). However, the sentence is also saying *She has climbed Everest*, and in an informal style many people would therefore say *She's one of the few women who **has** climbed Everest*. Although this is not strictly correct (the verb in the relative clause should agree with the subject of the relative clause, not with the subject of the main clause), structures of this kind are very common in informal English.
*One of the things that really **make/makes** me angry is people who don't answer letters.*
*Alice was one of the students that **were/was** late for the lecture.* ▶

2 singular subject, plural complement

In English a verb normally agrees with the subject of a sentence, not with a following complement.

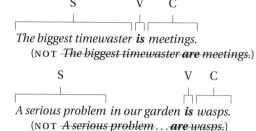

*The biggest timewaster **is** meetings.*
    (NOT ~~The biggest timewaster **are** meetings.~~)

*A serious problem in our garden **is** wasps.*
    (NOT ~~A serious problem . . . **are** wasps.~~)

However, if the subject is a long way from the verb, people sometimes make the verb agree with a complement.

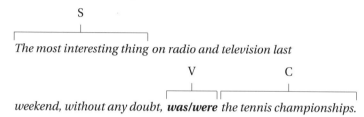

The most interesting thing on radio and television last

*weekend, without any doubt, **was/were** the tennis championships.*

This often happens, too, when the subject is a relative *what*-clause, especially when the complement is long.

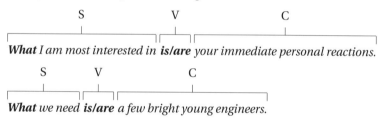

***What** I am most interested in **is/are** your immediate personal reactions.*

***What** we need **is/are** a few bright young engineers.*

For singular and plural verbs after interrogative *what* and *who*, see 509.3.

3 singular subject, plural continuation, plural verb

When a singular subject is modified by a following plural expression, people sometimes use a plural verb. This is not usually considered correct.

   ~~Nobody except his best friends like him.~~
      (More correct: *Nobody . . . **likes** him.*)
   ~~A good knowledge of three languages are necessary for this job.~~
      (More correct: *A good knowledge . . . **is** . . .*)

For problems with *kind, sort, type* etc, see 526.

507 **singular and plural** (8): distributive plural

1 **people doing the same thing**

To talk about several people each doing the same thing, English usually prefers a plural noun for the repeated idea.

*Tell the kids to bring **raincoats** to school tomorrow.*

(More natural than *Tell the kids to bring **a raincoat**...*)

Plural forms are almost always used in this case with possessives.

*Tell the children to blow **their noses**.* (NOT ...*to blow their nose*.)

*Six people lost **their lives** in the accident.*

Uncountable nouns cannot of course be used in the plural.

*They were all anxious to increase their **knowledge**.*

(NOT ...*their **knowledges**.*)

For singular and plural forms after *every*, see 199.

2 **repeated events**

In descriptions of repeated single events, singular and plural nouns are both possible. When no details are given, plural nouns are more natural.

*I often get **headaches**.* (NOT *I often get **a headache**.*)

*She sometimes goes for **rides** over the hills.*

When details of the time or situation are given, nouns are often singular.

*I often get **a headache** when I've been working on the computer.*

*She often goes for **a ride** over the hills before supper.*

Singular nouns may also be used to avoid misunderstanding.

*I sometimes throw **a stone** into the river and wish for good luck.*

(NOT *I sometimes throw **stones**...* – only one stone is thrown each time.)

To refer to the time of repeated events, both singular and plural expressions are often possible with little difference of meaning.

*We usually go and see my mother **on Saturday(s)**.*

*He's not at his best **in the morning(s)**.*

3 **generalisations and rules**

In generalisations and rules, singular and plural nouns are both possible.

*We use **a past participle** in **a perfect verb form**.*

OR *We use **past participles** in **perfect verb forms**.*

Mixtures of singular and plural are possible.

***Subjects** agree with their **verb**.*

***Children** usually inherit some characteristics from **their father** and some from **their mother**.*

This often happens when fixed singular expressions like *at the beginning* are used.

*Discourse **markers** usually come **at the beginning** of sentences.*

508 **singular and plural** (9): noun modifiers

1 **first noun singular**

In **noun + noun** structures (see 378), the first noun is normally singular in form even if it has a plural meaning.

*a **shoe** shop* (= *a shop that sells **shoes***)
*a **tooth**brush* (= *a brush for **teeth***)
trouser** pockets* (= *pockets in **trousers)
*a **ticket** office* (= *an office that sells **tickets***)

2 **exceptions**

Some nouns have the plural -*s* even when they modify other nouns. These include nouns which have no singular form (like *clothes*), nouns which are not used in the singular with the same meaning (like *customs*), and some nouns which are more often used in the plural than in the singular (like *savings*). In some cases (e.g. *sport(s), drug(s)*), usage is divided, and both singular and plural forms are found. In general, the use of plural modifiers is becoming more common in British English; American English often has singular forms where British has plurals. Some examples:

*a **clothes** shop*	*a **savings** account*
*a **glasses** case*	*the **accounts** department*
*a **customs** officer*	*the **sales** department*
***arms** control*	*an **antique(s)** dealer* (but *an **antique** shop*)

*the **outpatients** department* (of a hospital)
*a **greetings** card* (US ***greeting** card*)
*the **drug(s)** problem* (US ***drug** problem*)
*the **arrivals** hall* (US ***arrival** hall*)
*a **drinks** cabinet* (US ***drink** cabinet*)
*a **goods** train* (British English)
*a **sports** car   **sport(s)** shoes*

Note also that singular nouns ending in -*ics* can be used as modifiers.

***athletics** training   an **economics** degree*

We use the plurals *men* and *women* to modify plural nouns when they have a 'subject' meaning; *man* and *woman* are used to express an 'object' meaning. Compare:

– ***men** drivers* (= *men who drive*)
  ***women** pilots* (= *women who fly planes*)
– ***man**-eaters* (= *lions or tigers that eat people*)
  ***woman**-haters* (= *people who hate women*)

509 **singular and plural** (10): miscellaneous points

1 **uncountable nouns**

Certain English singular uncountable nouns correspond to plural nouns in some other languages.

*Your **hair is** very pretty.* (NOT ~~*Your **hairs are**...*~~)
*My **baggage has** been sent to Greece by mistake.*
    (NOT ~~*My **baggages have**...*~~)

For a list of words of this kind, see 148.3.

For plural uncountables, see 148.7.

2   co-ordinated subjects

When two singular subjects are joined by *and*, the verb is normally plural.

> ***Alice and Bob are*** *going to be late.*

But note that some phrases with *and* are treated like single ideas, and used with singular verbs (see 504.5).

> *'**Romeo and Juliet' is** one of Shakespeare's most popular plays.*
> (N O T *~~'Romeo and Juliet' are~~ . . .*)

When two subjects are joined by *as well as*, *together with* or a similar expression, the verb is usually singular if the first subject is singular.

> *The Prime Minister, **as well as** several Cabinet Ministers, **believes** in a tough financial policy.*
> *The Managing Director, **together with** his heads of department, **is** preparing a new budget.*

When two subjects are joined by *or* the verb is usually singular if the second subject is singular, and plural if it is plural. Compare:

> *The room's too crowded – either two chairs **or a table has** got to be moved out.*
> *The room's too crowded – either a table **or two chairs have** got to be moved out.*

When two singular subjects are joined by *neither . . . nor*, the verb is singular in a formal style, but is usually plural in an informal style.

> ***Neither she nor*** *her husband **has** arrived.* (formal)
> ***Neither*** *she **nor** her husband **have** arrived.* (informal)

3   *who* and *what*

When *who* and *what* are used to ask for the subject of a clause, they most often have singular verbs, even if the question expects a plural answer.

> *'**Who is** working tomorrow?' 'Phil, Lucy and Shareena (are working tomorrow).'* (More natural than *Who **are** working tomorrow?*)
> ***Who was*** *at the party?* (More natural than *Who **were** at the party?*)
> *'**What lives** in those little holes?' 'Rabbits (do).'* (N O T *~~What live~~ . . .*)

When *who* and *what* are used to ask for the complement of a clause, they can have plural verbs.

> *'**Who are** your closest friends?' '(My closest friends are) Naomi and Bridget.'*
> *'**What are** your politics?' '(My politics are) extreme left-wing.'*

Relative *what*-clauses are normally the subject of a singular verb.

> ***What*** *she needs **is** friends.* (More natural than *What she needs **are** friends.*)

However, plural verbs are often used before longer plural complements, especially if *what* is a long way from the verb (see 506).

> ***What*** *we need most of all **are** some really new ideas.*

4   *here's, there's* and *where's*

In an informal style, *here's, there's* and *where's* are often used with plural nouns. Some people consider this incorrect.

> ***Here's*** *your **keys**.*
> ***There's*** *some **children** at the door.*
> ***Where's those books** I lent you?*

▶

5   determiners

When *none, neither, either* and *any* are followed by **of + plural noun/pronoun**, they are normally used with singular verbs in a formal style in British English. Plural verbs are common in informal British usage and generally in American English.

> ***None of the cures*** *really **works**.* (formal British)
> ***None of the cures*** *really **work**.* (informal British; American)
> ***Neither of my brothers has/have*** *been outside England.*
> ***Has/Have either of them*** *been seen recently?*
> *If **any of the children gets/get** hungry, they can have an orange.*

6   *another, a/an* + adjective

Plural expressions of quantity can be used with *another* (see 53) and with *a/an* + **adjective**.

> *I want to stay for **another three weeks**.*
> *We'll need **an extra ten pounds**.*
> *He's been waiting for **a good twenty-five minutes**.*
> *She spent **a happy ten minutes** looking through the photos.*
> *I've had **a very busy three days**.*

Note also the expression ***a good many/few*** + **plural** (informal).

> *I've lain awake **a good many nights** worrying about you.*
> *I bet that house could tell **a good few stories**.*

7   *kind, sort* and *type*

In an informal style, we sometimes mix singular and plural forms when we use demonstratives with *kind, sort* or *type*. For details, see 526.

> *I don't like **those kind** of boots.*

8   *every* (frequency)

Every (which is normally used with singular nouns) can be used before plural expressions in measurements of frequency.

> *I go to Ireland **every six weeks**.*

9   fractions

Fractions between 1 and 2 are normally used with plural nouns.

> *It weighs **one and a half tons**.* (NOT *...~~one and a half ton~~.*)
> *The house has about **1.75 hectares** of land.*

For more about the grammar of fractions and other numbers, see 385.

510   slang

1   What is slang?

'Slang' is a very informal kind of vocabulary, used mostly in speech by people who know each other well. Examples:

> *See you down at the **boozer**.* (pub)   *He's a real **prat**.* (fool)
> *OK, let's **shove off**.* (go)   *Wait a minute – my shoelace has **bust**.* (broken)

Slang expressions are not usually written, and would be considered out of place in formal kinds of communication.

2 strong feelings

Many English slang expressions relate to things that people feel strongly about (e.g. sex, family and emotional relationships, drink, drugs, conflict between social groups, work, physical and mental illness, death).

> *She's got **tits** like ripe melons. (breasts)*
> *I spent the weekend at my **gran's**. (grandmother's)*
> *God, we got **smashed** last night. (drunk)*
> ***Prods** out! (Protestants)*
> *Can you get that **sitrep** to the **MD** by five?*
>   *(situation report; Managing Director)*
> *I've got some sort of **bug**. (illness)*
> *He's **lost his marbles**. (gone mad)*
> *When I **kick the bucket**, I want you all to have a big party. (die)*

Slang is often used in order to be offensive.

> *Shut your **gob**! (mouth)*
> *Kill the **wogs**! (coloured people)*

For more about 'taboo' words for subjects that some people find shocking, see 550.

3 group membership; using slang

Many slang expressions are used by members of particular social and professional groups, and nearly all slang is used between people who know each other well or share the same social background. So it is usually a mistake for 'outsiders' (including foreigners) to try deliberately to use slang. This can give the impression that they are claiming membership of a group that they do not belong to. There is also the danger that the slang may be out of date – when slang gets into books, it is often already dead. It is best to wait until one is really becoming accepted as part of a community; one will then start using their slang naturally and correctly along with the rest of their language.

511 small and little

Small simply refers to size. It is the opposite of *big* or *large* (see 105).

> *Could I have a **small** brandy, please?*
> *You're too **small** to be a policeman.*

Usually, the adjective *little* not only refers to size, but also expresses some kind of emotion.

> ***Poor little** thing – come here and let me look after you.*
> *'What's he like?' 'Oh, he's a **funny little** man.'*
> *What's that **nasty little** boy doing in our garden? Tell the **little bastard** to get out.*
> *They've bought a **pretty little** house in the country.*

In a few fixed expressions, *little* is used in the same way as *small* or *short*.

> **little** finger   the **little** hand of a clock
> a **little** while   a **little** way

▶

In British English, *little* is unusual in 'predicative' position (after a verb), and comparative and superlative forms are not normally used. In American English, predicative use is normal, and comparative and superlative forms are more common.

> *Sorry, honey, you're too **little** to watch horror movies.*
> > (GB ... *you're too **small** ...*)
>
> *He's the **littlest** baby I ever saw.* (GB ... *the **smallest** baby ...*)

For *little* used as a determiner (e.g. *There's **little** hope*), see 322.

512 smell

1 British and American forms

In British English, *smell* has an irregular past tense and past participle: *smelt*. American forms are usually regular.

2 copular verb

Smell can be used as a 'copular verb', followed by adjective or noun complements (see 147), to say what sort of smell something has. Progressive forms are not used.

> *Those roses **smell** beautiful.* (NOT ... ~~smell **beautifully**.~~)
> *The soup **smells** funny. What's in it?* (NOT ... ~~is smelling funny~~ ...)

Before a noun, *smell of* and *smell like* are used.

> *The railway carriage **smelt of** beer and old socks.*
> *His aftershave **smelt like** an explosion in a flower shop.*

Smell is sometimes used to mean 'smell bad'.

> *That dog **smells**.*

3 transitive verb: 'perceive'

Smell can be used as a transitive verb, followed by an object, to say what we perceive with our noses. Progressive forms are not used. We often use *can smell* (see 125).

> *As we walked into the house, we **smelt** something burning.*
> *I **can smell** supper.*

4 transitive verb: 'investigate'

Another transitive use is to say that we are using our noses to find out something. Progressive forms can be used.

> *'What are you doing?' 'I**'m smelling** my shirt to see if it will do for another day.'*
> *He picked the scarf up and **smelt** it carefully. 'Chanel No 5,' he said.*

513 so (degree adverb; substitute word)

1 degree

So can have a similar meaning to 'to that extent' or 'that much'. It is often used when we are talking about a high degree of some quality – in situations where *very* is also a suitable word.

*I'm sorry you're **so tired**.* (= *I know you're **very tired**, and I'm sorry.*)
*It was **so cold** that we couldn't go out.*
  (= *It was **very cold** weather, and because of that we couldn't go out.*)

2 before adjectives etc

We can use *so* before an adjective alone (without a noun) or an adverb.
  *He's **so silly**.*   *The milk was **so good** that we couldn't stop drinking it.*
  *Why are you driving **so fast**?*
So is not used with **adjective + noun**.
  *It's **such terrible weather**.* (NOT ~~It's **so terrible weather**.~~)
  *I enjoyed my stay in your country, which is **so beautiful**.*
    (NOT ~~I enjoyed my stay in your **so beautiful country**.~~)
So can be used before the quantifiers *much, many, few* and *little* (with or
without nouns).
  *There was **so much** to eat and **so few people** to eat it.*
We use *so much*, not *so*, before comparatives.
  *She's looking **so much older**.* (NOT *. . .**so older**.*)

For the difference between *such* and *so*, see 544.
For more about *so much* and *so many*, see 518.

3 *so* and *very*

Very is used when we are simply giving information. *So* is mainly used (in the
same way as *like this/that*) to refer to information which has already been
given, which is already known, or which is obvious. Compare:
– *You're **very** late.* (giving information)
  *I'm sorry I'm **so** late.* (referring to information which is already known)
– *It was **very** warm when we were in Scotland.* (giving information)
  *If I'd known it would be **so warm** I'd have taken lighter clothing.* (referring
    to information which is already known)

4 emphatic use

In an informal style, *so* can also be used like *very* to give new information,
when the speaker wishes to emphasise what is said. This structure is rather
like an exclamation (see 201).
  *He's **so** bad-tempered!* (= *How bad-tempered he is!*)   *You're **so** right!*

5 *that*-clauses

Structures with *very* cannot be followed directly by *that*-clauses. Instead, we
can use *so . . . that*.
  *It was **so cold that we stopped playing**.*
    (NOT ~~It was **very cold that we stopped playing**.~~)
  *He spoke **so fast that nobody could understand**.*

6 *so . . . as to . . .*

There is also a structure with *so* followed by **adjective + *as to* + infinitive**.
This is formal and not very common.
  *Would you be **so kind as to tell** me the time?* (= *. . . kind enough to . . .*)
    (NOT ~~Would you be **so kind and** . . .~~)
    (NOT ~~Would you be **so kind to** . . .~~)

▶

7   *so ... a ...*

There is a rather formal structure *so* + **adjective** + *a/an* + **singular countable noun** (see 16).

> *I had never before met **so gentle a person**.* (= ... *such a gentle person*.)

8   adverbial uses: *like that*

So is not normally used adverbially to mean 'like this/that', 'in this/that way'.

> *Look – hold it up in the air **like this**.* (N O T ... ~~hold it up in the air so~~.)
> *When he laughs **like that** I want to scream.* (N O T ~~When he laughs so~~ ...)
> *I don't think we should do it **in that way**.*
>   (N O T ~~I don't think we should do it so~~.)

9   substitute word

So can be used in some structures instead of repeating an adjective or adverb.

> *The weather is stormy and will remain **so** over the weekend.*
> *I read the front page very carefully, and the rest of the paper less **so**.*

For *so* as a clause substitute in *think so, hope so* etc, see 515.
For *so am I* etc, see 516.1.
For *so* after *say* and *tell*, see 514.
For *do so*, see 166.

10   *so-and-so, so-so*

Note these informal expressions.

> *What's happened to old **so-and-so** (= what's his name?) who you used to play chess with?*
> *She's an old **so-and-so**.* (replacing a swearword or insult)
> *'How are you feeling?' '**So-so**.'* (= 'Not too well.') (N O T ... ~~'So-and-so.'~~)
> *'Was the concert any good?' '**So-so**.'* (= 'Not too good.')

For the use of *this/that* to mean 'so', see 565.7.
For more about *very*, see 153.
For other ways of expressing the idea of degree, see 153–156.
For *so that* and *in order that*, see 519.

514   **so** after **say** and **tell**

1   instead of *that*-clauses

So can be used after *say* and *tell* instead of repeating information in a *that*-clause.

> *She's going to be the next president. Everybody **says so**.*
>   (= ... *Everybody **says that she's going to be the next president**.)*
> *'You've got to clean the car.' 'Who **says so**?'*
> *Taxes are going up. Bob **told** me **so**.*

Note that *so* is used in this way mostly when we are talking about the authority for statements, about reasons why we should believe them. When we simply want to identify the speaker, we prefer *that*. Compare:

> *'Jane's crazy.' 'Who **says so**?' 'Dr Bannister.'*
> *'Jane's crazy.' 'Who **said that**?' 'I did.'*

2 *I told you so*

The expression *I told you so* is generally used to mean 'I warned you, but you wouldn't listen to me'.

> *'Mummy, I've broken my train.' 'I told you so. You shouldn't have tried to ride on it.'*

3 other verbs

So cannot be used after all verbs of saying. We cannot say, for example, ~~She **promised** me so.~~

515 so and not with hope, believe etc

1 instead of *that*-clauses

We can often use *so* instead of repeating information in a *that*-clause. This happens with *believe, hope, expect, imagine, suppose, guess, reckon, think, be afraid.*

> *'Is Alex here?' 'I **think so**.'* (NOT ...~~'I think it.'~~)
> *'Do you think we'll have good weather?' 'Yes, I **hope so**.'*
> (NOT ...~~'Yes, I hope.'~~)
> *'Did you lose?' 'I'**m afraid so**.'*

We do not use *so* before a *that*-clause.

> *I hope **that** we'll have good weather.*
> (NOT ~~I hope so, that we'll have good weather.~~)

Note the special use of *I thought so* to mean 'my suspicions were correct'.

> *Show me what's in your pockets. Ah, **I thought so**! You've been stealing biscuits again.*

So is not used after *know* (see 306).

> *'You're late.' 'I know.'* OR *'I know that.'* (NOT ...~~'I know so.'~~)

2 negative structures

We can make these expressions negative in two ways.

> affirmative verb + *not*

> *'Did you win?' 'I'**m afraid not**.'*
> *'We won't be in time for the train.' 'No, I **suppose not**.'*

> negative verb + *so*

> *'You won't be here tomorrow?' 'I **don't suppose so**.'*
> *'Will it rain?' 'I **don't expect so**.'*

Hope and *be afraid* are always used in the first structure.

> *I **hope not**.* (NOT ~~I don't hope so.~~)

Think is more common in the second structure.

> *I **don't think so**.* (More common than *I **think not**.*)

3 *so* at the beginning of a clause

A structure is possible with *so* at the beginning of a clause, with *say, hear, understand, tell, believe* and a number of other verbs. This structure is used to say where the speaker's opinion comes from, or what evidence he/she has for it.

> *It's going to be a cold winter, or **so the newspaper says**.*
> *'Mary's getting married.' 'Yes, **so I heard**.'*
> *'The Professor's ill.' '**So I understand**.'*

This structure is not used with the verbs *think, hope* or *suppose*.

For *so* after *tell* and *say*, see 514.

516   so am I, so do I etc

1   *so* + auxiliary + subject

We can use *so* with a similar meaning to *also*, in the structure ***so* + auxiliary verb + subject**. The structure is used to answer or add to the sentence before, and uses the same auxiliary verb. Note the word order.

> *Louise **can** dance beautifully, and **so can her sister**.*
> *'**I've** lost their address.' '**So have I**.'*

The structure is also used with non-auxiliary *be* and *have*.

> *I **was** tired, and **so were** the others.*
> *'I **have** a headache.' '**So have I**.'*

After a clause with no auxiliary verb, we use *do/does/did*.

> *'He just **wants** the best for his country.' 'So **did** Hitler.'*

It is not normally possible to use a more complete verb phrase in this structure. We can say, for example, *So can her sister*, but not ~~So can her sister dance~~.

2   *so* + subject + auxiliary

So can also be followed by **subject + auxiliary verb** (note the word order) to express surprised agreement.

> *'It's raining.' 'Why, **so it is!**'*
> *'You've just put the teapot in the fridge.' '**So I have!**'*

For *neither/nor am I* etc, see 364.
For short answer structures, see 493.
For other examples of inverted word order, see 298–299.
For *do* with non-auxiliary *have*, see 240–241.

517   so and then

So and *then* can both be used to mean 'since that is so'. There is a slight difference. *Then* is most often used when one speaker replies to another: it means 'It follows from what you have said'. We do not normally use *then* when the same speaker wants to connect two ideas ('It follows from what I have said'). *So* can be used in both ways. Compare:

– *It's more expensive to travel on Friday, **so** I'll leave on Thursday evening.*
    (NOT *...**Then** I'll leave on Thursday evening.*)
  *'It's more expensive to travel on Friday.' '**Then/So** I'll leave on Thursday evening.'*

– *I'll be needing the car, **so** you'll have to take a taxi.*
  *'I'll be needing the car.' '**Then/So** I suppose I'll have to take a taxi.'*

   – *I'm off on holiday,* **so** *I won't be seeing you for a bit.*
   'I'm off on holiday.' '**Then/So** *I won't be seeing you for a bit. Have a good*
     time, **then.**'

518 so much and so many

1 the difference

The difference between *so much* and *so many* is the same as between *much*
and *many*. *So much* is used with singular (uncountable) nouns; *so many* is
used with plurals.

   I had never seen **so much food** *in my life.*
   She had **so many children** *that she didn't know what to do.*
     (NOT *...*~~*so much children*~~*...*)

Note that we use *so*, not *so much*, to modify adjectives and adverbs. For
details, see 513.

   You're **so beautiful.** (NOT ~~*You're* **so much** *beautiful.*~~)

But *so much* is used before comparatives (see 139).

   She's **so much more beautiful** *now.*

2 *so much/many* without a noun

We can drop a noun after *so much/many*, if the meaning is clear.

   I can't eat all that meat – there's **so much**!
   I was expecting a few phone calls, but not **so many**.
   I have **so much** *to tell you.*

3 *so much* as an adverb

So much can be used as an adverb.

   I wish you didn't smoke **so much**.

4 special structures with *so much*

We can use *not so much ... as* or *not so much ... but* to make corrections and
clarifications.

   *She did***n't so much** *wake up* **as** *explode out of the bed.*
   It's **not so much** *that I dislike her* **as** *that I'm just not interested.*
   It wasn't **so much** *his appearance I liked* **as** *his personality.*
   It's **not so much** *that I don't want to come,* **but** *I simply haven't got*
     the time.

In negative and non-assertive clauses, *so much as* can be used to mean 'even'.

   He didn't **so much as** *say thank you, after all we'd done for him.*
   If he **so much as** *looks at another woman, I'll kill him.*

For more details of the use of *much* and *many*, see 348.

519 so that and in order that

1 purpose

These structures are used to talk about purpose. *So that* is more common
than *in order that*, especially in an informal style. They are normally followed

by modal auxiliary verbs such as *can* or *will*; *may* is more formal.

> *She's staying here for six months **so that** she **can** perfect her English.*
> *I'm putting it in the oven now **so that** it'll be ready by seven o'clock.*
> *We send them monthly reports **in order that** they **may** have full*
> *information about progress.*

In an informal style, *that* can be dropped after *so*; this is very common in American English.

> *I've come early **so** I can talk to you.*

For more about omission of *that*, see 560.

2 present tenses for future

Present tenses are sometimes used to refer to the future after *so that* / *in order that*.

> *Send the letter express **so that** she **gets** / **she'll get** it before Tuesday.*
> *I'm going to make an early start **so that** I **don't**/**won't** get stuck in the traffic.*
> *We ought to write to him, **in order that** he **does not** / **will not** feel we are*
> *hiding things from him.*

3 past structures

In sentences about the past, *would, could* or *should* (British English only) are generally used with verbs after *so that* / *in order that*. *Might* is possible in a very formal style.

> *Mary talked to the shy girl **so that** she **wouldn't** feel left out.*
> *I took my golf clubs **so that** I **could** play at the weekend.*
> *They held the meeting on a Saturday **in order that** everybody **should** be*
> *free to attend. (US ... **in order that** everybody **would** be free ...)*
> *Whole populations of natives were wiped out **in order that** civilisation*
> ***might** advance.*

For the infinitive structures *in order to* and *so as to*, see 281.
For *so ... that* expressing result, see 513.5.
For *lest* meaning 'so that ... not', see 314.

520 'social' language

Every language has fixed expressions which are used on particular social occasions – for example when people meet, leave each other, go on a journey, sit down to meals and so on. Here are some of the most important English expressions of this kind.

1 introductions

Common ways of introducing strangers to each other are:

> *John, do you know Helen? Helen, this is my friend John.*
> *Sally, I don't think you've met Elaine.*
> *I don't think you two know each other, do you?*
> *Can/May I introduce John Willis?* (more formal)

When people are introduced, they usually say *How do you do?* (formal), *Hello*, or *Hi* (very informal). Americans often say *How are you?* Note that *How do you do?* is not a question, and the normal reply is *How do you do?* (It does not mean the same, in British English, as *How are you?*)

People who are introduced often shake hands.

For the use of first names, surnames and titles, see 353.

2 greetings

When meeting people (formal):
Good morning/afternoon/evening.
When meeting people (informal):
Hello.   *Hi.* (very informal)
When leaving people:
Good morning/afternoon/evening/night. (formal)
Goodbye. (less formal)   *Bye.* (informal)
Bye-bye. (often used to and by children)   *Cheerio.*
See you. (informal)   *See you later/tomorrow/next week/*etc. (informal)
Cheers. (informal – British only)   *Take care.* (informal)
It was nice to meet you.
Note that *Goodnight* is used only when leaving people, not when meeting them.

3 asking about health etc

When we meet people we know, we often ask politely about their health or their general situation.
How are you?   *How are things? / How's things?* (very informal)
How's it going? (informal)   *How (are) you doing?* (especially American)
Formal answers:
Very well, thank you. And you?   *Fine, thank you.*
Informal answers:
Fine/Great, thanks.   *Not too bad.*   *OK.*
So-so. (NOT ~~*So and so.*~~)   *All right.*   *(It) could be worse.*
British people do not usually ask *How are you?* when they are introduced to people. And neither British nor American people begin letters to strangers by asking about health (see 317).

4 special greetings

Greetings for special occasions are:
Happy birthday! OR *Many happy returns!*
Happy New Year/Easter!
Happy/Merry Christmas!

5 small talk

British people often begin polite conversations by talking about the weather.
'Nice day, isn't it?' 'Lovely.'   ▶

6 getting people's attention

Excuse me! is commonly used to attract somebody's attention, or to call a waiter in a restaurant. *I beg your pardon!* is also possible, especially in American English.

7 apologies

British people say *Excuse me* before interrupting or disturbing somebody, and *Sorry* after doing so. Compare:

>   **Excuse me**. Could I get past?   Oh, **sorry**, did I step on your foot?
>   **Excuse me**, could you tell me the way to the station?

Americans also use *Excuse me* to apologise after disturbing somebody.

I beg your pardon is a more formal way of saying 'Sorry'.

>   **I beg your pardon**. I didn't realise this was your seat.

8 asking people to repeat

If British people do not hear or understand what is said, they may say *Sorry?* (GB), *What?* (informal), *(I beg your) pardon?* or *Pardon me?* (US).

>   'Mike's on the phone.' **'Sorry?'** 'I said Mike's on the phone.'
>   'See you tomorrow.' **'What?'** 'See you tomorrow.'
>   'You're going deaf.' **'I beg your pardon?'**

9 journeys etc

Common ways of wishing people a good journey are:

>   *Have a good trip.*   *Have a good journey.* (GB)   *Safe journey home.* (GB)

After a journey (for example when we meet people at the airport or station), we may say:

>   *Did you have a good journey/trip/flight?*
>   *How was the journey/trip/flight?*

If somebody is leaving for an evening out or some kind of pleasant event, people might say *Have a good time!* or *Enjoy yourself!* (in American English sometimes just *Enjoy!*). *Good luck!* is used before examinations or other difficult or dangerous events.

When people return home, their friends or family may say *Welcome back.*

10 holidays

Before somebody starts a holiday, we may say:

>   *Have a good holiday.* (US . . . *vacation.*) OR *Have a good time.*

When the holiday is over, we may say:

>   *Did you have a good holiday?*

11 meals

We do not have fixed expressions for the beginnings and ends of meals. It is common for guests or family members to say something complimentary about the food during the meal (for example *This is very nice*), and after (for example *That was lovely/delicious; thank you very much*). Some religious people say 'grace' (a short prayer) before and after meals. Waiters often say *Enjoy your meal* after serving a customer.

For the names of meals, see 338.

12   drinking

When people begin drinking alcoholic drinks socially, they often raise their glasses and say something. Common expressions are *Cheers!* (GB) and *Your health!* When we drink to celebrate an occasion (such as a birthday, a wedding or a promotion), we often say *Here's to ...!*

> ***Here's to*** *Betty!*   ***Here's to*** *the new job!*
> ***Here's to*** *the happy couple!*

13   sending good wishes

Typical expressions are *Give my best wishes/regards/greetings/love to X* and *Remember me to X.* Americans often say *Say hello to X for me.* When the wishes are passed on, common expressions are *X sends his/her best wishes/regards* etc.

14   sympathy

Common formulae in letters of sympathy (for example on somebody's death) are *I was very/terribly/extremely sorry to hear about ...* and *Please accept my deepest sympathy.*

15   invitations and visits

Invitations often begin:

> *Would you like to ... ?*

Possible formal replies:

> *Thank you very much. That would be very nice.*
> *Sorry. I'm afraid I'm not free.*

It is normal to thank people for hospitality at the moment of leaving their houses.

> *Thank you very much. That was a wonderful evening.*

16   offers and replies

Offers often begin *Would you like ... ?* or *Can/May I get/offer you ... ?* (more formal). Offers to do things for people can begin *Would you like me to ... ?*, *Can/May I ... ?* or *Shall I ... ?* (British). Typical replies are *Yes please, No thank you, I'd love some, I'd love to, That's very nice/kind of you.*

Note that *thank you* can be used for accepting as well as refusing (see below).

17   asking for things

We normally ask for things by using *yes/no* questions. (For more details, see 483.)

> *Could you lend me a pen?* (NOT ~~*Please lend me a pen.*~~)

18   handing over things

We do not have an expression which is automatically used when we hand over things. We sometimes say *Here you are*, especially when we want to attract people's attention to the fact that we are passing something to them. Americans may also say *There you go* in this situation.

> *'Have you got a map of London?' 'I think so. Yes, **here you are.**' 'Thanks.'*   ▶

19   thanks

Common ways of thanking people are:

Thank you very much.   *Thank you.*   *Thanks (a lot).* (informal)

Possible replies to thanks are:

Not at all.   *Don't mention it.*   *That's OK.* (informal)
You're welcome.   *That's (quite) all right.*

But note that British people do not always reply to thanks, especially thanks for small things.

For more information about thanking and the use of *please,* see 429.

20   sleep

When somebody goes to bed, people often say *Sleep well.* In the morning, we may ask *Did you sleep well?* or *How did you sleep?*

For expressions used when telephoning, see 554.

521   some

1   meaning: indefinite quantity/number

Some is a determiner (see 157). It often suggests an indefinite quantity or number, and is used when it is not important to say exactly how much/many we are thinking of.

*I need **some** new clothes.*   *Would you like **some** tea?*

2   pronunciation

When *some* has this indefinite meaning, it usually has a 'weak' pronunciation /s(ə)m/ before **(adjective +) noun**.

some /s(ə)m/ *new clothes*   *some* /s(ə)m/ *tea*

For more about 'strong' and 'weak' pronunciations, see 588.

3   *some* and *any*

With this meaning, *some* is most common in affirmative clauses, and in questions which expect or encourage the answer 'Yes'. In other cases, *any* is generally used. For details, see 522. Compare:
– *There are **some** children at the front door.*
  *Do you mind if I put **some** music on?*
– *Did you meet **any** interesting people on holiday?*
  *She hasn't got **any** manners.*

4   *some* and *a/an*

Some (used in this sense) is quite similar to the indefinite article *a/an.* However, it is not normally used with the same kind of nouns (but see paragraph 6 below). Compare:

*I need **a new coat**.* (singular countable noun) (NOT ...~~some new coat.~~)
*I need **some new shirts**.* (plural countable noun)
*I need **some help** shopping.* (uncountable noun)

5 *some* and no article

With an uncountable or plural noun, *some* usually suggests the idea of an indefinite (but not very large) quantity or number. When there is no idea of a limited quantity or number, we usually use **no article**. For details, see 67. Compare:

- *We've planted **some roses** in the garden.* (a limited number)
  *We've decided to put **roses** under the back fence this year instead of* ***chrysanthemums***. (no idea of number)
- *Can you put **some blankets** in the back of the car in case the children get cold?*
  *The President has appealed for **blankets** and **warm clothing** for the earthquake victims.*

6 *some* and *some of*; *some* with no following noun

Before another determiner (article, demonstrative or possessive word) or a pronoun, we use *some of*. Compare:

- *I've got tickets for **some** concerts next month.* (NOT ... ~~*some of concerts*~~...)
  *Pete's coming to **some of the** concerts with me.*
  (NOT ...~~*some the concerts*~~...)
- ***Some** people want to get to sleep.* (NOT ...~~*some of people*~~...)
  ***Some of us** want to get to sleep.* (NOT ~~*Some us*~~...)

Some of the is possible before a singular countable noun in certain cases.
  *Move over and give me **some of the bed**.*

Nouns can be dropped after *some*, if the meaning is clear.
  *I've got too many strawberries. Would you like **some**?*

Before *of*, or with no following noun, *some* is pronounced /sʌm/.
  some /sʌm/ of us   *Would you like **some** /sʌm/ ?*

7 contrast with *others* etc

Some (pronounced /sʌm/) can have a more emphatic meaning, contrasting with *others*, *all* or *enough*.
  ***Some** people like the sea; **others** prefer the mountains.*
  ***Some** of us were late, but we were **all** there by ten o'clock.*
  *I've got **some** money, but not **enough**.*

8 with singular countable noun

With a singular countable noun, *some* (/sʌm/) can refer to an unknown person or thing.
  ***Some** idiot has taken the bath plug.*
  *There must be **some** job I could do.*
  *She's living in **some** village in Yorkshire.*

We can use this structure to suggest that we are not interested in somebody or something, or that we do not think much of him/her/it.
  *Mary's gone to America to marry **some** sheep farmer or other.*
  *I don't want to spend my life doing **some** boring little office job.*

In informal American English, *some* can also be used to show enthusiastic appreciation.
  *That's **some** bike you've got there!* (GB ... ***quite a** bike* ...)
  *It was **some** party!*

9 with numbers

Some (/sʌm/), with a number, is used to suggest that the number is a high or impressive one.

*We have exported **some four thousand** tons of bootlaces this year.*

For *somebody* and *anybody, something* and *anything* etc, see 523.
For *some time, sometime* and *sometimes,* see 524.
For *any,* see 54.

522 some and any

1 indefinite quantities

Both *some* and *any* can refer to an indefinite quantity or number. They are used when it is not easy, or not important, to say exactly how much/many we are thinking of.

*I need to buy **some** new clothes.*
*Is there **any** milk left?*

2 the difference

In this indefinite sense, *some* is most common in affirmative clauses. *Any* (used in this sense) is a 'non-assertive' word (see 374), and is common in questions and negatives. Compare:

*I want **some** razor blades.* (NOT *I want **any** razor blades.*)
*Have you got **any** razor blades?*
*Sorry, I haven't got **any** razor blades.*
      (NOT *Sorry, I haven't got **some** razor blades.*)

For other uses of *any,* see 54.

3 *some* in questions

We use *some* in questions if we expect people to answer 'Yes', or want to encourage them to say 'Yes' – for example in offers and requests.

*Have you brought **some** paper and a pen?*
      (The hearer is expected to bring them.)
*Shouldn't there be **some** instructions with it?*
*Would you like **some** more meat?*
*Could I have **some** brown rice, please?*
*Have you got **some** glasses that I could borrow?*

4 *any* in affirmative clauses

We use *any* in affirmative clauses after words that have a negative or limiting meaning: for example *never, hardly, without, little.*

*You **never** give me **any** help.*
*There's **hardly any** tea left.*
*We got there **without any** trouble.*
*There is **little** point in doing **any** more work now.*
*I **forgot** to get **any** bread.*

For other uses of *any* in affirmative clauses (e.g. ***Any** ten-year-old child could do this*), see 54.

5   *if*-clauses

Both *some* and *any* are common in *if*-clauses.
>*If you want **some/any** help, let me know.*

Sometimes *any* is used to suggest 'if there is / are any'.
>***Any** cars parked in this road will be towed away.*
>>(= ***If there are any** cars parked in this road, they will . . .*)

For more information about *some*, see 521.
For *somebody* and *anybody*, *something* and *anything* etc, see 523.

523   **somebody, someone, anybody, anyone** etc

1   *-body* and *-one*

There is no significant difference between *somebody* and *someone*, *anybody* and *anyone*, *everybody* and *everyone* or *nobody* and *no one*. The forms with *-one* are more common; those with *-body* are a little more informal.

2   *some-* and *any-*

The differences between *somebody* and *anybody*, *something* and *anything*, *somewhere* and *anywhere* etc are the same as the differences between *some* and *any* (see 522 for details). Compare:
– *There's **somebody** at the door.*
  *Did **anybody** telephone?*
– *Let's go **somewhere** nice for dinner.*
  *I don't want to go **anywhere** too expensive.*
– *Can I get you **something** to drink?*
  *If you need **something/anything**, just shout.*

3   singular

When these words are subjects they are used with singular verbs.
>***Everybody likes** her.* (N O T *Everybody like her.*)
>***Is everything** ready?* (N O T *Are everything ready?*)

Somebody normally refers to only one person. Compare:
>*There's **somebody** outside who wants to talk to you.*
>*There are **some people** outside who want to talk to you.*

4   use of *they*

They, them and *their* are often used with a singular meaning to refer back to *somebody* etc (see 505).
>*If **anybody** wants a ticket for the concert, **they** can get it from my office.*
>*'There's **somebody** at the door.' 'Tell **them** I'm busy.'*
>***Someone** left **their** umbrella on the bus.*   ***Nobody** phoned, did **they**?*

5   complementation

Somebody etc can be followed by adjectives or adverbial expressions.
>*I hope he marries **somebody nice**.*
>*She's going to meet **someone in the Ministry**.*
>*I feel like eating **something hot**.*
>*Let's go **somewhere quiet** this weekend.*   ▶

They can also be followed by *else* (see 187).
> *Mary – are you in love with **somebody else**?*
> *I don't like this place – let's go **somewhere else**.*

Note also the informal use of *much* after *any-* and *no-*.
> *We didn't do **anything much** yesterday.*
> *There's **nothing much** on TV tonight.*

6 *someplace*

Someplace is common in informal American English.
> *Let's go **someplace** quiet.*

7 *anyone* and *any one*; *everyone* and *every one*

Anyone means the same as *anybody*; *any one* means 'any single one (person or thing)'. Compare:
> *Does **anyone** know where Celia lives?*
> *You can borrow **any one video** at a time.*

There is a similar difference between *everyone* and *every one*. Compare:
> ***Everyone** had a good time at the party.*
> *There aren't any cakes left – they've eaten **every one**.*

For the difference between *no one* and *none*, see 373.
For question tags after *everything* and *nothing*, see 466.
For *some time, sometime* and *sometimes*, see 524.

524 some time, sometime and sometimes

Some time (with two stresses: /'sʌm 'taɪm/) means 'a considerable amount of time', 'quite a lot of time'.
> *I'm afraid it'll take **some time** to repair your car.*
> *She's lived in Italy for **some time**, so she speaks Italian quite well.*

Sometime (/'sʌmtaɪm/) refers to an indefinite time, usually in the future; it often means 'one day'.
> *Let's have dinner together **sometime** next week.*
> *When will I get married – this year, next year, **sometime**, never?*

Sometimes (/'sʌmtaɪmz/) is an adverb of frequency (see 23.2). It means 'on some occasions', 'more than once' (past, present or future).
> *I **sometimes** went skiing when I lived in Germany.*
> ***Sometimes**, in the long winter evenings, I sit and wonder what life is all about.*

525 soon, early and quickly

Not all languages have separate equivalents for these three words, and some students may confuse them.

1 *soon*

Soon usually relates to the time when one is talking or writing – it means 'a short time after now'.
> *Get well **soon**.* (NOT ~~*Get well **early**.*~~)

Soon can also relate to the time one is talking or writing about – it can mean 'a short time after then'.

*The work was hard, but she **soon** got used to it.*

For *no sooner... than,* see 237.

2 *early*

The adverb *early* means 'near the beginning of the time-period that we are talking or thinking about'. It does not usually mean 'a short time after now'.

*   **Early** that week, Luke was called to the police station.*
*   We usually take our holidays **early** in the year.* (NOT *...~~soon in the year.~~*)
*   I usually get up **early** and go to bed **early**.* (NOT *~~I usually get up soon~~...*)
Sometimes *early* means 'before the expected time'.

*   The plane arrived twenty minutes **early**.*
Early can also be used as an adjective (e.g. *an **early** train*). The adjective *early* can sometimes have the same kind of meaning as *soon.*

*   I should be grateful for an **early** reply.   Best wishes for an **early** recovery.*
Note the common use of *be early/late* to mean 'arrive early / late'.

*   That woman **is** never **early**.*
A watch or clock is *fast* or *slow*, not *early* or *late*.

*   My watch is five minutes **fast**.*

3 *quickly*

Quickly refers to the speed with which something is done. Compare:
–   *Come and see us **quickly**.* (= *Hurry – make the arrangements fast.*)
*   Come and see us **soon**.* (= *Come and see us before long.*)
–   *He did the repair **quickly** but not very well.*
*   I hope you can do the repair **soon** – I need the car.*

526 **sort of, kind of** and **type of**

1 **articles**

The article *a/an* is usually dropped after *sort of, kind of* and *type of*, but structures with articles are possible in an informal style.

*   That's a funny **sort of (a)** car.   What **sort of (a)** bird is that?*

2 **singular and plural;** *these sort of* **etc**

When we are talking about one sort of thing, we can use *sort of, kind of* or *type of* followed by a singular noun.

*   This **sort of car** is enormously expensive to run.*
*   I'm interested in any new **type of development** in computer science.*
Singular *sort of, kind of* and *type of* can also be followed by plural nouns, especially in an informal style.

*   I'm interested in any new **kind of developments** ...*
Plural demonstratives (*these* and *those*) can also be used.

*   **These sort of cars** are enormously expensive to run.*
*   Do you smoke **those kind of cigarettes**?*
This structure is often felt to be incorrect, and is usually avoided in a formal style. This can be done by using a singular noun (see above), by using plural

sorts/kinds/types, or by using the structure ... *of this/that sort/kind/type.*
This sort of car *is ...* **These kinds of car(s)** *are ...*
Cars of that type *are ...*

3 softeners

In an informal style, *sort of* and *kind of* can be used before almost any word or expression, or at the end of a sentence, to show that we are not speaking very exactly, or to make what we say less definite.

*We **sort of** thought you might forget.*
*Sometimes I **sort of** wonder whether I shouldn't **sort of** get a job.*
*I've had **sort of** an idea about what we could do.*
*She's **kind of** strange.*   *I've changed my mind, **kind of**.*

527 sound

Sound is a 'copular verb' (see 147). It is followed by adjectives, not adverbs.

*You **sound unhappy**. What's the matter?*

Progressive forms are not very common.

*Your idea **sounds** great.* (NOT ~~*Your idea's sounding great.*~~)

However, progressive forms are possible when there is an idea of change.

*The car **sounds / is sounding** a bit rough these days.*

Sound is often followed by *like* or *as if.*

*That **sounds like** Bill coming up the stairs.*
*It **sounds as if** he's had a hard day.*

528 speak and talk

1 little difference

There is not very much difference between *speak* and *talk*. In certain situations one or the other is preferred (though they are usually both possible).

2 formality

Talk is the more usual word to refer to conversational exchanges and informal communication.

*When she walked into the room everybody stopped **talking**.*
*Could I **talk** to you about the football match for a few minutes?*

Speak is often used for one-way communication and for exchanges in more serious or formal situations.

*I'll have to **speak** to that boy – he's getting very lazy.*
*They had a terrible row last week, and now they're not **speaking** to one another.*
*After she had finished reading the letter, nobody **spoke**.*

3 lectures etc

Talk is often used for the act of giving an informal lecture (a *talk*); *speak* is preferred for more formal lectures, sermons etc.

*This is Mr Patrick Allen, who's going to **talk** to us about flower arrangement.*

*This is Professor Rosalind Bowen, who is going to **speak** to us on recent developments in low-temperature physics.*
*The Pope **spoke** to the crowd for seventy minutes about world peace.*

4 languages

Speak is the usual word to refer to knowledge and use of languages, and to the physical ability to speak.
*She **speaks** three languages fluently.*
*We **spoke** French so that the children wouldn't understand.*
*His throat operation has left him unable to **speak**.*

5 other cases

One usually asks to *speak to* somebody on the phone (US also *speak with*).
*Hello. Could I **speak to** Karen, please?*
Talk is used before *sense, nonsense* and other words with similar meanings.
*You're **talking** complete **nonsense**, as usual.*
(NOT ~~You're **speaking** complete nonsense...~~)

529 spelling (1): capital letters

We use capital (big) letters at the beginning of the following kinds of words:

1 the names of days, months and public holidays (but not usually seasons)

Sunday	*March*	*Easter*
Tuesday	*September*	*Christmas*
(BUT *summer, autumn*)		

2 the names of people and places, including stars and planets

John	*Mars*	*The Ritz Hotel*
Mary	*North Africa*	*The Super Cinema*
Canada	*the Far East*	*the United States*
(BUT *the earth, the sun, the moon*)		

3 people's titles

Mr Smith	*Professor Blake*	*the Managing Director*
Dr Jones	*Colonel Webb*	

4 nouns and adjectives referring to nationalities and regions, languages, ethnic groups and religions

*He's **Russian**.*	*I speak **German**.*	*Japanese history*
Catalan cooking	*She's **Jewish**.*	*He's a Sikh.*

5 the first word (and often other nouns, verbs, adjectives and adverbs) in the titles of books, films, plays, pictures, magazines etc

*Gone with the **Wind*** OR *Gone with the wind*
New Scientist

For more about the use of capitals with *East, North* etc, see 176.

530 spelling (2): -ly

1 adverb formation

We normally change an adjective into an adverb by adding *-ly*.

late → lately   *real → really* (NOT ~~realy~~)
right → rightly   *definite → definitely*
hopeful → hopefully   *pale → palely*
complete → completely (NOT ~~completly~~)

Exceptions:

true → truly   *due → duly*   *whole → wholly*   *full → fully*

2 *y* and *i*

-y usually changes to *-i-* (see 534).

happy → happily   *easy → easily*
dry → drily or *dryly*   *gay → gaily*

Exceptions:

shy → shyly   *sly → slyly*   *coy → coyly*

3 adjectives ending in consonant + *le*

-le changes to *-ly* after a consonant.

idle → idly   *noble → nobly*   *able → ably*

4 adjectives ending in *ic*

If an adjective ends in *-ic*, the adverb ends in *-ically* (pronounced /ɪkli/),

tragic → tragically   *phonetic → phonetically*

Exception:

public → publicly

531 spelling (3): -ise and -ize

Many English verbs can be spelt with either *-ise* or *-ize*. In American English, *-ize* is preferred in these cases. Examples:

realise/realize (GB)   *realize* (US)
mechanise/mechanize (GB)   *mechanize* (US)
computerise/computerize (GB) *computerize* (US)
baptise/baptize (GB)   *baptize* (US)

Most words of two syllables, and some longer words, have *-ise* in both British and American English. Examples:

surprise (NOT ~~surprize~~)   *exercise*
revise   *improvise*
advise   *supervise*
comprise   *televise*
despise   *advertise* (US also sometimes *advertize*)
compromise

Capsize has *-ize* in both British and American English.

Note also *analyse* and *paralyse* (US *analyze* and *paralyze*).

If in doubt, remember that in British English *-ise* is almost always acceptable. For American English, consult an American dictionary.

532   spelling (4): hyphens

1   What are hyphens?

Hyphens are the short lines (-) that we put between words in expressions like *ticket-office* or *ex-husband*.

2   two-part adjectives

We usually put a hyphen in two-part adjectives in which the second part ends in *-ed* or *-ing*.
>*blue-eyed*   *broken-hearted*   *nice-looking*

We also often hyphenate two-part adjectives or noun modifiers which contain the sense of 'between'.
>*grey-green* (= *between grey and green*)
>*the London-Paris flight*
>*the Scotland-France match*
>*an Anglo-American agreement*

3   phrases used as adjectives

When we use a longer phrase as an adjective before a noun, we often use hyphens. Compare:
- *an **out-of-work** miner.*
  *He's **out of work**.*
- *a **shoot-to-kill** policy*
  *They were ordered to **shoot to kill**.*

4   two-part nouns; stress

In British English, hyphens are common in two-word compound nouns when the first word has the main stress.
>*a 'paper-shop* (compare *a paper 'bag*)
>*some 'make-up* (compare *to make 'up*)
>*'running-shoes* (compare *running 'water*)
>*'lorry-driver* (compare *hotel 'waiter*)

5   prefixes

The prefixes *co-*, *non-* and *ex-* are sometimes separated from what follows by hyphens.
>*It's a British and American **co-production**.*
>*We have a policy of **non-involvement**.*
>*He's one of her **ex-lovers**.*

And other prefixes may be separated by hyphens in order to avoid unusual or misleading combinations of letters.
>*un-American*   *pre-emptive*   *counter-revolution*   ▶

6 word division

We use a hyphen to separate the parts of a long word at the end of a written or printed line. (To see where to divide words, look in a good dictionary.)
> ... *is not completely in accordance with the policy of the present govern-*
> *ment, which was ...*

7 Are hyphens disappearing?

The rules about hyphens are complicated, and usage is not very clear. Perhaps because of this, people seem to be using hyphens less. Many common short compounds are now often written 'solid', with no division between the words (e.g. *weekend, wideawake, takeover*); other less common or longer compounds are now more likely to be written as completely separate words (e.g. *train driver, living room*). The situation at present is rather confused, and it is not unusual to find the same expression spelt in three different ways (e.g. *bookshop, book-shop, book shop*). If one is not sure whether to use a hyphen between words or not, the best thing is to look in a dictionary, or to write the words without a hyphen.

533 spelling (5): final e

1 when final *e* is dropped

When an ending that begins with a vowel (e.g. *-ing, -able, -ous*) is added to a word that ends in *-e*, we usually drop the *-e*.

hope → hoping	*note → notable*	*shade → shady*
make → making	*fame → famous*	

Some words have two possible forms before *-able* and *-age*. The form without *-e* is more common in most cases.

like → lik(e)able	*move → mov(e)able*
love → lov(e)able	*mile → mil(e)age* (more common with *e*)

Final *-e* is not dropped from words ending in *-ee*, *-oe* or *-ye*.

see → seeing	*canoe → canoeist*
agree → agreeable	*dye → dyeing*

2 when final *e* is not dropped

Before endings that begin with a consonant, final *-e* is not normally dropped.

excite → excitement	*complete → completeness*
definite → definitely	

Exceptions: words ending in *-ue*

due → duly	*true → truly*	*argue → argument*

In words that end with *-ce* or *-ge*, we do not drop *-e* before *a* or *o*.
> *replace → replaceable*   *courage → courageous*
> (BUT *charge → charging, face → facing*)

Judg(e)ment and *acknowledg(e)ment* can be spelt with or without the *-e* after *g*.

For words ending in *-ie*, see 534.4. For adverbs ending in *-ly*, see 530.

534   spelling (6): **y** and **i**

1   changing *y* to *i*

When we add an ending to a word that ends in -*y*, we usually change -*y* to -*i*-.

hurry → hurried	*fury → furious*	*merry → merriment*
marry → marriage	*easy → easier*	*busy → business*
happy → happily		

Generally, nouns and verbs that end in -*y* have plural or third person singular forms in -*ies*.

story → stories	*spy → spies*	*hurry → hurries*

Two spellings are possible for the nouns *dryer/drier* and *flyer/flier*, and for words made from the adjective *dry* (*dryer/drier*, *dryly/drily*, *dryness/driness*). Other exceptions: *slyer, slyest, slyly, slyness*.

2   no change before *i*

We do not change -*y* to -*i*- before *i* (for example when we add -*ing*, -*ism*, -*ish*, -*ise*).

try → trying	*Tory → Toryism*	*baby → babyish*

3   no change after a vowel

We do not change -*y* to -*i*- after a vowel letter.

buy → buying	*play → played*
enjoy → enjoyment	*grey → greyish*

Exceptions:

say → said	*pay → paid*	*lay → laid*

4   changing *ie* to *y*

We change -*ie* to -*y*- before -*ing*.

die → dying	*lie → lying*
(BUT *dye → dyeing*)	

535   spelling (7): doubling final consonants

1   doubling before vowels

We sometimes double the final consonant of a word before adding -*ed*, -*er*, -*est*, -*ing*, -*able*, -*y* (or any ending that begins with a vowel).

stop → stopped	*sit → sitting*	*big → bigger*

2   Which consonants are doubled?

We double the following letters:

b:	*rub → rubbing*	n:	*win → winnable*	
d:	*sad → sadder*	p:	*stop → stopped*	
g:	*big → bigger*	r:	*prefer → preferred*	
l:	*travel → travelling*	t:	*sit → sitting*	
m:	*slim → slimming*			

▶

We double final *-s* in *gassing, gassed* (but not usually in other words), final *-z* in *fezzes*, and final *-f* in *iffy* (a colloquial word for 'questionable', 'uncertain').

3   only at the end of a word

We only double consonants that come at the end of a word. Compare:

hop → *hopping* BUT *hope* → *hoping*
fat → *fatter* BUT *late* → *later*
plan → *planned* BUT *phone* → *phoned*

4   one consonant after one vowel letter

We only double when the word ends in *one* consonant after *one* vowel letter. Compare:

fat → *fatter* BUT *fast* → *faster* (NOT *fastter*)
bet → *betting* BUT *beat* → *beating* (NOT *beatting*)

5   only stressed syllables

We only double consonants in stressed syllables. We do not double in longer words that end in unstressed syllables. Compare:

up'set → *up'setting* BUT *'visit* → *'visiting*
be'gin → *be'ginning* BUT *'open* → *'opening*
re'fer → *re'ferring* BUT *'offer* → *'offering*

Note the spelling of these words:

'gallop → *'galloping* → *'galloped* (NOT *gallopping, gallopped*)
de'velop → *de'veloping* → *de'veloped* (NOT *developping, developped*)

6   exception: final *l* in unstressed syllables

In British English, we double *-l* at the end of a word after one vowel letter, in most cases, even in unstressed syllables.

'travel → *travelling*   *'equal* → *equalled*

In American English, words like this are normally spelt with one *l*: *traveling*.

7   other exceptions

Consonants are sometimes doubled at the end of final syllables that are pronounced with full vowels (e.g. /æ/), even when these do not carry the main stress.

kidnap → *kidnapped*
handicap → *handicapped*
worship → *worshippers* (US also *worshipers*)
combat → *combating* OR *combatting*

Final *-s* is sometimes doubled in *focus(s)ing, focus(s)ed, bias(s)ed* and similar words.

8   final *c*

Final *-c* changes to *ck* before *-ed, -er, -ing* etc.

picnic → *picnickers*   *panic* → *panicking*   *mimic* → *mimicked*

9 Why double?

The reason for doubling is to show that a vowel is pronounced short.
This is because, in the middle of a word, a stressed vowel letter before *one*
consonant is usually pronounced as a long vowel or as a diphthong
(double vowel). Compare:

hoping /ˈhəʊpɪŋ/   *hopping* /ˈhɒpɪŋ/
later /ˈleɪtə(r)/   *latter* /ˈlætə(r)/
diner /ˈdaɪnə(r)/   *dinner* /ˈdɪnə(r)/

536   spelling (8): **ch** and **tch, k** and **ck**

After one vowel, at the end of a word, we usually write *-ck* and *-tch* for the
sounds /k/ and /tʃ/.

*ba**ck** ne**ck** si**ck** lo**ck** stu**ck***
*ca**tch** fe**tch** sti**tch** bo**tch** hu**tch***

Exceptions:

*ya**k** ti**c*** (and many other words ending in *-ic*)
*ri**ch** whi**ch** su**ch** mu**ch** atta**ch** deta**ch***

After a consonant or two vowels, we write *-k* and *-ch*.

*ban**k** wor**k** tal**k** mar**ch** ben**ch***
*brea**k** boo**k** wee**k** pea**ch** coa**ch***

537   spelling (9): **ie** and **ei**

The sound /iː/ (as in *believe*) is often written *ie*, but not usually *ei*. However,
we write *ei* after *c*. English-speaking children learn a rhyme: 'i before e,
except after c'.

*bel**ie**ve ch**ie**f f**ie**ld gr**ie**f p**ie**ce sh**ie**ld*
*c**ei**ling dec**ei**ve rec**ei**ve rec**ei**pt*

Exceptions: *s**ei**ze, N**ei**l, K**ei**th.*

538   spelling and pronunciation

In many English words, the spelling is different from the pronunciation. This
is mainly because our pronunciation has changed a good deal over the last
few hundred years, while our spelling system has stayed more or less the
same. Here is a list of some difficult common words with their
pronunciations.

1   usually two syllables, not three

The letters in brackets are usually not pronounced.

asp(i)rin	*ev(e)ning*	*om(e)lette*
bus(i)ness	*ev(e)ry*	*rest(au)rant*
choc(o)late	*marri(a)ge*	*sev(e)ral*
diff(e)rent	*med(i)cine* (US three syllables)	

►

2   usually three syllables, not four

The letters in brackets are usually not pronounced.

comf(or)table	*temp(e)rature*
int(e)resting	*us(u)ally*
secret(a)ry (US four syllables)	*veg(e)table*

3   silent letters

The letters in brackets are usually not pronounced.

- *clim(b)   com(b)   dum(b)*
- *mus(c)le*
- *han(d)kerchief   san(d)wich   We(d)nesday*
- *champa(g)ne   forei(g)n   si(g)n*
- *bou(gh)t   cau(gh)t   ou(gh)t   thou(gh)t*
- *dau(gh)ter   hei(gh)t   hi(gh)   li(gh)t   mi(gh)t   nei(gh)bour   ni(gh)t   ri(gh)t   strai(gh)t   throu(gh)   ti(gh)t   wei(gh)*
- *w(h)at   w(h)en   w(h)ere   w(h)ether   w(h)ich   w(h)ip   w(h)y* (Some speakers use an unvoiced /w/ in these words.)
- *(h)onest   (h)onour   (h)our*
- *(k)nee   (k)nife   (k)nob   (k)nock   (k)now*
- *ca(l)m   cou(l)d   ha(l)f   sa(l)mon   shou(l)d   ta(l)k   wa(l)k   wou(l)d*
- *autum(n)   hym(n)*
- *(p)neumatic   (p)sychiatrist   (p)sychology   (p)sychotherapy   (p)terodactyl*
- *cu(p)board*
- *i(r)on* (British pronunciation)
- *i(s)land   i(s)le*
- *cas(t)le   Chris(t)mas   fas(t)en   lis(t)en   of(t)en   whis(t)le* (*Often* can also be pronounced /ˈɒftən/.)
- *g(u)ess   g(u)ide   g(u)itar*
- *(w)rap   (w)rite   (w)rong*
- *(w)ho   (w)hose   (w)hole*

4   *a* = /e/

- *any   many   Thames*

5   *ch* = /k/

- *ache   architect   **ch**aracter   **ch**emist   **Ch**ristmas   stoma**ch***

6 *ea* = /e/

☐ *bread breakfast dead death head health heavy instead lead* (the metal) *leather pleasure read* (past) *ready sweater*

7 *ea* = /eɪ/

☐ *break great steak*

8 *gh* = /f/

☐ *cough enough laugh rough*

9 *o* = /ʌ/

☐ *brother colour come comfortable company cover glove government honey London money month mother none nothing one onion other some son stomach ton wonder worry*

10 *ou* = /ʌ/

☐ *country couple cousin double enough trouble*

11 *u* = /ʊ/

☐ *butcher cushion pull push put*

12 **words pronounced with /aɪ/**

☐ *biology buy dial height idea iron microphone science society either* (many British speakers) *neither* (many British speakers)

13 **other strange spellings**

area /'eərɪə/
Australia /ɒs'treɪlɪə/
bicycle /'baɪsɪkl/
biscuit /'bɪskɪt/
blood /blʌd/
brooch /brəʊtʃ/
business /'bɪznɪs/
busy /'bɪzi/
Europe /'jʊərəp/
foreign /'fɒrən/
friend /frend/
fruit /fruːt/
heard /hɜːd/
heart /hɑːt/
juice /dʒuːs/
minute /'mɪnɪt/
moustache /mə'stɑːʃ/ (US /'mʌstæʃ/)
once /wʌns/
one /wʌn/
theatre /'θɪətə(r)/
two /tuː/
woman /'wʊmən/
women /'wɪmɪn/

►

14   silent *r*

In standard southern British English, *r* is not normally pronounced before a consonant or at the end of a word.

>*hard* /hɑːd/   *first* /fɜːst/   *order* /'ɔːdə/
>*car* /kɑː/   *four* /fɔː/   *more* /mɔː/

But *r* is pronounced at the end of a word if a vowel follows immediately.

>*four islands* /'fɔːr 'aɪləndz/   *more eggs* /'mɔːr 'egz/

Note the pronunciation of *iron*, and of words ending in *-ered* and *-re*.

>*iron* /aɪən/ (US /'aɪrən/)   *centre* /'sentə(r)/
>*wondered* /'wʌndəd/   *theatre* /'θɪətə(r)/
>*bothered* /'bɒðəd/

We often add /r/ after words ending in the sound /ə/ even when this is not written with *r*, if another vowel follows immediately.
>*India and Africa* /'ɪndɪər ənd 'æfrɪkə/

In most varieties of American English, and in many regional British accents, *r* is pronounced whenever it is written.

539   still, yet and already

1   meanings

Still, yet and *already* can all be used to talk about things which are going on, or expected, around the present. We use these words to say where something is in relation to the present moment.

2   *still*

Still is used to say that something is in the present, not the past – it has, perhaps surprisingly, not finished.
>*She's **still** asleep.   Is it **still** raining?*
>*I've been thinking for hours, but I **still** can't decide.*
>*You're not **still** seeing that Jackson boy, are you?*

For the use of *not any longer/more* or *no longer* to say that something has finished, see 372.

3   *yet*

Not yet is used to say that something which is expected is in the future, not the present or past.
>*'Is Sally here?' '**Not yet**.'   The postman hasn't come **yet**.*

In questions, we use *yet* to ask whether something expected has happened.
>*Is supper ready **yet**?   Has the postman come **yet**?*

Yet is normally used in questions and negative sentences, but it is occasionally used in affirmative sentences (with a similar meaning to *still*) in a formal style.
>*We have **yet** to hear from the bank.* (= We are **still** waiting to hear . . .)

4   *already*

Already is used to say that something is in the present or past, not the future. It may express some surprise – for example, because something has happened sooner than expected.

> *'When's Sally going to come?' 'She's **already** here.'*
> *'You must go to Scotland.' 'I've **already** been.'*
> *Have you **already** finished? That was quick!*

5 related to a past moment

All three words can be related to a past moment instead of to the present.

> *I **went** to see if she had woken up **yet**, but she was **still** asleep. This was*
> *embarrassing, because her friends had **already** arrived.*

6 tenses

Various tenses are possible with all three words. In British English, perfect
tenses are common with *already* and *yet*; Americans often prefer past tenses.
Compare:

- *– **Have you called** the garage **yet**?* (GB)
  ***Did you call** the garage **yet**?* (US)
- *– **She's already left**.* (GB)
  *She **already left**.* (US)

7 position

Already and *still* usually go in 'mid-position' (see 22).

> *Are you **already** here?*
> *She's **still** working.*

Already is not usually put with time adverbials.

> *When I was fourteen I **already** knew that I wanted to be a doctor.*
> (NOT *~~Already when I was fourteen~~*...)
> *In 1970 Britain's car industry was **already** in serious trouble.*
> (NOT *~~Already in 1970~~*...)

Already can also go at the end of a clause for emphasis.

> *Are you here **already**? You must have run all the way.*

Yet usually goes at the end of a clause, but it can go immediately after *not* in
a formal style.

> *Don't eat the pears – they aren't ripe **yet**.*
> *The pears are **not yet** ripe.* (more formal)

For other meanings of *still* and *yet*, see a good dictionary.
For the difference between these words and *ever*, see 197.

540 stress, rhythm and intonation

1 stress

Stress is the word for the 'strength' with which syllables are pronounced. In
speech, some parts of English words and sentences sound much louder than
others. For example, the first syllable of *CARpet*, the second syllable of
inSPECtion or the last syllable of *conFUSE* are usually stressed, while the
other syllables in these words are not. In the sentence *Don't look at HIM –
HE didn't do it*, the words *him* and *he* are stressed in order to emphasise
them. Stressed syllables are not only louder; they may also have longer
vowels, and they may be pronounced on a higher pitch.

▶

2 word stress

English words with more than one syllable mostly have a fixed stress pattern. There are not many rules to show which syllable of a word will be stressed: one usually has to learn the stress pattern of a word along with its meaning, spelling and pronunciation. Examples:

Stressed on first syllable:

AFter, CApital, HAPpen, EXercise, EAsy

Stressed on second syllable:

inSTEAD, proNOUNCE, aGREEment, parTIcularly

Stressed on third syllable:

enterTAIN, underSTAND, concenTRAtion

The stressed syllable of a word is the one that can carry an intonation movement (see paragraph 6 below).

Many short phrases also have a fixed stress pattern.

front DOOR (NOT ~~FRONT door~~)

LIVing room (NOT ~~living ROOM~~)

Related words can have different stress patterns.

to inCREASE   an INcrease

PHOtograph   phoTOgrapher   photoGRAphic

3 variable stress

Some words have variable stress. In these, the stress is at or near the end when the word is spoken alone, but it can move to an earlier position when the word is in a sentence, especially if another stressed word follows. Compare:

– *afterNOON* (stress at the end)

It's time for my AFternoon SLEEP. (stress at the beginning)

– *JapanESE*

JApanese COOking

– *nineTEEN*

The year NINEteen TWENty

Many short phrases – for instance, two-word verbs – have variable stress.

– *Their marriage broke UP.*

Money problems BROKE up their marriage.

– *It's dark BLUE.*

a DARK blue SUIT

4 stress and pronunciation

Unstressed syllables nearly always have one of two vowels: /ə/ or /ɪ/. Compare the first syllables in the following pairs of words:

– *CONfident* (/ˈkɒnfɪdənt/)

conFUSED (/kənˈfjuːzd/)

– *PARticle* (/ˈpɑːtɪkl/)

parTIcular (/pəˈtɪkjələ(r)/)

– *EXpert* (/ˈekspɜːt/)

exPERience (/ɪkˈspɪərɪəns/)

Many short words (mostly pronouns, prepositions, conjunctions and auxiliary verbs) have two quite different pronunciations: a normal 'weak' unstressed form, and a 'strong' form used when the word has special stress. (For details, see 588.)

'I was (/wəz/) *here first.' 'No you weren't.' 'Yes I was* (/wɒz/).'

5   stress in sentences; rhythm

Rhythm is the word for the way stressed and unstressed syllables make patterns in speech. In sentences, we usually give more stress to nouns, ordinary verbs, adjectives and adverbs, and less stress to pronouns, determiners, prepositions, conjunctions and auxiliary verbs.

She was SURE that the BACK of the CAR had been DAMaged.

Many linguists feel that the rhythm of spoken English is based on a regular pattern of stressed syllables. These follow each other at roughly regular intervals, and are pronounced more slowly and clearly. Unstressed syllables are pronounced more quickly and less clearly, and are fitted in between the regular stressed syllables. If several unstressed syllables come together, these are pronounced even more quickly so as not to disturb the rhythm. Compare the following two sentences. The second does not take much longer to say than the first: although it has three more unstressed syllables, it has the same number of stressed syllables.

She KNEW the DOCtor.

She KNEW that there was a DOCtor.

Note, however, that this is a very complicated question, and not all experts agree about the way English rhythm works.

6   intonation

Intonation is the word for the 'melody' of spoken language: the way the musical pitch of the voice rises and falls. Intonation systems in languages are very complicated and difficult to analyse, and linguists disagree about how English intonation works.

One way in which intonation seems to be used is to show how a piece of information fits in with what comes before and after. For instance, a speaker may raise his or her voice when taking over the conversation from somebody else, or to indicate a change of subject. A rise or fall on a particular word may show that this is the 'centre' of the message – the place where the new information is being given; or it may signal a contrast or a special emphasis. When a speaker ends on a falling tone, this often expresses some kind of conclusion or certainty; a rising tone at the end of a sentence may express uncertainty, suggest that there is more to be said, or invite another speaker to take over.

Intonation (together with speed, voice quality and loudness) can also say things about the speaker's attitude. For instance, when people are excited or angry they often raise and lower their voices more.

541 subjunctive

1 forms and meanings

The subjunctive is a special kind of present tense which has no *-s* in the third person singular. It is sometimes used in *that*-clauses in a formal style, especially in American English, after words which express the idea that something is important or desirable (e.g. *suggest, recommend, ask, insist, vital, essential, important, advice*). The same forms are used in both present and past sentences.

*It is essential that every child **have** the same educational opportunities.*
*We felt it was important that James **write** to Uncle Arthur as soon as possible.*
*Our advice is that the company **invest** in new equipment.*
*The judge recommended that Simmons **remain** in prison for at least three years.*

Do is not used in negative subjunctives. Note the word order.

*We considered it desirable that he **not leave school** before finishing his exams.*

2 *be*

Be has special subjunctive forms: *I be, you be* etc.

*It is important that Helen **be** present when we sign the papers.*
*The Director asked that he **be** allowed to advertise for more staff.*

The forms *I were* and *he/she/it were,* used for example after *if* (see 260.4) and *wish* (see 601) in a formal style, are also a kind of subjunctive.

*If I **were** you I should stop smoking.*   *I wish it **were** Saturday.*

3 fixed phrases

Subjunctives are also used in certain fixed phrases. Examples:

*God **save** the King/Queen!*   *Long **live** the bride and groom!*
*God **bless** you.*   *Heaven **forbid**.*
*He's a sort of adopted uncle, as it **were**. (= ... in a way.)*
***Be** that as it may ... (= Whether that is true or not ...)*
*If we have to pay £2,000, then so **be** it. (= We can't do anything to change it.)*

4 other structures

Most subjunctive structures are formal and unusual in British English. In *that*-clauses, British people usually prefer ***should* + infinitive** (see 497), or ordinary present and past tenses.

*It is essential that every child **should have** the same educational opportunities. (OR ... that every child **has** ...)*
*We felt it was important that James **should write** to Uncle Arthur as soon as possible. (OR ... that James **wrote** ...)*

5 older English

Older English had more subjunctive forms, and used them in many kinds of 'unreal' sense to talk about possible, desirable or imaginary situations. Many of these forms have disappeared from modern English, being replaced by uses of *should, would* and other modal verbs, by special uses of past tenses (see 422), and by ordinary verb forms.

542 substitution

1 What is substitution?

We often avoid repeating a word or expression that has been used before. One way of doing this is to use a general-purpose substitute word or 'proform' like *it, that, one, do, there, so.*

> She folded **the letter** and put **it** away in a drawer.
> (= ... put **the letter** away ...)
> 'How about **a swim**?' 'I'd like **that**.' (= ... 'I'd like **a swim**.')
> 'What sort of **cake** would you like?' '**One** with lots of cream.'
> 'Joe **thinks it's time to go**.' 'I **do** too.'
> 'Let's meet **at the station**.' 'OK, see you **there**.'
> 'Do you think **we'll win**?' 'I hope **so**.'

Substitute words are also used when the meaning is so clear from the situation that a more precise word is unnecessary.

> **Those** look nice. Can I have **one**?
> Isn't **she** beautiful!

For structures in which words are left out with no substitute ('ellipsis'), see 181–186.
For repetition (and avoidance of repetition) in general, see 479.

2 pronouns

Pronouns substitute for nouns or noun phrases. They include personal pronouns like *she, it* (see 425), reflexive pronouns like *himself, herself* (see 471), possessives like *her, theirs* (see 433), relatives like *who, that* (see 473), interrogatives like *what, who* (which substitute for unknown expressions – see 460), the demonstratives *this/that/these/those* (see 565), indefinite pronouns like *somebody* (see 523), and *one* (which replaces countable nouns – see 391).

> Liz went home because **she** was tired.
> He's started talking to **himself** again.
> Look at Mary with **her** new boyfriend.
> You ought to meet the people **who** live next door.
> **What** happened?
> Can I have a look at **that**?
> I'd like **somebody** to help me.

3 the pro-verb *do*

We can use *do so* and *do it/that* as substitutes to avoid repeating a verb and words that follow. For details, see 166.

> I asked him to **give me a contract**, but he wasn't prepared to **do so**.
> 'Could you **fix my bike**?' 'I'll **do it** at once.'

In British English, *do* can also be used alone as a substitute for a verb after an auxiliary (see 165).

> 'Do you think Phil will come?' 'He **might do**.' (US ... 'He might.') ▶

4 adverbial and adjectival substitutes

There and *then* are used as substitutes for adverbial expressions of place and time.

> *'Let's meet at the station.' 'OK, see you **there**.'*
> *'I got married in 1986.' 'How old were you **then**?'*

The question words *where, when, how* and *why* are used as substitutes for unknown adverbial expressions – for details, see 460.

> ***Where** did you hide the chocolates?*

Such and *so* substitute for expressions like 'of the kind already mentioned' or 'to the degree already mentioned or perceived'. For details, see 513 and 543.

> ***Such** a plan would be disastrous.*
> *I didn't realise you were **so** ill.*

So can sometimes substitute for an adjective.

> *The weather is stormy, and will remain **so** through the weekend.*
> *'Is she still depressed?' 'Less **so** than yesterday.'*

5 clause substitutes

So and *not* are used as substitutes for clauses in certain cases. For details, see 514, 515 and 261.12.

> *'You're in big trouble.' 'Who says **so**?'*
> *'Have we got enough bread?' 'I think **so**.'*
> *'We're not going to be in time.' 'No, I suppose **not**.'*
> *I may be free this evening. If **so**, I'll come round and see you.*

6 substitution with auxiliaries

An auxiliary verb can be used as a substitute for a complete verb phrase (and often for what follows). This is dealt with in the section on ellipsis: see 185.

> *'Give my love to Granny.' 'I **will**.'*

543 such

1 'of the kind just mentioned'

In a formal style, ***such* + noun** can be used to mean 'like this/that', 'of the kind that has just been mentioned'. *Such* comes before *a/an*.

> *The committee is thinking of raising the subscription. I would oppose **such a decision**.* (NOT *...a such decision.*)
> *There are various ways of composing secret messages. **Such systems** are called 'codes' or 'ciphers'.*
> *Many long-term prisoners come to regard prison as their home; when **such prisoners** are released they have serious problems.*

In an informal style we prefer other expressions, for example *like this/that* or *this/that kind of*.

> *... **systems like that** are called ...*
> *... when **this kind of prisoner** is released ...*

2 when *such* cannot be used

Such refers back to what has been said. It is not generally used demonstratively, to refer to things in the present situation. To express the idea 'of the kind that I am showing you' or 'of the kind that we can see/hear now', we prefer *like this/that* or *this/that kind/sort of.*

> *Look over there! Would you like to have **a car like that**?*
>> (NOT ~~Would you like to have **such a car**?~~)
> *Where can I get **trousers like those**?* (NOT ...~~**such trousers**?~~)
> *I don't like **this sort of music**.* (NOT ~~I don't like **such music**.~~)

3 high degree

Such is often used when we are talking about a high degree of some quality – in situations where *very* is also a suitable word (for the difference, see paragraph 4). In this sense, *such* is common before **adjective + noun**.

> *I'm sorry you had **such a bad journey**.*
>> (= *You had a **very** bad journey, and I'm sorry.*)
> *It was a pleasure to meet **such interesting people**.*

Such is also possible with this meaning before a noun alone, when the noun has an emphatic descriptive meaning.

> *I'm glad your concert was **such a success**.*
> *Why did she make **such a fuss** about the dates?*

4 *such* and *very*

Very is used when we are simply giving information. *Such* is mainly used (in the same way as *like this/that*), to refer to information which has already been given, which is already known, or which is obvious. Compare:

> – *I've had a **very** bad day.* (giving information)
> *Why did you have **such** a bad day?*
>> (referring to information which is already known)
> – *The weather was **very** cold.* (giving information)
> *I wasn't expecting **such** cold weather.*
>> (referring to information which is already known)

Used directly before nouns, *such* can be compared to words like *great, extreme* etc. Compare:

> – *There was **great** confusion.* (giving information)
> *Why was there **such** confusion?*
>> (referring to information which is already known)

5 emphatic use

In an informal style, *such* can also be used to give new information, when the speaker wishes to emphasise what is said.

> *He's **such** an idiot!*
> *She has **such** a marvellous voice!*
> *This is **such** wonderful soup – what do you put in it?*

6 *that*-clauses

Structures with *very* cannot be followed directly by *that*-clauses. Instead, we can use *such ... that.*

> *It was **such** a cold afternoon **that we stopped playing**.*
>> (NOT ~~It was a **very** cold afternoon **that**...~~)   ▶

7 *such ... as to ...*

There is also a structure with *such* followed by **... + as to + infinitive**. This is formal and not very common.

> It was **such a loud noise as to wake** *everybody in the house.*
> (Less formal: ... **such a loud noise that it woke** ...)

8 *such-and-such*

Note this informal expression.

> *When you're studying medicine, you learn that* **such-and-such** *a symptom* (= *one or other symptom*) *corresponds to* **such-and-such** *an illness.*

9 *such as*

Note the use of *such as* with a noun to introduce examples.

> *My doctor told me to avoid fatty foods* **such as** *bacon or hamburgers.*
> *In* **such** *areas* **as** *North Wales or the Lake District, there are now too many walkers and climbers.*

For the difference between *such* and *so*, see 544.
For more about *very*, see 153.
For other ways of expressing the idea of degree, see 153–156.

544 **such** and **so**

1 *such* **before (adjective +) noun**

We use *such* before a noun (with or without an adjective). *Such* comes before *a/an*.

> *She's* **such a baby.** (NOT *She's* **so a baby.**)
> *I'm surprised that he's got* **such patience.**
> *They're* **such fools.**
> *It was* **such good milk** *that we couldn't stop drinking it.*
> (NOT *It was* **so good milk that** ...)
> *I've never met* **such a nice person.** (NOT ... *a* **such/so** *nice person.*)
> *You've got* **such strange friends.**

2 *so* **before adjective, adverb etc**

We use *so* before an adjective alone (without a noun) or an adverb.

> *She's* **so babyish.** (NOT *She's* **such babyish.**)
> *He's* **so patient** *with her.*
> *The milk was* **so good** *that we couldn't stop drinking it.*
> *She's* **so nice.**
> *Why do you talk* **so slowly?**

We can also use *so* before *much, many, few* and *little.*

> *We've got* **so much** *to do, and* **so little** *time.*

We use *so much*, not *so*, before comparatives.

> *I'm glad you're feeling* **so much** *better.* (NOT ... **so better.**)

For *so beautiful a day* etc, see 16.
For more about the meaning and use of *such*, see 543. For more about *so*, see 513.

545 suggest

1 infinitive not used

Suggest is not followed by **object + infinitive**. *That*-clauses and -*ing* structures are common.

>*Her uncle **suggested that she (should) get** a job in a bank.*
>*Her uncle **suggested getting** a job in a bank.*
> (NOT ~~Her uncle suggested **her to get** a job in a bank.~~)

2 verb forms in *that*-clauses

In *that*-clauses after *suggest*, various verb forms are possible.

a   Ordinary present and past tenses can be used in British English.
>*Her uncle suggests that she **gets** a job in a bank.*
>*He suggested that she **got** a job in a bank.*

b   In a formal style, subjunctives are possible, especially in American English. See 541 for details.
>*He suggests that she **get** a job in a bank.*
>*He suggested that she **get** a job in a bank.*

c   In British English, ***should* + infinitive** is common. (This is rare in American English.)
>*He suggests that she **should get** a job in a bank.*
>*He suggested that she **should** get a job in a bank.*

3 direct suggestions

In direct suggestions ('*I suggest . . .*'), *should* is not generally used.
>*I suggest (that) you **get** . . .* (NOT ~~I suggest that you **should get**. . .~~)

4 objects

We can use a direct object after *suggest*.
>*'What shall we give the children?' 'I **suggest hamburgers**.'*

Suggest is not normally followed by an indirect object without a preposition.
>*Can you suggest a restaurant **to us**?* (NOT ~~Can you suggest **us a restaurant**?~~)

546 suppose, supposing and what if

Suppose, supposing and *what if* can all be used to introduce suggestions. (*Supposing* is less common in American English.) The verb can be present or past; a past form makes the suggestion sound less definite.
>*'I haven't got a table cloth.' '**Suppose** we use a sheet.'*
>***What if** we invite your mother next weekend and go away the week after?*
>*'Daddy, can I watch TV?' '**Supposing** you did your homework first?'*
>***What if** I came tomorrow instead of this afternoon?*

These expressions can also be used to talk about fears.
>*'Let's go swimming.' '**Suppose** there are sharks?'*
>*'I'm going to climb up there.' 'No! **What if** you slipped?'*

▶

In sentences about the past, past perfect tenses are used to talk about situations that did not occur.

That was very clever, but **supposing** *you* **had slipped**?

For other uses of *suppose*, see 451.2, 515, 359.
For other cases where past tenses are used with present or future meanings, see 422.

547 supposed to

Be supposed + **infinitive** can be used to talk about what is generally believed.
He's **supposed to be** *quite rich, you know.*
This stuff **is supposed to kill** *flies. Let's try it.*

Often, *be supposed to* is used rather like *should*, to talk about what people have to do according to the rules or the law, or about what is expected to happen.
You're **supposed to start** *work at 8.30 every morning.*
Catholics **are supposed to go** *to church on Sundays.*

Be supposed to can express a contrast between what should happen and what actually happens.
Lucy **was supposed to come** *to lunch. What's happened?*
Cats **are supposed to be** *afraid of dogs, but our Tibby has just chased Mr Glidewell's bulldog right down the road.*
That's a lovely picture, but what's it **supposed to be**?

Not supposed to can refer to prohibitions.
You're **not supposed to park** *on double yellow lines.*
People under eighteen **aren't supposed to buy** *alcoholic drinks.*

Note the pronunciation: / sə'pəʊst tə /, not / sə'pəʊzd tə / .

548 surely

1 not the same as *certainly*

Surely does not usually mean the same as *certainly*. Compare:
That's **certainly** *a plain-clothes policeman.*
   (= *I know that's a plain-clothes policeman.*)
Surely *that's a plain-clothes policeman?*
   (= *That really seems to be a plain-clothes policeman. How surprising!*)

2 meaning: belief in spite of ...

Surely is normally used to say that the speaker believes something in spite of appearances, in spite of reasons to believe the opposite, or in spite of suggestions to the contrary. Sentences with *surely* often have question marks.
Surely *that's Henry over there? I thought he was in Scotland.*
'I'm going to marry Sonia.' **'Surely** *she's married already?'*
'Is it tonight we're going out?' 'No, tomorrow, **surely**?'

Surely (with heavy stress) can suggest that the speaker would like to believe something, but is beginning to lose hope.
Surely *she's going to stop crying soon?*
   (*It looks as if she's going to go on for ever.*)
Surely *there's somebody in the house? Why don't they answer the door?*
Surely *somebody's going to help him? He'll drown!*

Surely not expresses difficulty in believing something.
> **Surely** you're **not** going out in that hat?
> 'Tim failed his exam.' 'Oh, **surely not**?'
> You **don't** think I'm going to pay for you, **surely**?

3 American English

In American English, *surely* can also be used in replies to mean 'certainly'.
> 'Do you want something to eat?' 'I **surely do**.'
> 'Could you help me for a moment?' '**Surely**.'

549 sympathetic

Sympathetic is a 'false friend' for speakers of certain languages. It does not usually mean the same as, for example, *sympathique, sympathisch, sympatisk* or *simpático*.
> The people in my class are all very **nice/pleasant/easy to get on with**.
> (NOT ...~~are all very sympathetic~~.)

Sympathetic usually means 'sharing somebody's feelings' or 'sorry for somebody who is in trouble'.
> I'm **sympathetic** towards the strikers.
> She's always very **sympathetic** when people feel ill.

550 taboo words and swearwords

1 introduction

Many languages have words which are considered dangerous, holy, magic or shocking, and which are only used in certain situations or by certain people. For instance, in some African tribes the names of dead chiefs must not be said; in many cultures, words associated with religious beliefs are used only on religious occasions, or only by priests. Words of this kind can be called 'taboo words'.

English has three main groups of taboo words and expressions:

a   A number of words connected with the Christian religion (e.g. the names *Christ, God*) are considered holy by some people. These people prefer to use such words only in formal and respectful contexts, and they may be upset or shocked by their 'careless' use.

b   Certain words relating to sexual activity and the associated parts of the body (e.g. *fuck, balls*) are regarded as shocking by many people. Thirty or forty years ago some of these words could not be printed or broadcast, and they are still comparatively unusual in public speech and writing. In polite or formal language these words are generally avoided, or replaced by other words and expressions (e.g. *make love* or *have sexual intercourse, testicles*).

c   Some words referring to the elimination of bodily wastes (what one does in the lavatory), and the associated parts of the body, are also regarded as 'dirty' or shocking (e.g. *piss, shit*). They are often replaced by more 'polite' words and expressions with the same meaning (e.g. *urinate, defecate*) or by substitutes (e.g. *go to the lavatory, wash one's hands*).   ▶

Because taboo words are shocking, they are common in situations where people want to express powerful emotions by using 'strong' language. This is called 'swearing'. When people swear, taboo words usually change their meanings completely. For example, *fuck off* and *piss off* have nothing to do with sex or urinating – they are simply violently rude ways of saying 'go away'. The strength of the original taboo word is borrowed for a different purpose.

Linguistic taboos in English-speaking countries are less strong than they used to be. Most taboo words and swearwords shock less than they did, say, twenty years ago. And increasingly, people are using informal taboo words which are felt to be amusingly 'naughty' rather than shocking, such as *bonk* instead of *fuck*, or *willy* instead of *prick* (= 'penis').

None the less, students should be very careful about using taboo words and swearwords. There are two reasons for this. First of all, it is not easy to know the exact strength of these expressions in a foreign language, or to know what kind of people are shocked by them, and in what circumstances. One may easily say something that is meant as a joke, but which seriously upsets the people one is talking to. And secondly, using this sort of language generally indicates membership of a group: one most often swears in the company of people one knows well, who belong to one's own social circle, age group etc. (Children usually avoid swearing in front of adults so as not to annoy or shock them, and adults avoid swearing in front of children for similar reasons.) So a foreigner who uses swearwords may give the impression of claiming membership of a group that he or she does not belong to.

2   taboo words

The following are some of the most common English taboo words, with explanations of their literal meanings where necessary. Their approximate 'strength' is shown by stars: a one-star word like *hell* will not upset many people, while a three- or four-star word may be very shocking if it is used in the wrong situation. Note, however, that individual reactions to particular words (and to swearing in general) vary enormously, and that attitudes are changing rapidly; so people are likely to disagree a good deal about the strength of the words listed.

The words associated with religion are not considered shocking when used with their literal meaning, and the stars show their strength when used as swearwords. The strength of the other words is mostly the same whether they are used literally or for swearing.

Religion

taboo word	meaning
damn *	condemn to hell (rare in literal sense; mainly used as swearword)
blast * (GB)	strike with divine punishment (rare in literal sense; mainly used as swearword)
hell *	
God *	
Jesus **	
Christ **	

page 574

Parts of the body

taboo word	meaning
arse *** (US ass **)	bottom, buttocks, anus
arsehole *** (US asshole **)	anus
balls ***	testicles
bollocks *** (GB)	testicles
cock ***	penis
dick***	penis
prick ***	penis
tits ***	breasts
cunt ****	woman's sex organs

Sexual activity

taboo word	meaning
fuck ***	have sex (with)
wank *** (US jerk off ***)	masturbate (have sex with oneself)
bugger *** (GB)	have anal intercourse with a person or animal; person who does so
come **	reach a sexual climax (orgasm)
sod ** (GB)	homosexual (abbreviation of *sodomite*; rare in literal sense)
bitch **	female dog; earlier used for 'immoral' woman
whore **	prostitute
bastard **	child of unmarried parents

Lavatory

taboo word	meaning
piss ***	urine; urinate
shit ***	excrement; defecate
crap **	excrement; defecate
fart **	let digestive gas out from the anus

3 swearwords

All of the words listed above, and a few others, are used in swearing. The meaning of a swearword is always different from its literal (taboo) meaning (see introduction above). Compare:

*What are you doing **fucking** in my bed?*

(= *Why are you making love in my bed?* – literal meaning of *fucking*)

*What are you **fucking** doing in my bed?*

(= *Why the hell are you in my bed?* – *fucking* used as a swearword)

The meaning of a swearword can also change with its grammatical form. For instance, *piss off* is an aggressive way of saying *go away*; *pissed* is British slang for *drunk*; *pissed off* is British slang for *fed up*. Many swearwords are grammatically very flexible. *Fucking*, for example, can act both as an adjective (e.g. **fucking** *idiot*) and as an intensifying adverb (e.g. **fucking** *good, **fucking** soon, it's **fucking** raining, **fucking** well shut up*). Swearwords are the only words in the language that have this grammatical range. The following list shows some of the most common expressions used in swearing; they are grouped according to meaning.

a   exclamation of annoyance

Damn (it)!	*Hell!*	*Bugger (it)! (GB)*
Blast (it)!	*(My) God!*	*Sod (it)! (GB)*
God damn it!	*Jesus!*	*Shit!*
God damn!	*Christ!*	*Fuck (it)!*
(especially US)	*Jesus Christ!*	

Examples of use:

> **Damn it!** *Can't you hurry up?*
> **Christ!** *It's raining again!*
> **Oh, fuck!** *I've lost the address!*

b   exclamation of surprise

> *(My) God!   Jesus!   Christ!   Jesus Christ!*
> *God damn! (especially US)   Well, I'll be damned!*
> *Son of a bitch! (especially US)   Damn me! Bugger/Fuck me! (GB)*
> *Well, I'm damned/buggered! (GB)*

Examples of use:

> **My God!** *Look at that!*
> **Well, I'm damned!** *What are you doing here?*
> **Bugger me!** *There's Mrs Smith. I thought she was on holiday.*

c   surprised question

> *Who/What/Why etc the hell . . . ?* (US also . . . *in hell . . . ?)*
> *Who/What/Why etc the fuck . . . ?*

Examples of use:

> **What the hell** *do you think you're doing?*
> **Where the fuck** *are the car keys?*

d   insult (noun)

Note that these nouns generally have no real meaning. They simply express a strong emotion such as hatred, anger, envy or contempt.

bastard	*shit*	*son of a bitch* (US)
fart	*sod* (GB)	*asshole* (US)
prick	*bugger* (GB)	*motherfucker* (US)
fucker	*wanker* (GB)	*cocksucker* (US)
cunt	*bitch* (applied to women)	*dickhead* (= 'idiot')

Examples of use:

> *You **bastard!***   *Lucky **sod!***
> *Stupid old **fart!***   *She's such a **bitch!***
> *He's a real **prick!***   *That guy's a real **asshole!***
> *Stupid **fucker!***

e   insult (imperative verb + object)

> *Damn ...!*   *Blast ...! (GB)*   *Sod ...! (GB)*
> *Bugger ...! (GB)*   *Fuck ...!*   *Screw ...!*

Examples of use:

> **Damn** *that child!*   **Fuck** *you!*   **Screw** *the government!*

f   insulting request to go away

> *Fuck off!*   *Bugger off! (GB)*   *Screw!*
> *Piss off!*   *Sod off! (GB)*

Examples of use:

> '*Can I have a word with you?*' '**Fuck off!**'
> *If Andy comes asking for money, tell him to* **piss off**.

g   expression of unconcern (= 'I don't care')

> *I don't give a damn/shit/fuck; ... a bugger (GB).*

Examples of use:

> *They can come and arrest me if they want to.* **I don't give a fuck**.
> '*Mary's very angry with you.*' '**I don't give a bugger.**'

h   violent refusal / rejection / defiance

> *(I'll be) damned/fucked if I will!*   *Get stuffed! (GB)*
> *... buggered if I will! (GB)*   *Balls!*
> *Stuff it (up your arse)! (GB)*   *Balls to ...! (GB)*
> *Stuff it up your ass! (US)*   *Bollocks! (GB)*

Examples of use:

> '*Mr Parsons wants you to clean out the lavatories.*' '**Fucked if I will!**'
> '*Management are offering another £8 a week.*' '*They can* **stuff it**.'
> '*Give me a kiss.*' '**Get stuffed!**'
> '*You're afraid to fight.*' '**Balls!**'
> **Balls to** *the lot of you! I'm going home.*

i   intensifying adjective / adverb (used to emphasise an emotion)

> *damn(ed)*   *goddam (US)*   *blasted (GB)*   *fucking*
> *bloody (GB)*   *sodding (GB)*   *bleeding (GB)*

Bloody has no literal taboo equivalent in modern English.
Examples of use:

> *That car's going* **damn(ed)** *fast.*   *She's a* **fucking** *marvellous singer.*
> *Where's the* **bloody** *switch?*   *Put the* **fucking** *cat out!*
> *It's* **bloody** *raining again.*

When these words are used before verbs, the word *well* is often added in British English.

> *I* **damn well hope** *you never come back.*
> *I'm not* **fucking well paying** *this time.*
> *It's* **bloody well raining** *again.*

►

j   miscellaneous

Fuck (up), screw (up) and *bugger (up)* (GB) can mean 'ruin', 'spoil' or 'destroy'.

> *Somebody's **fucked up** the TV.*   *You've **buggered** my watch.*

Fucked and *buggered* can mean 'exhausted' (GB).

> *'Want another game of tennis?' 'No, I'm **fucked**.'*

Screw (especially US) can mean 'cheat'.

> *Don't buy a car from that garage – they'll **screw** you.*

Cock up (GB), *balls up* (GB), *fuck up* and *screw up* can be used as verbs or nouns to refer to mistakes of organisation. (When used as nouns, they are often written with hyphens.)

> *That bloody secretary's **cocked up** my travel arrangements.*
> *Sorry you didn't get your invitation – Mary made a **balls-up**.*
> *The conference was a complete **fuck-up**.*
> *Well, we really **screwed up** this time, didn't we?*

Balls (GB), *bullshit* (US) and *crap* are used to mean 'nonsense'.

> *'What's his new book like?' 'A load of **balls**.'*   *Don't talk **crap**!*

In American English, *shit* can mean 'lies' or 'nothing'.

> *'Janie's getting married.' 'No **shit**?'*
> *He don't know his ass from a hole in the ground. He don't know **shit**.*

Bugger/fuck/damn/sod all are used in British English to mean 'nothing'.

> *There's **fuck all** in the fridge. We'll have to eat out.*

In British English, *pissed* means 'drunk' and *pissed off* means 'fed up'.

> *Steve was **pissed** out of his mind again last night.*
> *I'm getting **pissed off** with London.*

In American English, *pissed* is 'annoyed', 'angry'.

> *I'm **pissed** at him because of what he's been saying about me.*

For information about slang, see 510.

551   take

1   the opposite of *give*

One meaning of *take* is 'gain possession of' or 'receive'.

> *She **took** my plate and gave me a clean one.*
> *Who's **taken** my bicycle?*
> *Andrew's not in just now. Can I **take** a message?*

We take something *from/out of/off* a place, and *from* a person.

> *Could you **take** some money **out of** my wallet?* (NOT *...~~in my wallet.~~*)
> *She took the letter **from** the postman.*

Take cannot be used with two objects in this sense.

> *They **took** everything away **from** me.* (NOT ~~They took me everything.~~)

2   the opposite of *put*

Take can be used to talk about moving things away from their places.

> *I **took** off my coat and put on a dressing gown.*
> *He **took** a ring out of his pocket and put it on her finger.*

3   the opposite of *bring*

Take can also mean 'transport', 'carry'. In this sense, it is used for movements which are not towards the speaker or hearer. See 112 for details.

*Can you **take** me to the station tomorrow morning?*

(NOT ~~*Can you **bring** me to the station*...?~~)

***Take** this form to Mr Collins, ask him to sign it, and then bring it back.*

4   'have', 'experience'

***Take** + noun* is used in many common expressions referring to activities. In these expressions *take* generally means 'have', 'experience'; *have* is often preferred in British English (see 240).

*I think I'll **take a bath**. (GB also ... **have** a bath.)*

*Let's **take a break**. (GB also ... **have** a break.)*

Note that *have*, not *take*, is used with the names of meals (e.g. ***have** breakfast*).

For more about the use of nouns for activities, see 573.

5   two-word verbs

Take is used in a large number of common idiomatic two-word verbs (e.g. *take off, take down, take up, take over, take to*). For the meanings of these and other two-word verbs beginning with *take*, see a good dictionary. For more about two-word verbs, see 582.

6   time

We can use *take* to say how much time we need to do something. Four structures are common:

a   The person is the subject:

> person + *take* + time + infinitive

***I took** three hours to get home last night.*
***She takes** all day to get out of the bathroom.*
***They took** two hours to unload the ferry.*

b   The activity is the subject:

> activity + *take* (+ person) + time

***The journey took** me three hours.*
***Gardening takes** a lot of time.*
***Unloading the ferry took** them two hours.*

c   The object of the activity is the subject:

> object of activity + *take* (+ person) + infinitive

***The ferry took** them two hours to unload.*
***This house will take** all week to clean.*

▶

d   Preparatory *it* is the subject:

> *It* + *take* (+ person) + time + infinitive

> **It took** *me three hours to get home last night.*
> **It takes** *ages to do the shopping.*

7   *take* and *last*

Take and *last* are both used to talk about the length of experiences and events. In general, we say that something *takes* a certain time when we see it as an active experience – a job or task that somebody *does*, for which time is *needed* – and we say that it *lasts* a certain time when we see it as a more passive experience, which somebody goes through without controlling it. (Often, both words are possible with a slight difference of emphasis.) Compare:

> *It was a terrible job – I thought it would **take** forever.*
> *It was a wonderful holiday – I wished it would **last** forever.*

552   taste

1   copular verb

Taste can be used as a 'copular verb', followed by adjective complements (see 147), to say what sort of taste something has. Progressive forms are not used.

> *This **tastes nice**. What's in it?* (NOT *...tastes **nicely**.*)
> *The wine **tastes funny**.* (NOT *...is tasting funny...*)

Before a noun, *taste of* and *taste like* are used.

> *The fish soup **tasted** mostly **of** garlic.*
> *Her lips **tasted like** wild strawberries.*

2   transitive verb: 'perceive'

Taste can be used as a transitive verb, followed by an object, to say what we perceive with our sense of taste. Progressive forms are not used. We often use *can taste* (see 125).

> *I **can taste** garlic and mint in the sauce.* (NOT *I am tasting...*)

3   transitive verb: 'investigate'

Another transitive use is to say that we are using our sense of taste to find out something. Progressive forms can be used.

> *'Stop eating the cake.' 'I'm just **tasting** it to see if it's OK.'*

553   **technique** and **technology**

Technology is the normal word for 'scientific and industrial manufacturing processes and skills'.

> *Modern **technology** has improved our standard of living.*
>   (NOT *Modern technique...*)

A *technique* is a method of doing something.

> *Barnard developed a new **technique** in heart surgery.*

Technique can be used for the way an artist or athlete performs.
>*He's not only very fast, but he's also got marvellous **technique**.*
>*Joyce was not the first novelist to use the 'stream of consciousness'*
>***technique**.*

554 telephoning

1 answering a private phone

British people usually give their name or number.
>*Hello. Albert Packard.*
>*Hello. Ardington three seven oh double two.* (= 37022)
>(US *Hello. Packard residence. Albert Packard speaking.*)

2 asking for a person

>*Could I speak to Jane Horrabin?* (US also *Could I speak **with** ...?*)

3 saying who you are

>*Hello, **this is** Corinne.* (NOT USUALLY ...~~*I'm Corinne.*~~)
>*'Could I speak to Jane Horrabin?' '**Speaking.**'* (OR *This is Jane Horrabin*
>*(speaking).*) (US *This is she.*)

4 asking who somebody is

>*Who is **that**?* (US *Who is **this**/Who's there?*)
>*Who am I speaking to?*
>*Who is that speaking?*

5 asking for a number

>***Could I have** extension two oh four six?*
>*What's the **(dialling) code** for London?* (US ... *area code ...?*)
>*How do I call the **operator**?*

6 if you want the person that you are calling to pay for the call

>*I'd like to make a **reversed** (OR **transferred**) **charge call** to Bristol 37878.*
>(US *I'd like to make a **collect call** ...*)

7 if somebody is not there

>*I'm afraid she's not in at the moment.*
>*Can I **take a message**?*
>*Can I **leave a message**?*
>*I'll **ring/call** again later.* (US *I'll **call** ...*)
>*Could you ask her to **ring/call me back**?*
>*Could you ask her to ring/call me at/on Ardington 37022?*
>*Could you just tell her Jake called?*

8 asking people to wait

>*Just a moment.* *Hold the line, please.*
>*Hold on a moment, please.* *Hang on.* (informal) ▶

9 things the operator may say

One moment, please.   *(I'm) trying to connect you.*
(The number's) ringing for you.   *(I'm) putting you through now.*
I'm afraid the number/line is engaged (GB) / busy (US). Will you hold?
I'm afraid there's no reply from this number / from her extension.

10 wrong number

I think you've got the wrong number.
I'm sorry. I've got the wrong number.

11 problems

Could you speak louder? It's a bad line. (US ... bad connection.)
It's a very bad line. I'll hang up and call again.
I rang you earlier but I couldn't get through.

555 telling the time

1 saying what time it is

There are two common ways of saying what time it is.

8.05	*eight (oh) five* OR *five past eight*
8.10	*eight ten* OR *ten past eight*
8.15	*eight fifteen* OR *a quarter past eight*
8.25	*eight twenty-five* OR *twenty-five past eight*
8.30	*eight thirty* OR *half past eight*
8.35	*eight thirty-five* OR *twenty-five to nine*
8.45	*eight forty-five* OR *a quarter to nine*
8.50	*eight fifty* OR *ten to nine*
9.00	*nine o'clock*

Many British people prefer to say *minutes past/to* for times between the five-minute divisions (e.g. *seven minutes past eight, three minutes to nine*).

The expression *o'clock* is only used at the hour. Compare:
Wake me at seven (o'clock).
Wake me at ten past seven. (NOT *... ten past seven o'clock.*)
Past is often dropped from *half past* in informal speech.
OK, see you at half two. (= *... half past two.*)
In American English *after* is often used instead of *past* (e.g. *ten after six*); but Americans do not say *half after*. And in American English *of, before* and *till* are possible instead of *to* (e.g. *twenty-five of three*).

2 asking what time it is

Common ways of asking about time are:
What time is it?   *Have you got the time?* (informal)
What's the time?   *Could you tell me the time?* (more formal)
What time do you make it? OR *What do you make the time?*
   (GB; = *What time is it by your watch?*)
What time does the game start? (NOT USUALLY *At what time ...?*)

3 the twenty-four hour clock

The twenty-four hour clock is used mainly in timetables, programmes and official announcements. In ordinary speech, people usually use the twelve-hour clock. Compare:
- *Last check-in time is **20.15**.*
  *We have to check in by **a quarter past eight in the evening**.*
- *The next train from platform 5 is the **seventeen fifty-three** departure for Carlisle.*
  *'What time does it leave?' '**Seven minutes to six**.'*

If necessary, times can be distinguished by using *in the morning/afternoon/evening*. In a more formal style, we can use *am* (= Latin *ante meridiem* – 'before midday') and *pm* (= *post meridiem* – 'after midday').

  09.00 = *nine o'clock in the morning* (OR *nine am*)
  21.00 = *nine o'clock in the evening* (OR *nine pm*)

556 **tense simplification** in subordinate clauses

1 reasons for tense simplification

If the main verb of a sentence makes it clear what kind of time the speaker is talking about, it is not always necessary for the same time to be indicated again in subordinate clauses. Compare:
- *This discovery **means** that we **will spend** less on food.*
  *This discovery **will mean** that we **spend** less on food.*
- *It **is** unlikely that he **will** win.*
  *I **will pray** that he **wins**.*

Verbs in subordinate clauses are often simpler in form than verbs in main clauses – for example present instead of future, simple past instead of conditional, simple past instead of past perfect.

  *You'll find Coca-Cola wherever you **go**.* (NOT ... ~~wherever you will go~~.)
  *He would never do anything that **went** against his conscience.*
    (More natural than ... *that **would go** against his conscience*.)
  *I hadn't understood what she **said**.*
    (More natural than ... *what she **had said**.*)

2 present instead of future

Present tenses are often used instead of ***will* + infinitive** to refer to the future in subordinate clauses. This happens not only after conjunctions of time like *when, until, after, before, as soon as*, but in most other subordinate clauses – for instance after *if, whether* and *on condition that*, after question words and relatives, and in indirect speech.

  *I'll write to her **when** I **have** time.* (NOT ... ~~when I will have time~~.)
  *I'll think of you when **I'm lying** on the beach next week.*
    (NOT ... ~~when I will be lying~~...)
  *Will you stay here **until** the plane **takes** off?*
  *It will be interesting to see **whether** he **recognises** you.*
  *I'll have a good time **whether** I **win** or **lose**.*
  *I'll lend it to you **on condition that** you **bring** it back tomorrow.*
  *I'll go **where** you **go**.*

▶

*He says he'll give five pounds to anybody **who finds** his pen.*
*One day the government will really ask people **what** they **want**.*
*If she **asks** what I**'m doing** in her flat, I'll say I**'m checking** the electricity meter.*
*I think you'll find the wind **slows** you down a bit.*

This can happen even if the main verb does not have a future form, provided it refers to the future.

*__Phone__ me when you **arrive**. __Make sure__ you **come** back soon.*
*You **can** tell who you **like** next week, but not until then.*

Present perfect tenses can be used to express the idea of completion.

*I'll tell you when I**'ve finished**.*

In comparisons with *as* and *than*, present and future verbs are both possible.

*She'll be on the same train **as** we **are/will** tomorrow.*
*We'll get there sooner **than** you **do/will**.*

3   future in subordinate clauses

A future verb is necessary for future reference in a subordinate clause if the main verb does not refer to the future (or to the same time in the future).

*I **don't know** where she **will be** tomorrow.*
*I'm sure I **won't understand** a word of the lecture.*
*I'll **hide** it somewhere where he**'ll** never **find** it.* (two different future times)
*If she rings, I'll **tell** her that I**'ll** ring back later.* (two different future times)

Future verbs are used in *if*-clauses when *if* means 'if it is true that ...' (see 261.1).

*If the office **will be** open until five o'clock, then we**'ll have** plenty of time to go there this afternoon.*

4   *in case, I hope, I bet, it doesn't matter* etc

A present tense is normally used with a future meaning after *in case* even if the main verb is present or past. For details, see 271.

*I've got my tennis things **in case** we **have** time for a game tomorrow.*

In an informal style, present verbs are often used with future meanings after *I hope* (see 252) and *I bet* (see 102).

*I **hope** you **sleep** well.*
*I **bet** he **gets** married before the end of the year.*

Present tenses are also used with future reference after *it doesn't matter, I don't care, I don't mind, it's not important* and similar expressions.

*It **doesn't matter** where we **go** on holiday.*
*I **don't care** what we **have** for dinner if I **don't** have to cook it.*

5   past instead of conditional

Just as *will* is avoided in subordinate clauses referring to the future, *would* is avoided in subordinate clauses referring to the past. Instead of **would + infinitive**, past verbs are generally used with conditional meanings in subordinate clauses. This happens not only in *if*-clauses, but also after most other conjunctions.

*If I **had** lots of money, I would give some to anybody **who asked** for it.*
    (NOT ~~If I **would have** ... who **would ask** for it.~~)
*Would you follow me **wherever** I **went**?* (NOT ... ~~wherever I **would go**?~~)

*In a perfect world, you would be able to say exactly what you **thought**.*
(NOT ... ~~what you **would think**~~.)
*I would always try to help anybody who **was** in trouble, whether I **knew***
them or not.
*To see him walk down the street, you'd never know he **was** blind.*

6 exceptions

These rules do not usually apply to clauses beginning *because, although, since* or *as* (meaning 'because').

*I won't mind the heat on holiday **because** I **won't have** to move about*
much.
*I'll come to the opera with you, **although** I probably **won't enjoy** it.*

7 simplification of perfect and progressive verbs

Simple past verb forms are used quite often in subordinate clauses instead of present perfect and past perfect tenses, if the meaning is clear.

*It's been a good time while it('s) **lasted**.*
*I've usually liked the people I('ve) **worked** with.*
*For thirty years, he had done no more than he **(had) needed** to.*
*He had probably crashed because he had gone to sleep while he **was***
driving. (More natural than ... *while he **had been** driving*.)

Progressive forms are quite often replaced by simple forms in subordinate clauses. Compare:

*He's **working**. But at the same time as **he works**, he's exercising.*
(OR ... *at the same time as he's **working**...*)

For tenses in indirect speech, see 481.
For past tenses with present or future meanings, see 422.

557 than, as and that

1 *than* after comparatives

Than is used after comparative adjectives and adverbs (see 135). *As* and *that* are not used after comparatives.

*My sister's **taller than** me.*
(NOT ... ~~**taller as** me~~.)
(NOT ... ~~**taller that** me~~.)
*She's got **longer** hair **than** I have.* (NOT ... ~~**longer hair as/that I have**~~.)

2 *as ... as*

As is used in 'comparisons of equality' (*as ... as ...*; *the same ... as ...*). *Than* and *that* are not used in this way.

*My hands are **as cold as** ice.* (NOT ... ~~**as cold than/that ice**~~.)
*Your eyes are **the same colour as** mine.*
(NOT ... ~~**the same colour than/that mine**~~.)

▶

3 *as-* and *than*-clauses with missing subject or object

As and *than* can introduce clauses in which there is no subject or object pronoun (rather as if *as* and *than* were relative pronouns). Clauses with no subject pronoun are mainly used in a formal style.

*Their marriage was as stormy **as had been expected**.*
(NOT ...*as ~~it~~ had been expected.*)
*Anne's going to join us, **as was agreed last week**.*
(NOT ...*as ~~it~~ was agreed last week.*)
*He worries more **than is good for him**.*
(NOT *He worries more than ~~it/what~~ is good for him.*)
*Don't lose your passport, **as I did** last year.*
(NOT ...*as I did ~~it~~ last year.*)
*They sent more **than I had ordered**.*
(NOT ...*more than I had ordered ~~it~~.*)
*She gets her meat from the same butcher **as I go to**.*
(NOT ...*as I go to ~~him~~.*)

For subject and object pronouns after *than*, see 138.8.
For *that*-clauses, see 559.
For the pronunciation of *than*, *as* and *that*, see 588.

558 **thankful** and **grateful**

Grateful is the normal word used to talk about people's reactions to kindness, favours etc.

*I'm very **grateful** for all your help.* (NOT *~~I'm very thankful~~...*)
*She wasn't a bit **grateful** to me for repairing her car.*

Thankful is used especially to talk about people's feelings of relief at having avoided a danger of some kind, or at having come through an unpleasant experience.

*I'm **thankful** that we got home before the storm started.*
*We feel very **thankful** that she didn't marry him after all.*
*Well, I'm **thankful** that's over.*

559 **that**-clauses

1 *that* as a connector

That is a conjunction with little real meaning. It is simply a connector – it shows that a declarative clause forms part of a larger sentence. Compare:

I understood. He was innocent. (two separate sentences)
*I understood **that** he was innocent.* (The clause *he was innocent* has become the object of the verb in the larger sentence.)

2 *that*-clauses in sentences

That-clauses can have various functions in sentences. A *that*-clause can be the subject.

That she should forget me so quickly *was rather a shock.*
It can be the complement.
*The main thing is **that you're happy**.*

Many verbs can have *that*-clauses as objects.

> We **knew that** the next day would be difficult.
>
> I **regretted that** I was not going to be at the meeting.

And many nouns and adjectives can be followed by *that*-clauses as complements.

> I admire your **belief that** you are always right.
>
> The Minister is **anxious that** nothing should get into the papers.

3   *the fact that ...*

It is unusual for *that*-clauses to stand alone as subjects. They are more often introduced by the expression *the fact*.

> **The fact that** she was foreign made it difficult for her to get a job.
> (NOT ~~That she was foreign made it difficult~~...)
>
> **The fact that** Simon had not been home for three days didn't seem to worry anybody. (More natural than **That** Simon had not been home for three days didn't...)

The fact also introduces *that*-clauses after prepositions (*that*-clauses cannot follow prepositions directly).

> The judge paid no attention **to the fact that** she had just lost her husband.
> (NOT ...~~paid no attention to that she had just~~...)
>
> He held her completely responsible **for the fact that** she took food without paying for it. (NOT ...~~responsible for that she took~~...)
>
> **In spite of the fact that** she had three small children, he sent her to prison for six months. (NOT ~~In spite of that she had~~...)

For cases when prepositions are dropped before *that*-clauses, see 441.

4   **preparatory** *it*

In many cases, *it* is used as a 'preparatory' subject or object for a *that*-clause. For details, see 301–302.

> **It** surprised me **that he was still in bed**.
> (More natural than *That he was still in bed surprised me.*)
>
> She made **it** clear **that she was not interested**.
> (NOT ~~She made that she was not interested clear.~~)

For reasons why *that*-clause subjects and objects are often moved to the end of sentences, see 289.

5   *that*-clauses after verbs, nouns and adjectives

Not all verbs, nouns or adjectives can be followed by *that*-clauses. Compare:

> – I **hope that you'll have** a wonderful time.
>   I **want you to have** a wonderful time. (NOT ~~I want that you'll have~~...)
> – I understood his **wish that we should be** there.
>   I understood the **importance of our being** there.
>   (NOT ...~~the importance that we should be there.~~)
> – It's **essential that you visit** the art museum.
>   It's **worth your visiting** the art museum. (NOT ~~It's worth that you visit~~...)

For complementation in general, see 140.

For complementation of verbs, see 579. For nouns, see 377. For adjectives, see 12.

For the structures that are possible after particular verbs, nouns and adjectives, see a good dictionary.

▶

6   verbs in *that*-clauses

In some kinds of *that*-clause, ***should* + infinitive** or subjunctives are often used instead of ordinary verb forms. For details, see 497, 541.

> *I insisted **that** she **(should) see** the doctor at once.*

7   compound conjunctions

Some conjunctions are made up of two or more words, including *that*. Common examples: *so that, in order that, provided that, providing that, seeing that, given that, now that.*

> *I got here early **so that** we could have a few minutes alone together.*
> *I'll come with you **providing that** Bill doesn't mind.*
> ***Now that** the kids are at school, the house seems very quiet.*

8   omission of *that*

That can be left out in some cases, especially in an informal style. For details, see 560.

> *She said **(that)** she didn't mind.*
> *I'm surprised **(that)** she hasn't phoned.*
> *He was so cold **(that)** he couldn't feel his fingers.*

For *that*-clauses after reporting verbs ('indirect speech'), see 480–482.
For the relative pronoun *that*, see 473.

560   **that**: omission

We can often leave out the conjunction *that*, especially in an informal style.

1   indirect speech

That can be left out informally after many common reporting verbs.

> *James **said (that)** he was feeling better.*
> *I **thought (that)** you were in Ireland.*
> *The waiter **suggested (that)** we should go home.*

That cannot be dropped after certain verbs (e.g. *reply, telegraph, shout*), and it is not usually dropped after nouns.

> *James **replied that** he was feeling better.*
> (NOT ~~James replied he was feeling better.~~)
> *She **shouted that** she was busy.* (NOT ~~She shouted she was busy.~~)
> *He disagreed with Copernicus' **view that** the earth went round the sun.*
> (NOT ~~...Copernicus' view the earth went...~~)

For omission of *that* in questions referring to *that*-clauses, see 461.8.

2   after adjectives

We can use *that*-clauses after some adjectives (see 12). *That* can be left out in more common expressions.

> *I'm **glad (that)** you're all right.*
> *It's **funny (that)** he hasn't written.*
> *We were **surprised (that)** she came.*

3 conjunctions

That can be left out in an informal style in some common two-word conjunctions, such as *so that, such ... that, now that, providing that, provided that, supposing that, considering that, assuming that.*

> *Come in quietly **so (that)** she doesn't hear you.*
> *I was having **such** a nice time **(that)** I didn't want to leave.*
> *The garden looks nice **now (that)** we've got some flowers out.*
> *You can borrow it **provided (that)** you bring it back tomorrow.*
> ***Assuming (that)** nobody gets lost, we'll all meet again here at six o'clock.*

4 relative structures

We can usually leave out the relative pronoun *that* when it is the object in a relative clause (see 474).

> *Look! There are the people **(that)** we met in Brighton.*
> *Do it the way **(that)** I showed you.*

561 the matter (with)

The expression *the matter (with)* is used as a complement after *be.*
It follows *something, anything, nothing* and *what,* and means something like 'wrong (with)'.

> *Something's **the matter with** my foot.*
> *Is anything **the matter**?*
> *Nothing's **the matter with** the car – you're just a bad driver.*
> *What's **the matter with** Frank today?*

There is often used as a 'preparatory subject' for *anything, something* and *nothing* (see 563).

> *Is **there** anything **the matter**?*
> ***There's** something **the matter with** the TV.*

562 there

The spelling *there* is used for two words with completely different pronunciations and uses.

1 adverb of place

There (pronounced /ðeə(r)/) is an adverb meaning 'in that place'.

> *What's that green thing over **there**?*
> ***There's** the book I was looking for.*

For the difference between *here* and *there,* see 248.

2 introductory subject

There (pronounced /ðə(r)/) is used as an introductory subject in sentences beginning *there is, there are, there seems to be, there might be* etc. For details, see 563.

> ***There's** a book under the piano.*

563 there is

1 use

In sentences which say that something exists (or does not exist) somewhere, we usually use *there* as a kind of preparatory subject, and put the real subject after the verb. Note the pronunciation of *there*: usually /ðə(r)/, not /ðeə(r)/.

> **There's** *a hole in my tights.* (More natural than *A hole is in my tights.*)
> **There's** *ice on the lake.* (More natural than *Ice is on the lake.*)

It cannot be used in this way.

> **There is** *a lot of noise in the street.* (NOT ~~It is a lot of noise in the street.~~)

There are is used with plural subjects.

> *I don't know how many people* **there are** *in the waiting room.*
> (NOT *...* ~~how many people *there is*...~~)

However, *there is* is also common before plural subjects in informal speech.

> **There's two policemen** *at the door, Dad.*
> **There's some grapes** *in the fridge, if you're still hungry.*

2 indefinite subjects

We use *there* in this way particularly with subjects that have indefinite articles, no article, or indefinite determiners like *some, any, no*; and with indefinite pronouns like *somebody, nothing*.

> **There are some** *people outside.*   **There were no** *footsteps to be seen.*
> **Is there anybody** *at home?*   **There's something** *worrying me.*

Note the use of *wrong* and *the matter* after *something, anything* and *nothing*.

> *There's* **something wrong**.   *Is there* **anything the matter**?

Note also the structures with *sense, point, use* and *need*.

> **There's no sense** *in making him angry.*
> **Is there any point** *in talking about it again?*
> *Do you think* **there's any use** *trying to explain?*
> **There's no need** *to hurry – we've got plenty of time.*

For more about *the matter*, see 561.
For more about *any/no use*, see 56.

3 all tenses

There can be used in this way with all tenses of *be*.

> *Once upon a time* **there were** *three wicked brothers.*
> **There has** *never* **been** *anybody like you.*
> **There will be** *snow on high ground.*

And *there* can be used in tags.

> *There'll be enough for everybody,* **won't there**?

4 structures with auxiliary *be*

There can also be used in structures where *be* is a progressive or passive auxiliary. Note the word order.

> **There was** *a girl* **water-skiing** *on the lake.* (= *A girl was water-skiing...*)
> (NOT ~~There was water-skiing a girl...~~)

There have been more Americans **killed** *in road accidents than in all the wars since 1900.* (= *More Americans have been killed . . .*)
(NOT ~~*There have been killed more Americans . . .*~~)
There'll be somebody **meeting** *you at the airport.*

5 more complex structures

There can be used with **modal verb + *be*** and with some other verbs (e.g. *seem, appear, happen, tend*) before *to be*.
There might be *drinks if you wait for a bit.*
There must be *somebody at home – ring again.*
If the police hadn't closed the road **there could have been** *a bad accident.*
There seem to be *some problems.* (NOT ~~*There seems to be . . .*~~)
Could you be quiet? **There happens to be** *a lecture going on.*
There tends to be *jealousy when a new little brother or sister comes along.*
Note also the structure *there is certain/sure/likely/bound to be*.
There is sure to be *trouble when she gets his letter.*
Do you think **there's likely to be** *snow?*
Structures with infinitives (*there to be*) and *-ing* forms (*there being*) are also possible.
I don't want **there to be** *any more trouble.*
What's the chance of **there being** *an election this year?*

6 other verbs

In a formal or literary style, some other verbs can be used with *there* besides *be*. These are verbs which refer to states, or to the arrival of somebody or something.
In a small town in Germany **there** *once* **lived** *a poor shoemaker.*
There remains *nothing more to be done.*
Suddenly **there entered** *a strange figure dressed all in black.*
There followed *an uncomfortable silence.*

7 definite subjects

There is not normally used in a sentence with a definite subject (e.g. a noun with a definite article, or a proper name).
The door *was open.* (NOT ~~**There was the door open.**~~)
James *was at the party.* (NOT ~~**There was James at the party.**~~)
One exception to this is when we simply name people or things, in order to draw attention to a possible solution to a problem.
'Who could we ask?' 'Well, **there's James**, *or Miranda, or Ann, or Sue, . . .'*
'Where can he sleep?' 'Well, **there's** *always the attic.'*
Another apparent exception is in stories that begin *There was this . . .*, when *this* has an indefinite sense.
There was this *man, see, and he couldn't get up in the mornings. So he . . .*

564 think

1 'have an opinion'

When *think* is used to talk about opinions, progressive forms are not normally used.

>*I **don't think** much of his latest book.* (NOT ~~I'm not thinking much~~...)
>*Who **do you think** will win the election?* (NOT ~~Who are you thinking~~...?)

2 other meanings

When *think* has other meanings (e.g. *plan* or *consider*) progressive forms are possible.

>*You're looking worried. What **are** you **thinking** about?*
>   (NOT ...~~What **do you think about?**~~)
>*I'm **thinking** of changing my job.*

3 *-ing* forms

After *think*, *-ing* forms can be used, but infinitives are not usually possible unless there is an object (see paragraph 4 below).

>*She's thinking **of going** to university next year.*
>   (NOT ~~She's thinking **to go**~~...)

However, ***think* + infinitive** is used when we talk about remembering to do something, or having the good sense to do something.

>*Did you **think to close** the windows when it started raining?*

4 *think* + object (+ *to be*) + complement

In a very formal style, *think* is sometimes followed by an object and an adjective or noun complement.

>*They **thought her fascinating**.*
>*We **thought him a fool**.*

It can be used as a preparatory object for an infinitive.

>*I thought **it** better **to pretend that I knew nothing**.*

To be is occasionally used before the complement (suggesting objective judgement rather than subjective impression), but this is very unusual.

>*They thought him **to be a spy**.*

In more normal styles, *that*-clauses are preferred after *think*.

>*They thought **that she was fascinating**.*
>*We thought **that he was a fool**.*

However, the passive equivalent of the **object + complement** structure is reasonably common, usually with *to be*.

>*She **was thought to be** a terrorist.*

5 transferred negation

When *think* is used to introduce a negative clause, we most often put *not* with *think*, rather than with the following clause (see 359).

>*I **don't think** it will rain.* (More natural than *I think it won't rain.*)
>*Mary **doesn't think** she can come.*

However, we can express surprise with *I thought ... not*.

>*Hello! I **thought** you **weren't** coming!*

6 indirect speech

Think does not usually introduce indirect questions.

*I was **wondering if** I could do anything to help.*
(More natural than *I was thinking if . . .*)

7 *I thought . . .*

Note the use of stressed *I thought . . .* to suggest that the speaker was right. Compare:

'It isn't very nice.' 'Oh, dear. I thought you'd <u>like</u> it.' ('But I was wrong.')
'It's beautiful!' 'Oh, I am glad. I <u>thought</u> you'd like it.' ('And I was right.')

8 *I had thought . . . , I should think* etc

Past perfect forms can suggest that the speaker was mistaken or disappointed.

*I **had thought** that we were going to be invited to dinner.*
I should think and *I should have thought* (US *I would . . .*) can introduce guesses.

*I **should think** we'll need at least twelve bottles of wine.*
*I **should have thought** we could expect at least forty people.*
I should have thought can also introduce criticisms.

*I **should have thought** he could have washed his hands, at least.*

For *I (don't) think so* and *I thought so*, see 515.
For *it* as a preparatory object in sentences like *I think it strange that . . .*, see 302.

565 **this** and **that** (demonstrative pronouns and determiners)

1 people and things

This/that/these/those can be used as determiners with nouns that refer to either people or things.

this *child*   **that** *house*

But when they are used as pronouns without nouns, *this/that/these/those* normally only refer to things. Compare:

– **This** *costs more than* **that**.
 This little boy *says he's tired.* (NOT ~~This says he's tired.~~)
– *Put* **those** *down – they're dirty.*
 Tell **those men** *to go away.* (NOT ~~Tell those to go away.~~)

However, *this* etc can be used as pronouns when we are identifying people.

Hello. **This** *is Elisabeth. Is* **that** *Ruth?*
Who's **that**?
That *looks like Mrs Walker.*
These *are the Smiths.*

Note also *Those who . . .* (see paragraph 6 below).

For a similar use of *it* to refer to people, see 424.5.   ▶

2   the difference

We use *this/these* to talk about people and things which are close to the speaker.

> **This** *is very nice – can I have some more?*
> *Get* **this** *cat off my shoulder.*
> *Do you like* **these** *ear-rings? Bob gave them to me.*
> *I don't know what I'm doing in* **this** *country.* (NOT *...~~in that country.~~*)

We use *that/those* to talk about people and things which are more distant from the speaker, or not present.

> **That** *smells nice – is it for lunch?*   *Get* **that** *cat off the piano.*
> *I like* **those** *ear-rings. Where did you get them?*
> *All the time I was in* **that** *country I hated it.*

3   time

This/these can refer to situations and experiences which are going on or just about to start.

> *I like* **this** *music. What is it?*
> *Listen to* **this**. *You'll like it.* (NOT ~~*Listen to that*...~~)
> *Watch* **this**.   **This** *is a police message.*

That/those can refer to experiences which have just finished, or which are more distant in the past.

> **That** *was nice. What was it?* (NOT ~~*This was nice*...~~)
> *Did you see* **that**?   *Who said* **that**?
> *Have you ever heard from* **that** *Scottish boy you used to go out with?*
>   (NOT *...~~this Scottish boy you used to go out with.~~*)

That can show that something has come to an end.

> *... and* **that**'s *how it happened.*
> *'Anything else?' 'No,* **that**'s *all, thanks.' 'Right,* **that**'ll *be £7.50 altogether.'*
>   (in a shop)
> *OK.* **That**'s *it. I'm leaving. It was nice knowing you.*
> *Well,* **that**'s *that. Another day's work finished. Let's go home.*

Note that *this morning* can refer to a finished period (if one is speaking later the same day); *this afternoon* and *this spring/summer/autumn* are used in similar ways.

For *this, that* and *it* used to refer back to what has just been said or written, see 566.

4   acceptance and rejection

We sometimes use *this/these* to show acceptance or interest, and *that/those* to show dislike or rejection. Compare:

> *Now tell me about* **this** *new boyfriend of yours.*
> *I don't like* **that** *new boyfriend of yours.*

5   on the telephone

On the telephone, British people use *this* to identify themselves, and *that* to ask about the hearer's identity.

> *Hello.* **This** *is Elisabeth. Is* **that** *Ruth?*

Americans can also use *this* to ask about the hearer's identity.

> *Who is* **this**?

6 *that, those* meaning 'the one(s)'

In a formal style, *that* and *those* can be used with a following description to mean 'the one(s)'. *Those who ...* means 'the people who ...'

> *A dog's intelligence is much greater than **that** of a cat.*
> ***Those who** can, do. **Those who** can't, teach.*

7 *this* and *that* meaning 'so'

In an informal style, *this* and *that* are often used with adjectives and adverbs in the same way as *so*.

> *I didn't realise it was going to be **this** hot.*
> *If it goes on raining **this** hard, we'll have to swim to work.*
> *If your boyfriend's **that** clever, why isn't he rich?*

In standard English, only *so* is used before a following clause.

> *It was **so** cold **that I couldn't feel my fingers.***
>   (NOT ~~It was **that** cold that...~~)

Not all that can be used to mean 'not very'.

> *'How was the play?' '**Not all that** good.'*

8 other uses

Note the special use of *this* (with no demonstrative meaning) in conversational story-telling.

> *There was **this** travelling salesman, you see. And he wanted ...*

That/those can suggest that an experience is familiar to everybody.

> *I can't stand **that** perfume of hers.*

This use is common in advertisements.

> *When you get **that empty feeling** – break for a biscuit.*
> *The perfect hobby for **those long winter evenings** – astrology. Send for our free brochure ...*

The differences between *this* and *that* are similar to the differences between *here* and *there* (see 248), *come* and *go* (see 134) and *bring* and *take* (see 112).
For *this one, that one* etc, see 391.
For *these* and *those* with singular *kind of, sort of,* see 526.
For *these* and *those* with singular *kind of, sort of,* see 526.
For *that which,* see 476.5.
For the difference between *this/that* and *it,* see 566.

566 **this/that** and **it** in discourse

This, that and *it* can all be used to refer back to things that have been talked or written about earlier. The differences between them are not well understood, but the following suggestions may be useful.

1 things mentioned

All three words can be used in the sense of 'the thing or situation I have just mentioned'.

It does not give any special emphasis to the thing or situation.

> *So she decided to paint her house pink. **It** upset the neighbours a bit.*   ▶

This and *that* are more emphatic; they seem to suggest 'an interesting new fact has been mentioned'.

> *So she decided to paint her house pink.* **This/That** *really upset the neighbours, as you can imagine.*

This seems to be preferred when the speaker has *more to say* about a new subject of discussion.

> *So she decided to paint her house pink.* **This** *upset the neighbours so much that they took her to court, believe it or not. The case came up last week . . .*
> *Then in 1917 he met Andrew Lewis.* **This** *was a turning point in his career: the two men entered into a partnership which lasted until 1946, and . . .*
> (More natural than . . . **That** *was a turning point . . .*)

2 last thing mentioned

When more than one thing has been mentioned, *it* generally refers to the main subject of discussion; *this* and *that* generally select the last thing mentioned. Compare:

> *We keep the ice-cream machine in the spare room.* **It** *is mainly used by the children, incidentally.* (The machine is used by the children.)
> *We keep the ice-cream machine in the spare room.* **This/That** *is mainly used by the children, incidentally.* (The spare room is used by the children.)

3 focus

It is only used to refer to things which are 'in focus' – which have already been talked about. *This* can be used to 'bring things into focus' before anything has been said about them. Compare:

> *I enjoyed 'Vampires' Picnic'.* **It/This** *is a film for all the family . . .*
> *VAMPIRES' PICNIC:* **This** *is a film for all the family . . .*
> (NOT ~~VAMPIRES' PICNIC: **It is a film for all the family**~~ . . .)

4 referring forward

Only *this* can refer forward to something that has not yet been mentioned.

> *Now what do you think about* **this**? *I thought I'd get a job in Spain for six months, and then . . .* (NOT ~~Now what do you think about **that/it**~~ . . .)

For more about *this* and *that* and the differences between them, see 565.
For more about *it*, see 424.

567 **through** (time)

In American English, *through* can be used in time expressions to mean 'up to and including'.

> *The park is open from May* **through** *September.*

In British English, *through* is not used in this way. When it is necessary to be precise, British people generally use *to . . . inclusive*, or structures like *until the end of . . .*

> *The park is open from May* **to** *September* **inclusive**.
> OR *. . . from May* **until the end** *of September.*

568   time

1   countability and article use

Time has various uses, some countable and some uncountable (for full details see a good dictionary). Most of these are straightforward, but there are problems in two areas.

a   measure of duration

When we talk about the number of hours, days etc that are needed to complete something, *time* is generally uncountable.

> *How much **time** do we need to load the van?*
> *It took quite some **time** to persuade her to talk to us.*
> *Don't worry – there's plenty of **time**.*   *This is a complete waste of **time**.*

However, *time* is countable in certain expressions like *a long/short time* and *quite a time*.

> *I took **a long time** to get to sleep.*   *She was away for **quite a time**.*

The time can be used to mean 'enough time'; *the* is often dropped.

> *Just come with me – I haven't got **(the) time** to explain.*

b   clock times

When we talk about clock times, *time* is countable.

> *Six o'clock would be **a good time** to meet.*
> *She phoned me at various **times** yesterday.*

However, *the* is dropped in the expression *it's time*.

> ***It's time** to stop.* (NOT ~~It's **the** time to stop.~~)
> *I'm hungry. **It's time** for a little something.*

For the use of *take* with expressions of time, see 551.

2   without preposition

Prepositions are often dropped before common expressions with *time* meaning 'occasion'.

> *He's busy. Why don't you come **another time**?*
>   (More natural than ... **at** *another time*.)
> ***What time** does the match start?*
>   (More natural than *At what time ...?*)
> *You won't fool me **this time**.*

In relative structures after *time*, *that* is often used instead of *when* in an informal style (or dropped).

> *Do you remember the **time (that)** Freddy pretended to be a ghost?*
> *You can come up and see me any **time (that)** you like.*
> *The first **time (that)** I saw her, my heart stopped.*

For similar structures with other time words, and with *place, way* and *reason*, see 477.3.

3   *on time* and *in time*

On time means 'at the planned time', 'neither late nor early'. The opposite is 'early' or 'late'. It is often used to refer to timetabled events.

> *Only one of the last six trains has been **on time**.* (NOT *... ~~in time~~.*)
> *Peter wants the discussion to start exactly **on time**.* (NOT *... ~~in time~~.*)   ▶

In time means 'with enough time to spare', 'before the last moment'. The opposite is *too late*.

> *We arrived **in time** to get good seats.*
> (NOT ~~We arrived **on** time to get good seats.~~)
> *He would have died if they hadn't got him to hospital **in time**.*
> (NOT ...~~got him to hospital **on** time.~~)
> *I nearly drove into the car in front, but I stopped just **in time**.*

For structures after *It's time*, see 304.
For ways of telling the time, see 555.
For *by the time*, see 118.
For tenses with *this is the first time*... and similar structures, see 419.7.
For *this is the last time* etc, see 307.5.

569 tonight

Tonight refers to the present or coming night, not to the past night (*last night*). Compare:

> *I had a terrible dream **last night**.* (NOT ~~I had a terrible dream **tonight**.~~)
> *I hope I sleep better **tonight**.*

570 too

1 structures

We can use an infinitive structure after ***too* + adjective / adverb / determiner**.

> *He's **too old to work**.*
> *It's far **too cold to play** tennis.*
> *We arrived **too late to have** dinner.*
> *There was **too much snow to go** walking.*

If the infinitive has its own subject, this is introduced by *for* (see 280).

> *It's too late **for the pubs to be** open.*
> *The runway's too short **for planes to land**.*
> *There was too much snow **for us to go** walking.*

The subject of a sentence with *too* can also be the object of the following infinitive. (For more about this structure, see 285.4.) Object pronouns are not normally used after the infinitive in this case.

> *The water is **too salty to drink**.* (NOT ~~The water is too salty to drink **it**.~~)

However, object pronouns are possible in structures with *for*.

> *The water is **too salty for us to drink (it)**.*

Note the two possible meanings of sentences like *He's too stupid to teach* (= *He's too stupid to be a teacher* OR *He's too stupid for anyone to teach – he can't be taught*).

2 modification

Expressions which modify comparatives (see 139) also modify *too*.

***much** too old* (NOT ~~*very too old*~~)	*a little too confident*
***a lot** too big*	***a bit** too soon*
***far** too young*	***rather** too often*

3 *too* and *too much*

Before adjectives without nouns and before adverbs we use *too*, not
too much.

> You're **too kind** to me. (NOT ~~You're too **much** kind to me.~~)
> I arrived **too early**. (NOT ~~I arrived too **much** early.~~)

4 other determiners

Too is not normally used before **adjective + noun**.

> I put down the bag because it was **too heavy**.
>> (NOT ~~I put down the **too heavy bag**.~~)
> She doesn't like men who are **too tall**.
>> (NOT ~~She doesn't like **too tall men**.~~)
> Let's forget this problem – it's **too difficult**.
>> (NOT ~~Let's forget this **too difficult problem**.~~)

In a rather formal style, *too* can be used before **adjective + *a/an* + noun**
(see 16). Note the word order.

> It's **too cold a day** to go out.

5 *too* and *very*

Too is different from *very* – *too* means 'more than enough', 'more than
necessary' or 'more than is wanted'. Compare:

– He's a **very** intelligent child.
  He's **too** intelligent for his class – he's not learning anything.
– It was **very** cold, but we went out.
  It was **too** cold to go out, so we stayed at home.

However, in informal speech *too* can sometimes be used to mean 'very'.

> Oh, that's really **too** kind of you – thank you so much.
> I'm not feeling **too** well.

The expression *only too* is used to mean 'very', 'extremely'. It is common in
formal offers and invitations.

> We shall be **only too** pleased if you can spend a few days with us.

For more about *too much*, see 571.
For *too* meaning 'also', see 45.

571 **too much** and **too many**

1 the difference

The difference between *too much* and *too many* is the same as the difference
between *much* and *many*. *Too much* is used with singular (uncountable)
nouns; *too many* is used with plurals.

> You put **too much salt** in the soup.
> I've had **too many** late nights recently. (NOT ...~~too **much** late nights~~...)

For more details of the use of *much* and *many*, see 348. ▶

2 modification

Expressions which modify comparatives and *too* (see 139) can also modify *too much* and *too many*.

> *She's wearing **a bit too much** make-up for my taste.*
> *I've been to **rather too many** parties recently.*

However, *much too many* is unusual.

> *You ask **far too many** questions.* (NOT ...*much too many questions.*)

3 *too much/many* without a noun

We can drop a noun after *too much/many*, if the meaning is clear.

> *You've eaten **too much**.*
> *'Did you get any answers to your advertisement?' '**Too many**.'*

For *too* and *too much*, see 570.3
For structures like *too much of an effort*, see 154.

572 travel, journey, trip and voyage

Travel means 'travelling in general'. It is normally uncountable.

> *My interests are music and **travel**.*

The plural form *travels* is sometimes used for a long tour in which several places are visited.

> *Did you meet anybody interesting on your **travels**?*
> *'**Travels** with a Donkey' (book by R L Stevenson)*

A *journey* (mainly British English) is one 'piece' of travelling.

> *Did you have a good **journey**?* (NOT *Did you have a good **travel**?*)

A *trip* is a return journey together with the activity which is the reason for the journey.

> *I'm going on a business **trip** next week.*
> *(= I'm going on a journey and I'm going to do some business.)*

Compare:

> *'How was your **journey**?' 'The train broke down.'*
> *'How was your **trip**?' 'Successful.'*

We do not so often use *trip* for expeditions which have a very serious purpose, are very hard and / or take a very long time.

> *In 1863 the President travelled to Dakota to make peace with the Indians.*
> *(NOT ...made a **trip** to Dakota to make peace...)*
> *Amundsen made his **journey** to the South Pole in 1911.*
> *(NOT Amundsen made his trip to the South Pole...)*

A long sea journey is often called a *voyage*.

573 turning verbs into nouns

1 using nouns for actions

It is very common to refer to an action by using a noun instead of a verb. Nouns of this kind often have the same form as the related verbs. The structure is especially common in informal British English.

> *There was a loud **crash**.*   *Did I hear a **cough**?*

*I need a **wash**.* (GB)   *Let's have a **talk** about your plans.*
*Let your sister have a **go** on the swing.* (informal GB)
*Just take a **look** at yourself.*   *What about a **drink**?*
*Would you like a **taste**?*   *Come on – one more **try**!*

2 common structures

Nouns of this kind are often introduced by 'general-purpose' verbs such as
have, take, give, make, go for.
> *I'll **have a think** and let you know what I decide.* (informal GB)
> *I like to **take a bath** before I go to bed.* (especially US – see 551.4)
> *If it won't start, let's **give it a push**.*
> *I don't know the answer, but I'm going to **make a guess**.*
> *I try to **go for a run** every day.*

We can use *-ing* forms in a similar way, for example after *go* and *do.*
> *Would you like to **go swimming** tomorrow?*
> *She **does** a bit of **painting**, but she doesn't like to show people.*

For details of 'action-nouns' with *have*, and a list of common expressions, see 240.
For *give*, see 230. For *go for*, see 231. For *go . . . ing*, see 232. For *do . . . ing*, see 164.3.

3 clauses ending with verbs

Clauses that end with simple tenses or infinitives of intransitive verbs can
seem unnatural in English, as if they end too suddenly. In an informal style,
people often prefer to avoid this structure by using nouns for actions.
Compare:
> *I'd like to **have a drink**.* (More natural than *I'd like to **drink**.*)
> *Do you want to **go swimming**?* (More natural than *Do you want to **swim**?*)
> *'What did you do this afternoon?' 'I **went for a walk**.'*
>   (More natural than *I **walked**.*)

574 unless

1 meaning

Unless has a similar meaning to *if not*, in the sense of 'except if'.
> *Come tomorrow **unless** I phone.* (= . . . **if** I **don't** phone / **except if** I phone.)
> *I'll take the job **unless** the pay is too low.*
>   (= **if** the pay **isn't** too low / **except if** the pay is too low.)
> *I'll be back tomorrow **unless** there's a plane strike.*
> *Let's have dinner out – **unless** you're too tired.*
> *I'm going to dig the garden this afternoon, **unless** it rains.*

2 when *unless* cannot be used

Unless (= 'except if') can be used instead of *if not* when we refer to
exceptional circumstances which would change a situation (see above
examples). We do not use *unless* to refer to something negative that would
be the **main cause** of the situation that we are talking about.
> *My wife will be very upset **if** I **don't** get back tomorrow.*
>   (NOT *~~My wife will be very upset **unless** I get back tomorrow.~~*
>   If the speaker does not get back, this will be the **main cause** of his
>   wife's unhappiness – *if not* doesn't mean 'except if' here.)

*She'd look nicer **if** she did**n't** wear so much make-up.*
(NOT ~~She'd look nicer **unless** she wore so much make-up.~~ *If not* doesn't
mean 'except if' here.)
*I'll be surprised **if** he does**n't** have an accident soon.*
(NOT ~~I'll be surprised **unless** he has an accident soon.~~)

3 tenses

In clauses with *unless*, we usually use present tenses to refer to the future.
*I'll be in all day unless the office **phones**.*
(NOT ... ~~unless the office **will phone**.~~)

For more about sentences with *if*, see 258–264.
For more about tenses in subordinate clauses, see 556.

575 until

1 *until* and *till*

These two words can be used both as prepositions and conjunctions. They
mean exactly the same. *Till* is informal British English (in American English,
'til is the preferred informal spelling).
*OK, then, I won't expect you **until/till** midnight.*
*I'll wait **until/till** I hear from you.*
*The new timetable will remain in operation **until** June 30.*

2 *until/till* and *to*

To can sometimes be used as a preposition of time with the same meaning as
until/till. This happens after *from* ...
*I usually work **from** nine **to** five.* (OR ... ***from** nine **until/till** five.*)
We can also use *to* when counting the time until a future event.
*It's another three weeks **to** the holidays.* (OR ... ***until/till** the holidays.*)
In other cases, *to* is not generally used.
*I waited for her **until** six o'clock, but she didn't come.*
(NOT ~~I waited for her **to** six o'clock...~~)

For American *from* ... *through*, see 567.

3 place and quantity: *until/till* not used

Until/till is used only to talk about time. To talk about distance, we use *to, as
far as* or *up to*; *up to* is also used to talk about quantity.
*We walked **as far as** / **up to** the edge of the forest.*
(NOT ... ~~**till** the edge of the forest.~~)
*The minibus can hold **up to** thirteen people.*
(NOT ... ~~**until** thirteen people.~~)
*You can earn **up to** £500 a week in this job.*
It is sometimes possible to use *until/till* before a place name in the sense of
'until we get to ...'.
*You drive **until** Phoenix and then I'll take over.*

4 tenses with *until*

Present tenses are used to refer to the future after *until* (see 556).
> *I'll wait **until** she **gets** here.* (NOT *...until she **will get** here.*)

Present and past perfect tenses can emphasise the idea of completion.
> *You're not going home **until** you've **finished** that report.*
> *I waited **until** the rain **had stopped**.*

5 structure with *Not until ...*

In a literary style it is possible to begin a sentence with *Not until ...*, using inverted word order in the main clause (see 298).
> ***Not until** that evening **was she** able to recover her self-control.*
> ***Not until** I left home **did I begin** to understand how strange my family was.*

6 *until* and *by*: states and actions

We use *until* to talk about a **situation or state** that will continue up to a certain moment. We use *by* to say that an **action or event** will happen at or before a future moment. Compare:
- *'Can I stay **until** the weekend?'*
  *'Yes, but you'll have to leave **by** Monday midday at the latest.'*
  *(= **at** twelve on Monday **or before**.)*
- *'Can you repair my watch if I leave it **until** Saturday?'*
  *'No, but we can do it **by** next Tuesday.'* (NOT *...until next Tuesday.*)

7 *until* and *before*

Not until/till can mean the same as *not before*.
> *I won't be seeing Judy **until/before** Tuesday.*

And both *until* and *before* can be used to say how far away a future event is.
> *It'll be ages **until/before** we meet again.*
> *There's only six weeks left **until/before** Christmas.*

576 up and down

1 'towards/away from the centre'

Up and *down* are not only used to refer to higher and lower positions (or movements to and from these positions). They can also refer to more or less important or central places. (Trains to London used to be called 'up trains', and trains from London 'down trains').
> *The ambassador walked slowly **up** the room towards the Queen's throne.*
> *She ran **down** the passage, out of the front door and **down** the garden.*
> *We'll be going **down** to the country for the weekend.*

But note that in the US *downtown* usually means '(in/to) the central business/entertainment area'.

2 north and south

People often use *up* for movements towards the north, and *down* for movements towards the south (perhaps because north is at the top of a map page).
> *I work in London, but I have to travel **up** to Glasgow every few weeks.*   ▶

3 'along'

Sometimes both *up* and *down* are used to mean 'along', 'further on', with little or no difference of meaning.

*The nearest post office is about half a mile **up/down** the road.*

577 **used** + infinitive

1 meaning

We use ***used* + infinitive** to talk about past habits and states which are now finished.

*I **used to smoke**, but now I've stopped.* (NOT ~~I was used to smoke...~~)
*That bingo hall **used to be** a cinema.*

2 only past

Used to ... has no present form (and no progressive, perfect, infinitive or *-ing* forms). To talk about present habits and states, we usually just use the simple present tense (see 444).

*He **smokes**.* (NOT ~~He uses to smoke.~~)
*Her brother still **collects** stamps.*

3 question and negative forms

In a formal style, *used to ...* can have the forms of a modal auxiliary verb (questions and negatives without *do*), especially in British English. The modal question forms are rare.

*I **used not** to like opera, but now I do.* (OR *I **used to not like** opera ...*)
***Used you** to play football at school?*

These forms are not used in tags.

*You **used not** to like him, **did you**?* (NOT ~~...used you?~~)

In an informal style, it is more common to use ordinary question and negative forms with auxiliary *do*.

***Did you use** to play football at school?*
*I **didn't use** to like opera, but now I do.*

These forms are not often written; when they are, they are sometimes spelt *did ... used to* and *didn't used to*; many people consider these spellings incorrect.

The contraction *use(d)n't* is also occasionally used.

4 when *used to ...* is not used

Used to refers to things that happened at an earlier stage of one's life and are now finished: there is an idea that circumstances have changed. It is not used simply to say what happened at a past time, or how long it took, or how many times it happened.

*I **worked** very hard last month.* (NOT ~~I used to work very hard last month.~~)
*I **lived** in Chester for three years.*
    (NOT ~~I used to live in Chester for three years.~~)
*I **went** to France seven times last year.*
    (NOT ~~I used to go to France seven times last year.~~)

5   word order

Mid-position adverbs (see 22–23) can go before or after *used*. The position before *used* is more common in an informal style.

> I *always* **used** to be afraid of dogs. (informal)
> I **used** *always* to be afraid of dogs. (formal)

6   pronunciation

Note the pronunciation of *used* /juːst/ and *use* /juːs/ in this structure.

7   *used* + infinitive and *be used to . . .ing*

Used + **infinitive** has a quite different meaning from *be used to . . .ing* (see next section). Compare:

> I **didn't use to drive** a big car.
>   (= Once I didn't drive a big car, but now I do.)
>   (NOT ~~I wasn't used to drive a big car.~~)
> I **wasn't used to driving** a big car. (= Driving a big car was a new and difficult experience – I hadn't done it before.)

For the difference between *used to* and *would*, see 604.8.

578   (be) used to

1   meaning

If a person *is used* to something, it is familiar; he or she has experienced it so much that it is no longer strange or new.

> I've lived in Central London for six years now, so **I'm used to** the noise.
> At the beginning I couldn't understand Londoners because I **wasn't used to** the accent.

2   structures

Be used to can be followed by nouns or *-ing* forms (NOT infinitives).

> **I'm used to driving** in London now, but it was hard at the beginning.
>   (NOT ~~I'm used to drive in London. . .~~)
> It was a long time before she **was** completely **used to working** with old people.

Used is an adjective in this structure, and can be modified by adverbs such as *quite* or *very*.

> I'm **quite used to** her little ways.

3   *get used to . . .ing* etc

Get, *become* and *grow* can also be used before *used to* (*. . .ing*).

> You'll soon **get used to living** in the country.
> I lived in France for six years, but I never **got used to shaking** hands with people all the time.
> Little by little, he **became used to** his new family.
> It took them a long time to **grow used to getting** up in the middle of the night.

▶

4 **pronunciation**

Note that *used* is pronounced /juːst/ in this structure.

For more about *-ing* forms after the preposition *to*, see 295.2.
For the differences between *get, become* and *grow*, see 129.

579 verb complementation: what can follow a verb?

1 different verbs, different structures

Different verbs can be followed by different kinds of word and structure. This is partly a matter of meaning: after a verb like *eat* or *break*, for instance, it is normal to expect a noun; after *try* or *stop*, it is natural to expect a verb. It is also partly a matter of grammatical rules that have nothing to do with meaning. Before an object, *wait* is followed by the preposition *for*; *expect* has no preposition. One can *tell somebody something*, but one cannot ~~explain somebody something~~. One *hopes to see somebody*, but one *looks forward to seeing somebody*. One *advises somebody to see the doctor* but one does not ~~suggest somebody to see the doctor~~. There are no simple rules for this kind of problem; it is necessary to learn, for each verb, what kind of structures can follow it.

2 verb + object; transitive and intransitive verbs

Some verbs are usually followed by nouns or pronouns that act as direct objects. In grammars these verbs are called 'transitive'. Examples are *invite, surprise*.

> Let's **invite Sally and Bruce**. (BUT NOT ~~Let's invite.~~)
> You **surprised me**. (BUT NOT ~~You surprised.~~)

Some verbs are not normally followed by direct objects. These are called 'intransitive'. Examples are *sit, sleep*.

> Do **sit down**. (BUT NOT ~~Do sit that chair.~~)
> I usually **sleep** well. (BUT NOT ~~She slept the baby.~~)

Many verbs can be both transitive and intransitive.

> England **lost**. Let's **eat**.
> England **lost the match**. I can't **eat this**.

Some transitive verbs can be followed by two objects (indirect and direct). For details, see 583.

> **Send me the form** when you've filled it in.
> I'm going to **buy Sarah some flowers**.

3 ergative verbs

Some verbs are used transitively and intransitively with different kinds of subject; the intransitive use has a meaning rather like a passive (see 407) or reflexive (see 471) verb. Modern grammarians call these verbs 'ergative'. Compare:

– She **opened** the door.   – The wind's **moving** the curtain.
  The door **opened**.   The curtain's **moving**.
– Something **woke** her.   – I can't **start** the car.
  Suddenly she **woke**.   The car won't **start**.

– *Marriage has really **changed** her.*
  *She's **changed** a lot since she got married.*
– *We're **selling** a lot of copies of your book.*
  *Your book's **selling** well.*

For verb structures used as objects, see paragraphs 7–9 below.
For structures with object complements, see paragraph 10 below.

4   verbs with prepositions and particles

Many verbs need prepositions before their objects.
  *Why are you **looking at** me like that?* (NOT ~~Why are you looking me~~ ...?)
  *I'd like you to **listen to** this.* (NOT ... ~~to listen this.~~)
  *Let's **talk about** your plans.* (NOT ~~Let's talk your plans.~~)
The preposition is dropped when there is no object.
  Look! (NOT ~~Look at!~~)
Other verbs are used with adverb particles. Some of these combinations are transitive; others are intransitive.
  *We'll have to **put off** our visit to Scotland.*   *It's time to **get up**.*

For more about two-part verbs like these, see 582.

5   complements of place

Usually, a preposition is necessary before an expression of place.
  *She arrived **at the station** last night.* (NOT ~~She arrived the station~~...)
  *Don't walk **on the grass**.* (NOT ~~Don't walk the grass.~~)
A few verbs can be used with direct objects referring to place.
  *I like **climbing mountains**.* (NOT ~~I like climbing on mountains.~~)
Some verbs are incomplete without an expression of place.
  *He **lives in York**.* (BUT NOT ~~He lives.~~)
  *She **got off the bus**.* (BUT NOT ~~She got.~~)

For information about the position of place and other adverbials, see 23.

6   copular verbs

Some verbs are followed not by an object, but by a subject complement – an expression which describes the subject. These are called 'copular verbs'. For details, see 147.
  *Your room **is a mess**.*   *That **looks nice**.*
  *The toilets **are upstairs**.*   *I felt **a complete idiot**.*

7   verb + verb structures: auxiliaries

Many verbs can be followed by forms of other verbs. Auxiliary verbs are used with other verbs to make questions and negatives, progressive forms, perfect forms, and passives. For details, see 84.
  ***Do** you **want** some tea?*
  *It **doesn't matter**.*
  ***Is** it **raining**?*
  *Where **have** you **been**?*
  *These **are made** in France.*

▶

Modal auxiliary verbs are used with other verbs to add ideas such as certainty, probability, futurity, permission and obligation. For details, see 344–345.

>You **must be** tired.
>The car **may need** a new engine.
>The lecture **will start** at ten.
>**Can** I **borrow** your paper?
>We **ought to invite** the Maxwells this weekend.

8 verb + verb structures: other verbs

Many verbs besides auxiliaries can be followed by forms of other verbs (or by structures including other verbs). This can happen, for example, if we talk about our attitude to an action: the first verb describes the attitude and the second refers to the action. The second verb structure is often rather like the direct object of the first verb.

>I **enjoy playing** cards.   I **hope to see** you soon.
>I **saw that she was crying**.

Different structures are possible, depending on the particular verb. Some verbs can be followed by infinitives (with or without *to*), some verbs can be followed by *-ing* forms, some by past participles, and some by clauses. Many verbs can be followed by two or more of these structures, often with a difference of meaning or use. For each verb, it is necessary to know which structures are possible.

>We **seem to have** a problem. (NOT *We **seem having a problem.***)
>Can I **help wash up**?
>It's not very easy to **stop smoking**. (NOT *...to **stop to smoke.***)
>Did you see that the police station **got burnt** down?
>I **suggest that you see** a solicitor. OR I **suggest seeing** a solicitor.
>   (NOT *I **suggest you to see a solicitor.***)

In some cases, the first verb does not really say what the subject does – it simply gives more information about the action which the second verb refers to.

>I **happened to see** Alice the other day.
>Now he's getting older he **tends to forget** things.
>We're **starting to get invited** to some of the neighbours' parties.
>My keys **seem to have disappeared**.

It is possible to have 'chains' of verbs following each other.

>I **keep forgetting to go shopping**.   Don't **let** me **stop** you **working**.
>He **seems to be trying to sit** up.
>I don't **want to have to get** her **to start telling** lies.

For more about verbs followed by infinitives, see 283–284. For verbs followed by *-ing* forms, see 293. For *it* as a preparatory subject, see 301.
See the Index for problems with the structures after some common verbs.
For information about other verbs, see a good dictionary.

9 verb + object + verb structure

Many verbs can be followed by an object as well as a verb structure.

>Can I **help you wash up**?   I'd **like you to meet** Sally.
>We all **want you to be** happy. (NOT *We all **want that you are happy.***)

*We've got to **stop him making** a fool of himself.*
*When are you going to **get the clock repaired**?*
*Nobody **told me that you were here**.*

For more about **verb + object + infinitive**, see 284.
For structures with **object + -*ing* form**, see 293.

10 verb + object + complement

Some transitive verbs can be followed by an object together with an object
complement (an expression that gives more information about the object).
For details, see 580.

*You **make me nervous**.*
*Let's **paint it blue**.*
*That cat **regards Bill as his father**.*
*The police **believe him to be dangerous**.*

11 short verbs without complements

A short verb form without any kind of following complement can sometimes
sound unnatural in English, and structures like this are avoided in some
cases.

*Let's **go swimming**.* (More natural than *Let's **swim**.*)
*Why don't you **go shopping**?* (More natural than *Why don't you **shop**?*)
*I think I'll **have a shower**.* (More natural than *I think I'll **shower**.*)

For more about structures like these, see 573.3.
For the structures that are possible after a particular verb, see a good dictionary.

580 verb + object + complement

1 adjective and noun complements

Some transitive verbs can be followed by an object together with an object
complement (an expression that gives more information about the object).
This is often an adjective or noun phrase.

*You **make me nervous**.*
*She's **driving us crazy**.*
*Let's **cut it short**.*
*I **find her attitude strange**.*
*Don't **call me a liar**.*
*I don't know why they **elected him President**.*
*'Would you like to join the committee?' 'I would **consider it an honour**.'*

2 structures with *as*

After some verbs, an object complement is introduced by *as*. This is common
when we say how we see or describe somebody / something.

*I see you **as** a basically kind person.*
*She described her attacker **as** a tall dark man with a beard.*
*His mother regards him **as** a genius.*
*After tests, they identified the metal **as** gold.*

The structure is also possible with *as being*.

*The police do not regard him **as being** dangerous.*

▶

3 verbs of thinking and feeling

Some verbs that refer to thoughts, feelings and opinions (e.g. *believe, consider, feel, know, find, think, understand*) can be followed by **object + infinitive** (usually *to be*) in a formal style. In an informal style, *that*-clauses are more common.

> *I **considered him to be** an excellent choice.*
>> (Less formal: *I **considered that he was**...*)
> *We **supposed them to be** married.*
>> (Less formal: *We **supposed that they were**...*)
> *They **believed her to be** reliable.*

This structure is very unusual with *think*.

> *I **thought that she was** mistaken.*
>> (More natural than *I **thought her to be** mistaken.*)

After *believe, consider, find* and *think*, it is often possible to drop *to be* before adjectives, and sometimes (especially with *consider*) before nouns.

> *We **found her delightful.***
> *I **considered him an excellent choice.***

Passive forms of these structures may be less formal than active forms (see paragraph 5 below).

For more details of structures with *feel*, see 208; for *know*, see 306; for *think*, see 564.

4 structures with preparatory *it*

When the object of a verb is a clause, infinitive structure or *-ing* structure, and there is an object complement, it is common to use *it* as a preparatory object.

> *He thought **it** strange **that she had not written.***
>> (More natural than *He thought that she had not written strange.*)
> *The government regard **it** as necessary **to raise taxes.***
> *We found **it** impossible **to understand her.***
> *She felt **it** necessary **to put her views in writing.***
> *He considered **it** his duty **to call the police.***
> *I found **it** interesting **being back at school again.***

5 passive structures

Passive versions of these structures are common.

> *It was painted blue.*
> *He was elected President.*
> *Her attacker was described as a tall man with a beard.*
> *The metal was identified as gold.*
> *He is not regarded as being dangerous.*
> *For a long time he was thought to be a spy.*
> *She was believed to belong to a revolutionary organisation.*
> *Seven people are understood to have been injured in the explosion.*
> *It was considered impossible to change the date.*

For more about the structures that can follow verbs, see 579.
For the structures that are possible after a particular verb, see a good dictionary.

581   verbs of movement

When we want to talk about a movement, its direction and its nature, there are various ways of doing this. We can use three separate words for the three ideas:

*She **came out dancing**.*

We can use a verb which includes the idea of direction, and describe the nature of the movement separately:

*She **entered dancing**.*

Or we can use a verb which makes clear the nature of the movement, and describe the direction separately:

*She **danced in**.*

In English, the third of these solutions is the most common.

*She **danced across** the garden.*

(More natural than *She **crossed** the garden **dancing**.*)

*I **jumped down** the stairs.*

(More natural than *I **came down** the stairs **jumping**.*)

*He **ran into** the room.*

(More natural than *He **entered** the room **running**.*)

*They **crawled out of** the cellar.*

(More natural than *They **left** the cellar **crawling**.*)

*We **flew past** Mont Blanc.*

(More natural than *We **passed** Mont Blanc **flying**.*)

582   verbs with prepositions and particles

1   two-word verbs

Many English verbs can be followed by prepositions or adverb particles (for the difference, see 19).

*Alan **walked down** the road without **looking at** anybody.*

*Do **sit down**.*

Some verbs and prepositions / particles are regularly used together: for example *look at, listen to, stand up, switch off.* These combinations are rather like two-word verbs. They are often called 'phrasal verbs' in grammars. The meaning of a two-word verb is sometimes very different from the meanings of the two parts taken separately.

*Could you **look after** the kids while I'm out?*

(*Look after* is not the same as *look + after.*)

*We had to **put off** the meeting till Tuesday.*

(*Put off* is not the same as *put + off.*)

2   verbs with prepositions and particles together

Some verbs can be used with both an adverb particle and a preposition.

*I **get on with** her quite well.*

*If you're on the road on Saturday night, **look out for** drunk drivers.*   ▶

3 word order with objects

Prepositions and particles do not always go in the same place in clauses with objects. Prepositions normally go before objects.

*He fell **off the bridge**.* (NOT ~~He fell **the bridge off**.~~)

Particles can go before or after noun objects.

*She switched **off the light**.* OR *She switched **the light off**.*

But particles can only go after pronoun objects.

*She switched **it off**.* (NOT ~~She switched **off it**.~~)

*Is that the light **which** you switched **off**?*

(NOT ... ~~the light **off which** you switched?~~)

*Give **me back** my watch.* OR *Give **me** my watch **back**.*

(NOT ~~Give **back me** my watch.~~)

4 objects at the beginning of clauses

When an object comes at the beginning of a clause (e.g. in a question or relative clause), a two-word verb usually stays together, so that a preposition can be separated from its object and go at the end of the clause. For details of this and other preposition-final structures, see 440.

***What** are you **thinking about**?* (NOT ~~**About what** are you **thinking**?~~)

*I've found the book **which** I was **looking for**.*

(More natural in an informal style than ... *the book **for which** I was looking.*)

5 stress

At the end of a clause, a preposition is usually unstressed, while an adverb particle is usually stressed. Compare:

They were 'called on. (preposition)

They were called 'up. (particle)

For details of particular two-word verbs, see the *Oxford Dictionary of Phrasal Verbs* Volume 1, or the *Longman Dictionary of Phrasal Verbs.*

583 verbs with two objects

1 indirect and direct objects

Many verbs can be followed by two objects – one indirect and one direct. Usually the indirect object refers to a person, and comes first.

*He gave **his wife a camera** for Christmas.*

*Could you send **me the bill**?*

*I'll lend **you some**.*

*I wish **you a Merry Christmas**.*

*Let me make **you some tea**.*

Some common verbs which are used like this:

bring	leave	pass	refuse	teach
buy	lend	pay	send	tell
cost	make	play	show	wish
get	offer	promise	sing	write
give	owe	read	take	

2   indirect object last

We can also put the indirect object after the direct object. In this case it normally has a preposition (usually *to* or *for*).

*I handed **my licence to the policeman**.*

*Mrs Norman sent **some flowers to the nurse** who was looking after her daughter.*

*Mother bought **the ice-cream for you**, not for me.*

3   two pronouns

When both objects are pronouns, it is common to put the indirect object last. *To* is occasionally dropped after *it* in informal British English.

*Lend **them to her**.*

*Send **some to him**.*

*Give **it (to) me**.*

It is also possible to put the indirect object first.

*Give **her one**.*

*Send **him some**.*

However, this structure is avoided in some cases: phrases ending with *it* or *them* (e.g. *He gave you **it*** or *Send them **them***) are often felt to be unnatural.

4   *wh*-questions

Prepositions are used in *wh*-questions referring to the indirect object.

***Who** did you buy it **for**?* (NOT ~~*Who did you buy it?*~~)

***Who** was it sent **to**?* (NOT ~~*Who was it sent?*~~)

5   passives

When these verbs are used in passive structures, the subject is usually the person who receives something, not the thing which is sent, given etc. In this case the prepositions *to* and *for* are not used.

***I've** just been given a lovely picture.*

(NOT ~~*I've just been given a lovely picture to.*~~)

***We** were all bought little presents.*

(NOT ~~*We were all bought little presents for.*~~)

***Mr Fairfax** was paid £300 last month.*

Write is not normally used in this structure.

(NOT USUALLY ~~*I was **written** a letter.*~~)

The thing which is given, sent etc can be the subject if necessary.

A preposition is most often used before the indirect object in this case.

*'What happened to the stuff he left behind?' 'Well, **the picture** was given **to** Mr Ferguson.'*

6   structures with *explain, suggest* and *describe*

We do not generally use *explain, suggest* or *describe* with the structure **indirect object + direct object**.

*I'd like him to **explain his decision to us**.*

(NOT ... ~~*to explain us his decision.*~~)

*Can you **suggest a good dentist to me**?*

(NOT ~~*Can you **suggest me a good dentist**?*~~)

*Please **describe your wife to us**.* (NOT ~~*Please **describe us your wife**.*~~)   ►

7 one object or two

Some verbs can be followed by either a direct object, or an indirect object, or both.

> *I asked **John**.*
> *I asked **a question**.*
> *I asked **John a question**.*

Other verbs like this include *teach, tell, pay, show, sing, play* and *write*. Note that when *sing, play* and *write* have no direct object, we put *to* before the indirect object. Compare:

– *Sing **her** a song.*
   *Sing **to her**.* (NOT ~~Sing **her**.~~)
– ***Write me** a letter.*
   *Write **to me** when you get home.*
> (More common than *Write me ...* in standard British English.)

For structures with object complements (e.g. *They made him captain*), see 580.

584 wait

Wait can be followed by an infinitive.

> *I'll **wait to hear** from you before I do anything.*

Before a direct object, *wait for* is used.

> *Please **wait for** me here.* (NOT ~~Please **wait me here**.~~)

That-clauses are not used after *wait*, but an **object + infinitive** structure is possible.

> *We'll have to wait **for the photos to be ready**.*
> (NOT *... **wait that the photos are ready**.*)

The time preposition *for* is often dropped after *wait*.

> *I waited **(for)** a very long time for her answer.*

The transitive verb *await* is formal, and is used with abstract objects.

> *We're still **awaiting instructions**.*

For the difference between *wait for* and *expect*, see 202.

585 want

1 infinitive with *to*

After *want*, we normally use an infinitive with *to*.

> *I don't **want to come** back here ever again.*
> (NOT ~~I don't **want come back** ...~~)

That-clauses are not normally used after *want*, but an **object + infinitive** structure is possible.

> *Do you **want me to make** you some coffee?*
> (NOT ~~Do you **want (that) I make** you some coffee?~~)
> *I don't **want that woman to come** here ever again.*
> *I **want you to be** my wife.*

2   structure with object complement

Want can be followed by an object together with a complement (adjective, adverb or past participle) to express ideas such as change or result.

> They **wanted him dead**.   She doesn't **want him back**.
> I **want her out of there** now.   We **want the job finished** by Tuesday.
> Do you **want your grass cut**?

To be or *as* is used before a noun complement.

> I **want you to be my friend**. (OR I **want you as my friend**.)
>   (NOT ~~I want you my friend.~~)

3   *want* meaning 'need'

In informal British English, *want* is often used to mean 'need', particularly with reference to actions.

> That car **wants** a clean.   Your hair **wants** a good brush.

In this case, *want* can be followed by an *-ing* form.

> This coat **wants cleaning**. (= ... **needs to be cleaned**.)
> The grass **wants cutting**.

4   politeness

Want is not used in polite expressions of wishes.

> **Would** you **like** some help? (NOT ~~Would you want some help?~~)

Need can be used in the same way. See 357.
For other verbs followed by **object + infinitive**, see 284.
For *to* used instead of a whole infinitive (e.g. *I don't want **to**, thanks*), see 186.
For *want* and *will*, see 600.7.

586 -ward(s)

Backward(s), forward(s), northward(s), outward(s) and similar words can be used as adjectives or adverbs.

1   adjectives

When they are used as adjectives, they do not have *-s*.

> This country is very **backward** in some ways.
> You're not allowed to make a **forward** pass in rugby.
> He was last seen driving in a **northward** direction.

2   adverbs

When these words are adverbs, they can generally be used with or without *-s*. The forms with *-s* are probably more common in British English, and the forms without *-s* in American English.

> Why are you moving **backward(s) and forward(s)**?
> If we keep going **upward(s)** we must get to the top.
> Let's start driving **homeward(s)**.

In figurative expressions such as *look forward to, bring forward, put forward,* the form without *-s* is always used.

> I **look forward to** hearing from you.
> She **put forward** a very interesting suggestion.

▶

3 other words

Towards is normally used in British English; *toward* is more common in American English. *Afterwards* is normal in British English; both *afterward* and *afterwards* are used in American English.

587 way

1 preposition dropped

Way can mean 'method', 'manner' or 'route', 'road'. In an informal style, we usually drop the prepositions *in* or *by* before common expressions with either meaning.

> *You're doing it **(in) the wrong way**.*
> *You don't put in the cassette **that way**.*
> *Do it **(in) any way** you like.*
> *Come **this way**.*
> *We went there **the usual way**.*

2 relative structures

In informal relative structures, *that* is often used instead of *in which* or *by which* after *way*. *That* can also be dropped.

> *I don't like the way **(that)** you talk to me.*
> *The way **(that)** they organised the meeting was completely crazy.*
> *Let's go the way **(that)** we went yesterday.*

3 infinitive or -*ing*

After *way* (meaning 'method'/'manner') we can use an infinitive structure or *of*. . .*ing*. There is no important difference between the two structures.

> *There's no way **to prove / of proving** that he was stealing.*

4 *way of* and *means of*

Way of is unusual before a noun. We use *means of* or *method of* instead.

> *We tried all possible **means of communication**, but we couldn't get in*
> *touch with him.* (NOT . . .*ways of communication*. . .)
> *The 19th century saw a revolution in **methods of transport**.*
> (NOT . . .*ways of transport.*)

5 *in the way* and *on the way*

These expressions are quite different. *In the/my/etc way* is used for obstacles – things that stop people getting where they want to.

> *I can't get the car out because those boxes are **in the way**.*
> *Please don't stand in the kitchen door – you're **in my way**.*

On the/my etc *way* means 'during the journey/movement' or 'coming'.

> *Spring is **on the way**.*
> *She's got five children, and another one **on the way**.*
> *We'll have lunch **on our way**.*
> *Close the door **on your way** out.*

For *by the way*, see 159.8.

588 weak and strong forms

1 What are weak and strong forms?

Some English words have two pronunciations: one is used when they are
stressed, and the other when they are not. Compare:

> *What are you looking* **at** */æt/?*
> *I'm looking* **at** */ət/ you.*

Most of these words are prepositions, pronouns, conjunctions, articles and
auxiliary verbs. Such words are not usually stressed, so the unstressed
('weak') pronunciation is the normal one. This usually has the vowel /ə/ or
no vowel; a few weak forms are pronounced with /ɪ/. The 'strong'
pronunciation has the vowel that corresponds to the spelling. Compare:

– *I was /wəz/ late.*
  It was /wəz/ raining.
  Yes, it **was** */wɒz/.* (stressed at end of sentence)
– *I must /məs/ go now.*
  I really **must** */mʌst/ stop smoking.* (stressed for emphasis)
– *Where have /əv/ you been?*
  You might have /əv/ told me.
  What did you **have** */hæv/ for breakfast?* (non-auxiliary verb)

Contracted negatives always have a strong pronunciation.

> *can't /kɑːnt/   mustn't /ˈmʌsnt/   wasn't /ˈwɒznt/*

2 list of words with weak and strong forms

The most important words which have weak and strong forms are:

	Weak form	Strong form
a	/ə/	/eɪ/ (unusual)
am	/(ə)m/	/æm/
an	/ən/	/æn/ (unusual)
and	/(ə)n(d)/	/ænd/
are	/ə(r)/	/ɑː(r)/
as	/əz/	/æz/
at	/ət/	/æt/
be	/bɪ/	/biː/
been	/bɪn/	/biːn/
but	/bət/	/bʌt/
can	/k(ə)n/	/kæn/
could	/kəd/	/kʊd/
do	/d(ə)/	/duː/
does	/dəz/	/dʌz/
for	/fə(r)/	/fɔː(r)/
from	/frəm/	/frɒm/
had	/(h)əd/	/hæd/
has	/(h)əz/	/hæz/
have	/(h)əv/	/hæv/
he	/(h)ɪ/	/hiː/
her	/(h)ə(r)/	/hɜː(r)/
him	/(h)ɪm/	/hɪm/
his	/(h)ɪz/	/hɪz/

▶

	Weak form	Strong form
is	/z, s/	/ɪz/
must	/m(ə)s(t)/	/mʌst/
not	/nt/	/nɒt/
of	/əv/	/ɒv/
our	/ɑː(r)/	/aʊə(r)/
Saint	/s(ə)nt/ (GB only)	/seɪnt/
shall	/ʃ(ə)l/	/ʃæl/
she	/ʃɪ/	/ʃiː/
should	/ʃ(ə)d/	/ʃʊd/
sir	/sə(r)/	/sɜː(r)/
some (see 521)	/s(ə)m/	/sʌm/
than	/ð(ə)n/	/ðæn/ (rare)
that (conj.)	/ð(ə)t/	/ðæt/
the	/ðə, ðɪ/	/ðiː/
them	/ð(ə)m/	/ðem/
there (see 562)	/ðə(r)/	/ðeə(r)/
to	/tə/	/tuː/
us	/əs/	/ʌs/
was	/w(ə)z/	/wɒz/
we	/wɪ/	/wiː/
were	/wə(r)/	/wɜː(r)/
who	/hʊ/	/huː/
would	/wəd, əd/	/wʊd/
will	/(ə)l/	/wɪl/
you	/jʊ/	/juː/
your	/jə(r)/	/jɔː(r)/

589 well

1 *well* and *good*

Well and *good* can have similar meanings, but in this case *well* is an adverb, while *good* is an adjective. Compare:
- *The car runs **well**.* (adverb modifying *runs*) (NOT *The car runs **good**.*)
  *It's a **well**-made car.* (adverb modifying *made*)
  *It's a **good** car.* (adjective modifying *car*)
- *He teaches very **well**.*
  *I like that teacher. He's **good**.* (NOT *He's **well**.*)
- *She speaks English **well**.* (NOT *She speaks English **good**.*)
  *She speaks **good** English.*
  *Her English is **good**.*

Note that we cannot say *She **speaks well** English*. (Adverbs cannot usually go between the verb and the object – see 22.)

2 *well* = 'in good health'

There is also an adjective *well*, meaning 'in good health'.
  *'How are you?' 'Quite **well**, thanks.'*
  *I don't feel very **well**.*

Note that the adjective *well* is only used to talk about health. Compare:
> *When I'm in the mountains I am always **well**.*
> *When I'm with you I'm **happy**.* (NOT ~~When I'm with you I'm **well**.~~)

Well is not common before a noun in British English. We can say *She's **well***, but it is less usual to say, for example, *She's a **well girl***.

For *ill* and *sick*, see 266.
For *well* as a discourse marker, see 159.16, 17, 20.
For more complete information about uses of *well*, see a good dictionary.

590 **when** and **if**

A person who says *when* (referring to the future) is sure that something will happen. A person who says *if* is unsure whether it will happen or not. Compare:
> *I'll see you at Christmas **when** we're all at Sally's place.*
> (*We are certain to be at Sally's place.*)
> *I'll see you in August **if** I come to New York.*
> (*Perhaps I'll come to New York, perhaps not.*)

To talk about repeated, predictable situations and events (in the sense of 'whenever'), both *when* and *if* can be used with little difference of meaning.
> ***When/If** you heat ice it turns to water.*
> ***When/If** I'm in Liverpool I usually stay with my sister.*

For past perfect with *when*, see 421.5; for future reference, see 556.
For *when* in relative clauses, see 143.3.

591 **where (to)**

To is often dropped in questions after *where*.
> ***Where** are you going **(to)**?*   ***Where** does this road lead **(to)**?*
> ***Where** do you want me to take these files **(to)**?*

To is not normally dropped in the short question *Where to?*
> *'Could you send this off for me?' '**Where to?**'*

For *where* in relative clauses, see 473.3.

592 **whether . . . or . . .**

We can use *whether . . . or . . .* as a double conjunction, with a similar meaning to *It doesn't matter whether . . . or . . .*
> ***Whether** we go by bus **or** train, it'll take at least six hours.*
> *We'll have to pay the same for the hotel room, **whether** we leave today **or** stay till the end of the week.*

When the second part of the structure is negative there are several possibilities.
> ***Whether** you like it **or not**, . . .*   ***Whether or not** you like it, . . .*
> ***Whether** you like it or **whether you don't**, . . .*

For *whether* and *if*, see 593.

593 **whether** and **if**

1 indirect questions

We can generally use both *whether* and *if* to introduce indirect *yes/no* questions.

> *I'm not sure **whether/if** I'll have time.*
> *I asked **whether/if** she had any letters for me.*

After some verbs, *whether* is preferred to *if*.

> *We **discussed whether** we should close the shop.*
> (More normal than *We discussed **if**...*)

In a formal style, *whether* is usually preferred in a two-part question with *or*.

> *Let me know **whether** you can come **or** not.* (... ***if** you can come or not* is also possible.)
> *The Directors have not decided **whether** they will recommend a dividend **or** reinvest the profits.*

If an indirect question is fronted (see 217), *whether* is used.

> ***Whether** I'll have time I'm not sure at the moment.*

2 not used in echo questions

If and *whether* are not normally used in 'echo questions' (see 463.2).

> *'Are you happy?' **Am I happy**? No!'* (NOT *'...~~If/Whether I'm happy?~~...'*)

3 prepositions

After prepositions, only *whether* is possible.

> *There was a big argument **about whether** we should move to a new house.*
> (NOT *...~~about if we should move~~...*)
> *I haven't settled the question **of whether** I'll go back home.*
> (NOT *...~~question of if~~...*)

For cases when prepositions can be dropped before conjunctions, see 441.

4 infinitives

Whether, but not *if*, is used before *to*-infinitives.

> *They can't decide **whether to get** married now or wait.*
> (NOT *~~They can't decide **if to get** married~~...*)

5 subject, complement and adverbial clauses

When a question-word clause is a subject or complement, *whether* is normally preferred.

> ***Whether we can stay with my mother** is another matter.* (subject)
> *The question is **whether the man can be trusted**.* (complement)

If is sometimes possible in a very informal style.

> *The question is **if** the man can be trusted.*
> ***Whether you like it or not**, I'm staying here.*

594 *which*, **what** and **who**: question words

1 *which* and *what:* the difference

Which and *what* are often both possible, with little difference of meaning.
Which/What is the hottest city in the world?
Which/What train did you come on?
Which/What people have influenced you most in your life?
Which is preferred when the speaker has a limited number of choices in mind.
*We've got white or brown bread. **Which** will you have?*
(More natural than . . . *What will you have?*)
***Which** size do you want – small, medium or large?*
When the speaker is not thinking of a limited number of choices, *what* is used.
***What** language do they speak in Greenland?*
(More natural than *Which language . . .*)
***What**'s your phone number?* (NOT ~~*Which is your phone number?*~~)

2 determiners: *which* and *what*

Before nouns, *which* and *what* can be used to ask questions about both things and people.
***Which teacher** do you like best?*
***Which colour** do you want – green, red, yellow or brown?*
***What writers** do you like?*
***What colour** are your baby's eyes?*

3 *which of*

Before another determiner (e.g. *the, my, these*) or a pronoun, we use *which of*. *Who* and *what* are not normally used with *of* like this in modern English.
***Which of** your teachers do you like best?*
(NOT ~~*Who/What of your teachers . . .*~~)
***Which of** us is going to do the washing up?* (NOT ~~*Who of us . . .?*~~)
***Which** of these coats is yours?* (NOT ~~*What of these . . .?*~~)

4 without nouns: *who, which* and *what*

When these words are used as pronouns, without nouns immediately after them, we generally use *who*, not *which*, for people.
***Who** won – Smith or Fitzgibbon?* (NOT ~~*Which won . . .?*~~)
***Who** are you going out with – Lesley or Maria?*
However, *which* can be used in questions about people's identity, and *what* can be used to ask about people's jobs and functions.
*'**Which** is your husband?' 'The one in jeans.'*
*'So Janet's the Managing Director. **What's** Peter?' 'He is the Company Secretary.'*
And *which* is sometimes used instead of *who* in questions about *classes* of people.
***Which** is more valuable to society – a politician or a nurse?*   ▶

Which and *what* can both be used to ask about things (for the difference, see above).

> **Which** *do you prefer – electric cookers or gas?*
> **What** *have you got in your pockets?*

For the difference between *who* and *whom*, see 425.4–6.
For relative *who* and *which*, see 473. For relative *what*, see 476.
For singular and plural verbs after *who* and *what*, see 509.3.
For the grammar of clauses beginning with question words, see 460.

595 who ever, what ever etc

These expressions are used to show surprise or difficulty in believing something.

> **Who ever** *is that strange girl wịth Roger?*
> **What ever** *are you doing?*
> **How ever** *did you manage to start the car? I couldn't.*
> **How ever many** *people have you invited?*
> **When ever** *will I have time to write some letters?*
> **Why ever** *did I marry you?*

The expressions can also be written as single words: *whoever, whatever* etc. Note that *whose* and *which* are not used with *ever* in this way.

In an informal style, *on earth, the hell* (US also *in hell*) or *the fuck* (taboo) can be used instead of *ever*.

> **Who on earth** *is that strange girl?*
> **How on earth** *did you manage to start the car?*
> **Why the hell** *did I marry you?*
> **What the fuck** *is she talking about?*

Note that *on earth* etc are not used with longer question-word expressions.

> N O T ~~*How long the hell is this going to take?*~~ O R ~~*How the hell long*~~ . . . ?

For *whoever* etc, see 596.
For more about *ever*, see 197.
For *hell* and other taboo words, see 550.

596 whoever, whatever etc

1 meaning and use

The words *whoever, whatever, whichever, however, whenever* and *wherever* have similar meanings to 'it doesn't matter who/what/which etc', 'any person who' / 'any thing that' etc, or 'the unknown person who' / 'the unknown thing that' etc.

A word of this kind has a double function, like a relative pronoun or adverb (see 473): it acts as a subject, object or adverb in its own clause, but it also acts as a conjunction, joining its clause to the rest of the sentence.

> **Whoever** *comes to the door, tell them I'm out.*
> **Whoever** *phoned just now was very polite.*
> *I'm not opening the door,* **whoever** *you are.*
> *Send it to* **whoever** *pays the bills.*

Whatever you do, I'll always love you.
Whatever is in that box is making a very funny noise.
Keep calm, whatever happens.
Spend the money on whatever you like.
Whichever of them you marry, you'll have problems.
We're free all next week. You'll be welcome whichever day you come.
However much he eats, he never gets fat.
People always want more, however rich they are.
However you travel, it'll take you at least three days.
Whenever I go to London I try to see Vicky.
You can come whenever you like.
Wherever you go, you'll find Coca-Cola.
The people were friendly wherever we went.

2   *whoever, whichever* and *whatever*: subjects and objects

Whoever, whichever and *whatever* can be the subjects or objects of the verbs
in their clauses. (Note that *whomever* is not used in modern English.)
Whoever directed this film, it's not much good. (subject)
Whoever you marry, make sure he can cook. (object)
Whatever you say, I don't think he's the right man for you. (object)
Whichever and *whatever* can also go with nouns as determiners. Note the
word order when they go with objects.
Whichever room you use, make sure you clean it up afterwards.
Whatever problems you have, you can always come to me for help.
If you change your mind for whatever reason, just let me know.

3   clauses as subjects or objects

A clause with *whoever, whichever* and *whatever* can be the subject or object
of the verb in the other clause.
Whoever told you that was lying.
I'll marry whoever I like.
Whatever you want is fine with me.
Prisoners have to eat whatever they're given.
Whichever climber gets to the top first will get a £5,000 prize.
I'll take whichever tent you're not using.

4   *whenever* = 'every time that'

Whenever can suggest repetition, in the sense of 'every time that'.
Whenever I see you I feel nervous.
I stay with Monica whenever I go to London.

5   *whoever* etc ... *may*

May can be used after some of these words to suggest ignorance or
uncertainty.
He's written a book on the philosopher Matilda Vidmi, whoever she may be.
She's just written to me from Llandyfrdwy, wherever that may be. ▶

6 leaving out the verb

In a clause like *whatever his problems may be*, where *whatever* is the complement of the verb *be*, it is possible to leave out the verb. This happens mostly with *whatever* and *however*. Examples:

Whatever his problems, *he has no right to behave like that.*
A serious illness, **whatever its nature**, *is almost always painful.*
A grammar rule, **however true**, *is useless unless it can be understood.*

7 informal uses

In an informal style, these conjunctions are sometimes used as short answers.

'When shall we start?' **'Whenever.'** (= *'Whenever you like.'*)
'Potatoes or rice?' **'Whichever.'** (= *'I don't mind.'*)
Whatever can mean 'or anything else'.
Would you like some orange juice or a beer **or whatever**?
If you play football or tennis **or whatever**, *it does take up a lot of time.*

8 *whatever* meaning 'at all'

After *any* and *no*, *whatever* can be used to mean 'at all'.

Don't you have **any** *regrets* **whatever**?
I can see **no** *point* **whatever** *in buying it.*

In a formal style, *whatsoever* is sometimes used as an emphatic form of *whatever* in this structure.

For other uses of *whatever* and *however*, see a good dictionary.
For *who ever*, *what ever* etc, see 595.
For *no matter who/what/* etc, see 371.

597 whose (question word)

1 with a noun or alone

The question word *whose* can be used with a noun as a determiner like *my*, *your* etc.

Whose car *is that outside?*
Whose garden *do you think looks the nicest?*
Whose can also be used alone, like *mine*, *yours* etc.
Whose *is that car outside?*
'Whose *is this?'* *'Mine.'*

2 prepositions

Prepositions can normally come either before *whose* (more formal) or at the end of the clause (less formal). See 440 for details.

For whose *benefit were all these changes made?*
Whose *side are you* **on**?
In short questions with no verb, prepositions can only come before *whose*.
'I'm going to buy a car.' **'With whose** *money?'* (NOT *Whose money with?*)

For the relative pronoun *whose*, see 475.
For *whose and who's*, see 598.

598 **whose** and **who's**

Whose is a possessive word meaning 'of whom / which', used in questions and relative clauses. *Who's* is the contraction of *who is* or *who has*. Compare:
- **Whose** *is that coat?* (NOT ~~*Who's is that coat?*~~)
  *It was a decision **whose** importance was not realised at the time.*
    (NOT ...~~*who's importance*~~...)
- *Do you know anybody **who's** going to France in the next few days?*
    (NOT ...~~*anybody whose going*~~...)
  *I've got a cousin **who's** never been to London.*
    (NOT ...~~*whose never been*~~...)

There is a similar confusion between *its* and *it's*: see 303.

599 **why** and **why not**

1 **replies**

We generally use *Why not?*, not *Why?*, in short replies to negative statements. Compare:
  *'They've decided to move to Devon.' '**Why?**'*
  *'I can't manage tomorrow evening.' '**Why not?**'*
  (More natural than *Why?*)
Why not? can also be used to agree to a suggestion.
  *'Let's eat out this evening.' 'Yes, **why not?**'*

2 *why should ...?*

A structure with *why* followed by *should* can suggest surprise.
  *I wonder **why** she **should** want to go out with me.*
    (US ... *why she **would**...*)
The structure can also suggest anger or refusal to do something.
  *I don't see **why** we **should** have to pay for your mistake.*
  *'Give me a cigarette.' '**Why should** I?'*

For a similar structure with *how*, see 464.2.

3 **infinitive structures**

Why can be followed by an infinitive without *to*. This structure can be used to suggest that an action is unnecessary or pointless.
  ***Why argue** with him? He'll never change his mind.*
    (NOT ~~*Why arguing*~~...? OR ~~*Why to argue*~~...?)
  ***Why pay** more at other shops? We have the best value.*
***Why not** + infinitive without to** is used to make suggestions.
  *'Sandy's in a bad mood.' '**Why not give** her some flowers?'*
    (NOT ~~*'Why not giving*~~...?')
Why don't ...? can be used in the same way.
  ***Why don't** you give her some flowers?*
  ***Why don't** we go and see Julie?*

600 will

1 forms

Will is a modal auxiliary verb (see 344–345). It has no *-s* in the third person singular; questions and negatives are made without *do*; after *will*, we use an infinitive without *to*.

Will the train be on time?

Contractions are *'ll, won't*.

Do you think it'll rain?   *It won't rain.*

Would is used as a past or less definitive form of *will* for some of its meanings; for details, see 604.

2 future auxiliary

We can use *will* as an auxiliary verb when we make predictions about the future. For details, see 221.

I will be happy when this is finished.
This time tomorrow I'll be sitting in the sun.
He will have finished the whole job by this evening.

For the use of *shall* as a future auxiliary, see 221.

3 certainty

Will can express certainty or confidence about present or future situations.

As I'm sure you will understand, we cannot wait any longer for our order.
Don't phone them now – they'll be having dinner.
'There's somebody coming up the stairs.' 'That'll be Mary.'

Will have + past participle can express certainty or confidence about the past.

Dear Sir, You will recently have received a form . . .
I wonder why we haven't heard from him – do you think he won't have got our letter yet?
We can't go and see them now – they'll have gone to bed.

For more about the use of *will* and other modal verbs to express certainty, probability and logical deductions, see 345.

For modal verbs with perfect infinitives (e.g. *won't have got*), see 278.3.

4 willingness and decisions

We can use *will* to express the speaker's willingness, or a decision to do something.

'Can somebody help me?' 'I will.'   *'There's the doorbell.' 'I'll go.'*

Will can express a firm intention, a promise or a threat.

I really will stop smoking.   *I'll definitely pay you back next week.*
I'll kill her for this.

We can use *will not* or *won't* to talk about unwillingness or refusal.

She won't open the door.   *'Give me a kiss.' 'No, I won't.'*
The car won't start.

Would not can refer to past refusal.

She wouldn't open the door.   *The car wouldn't start this morning.*

5 requests, orders and offers

We use *will you* to tell people what to do.

> ***Will you*** *send me the bill, please?*   *Come this way,* ***will you****?*
> ***Will you*** *be quiet!*

Would you is 'softer', more polite.

> ***Would you*** *send me the bill, please?*   *Come this way,* ***would you****?*

Will can be used in affirmative structures to give impersonal, military-type orders.

> *All staff* ***will*** *submit weekly progress reports.*

Will you ... ? can be used to ask about people's wishes.

> ***Will you*** *have some more potatoes?*   *What* ***will you*** *drink?*

Won't you ... ? expresses a pressing offer.

> ***Won't you*** *have some more wine?*

For more about requests, see 483.

6 habits and characteristics

We can use *will* to talk about habits and characteristic (typical) behaviour.

> *She***'ll** *sit talking to herself for hours.*
> *When you look at clouds they* ***will*** *often remind you of animals.*
> *If something breaks down and you kick it, it* ***will*** *often start working again.*
> *Sulphuric acid* ***will*** *dissolve most metals.*

Sentences with stressed *will* can be used to criticise people's typical behaviour.

> *She* ***WILL*** *fall in love with the wrong people.*
> *Well, if you* ***WILL*** *keep telling people what you think of them ...*

Would is used in a similar way to refer to the past. For details, see 604.7.

> *On Saturdays, when I was a child, we* ***would*** *all get up early and go fishing.*
> *He was a nice boy, but he* ***WOULD*** *talk about himself all the time.*

7 *will* and *want*

Will and *want* can both be used to talk about wishes, but they are rather different. *Will* is used mostly in 'interpersonal' ways, to express wishes that affect other people through orders, requests, offers, promises etc. *Want* simply refers to people's wishes – nothing more. *Will* is to do with actions, *want* is to do with thoughts. Compare:

– ***Will*** *you open the window?* (an order)
  Do you ***want*** *to open the window?* (a question about somebody's wishes)
– *She* ***won't*** *tell anybody.* (= *She refuses to ...*)
  She doesn't ***want*** *to tell anybody.* (= *She prefers not to ...*)

Note that *will* cannot be used with a direct object.

> *Do you* ***want*** */ ***Would you like*** an aspirin?* (NOT ~~*Will you an aspirin?*~~)

601 wish

1 *wish* + infinitive

We can use ***wish*** + **infinitive** to mean *want. Wish* is very formal in this sense. Note that progressive forms are not used.

> *I* ***wish to see*** *the manager, please.* (NOT ~~*I'm wishing to see ...*~~)
> *If you* ***wish to reserve*** *a table, please telephone after five o'clock.*   ▶

An **object + infinitive** structure is also possible.

>*We do not **wish our names to appear** in the report.*
>*Do you **wish me to serve** drinks on the terrace, madam?*

Note that ***wish* + direct object** is not normally possible without a following infinitive.

>*I **want/would like an appointment** with the manager.*
>(NOT ~~*I wish an appointment with the manager.*~~)

2   *I wish you . . .*

Wish is used with two objects in some fixed expressions of good wishes.

>*I **wish you a Merry Christmas**.   We all **wish you a speedy recovery**.*
>*Here's **wishing you all the best** in your new job.*

3   *wish* + *that*-clause: meaning

We can also use *wish* with a *that*-clause (*that* can be dropped in an informal style). In this case, *wish* does not mean 'want' – it expresses regret that things are not different, and refers to situations that are unreal, impossible or unlikely. Tenses are similar to those used with *if* (see below).

>*I **wish (that)** I was better looking.   Don't you **wish (that)** you could fly?*
>*We all **wish (that)** the snow would stay forever.*

***Wish* + *that*-clause** is not generally used for wishes about things that seem possible in the future. We often use *hope* in this sense (see 252).

>*I **hope** you pass your exams.* (NOT ~~*I wish you would pass your exams.*~~)
>*I **hope** you feel better tomorrow.* (NOT ~~*I wish you felt better tomorrow.*~~)

4   *wish* + *that*-clause: tenses

In a *that*-clause after *wish*, we generally use the same tenses as we would use, for instance, after 'It would be nice if . . .' (see 260). Past tenses are used with a present or future meaning.

>*I wish I **spoke** French.* (= *It would be nice if I **spoke** French.*)
>*I wish I **had** a yacht.   I wish tomorrow **was** Sunday.*
>*All the staff wish you **weren't** leaving so soon.*
>*Do you ever wish you **lived** somewhere else?*

Many people use *were* instead of *was* in this structure, especially in a formal style.

>*I wish that I **were** better looking.*

Past perfect tenses are used for wishes about the past.

>*I wish you **hadn't said** that.* (= *It would be nice if you **hadn't said** that.*)
>*Now she wishes she **had gone** to university.*

In informal speech, sentences like *I wish you'**d have seen** it* sometimes occur. For similar structures with *if*, see 261.9.

5   *wish . . . would*

Would is very common in *that*-clauses after *wish* (more common than it is in *if*-clauses). *Would* is used as a 'softened' equivalent of *will*, referring to people's willingness, unwillingness, insistence or refusal to do things (see 604.2).

>*Everybody wishes you **would** go home.* (= *Why **won't** you go home?*)
>*I wish you **would** stop smoking.* (= *Why **won't** you stop smoking?*)

Wish ... would usually expresses regret, dissatisfaction, impatience or irritation because somebody ***will** keep doing something* or ***won't** do something*.

> *I wish she **would** be quiet.*
> *I wish you **wouldn't** keep making that stupid noise.*
> *I wish the postman **would** come soon.*

Sometimes we talk as if things and situations could be willing or unwilling, or could insist or refuse to do things.

> *I wish it **would** stop raining. (It **will** keep on raining!)*
> *Don't you wish that this moment **would** last for ever?*

Wish ... would can be like an order or a critical request. Compare:

- *I **wish** you **wouldn't** drive so fast.* (Similar to *Please don't drive so fast.*)
  *I **wish** you **didn't** drive so fast.* (More like *I'm sorry you drive so fast.*)
- *I **wish** you **wouldn't** work on Sundays.* (= *Why don't you stop?*)
  *I wish you **didn't** work on Sundays.* (= *It's a pity.*)

6 *would* not used

When we are not talking about willingness, unwillingness, insistence or refusal, *wish ... would* is not normally used.

> *I wish today **was** Saturday.*
> > (NOT ~~I wish today **would be** Saturday~~ – Nothing to do with willingness.)
> *I wish I **could** manage to give up smoking.*
> > (NOT ~~I wish I **would** give up smoking~~ – It is strange to wish for oneself to be willing.)
> *I **hope** she doesn't have an accident.*
> > (NOT ~~I wish she **wouldn't** have an accident~~ – Nothing to do with willingness.)
> *I **hope** there's a strike tomorrow.*
> > (NOT ~~I wish there **would be** a strike tomorrow~~ – We can't say that *'there'* is willing to strike.)

For more about *hope*, see 252.
For similar structures with *if only*, see 265.
For other cases where past tenses have present or future meanings, see 422.

602 with

1 *trembling with rage, blue with cold* etc

With is used in a number of expressions which say how people are showing their emotions and sensations.

> *My father was trembling **with** rage.*
> *Annie was jumping up and down **with** excitement.*
> *When I found her she was blue **with** cold.*
> *white **with** fear/rage*
> *red **with** anger/embarrassment*
> *green **with** envy*
> *shivering **with** cold*

▶

2 *angry with* etc

With is also used after a number of adjectives which say how people are feeling towards others.

> *I'm cross **with** you.   You're very patient **with** me.*
> *angry **with**   furious **with**   pleased **with**   upset **with***

Note that *with* is not generally used after words like *kind, nice, polite, rude, good,* which say how people *act* towards others.

> *She was very **nice to** me.* (NOT *...~~nice with me.~~*)

3 *with* meaning 'against'

After *fight, struggle, quarrel, argue, play* and words with similar meanings, *with* can be used with the same meaning as *against.*

> *Don't fight **with** him – he's bigger than you are.*
> *Will you play chess **with** me?*

4 accompanying circumstances and reasons

With can introduce accompanying circumstances (rather like *and there is/was*).

> *The runners started the race **with a light following wind**.*

With can also introduce the reasons for a situation (rather like *because there is/was*).

> ***With all this work to do**, I won't have time to go out.*
> ***With three people away ill**, we'll have to close the shop.*
> ***With friends like you**, who needs enemies?*

Without can be used in similar ways.

> *The meeting finished **without a single disagreement**.*
> ***Without Sue and Jake**, we're going to have trouble finishing the repairs.*

5 possession

With is very often used, like *have,* to indicate possession and similar ideas.

> *There are so many people around **with** no homes.*
>   (= ... *who **have** no homes.*)
> *We need a computer **with** a huge memory.*
> *They've bought a house **with** a big garden.*
> *He didn't just look like a fish: he looked like a fish **with** a headache.*

6 clothing, voices, transport etc

Note that *in* is often used instead of *with* to refer to articles of clothing.

> *Who's the man **in the funny hat**?*
> *Could you go and give this paper to the woman **in glasses**?*

We say ***in** a ... voice,* not *~~with a ... voice.~~*

> *Why are you talking **in such a loud voice**?*

Note also: ***by** car/train/* etc (NOT *~~with the car~~* etc), and *write **in** pencil/ink.*

For other uses of *with,* see a good dictionary.
For the difference between *by* and *with,* see 117.
For omission of pronouns in expressions like *a cake with cream on (it),* see 181.13.

603 worth

1 *worth a few pounds*

Worth can be followed by a noun phrase which describes the value of something.

> *That piano must be **worth a few pounds**.*
> *I don't think their pizzas are **worth the money**.*
> *'Shall I talk to Rob?' 'It's not **worth the trouble**.'*

In questions about the value of something, either *what* or *how much* can be used.

> ***What/How much** is that painting worth?*

2 *five pounds' worth of...*

A possessive structure can be used before *worth* in measurement expressions.

> *Could I have **five pounds' worth** of petrol, please?*
> *They've ordered **a million dollars' worth** of computer software.*

For more about possessives in measurement expressions, see 382.7.

3 *It's worth talking to Joe*

When we talk about the value of an activity, we can use an *-ing* form with *worth*. The *-ing* clause cannot be the subject, but we often use a structure with preparatory *it*. (This structure is more common in British than in American English.)

> ***It**'s worth talking to Joe.* (NOT ~~Talking to Joe is worth.~~)
> ***It** isn't worth **repairing** the car.* (NOT ~~Repairing the car isn't worth.~~)
> *Is **it** worth **visiting** Leicester?*

It can be used to refer to an action mentioned earlier.

> *'Shall we take the car?' 'No, it's not worth **it**.'*

4 *Joe's worth talking to*

Ideas like the ones in paragraph 3 can also be expressed by a structure in which the object of the *-ing* form (*Joe, the car, Leicester*) is made the subject of the sentence.

> ***Joe**'s worth talking to.*
> ***The car** isn't worth repairing.*
> (NOT ~~The car isn't worth repairing **it**.~~)
> (NOT ~~The car isn't worth **to be repaired**.~~)
> *Is **Leicester** worth visiting?*
> ***She**'s not worth getting angry with.*

For more about structures in which the object of a verb is the subject of the sentence (e.g. *She's easy to amuse*), see 285.4.

5 *worthwhile*

In structures with *-ing* forms, *worthwhile* (or *worth while*) is sometimes used instead of *worth*, particularly to express the idea 'worth spending time'.

> *Is it **worthwhile** visiting Leicester?* ▶

Infinitives are also possible after *worthwhile*.

> We thought it might be **worthwhile to compare** this year's accounts with
>   last year's.

Note also the structure *worth somebody's while*.

> Would you like to do some gardening for me? I'll make it **worth your while**.
>   (= ... I'll pay you enough.)

6 *well worth*

Worth can be modified by *well*.

> Leicester's **well worth** visiting. (NOT ... ~~very worth~~...)

604 would

1 forms

Would, the past form of *will*, is a modal auxiliary verb (see 344–345).
Questions and negatives are made without *do*; after *would*, we use an
infinitive without *to*.

> **Would** your daughter like to play with my little girl?

Contractions are *'d*, *wouldn't*.

> **I'd** like some advice, please.
>
> I wish she **wouldn't** take things so seriously.

2 *would* and *will*

Would is often used in similar ways to *will*; it can act as a past of *will* in
indirect speech, for example, and as a softer, less definite form of *will* in
other cases.

3 indirect speech

In indirect speech, *would* is used after past reporting verbs where *will* was
used in direct speech. For details, see 481.

> Direct speech: Tomorrow **will** be fine.
> Indirect speech: The forecast said the next day **would** be fine.

Would itself does not usually change in indirect speech (see 482).

> Direct speech: **Would** you like some help?
> Indirect speech: She asked if I **would** like some help.

4 future in the past

Would is also used to express the idea of 'future in the past' – to talk about
a past action which had not yet happened at the time we are talking about.
For details, see 226.

> In Berlin, he first met the woman whom he **would** one day marry.
>
> There was a chance that my letter **would** arrive in time.

5 interpersonal uses

Would is used in polite requests and offers; it often acts as a softer form
of *will*.

> **Would you** open the window, please?
>
> If you **would** come this way ...

Would you mind standing up for a moment?
Would you like tea, or would you prefer coffee?
I'd like to speak to John for a moment, please.

6   past willingness and refusals

Would can refer to past willingness of a general kind, but not to willingness
to do something on a particular past occasion. Compare:
  She would hoover, dust and iron, but she didn't like doing windows.
  She agreed to come and see me. (NOT ~~She would come and see me.~~)
But *would not* can be used to refer to a refusal on a particular past occasion.
  I asked him very politely, but he wouldn't tell me.
  The car wouldn't start again this morning.

For present refusals with *will not*, see 222.

7   past habits

Would is used as the past of *will* (see 600.6) to talk about past habits and
typical characteristics.
  When she was old, she would sit in the corner talking to herself for hours.
  Sometimes he would bring me little presents without saying why.
  On Sundays when I was a child we would all get up early and go fishing.
Sentences with stressed *would* can be used to criticise people's behaviour.
  He was a nice boy, but he WOULD talk about himself all the time.
Stressed *would* can also be used to criticise a single past action – the
meaning is 'that's typical of you'.
  You WOULD tell Mary about the party – I didn't want to invite her.

8   *would* and *used to*

Both *would* and *used to* (see 577) can refer to repeated actions and events in
the past, but only *used to* can refer to past states. Compare:
  When we were children we would/used to go skating every winter.
  I used to have an old Rolls-Royce.
      (BUT NOT ~~I would have an old Rolls-Royce.~~)

9   conditional auxiliary

The mixed verb *would/should* (see 498) is often used as an auxiliary with
verbs that refer to unreal or uncertain situations – for example in sentences
with *if*. (Compare the use of *will/shall* to refer to more definite situations.)
  I should/would tell you if I knew.
  It would have been nice if he'd thanked you.

For *would* after *wish*, see 601.5.
For *would* after *if only*, see 265.
For *will*, see 600.

605 **yes** and **no**

1 answers to negatives

In English, *yes* is used with affirmative sentences and *no* with negative sentences. In answers to negative questions and statements, *yes* and *no* are chosen according to the form of the answer, not in order to show agreement or disagreement with the speaker.

> *'Aren't you going out?' 'No, I'm not.'* (NOT ~~*'Yes, I'm not.'*~~)
> *'I have no idea what's happening.' 'No, I haven't either.'*
> (NOT ~~*'Yes, I haven't too.'*~~)
> *'Haven't you got a raincoat?' 'Yes, I have.'* (NOT ~~*'No, I have.'*~~)

2 contradicting

Some languages have a special word for contradicting negative statements or suggestions (e.g. French *si* or German *doch*). English does not have a word like this. Negative statements are generally contradicted with a short answer structure (see 493).

> *'The phone isn't working.' '(Yes,) it is.'*
> (NOT ~~*'The phone isn't working.' 'Yes.'*~~)

Affirmative statements or suggestions are contradicted with negative short answers.

> *'It's raining.' '(No,) it isn't.'*

For more about negative questions, see 360.
For *yes* and *no* in answers to *Do/Would you mind . . . ?*, see 342.

Index

a/an 63–64; 66; 68–69
  and *any* 54.4
  and *some* 521.4
  in measuring expressions 69.17
  meaning 'per' 385.19
  with uncountables 148.6
  position with *as/how/so/too* + adjective 16
  see also **articles**
a bit 106
  modifying adjectives/adverbs 153
  with comparatives 139.1
a bit of a 154.3
a couple of . . . with plural verb 503.2
a few and *a little* 322
a friend of mine etc 434
a good three weeks etc 509.6
a great deal 326
a group of . . . with plural verb 503.2
a large number 326
a little and *a few* 322
a little modifying adjectives/adverbs 153
  with comparatives 139.1
a long time and *long* 323
a long way and *far* 206
a lot 326
  with comparatives 139.1
a lot of . . . with plural verb 503.2
a number of . . . with plural verb 503.2
abbreviated styles 1
abbreviations 2
able 3
  was able and *could* 122.3
about adverb particle 19
about and *(a)round* 60
  and *on* 4
about to 5
above adverb particle 19
above and *over* 6
accept and *agree* 7
accommodation uncountable 148.3
according to 8
accuse preposition 437
accustomed to + *-ing* form or infinitive 296.11
ache simple or progressive 445.7
acronyms 2
across adverb particle 19
across and *over* 6.3; 9
  and *through* 9.5
active and passive reasons for choice 289.3
  see also **passive**
active and passive infinitive with similar
  meaning 287
active past participles 404.3
active verb forms 10
actor, *actress* 227.4
actual(ly) 11
  discourse marker 159.15,16,20

AD and *BC* 151.3
addresses prepositions 80.5
adjectives + *-ing* forms 294
  + infinitives 285
  after copular verbs 147.2
  after nouns 15.4
  with pronouns (e.g. *poor you*) 424.3
  after verbs in descriptions 147.5
  and adverbs 20; 21
  attributive and predicative position 15
  commas 14.5
  comparison 135–139
  complementation 12
  position of complements 15.7
  ending in *-ed*: pronunciation 13
  modification 153
  order before nouns 14
  position after *as, how, so, too* 16
  position after nouns 15.4
  position in expressions of measurement 15.6
  with *and* 17; 51.3
  without nouns (e.g. *the accused, the beautiful,*
    the blind, the former) 18
admit . . .*ing* 293.1
adopted position and meaning 405.3
advanced active past participle 404.3
adverb particles 19; 582
  modification for degree 156.1
adverbs comparison 137
  modification 153
  position 22; 23; 217.4 (fronting)
  spelling of adverbs in *-ly* 530
  -ically 256.5
  adverbs and adjectives 20; 21
advertisements abbreviated style 1.1
advice uncountable 148.3
advise + *-ing* form or infinitive 296.4
affect and *effect* 24
afloat position, and *floating* 15.3
afraid 25
  position, and *frightened* 25.3
  + *-ing* form or infinitive 296.13
  preposition 437
  afraid so/not 515
  very much afraid 25.3
after adverb 26
  after and *afterwards, then* etc 26.2
after (preposition) and *according to* 8
after conjunction 27
  tenses 27.2, 3; 421.5; *after* . . .*ing* 27.4; 406.6
after all 28; 159.19
  after all and *finally* 28.2
afternoon, *evening* and *night* 29
afterwards and *after* 26.2
again and *back* 86
age 30

age marked and unmarked uses 341
  prepositions 30
aged pronunciation 13
agent in passive structures 408
ago 31
  position 31.1
  tenses 31.2
  and *before* 31.4; 95.2
  and *for* 31.3
agree non-progressive verb 451.2
  preposition 437
  structures 295.2
  and *accept* 7
ahead adverb particle 19
ain't 144.4 (notes)
alight position 15.3
alike 32
  position 15.3
alive position 15.3
all 33–38
  subject, object or complement 34
  with nouns and pronouns 35
  with verbs 36
  omission of article 69.6
  and *every* 37
  and *whole* 38
  all, everybody and *everything* 34
  all I want is . . . etc 131.5
  all the + comparative 138.6
all ready and *already* 44
all right and *alright* 39
  all right (change of subject) 159.8
all the same 159.5
all together and *altogether* 49
allow structures 40.1
  + *-ing* form or infinitive 296.4
  allow, permit and *let* 40
almost with superlatives 139.3
  and *nearly* 41
alone position 15.3
  alone, lonely, lonesome and *lone* 42
along adverb particle 19
along and *through* 43
already with present perfect 418.5
  already, yet and *ever* 197.7
  already, yet and *still* 539
  already and *all ready* 44
alright and *all right* 39
also, *as well* and *too* 45; 46
  also and *even* 195.3
alternate(ly) and *alternative(ly)* 47
although and *though* 48
altogether and *all together* 49
always with progressive forms 452
  and *ever* 197.2
  position 23
  position with imperatives 268.7
American 354 (notes)
American and British English 50
among and *between* 104
amount (of) 326.4
  omission of article 69.8

and after *try, wait, go* etc 52
  in numbers 385.9
  with adjectives 17
  commas 455.1, 5
angry preposition 437; 602.2
annoyed by/with 405.5
another and *other(s)* 53
  another three weeks etc 53.2; 509.6
another thing is 159.11
anxious preposition 437
any 54
  non-assertive word 374.1
  and *some* 522
  and *a/an* 66.2
  and *every* 55
  and no article 67
  not any and *no* 369
  any different, any good/use 56
  with comparatives 139.1
  any the + comparative 138.6
  after superlatives 138.13
  singular or plural verb 509.5
  if any 261.11
  hardly any 41.3
any more and *anymore* 57
  not any more 372
anybody etc 523
  non-assertive words 374.1
  anybody and *anyone* 523
  position with adjectives 15.5
anyhow 159.7
anyone and *any one* 523.7
anything non-assertive word 374.1
  position with adjectives 15.5
  anything much 523.5
anyway 159.7
anywhere non-assertive word 374.1
  position with adjectives 15.5
apart from 159.12
  apart from, besides and *except* 101
apologies 520.7
apologise preposition 437
apostrophe 453
  in abbreviations 2.5
apparently 159.16
appear 58; 147
  non-progressive verb 451.2
  and *seem* 58.2
  + infinitive (negative structure) 359.4
  there appears to be 563.5
appreciate . . . *ing* 293.1
approach no preposition 439
Arab, *Arabian, Arabic* 354 (notes)
areas 385.18
aren't I? 466.1
arise and *rise* 59
around, *round* and *about* 60
arouse and *rouse* 61
arrange structures 295.3
arrive preposition 79.3; 437
arrived active past participle 404.3
art older English form of *are* 388

articles 62–69
and possessives 433.6
as determiners 157
left out in abbreviated styles 1
with abbreviations 2.3, 4
see also **a/an, the**
as + adjective + article + noun 16
+ object complement 580.2
+ object pronouns 70.4
modifying adjectives/adverbs 153
replacing subject/object 320.4; 70.11; 557.3
inversion after *as* 298.6
as I or *as me* etc 425.9
as and *as much* 153
and *how* 254.2
and *like* 320
as, because, since and *for* 72
as, than and *that* 557
as, when and *while* 73
special word order after *as* and *though* 71
as ... as 70
as a matter of fact 159.20
as a result 159.14
as far as ... is concerned 159.1
as few 156.2
as for 159.1
as I was saying 159.9
as if and *as though* 74
as it were 541
as little 156.2
as long as 75; 262
as much/many 156.2
as much/many as 70.5
as regards 159.1
as soon as 556
as though and *as if* 74
as usual 76
as well, *also* and *too* 45; 46
as well as 77
as well as that 159.11
as you know 320.5
aside adverb particle 19
ask 78
asleep position, and *sleeping* 15.3
astonish non-progressive verb 451.2
at, *on* and *in* (place) 80
at, *on* and *in* (time) 81
at/in and *to* 79
at all 82
at any rate 159.7
at first and *first* 83
at home 251.1; 69.1
at last, *finally* and *in/at the end* 210
at least 311.6
discourse marker 159.7, 16
at/in the end, *at last* and *finally* 210
(at) what time preposition left out 439.5
ate British and American pronunciations 300.3
attempt + *-ing* form or infinitive 296.11
attention signals 463.3
author, *authoress* 227

autumn article 69.10
auxiliary verbs 84
emphasis 189.2
available position 15.4; 477.6
avoid ...*ing* 293.1
await 584
awake and *asleep* 85.3
position 15.3
awake, wake and *(a)waken* 85
away adverb particle 19

back adverb particle 19
and *again* 86
backward(s) 586
bad comparative and superlative 136.2
preposition 437
badly comparative and superlative 137
baggage uncountable 148.3
bath and *bathe* 87
BC and *AD* 151.3
be copular verb 147
progressive forms 88
subjunctive forms (*I be, I were* etc) 541
with auxiliary *do* 89
left out in abbreviated styles 1
with ages 30
in measurements 91
be and *have* 91
be + infinitive (*am to* ...) 90
future in the past (*was to* ...) 226
be able 3
be afraid and *fear* 25.1
be born 107.1
be finished 211
be going to 220
be gone 233
be supposed to 547
be sure and ... 52
be that as it may 541
be used *to* ...*ing* 295.2; 578
bear verb 107.2
can't bear 296.11
beat and *win* 92
because and *because of* 93
because, as, since and *for* 72
position of *because*-clauses 93.2
become copular verb 147
changes 129.1
bed expressions without article 69.1
been meaning 'come' or 'gone' 94
before adverb 95
with perfect tenses 95; 418.5
and *ago* 31.4; 95.2
and *ever* 197.8
before (that) and *first* 95.3
before adverb particle 19
before conjunction 96
position of *before*-clauses 96
tenses 96.2, 3
before ...*ing* 406.6

before (preposition) and *in front of* 97
  and *until* 575.7
  before . . . ing 96.4
begin + *-ing* form or infinitive 296.10
  begin and *start* 98
behind adverb particle 19
believe non-progressive verb 451.2
  negative structures 359.1
  with *so* and *not* 359.3
  preposition 437
  believe somebody/something to be . . . 580.3
belong non-progressive verb 451.2
  preposition 437
beloved pronunciation 13
below adverb particle 19
below and *under* 99
besides 159.11
  beside and *besides* 100
  besides, except and *apart from* 101
best 136.2; 137
bet 102
better 103
  had better 234
between and *among* 104
bicycle expressions without article 69.1
big, *large* and *great* 105
billion 385.13
  billion(s) (of) 385.14
binoculars 501.7
bit 106; 426
  a bit of a 154
blessed pronunciation 13
blind *the blind* 18
bloody adjective and adverb 21.2; 550
blue *with cold* etc 602.1
boat expressions without article 69.1
body parts article use 69.16
bored and *boring* 404.2
born and *borne* 107
borrow and *lend* 108
both (of) with nouns and pronouns 109
  omission of article 69.6
  with verbs; (word order) 110
both . . . and 111
bread uncountable 148.3
break meaning of passive 414
bride, *bridegroom* 227.4
briefly 159.21
bring verb with two objects 583
  bring and *take* 112
bring up and *educate* 113
Britain, *the United Kingdom, the British Isles* and *England* 114
British 354.3
  the British 18.2
British and American English 50
Briton 354 (notes)
broad and *wide* 115
broadly speaking 159.12
build meaning of passive 414
burn British and American forms 300.3
burst out . . . *ing* 293.1

bus expressions without article 69.1
but meaning 'except' 116
  but I or *but me* etc 116; 425.9
  meaning 'only' 116.4
  ellipsis after *but* 182
buy verb with two objects 583
by adverb particle 19
by with agent in passive clauses 408
  by and other prepositions with past participles 405.5
  time 118
  by and *near* 119
  and *until* 575.6
  by (method, agent) and *with* (tools, etc) 117
by all/any/no means 340.2
by and large 159.12
by car, *bus* etc and other expressions without article 69.1
by far with superlatives 139.3
by oneself 471.6
by the kilo etc 69.17
by the time (that) 118
by the way 159.8

calculations in speech 385.21, 22
call meaning 'telephone' or 'visit' 120
can and *could* 121–125
  introduction 121
  ability 122
  possibility and probability 123
  interpersonal uses (requests, etc) 124
  with *see, hear* etc 125
  can and *be able* 3
  could and *was able* 122.3
  can and *must* (certainty) 350.2
  can't pronunciation 144.4 (notes)
  distancing use of *could* 161.3
  can, could, may and *might* 331.10, 11
can't bear + *-ing* form or infinitive 296.11
can't help 126
  cannot (help) but 116.3
can't seem to . . . 490.4
can't stand . . . ing 293.1
capital letters 529
  in *East, North* etc 176.3
car expressions without article 69.1
care *take care (of), care (about)* and *care for* 127
case (subject and object forms) 425
cattle 501.7
centuries *18th century* etc 385.7
certain + *-ing* form or infinitive 296.15
certainly and *surely* 548
certainly structuring argument 159.5
chair, *chairman, chairperson* 227.5
chance countable or uncountable 148.5
change countable or uncountable 148.5
  followed by plural 128
changes verbs 129
chess uncountable 148.3
chewing gum uncountable 148.3
church expressions without article 69.1

cinema article use 69.12
 preposition 438
city and *town* 130
classic and *classical* 256.4
classifying genitives 380
clean adverb 21.2
cleft sentences 131
clever preposition 437
close meaning of passive 414
 close and *shut* 132
cloth and *clothes* 133
collapsed active past participle 404.3
collective nouns singular or plural 503
college expressions without article 69.1
collocations 257.3
colon 454
colour with *be* 91
come and *go* 134
 come and . . . 52
 come changes 129.5
 come/go for a . . . 231
 come/go . . . ing 232
 come from 134.3
 come to 134.3
comic and *comical* 256.4
commas 455
 with adjectives 14.5
 in numbers 385.9
 in relative clauses 474
 with *and* 455.1, 5
commentaries abbreviated style 1.3
committed to + -*ing* form or infinitive 296.11
comparatives and superlatives 135–139
 adjectives 136
 adverbs 137
 the difference between comparatives and
  superlatives 138
 double comparatives 138.4
 comparatives with *the . . . the* 138.5
 three times more etc 138.7
 comparative with *all/any/none the* 138.6
 much, far etc with comparatives and
  superlatives 139.1,2
 non-assertive words after superlatives 138.13
 possessive *'s* after superlatives 138.9
 prepositions after superlatives 138.9
 the with superlatives 138.12
comparison structures 135
 as . . . as 70
 ellipsis in comparative structures 138.10
 see also **comparatives and superlatives**
complements of verbs, nouns and adjectives 140.2
 of verbs 579
 of nouns 377
 of adjectives 12
 clause and subject/object complements 140.1
compound nouns 379–382
concentrate not used with reflexive pronouns 471.9
concern non-progressive verb 451.2
concerned position and meaning 405.3
conditional clauses and verbs (terminology) 141.1
 distancing use 161.4

 in indirect speech 482.6
 not used in subordinate clauses 556.5
 see also **if**
congratulate, congratulations preposition 437
conjunctions general points 142
 problems 143
 conjunction + participle 406.6
consequently 159.14
consider . . . *ing* 293.1
 consider somebody/something to be . . . 580.3
 passive structures with *consider* 413
consist non-progressive verb 451.2
contain non-progressive verb 451.2
contemplate . . . *ing* 293.1
continually with progressive forms 452
continue + -*ing* form or infinitive 296.11
continuous see **progressive**
contractions 144
contrary *on the contrary / other hand* 145
 contrary and *opposite* 145.2
contrastive emphasis 189
control 146
co-ordinating conjunctions 142.2
copular verbs 147
costly 21
could see **can**
countable and uncountable nouns 148
 article use 64
countries and regions 354
country 149
court martial 15.4
cowardly 21
crash preposition 437
crooked pronunciation 13
cursed pronunciation 13
cut meaning of passive 414

daily adjective and adverb 21.1
dangling participles 406.4
dare 150
 I dare say 150.3
dashes 456
data 501.3
dates 151
day expressions without article 69.1
 the day we met etc 477.3
 articles with *Sunday* etc 69.10
dead and *died* 152
 dead slow etc 21.2
 dead and *deadly* 21.2
decimals 385.1
declarative questions 462
definite article 63–65, 68–69 and see **the**
degree modification of adjectives/adverbs 153
 of nouns 154
 of verbs 155
 of particles 156.1
 of prepositions 156.1
delay . . . *ing* 293.1
demonstratives 565
 as determiners 157

deny non-progressive verb 451.2
  deny...ing 293.1
depend non-progressive verb 451.2
  preposition 437
describe structures 583.6
  describe somebody/something as ... 580.2
deserve non-progressive verb 451.2
  deserve...ing passive meaning 293.3
details preposition 437
determiners 157
detest...ing 293.1
developed active past participle 404.3
diary entries abbreviated style 1.2
dice 501.3
die preposition 437
died and *dead* 152
difference countable or uncountable 148.5
  difference between 104.4
different 158
  and *other* 53.5
difficult to please etc 285.4
difficulty countable or uncountable 148.5
  preposition 437
dinner, *lunch* and *supper* 338
direct adverb 21.2
direct speech see **reporting**
directly, *immediately* etc (conjunctions) 267
disagree non-progressive verb 451.2
disappointed preposition 437
discourse markers 159
discuss(ion) preposition 437; 439
disinterested 160
dislike non-progressive verb 451.2
  structures 293.1,2
distancing 161
dive British and American forms 300.3
divide *between/among* 104.3
  into 437
divorce 329
do 162
  auxiliary verb 163
  general-purpose verb 164
  and *make* 164
  do...ing 164.3
  substitute verb 165
  stressed 159.5
  emphasis 189.2
  with *be* 89; 268.4
  do so, do it and *do that* 166
do you mind ... ? 342
dogged pronunciation 13
dost, *doth* older English forms of *do* 388
double comparatives 138.4
double negatives 361
doubling final consonants 535
doubt 167
  non-progressive verb 451.2
down adverb particle 19
  down and *up* 576
dozen(s) of 385.14
Dr 353.3

dream British and American forms 300.3
  preposition 437
dress 168
  not used with reflexive pronouns 471.9
drinking polite formulae 520.12
drive preposition 437
drown 169
drunken 405.6
duchess, *duke* 227.4
due to and *owing to* 170
during position 440.6
  and *for* 171
  and *in* 172

each 173
  between each 104.6
  each and *every* 174
each other and *one another* 175
early adjective and adverb 21.1
  comparative and superlative 137
  early, soon and *quickly* 525
easily with superlatives 139.3
east(ern), *north(ern)* etc 176
easy comparative and superlative 137
  adverb 21.2
  easy to amuse etc 285.4
echo questions 463.2
economic and *economical* 256.4
-ed and *-ing forms* 403–406
-ed pronunciation 13
  pronunciation of *aged, naked* etc 13
educate and *bring up* 113
effect and *affect* 24
effective and *efficient* 177
e.g. 159.13
either determiner 178
  singular or plural verb 509.5
either adverb: *not either* 364
  either, also, as well and *too* in negative
    sentences 46
either ... or 179
elder and *eldest* 15.2; 180
elect passive 413
electric and *electrical* 256.4
ellipsis (leaving out words) 181–186
  general 181
  with *and, but* and *or* 182
  in co-ordinate clauses 142.5
  at the beginning of a sentence 183
  after adjectives and determiners 184
  after comparatives and superlatives 138.10
  after auxiliary verbs 185
  after *if* 261.10
  of subject/object after *as* 70.10
  of subject/object after *than* 138.14
  to used instead of whole infinitive 186
  adjectives without nouns 18
  in abbreviated styles 1
  omission of *that* 560
else 187
elsewhere 187.6

embedding 188
emphasis 189
  cleft sentences 131
enable 190
end and *finish* 191
  at/in the end 210
end preposition 438
end-weight 289.4
endure *...ing* 293.1
England, *Britain*, *the United Kingdom* and *the British Isles* 114
English, *Englishman/woman* 354.3
  the English 18.2
enjoy 192
  enjoy...ing 293.1
enough 193
  modifying adjectives/adverbs 153
  + *for* + infinitive 280.8
enter preposition 437; 439
equipment uncountable 148.3
ergative verbs 579.3
escape *...ing* 293.1
escaped active past participle 404.3
especial(ly) and *special(ly)* 194
even 195
  with comparatives 139.1
even if/though 195.4
even so 195.5
evening *afternoon* and *night* 29
eventual(ly) 196
ever 197
  non-assertive word 374.1
  with present perfect 418.5
  after superlatives 138.13
  used for emphasis 189.3
  hardly ever 41.3
  ever and *before* 197.8
  ever, yet and *already* 197.7
  who ever etc 595
  whoever etc 596
ever so, *ever such* 198
every (one) 199
  every and *all* 37
  and *any* 55
  and *each* 174
every now and then 199.9
every other 199.9
every single 199.9
every six weeks etc 509.8
every so often 199.9
everybody + singular 199.7
  everybody and *all* 34.1,3
  and *everyone* 523
everyday 199.8
everyone and *every one* 523.7
everything + singular 199.7
  and *all* 34.2,3
  position with adjectives 15.5
example preposition 437
except (for) 159.12; 200
  except and *without* 200.6
  except I or *except me* etc 425.9

except, besides and *apart from* 101
excited by/about 405.5
  excited and *exciting* 404.2
exclamation mark 457
exclamations 201
  article use 69.14
excuse *...ing* 293.1
excuse me 520.6,7
expect + infinitive (negative structure) 359.4
  expect so/not 515
  expect, hope, wait and *look forward* 202
experience countable or uncountable 148.5
  experience and *experiment* 203
explain 204
extremely modifying adjectives/adverbs 153

face *...ing* 293.1
facing, *opposite* and *in front of* 272
fact *the fact that* 441.2; 559.3
faded active past participle 404.3
fair adverb 21.2
fairly modifying adjectives/adverbs 153
  fairly, quite, rather and *pretty* 205
fall (meaning 'autumn') article 69.10
fall with adjectives 129.8; 147.5
  fall, feel and *fill* 300.2
fallen active past participle 404.3
fancy *...ing* 293.1
far and *a long way* 206
far comparative and superlative 136.2; 207
  used to modify comparatives 139.1
  far too much etc 156.2
farther and *further* 207
fast and *slow* (marked and unmarked words) 341
fast comparative and superlative 137
  adverb 21.2
fear and *be afraid* 25.1
feel 147; 208
  simple and progressive forms 445.7
  can feel 125.1
  not used with reflexive pronouns 471.9
  feel somebody/something to be ... 580.3
  there is felt to be ... 412.3
  feel, fall and *fill* 300.2
feel like *...ing* 293.1
female and *feminine* 209
feminine and masculine words and pronouns: see **gender**
few and *a few* 322.3
  (a) few and *(a) little* 322
fewer and *less* 313
fewest and least 311
fight preposition 437
fill, *feel* and *fall* 300.2
finally 159.10
  and *after all* 28.2
  finally, at last and *in/at the end* 210
find *somebody/something to be* ... 580.3
  find and *found* 300.2
fine adverb 21.2

finish ...*ing* 293.1
  finish and *end* 191
finished adjective 211
  active past participle 404.3
first position with cardinal numbers 14.4
  first and *at first* 83
  and *before (that)* 95.3
  very first 139.4
  this is the first time etc + present perfect 419.7
first floor 385.8
first of all 159.10
first(ly), *second(ly)*, etc (structuring discourse) 159.10
fit non-progressive verb 451.2
  British and American forms 300.3
  fit and *suit* 212
flat and *flatly* 21.2
floating and *afloat* 15.3
floor *ground floor* etc 385.8
flow and *fly* 300.2
flu uncountable 148.4
fly and *flow* 300.2
follow *can follow* 125.3
foot as plural 385.14
  expressions without article 69.1
for purpose and cause 213
  for ...*ing* 294
  for, as, because and *since* 72
for time preposition left out 439.7; 584
  for and *ago* 31.3
  and *during* 171
  for, in, since and *from* 214
for + noun/pronoun + infinitive 280
  for there to be 280.10
  + object + infinitive after ask 78.3
for a long time and *long* 323
for example 159.13
for instance 159.13
for one/another thing 159.10
forbid + -*ing* form or infinitive 296.4
forever 197.2; with progressive forms 452
forget + -*ing* form or infinitive 296.1
  forget and *leave* 215
forgive ...*ing* 293.1
formality and politeness 216
former *the former* 18
forward adverb particle 19
  forward(s) 586
found and *find* 300.2
fractions 385.1
  with plural nouns 509.9
frankly 159.18
free adverb; *free* and *freely* 21.2
friendly 21
frightened and *afraid* 15.3
  frightened by/of 405.5; 437
from school, *university* etc (expressions without article) 69.1
from, since, for and *in* 214
from ... *to* 575.2
front *in front of* 97; 272

fronting 217
frown preposition 79.3
full stops 457
  in abbreviations 2.1
fun and *funny* 218
furniture uncountable 148.3
further and *farther* 207
furthermore 159.11
future 219–226
  introduction 219
  present progressive and *going to* 220
  shall/will 221 (future auxiliary)
    222 (interpersonal uses)
  shall/will contrasted with present 221.6, 7
  will with *if* 259.3
  future perfect 224
  future progressive 225
  future in the past 226
  be + infinitive 90
  simple present with future reference 223
  present tense with future reference in
    subordinate clauses 556; 102 (after *bet*);
    252 (after *hope*)
  distancing use of future verb forms 161.2

game and *play* 428
gather *I gather (that)* 246
gender 227
genitive see **possessive** *'s*
geographical expressions article use 69.18
gerunds see -**ing forms**
get structures and meanings 228
  got and *gotten* 228.7
  copular verb 147
  changes 129.2, 3
  two objects 583
  passive auxiliary 228.4
  in passive imperatives 268.3
  prepositions 437
  get and *go* (movement) 229
  have got see **have**
get divorced 329
get dressed 168.2
get married 329
get round *to* ...*ing* 295.2
get up and *rise* 59
get used to 578.3
give passive 410
  two objects 583
  give a cough, push, smile etc 230
give up ...*ing* 293.1
giving things polite formulae 520.18
glasses 501.7
go and *come* 134
go and *get* movement 229
go changes 129.4
  go and ... 52
  go/come for a ... 231
  go/come ...*ing* 232

go on + -*ing* form or infinitive 296.2
God Almighty 15.4
God save . . . 541
going to 220
  was going to 226
  gonna 220.7
gone active past participle 404.3
  gone with *be* 233
good comparative and superlative 136.2
  good and *well* 589.1
  any/no good . . . ing 292.5
  a good six weeks etc 509.6
good evening and *good night* 29
gotta 243.4
gotten 228.7
grass uncountable 148.3
grateful and *thankful* 558
Great Britain, *the United Kingdom, the British Isles* and *England* 114
great *a great deal* 326
great, *big* and *large* 105
greetings 520.2, 4
ground floor 385.8
group nouns singular or plural 503
grow changes 129.6
grown-up active past participle 404.3
guess *can guess* 125.2
  guess so/not 515

had better 234
had rather (obsolete form) 469.3
hair uncountable 148.3
half 235
  half as . . . as 70.6
  half seven (meaning 'seven thirty') 555.1
happen 236
  happen to with *if* 261.2
  negative structure 359.4
  there happens to be 563.5
hard comparative and superlative 137
  hard and *hardly* 21.2
hardly 21.2
  hardly, scarcely and *no sooner* 237
  hardly any, ever etc 41.3
hast older English form of *have* 388
hate non-progressive verb 451.2
  + -*ing* form or infinitive 296.9
hath older English form of *has* 388
have 238–243
  introduction 238
  auxiliary verb 239
  actions (*have a drink/bath* etc) 240
  have (got) possession, relationships, etc 241
  have + object + verb form 242
  have (got) to 243
  gotta 243.4
  have (got) to and *must* 352
  have and *be* 91
have a good *trip/journey* etc 520.9,10
have on *clothes* 168.3
he and *him* 425
  he or she 227.2

he and *she* for animals 227.1
headache, *toothache* etc countable or uncountable 148.4
headings abbreviated style 1.4
headlines 366
health social enquiries 520.3
hear non-progressive verb 451.2
  + object + infinitive or -*ing* form 245
  + object + past participle 245.3
  + infinitive with *to* in passive 412.2
  can hear 125.1
  hear and *listen (to)* 244
  I hear (that) 246
heavy and *light* marked and unmarked words 341
hell *what the hell* etc 595
help structures 247
  help . . . ing 293.1
  infinitive with *to* in passive 412.2
  can't help 126
here and *there* 248
  here's + plural 509.4
  here comes . . . 444.6
  here you are 520.18
hero, *heroine* 227.4
high comparative and superlative 137
  high and *highly* 21.2
  high and *tall* 249
historic and *historical* 256.4
holiday(s) 250
home 251
  expressions without article 69.1
home adverb particle 19
homeward(s) 586
honestly 159.18
hope structures 252
  negative structures 359.2
  hope so/not 515
  hope, expect, wait and *look forward* 202
hopefully 253
hospital expressions without article 69.1
host, *hostess* 227.4
house and *home* 251.2
how long are you here for? 323.5
how 254; 460
  in exclamations 201.1
  in questions and exclamations 254.1
  modifying adjectives/adverbs 153
  how + adjective + article + noun 16
  nominal relative pronoun 476.4
  how should . . . ? 464.2
  how to . . . 288
  how and *as* 254.2
  and *how much* 153
  and *what . . . like* 255
  how, what and *why* 254.3
how dare you? 150.3
how do you do? and *how are you?* 520.1
how ever, *the hell* etc 595
how few/little 156.2
how much/many 156.2
  how much of a 154.3
however discourse marker 159.3

however meaning 'it doesn't matter how' 596
hundred *a hundred* and *one hundred* 385.10
   hundred(s) (of) 385.14
hurry not used with reflexive pronouns 471.9
hurry up and . . . 52
hurt simple and progressive forms 445.7
hyphens 532

I and *me* etc 425, and see **personal pronouns**
I'm afraid meaning 'I'm sorry to tell you' 25.2;
   159.16
I beg your pardon 520.6, 7, 8
I bet + present tense with future meaning 102
I dare say 150.3
I don't know discourse marker 159.17
I feel discourse marker 159.16
I gather (that) . . . 246
I guess discourse marker 159.16
I hear (that) . . . 246
I hope + present tense with future meaning 252.1
I mean 159.15–17; 339.4
I reckon 159.16
I see (that) . . . 246
I should . . . meaning 'If I were you, I should . . .'
   264.2
I suppose 159.16
I think 159.16
I thought + negative expressing surprise 359.1
I understand (that) . . . 246
I wish 601
-ic and *-ical* 256
-ics singular words ending in *-ics* 501.3
idea countable or uncountable 148.5
   preposition 437
identifying relative clauses 474
idioms 257
if 258–265
   introduction 258
   ordinary tense-use 259
   special tense-use 260
   advanced points 261
   extra negative 261.7
   if I were 260.4
   had I . . . , were I . . . etc 261.6
   would in both clauses 261.8
   'd have in *if*-clause 261.9
   if . . . could/might 260.8
   if . . . should/happen to 261.2
   if . . . was/were to 261.3
   if with *will* 259.3; 261.1
   if structuring argument 159.5
   if and *in* case 271
   if and *when* 590
   if in reported questions 481.6
   if and *whether* 593
   if meaning 'although' 263
   other words with the same meaning as *if* 262
if any 261.11
if I were you 264
if in doubt etc 261.10

if it was/were not for 261.4
if not and *unless* 574.2
if only 265
if so/not 261.12
if you like etc 319.6
ill comparative and superlative 136.2
   preposition 437
   ill and *sick* 266
illnesses article use 69.15
   uncountable words 148.4
imagine (that) 262
   non-progressive verb 451.2
   imagine . . . ing 293.1
   imagine . . . + object + *-ing* 293.2
   negative structures 359.1
   imagine so/not 515
immediately conjunction 267
imperatives 268
   introduced by *let* 315
   question tags 466.2
   get in passive imperative 268.3
impossible to please etc 285.4
impress non-progressive verb 451.2
impressed preposition 437
in adverb particle 19
   with time expression and *later* 308
in, *at* and *on* (place) 80
   in and *into* 269
   in and *to* 79; 270
in, *at* and *on* (time) 81
   in and *during* 172
   in, for, since and *from* 214
in addition 159.11
in all/most/etc cases 159.12
in any case 159.11
in case and *if* 271
   in case of 271.4
in conclusion 159.21
in fact 159.20
in front of and *before* 97
   in front of, facing and *opposite* 272
in general 159.12
in my view/opinion 159.16
in order to 281
in order that 519
in other words 159.15
in particular 159.13
in short 159.21
in spite of 273
   in spite of this 159.3
in the first place 159.10
in/at the end, *at last* and *finally* 210
in the same way 159.4
in the way and *on the way* 587.5
in time and *on time* 438
incidentally 159.8
include non-progressive verb 451.2
increase preposition 437
increased active past participle 404.3
indeed 274
indefinite article 63–64; 66; 68–69 and see **a/an**
independent preposition 437

indirect object position 583.2,3
indirect speech 480–482
infinitive 275–288
  introduction 275
  negative, progressive, perfect and passive
    infinitive 276
  split infinitive 276.7
  infinitives without *to* 277; 77.2 (after *as well*
    as); 116.3 (after *but*)
  use of perfect infinitive 278
  active and passive infinitive with similar
    meaning 287
  infinitive after adjective 285
  after superlative 285.3
  after noun/pronoun 286
  after verb 283
  after verb + object 284
  after *who, what, how* etc 288
  after *why* 599.3
  after *as* 70.8
  to used instead of whole infinitive 186
  infinitive with its own subject 279.4
  the life to come etc 286.6
  easy to please etc 285.4
  a friend to play with / with whom to play etc
    286.5
  infinitive structure after *ask* 78.3
  be + infinitive 90
  infinitive or *-ing* form 296
infinitive clause as subject, object or
    complement 279
  introduced by *for* ... 280
  expressing purpose 281
  other uses 282
  position of preposition 440.5
  it as preparatory subject/object 301–2
information structure 289
  with *as well as* 77
information uncountable 148.3
-ing and -ed forms (verbal and adjectival uses)
    403–406
-ing forms (noun-like uses) 290–296
  introduction 290
  used as modifiers before nouns 291
  subject, object or complement 292
  me/my going, etc 292.4
  it as preparatory subject/object 292.5; 301–2
  -ing forms after verbs 293
  with passive meaning 293.3
  after noun or adjective 294
  after preposition 295
  after *to* 295.2
  after *as well as* 77.2
  after *before* 96.4
  after do etc 164.3
  -ing form or infinitive 296
initials names of organisations 2.2
insist preposition 437
instant *the instant* (conjunction) 267
instead (of) 297
instructions abbreviated style 1.1
intend + infinitive (negative structure) 359.4
  + *-ing* form or infinitive 296.11

interest(ed) preposition 437
  + *-ing* form or infinitive 296.16
  interested and *interesting* 404.2
interrogative pronouns see **question words**
interrogative structures 461–466 (see also
    questions)
into and *in* 269
intonation 540
intransitive verbs 579.2
introductions 520.1
inversion auxiliary verb etc before subject 298
  whole verb before subject 299
  after *as* 320.4
  in conditionals 261.6
inverted commas 458
invitations polite formulae 520.15
involve non-progressive verb 451.2
  involve...ing 293.1
involved position and meaning 405.3
Irish, *Irishman/woman* 354.3
irregular verbs 300
it empty subject 424.7
  referring to *nothing, everything, all* 424.6
  used to identify 424.5
  preparatory subject 301
  preparatory object 302
  preparatory subject/object for *-ing*
    forms 292.5
  cleft sentence structure with *it is ... that* 131.4
  it is I who am ... / It's me that is ... 477.5
  It is/was I/me who ... etc 425.7
  it and *one* 391.9
  it and *this/that* 566
it doesn't matter 371.4
it is true 159.5
it was not until ... 131.5
it was only when ... 131.5
it's no good/use ...ing 292.5
it's time structures 304
it's worth ...ing 603
its and *it's* 303

jeans 501.7
jobs article use 69.13
journey, *travel, trip* and *voyage* 572
just (time) 305
  just now 305.2
just used for emphasis 189.3
just and *justly* 21.2

keep + adjective 129.10
  keep (on) ...ing 293.1
kind preposition 437
kind of 159.16,17; 526
know 306
  know somebody/something to be ... 580.3
  known to 405.5
  I know and *I know it* 306
knowledge uncountable 148.3

labels abbreviated style 1.4
lack 343.4
  non-progressive verb 451.2
  preposition 437; 439
large *a large number of* 326.4
  large and *wide* 105.6
  large, big and *great* 105
last tenses with *this is the last* ... etc 307.5
  very last 139.4
  position with numbers 14.4
  last and *latest* 307.4
  last and *the last* 307
  at last 210
  last but one etc 116.1
lastly 159.10
late comparative and superlative 136.1
  late and *lately* 21.2
later and *in* 308
latter *the latter* 18
laugh preposition 79.3; 437
lay and *lie* 309
lean British and American forms 300.3
learn structures 310
  + *-ing* form or infinitive 296.8
  British and American forms 300.3
learned (adjective) pronunciation 13
least and *fewest* 311
leave two objects 583
  leave and *forget* 215
  leave it to somebody to ... 302.4
  leave and *live* 300.2
  see also **left**
leave off ...*ing* 293.1
leaving words out see **ellipsis**
left meaning 'remaining' 312
leisurely adjective and adverb 21.1
lend two objects 583
  passive 410
  lend and *borrow* 108
length marked and unmarked uses 341
less and *fewer* 313
less of a 154.3
lesser 313.4
lest 314
let structures 40.2; 316
  let, allow and *permit* 40
let introducing imperatives 268.8; 315
  let me see 268.8
  let's 315
  let's see 159.17
  let's question tag 466.3
letter expressions without article 69.1
letters 317
  abbreviated style 1.2
lie with adjectives 147.5
  lie and *lay* 309
life 318
lightning uncountable 148.3
like and *as* 320
  and *as if/though* 74
like (verb) 319; 186.3
  non-progressive verb 451.2
  like + *-ing* form or infinitive 296.9

likely 21; 321
listen preposition 437
  listen (to) and *hear* 244
little and *small* 511
little comparative and superlative 136.2
  little and *a little* 322.3
  (a) little and *(a) few* 322
live and *leave* 300.2
live adjective and *alive* 15.2
lively 21
lonely 21; *lone, lonely, lonesome* and *alone* 42
long live ... 541
long comparative and superlative
  (pronunciation) 136.1
  long and *for a long time* 323
  a long way and *far* 206
  as long as 75; 262
  no longer 372
look 147; 324
  non-progressive verb 451.2
  look (at), see and *watch* 489
  look at + object + *-ing* form 245.4
  preposition 79.3; 437
  discourse marker 159.19
look after and *look for* 324.4
look forward *to* ...*ing* 295.2
  look forward, expect, hope and *wait* 202
look here 159.19
lose and *loose* 325
lot see **a lot**
lots 326
  with comparatives 139.1
loud comparative and superlative 137
  adverb 21.2
love meaning 'zero' 385.3
love non-progressive verb 451.2
  + *-ing* form or infinitive 296.9
lovely 21
low comparative and superlative 137
  adjective and adverb 21.2
luck uncountable 148.3
luggage uncountable 148.3
lunch and *dinner* 338

made preposition 328
magazines and newspapers article use 69.19
magic and *magical* 256.4
mail expressions without article 69.1
majority *the majority* 326
make structures 327
  two objects 583
  prepositions 328
  + infinitive with *to* in passive 412.2
  + object complement 580
  object complement in passive 413
  make and *do* 164
male and *masculine* 209
man omission of article 69.9
  man meaning 'people in general', 'the human
    race' 69.9; 227.6
man-eaters, *men drivers* 508.2

man-made 227.6
mankind 227.6
many and *much* 348
  comparative and superlative 136.2
  as much/many as 70.5
  many with comparatives 139.2
  see also *much*
marked and unmarked uses (*tall/short* etc) 341
marriage preposition 437
married preposition 437
  get married 329
marry 329
  preposition 437, 439
masculine and feminine words and pronouns
  see **gender**
matter non-progressive verb 451.2
  no matter who etc 371
may and *might* 330–336
  introduction 330
  mayn't 144.4 (notes)
  possibility 331
  permission 332
  may, might and *can* 331.10
  may, might and *could* 331.11
  may in wishes and hopes 333
  may structuring argument 159.5
  may . . . but 334
  may/might as well 335
  distancing use of *might* 161.3
  might in requests, suggestions and criticisms
    336
maybe and *perhaps* 337
mayor, *mayoress* 227.4
me too 45.3
meals 338
  polite formulae 520.11
mean 339
  non-progressive verb 451.2
  + -*ing* form or infinitive 296.7
  mean and *think* 339.2
meaning and *opinion* 339.2
means 340
  means and *way* 587.4
measles uncountable 148.4
measure non-progressive verb 451.2
measurement marked and unmarked uses of
    measurement words 341
  use of *be* 91
  article use 69.17
  measurement expressions 382.7, 8
  word order 15.6
  British and American measures 385.17
mention . . . *ing* 293.1
method and *way* 587.4
might see **may**
million(s) (of) 385.14
mind 342
  mind . . . ing 293.1
  I don't mind you/your . . . ing 292.4
mind you 159.3
mine, **yours** etc 433
  a friend of mine etc 434

minute *the minute* (conjunction) 267
misrelated participles 406.4
Miss 353.3
miss 343
  miss . . . ing 293.1
missing 343.5
modal auxiliary verbs 344–345
  with perfect infinitives 278.3
  in indirect speech 482.5
moment *the moment* (conjunction) 267
money British and American currency 385.15, 16
  singular verbs with sums of money 504.1
money uncountable 148.3
monthly adjective and adverb 21.1
months article use 69.10
more 346
  in comparative structures 135–139
  any more 57
  more of a 154.3
  more and more . . . 138.4
  no more and *no longer* 372
  more and *another* 53.2
  more than one + singular 504.3
more or less 159.16
moreover 159.11
most 347
  in superlative structures 135–139
  modifying adjectives / adverbs 153
  meaning 'very' 153.2
  most and *mostly* 21.2
Mr 353.3
  punctuation 2.1
Mrs 353.3
Ms 227.7; 353.3
much and *many* 348
  comparative and superlative 136.2
  much before verbs 155.1
  with comparatives 139.1
  with superlatives 139.3
  anything/nothing much 523.5
  as much/many as 70.5
  too much etc 156.2
  much, very and *very much* with past
    participles 405.4
  see also **many**
musical instruments article use 69.11
must 349–352
  introduction 349
  concluding that something is certain 350
  must and *can* (certainty) 350.2
  must not and *need not* 350.3; 357.6
  necessity and obligation 351
  must and *have (got) to* 352
  must, should and *ought* 496
my, your etc 433
myself, *yourself* etc 471
  and see **reflexive pronouns**

naked pronunciation 13
names and titles 353
nationalities 354

nature no article 68.3a
near adverb particle 19
near comparative and superlative 137
   near (to) 355; 437
   near and *by* 119
nearest and *next* 356
nearly with superlatives 139.3
   nearly and *almost* 41
need 357
   non-progressive verb 451.2
   need . . . ing passive meaning 293.3; 357.4
   need not and *must not* 350.3; 357.6
   need not have . . . and *did not need to . . .* 357.5
   there is no need to . . . 563.2
negative structures 358–362
   basic rules 358
   negative infinitive 276.5
   transferred negation 359
   negative questions 360
   negative questions as exclamations 201.4
   negative questions in indirect speech 482.7
   double negatives 361
   ambiguous sentences 362
   extra negative in *if*-clauses 261.7
   distancing use of negative structures 161.4
neither (of) 363
   neither and *none* 368.3
   neither and *both . . . not* 109.4
   singular or plural verb after *neither* 509.5
neither can I/do I etc 364
neither . . . nor 365
never with present perfect 418.5
   position with imperatives 268.7
   never and *not ever* 361.2
nevertheless 159.3
news uncountable 148.3
newspaper headlines 366
newspapers and magazines article use 69.19
next position with numbers 14.4
   very next 139.4
   next and *the next* 367
   and *nearest* 356
   next but one etc 116.1
nice preposition 437
   nice and . . . 51.4
night expressions without article 69.1
   night, afternoon and *evening* 29
nil 385.3
no and *not* 375
   no and *none* 368
   no/none and *not a/any* 369
   no and *not all* 35.5
   no with comparatives 56; 139.1
no and *yes* 605
   in answers to negative questions 360.4
no doubt 159.18,19; 370
no good 56
   no good . . . ing 292.5
   no . . . ing 292.3
no matter who/what etc 371
no more and *no longer* 372

no one and *nobody* 523
   no one and *none* 373
no sooner, *scarcely* and *hardly* 237
no use 56
   no use . . . ing 292.5
nobody position with adjective 15.5
   nobody and *no one* 523
   and *not anybody* 361.2
nominal relatives 476
nominalisation 573
non-assertive words 374
   after superlatives 138.13
non-identifying relative clauses 474
non-progressive verbs 451
none singular or plural verb 509.5
   none the + comparative 138.6
   none of which 477.1
   none and *neither* 368.3
   and *no* 368
   and *no one* 373
nor *can I / do I* etc 364
   not . . . nor 364.3
north(ern), *east(ern)* etc 176
northward(s) 586
not referring to different parts of a sentence 362
   with *believe, hope* etc 515
   not and *no* 375
   if not 261.12
   not . . . either 364.2
   not . . . nor 364.3
not a/any and *no/none* 54.3; 369
not a bit 106.3
not all and *no* 35.5
not any more and *not any longer* 372
not at all 82.3
   modifying adjectives/adverbs 153
   answer to thanks 520.19
not even 195.2
not in the least 311.7
not much of a 154.3
not only 376
not quite 467.6
(not) so . . . as 70.2
   not so much . . . as/but 518.4
not until inverted word order 575.5
not very modifying adjectives/adverbs 153
notes abbreviated style 1.2
nothing position with adjectives 15.5
   nothing and *not anything* 361.2
   nothing much 523.5
   nothing to do and *nothing to be done* 287.3
   nothing but 116.1
notice + object + infinitive or *-ing* form 245
   + object + past participle 245.3
notices abbreviated style 1.4
nought 385.3
nouns complementation 377
   countable and uncountable 148
   plurals 500–502
   noun + *-ing* form 294
nouns in groups 379–382
   noun modifiers 378; 382

nouns modification for degree 154
nouns used for actions 573
now (*that*) 383
now to show change of subject 159.8
nowadays 384
number see **singular and plural**
number *a large number* 326
   omission of article after *number of* 69.8
numbers 385
   position of numbers 14.4

object *to ... ing* 295.2
of course 386
   structuring argument 159.5
of whom / which 477.1
of with determiners 157.4
   with *all* 35
   with *both* 109
   compound nouns with *of*-structure and
      possessive *'s* 379–382
off adverb particle 19
offer two objects 583
   passive 410
offers polite formulae 520.16
often 387
OK used to show change of subject 159.8
old position and meaning 15.2
   comparative and superlative 136.2
   old and *young* (marked and unmarked) 341
   the old 18
older and *elder, oldest* and *eldest* 180
older English verb forms 388
omission of relative pronouns (comprehension
   problems) 188
omission of words see **ellipsis**
on adverb particle 19
on, *at* and *in* (place) 80
   (time) 81
   on and *onto* 269
   on ... ing 406.6
on and *about* 4
on condition (that) 262
on earth used for emphasis 189.3
on foot 69.1
on holiday 250
on one's own 400.5
on the contrary 159.6
   and *on the other hand* 145.1
on the other hand 159.2
   and *on the contrary* 145.1
on the way and *in the way* 587.5
on the whole 159.12
on time and *in time* 438
once, *sometime* and *one day* 389
once conjunction meaning 'after' 390
one and *a* with numbers 385.10
one and a half 235.5
one and *it* 391.9
one another and *each other* 175
one day and *once* 389
one of ... 393

one of the ... + relative clause (singular or
   plural) 506.1
one personal pronoun 392
   distancing use 161.6
   one, you and *they* 392
one substitute word 391
only referring to different parts of a sentence 394
   inversion after *only ...* 298
   only today etc 394.4
   if only 265
   the only thing is 131.5
onto and *on* 269
open (adjective) and *opened* 395
open (verb) not used with reflexive pronouns
   471.9
operate preposition 437
opinion preposition 438
   opinion and *meaning* 339.2
opportunity and *possibility* 396
opposite position 397
   opposite and *contrary* 145.2
   opposite, in front of and *facing* 272
or words left out after *or* 182
or else 187.5
or rather 159.16; 469.4
other(s) and *another* 53
   other and *different* 53.5
   on the other hand 159.2; 145.1
ought 398
   ought, should and *must* 496
out adverb particle 19
out of 399
outward(s) 586
over adverb particle 19
over and *above* 6;
   and *across* 6.3, 9
owe non-progressive verb 451.2
   two objects 583
   owe it to somebody to ... 302.4
owing to and *due to* 170
own 400; non-progressive verb 451.2

pack meaning of passive 414
page preposition 438
pair 426.3
pants 501.7
paragraphs 401
pardon, *excuse me* and *sorry* 520.6–8
part no article 402
participles 403–406
   introduction 403
   active and passive participles 404
   details of participle use 405
   participles used as adjectives 405
   participle clauses 406
   dangling participles 406.4
particles modification for degree 156.1
parts of the body article use 69.16
party preposition 438
passives 407–14
   structures and verb forms 407

get as passive auxiliary 228.4
get in passive imperatives 268.3
passive infinitive 276.3
passive infinitive after *be* 90
passive infinitive not used after *able* 3
agent 408
by and *with* 117.2
choice between active and passive 409; 289.3
verbs with two objects 410
verbs with infinitive and clause objects 411
verbs with object + infinitive 412
there as preparatory subject 412.3
verbs with object complements 413
finished-result verbs (e.g. *cut, close*) 414
position of preposition in passive clauses
440.4
past adverb particle 19
past continuous see **past progressive**
past participles 403–406
confusion between past participles and past
tenses 188
past participles with *very, much* and *very
much* 405.4
past perfect tenses 421
past progressive tense 417
future in the past 226
past progressive and simple past 417.3–5
past simple see **simple past**
past tenses introduction 415
distancing use 161.2
past verb forms with present or future
meaning 422
past with conditional meaning in subordinate
clauses 556
see also **simple past**, **present perfect** etc
pay passive 410
preposition 437
two objects 583
pen/pencil/ink preposition 438
pennies and *pence* 385.15, 16; 501.2
people 501.2
per 385.19
perfect verb forms 423
perfect infinitive 276.2; 278
see also **present perfect**, **past perfect,
future perfect**
perhaps and *maybe* 337
periods see **full stops**
permission uncountable 148.3
permit structures 40.1
+ -*ing* form or infinitive 296.4
permit, allow and *let* 40
personal pronouns general 424
subject and object forms 425
with adjectives (e.g. *poor you*) 424.3
object pronouns after *as* 70.4
after *but* 116
after *than* 138.8
pronouns left out in abbreviated styles 1
pronouns left out in informal speech 183
me/my going etc 292.4
phone expressions without article 69.1

preposition 438
phrasal verbs 19.2; 257.2; 582
picture preposition 438
piece 426
piece- and group-words 426
place + infinitive or relative 427
a place we can stay etc 477.3
prepositions 80; 439.11
place names article use 69.18
plane expressions without article 69.1
play and *game* 428
please 429
please non-progressive verb 451.2
pleased preposition 437
plenty 326
plural see **singular**
plural uncountables 148.7
plurals of abbreviations 2.5
Poet Laureate 15.4
poet, poetess 227.4
poetry uncountable 148.3
point countable or uncountable 148.5
preposition 79.3
point of view 430
preposition 438
police *the police* 68.3b; 501.7
policeman/woman 227.4
polite conversational formulae 520
polite preposition 437
politeness and formality 216
politic and *political* 256.4
politics and *policy* 431
politics and *policy* 18
poor *the poor* 18
position of adjectives, adverbs, prepositions etc:
see **adjectives**, **adverbs**, **prepositions** etc
possess non-progressive verb 451.2
possessive 's forms and grammar 432
article use 69.3
used to make compound nouns 379–382
with superlatives 138.9
possessives *my, mine* etc 433
possessives as determiners 157
possessives with *of*: *a friend of mine* etc 434
possessives and object pronouns with -*ing*
forms 292.4
possibility and *opportunity* 396
possible position 15.4; 477.6
postcards abbreviated style 1.2
postpone ... *ing* 293.1
practically with superlatives 139.3
practise ... *ing* 293.1
prefer 435; non-progressive verb 451.2
+ -*ing* form or infinitive 296.9
prefer ... *to* ... *ing* 295.2
prepositions 436–442
introduction 436
prepositions after particular words and
expressions 437
after past participles 405.5
before particular words and expressions 438
expressions without preposition 439
prepositions at the ends of clauses 440

before conjunctions 441
with -*ing* forms 295, 406.6; 442
with infinitives 442
left out in abbreviated styles 1
modification for degree 156.1
prepositional verbs the difference between
  prepositions and adverb particles 19
  idiomatic prepositional verbs 257.2
present position and meaning 15.4
present continuous see **present progressive**
present participles 403–406
present perfect tenses 418–420
  present perfect simple 418
  present perfect and simple past 418.3–8; 419
  present perfect progressive 420
  comparison between simple and progressive
    420.4–7
  comparison between present and present
  perfect progressive 420.3
present progressive 445 and see **present tenses**
present simple 444 and see **present tenses**
present tenses 443–446
  introduction 443
  simple present 444
  present progressive 445
  present progressive and simple present
    445.5–8
  present tenses in stories, commentaries and
  instructions 446
  present tenses with future reference: see
    future
presently 447
President article use 69.13
President elect 15.4
presume *there is presumed to be* ... 412.3
pretty and *prettily* 21.2
  pretty modifying adjectives/adverbs 153
  pretty, rather, quite and *fairly* 205
prevent preposition 437
price and *prize* 448
prince, *princess* 227.4
principal and *principle* 449
prison expressions without article 69.1
prize and *price* 448
Professor 353.3
progress uncountable 148.3
progressive verb forms general 450
  with *always* etc 452
  distancing use of progressive forms 161.2
  progressive infinitive 276.1
  progressive forms of *be* 88
  non-progressive verbs 451
  see also **present progressive,**
    past progressive, future progressive
promise non-progressive verb 451.2
  two objects 583
  passive 410
pronouns see **personal pronouns, relative**
  pronouns etc
pronunciation British-American differences 50.4
  -*ed* 416.2
  adjectives ending in -*ed* 13
  regular plural endings 502

third person singular endings 444.3
  possessive '*s* 432
  the 65.9
  intonation in question tags 465
  pronunciation and spelling 538
proof preposition 437
proper position and meaning 15.4
provided/providing (that) 262
publicity uncountable 148.3
punctuation 453–459
  apostrophes in abbreviations 2.5
  full stops in abbreviations 2.1
  punctuation between clauses 142.4
  commas with adjectives 14.5
  punctuation of numbers 385.9
put off ...*ing* 293.1
put on *clothes* 168.2
pyjamas 501.7

Queen article use 69.13
question countable or uncountable 148.5
question mark 457
question tags 465–466
  with imperatives 268.6
question words 460
  question word clauses 460.5
questions 461–466
  basic rules 461
  questions with non-interrogative word order
    462
  negative questions 360
  negative questions as exclamations 201.4
  negative questions in indirect speech 482.7
  reply questions 463
  rhetorical questions 464
  question tags 465–466
  questions used for 'distancing' requests and
  statements 161
  position of prepositions 440.2
  indirect questions 481.6
quick comparative and superlative 137
  adverb 21.2
quickly, *soon* and *early* 525
quit British and American forms 300.3
quite 467
  modifying adjectives/adverbs 153
  with comparatives 139.1
  quite a before nouns 154.2,5
  quite, fairly, rather and *pretty* 205
quite a bit etc 467.5
  quite a few / a lot / enough 156.2
quotation marks 458

radio article use 69.1,12
  preposition 438
ragged pronunciation 13
rain etc preposition 438
raise and *rise* 300.2
rather adverb of degree 468
  modifying adjectives/adverbs 153
  with comparatives 139.1

rather a before nouns 154.2
rather few / little / many / much / too much / a lot 156.2
rather, fairly, quite and *pretty* 205
rather preference 469
rather than 469.1
or rather 159.16; 469.4
read two objects 583
real adverb 21.2
really discourse marker 159.16
used for emphasis 189.3
reason structures 470
countable or uncountable 148.5
preposition 438
reckon so/not 515
recognise non-progressive verb 451.2
recovered active past participle 404.3
reduced relative clauses 406.2; 477.6
reflexive pronouns 471
and *each other* 471.7
refuse passive 410
regard passive 413
regard somebody/something as ... 580.2
regarding 159.1
regret + *-ing* form or infinitive 296.3
reinforcement tags 472
relative pronouns and clauses 473–477
introduction 473
identifying and non-identifying clauses 474
punctuation 474
whose 475
what and other nominal relatives 476
advanced points 477
relative pronouns like conjunctions 143.2
reduced relative clauses 406.2; 477.6
omission of relative pronouns and
comprehension problems 188
position of preposition 440.3
relatives and indirect statements combined
(e.g. *somebody I know you'll like*) 477.10
relatives and indirect questions combined
(e.g. *a car that I didn't know how fast it would go*) 477.11
remain + adjective 129.10
remember non-progressive verb 451.2
+ *-ing* form or infinitive 296.1
can remember 125.3
remember and *remind* 478.3
remind 478
preposition 437
repetition 479
for emphasis 189.4
reply questions 463
report *there is reported to be* ... 412.3
reported speech see **reporting**
reporting 480–482
introduction 480
basic rules for indirect speech 481
advanced points 482
reporting expressions and comprehension
problems 188
requests 483

require ... *ing* passive meaning 293.3
research uncountable 148.3
resemble no preposition 439
resent ... *ing* 293.1
resist ... *ing* 293.1
responsible/responsibility preposition 437
rest the rest 484
retired active past participle 404.3
rhetorical questions 464
rhythm 540
rich *the rich* 18
right adverb; showing change of subject 159.8
right and *rightly* 21.2
rise and *arise* 59
rise and *raise* 300.2
risk ... *ing* 293.1
road and *street* 485
Roman numbers 385.5
round, *around* and *about* 60
rouse and *arouse* 61
rubbish uncountable 148.3
rude preposition 437
rugged pronunciation 13
run preposition 437
run and ... 52

's genitive see **possessive** *'s*
sacred pronunciation 13
same *the same* 486
satisfy non-progressive verb 451.2
say and *tell* 487
say so 514
there is said to be ... 412.3
scales 501.7
scarcely, *hardly* and *no sooner* 237
school expressions without article 69.1
scissors 501.7
Scot, *Scottish, Scotch* 354 (notes)
sea *the sea* 68.3a
expressions without article 69.1
search preposition 437
seasons article use 69.10
second *the second* (conjunction) 267
Secretary General 15.4
see 488
non-progressive verb 451.2
can see 125.1
+ object + infinitive or *-ing* form 245
+ object + past participle 245.3
+ infinitive with *to* in passive 412.2
I see (that) 246
see somebody as ... 580.2
see, look (at) and *watch* 489
see above/over 6.6
seem copular verb 147; 490
non-progressive verb 451.2
+ infinitive (negative structure) 359.4
can't seem to ... 490.4
there seems to be 563.5
seem and *appear* 58.2

-self see **reflexive pronouns**
sell not used with reflexive pronouns 471.9
semi-colon 459
send passive 410
  with two objects 583
sensible and *sensitive* 491
several 157.3
shade and *shadow* 492
shall future auxiliary 221
  interpersonal uses 222
share *between/among* 104.3
sharp and *sharply* 21.2
shave not used with reflexive pronouns 471.9
she for cars, ships, countries etc 227.1
  she and *her* 425
shocked by/at 405.5; 437
shone British and American pronunciations 300.3
shoot preposition 79.3
short and *shortly* 21.2
short answers 493
shorten 129.9
should 494–498
  should and *would* 494
  should obligation, deduction etc 495
  should, ought and *must* 496
  should in subordinate clauses 497
  with *in case* 271.2
  should/would auxiliary in conditional clauses
    etc 498
  if... should 261.2
  I should ... meaning 'If I were you,
    I should ...' 264.2
shout preposition 79.3; 437
show passive 410
  two objects 583
shrunken 405.6
shut and *close* 132
sick and *ill* 266
silly 21
similarly 159.4
simple past tense 416
  simple past and past progressive 417.3–5
  simple past and present perfect 418.3–8; 419
  simple instead of progressive in subordinate
    clauses 556.7
  simple past instead of perfect in subordinate
    clauses 556.7
  see also **past tenses**
simple present tense 444
  simple present and present progressive
    445.5–8
  future use 223
  simple instead of progressive in subordinate
    clauses 556.7
since tenses 499
  since (preposition) position 440.6
  since, in, from and *for* 214
since, *as, because* and *for* 72
singular and plural 500–509
  regular plurals 500
  irregular and special plurals 501
  pronunciation of regular plurals 502

singular nouns with plural verbs 503
plural expressions with singular verbs 504
they with singular reference 505
mixed structures 506
distributive plural 507
noun modifiers (e.g. *antique shop, ten-pound
  note, sports car*) 508
miscellaneous points 509
fractions and decimals 385.2
abbreviations 2.5
plural uncountables 148.7
sit with adjectives 147.5
slang 510
sleep well etc 520.20
sleeping and asleep 15.3
slogans abbreviated style 1.4
slow comparative and superlative 137
  adverb 21.2
small and *little* 511
smell 512
  British and American forms 300.3
  can smell 125.1
smile preposition 79.3; 437
so degree adverb 513.1–7
  modifying adjectives/adverbs 153
  substitute word 513.8–10
  used for emphasis 189.3
  exclamations 201.3
  logical consequence 159.14
  inversion 298.6
  so am I etc 516.1
  so I am etc 516.2
  so + adjective + article + noun 16
  if so 261.12
  so after *say* and *tell* 514
  so she says, so I hear etc 515.3
  so and *not* with *believe, hope* etc 515
  so and *so much* 153
  so and *such* 544
  so and *then* 517
  so and *very* 513.3
  not so... as 70
  so... as to... 513.6
so be it 541
so few/little/many/much 156.2
so long as condition 262
so many and *so much* 518
so that 519
so to speak 159.16
so-and-so 513.10
so-so 513.10
social language 520
society no article 68.3a
some 521
  and *a/an* 521.4
  and no article 521.5
  and *any* 522
  some of whom /which 477.1
some time, *sometime* and *sometimes* 524
  sometime and *once* 389
somebody position with adjectives 15.5
  somebody and *someone* 523

something position with adjectives 15.5
sometime and *once* 389
somewhere position with adjectives 15.5
  somewhere we can stay etc 477.3
soon comparative and superlative 137
  soon, early and *quickly* 525
sorry 520.7,8
  + *-ing* form or infinitive 296.14
  preposition 437
sort of 159.16,17; 526
  omission of article 69.7
sound and *soundly* 21.2
sound (verb) 527
south(ern), *north(ern)* etc 176
spaghetti uncountable 148.3
speak preposition 437
  speak and *talk* 528
  speaking of/about 159.1
special(ly) and *especial(ly)* 194
spell British and American forms 300.3
spelling 529–537
  capital letters 529
  -ly 530
  -ise and *-ize* 531
  hyphens 532
  hyphens in compound nouns 379.7
  final *-e* 533
  y and *i* 534
  doubling final consonants 535
  ch and *tch, k* and *ck* 536
  ie and *ei* 537
  spelling and pronunciation 538
  British-American differences 50.3
  its and *it's* 303
  whose and *who's* 598
  regular past tenses 416.3
  third person singular forms 444.2
spend ... + object + *-ing* 293.2
spill British and American forms 300.3
spit British and American forms 300.3
split infinitive 276.7
spoil British and American forms 300.3
spokesman/woman, *spokesperson* 227.5
spring article 69.10
stand with adjectives 147.5
start + *-ing* form or infinitive 296.10
  start and *begin* 98
stay + adjective 129.10
  stay and ... 52
steward, *stewardess* 227.4
still 159.3
  still, yet and *already* 539
stop + *-ing* form or infinitive 296.12
  + object + *-ing* 293.2
stopped active past participle 404.3
straight adjective and adverb 21.2
street and *road* 485
stress 540
  in abbreviations 2.3
  for emphasis 189.2
strike and *stroke* 300.2
strong and weak forms 588

subjunctive 541
subordinate clauses position 142.3
  tenses 556
subordinating conjunctions 142.2
substitution 542
such 543
  modifying nouns 154.4
  used with adjective + noun 543.3; 544.1
  used for emphasis 189.3
  exclamations 201.3
  such and *like this/that* 543.2
  such and *so* 544
  such and *very* 543.4
  such as 543.9
  such ... as to 543.7
such-and-such 543.8
suffer preposition 437
suggest 545
suit and *fit* 212
summer article 69.10
Sunday etc no preposition 439
sunken 405.6
superlative see **comparison, comparative**
superlatives with *much, far* etc 139.3,4
  with *ever* 197.4
  prepositions 138.9
  + infinitive 285.3
  with non-assertive words 138.13
  with *the* 65.4; 138.10
  with *very* 139.4
  see also **comparatives and superlatives**
supper and *dinner* 338
suppose non-progressive verb 451.2
  suppose (that) 262
  suppose so/not 515
  I don't suppose so and *I suppose not* 359
suppose, *supposing* (conjunctions) 546
  that after *supposing* 262
supposed to 547
sure + *-ing* form or infinitive 296.15
  sure (adverb) 21.2
surely 548
surprise non-progressive verb 451.2
surprised by/at 405.5
swearwords 550
swollen active past participle 404.3
sympathetic 549
sympathy polite formulae 520.14

taboo words 550
tag questions see **question tags**
tags see **question tags** and **reinforcement tags**
take 551
  two objects 583
  take and *bring* 112
take care (of) 127
take off clothes 168.2
take part preposition 437
talk and *speak* 528
  talking of/about 159.1

tall and *high* 249
  tall and *short* (marked and unmarked) 341
taste 552
  can taste 125.1
tea meal 338
teach + *-ing* form or infinitive 296.8
  two objects 583
technique and *technology* 553
telephoning 554
  telephone numbers 385.4
television article use 69.12
  preposition 438
tell passive 410
  two objects 583
  tell somebody how to … 288
  tell and *say* 487
  I told you so 514
  can tell 125.2
telling the time 555
tend *there tends to be* 563.5
tenses list of all active verb forms 10
  passive verb forms 407
  tenses in subordinate clauses 556
  in indirect speech 481.4
  in as-clauses 70.9
  in *before* -clauses 96.2,3
  with *as if* and *as though* 74.2
  with *as long as* 75
  with *as, when* and *while* 73
  with *since* 499
  with *before* (adverb) 95
  see also **present tenses, past tenses** etc
than *than I* or *than me* etc 138.8; 425.9
  than replacing subject/object 138.14
  inversion 298.6
  than, as and *that* 557
than ever 197.6
thank you 429
thankful and *grateful* 558
thanks 520.19
that (conjunction) omission 560
  dropped in indirect speech 481.5
  that, than and *as* 557
that demonstrative: see **this**
that relative pronoun 473–474; 477
  that which (older English) 476.5
  that, where and *when* (relative) 143.3
that-clauses 559
that is to say 159.15,16
that/those of … 391.8
the British Isles, *Britain, the United Kingdom*
  and *England* 114
the 63–65, 68–69
  the … the with comparatives 138.5
  the with superlatives 65.4; 138.12
  the meaning 'enough' 193.7
  see also **articles**
the accused, *the beautiful, the blind, the former*
  etc 18
the British, the Dutch etc 354
the fact that 441.2; 559.3
the hell used for emphasis 189.3

the majority 326
the matter (with) 561
the moment, *the minute* etc (conjunction) 267
the police 68.3b
the rest 484
the sea 68.3a
the way and *how* 254.6
the weather 68.3a
theatre article use 69.12
  preposition 438
thee older English 388
then logical consequence 159.14
  then and *so* 517
there 562; *there is* 563
  there is said/thought/ etc *to be* 412.3
  there in question tags 466.4
  there's + plural 509.4
  there goes … 444.6
  there and *here* 248
therefore 159.14
they and *them* 425
  they with singular reference 227.3; 505
  they, one and *you* 392
thicken 129.9
think 564
  negative structures 359.1,3
  think somebody/something to be 580.3
  there is thought to be 412.3
  preposition 437
  think so/not 515
  I thought so 515
  think and *mean* 339.2
this and *that* 565
  this/that and *it* 566
  this and *that* meaning 'so' 565.7
  this/these sort of etc 526
this is the first time etc + present/past perfect
  419.7
  this is the last … + present 307.5
thou older English 388
though and *although* 48
  though and *as*: special word order 71
thought preposition 437
thousand *a thousand* and *one thousand* 385.10
  thousand(s) (of) 385.14
through 567
  adverb particle 19
  through and *across* 9.5
  through and *along* 43
throw preposition 79.3; 437
thunder uncountable 148.3
thy older English 388
tight adverb 21.2
till 575
time 568
  countable or uncountable 148.5; 568
  in time and *on time* 438
  (at) what time …? 439
  any time you're in town etc 477.3
  this is the first time etc + present perfect 419.7
time telling the time 555

titles 353
  abbreviated style 1.4
to and *at/in* 79
  to and *in* 270
  to and *until/till* 575.2
  to dropped after *where* 591
  to school, university etc (expressions without
    article) 69.1
to . . . ing 295.2
to used instead of whole infinitive 186
to a great/some extent 159.12
to begin/start with 159.10
to sum up 159.21
to tell the truth 159.20
tonight 569
too 570
  modifying adjectives/adverbs 153
  + adjective + article + noun 16
  too . . . for . . . + infinitive 280.8
  too and *too much* 153; 570.3
  too and *very* 570.5
too, *also* and *as well* 45, 46
too few/little/much/many 156.2
too much and *too many* 571
toothache 148.4
town expressions without article 69.1
  town and *city* 130
traffic uncountable 148.3
train expressions without article 69.1
transferred negation 359
transitive and intransitive verbs 579.2
translate preposition 437
travel uncountable 148.3
  travel, journey, trip and *voyage* 572
  travels 148.5
travelled active past participle 404.3
trip preposition 437
  trip, journey, travel and *voyage* 572
trousers 501.7
try + *-ing* form or infinitive 296.6
  try and 52
tube expressions without article 69.1
turn changes 129.7
turning verbs into nouns 573
TV preposition 438
twice as . . . etc 70.6
type of 526
  omission of article 69.7
typical preposition 437

ugly 21
UK 114
unable 3
uncountable see **countable**
under adverb particle 19
  under and *below* 99
underneath 99.6
understand non-progressive verb 451.2
  can understand 125.3
  understand how to 288
  understand . . . ing 293.1

understand somebody/something to be 580.3
  there is understood to be 412.3
  I understand (that) . . . 246
uninterested and *disinterested* 160
United Kingdom 114
university preposition 438
  expressions without article 69.1
unless 574
  and *if not* 574.2
unlikely 21
until 575
  and *before* 575.7
  and *by* 575.6
  and *to* 575.2
up adverb particle 19
  up and *down* . . . 576
us meaning 'me' 424.9
use *any/no use* 56
  any/no use . . . ing 292.5
  there's no use 563.2
used + infinitive 577
  used to and *would* 604.8
used *be used to . . . ing* 578
usual *as usual* 76

vacation 250
vanished active past participle 404.3
verb forms active 10
  passive 407
  verb complementation 579
  verb + infinitive 283
  verb + *-ing* form 293
  verb + object + complement 15.8; 580
  verb + object + infinitive 284
  verbs with two objects 583, 410 (passive
    structures)
  verbs not used in progressive forms 451
  modification of verbs 155
  verbs with prepositions and particles 582
  verbs of movement (e.g. *she danced in*) 581
verbs left out in commentaries 1.3
very modifying adjectives/adverbs 153
  very with superlatives, *first* etc 139.4
  very and *very much* 153
  very and *(very) much* with past participles
    405.4
  with *afraid* 25.3
  very . . . indeed 274
  very and *so* 513.3
  very and *such* 543.4
  very and *too* 570.5
very few/little/much/many 156.2
  very much with comparatives 139.1
  very much afraid 25.3
  very much of a 154.3
  position of *very much* 22.2
  very much, very and *much* with past
    participles 405.4
voice preposition 438
voyage, *travel, journey* and *trip* 572

wait 584
  wait and ... 52
  wait, expect, hope and *look forward* 202
waiter, *waitress* 227.4
wake British and American forms 300.3
  wake, awake and *(a)waken* 85
want 585
  non-progressive verb 451.2
  negative structure 359.4
  want (to) 186.3
  want ... ing passive meaning 293.3
  want and *will* 600.7
-ward(s) 586
wash *(oneself)* 471.9
watch + object + infinitive or -*ing* form 245
  + object + past participle 245.3
  watch, look (at) and *see* 489
wave preposition 79.3
way prepositions, relative and other structures
    587
  way and *means/method* 587.4
  the way she spoke etc 477.3
  by the way 159.8
we inclusive or exclusive 424.8
  we and *us* 425
weak and strong forms 588
wear 168.3
weather *the weather* 68.3a
  weathers 148.5
weekly adjective and adverb 21.1
weigh non-progressive verb 451.2
well 589
  position 589; 22.1
  well and *fit/healthy* 15.3
  comparative and superlative 137
  discourse marker 159.16,17,20
  well and *good* 589.1
  as well 45–46
  as well as 77; 159.11
well-read active past participle 404.3
Welsh, *Welshman/woman* 354.3
were instead of *was* 260.4; 541
wert older English form of *were* 388
west(ern), *north(ern)* etc 176
wet British and American forms 300.3
what question word 460
  nominal relative pronoun 476.1
  exclamations 201.2
  singular or plural verb 509.3
  what I need is ... etc 131
  what to ... 288
  what and *pardon* 520.8
  what, how and *why* 254.3
  what, which and *who* (question words) 594
  see also **question words** and **relative
    pronouns**
what do you mean? 339.5
what ever, *on earth, the hell* etc 595; 189.3
what if 546
what is more 159.11
what ... like and *how* 255
what time no preposition 439

whatever 476.4; 596
when question word 460
  relative use 473.3
  when and *that* (relative) 143.3
  nominal relative pronoun 476.4
  conjunction with past perfect 421.5
  when ... ing 406.6
  when, as and *while* 73
  when and *if* 590
  see also **question words**
when ever, the hell etc 595
whenever 476.4; 596
where question word 460
  relative use 473.3
  where and *that* (relative) 143.3
  nominal relative pronoun 476.4
  where (to) 591
  where's + plural 509.4
  see also **question words**
where ever, *the hell* etc 595
whereas 159.2
wherever 476.4, 596
whether and *if* 593
  whether ... or 592
  preposition + *whether* 441
which question word 460
  relative pronoun 473–477
  nominal relative pronoun 476.2
  which, what and *who* 594
  see also **question words** and **relative
    pronouns**
whichever 596
while contrast 159.2
  while, as and *when* 73
  while ... ing 406.6
who question word 460
  relative pronoun 473–477
  who and *whom* 425.4–6
  singular or plural verb 509.3
  who to ... 288
  who, what and *which* 594
  see also **question words** and **relative pronouns**
who ever, *the hell* etc 595
whoever 476.4; 596
whole and *all* 38
  on the whole 159.12
whose question word 433.4; 460; 597
  relative pronoun 475
  whose and *who's* 598
why question word 460
  relative use 473.3
  + infinitive 599.3
  why should ...? 464.2; 599.2
  why and *why not* 599.1
  why, what and *how* 254.3
why ever, *the hell* etc 595
wicked pronunciation 13
wide and *widely* 21.2
  wide and *broad* 115
  wide and *large* 105.6
widen 129.9
widow, *widower* 227.4

will 600; future auxiliary 221
  interpersonal uses 222
  will you . . .? (meanings) 221.9
  will with *if* 259.3
  will and *want* 600.7
win and *beat* 92
wind and *wound* 300.2
winter article 69.10
wish 601
  non-progressive verb 451.2
wishes *best wishes* etc 520.13
with 602
  possession 602.5
  acompanying circumstances 602.4
  clothing, voices, transport 602.6
  meaning 'against' 602.3
  with (tools) and *by* (method, agent) 117
with reference to 159.1
without and *except* 200.6
  and *instead of* 297.2
  article not dropped 69.2
woman omission of article 69.9
woman-haters, women drivers 508.2
wonder *I wondered / I was wondering* (polite requests) 161.2
won't refusals 222.3
word order adjectives after nouns 15.4
  adjectives after *something* etc 15.5
  adverb position 22–23
  verb not separated from object 22.1
  as and *though* after adjective/adverb 71
  auxiliary verb etc before subject 298
  whole verb before subject 299
  fronting 217
  questions 461, 462
  position of subordinate clauses 142.3
  prepositions at the ends of clauses 440
  direct and indirect object 583
  object of phrasal verb 582.3
  all 35–36
  both 110
  enough 193
  even 195
  how 254.1
  quite 467.3
  rather 468.3
  well 22.1
  very much 22.2
  yet, still and *already* 539
work uncountable 148.3
  expressions without article 69.1
worried about/by 408
worry active and passive with similar meanings 404.3
worse, worst 136.2; 137
worth 603
worthwhile 603
would 494; 498; 604
  distancing use 161.3
  future in the past 226
  would and *should* with *if* 260.3
  would and *used to* 604.8

would rather 469.2,3
would you mind . . .? 342
wound and *wind* 300.2
wretched pronunciation 13
write direct and indirect objects 583
wrong adverb 21.2
  prepositions 437

ye older English form of *you* 388
yearly adjective and adverb 21.1
years old 30
yes and *no* 605
  in answers to negative questions 360.4
yet 159.3
  non-assertive word 374.1
  with present perfect 418.5
  after superlatives 138.13
  yet, already and *ever* 197.7
  yet, still and *already* 539
you and I etc 424.11; 425.3
you know 159.17
you meaning 'people in general' 392
  you, one and *they* 392
  you guys, you all (US) 424.2
your health 520.12
you're welcome 520.19
yours faithfully/sincerely 317

zero 385.3